Redefining EU Membership

Redefining EU Membership

Differentiation In and Outside the European Union

Edited by

DIANE FROMAGE

OXFORD
UNIVERSITY PRESS

OXFORD
UNIVERSITY PRESS

Great Clarendon Street, Oxford, OX2 6DP,
United Kingdom

Oxford University Press is a department of the University of Oxford.
It furthers the University's objective of excellence in research, scholarship,
and education by publishing worldwide. Oxford is a registered trade mark of
Oxford University Press in the UK and in certain other countries

Published in the United States of America by Oxford University Press
198 Madison Avenue, New York, NY 10016, United States of America

British Library Cataloguing in Publication Data

Data available

Library of Congress Control Number: 2024936312

ISBN 9780192857347

DOI: 10.1093/9780191948145.001.0001

Printed and bound by
CPI Group (UK) Ltd, Croydon, CR0 4YY

MIX
Paper | Supporting
responsible forestry
FSC® C013604

Acknowledgement

The origin of this edited volume dates back to 2018, when Johan Adriaensen, Thomas Christiansen, Ellen Vos, and I began to wonder about EU membership from a multidisciplinary perspective, within the framework of the Centre for European Research in Maastricht (CERiM). Two conferences followed in 2018 and 2019, and all speakers, discussants, chairs, and participants should be thanked for contributing to the success of these events, as should CERiM, the Law Faculty, and the Faculty of Arts and Social Science (FASoS) for their generous support. Generous support by the European Commission through the Jean Monnet Programme should, furthermore, be acknowledged, as CERiM was a Jean Monnet Centre of Excellence at the time. These events would not have been as successful without Elke Hundhausen's efficient help in their organization.

The authors of this edited volume should also be warmly thanked for their valuable and thought-provoking contributions, as should Vanessa Aichstill, Martin Dippe, Franziska Federspieler, and David Fitza for their assistance in preparing the submission of this edited volume.

Last but not least, I am very grateful to the editorial team at Oxford University Press (in particular Lane Berger, Imogen Hill, and Luise Wilde) for supporting this project and for their continuous and kind help.

Diane Fromage

Contents

Brief Contents

Figures and Tables

Figures

Tables

Abbreviations

AA	Association Agreement
ACER	Agency for the Cooperation of Energy Regulators
AFSJ	Area of Freedom, Security and Justice
AFTR	Agriculture and Fisheries Trade Regime
AGS	Annual Growth Survey
BTI	Bertelsmann Stiftung's Transformation Index
CCP	Common Commercial Policy
CEE	Central and Eastern European
CEECs	Central and Eastern European countries
CEPA	Comprehensive Enhanced Partnership Agreement
CERiM	Centre for European Research in Maastricht
CFSP	Common Foreign and Security Policy
CIB	Comprehensive Institution Building Programmes
CIF	chamber investment forum
CJEU	Court of Justice of the European Union
COSME	Programme for the Competitiveness of Enterprises and SMEs
CR	Country Report
CSA	Agreement on Coal and Steel
CSDP	Common Security and Defence Policy
CSR	country-specific recommendation
CSTO	Collective Security Treaty Organization
CTA	Common Travel Area
CU	Customs Union
CUA	Customs Union Agreement
DBP	draft budgetary plan
DCFTA	Deep and Comprehensive Free Trade Area
DCFTAs	Deep and Comprehensive Free Trade Agreements
DG	Directorates General
DI	differentiated integration
EAEU	Eurasian Economic Union
EAN	European Administrative Network
EaP	Eastern Partnership
EASA	European Union Aviation Safety Agency
EaSI	EU Programme for Employment and Social Innovation, Progress and Social Entrepreneurship
EBCG	European Border and Coast Guard
EC	European Communities
ECB	European Central Bank
ECHA	European Chemicals Agency

ECJ	European Court of Justice
ECU	Eurasian Customs Union
EDA	European Defence Agency
EDP	excessive deficit procedure
EDU	Europol Drugs Unit
EEA	European Economic Area
EEA	European Environment Agency
EEAS	European External Action Service
EEC	European Economic Community
EFTA	European Free Trade Association
EFTA	European Free Trade Association
EMA	European Medicines Agency
EMU	Economic and Monetary Union
ENP	European Neighbourhood Policy
ENPI	European Neighbourhood and Partnership Instrument
ENTSO-E	European Network of Transmission System Operators for Electricity
EPF	European Peace Facility
EPPO	European Public Prosecutor Office
ESA	EFTA Surveillance Authority
ESM	European Stability Mechanism
EU	European Union
EUIPO	European Union Intellectual Property Office
EULEX	European Union Rule of Law Mission in Kosovo
EUMA	European Union Mission in Armenia
EUSS	EU Settlement Scheme
FASoS	Faculty of Arts and Social Science
fsQCA	fuzzy-set qualitative comparative analysis
FTA	free trade agreement
GB	Great Britain
GDP	gross domestic product
GDPR	General Data Protection Regulation
GFA	Good Friday Agreement
IGA	intergovernmental agreement
IMA	Independent Monitoring Authority for Citizens' Rights in the UK
IMF	International Monetary Fund
JC	Joint Committee
JHA	justice and home affairs
JPSG	Joint Parliamentary Scrutiny Group
LED	Law Enforcement Directive
LIBE	Committee on Civil Liberties, Justice and Home Affairs
MEP	Member of the European Parliament
MFA	ministries of foreign affairs
MIP	macro-economic imbalances procedure
MP	Member of Parliament
MRA	mutual recognition agreement

NATO	North Atlantic Treaty Organization
NEC	Neighbourhood Economic Community
NI	Northern Ireland
NP	national parliament
NPM	New Public Management
NRP	national reform programme
NSD	Norwegian Centre for Research Data
OCT	Overseas Country or Territory Associated with the Union
OECD	Organisation for Economic Co-operation and Development
OMC	open method of coordination
OR	Outermost Region
PC	Partnership Council
PCA	Partnership and Cooperation Agreement
PD	Political Declaration
PESCO	permanent structured cooperation
PNR	Passenger Name Record
QCA	qualitative comparative analysis
RoC	Republic of Cyprus
SAA	Stabilisation and Association Agreement
SAP	Stabilisation and Association Process
SBA	Sovereign Base Area
SC	Specialised Committee
SCA	EFTA Surveillance and Court Agreement
SCP	stability/convergence programme
SIS	Schengen Information System
SPS	sanitary and phyto-sanitary standards
SSM	single supervisory mechanism
TAIEX	Technical Assistance and Information Exchange instrument
TBT	technical barriers to trade
TCA	Trade and Cooperation Agreement
TCN	third-country national
TEU	Treaty on European Union
TFEU	Treaty on the Functioning of the European Union
UK	United Kingdom
UNSC	United Nations Security Council
VLAP	visa liberalisation action plan
WA	Withdrawal Agreement
WTO	World Trade Organization

Contributors' Biographies

Giselle Bosse is Associate Professor and Jean Monnet Chair in EU International Relations at the Faculty of Arts and Social Sciences, Maastricht University. She is Co-Director of the Centre for European Research (CERiM), a fellow at the European Democracy Hub in Brussels and visiting professor at the College of Europe (Bruges) and the Diplomatic School of Armenia (Yerevan). Her research focuses on EU relations with countries in the post-Soviet area, EU democracy promotion through the European Neighbourhood Policy (ENP) and the Eastern Partnership (EaP) and the role of norms and values in the EU's international relations more broadly.

Deirdre Curtin is Professor of European Law at the European University Institute of Florence, Italy. She is Dean of Graduate Studies and Director of the Centre for Judicial Cooperation at the Robert Schuman Centre. Prior to joining the EUI, Prof Curtin held the Chair in European Law and Governance at the University of Amsterdam, where she was also the founding Director of the Amsterdam Centre of European Law and Governance (2008–16). Her specialist fields are European law and governance of the European Union. She studies phenomena such as democracy, legitimacy, and accountability, in particular in the digital context.

Mark Dawson is Professor of European Law and Governance at the Hertie School and Co-Director of the Jacques Delors Centre. His research focuses on the relationship between law and policy-making in the EU, particularly in the fields of economic governance and human rights protection. Dawson was previously an Assistant Professor at Maastricht University, and completed his PhD at the European University Institute in Florence in 2009. He has held visiting positions at the London School of Economics and Political Science (LSE), the University of Wisconsin, Sydney Law School, and the Harvard Kennedy School. He is co-editor of the series Cambridge Studies in European Law and Policy.

Laure Delcour is an Associate Professor, Université Sorbonne Nouvelle and a Visiting Professor, College of Europe. rHer research focuses on the diffusion and reception of EU norms and policies to Eastern European and South Caucasus countries as part of the European Neighbourhood Policy/Eastern Partnership.

Alvaro de Elera is Member of Cabinet and Legal Advisor to Commission Vice-President Vera Jourova, dealing, in her team, with rule of law and external relations. He was also Member of Cabinet and Legal Advisor to Commission First Vice-President Frans Timmermans and member of the Private Office of the EU Council Secretary-General. Prior to that, he was a member of the Council Legal Service (CLS) from 2008, after finishing graduate and postgraduate law studies in Spain, and having been visiting researcher at Amsterdam University, the European University Institute in Florence, and the Max Planck Institute for International law in Heidelberg. His areas of specialization include EU external relations policy in general, as well as the rule of law.

Christian N. K. Franklin is a Professor of EU/EEA law at the University of Bergen, and Director of its EEA law centre CENTENOL. He has published broadly on a range of methodological, institutional, and constitutional EU and EEA law issues, with a particular focus, in recent years, on issues related to the free movement of persons.

Diane Fromage is Professor of European Union Law at the University of Salzburg (Austria), where she is also the Vice-director of the Salzburg Centre of European Union Studies. She is the Principal Investigator of the European Commission-funded Jean Monnet Centre of Excellence EUCHALLENGES (2023–2026). She is an Affiliated Researcher at the Law School of Sciences Po, Paris (France). She has published extensively on EMU-related topics, and especially on the Banking Union. Other areas of her research include parliaments and democracy within the EU and EU institutional matters generally.

Katerina Kalaitzaki has been a Lecturer in EU public law at the University of Central Lancashire (UCLan) Cyprus since September 2021, teaching and researching in the areas of EU constitutional law, fundamental rights, EU citizenship, and European values. She previously held an academic position in EU law at the University of Edinburgh with research and teaching responsibilities (September 2019–September 2021). She was awarded her PhD for her thesis, 'EU citizenship as a means of reinforcement of EU fundamental rights: challenges, developments, limits', in June 2019.

Nadja Sophia B. Kühn is Senior Researcher at NORCE Norwegian Research Centre, and holds a PhD in public administration (2020) from the University of Agder. Her research interests include public administration and governance, multilevel administration, European integration, international public administration, and decision-making behaviour, as well as institutional and organizational studies.

Stéphanie Laulhé Shaelou has lectured, researched, supervised, transferred knowledge, and run externally funded projects in several universities throughout Europe, including in the UK, for the past fifteen years. Her teaching and research cover multiple aspects of European law in an interdisciplinary setting, with a particular focus on aspects of European integration and fundamental rights, including in times of crisis. She is currently Professor of European Law and Reform and Head of the School of Law of the University of Central Lancashire, Cyprus.

Adam Łazowski is a Professor of EU law at the Westminster Law School, University of Westminster, as well as a Visiting Professor at the College of Europe (Natolin), and at the Ivan Franko National University of Lviv. His research focuses on EU pre-accession policy, EU external relations, the internal market, and EU Criminal Law, as well as withdrawal from the EU.

Dirk Leuffen is Professor of International Politics at the Department of Politics and Public Administration at the University of Konstanz. He has published widely on issues of (differentiated) European integration and decision-making. His current research interests include the role of fairness in public opinion, and international solidarity.

Petra Mahnič has been a member of the Council Legal Service (CLS) since 2004, following her graduate studies in law in Ljubljana and Amsterdam, postgraduate studies of EU law at the College of Europe in Bruges (LLM), and a tenure as legal adviser in the Constitutional Court of Slovenia. Her areas of specialization include EU common foreign and security policy (CFSP), common security and defence policy, EU restrictive measures, and public international law. She provides legal advice to various Council preparatory bodies, and acts as Council agent before the EU Courts. Since 2021, she has co-organized the annual executive training seminar on EU restrictive measures at the European University Institute of Florence (Florence School of Transnational Governance), Italy.. She is also a visiting professor at the College of Europe (Legal Department).

Marko Milenković is a Jean Monnet Fellow at the European University Institute in Florence. He is a Senior Research Fellow at the Institute of Social Sciences in Belgrade, Serbia, and an Affiliated Research Fellow at the Center for Constitutional Studies and Democratic Development (CCSDD), part of Johns Hopkins University School of Advanced International Studies (SAIS) in Bologna. His main research interests include legal transformation in the context of the European integration process, public administration reforms, and EU agency governance. He has also published in areas of environmental law, energy law, health law, and state aid.

Meltem Müftüler-Bac is currently Dean of Faculty of Arts and Social Sciences, and Professor of International Relations/Jean Monnet Chair at Sabanci University, Istanbul, Turkey. Prof Müftüler-Baç received her PhD (1992) in political science/international relations from Temple University, USA. She has authored more than fifty journal articles published in indexed, refereed journals; twenty-three book chapters in edited books with prestigious international presses; and her publications have appeared in numerous international outlets. She is widely cited in the fields of European integration, Turkish foreign policy, and international relations.

Andrea Ott is Professor of EU External Relations Law at the Law Faculty of Maastricht University. Since 2011, she has held a Jean Monnet Chair in EU law. She is co-director of CERIM (Centre for European Research in Maastricht) and a scholar at the Maastricht Centre for European Law (MCEL). She has wide experience in legal consultancy for Dutch ministries and the European Commission in Central and Eastern Europe, and teaches regularly on EU institutional law, EU external relations, enlargement, and WTO law in the Netherlands, Central and Eastern Europe, and Southeast Asia and China.

Maria Patrin is an Adjoint Lecturer and Research Fellow at the University of Florence. She holds an LLM and a PhD in law from the European University Institute (EUI) and a postgraduate master's degree from the College of Europe in Bruges. She has been Research Associate at the EUI. Prior to her academic career, Maria worked for several years in Brussels in the field of EU Public Affairs.

Benedikt Pirker is a Titularprofessor and Senior Lecturer at the Chair for European Law, International Law and Public Law of the University of Fribourg, and a Legal Advisor at the Swiss Federal Department of Foreign Affairs. He has taught, among others, at the Universities of St. Gallen, Bern, and Ottawa, and has conducted research at the European University Institute, Hebrew University Jerusalem, the Max Planck Institute for Comparative Public Law and International Law, and the University of Michigan. He is treasurer of the International

Language & Law Association (co-president 2021-2023) and is member of the editorial board of the 'Forum' of European Papers, and associate editor of the European Law Blog.

Jarle Trondal is a Professor in Political Science at University of Oslo and University of Agder, Norway. He is also a Senior Fellow at University of California, Berkeley. He holds a PhD in political science (2001) from the University of Oslo. His research interests include public policy and administration, organization theory, decision-making behaviour, and regional and international (dis)integration.

Tomasz P. Woźniakowski is an Assistant Professor at the Institute of Political Science, University of Wrocław, and Bekker Fellow at LUISS. He leads research projects on legitimacy of EU economic governance and fiscal solidarity in the EU and the US. His monograph *Fiscal Unions* was published by Oxford University Press in 2022.

Kathryn Wright is Senior Lecturer (Associate Professor) in Law at the University of York, UK. She supported and advised UK and Welsh parliamentary committees on scrutiny of the Brexit negotiations and outcomes, and earlier in her career worked at the European Parliament. Her research interests include EU administrative law, regulation and competition, and the role of courts in governance.

A Prologue

The Peoples of Europe: Ways that Unite and Ways that Divide

By Hubert Legal[*]

If the devil hides in the details,
prologues must be words of mercy.
(Secular Wisdom)

Once upon a time there were states in Europe which, in the exercise of their sovereignty, waged wars against each other as a continuation of politics by other means and concluded bilateral treaties to consolidate victories, facilitate trade, and encourage other forms of commerce. With the increased possibilities that capitalization and industry offered, this combined taste for conquest and law-making started to affect other continents. After two wars in the twentieth century that imperilled stability and prosperity worldwide, the 'Old World' was summoned by its most influential liberators to organize its reconstruction in ways that would contribute to peace, eliminate imperial designs, and open the continent to the activities of external economic and intellectual operators. For the part of Europe that found itself placed under the US umbrella, the influence of the federal model of supra-national institutions enjoyed a significant degree of attention, but little popular support. The idea was to transfer political authority from national constitutional bodies that had either contributed to or at least not prevented the conflicts and their atrocities to new collective institutions free from nefarious traditions and ruled by elevated morals, modern and rational methods, and the will to carry forward a liberal and federalist design against all local objections, which would prove mistaken over time.

* Former Councillor of State (France), former Judge at the General Court (Court of Justice of the European Union), former Legal Adviser of the Council and of the European Council. The opinions here expressed are purely personal, and in no way reflect either the views of these institutions or the past activities of the contributor in any of them.

But they have not, so far, proven mistaken. Part one of the plan worked and, with few if notable exceptions, the sense of pride and confidence that national institutions generally enjoyed in the populations concerned—thus contributing to the social link within each nation—has largely vanished, and for good reasons. Why put your trust in entities that are unable to deliver—be it for lack of will, lack of means, or lack of competence—the performance of the duties that justify their existence? But part two has so far failed and, on the receiving end of the planned transfer, no constitutional framework has, as yet, demonstrated its ability to offer a satisfactory substitute, both technically and politically, to exercise the sovereignty that has in part been removed from the national capitals. A collective European ethos has not yet taken shape as a political reality; the peoples have remained mentally far apart and put little hope in each other's support. No one should be blamed for that: we have put our common destinies on a bark that has left one side of a very broad river, while the other side is not yet in sight, and the water is getting shaky.

In a way, this situation offers a satisfaction to those around the world who regarded the involvement of European powers in international affairs as a cause for concern, since their potential to act as credible destabilizing factors has been seriously limited.

But seen from inside, and although dangerous times are not the best ones to undertake existential reviews, it is inevitable that the question comes to the minds of Union members of what the purpose is they want to achieve together. This is number one of all institutional issues. The choice of adequate organizational arrangements depends entirely on what objective they are intended to support. Today's is not smooth sailing and the crew should know where we are heading before grumbling becomes nasty. Moving to smaller boats may prove less dangerous, but it will not take us far, at least as a united entity. Unmanning the flagship, be it partially, may take us back to times when the Union did not exist.

There is a multiplicity of forms under which the EU currently operates or could operate, in some sectors. Does this imply that the distinction between members and non-members of the Union, as such, has lost its cardinal character, and that the attributes of membership should be reconsidered to reflect this diversity? In other words, does the coexistence of numerous ad hoc structures with special operating rules and variable participation essentially affect the unitary nature of the European political project? After twenty-two years of service in three institutions of the Union, and in spite of five years of effective retirement, my answer to that is clearly in the negative.

I come to this view after a bit of hesitation on the value of this personal judgement. Constitutional debates can be such a compound of reconstructed history and of institutional idealism that it is easy to get carried away for no valid reason. Taking care of this risk requires a degree of peace and serenity that is seldom available. Is it megalomania to think that nation-building is the only worthwhile constitutional effort? Is it paranoia to suspect that, the UK no longer being a member, some commentators will find that any distinction based on membership *of the Union* is overrated and that there is more than one way of working together? Is it being a populist to imagine that a degree of confusion might be viewed by some Euro-enthusiasts as a convenient way to circumvent the limitations put by the Treaties on political developments they desire? Is it ludicrous to suppose that, some promises of future membership having been made to third countries unlikely to obtain it, a formula of 'quasi-membership' could have been devised as a possible way out?

With the numerous elements of suspicion and prejudice surrounding the issue, the mental landscape is in a somewhat messy condition and may need some tidying up. To this end, an effort to eliminate clichés cannot be spared. After all, the meaning of membership is the meaning of the Union.

The statute of members of any entity, with the rights and obligations it entails, is normally designed in view of the aims and purpose of said entity. Why should your fishing society dictate that you change your car every year? The problem with the EU is that what is viewed by many, including myself, as essential in its ultimate objective is expressed by the founding documents in terms that are not most explicit—to say the least—to the lay reader and that, even to the expert, are subject to interpretation. You may indeed count on the competent judge to elucidate with authority the concepts and values in question. But, to put it bluntly, have we been heading from day one towards a federation and is it for a judge, however inspired by the US Supreme Court, to determine whether this is the case or not? Especially when the answer you may expect to receive is that it depends on what you mean by a federation! '*What you mean*'? Is it so difficult to understand? Have members entered a church or a shopping centre?—just to allow them to adjust their attitudes accordingly.

When the UK joined the European project, it was obviously not to participate in an exercise of fusion of the souls with continental partners but to be relieved of the economic disadvantages of staying outside the single market. This required the acceptance, on balance, of certain circumscribed transfers of competence. But it proved an impossible task to keep them circumscribed. One of the reasons for Brexit was a disagreement with the idea that the notion of an ever-closer union of the peoples of Europe could have any legal or material consequences. The European Court of Justice (ECJ) did rule that it had such consequences, which implies that an eventual weakening of the national bond between the Member States and their citizens forms part of the constitutional prospects for Europe. The UK did not accept this extension of the legal landscape of the Union beyond the material competences inscribed in the Treaties. It is clear that, on this particular issue, which is not as theoretical as it appears at first sight, the UK was not alone among the Member States. Acting with the aim of bringing peoples of different nations ever closer in their union requires an adequate attitude, including, for example, a consideration of what their respective cultural heritages can and cannot live with. Although it is clear that the passing of time and the successive enlargements have considerably reduced the reverence that was once due to the integrative process, a purely mercantilist approach is certainly not what the Treaties are about.

The aim of an ever-closer union of the peoples being an essential character of the Union, the operating methods imposed on members should be determined in view of their contribution to this aim and not, vice versa, the aim chosen on the basis of the availability of politically convenient organizational models. Institutional reforms for the sake of institutional reforms are a poor textbook recipe to address the crises caused by unwise politics, weak leadership, and the fear of facing the essential question of purpose.

'I'm only here for the beer...' is what I could read in London on posters advertising a famous brand during my linguistic holidays as a French schoolboy in the late sixties or early seventies, together with 'There's a terrific draught in here...'. I took it as a sarcastic lesson in no-nonsense materialism directed against romantic mythologies, as a tribute to the provocative attitude of the deliberate beer drinker unamused by the conventional *ritournelles* of the lovely old pub with a sloping meadow and gentle patrons. It was, to me, a cruel and naive joke in the spirit of the times, not a literal message. As a teenager, I tended to over-rationalize. There are dreamers; there are also thirsty people.

Some people just need the drink, or are too focused on themselves to see another light or hear another voice, heavy with a heart that belongs elsewhere; or they are just casual bullies inaccessible to any form of beauty—unless there is a terrific spirit around. No reason for not joining, of course. Some are only here for the single market; NATO for military protection and the EU for liberal economics, full stop. Why not? And why not, on top of it, accommodate their requests of private lounges for their special needs, inside or outside the premises?

You may appreciate that I do not attribute any scientific merit to this undiplomatic analogy, which was only formulated as an illustration of a subliminal message present at the back of many minds. Anyway, pick and choose may be fine, but it is far from the idea that has been put together by the founders and maintained by the Court—by which I do not mean to say that the first entrants must have the last word or that their idea is beyond reproach.

To think of it, it takes a lot of the teleological touch to find the whole project very attractive regarding the legal guarantees offered to the contracting parties, namely the Member States. The official story narrated to students of European institutional law is that the first fifty years of development of the Union, via the Communities and the Community, have been guided by a hidden agenda: the 'plan Schuman', which, *in the form of* a mere statement made in 1950 on behalf of the government of France, offered a road map *à la Moses*, eventually sanctified by politicians and academics, from limited steps of economic cooperation to the creation of irreversible bonds between the peoples, bringing about unobtrusively the inevitable erection of a sovereign constitutional order which, had it been submitted to a popular vote, would have been rejected—which, by the way, it was.

'In the form of...' says it all. Although formally a set of international agreements with a defined scope, neatly restricted over time by conferral, subsidiarity, and proportionality, the founding Treaties, 'unlike ordinary international treaties', constitute 'the basic constitutional charter' of a legal order which is 'new', 'independent from any other source of law', enjoys primacy and direct effect, and benefits from the transfer of sovereign rights 'in ever wider fields', in the Court's constant (or almost constant) language since 1963.[1] You may as well say that, by becoming a member, you take from the landlord the door key of a building yet to be constructed, and for which plans exist, but with more small print than actual drawings. Some judiciously located *passerelles* fail (or should fail) to reassure the perplexed candidate. It takes a lot of trust to go ahead. Fortunately, trust is a mandatory rule of the house, as a component of the principle of sincere cooperation with full mutual respect.

Moreover, it was only very late that a mention of the possibility to exit the new legal order was inserted in the Treaties. Admittedly, withdrawal is a sovereign right which Article 50, when it came, only 'enshrined',[2] but considering such a move without any arrangements in place regarding the process was a tall order in view of the 'structured network of principles, rules and mutually interdependent legal relations binding the European Union and its Member States' that the Treaties imply.

Certainly, the EU Treaties differ from 'ordinary' international law, or even from ordinary law altogether, insofar as the essential purpose of the law (if I may be excused for the pomposity) is to ensure the degree of stability in social relations without which no valuable human undertaking may durably flourish. For this purpose, the law must be certain in its requirements and predictable in its application. No party to a convention should, therefore, be bound by rules it has not voluntarily subscribed to in full and conscious understanding of what they mean. If the convention allows for the elaboration of norms secondary to it, the making and the effect of such norms must remain in strict accordance with the primary law that offers them a scope for existence within pre-established limits.

It is open to discussion to what extent this predicament is compatible with the narrative according to which the Union and its precursors have been designed as organizations with a limitative set of material competences, but also with a purpose reaching beyond the competences conferred upon them and *providing a basis for their interpretation*. This purpose is undoubtedly, in my view, the political and societal integration of European nations, for which, however, the Union was—and remains—mainly devoid of direct legal authority.

[1] Judgment of the ECJ (Full Court) of 10 December 2018 in Case C-621/18 *Wightman and others*, EU:C:2018:999, at points 44 and 45 and the case law cited therein.

[2] ibid at point 57. The French word used is '*consacré*'.

If the Union does not (or does not yet) have this authority, it is solely because this would require Treaty bases, and to this effect Treaty changes, for which political support is manifestly lacking. This became very notable at the end of the Juncker Commission, during the drafting of its last State of the Union speech, and was further confirmed on 9 May 2022, when the representatives of thirteen Member States formally declared, regarding the outcome and follow-up of the Conference on the Future of Europe, that they did not regard the launching of a process of institutional reforms as timely. Even more Member States seemed to share this view.

An imbalance is thus permanently in place between deliberately conservative and mainly modest Treaty texts and a more aggressive political ambition, claiming that mere legal or procedural obstacles should not prevent the Union from accomplishing what it is best placed to accomplish in the general interest. To address this tension, the institutions have either consciously, unconsciously, or reluctantly acted along several trends, the first being the tendency to occupy as much material ground as possible by legislating very close to the limits of what is allowed by primary law, even broadly interpreted; the second the reliance on concepts elaborated upon by jurisprudence and building on the common values to extend the realm of EU control without having to amend the Treaties; the third the credo propagated by European schools and scholars that there is a sub-text in the EU Treaties by virtue of which there are some unwritten rules which are implied by practical provisions that have been inserted over time (like liberal economics and liberal democracy) and, conversely, some explicit clauses which have been inserted for the sake of compromise only and which are not meant to be effectively made use of (like subsidiarity and the respect of national traditions); the fourth the will to minimize unobtrusively but systematically the capacity of Member States to act autonomously at national level; and the fifth the sustained political effort to marginalize anti-federalist opinions by calling them 'Eurosceptic' and assimilating them to extremist nationalism, 'illiberalism', or populism, thus justifying procedural devices to bypass their supporters.

Sixth, but not least, recourse to structures and procedures placed outside the ordinary legislative framework or, more radically, outside the Treaty bases has also contributed to satisfy frustrated ambitions without violating EU law or changing its basic rules.

All these examples (on which my intention is not to pass judgement) manifestly reveal a continuous will to maintain a firm integrative purpose in legislative and executive action in spite of difficulties of a legal nature. Opponents may call it manipulation and complacency and the abstract (or literal) lawyer may well take issue with certain far-fetched constructions that are not technically rock-solid. I have had my share of that. However, if certain 'short-cuts' are able to be accepted by all Union members and to be blessed by the Court in its teleological benevolence, there are moments when an excessive confidence placed on theoretical reasoning might prove inopportune or plainly nonsensical. But, to me, the political red line for such facilities is that there is, whatever the voting rules, a consensus among Member States to use them and that no Member is pressured to join such a consensus by unfair methods. Such unfairness on matters of high political importance at national level would create durable frustrations and ruin the objective of long-term integration that the above-named efforts are meant to serve.

Seen from this angle, the multiplicity of forms of action available ought to be regarded as a means to avoid confrontation and, in so doing, to protect the process of integration, rather than as a dissolution of the common purpose into a myriad of unrelated circumstantial devices. But there are conditions for this to work properly, on which the Court set its views clearly, following the referral to it of the ESM Treaty,[3] concluded as an intergovernmental agreement (IGA) between Member States.[4] In essence, the perception of this judgment by the legal services of the institutions was, at the time, in my memory, that the Court looked at the purpose and effects of an IGA, rather than its form, to assess whether it could hamper the development of EU legislation proper or jeopardize its objectives or whether it could contribute, while respecting existing EU law and the rights of all members, to improve the coherence of the approaches of Member States when delivering their responsibilities outside the Union's exclusive competence, and thus facilitate the intellectual and practical integration of their national bodies.

Ad hoc legal tools supplementing the action of standard EU mechanisms where they cannot work effectively are not, per se, to be regarded as carrying a risk for the integrity of the Union. That the ordinary legislative procedure, aka the 'Community method', could be the only reliable and pure form of collective action of the Union and its members is something I have never believed. Special instruments do not necessarily conduce to a change of methods for the processes and bodies they create, as compared with orthodox instruments of EU law; rather the opposite. The Court has always accepted that EU institutions could be tasked by non-EU mechanisms in the strict sense, as long as this did not alter the nature of their functions.[5] As to agencies, there is no evidence that the legal form of the decisions creating them systematically generates a difference in their modus operandi. All this is subject to the conditions that EU law is applied and that a judicial review by the ECJ is foreseen.

In few words, by allowing rivulets to encircle and bypass the institutional and procedural obstacles along the road, the fluid or informal method providing for a multiplicity of organizational designs has created a differentiated approach leading to the objective of furthering economic, social, and societal integration, or at least

[3] Treaty establishing the European stability mechanism between the Member States whose currency is the euro, signed on 2 February 2012.

[4] Judgment of the ECJ of 27 November 2012 in Case C-370/12 *Pringle v Government of Ireland*, EU:C:2012:756.

[5] Judgment of the ECJ of 30 June 1993 in Joined Cases C-181/91 and C-248/91 *Parliament v Council* (the '*Bangladesh*' case), EU:C:1993:271.

protecting it from a radical questioning. It has, in my own perception, not made membership of the Union proper less relevant.

Admittedly, it is not such a big deal to accept that one may take the high road rather than the low road to go to Scotland, as long as it is only a matter of how much time you need to get there. But that takes it for granted that all concerned are actually on their way to Scotland, which is in the present case, and with my apologies to the Scots, a largely undefined or partly unaccepted concept. If the destination vanishes, the purpose goes with it, and the sense of direction is replaced by a myriad of fruit-pickers garnishing their baskets and oblivious of the promised land.

If it is the case that not everybody is on board, and that Britain was not the only state for which the main question was not when but what or where to (as the pre-Brexit discussions made clear), the EU is faced with the need to choose the right strategy to deal with this internal conflict: to diminish its original ambitions (and there the option of a fallback into a generalization of specialized agreements with varying composition becomes pertinent), to reduce its membership (which would come a bit late, since no Member State may be forced to go!)[6], to separate gently those who want more from those who have enough (by a special treaty topping the EU and designed for the federalists only), or by pushing ahead unheeded. In this last and most probable case, there is a secondary choice of going about it patiently, carrying on with the small-step method without exerting force against any member, or of doing it brutally, with the element of violence against national sovereignty present in the episodes of crisis management we have extensively experienced recently (spare a thought for Greece) and with the idea that the panic mode will bring about, in fact if not in law—or at least in good law—further sovereignty transfers. I have never made a mystery of where I stood on this division, but this is not the point here.

The brutal handling could take a form which I find at odds with equal treatment and mutual respect but would not call illegal, in view of where the Court stands on the subject[7], ie the form of the differentiated perimeters that institutions have given themselves the right to introduce in legislation or implementation by carving out from the benefits of EU funding the territories of Member States that have been categorized as disrespectful of the rule of law. This legal concept stems from two traditions: the German (and French) one, following which the law must be universally applied and respected, and the authority of lawmakers and courts of justice ensured; and the British one, which goes further to say that guaranteed situations (including privileges) must be safeguarded against the possible effects of political change, including those brought about by a democratic choice. A confusion

[6] *Wightman* (n 1) at points 66 and 67: 'It would be inconsistent with the Treaties' purpose of creating an ever-closer union among the peoples of Europe to force the withdrawal of a Member State.'

[7] Judgments of the ECJ (Plenary Assembly) of 16 February 2022 in Cases C-156/21 *Hungary v Parliament and Council, EU:C:2022:97*, and C-157/21 *Poland v Parliament and Council, EU:C:2022:98*.

between the two very different branches—one limiting the democratic principle, the other not necessarily so—led to an abusive and politically motivated recourse to the notion, in particular to attack 'populist' tendencies.[8]

Differentiations on this basis, which I am tempted to regard as punitive in disguise and consequential upon the difficulties inherent to the use of Article 7, may, incidentally, have the practical effect of putting pressure on a Member State reluctant to support an act requiring unanimity in Council for its adoption. Unlike other measures of differentiation, it is improbable that it may bring about an elevation of the global spirit of solidarity.

It is not, however, as if all other measures of territorial differentiation were in principle voluntary, as the familiar terminology of 'opt-ins' and 'opt-outs' could suggest. Quite to the opposite, in many of the cases when not all EU members participate in a restricted mechanism, there is no free choice either to take it or to leave it.

Just look at two of the major cases, namely the euro and Schengen. The euro is the currency of the Union as a whole and only the Member States 'in respect of which the Council has not decided that they fulfil the necessary conditions for the adoption of the euro'[9] shall have a derogation of transitional character (save one Member State that has an exception instead). The single currency is a full-fledged policy of the Union. As to the Schengen rules, although originally based on specific agreements under international law, they are fully integrated within the provisions of the area of freedom, security, and justice and, with one exception again, the only Member States that are not free from controls at internal borders are the new partners that have not yet been found to meet the conditions. Related measures are adopted as policies of the Union.

Have a look also at the system of enhanced cooperations, which was intended to be the standard device to allow the smooth integration of a regrouping of the willing into the global EU policies. It certainly succeeded in keeping the lawyers busy for a while trying to clarify the implications of Articles 326 to 334 TFEU, but in practice it has remained totally marginal, not to say unsuccessful.

There is a good reason for the Member States' wish to stay together in a single framework, which is that the fundamental asset of being an EU member is to sit around the Council table. If you are not there, you do not exist. Ask the states bound to apply EU law without being associated with the decision-making with full voting rights whether this is an attractive situation. There are examples of this, including EFTA states, who often make their frustration heard, or even the UK

[8] This was made sadly evident when the President of the Commission publicly declared on 24 September 2022, on the occasion of elections about to take place in a Member State and with reference to the use of the 'rule of law conditionality' vis-à-vis two other Member States: '[i]f things go in a difficult direction, we have the tools' which cast a strong doubt on whether, in her eyes, the purpose of the conditionality really is good spending.

[9] Article 139, paragraph 1, TFEU.

during the separation process, who tolerated the humiliation of forced absence from the table only because it was a short prelude to its complete independence.

It may sound improper to single out one institution as being more essential than others, but if we talk about membership there is no equality, and it is the Council that matters, even more in my view (and I know many observers do not agree, for perfectly acceptable reasons) than the European Council, which has no legislative role, and, for most of its deliberations, does not proceed by votes but by consensus (which is something totally different from unanimity), and whose conclusions, not being legal acts of the Union but essentially political documents, are not enforceable.[10]

But whether it is the Council or the European Council that matters most makes little difference to the point here, which is that the association of third countries with Union actions and their participation in the work of the organs put in place to manage them, on a permanent or temporary basis, does not—and in my view cannot—offer an equivalent or a substitute to full EU membership, which has much more in it than the collective management of policies. Things would, of course, be different if political integration was no longer on the agenda, in spite of the Court's interpretation of the objectives of the Union in the Treaties.

It was an urban legend before Brexit that, instead of the rigidity of a centralized structure of power of the Soviet style, there was room for a more relaxed future with a flowering conglomerate of autonomous spheres of action, informally or lightly connected in the form of networks, and without a hierarchy ('clusters' as opposed to 'vertical authority'). This tempting and ever-so-poetic political dream (so remote, by the way, from the British system of government) was offered by the UK and its not so few supporters, in search of modernism as an alternative to the final goodbye. The centre would disappear (only at EU level of course), and it would not matter whether you were in or out globally; the truth is in details, hierarchy is totalitarian and diversity is equalitarian. The ensemble would be fluid and wide open to third parties; in other words (the world being as it is), inexistent as an autonomous political agent.

The situation convincingly described in 2011 by Jean-Claude Piris[11] was one where, in the context of the recent enlargements, of the failed constitution, and of the implementation of the Lisbon Treaty, the prospects of further transfers of competence had become uncertain, and the notion of '*Europe à la carte*' had started gaining popularity. To avoid a dilution of the process of integration in a myriad of autonomous arrangements with their own rules and memberships, it was wise to consider the option of a two-speed Europe, with the current setting of material and

[10] And which has been designed as a Heads-only setting, making it quite difficult for individual leaders to resist the pressure of their peers and to put the interests of their country before their alleged duties as members of the so-called 'club'.

[11] J.-C. Piris, *The Future of Europe: Towards a Two-Speed EU?* (CUP 2011). The author was the Director-General of the Council Legal Service. Apologies are offered for the oversimplification.

institutional rules remaining in place for all members, but with a possibility for those interested to move further and faster in their integration while remaining in the Union, but without forcing their views on the rest of the membership.

This would certainly have been a model of great merit and attractiveness had the UK remained a member. The UK's continued membership would have entailed for the Union as a whole, in terms of structures and mechanisms, considerable consequences, described in the 'New Settlement for the United Kingdom within the European Union',[12] which, before ceasing to be in existence, after the UK's vote to leave, had been conditionally but unanimously adopted as a matter of international law by the Members of the European Council, on 18–19 February 2016. Among detailed arrangements institutionalizing differentiated regimes on a permanent basis in several areas, irrespective of any prospect of an eventual uniformization, and aiming to protect the rights of non-participants, this document went as far as to state that the Treaty reference to an ever-closer union of the peoples of Europe was neither a rule as such nor an instrument of interpretation of other EU rules.

If representatives of certain Member States joined the Commission in pinching their noses when accepting such language, others manifestly had nothing against it in principle, and, rather, perceived it as a reassurance for themselves. The result would not only have been a multi-speed Europe, which implies only a diversity

[12] A New Settlement for the United Kingdom within the European Union, Extract of the conclusions of the European Council of 18–19 February 2016 (2016/C 69 I/01): 'Intending to clarify in this Decision certain questions of particular importance to the Member States so that such clarification will have to be taken into consideration as being an instrument for the interpretation of the Treaties; . . . Recalling that the Treaties, together with references to the process of European integration and to the process of creating an ever closer union among the peoples of Europe, contain also specific provisions whereby some Member States are entitled not to take part in or are exempted from the application of certain provisions or chapters of the Treaties and Union law as concerns matters such as the adoption of the euro, decisions having defence implications, the exercise of border controls on persons, as well as measures in the area of freedom, security and justice. Treaty provisions also allow for the non-participation of one or more Member States in actions intended to further the objectives of the Union, notably through the establishment of enhanced cooperation. Therefore, such processes make possible different paths of integration for different Member States, allowing those that want to deepen integration to move ahead, whilst respecting the rights of those which do not want to take such a course; . . . SECTION CSOVEREIGNTY. The references in the Treaties and their preambles to the process of creating an ever closer union among the peoples of Europe do not offer a legal basis for extending the scope of any provision of the Treaties or of EU secondary legislation. They should not be used either to support an extensive interpretation of the competences of the Union or of the powers of its institutions as set out in the Treaties. These references do not alter the limits of Union competence governed by the principle of conferral, or the use of Union competence governed by the principles of subsidiarity and proportionality. They do not require that further competences be conferred upon the European Union or that the European Union must exercise its existing competences, or that competences conferred on the Union could not be reduced and thereby returned to the Member States. The competences conferred by the Member States on the Union can be modified, whether to increase or reduce them, only through a revision of the Treaties with the agreement of all Member States. The Treaties already contain specific provisions whereby some Member States are entitled not to take part in or are exempted from the application of certain provisions of Union law. The references to an ever-closer union among the peoples are therefore compatible with different paths of integration being available for different Member States and do not compel all Member States to aim for a common destination. The Treaties allow an evolution towards a deeper degree of integration among the Member States that share such a vision of their common future, without this applying to other Member States.'

of rhythm that the UK could not have been satisfied with, but, more fundamentally, a multidimensional scope, a variety of statuses open to national choice, and a relegation of the 'ever-closer' purpose to a merely optional and non-binding credo having no concrete effect concerning the law or its interpretation.[13]

This is why the protracted and painful process of separation of the UK was a traumatic event for many, but also offered some amount of relief to those, in the institutions and in the Member States at government level, who value the cultural and institutional unification as much as—or more than—the down-to-earth regulatory achievements; the big design as much as—or more than—the little steps patiently negotiated.

For the orphans left behind by the UK among their traditional allies in institutional games, the time was ripe to rethink their tactics, if not their strategies. This was made all the more necessary, for them as well as for all, by the occurrence of new crises of which the effects still remain to be assessed. Except for the happy and obstinate few, politicians may well now have on their minds more pressing activities than cherry-picking and rocket-launching in the field of institutions. Beyond circumstantial claims of unity, conflicts between real national interests are perceptible even to the outsider, so that the Union may be heading towards its most radical existential challenges ever. It cannot simply collapse, in particular because the Member States—even those who could in earlier days count on robust national institutions—have probably lost the ability to operate on their own; but it could be confronted with major political setbacks, annihilating whatever it possesses of the power of self-determination and initiative. This could be the case if trust between Member States and between Member States and institutions was no longer there, except on paper, and if the Court, although attempting to accomplish its traditional duty to stabilize and consolidate the long-term process, was unable to restart it, as it did in the past.

This might, of course, be the case if enlargements on a major scale were again organized, after the fall in the degree of empathy and mutual understanding which followed the previous ones, and, even more so, if new accessions were preceded by institutional reforms intended to differentiate the application of EU law in the broadest sense and to deprive Member States of the guarantee of control they retain in sensitive areas through unanimity and consensus.

In the catastrophic case of a complete collapse of mutual trust, a transfer of authority from the single centre—having become a hindrance rather than an asset—towards diverse and autonomous sectorial focal points might be the only remaining rational choice to contain the damage in the general interest. But this

[13] The Court's position was made abundantly clear, however, when it stated (once the 'settlement' had disappeared from the legal landscape) that the objective of an ever-closer union was indeed a source to be used to give EU rules their proper interpretation (*Wightman* (n 1) at points 61 and 65), which, incidentally, proved the British concern to be justified, from their viewpoint.

would be the end of an important episode in European history. Such things have happened before to major undertakings; but we may not be there yet. This is, in my view, fortunate since we have nothing on offer that can decently replace the 'ever-closer' guideline, however clumsy its legal construction, unfair its methods, and irritating the way some of its supporters behave.

I express the strongest reservation about the idea that, in the face of the perils brought about by massive uncontrolled migration, epidemic diseases, intensifying military activities, fragility of the financial system, radicalization of geopolitical tensions, and climate change, any form of collective reaction by the Union, whatever its substance, its form, or its methods, will necessarily unite us; it may divide us. Unguided projection in an uncertain future, on the assumption that shouting together in the dark will make us stronger anyway, is an adventurous, almost irresponsible, course of action for a sovereign agent.

To gain or regain a status as a first-rank interlocutor in world affairs, and not as a mere subsidiary of the 'global West', with institutions receiving and deserving little interest, the EU should primarily re-establish trust in its own merits by avoiding the return of the violent and punitive rhetoric that has, in the past, justified its creation, showing belief in its legal personality, and persisting in its fundamental character of a union based on law, meaning that its rules are not to be found in circumstantial political pronouncements but in proper legal norms—certain in their sources, adopted through established and verifiable procedures, and linked together by a clear hierarchy. Indifference to form leads to tyranny, because it blurs the difference between opinions and legal norms by giving the former the authority of the law and depriving the latter of their full and unconditional force. Therefore, as things currently stand, it is the lawyers' duty to differentiate, between different bodies and fora revolving around the Union and its members, those which contribute to the making of elements of the law of the Union and those which, rather, serve a purpose of communication or diplomacy or create associations without a normative character.

The day when 'communities' with associate third parties—whatever the attractive terminology used to describe them—will be essential tools of our collective being as an institutional order, rather than important but accessory discussion fora, will be the time to realize that this order is in pretty bad shape.

To keep it in good shape, it has to be better understood that the pursuit of the objective of an ever-closer union can and must go hand in hand with the scrupulous respect of Treaty-based requirements, notably as regards authority and procedure which are the guardians of fairness. Progressive integration requires respect and patience, with a careful and attentive implementation of existing rules, more than the constant and sometimes brutal search for new transfers of competence even when the time is not ripe for their smooth achievement.

As regards diversity of forms of collective action among Member States, ranging from sheer cooperation to exclusive Union competence, including with differentiated application, these are all instruments that may be used for a long-term incremental process respecting the traditions, structures, economies, and political intentions of the European nations concerned and building on them a collective future—if there is sufficient will and reason to carry on calmly and decently in this direction.

1

Introduction—(Re)defining Membership? Current and Future Perspectives for EU Differentiated Integration

Diane Fromage[*]

I. Why Seek to (Re)define European Union Membership? And Why Do so Now?

At first sight, it would appear as though the question of the definition of membership of the European Union (EU) is superfluous. The Treaty on EU (TEU) unequivocally defines in its Article 1 that the contracting parties are the Member States of the EU. As such, what membership of the EU entails seems to be straightforward, and states are either members of it or they are not.

However, closer examination could cast some doubt on this unitary status of Member States, or at the very least it could reveal that it needs nuancing.[1] While diversity, and to some extent differentiation or even fragmentation, have been part and parcel of the European integration process since its very beginning, several developments invite a new reflection on *membership within the EU*, and relatedly on *differentiation in and outside the EU today*.

There is little doubt that the EU has been characterized by growing diversity within its territory over time. This diversity has been induced by several factors, the most obvious of which is the growing number of Member States because of the seven waves of enlargement that have happened since the 1970s, when the European Communities first opened their doors to Denmark, Ireland, and the UK. This growth in the number of EU Member States has resulted in an ever-increasing variety of, inter alia, cultural understandings and traditions, and economic and geopolitical interests, having to be accommodated. Consequently, differentiation—which can be defined as 'the process that allows some EU member

* Warm thanks are owed to Jonathan Bauerschmidt, Andreas Schirk, and Bruno de Witte for their insightful comments on an earlier version of this Introduction.

[1] This introduction, and this edited volume, do not consider the role EU membership may play for its Member States. Indeed, some have argued that '"member statehood" is both a simple juridical term and a distinctive and new kind of state, where membership of the EU plays a constitutive role in the life of the state': Christopher J Bickerton, 'Member States in European Integration' in Simon Bulmer and Christian Lequesne (eds), *The Member States of the European Union* (3rd edn, OUP 2018) 30.

Diane Fromage, *Introduction—(Re)defining Membership? Current and Future Perspectives for EU Differentiated Integration* In: *Redefining EU Membership*. Edited by: Diane Fromage, Oxford University Press. © Diane Fromage 2024.
DOI: 10.1093/9780191948145.003.0001

states to go further in the integration process, while allowing others to opt not to do so',[2] or as 'the facilitation or accommodation of a degree of difference between Member States or regions in relation to what would otherwise be common . . . Union policy'[3]—has become a more visible and widespread feature of the EU as the process of European integration has progressed. Differentiation exists in an external and an internal dimension, whereby some non-EU states participate in some EU policies (external differentiation), while EU rules do not apply uniformly to all Member States (internal differentiation).[4] In other words, some Member States have opted out of certain policy areas, such as border controls or the single currency, while various non-Member States (third states) participate frequently in selected EU policies, such as the Schengen area. Beyond this, EU norms are diffused in various ways outside of the EU.

It therefore appears that even if membership to the EU is clearly defined in the Treaties (Art. 1 TEU), in practice this unitary status does not fully materialize.

As a consequence, EU Membership could seem to have become a somewhat fuzzy concept in practice, and if considered from a non-legal and, especially, a political science perspective. The use of the term 'membership' in a strictly legally accurate manner by the European Commission itself adds to this impression of confusion.[5]

Against this background, and also with a view to the greater complexity that the EU is confronted with post-Brexit, and with the prospect of possible future enlargements, a new reflection on the issue of membership within the EU appears necessary.

In particular, the question should be asked as to *what differentiates EU Member States from states that merely participate in some of the EU's policies, ie what EU membership means in today's EU.* More generally, the question arises as to whether the concept of membership needs to be redefined: should we go beyond the concept of unitary membership as it has existed so far? Also, is, for instance, the requirement set on any new Member State to adopt the whole *acquis communautaire*, first imposed by France when the UK joined the European Economic Community, still justifiable and appropriate? Beyond the sole question of membership, what is the current status of differentiated integration within the EU, and how can and

[2] Thierry Chopin and Christian Lequesne, 'Differentiation as a Double-edged Sword: Member States' Practices and Brexit' (2016) 92(3) International Affairs 531–45, 531.

[3] Bruno de Witte, Dominik Hanf, and Ellen Vos, 'Introduction' in Bruno de Witte, Dominik Hanf, and Ellen Vos (eds), *The Many Faces of Differentiation in EU Law* (Intersentia 2001) xii.

[4] Dirk Leuffen, Berthold Rittberger, and Frank Schimmelfennig, *Differentiated Integration: Explaining Variation in the European Union* (Palgrave Macmillan 2013) 18–19.

[5] The European Commission indeed referred to Ukraine's 'full membership' in the EU's civil protection mechanism in April 2023, whereas Ukraine is formally 'only' a participating state to it: European Commission, 'Ukraine Joins the EU Civil Protection Mechanism'. <https://civil-protection-humanitarian-aid.ec.europa.eu/news-stories/news/ukraine-joins-eu-civil-protection-mechanism-2023-04-20_en> accessed 23 April 2023.

should it evolve going forward? These are the main questions that this edited volume seeks to answer.

This is not only a pressing academic agenda, but in the context of current debates about the future shape of the EU (as discussed during the Conference on the Future of Europe (2022))[6] and its relationship to its neighbours (inter alia in the framework of the recent European Political Community)[7] it is also an important practical consideration. On the one hand, former Commission President Juncker had clearly expressed his preference that the EU should remain united (notably in his State of the Union speeches of 2017 and 2018),[8] thereby rejecting the perspective of a multi-speed or differentiated EU, called for by others at the time, such as French President Macron.[9] On the other hand, in a Union facing the prospect of further diversity with the arrival of new Member States, as well as centrifugal tendencies among the existing members—most prominently expressed in the withdrawal of the UK and the recurring violation of the EU's values by Hungary and Poland—the question arises whether the idea of a single united membership, as currently foreseen in the Treaty, is still fit to facilitate effective governance and accommodate growing diversity.

This edited volume addresses these issues by asking what membership means in the current practice of the EU, and thus what the current status of differentiation is. It provides a reflection on what is required for the future EU, and is organized around *four aspects* of the tensions faced by the concept of a unitary and formal EU membership: first, an examination of key policy areas which have already witnessed various forms of differentiated integration; second, an analysis of 'special statuses' within the EU; third, important examples of non-Member States in which EU law is applied (with and without their participation in the EU's decision-making process); and, fourth, the situation of states under accession or secession procedures which oblige them to accept EU norms and policies even prior to/after formal membership. These analyses are complemented by a reflection on the concept of membership in itself.

II. EU Membership and Differentiation in and outside the Union: Definition, Evolution, and State of the Art

The concept of *EU Membership* and what it entails was clarified with the adoption of the Lisbon Treaty. Article 4 TEU now details the characteristics inherent to the

[6] https://wayback.archive-it.org/12090/20230216155930/https://futureu.europa.eu/en/ accessed 26 April 2023.

[7] European Political Community (europa.eu) accessed 26 April 2023.

[8] https://ec.europa.eu/commission/presscorner/detail/en/SPEECH_17_3165; https://commission.europa.eu/system/files/2018-09/soteu2018-speech_en_0.pdf both accessed 26 April 2023.

[9] Emmanuel Macron, 'Initiative for Europe' (Sorbonne speech, Paris, 26 September 2017) https://international.blogs.ouest-france.fr/archive/2017/09/29/macron-sorbonne-verbatim-europe-18583.html accessed 26 April 2023.

statute of EU Member States. It clarifies the domain of their competence, ie all of the competences that have not been conferred upon the EU. It establishes equality among them,[10] and states the respect for their identity,[11] as well as the principle of sincere cooperation. It also defines Member States' obligations towards the Union, as they are to 'take any appropriate measure, general or particular, to ensure fulfilment of the obligations arising out of the Treaties or resulting from the acts of the institutions of the Union', and to 'facilitate the achievement of the Union's tasks and refrain from any measure which could jeopardise the attainment of the Union's objectives' (Art. 4(3) TEU). At first sight, being an EU Member State is thus characterized by the existence of a series of rights and obligations,[12] but this edited volume will seek to identify whether there are other features inherent to that status, as will be further detailed.

Differentiation, on the other hand, is one of the defining features of European integration, as it has arguably always existed within the European Communities, and still characterizes today's EU. Differentiation took, and still takes, various forms, including derogations at primary law level, as well as differentiation in the implementation of European norms, most notably in the transposition of directives, which leave it up to the Member States to define how to reach the defined objective.[13] A proper debate on differentiation within the EU, understood as 'multi-speed Europe', started to arise in the 1970s, notably when the *Tindemans Report* was adopted in 1975.[14] At that point in time, the possibility for some of the Member States to integrate faster than others was envisaged, while all of them were still expected to catch up at a later stage. Differentiation was formally anchored in primary law, for the first time, in the Single European Act (Art. 8c), and became much more extended at Maastricht, when several opt-outs were permitted to the UK and Denmark. A further step towards differentiation was taken at Amsterdam, when the possibility of enhanced cooperation was introduced in the Treaties.[15] Lisbon

[10] On this concept, see Pauline Corre-Dumoulin, 'L'égalité entre Etats membres de l'Union européenne et la differentiation: de la compatibilité affirmée à l'inconciabilité exacerbée' in Laurence Potvin-Solis (ed), *Le statut d'Etat membre dans l'Union européenne* (Bruylant 2018) 531–63; Jan Wouters, 'Constitutional Limits of Differentiation: The Principle of Equality' in de Witte, Hanf and Vos (eds) (n 3) 301–45.

[11] Further, on the concept of national identity, see Diane Fromage and Bruno de Witte (eds), 'Special Issue in European Public Law'; Diane Fromage and Bruno de Witte, 'National Constitutional Identity Ten Years on: State of Play and Future Perspectives' (2021) 27(3) European Public Law 411–26.

[12] See, further, Paul Craig, 'EU Membership: Formal and Substantive Dimensions' (2020) 22 Cambridge Yearbook of European Legal Studies 6ff.

[13] Bruno de Witte, 'Variable Geometry and Differentiation as Structural Features of the EU Legal Order' in Bruno de Witte, Andrea Ott, and Ellen Vos (eds), *Between Flexibility and Disintegration: The Trajectory of Differentiation in EU Law* (Edward Elgar 2017).

[14] Tindemans Report on European Union of 29 December 1975: https://www.cvce.eu/en/collections accessed 26 April 2023.

[15] On the debates existing at the time, see Alexander Stubb, 'Negotiating Flexible Integration in the Amsterdam Treaty' in Antje Wiener and Karlheinz Neureither (eds), *European Integration after Amsterdam: Institutional Dynamics and Prospects for Democracy* (OUP 2000).

confirmed this trend, inter alia by foreseeing various possibilities of enhanced co-operation and permanent cooperation, and by formalizing the distinction between the euro area and the EU27.[16] Differentiation hence covers a variety of concepts and situations that include 'multi-speed Europe', 'Europe à la carte', 'variable geometry Europe', opt-outs, and enhanced cooperation of various kinds,[17] and is generally 'the general mode of integration strategies which try to reconcile heterogeneity within the European Union'.[18] Differentiation may, in some cases, be temporary, as is for instance the case when transitional arrangements are made for new Member States entering the Union, or when Member States do not yet comply with the criteria to join a specific policy area, and are, therefore, temporarily excluded from it, as happens in the euro area. Differentiation may, however, be more long-lasting or permanent, for instance where Member States are granted opt-outs, or where Member States integrate outside of the EU Treaty framework, as under those circumstances no obligation exists that would force the participating Member State to admit another state at a later stage (or would force non-participating Member States to join eventually). Beyond the formal legal status of permanent and temporary differentiation, practice—and the contributions to this edited volume—additionally show that, in no few cases, differentiation that is meant to be temporary in fact becomes permanent. Moreover, differentiation (or differentiated integration) is perceived differently by the various actors involved, and by Member States in particular:

> in some Member States that have been members of the Union for longer, it can have positive connotations and be associated with the idea of creating a "pioneer group" designed to achieve more rapid progress in deepening integration, while in the Member States that joined the Union more recently it is often perceived as a path towards the creation of first- and second-class Member States.[19]

For all the reasons mentioned, as some have noted, 'there are . . . reasons to assume that European integration will remain differentiated'.[20] Some have gone as far as to claim that '[t]he future of Europe will be one of differentiated integration',[21] a prediction which the fact that there are hardly any policy areas where there are

[16] Reference is made here to the possibility, provided for in Art 136(2) TFEU, that only euro-area representatives in the Council partake in the voting process. On the various forms of enhanced cooperation provided for by the Lisbon Treaty, see 'The Implementation of Enhanced Cooperation in the EU' (europa.eu) accessed 26 April 2023.

[17] See further on these models, Daniel Thym, 'Competing Models for Understanding Differentiated Integration' in de Witte, Ott, and Vos (eds) (n 13) 28–75.

[18] Alexander Stubb, 'A Categorization of Differentiated Integration' (1996) 34 Journal of Common Market Studies 283–95, 283.

[19] European Parliament Resolution on differentiated integration, Recital C.

[20] Dirk Leuffen, Berthold Rittberger, and Frank Schimmelfennig, 'Introduction' in Leuffen, Rittberger, and Schimmelfennig (eds) (n 4) xx.

[21] Vivien A Schmidt, 'The Future of Differentiated Integration: A "Soft-Core" Multi-Clustered Europe of Overlapping Policy Communities' (2019) 17 *Comparative European Politics* 294.

no instances of internal and/or external differentiation, as shown by Dirk Leuffen, appears to support.

Differentiation in the European integration process has given rise to a significant strand of research, both in law and political science. [22] By contrast, the concept of *EU membership* has so far attracted only limited scholarly attention.[23] This edited volume adds to the existing literature on differentiated integration, which it updates and complements, while devoting enhanced attention to the concept of membership and its future.

Among the most recent publications on differentiated integration are the volumes edited by Benjamin Leruth, Stefan Gänzle, and Jarle Trondal;[24] the volume edited by Richard Bellamy, Sandra Kröger, and Marta Lorimer;[25] the one by Frank Schimmelfennig and Thomas Winzen;[26] and the ones by Bruno de Witte, Andrea Ott, and Ellen Vos;[27] Thomas Giegerich and others;[28] by Benjamin Leruth and Christopher Lord;[29] and by Stefan Gänzle, Benjamin Leruth, and Jarle Trondal.[30] Dirk Leuffen, Bertold Rittberger, and Frank Schimmelfennig also published a seminal book on this issue.[31]

The EU's relationship to third states, and the different policies it has developed in this field, have equally been the object of several (recent) publications, including

[22] Several book chapters and journal articles have regularly addressed the topic of differentiated integration as well. These include, among others, from a political science perspective: Thomas Duttle and others, 'Opting out from European Union Legislation: The Differentiation of Secondary Law' (2017) 24(3) Journal of European Public Policy 406–28; Benjamin Leruth and Christopher Lord, 'Differentiated Integration in the European Union: A Concept, a Process, a System or a Theory?' (2015) 22(6) Journal of European Public Policy 754–63; Frank Schimmelfennig, 'Good Governance and Differentiated Integration: Graded Membership in the European Union' (2016) 55(4) European Journal of Political Research 789–810; and, from a legal perspective: Alberto Miglio, 'ye' (2018) 14(3) European Constitutional Law Review 475–498; Bruno de Witte, 'An Undivided Union? Differentiated Integration in Post-Brexit Times' (2018) 55 Common Market Law Review 227–50.

[23] In fact, some went as far as arguing that the question of the statute of EU member state was outdated or had been surpassed, or that it had already been sufficiently clarified by the Treaties and the Court's case law: Cécile Rapoport, Isabelle Bosse-Platière, 'L'Etat tiers appréhendé par le droit de l'Union européenne' in Cécile Rapoport and Isabelle Bosse-Platière (eds), *L'Etat tiers en droit de l'Union européenne* (Bruylant 2014) 9.

[24] Benjamin Leruth, Stefan Gänzle, and Jarle Trondal (eds) *Routledge Handbook of Differentiation* (Routledge 2022).

[25] Richard Bellamy, Sandra Kröger, and Marta Lorimer, *Flexible Europe: Differentiated Integration, Fairness, and Democracy* (Bristol University Press 2022).

[26] Frank Schimmelfennig and Thomas Winzen, *Ever Looser Union? Differentiated European Integration* (OUP 2020).

[27] Bruno de Witte, Andrea Ott, and Ellen Vos, Between Flexibility and Disintegration: The Trajectory of Differentiation in EU Law (Edward Elgar 2017).

[28] Thomas Giegerich and others, Flexibility in the EU and Beyond: How Much Differentiation Can European Integration Bear? (Nomos 2017).

[29] Benjamin Leruth and Christopher Lord, *Differentiated Integration in the European Union* (Routledge 2016),

[30] Stefan Gänzle, Benjamin Leruth, and Jarle Trondal, *Differentiated Integration and Disintegration in a 'Post-Brexit' era* (Routledge 2020).

[31] Dirk Leuffen, Bertold Rittberger, and Frank Schimmelfennig, *Differentiated Integration: Explaining Variation in the European Union* (Palgrave Macmillan 2013).

the volumes edited by Serena Giusti and Irina Mirkina;[32] Peter van Elsuwege and Roman Petrov;[33] and Sandra Lavenex and Frank Schimmelfennig.[34]

However, this *edited volume adds value to this existing literature for at least four reasons.* First, research so far has failed to devote specific attention to the concept of EU membership, and has instead focused solely on differentiated integration, on specific derogations, or on the application of EU norms by third states. Second, this edited volume is unique in that it combines both a theoretical approach (Part I) and a policy-focused perspective (the following parts), while most of the pre-existing publications tend to focus on either one or the other aspect. Thirdly, it covers a large variety of cases of internal and external differentiation. Finally, this edited volume is novel because it offers a reflection on recent developments, including Brexit and its consequences, the creation of PESCO, and the renegotiations of EU–Swiss relationships, which, to date, have been analysed only to a limited extent, and have not yet been considered in an aggregate manner, in terms of the overall consequences they could have for the EU and its future development.

III. Research Question and Structure of this Book

To contribute to bridge this gap in the existing research, this edited volume seeks to (re)define EU membership today, and to provide an up-to-date account of the status of differentiation within the EU.

A. Common research framework

The various authors were invited to consider a series of questions, which they answer from the perspective of the individual case study or specific policy area that they focus on. In particular, the *main aim* of this edited volume is, in a nutshell, to *(re)define what characterizes EU Membership today*, in a context in which this appears to have become a fuzzy concept, and to *consider whether we should go beyond the concept of unitary membership as it is currently defined in the EU.* It also *provides a reflection on the current status of differentiated integration within the EU*, and *considers how it should continue to evolve in the future.*

[32] Serena Giusti and Irina Mirkina, The EU in a Trans-European Space: External Relations across Europe, Asia and the Middle East (Palgrave Macmillan 2019).

[33] Peter van Elsuwege and Roman Petrov, Legislative Approximation and Application of EU Law in the Eastern Neighbourhood of the European Union: Towards a Common Regulatory Space? (Routledge 2014).

[34] Sandra Lavenex and Frank Schimmelfennig, *EU External Governance: Projecting EU Rules beyond Membership* (Routledge 2010).

Against this background, this edited volume seeks to answer these questions by: (a) looking at *membership within the EU and outside of it, from a theoretical, a policy-specific, and a general perspective*; and (b) by examining various policy areas within which differentiation exists.

First, authors were invited to reflect upon some of the concepts which have been developed with regard to differentiated integration. These include *internal and external differentiation*, ie the possibility for some EU Member States to opt out of, and the possibility for some non-EU Member States to participate in, EU policies, respectively. In this regard, the external consequences of internal (policy) differentiation should also be considered, ie the consequences for the EU's relations with third states and organizations of the fact that not all Member States participate in certain policies. To what extent does differentiation spill over into the EU's external policies?

Secondly, in addition to an analysis of the level of integration in the different policy areas (also referred to as 'vertical differentiation'),[35] the authors were called on to provide an analysis that *distinguishes between 'membership' and 'participation'* in the decision-making procedures governing a specific policy area, wherein membership also implies full involvement in the enforcement procedures. Indeed, the distinction between those states that are full participants in the whole decision-making procedure, and those that only partially do so, is key to understanding what distinguishes an EU Member State from a third state that is involved in a specific EU policy. European Economic Area (EEA)/European Free Trade Association (EFTA) states, which only participate to a certain extent, are a clear illustration of this distinction.

In this context, it is also important to bear in mind that the status of EU Member States entails *specific features*. Member States are indeed *equal before the Treaties* (Art 4(2) TEU). Being an EU Member State entails *a series of rights and obligations*, both vis-à-vis EU institutions and vis-à-vis other Member States;[36] this clearly distinguishes the EU from other international organizations, while also determining the relationships EU Member States may establish with third states. The rights and obligations attached to the status of Member States (among which, for instance, are primacy, direct effect, and the duty of loyal cooperation) are at the very basis of the EU's constitutional order, and allow a distinction to be drawn between Member States and third states. At the same time, the EU legal order, contrary to other international organizations, only foresees two statuses for states: either a state is a member of the EU and, therefore, has a series of rights and obligations as regards, inter alia, its rights of participation in the EU institutional system and its

[35] Leuffen, Rittberger, and Schimmelfennig (eds) (n 4) 1.

[36] Koen Lenaerts, 'No Member State is More Equal than Others: The Primacy of EU law and the Principle of the Equality of the Member States before the Treaties' (*VerfBlog*, 8 October 2020) https://verfassungsblog.de/no-member-state-is-more-equal-than-others/ accessed 10 May 2023.

obligations to respect the general principles that govern the EU legal order as developed by the Court of Justice, or it is a third state.[37] This notwithstanding, the relationships the EU has with third states have become increasingly diverse over time, and vary greatly, from full participation in certain policy areas to cooperation.[38] The Treaties now identify several kinds of third states, too. Considering third states' participation in EU policies allows the precise content of the Member State status to be better defined, its attractiveness to third states to be reflected upon, and its very existence in practice, and for the future, to be questioned.

This is, in a nutshell, the background against which the authors were called upon to conduct their individual analyses. Specifically, their contributions were invited to consider the following questions, where appropriate:

1. Have the forms and the degree of (internal and external) differentiation in the domain examined varied over time? For what reasons (drivers), and with what consequences? (Consequences may, for instance, be visible in terms of the practical implementation of the policies in question, or of the applicable decision-making procedures.)
2. What is it that differentiates EU Member States from third states that participate in an EU policy/ cooperate with the EU? What is the status of third states: are they involved in the decision-making procedures, for instance? How does this distinction between EU and third states materialize in the domain you examine, and are there any specific challenges in this regard?
3. Can/does this contribute to define any core values/features that are inherent to the status of (EU) Member State?
4. Art 4 TEU currently establishes the principle of equality among EU Member States, and the Treaties, therefore, currently only foresee one type of membership: should this be reconsidered? Both internal and external differentiation could be considered here.
5. Do the different statuses existing within the EU (internal differentiation) have any consequences for the EU's relationship to third states? In other words, does the fact that not all Member States participate in certain policies affect the relationship with third states and international organizations? To what extent does differentiation spill over into the EU's external policies?
6. In practice, temporary and permanent opt-outs exist, as do derogations, which were sometimes meant to be temporary and ended up being quasi-permanent. Yet, the different forms of differentiation that exist within the EU have, so far, not questioned the unitary status of EU Member State. How can

[37] On this aspect and its rationale, see Cécile Rapoport and Isabelle Bosse-Platière, 'L'Etat tiers appréhendé par le droit de l'Union européenne' in Cécile Rapoport and Isabelle Bosse-Platière (eds), *L'Etat tiers en droit de l'Union européenne* (Bruylant 2014) 9.

[38] On third states and EU law in general, see Cécile Rapoport and Isabelle Bosse-Platière (eds), *L'Etat tiers en droit de l'Union européenne* (Bruylant 2014).

and should this affect a reflection on EU membership (and future enlargement procedures) going forward? In particular, should the obligation set on all new Member States to adopt the whole *acquis* continue to be upheld? Or should we, rather, opt for the definition of a common minimum, which all Member States must abide by, while allowing them to cherry-pick as regards their participation in other (non-core) policy areas? More generally, what sort of evolution might we anticipate for the future? Should the current Treaty framework be amended in the future to cater for current needs/weaknesses?

In this regard, one of the proposals authors were invited to consider was that made by MEP Pascal Durand, in his draft report on differentiated integration: 'As a step beyond the existing Treaty limitations, the Rapporteur considers useful to consider the possibility to introduce two sorts of Union memberships: full and associate membership. Full membership would mean full compliance with primary law and with the policies that are excluded from the possibility of launching enhanced cooperation. Associated members would participate in certain policies only and would not be fully integrated into the EU decision-making processes.'[39]

7. (How) can the UK's decision to leave the EU, and the content of the Brexit negotiations, contribute to the reflections on the future of the status of EU Member State?
8. The pandemic led to significant changes within the EU, visible, inter alia, in a unique shift towards more (economic) solidarity among Member States. May we anticipate the pandemic and the EU's response to it bringing about any form of (temporary or long-lasting) change in the domain you examine?

Answering these questions allows three dimensions of the overall reflection on EU membership and differentiated integration to be covered: a historical one; a contemporary one, which offers a critical evaluation of the current state of play; and a forward-looking one, which examines the resilience of the current situation for the future, and the need for reform, especially post-Brexit, and in the perspective of additional future enlargements.

B. Introducing the contributions to this edited volume

The first part of this edited volume sets the theoretical framework to the inquiry pursued therein.[40] It contains one chapter by Dirk Leuffen, which considers what membership entails from the perspective of equality and fairness.[4129]

39 Pascal Durand, 'Draft Report on Differentiated Integration', 2018/2093(INI), 2 August 2018, 10.
40 All chapters were concluded in 2021, and some were updated in 2023.
41 .

Dirk Leuffen's contribution builds on internationalist republicanism to claim that differentiation does not, per se, violate the principle of equality among Member States. For him, though, 'differentiated integration must be designed not to violate, but instead honour the principle of freedom as non-domination', an approach which, in his view, leads to differentiated integration ensuring Member States' and thus citizens' equality, instead of posing a threat to it. In Leuffen's view, Member States are set under an 'associative obligation' towards each other. This obligation does not, however, translate to non-EU members involved in initiatives of external differentiated integration. In his opinion, therefore, 'differentiated integration must not violate the principle of freedom as non-domination', and Member States are under the 'obligation to respect freedom as non-domination of all Member States' when acting in and outside the EU legal framework, but this obligation does not exist vis-à-vis third states, ie in cases of external differentiation. Furthermore, Leuffen stresses the necessity for the process leading to differentiation to be perceived as fair by citizens, and for it to be transparent; he also proposes, among other things, an original mechanism to introduce *ex post* opt-outs.

The following chapters (3 to 5) form the second part of this edited volume, which looks at differentiated integration in specific policy areas.

Mark Dawson and Tomasz P Woźniakowski focus on the Economic and Monetary Union (EMU) as the example where differentiation is most acute. They show that both centrifugal and centripetal forces may be observed among Member States in this policy area, and that the existing centripetal forces lead to the EMU being 'less differentiated than it (formally) appears'. This is notably shown by analyzing the specific case of the Polish parliament in the European Semester. The distinction between full and partial EMU membership is found to be diminishing, and it is also found that the 'direction of travel is thus contrary to what one might have expected given the increasing widening and deepening of the Union since Maastricht'.

The following chapter, by Petra Mahnič and Álvaro de Elera, focuses on another policy area in which differentiation is inherent, namely the Common Foreign and Security Policy (CFSP). Like the EMU, the area of the CFSP has always been differentiated, and the authors start by showing how internal and external differentiation materialize in this field. They emphasize the fact that there is a crucial distinction between the internal and external differentiation in this field, as participation in decision-making processes is only open to EU Member States in this field, as in all policy areas. Mahnič and de Elera usefully distinguish between, on the one hand, differentiated *integration* as it exists in the field of the Common Security and Defence Policy (CSDP); Danish opt-out, and the permanent structured cooperation (PESCO), which was instituted based on an inbuilt possibility of enhanced integration). On the other hand, they pin down the concept of differentiated *convergence* in the field of CFSP in general (ie without CSDP). Indeed, '[t]he CFSP is not about integration, rather it is about the convergence of national foreign policy preferences that result in EU positions, where other actors of international law deal with, and perceive, the Union as a separate international actor'. Hence, even if Member States could legally envisage proceeding with enhanced cooperation in the field of CFSP, this 'would defeat the very purpose of the CFSP policy and the credibility of the EU as a "collective external policy actor".[42] Therefore, only mechanisms that allow for the adoption of Union instruments constitutive of the *acquis* of the Union, and which, while maybe not committing all Member States, allow the Union to act, are capable of fulfilling the very objective of the policy.'[43] These two categories of differentiation should, additionally, be distinguished from differentiated *implementation* whereby not all Member States implement EU actions, or where third states which have not been involved in the decision-making processes that led to their adoption decide to implement EU measures. Differentiated implementation is most common in the CSDP, where civilian and military assets are deployed in the framework of peacekeeping or conflict-prevention operations, for example. The authors conclude that the existing legal framework would allow for a more effective and efficient EU policy to be built, and that it should be exploited to the full of its potential, along the lines they outline.

In the next chapter, Deirdre Curtin and Maria Patrin turn to the Area of Freedom, Security and Justice (AFSJ) which, too, is characterized by fragmentation, and by both internal and external differentiation. Like in the area of the CFSP, the forms taken by differentiation in the AFSJ are indeed very varied. Against this backdrop, Curtin and Patrin show that 'the overlap of various forms of differentiation creates a space in which the distinction between participating and non-participating Member States, as well as external and EU members, tends to get blurred and diluted within the many different participation patterns'. They illustrate how a variety of flexible memberships and 'different ways of "being members"' already exist, although they also ask what the limits of this flexibility should be. They additionally highlight the existence of some transparency and flexibility issues that derive from this flexibility.

The third part of this edited volume focuses on membership and special statuses in and of EU Member States.

Stéphanie Laulhé-Shaelou and Katerina Kalaitzaki examine the situation in specific territories located in or outside the EU that remain *de facto* or *de jure* integrated in EU policies, namely Greenland, the occupied territories that remain *de facto* outside of the control of the Cypriot government, and the British Sovereign Base Areas in Cyprus, as well as Gibraltar and Northern Ireland. They first underline that EU Treaties, contrary to ordinary treaties of international law, do not

[42] Annegret Bendiek, Ronja Kempin, and Nicolai von Ondarza, 'Qualified Majority Voting and Flexible Integration for a More Effective CFSP? A Critical Examination of the EU's Options' (2018) 25 SWP Comment 7.

[43] Mahnič and de Elera in this volume.

define their territorial scope. Instead, their scope is dependent on the territory of the Member States, and hence may vary as a result of changes internal to them, as was the case in Denmark as a result of Greenland having become an autonomous territory in 1979. Furthermore, they specifically analyze what the consequences of Brexit have been for the application of EU policies in Gibraltar and Northern Ireland, and in the military bases in Cyprus. The situation in the territories Stéphanie and Katerina consider in their chapter shows that membership 'is more nuanced than ever before'.

Adam Łazowski considers the various waves of EU enlargements and their consequences, in particular how 'new accessions have always come at the price of ever-increasing differentiation within the EU'. This differentiation takes the form of the well-known phenomena of opt-out and enhanced cooperation, but also results from permanent derogations and transitional arrangements defined in the various Acts on Conditions of Accession. Łazowski's chapter examines the two (less well-known) forms of differentiation. He shows, in particular, how temporary arrangements are part and parcel of the EU enlargement processes, but how they may also tend to become permanent, especially in the areas of Economic and Monetary Union (EMU) and Schengen.

The fourth part, finally, turns to the relationship of third states with the EU, and what it tells us about EU membership. It starts by considering the UK as a former EU Member State, before turning to candidate countries and state partners of the EU.

Kathryn Wright's analysis considers the unique case of the UK, which is the first state ever to have left the EU. Kathryn focuses, in particular, on the governance arrangements for the EU–UK future trade relationship. The UK's relationship with the EU is not only peculiar because of its quality as a former Member State; this peculiarity also derives from the fact that, even when it was part of the EU, the UK had a special status owing to the numerous opt-outs it had managed to secure for itself. As such, the British case is particularly useful in the attempt to define what EU membership entails. Contrary to the situation with other third states, the UK aims to cooperate with (some) EU agencies, as opposed to being a member thereof or participating therein. This cooperation takes, for instance, the form of exchange of information, and reaches deeper in certain areas, including energy, medicinal products, and aviation. Crucially, Wright finds that, '[t]he UK will experience mechanisms of European integration even without membership, given the interdependence of the EU and UK markets'. Further to mechanisms of transfer similar to those that exist in the case of the EEA, it bears emphasizing that the UK, as a former EU Member State, 'starts from a position of even greater integration'.

The next chapter, by Nadja S Kühn and Jarle Trondal, considers another example of a third state that is closely integrated to the EU by means of external differentiated integration: Norway. In their view, Norway is actually 'an extreme case of high integration without formal EU membership'. Kühn and Trondal focus specifically on cooperation at administrative level, and show that it is not only of crucial importance, but that is also expanding. Furthermore, they highlight that these processes, in turn, commonly influence domestic-level processes and policy outcomes. Based on questionnaires circulated among Norwegian officials over more than three decades, they interestingly find that the EU has contributed to reinforcing the administrative state in Norway, whereby 'Norwegian government officials who deal with the EU are also increasingly loosely coupled to the political level (low-ranked staff) and (surprisingly) and tightly interwoven and influenced by EU institutions'.

Christian NK Franklin analyses the Norwegian case from a legal standpoint. Franklin highlights how participation in the EEA Agreement allows access to, and indeed participation in, core areas of the internal market, which necessarily 'involves a high degree of diffusion of EU rights and obligations in the EFTA States'. Even if, theoretically, significant differentiation at the levels of policy-making, implementation, and enforcement of EU law in the EFTA States would be possible, his analysis demonstrates how, in practice, differences are kept to a minimum. Also, Franklin demonstrates how pragmatic solutions to the absence of updates to the EEA Agreement, since its conclusion in 1994, could contribute to bringing EEA and EU states closer over time, and could allow the expansion to some areas since introduced in the EU legal order, such as the EU Charter of Fundamental Rights or EU citizenship. However, these dynamics are found to have given rise to some criticism, by the Norwegian government in particular, for they appear to depart from the original EEA Agreement's original intention of economic cooperation, and in any event raise certain democratic issues, since EEA states have no say in the EU's decision-making process.

Andrea Ott and Benedikt Pirker look at another case of 'integration without membership': the Swiss example. They highlight the peculiarities of Switzerland, which, despite being part of EFTA, does not belong to the EEA, unlike EFTA's other members: Iceland, Liechtenstein, and Norway. Instead, the EU–Swiss relationship is governed by a series of numerous bilateral agreements, and Ott and Pirker show that norm diffusion exists between the two parties. This situation is largely unsatisfactory and outdated, since the EU increasingly wants to prevent cherry-picking by third states, especially after Brexit. A draft institutional framework agreement that would have improved this situation failed to be approved in May 2021, after the Swiss Federal Court declared that interpretation differences on the EU Citizens Rights Directive, wage protection in Switzerland, and state aid provisions, prevented any compromise. Ott and Pirker highlight the various forms which norm diffusion takes in Switzerland, namely *de jure* and *de facto* norm transfer, and how these vary across the various agreements. In fact, they argue that this kind of relationship, as an alternative to full membership, presents both pitfalls and advantages, although it has come under increased pressure over time.

The contribution by Meltem Müftüler-Baç first looks at the example of Turkey through the lens of differentiated integration, ie the situation where third states enter into agreements with the EU to participate in EU policies and where they are incorporated into the EU *acquis*. She finds the EU's relationship with Turkey to be 'at a rocky stage' at present because of internal and external factors, although Turkey is set to remain a key partner for the EU. This leads her to wonder how the relationship between the EU and Turkey may be conceptualized beyond Turkey's membership of the EU, as this option appears currently to be off the table. To this end, Müftüler-Baç examines Turkey's functional cooperation with the EU, which takes multiple forms (participation in two EU agencies, owing to its status as candidate country; participation in EU programmes and policies; Customs Union Agreement; alignment with EU norms). Some of these were established as part of Turkey's path towards EU accession, while others stem from the European Economic Community–Turkey 1963 Association Agreement. Several setbacks in the EU's relationship with Turkey have been witnessed over the past years because of political reasons, and in any event reforms, in the form of the creation of an efficient dispute settlement mechanism or a resumption of the bilateral summits headed by the Council, are found to be necessary. In summary, Turkey now appears to permanently embody a form of relationship alternative to EU membership, following its status as a candidate country having been officially recognized.

In the following chapter, Marko Milenković turns to the Western Balkans, the nations of which also aspire(d) to EU membership, but whose entry into the EU seems to have come to a halt as well. Milenković shows that enlargement fatigue on the EU's side has been mirrored by accession fatigue on the Western Balkans' side, and that, therefore, it is wise to explore political and legal alternatives to membership. As is also the case between the EU and Turkey, external differentiated integration is visible in that region as well. It takes, for instance, the form of Stabilization and Association Agreements, which enable free trade but demand comprehensive reforms and alignment with the *acquis* and its subsequent developments in several EU policy areas, or the form of the Treaty establishing the Energy Community. Milenković argues that other arrangements, in the form of broader access to EU funds and programmes, could represent an alternative to the (currently unpopular) enlargement, while also contributing to the development of the region.

The two last chapters of this edited volume consider third states which are further estranged from the EU (legal) space, and do not necessarily aspire to become EU Member States, yet are influenced by the EU.

Laure Delcour considers the European Neighbourhood Policy (ENP), launched in 2004 with the new neighbours the EU gained following its Eastern enlargement. The ENP differs from enlargement policy in that EU regulatory expansion and institutional inclusion are decoupled in the former case. ENP states adopt and apply EU norms, but not as part of their preparation for accession. Delcour examines how the ENP has evolved over time, and shows that it can no longer be regarded as a single model for the relationship between the EU and its neighbours. Instead, it is characterized by diversity, even within the ENP's sub-initiative, the Eastern Partnership, which brings together the EU's eastern neighbours. This is because the ENP's conditionality and incentives are unclear, and because it relies on joint ownership and differentiation between the states involved. This, in turn, raises the question of the viability of this policy framework. Delcour illustrates how the Eastern Partnership, launched in 2009, despite being an improvement on the general ENP, owing to its more result-oriented approach to legal approximation, is still unsatisfactory. It has been implemented in a fragmentary manner. Beyond this, Delcour highlights how this form of relationship of third states to the EU may resemble, or even reach deeper than, the bonds existing with candidate countries, thus calling for a potential need to redefine EU external differentiation altogether.

In the final chapter of this collection, Giselle Bosse's analysis is on the EU's influence (mainly by means of its ENP) on democratic standards in post-Soviet Europe and Eurasian countries, amid an absence of perspective of accession to the EU. More specifically, Bosse looks at the factors that explain the variation of democratic effort among the countries of the post-Soviet space, and how many of these are EU-induced. To this end, she considers EU-specific factors (levels of EU conditionality and EU financial assistance), domestic factors (democratic legacy and level of autonomous social capital), and external factors (dependence on external autocracy promoter). Giselle's analysis, interestingly, highlights that 'the majority of causal paths confirm the expectation that democratic reform progress in the post-Soviet space is the result of a mix of EU conditionality/assistance, favourable domestic factors and limited dependence on an external autocracy promoter (i.e. the Russian Federation)'. However, she also finds, for instance, that there is not one but several paths to democratic reform progress that may or not involve EU conditionality and assistance. Also, she finds that aspiration to EU membership, even in the absence of clear prospects thereof for the time being, can impact on democratic reform progress. All in all, the EU appears still to be a crucial factor in this respect, even at a time when democratic standards are not being upheld by some of the EU's own Member States.

IV. Conclusion: Where does 'EU Membership' Stand Today?

The chapters included in this edited volume have shown that the concept of EU membership is not as blurred as it may seem at first sight (from a non-legal perspective, as (EU) law clearly distinguishes between Member States and third states, as recalled at the beginning of this Introduction).

While differentiation in and outside the EU is, without any doubt, a defining feature of today's EU, it remains the case that membership of the Union still decisively differentiates between those who are in the EU and those who are not.

There are still certain elements that clearly distinguish EU Member States from (participating) third or partner states. EU-wide institutions are also always involved in decision-making to ensure that EU integration as a project is preserved,[44] ie that it is not threatened at its core by those (differentiated) initiatives. Even where a distinction in the membership of the responsible bodies or agencies is made, and where third states are involved in those bodies to mirror differentiated internal and external participation in some policy initiatives, EU-wide institutions, and especially the Council, are always involved with all their members, and are tasked with designing the applicable legal framework, although states with an opt-out may not have any voting right. For instance, the Lisbon Treaty introduced the possibility for decisions to be made with the votes of euro-area representatives only (Art 136(2) TFEU), but all other Member States are involved, at Council and lower levels. Even where Ministers of Finance meet in the Eurogroup, they often hold the meeting as 'Eurogroup in inclusive format'. Actually, as also highlighted by Mark Dawson and Tomasz P Woźniakowski, the divide between euro area and non-euro area, which is the deepest area of differentiated integration within the EU, may be less pronounced than it might seem at first sight. Beyond the arguments brought by these authors, informal mechanisms exist that contribute to reducing the gap between the two groups of Member States (such as the resort to 'inclusive formats'), and one may observe a convergence towards EU-wide policies in the field of EMU since the COVID-19 pandemic, contrary to what happened following the euro-area crisis.[45] Also, the divide between these two groups of states is becoming smaller as an ever-growing number of Member States adopt the common currency. However, the existing divide appears to be becoming ever more entrenched, as those states that are not part of the euro area and have not expressed any interest in joining (ie the Czech Republic, Denmark, Poland, and Sweden) are unlikely to take steps in this direction in the future. This is but one of the illustrations of the phenomenon, depicted earlier, of a long-lastingly differentiated Union. The clear distinction that exists in the membership of EU decision-making organs does not, however, imply that third states are not involved in the preparation of EU decisions and, relatedly, that participation in EU policies does not have any consequences for those states' institutional frameworks. Their role is, nonetheless, bound to remain limited, and may never equate to that of EU Member States, which, as highlighted by Deirdre Curtin and Maria Patrin, are the only states that may participate in both decision-making and implementation.

[44] A feature which is very much in line with what the European Parliament envisaged for the future of differentiated integration as well: European Parliament, 'Resolution of 17 January 2019 on Differentiated Integration' (2018/2093(INI)).

[45] Diane Fromage, 'Post-COVID-19 E(M)U Interinstitutional Balance: Assessment and Outlook' in European Central Bank, *Continuity and Change—How the Challenges of Today Prepare the Ground for Tomorrow*, ECB Legal Conference 2021, 421–35.

As such, the unitary status of EU membership still appears to be appropriate. As will be further detailed, this does not, however, automatically imply that a reflection on this state of facts is superfluous.

The contributions to this edited volume have, furthermore, shed some new light on the various existing forms of differentiation within today's EU. They have shown that internal and external differentiation exist, but also that a distinction between differentiated integration, differentiated convergence, and differentiated implementation may be warranted. As a consequence of the existing 'many faces of differentiation'[46] that are currently visible, the distinction between participation and non-participation is, in fact, not strictly evident at times.

This edited volume also evidences phenomena which are often ignored in the analysis of differentiation. These concern, in particular, the situation in specific territories in and outside the EU, and the reality of the *de facto* quasi-permanent differentiation that follows states' accessions to the EU where the existing derogations had been meant to remain temporary, ie limited in time following accession.[47]

This edited volume, furthermore, offers a critical evaluation of the EU's relationship to third states by considering states that are closely related to the EU, and states that (may have) aspire(d) to join the EU, as well as states with which the EU entertains a close relationship without any perspective of membership. It shows that participation in EU policies has an impact on those states. It also highlights that the relationships which the EU entertains with its neighbours are (increasingly) diverse, and that membership of the EU may no longer seem as attractive as it used to, although perhaps changes may be expected in this respect in the future, and are already beginning. This finding is, in fact, particularly insightful at a time when the debate on the EU's enlargement has regained vividity following the Russian invasion of Ukraine, having been stalled for a long time. While little to no progress had been made towards the accession of Turkey and the Western Balkan states over the past decade, or, better said, while the prospects of their accession had even worsened over time, the new geopolitical situation resulting from the war in Ukraine raises this question again. Actually, this questions anew what the very meaning of the European integration process is. European integration appeared to have become more about economic integration over time, thereby departing from its original purpose to guarantee peace and security across the European continent. However, with war having (sadly) returned to this part of the world, it could be that European integration is called upon to return to its original purpose, or at least that the balance between its economic and security-related objectives needs to be reassessed and amended in favour of the latter.

[46] de Witte, Hanf, and Vos (eds) (n 3).

[47] This issue was indeed picked up by the European Parliament in 2019: 'Resolution on Differentiated Integration' (2018/2093(INI)).

This, I would argue, should not happen at any cost, or without certain reforms being implemented first; nor should it necessarily obviate the debate on the potential necessity to adapt the EU's institutional framework to the reality of differentiation, or to introduce various kinds of memberships if diversity grows significantly or happens at a fast pace.

V. Outlook: The Future of Differentiation in an EU Post-Brexit, Post-COVID and Post-Ukraine

The idea of introducing various kinds of memberships, or more simply of departing from the unitary status of EU Member State as we have known it to date, is certainly not new, and its conceptualization has ranged from the possibility to have a 'soft-core Europe' to that of having 'full' and 'associate' memberships.[48] As regards the latter possibility, '[f]ull membership would mean full compliance with primary law and with the policies that are excluded from the possibility of launching enhanced cooperation [. . . whereas a]ssociated members would participate in certain policies only and would not be fully integrated into the EU decision-making processes'.[49] This proposal resembles that of the Spinelli Group,[50] which also foresaw the existence of associate membership for those states unwilling to accept the terms of the new constitution proposed. 'Soft-core Europe' would entail that 'multiple cluster[s] of member states [exist] that overlap in their participation in the EU's many policy communities [. . . whereby] a large majority of member states w[ould] continue to belong to a plurality of policy communities, including the Eurozone, security and defense, and Schengen, in addition to more specialized cooperative arrangements'.[51] Others, such as Jean-Claude Piris, have instead argued in favour of a two-speed EU, which is similar to the concept of 'core Europe', although it would require the prior approval of a new Treaty parallel to the Lisbon Treaty, and the introduction of a new institutional framework involving the institutions already in place.[52] Finally, the European Commission itself identified six possible scenarios for the future of the EU, back in 2017: five in its *White Paper on the Future of Europe*,[53] and one in then President Juncker's

[48] Many more proposals have been made regarding this issue that cannot be examined here.
[49] Pascal Durand MEP, 'Explanatory Statement to the EP Report on Differentiated Integration' (2018/2093(INI)) 11.
[50] Spinelli Group Manifesto, point 14, available at The Spinelli Group https://thespinelligroup.eu/wp-content/uploads/2021/04/Manifesto_EN.pdf accessed 27 April 2023.
[51] Schmidt (n 21) 295.
[52] Jean-Claude Piris, *The Future of Europe: Towards a Two-speed EU?* (CUP 2012).
[53] European Commission, Directorate-General for Communication, 'White Paper on the Future of Europe: Reflections and Scenarios for the EU27 by 2025' (2017) https://op.europa.eu/en/publication-detail/-/publication/ba81f70e-2b10-11e7-9412-01aa75ed71a1/language-en accessed 27 April 2023.

State of the Union speech.[54] The first scenario, 'Carrying on', suggested keeping the status quo, and the second scenario, 'Nothing but the single market', was inclined to recentre the institutional balance in favour of supranational institutions on the internal market only while excluding them from a series of key policy areas, like international trade, which would have been defined by Member States on a bilateral basis. The third scenario, 'Those who want more do more', would have allowed different groups of Member States to strengthen their cooperation. The fourth scenario, 'Doing less more efficiently', was very close to the second one. It would have given powers back to Member States, and they, together with the EU institutions, would have defined a focus on a selected number of policy priorities related but not limited to the internal market, in order to deliver better. The fifth scenario, 'Doing much more together', was geared towards an 'ever-closer Union'. In his own 'sixth scenario', President Juncker presented a 'reformist vision' of the EU, described as 'Doing much more together', and he rejected further differentiation. It is, however, important to note that interest in this debate on the future of the EU and differentiation among its members has faded over time, and is no longer as vivid as it was a few years back.

Next to this debate on the future of membership per se, a discussion arose at approximately the same time regarding the modalities for accession to the EU, which has proven to be in need for reform in many respects. To name but a few of the existing issues, the procedure for accession creates frustration on both sides, as illustrated by the chapters by Marko Milenkovic and Meltem Müftüler-Baç in this volume. Additionally, as shown by Adam Łazowski, temporary derogations in some cases become permanent. And the absence of respect for the core of the EU's values, most prominently, but not only, by Hungary and Poland, as well as the need to adopt pecuniary sanctions and to introduce new mechanisms (Rule of Law conditionality mechanism),[55] amid the absence of effective procedures to constrain those states violating EU values, clearly shows that the procedures for accession to the EU are not fit for purpose. France proposed reforming the existing procedures,[56] a proposal which was met by the opposition of other Member States, thus leading the Commission to craft a compromise solution in the form of a revised enlargement methodology, in 2020 (later endorsed by the Council).[57] Even if the EU may, therefore, be better equipped to prepare for the accession of new states, and to ensure the guarantee of its values, it remains the case that numerous shortcomings continue to exist, be it only because the three avenues to guarantee the respect of

[54] https://ec.europa.eu/commission/presscorner/detail/en/SPEECH_17_3165 accessed 27 April 2023.

[55] https://commission.europa.eu/strategy-and-policy/policies/justice-and-fundamental-rights/upholding-rule-law/rule-law/rule-law-mechanism_en accessed 27 April 2023.

[56] https://www.politico.eu/wp-content/uploads/2019/11/Enlargement-nonpaper.pdf accessed 27 April 2023.

[57] Commission lays out its proposals for EU accession process: https://ec.europa.eu/commission/presscorner/detail/en/IP_20_181 accessed 27 April 2023.

the EU's values once a state has joined the EU (legal procedures before the Court of Justice, Article 7 procedures, and budgetary conditionality (for the rule of law only)) all present deficiencies.[58] This is particularly worrisome as clear definitions of what those values (respect for the rule of law and respect for democracy, to name only two) entail, and what their relationships among each other are, are lacking.[59] Despite this, they could (or should) not admit any differentiation in their application.[60] And this is also extremely worrisome because the absence of respect of those values in fact never puts the status of a state as Member State into question.[61] Relatedly, and even if this question may not be examined at length here for reasons of space, a reflection may be needed on the modalities of secession from the Union, after the Brexit experiment revealed its risks and complexity. Should there also be a minimum threshold below which a Member State which consistently violates founding values would be obliged to leave the EU altogether?[62] Currently, the closest to such a demotion within the Treaties is probably the Article 7(3) TEU procedure, which, after a unanimous determination by the European Council that there has been a serious and persistent breach of the founding values in Article 2 TEU, allows the Council to suspend certain rights deriving from the Treaties, including the voting rights of the Member State in question. As will be further argued, Member States should all have to adhere to a minimum set of values and agree to participate in some core policy areas. Should they change their mind and cease to comply with those requirements, their continuing belonging to the Union (or their status as full member) could, arguably, be questioned. Furthermore, the question must be asked as to whether existing opt-outs (in whatever form they may exist) should not be open to states that no longer want (or are able) to participate in a specific policy area. This question arose during the Greek economic crisis, in relation to the possibility for a Member State to exit the euro area only,[63] and it is also raised by some Member States' systematic disrespect of their obligations stemming from their belonging to the Schengen area.[64]

As regards the future of membership and of differentiation, as posited by Paul Craig, membership itself sets boundaries to the possibilities of differentiated

[58] András Jakab and Dimitry Kochenov (eds), *The Enforcement of EU Law and Values: Ensuring Member States' Compliance* (OUP 2017); András Jakab, 'Wie die EU durch das Spitzenkandidatensystem ihre illiberalen Regime in Ungarn und Polen bekämpfen könnte' (*VerfBlog*, 12 April 2023) https://verfassungsblog.de/wie-die-eu-durch-das-spitzenkandidatensystem-ihre-illiberalen-regime-in-ungarn-und-polen-bekampfen-konnte/ accessed 10 May 2023.

[59] Bruno de Witte, 'Constitutional Challenges of the Enlargement: Is Further Enlargement Feasible without Constitutional Changes?', Study for the EP AFCO Committee 2019.

[60] For one of these values, see R Daniel Kelemen, 'Is Differentiation Possible in Rule of Law?' (2019) 17 Comparative European Politics 246–60.

[61] Laurence Potvin-Solis, 'Propos introductifs. Le statut d'Etat membre et le cadre constitutionnel de l'Union européenne' in Potvin-Solis (ed) (n 10) 47.

[62] Question raised by Marie Gautier, 'Le statut d'Etat membre: L'etat membre de l'Union dans l'ELSJ' in Potvin-Solis (ed) (n 10) 426.

[63] Pheobus Athanassiou, 'Withdrawal and Expulsion from the EU and EMU: Some Reflections' (2009) 10 ECB Legal Working Paper Series.

[64] Some Member States have *de facto* reintroduced systematic border checks.

integration: 'Membership properly understood imposes decisional constraints on differentiated integration. It demands that the uneven application of Treaty obligations as between the Member States has foundation in a source that is regarded as formally legitimate within the legal order. This is so irrespective of the content of the differential application or reach of EU law.'[65] This notwithstanding, instances exist where legitimacy is lacking, as a result of differentiation stemming from administrative practice, power politics, or inadequate enforcement.[66] For the time being, '[t]he Member States join a club when acceding to the EU'.[67]

Therefore, if it were to be the case that not all (newer or older) Member States were in a position (or willing) to comply with the obligations deriving from their status as EU Member States, Member States and EU institutions alike would be best advised to introduce a second kind of membership. The possibility to join the more closely integrated states would, naturally, remain, provided that the necessary conditions to this end were complied with. And the possibility of enhanced cooperation within the group of more closely integrated Member States should also be provided, to allow integration to go deeper, while catering for the need to accommodate diverging policy preferences and national capacities. I acknowledge the risk of increased instability, and the shortcomings outlined by Paul Craig with respect to Piris' idea of a two-speed Europe,[68] which are also inherent to the proposal made here, and am conscious of the departure from the current regime of equality among Member States. Yet, I still argue that it would, nevertheless, be more satisfactory than the currently existing regime, which is not only messy and difficult to govern, but is also—and most importantly—unfit for a Union which may be composed of a larger number of Member States, and in which diversity may, hence, continue to grow. Brexit did not trigger disintegration within the remaining EU27, as some had feared. But contestation is on the rise, and this phenomenon is not limited only to the states that joined during the latest enlargements. It reaches to the very founding Member States, as illustrated by the German Federal Constitutional Court's defiance towards the Court of Justice and one of the very core principles of EU law, EU primacy. One is thus faced with a very paradoxical situation: EU integration has, arguably, never reached as deep as it currently does, as prominently illustrated by Member States' approval of the Next Generation EU Programme and the REPowerEU Plan.[69] At the same time, EU integration has never been as contested as it currently is, both by citizens—as illustrated by the success of Eurosceptic parties in national and European

[65] Craig (n 12) 22.
[66] ibid 23.
[67] ibid.
[68] ibid 26.
[69] NextGenerationEU (europa.eu); European Commission, 'Communication from the Commission to the European Parliament, the European Council, the Council, the European Economic and Social Committee and the Committee of Regions', COM(2022) 230 final, 18 May 2022.

elections—and by national institutions. While this growing contestation may just be an unavoidable (side) effect of further integration, since citizens in a democracy should be allowed to show their discontent, and while differentiation, by—among other things—creating inequality, may contribute to this phenomenon, it may entail important limitations for the existing system of differentiation in order for the EU not to lose its constitutional identity as embodied in its founding values.

As already highlighted, the current situation is extremely complex; it is characterized by a lack of full compliance with the obligations that stem from the status of EU Member States. Also, the EU's relationship to third countries is particularly complicated, as it takes many different forms, and the boundaries between accession, European Neighbourhood Policy, and Eastern Partnership are increasingly blurred, as shown by Laure Delcour. In this domain, too, the need for an updated framework, or at least for revamped agreements, for instance in the Swiss and the Norwegian cases, is thus visible. The introduction of the European Political Community, in June 2022, is certainly a step in the right direction, though its informal character and the large number of, and variety across, its members could threaten possible tangible outcomes and its possible role as a first step on the road towards EU membership. It will, therefore, have to be seen if and to what extent it is formalized, and if so, under what form, and whether it may thus bring value added.[70] In the redefinition of its relationship to its neighbouring countries, the EU is, in any event, not free to decide the forms that it should take, for it depends on the other states' willingness and expectations. The lengthy negotiations and recent renegotiation of the EU–UK agreement, as well as the failure to revamp the EU–Swiss framework for relationships, are illustrations of the possible difficulties that may arise, and of the EU's limited influence.

In contrast to this, the EU (or, better said, its Member States) may redefine what membership means, how one accedes to it, and what kind of differentiation may (or may not) be permissible. The legal framework currently in place has evidenced some shortcomings, with regards to these aspects of EU integration and beyond. For instance, the unanimity requirement that still exists in some cases has prevented further integration and a satisfactory level of EU foreign policy-making. Also, the institutional framework in place has proven worthy of reform, notably because neither the Council nor the European Council are held to account, as collective bodies, for their decisions, and because it is still unclear who 'the President of the EU' is. The crises which the EU has continuously faced since the outbreak of the Great Financial Crisis have only reinforced executive, and especially Member States', dominance, to the detriment of national and European legislatures, and to some extent to the detriment of the European Commission. The attempt at better

[70] For some reflection on the European Political Community and the legal form it could take, see Bruno de Witte, 'The European Political Community and the Future of the EU' (Conference Paper: The Impact of War (in Ukraine) on the EU, College of Europe, 27 and 28 March 2023).

defining the EU's competences at Lisbon may not have totally succeeded; and, more crucially, the divide in operation between the EU's and its Member States' spheres of competence may not (or may no longer) be suitable. These are but a few examples of the points for attention which have come to light in recent years, and which should be addressed to ensure that the EU remains resilient, and up to future challenges. Member States and EU institutions alike should, arguably, conduct a reflection in this sense in any event (and they may, admittedly, be pursuing this goal in their follow-up to the work of the Conference on the Future of Europe).[71] But this is almost a necessity if enlargement to encompass new states materializes, as otherwise the risks of future blockages would be high.

In a nutshell, the argument is made here that if the EU is to return to its original purpose by becoming an integration process in defence of peace and security in Europe, and if it is, therefore, to enlarge quickly, then it will not be sufficient for it to maintain both its unitary membership and tidier relationships with third (European) states, as was advocated for earlier in this chapter. It will have to introduce the status of associated member, next to the already existing full membership. Both will be governed by a single set of institutions, while the decision-making process and participation therein will continue to be adapted to the different types of membership. In consequence, voting rights in the Council will vary, while the composition of Commission, Parliament, and Court of Justice will remain unaffected,[72] ie both full and associate members will designate and be represented in these EU institutions. Respect for the EU's values and fundamental rights, as well as participation in the internal market, would be required by all, whereas participation in other policy areas/initiatives of integration would be reserved to full members. Single opt-outs (or derogations) would not be possible, to avoid further fragmentation and absence of readability. There would, hence, only be three categories of states within Europe: full members (with the possibility of enhanced cooperation for those willing to integrate deeper); associate members, bound to respect the EU's values and fundamental rights, and participating in some of the EU's policies; and third states (in a revised, neater framework). The substance of associated membership could vary over time and among members, to include, for instance, the EU's energy and defence policies, and/or the internal market. It is anticipated that associated membership could be attractive to EEA states (and candidate countries), although compliance with internal market rules and the EU's values and fundamental rights have proven to be the most difficult to respect for

[71] For instance, the European Parliament made some proposals for Treaty change: https://www.europarl.europa.eu/news/en/press-room/20220603IPR32122/parliament-activates-process-to-change-eu-treaties accessed 27 April 2022.

[72] Further, on the issue of institutional unity and the inadequacy of institutional adaptation, see Diane Fromage, 'Moving beyond 'Institutional Unity' within the EU? Euro Area versus Non-Euro area Representation in the EU Institutions' (2019) 03 Maastricht University Law Faculty Working Paper 61–74.

new entrants. However, the EU (and its Member States) should not give in on these elements, for they are part of its identity: countries that are not willing or able to comply with those minimum requirements should remain third states (closely cooperating with the Union where appropriate). Moreover, to guarantee fairness among members, and to avoid free-riders, associated membership would only be available to those states that are not able to be full members.

Introducing two kinds of membership, with the possibility of enhanced cooperation among the full members, is obviously only a second-best solution. First, it is perhaps more difficult to defend politically than the existence of the sole unitary membership. Second, it is necessarily complex, and would solve the currently existing issue of readability by citizens only to a certain extent. But if one accepts that the states that would aspire to join would not be in a position to align with the EU's standards in all domains as fast as they would wish, in order to join the Union, and, most importantly, if one accepts that the EU should go back to playing its original role as guardian of peace and security across the European continent, it is probably the best possible option. Indeed, the present situation, which is characterized by complexity, lack of transparency, and insufficient (or even absent) legitimacy of the differentiated treatment awarded to Member States in practice, is hardly satisfactory and viable in the longer term. In other words, if they want to safeguard the EU's legitimacy[73] and continued existence, Member States should not repeat the mistakes they made in the past, and should refrain from allowing states to fully enter the Union without having had the time required to comply with the whole of the EU's values and requirements. Instead, they should design solutions to allow new entrants to join progressively (ie as associated members) under clearly defined conditions.

[73] On the impact of differentiated integration on EU legitimacy, see Daniel Thym, 'Supranational Differentiation and Enhanced Cooperation' in Robert Schütze and Takis Tridimas (eds), *Oxford Principles of European Union Law: The European Union Legal Order: vol I* (OUP 2018) 847–84.

2

Member State Equality and Procedural Fairness in Differentiated Integration: A Republican Perspective

Dirk Leuffen[*]

I. Introduction

In November 2020, at the peak of the second COVID-19 wave,[1] the EU's political system was at a stalemate: Hungary and Poland had blocked the adoption of the multi-annual financial framework and the desperately needed pandemic recovery fund 'Next Generation EU', together amounting to more than 1.8 trillion euros.[2] The two states opposed the introduction of a 'rule of law mechanism' that foresees financial redistribution to be rendered conditional on the adherence to Community norms, as demanded by the European Parliament and most other Member States. To circumvent Hungarian and Polish opposition, suggestions were made to pass the recovery fund via the 'enhanced cooperation' procedure or, alternatively, as an intergovernmental agreement of the remaining twenty-five Member States.[3] Thus, differentiated integration (DI), defined as the incongruence of 'the territorial extension of European Union (EU) membership and EU rule validity',[4] was considered to overcome the gridlock and free up the desperately needed financial resources. Eventually, the European Council, on 10 December 2020, agreed on

* I thank Paul Craig, Bruno de Witte, John Erik Fossum, Diane Fromage, Max Heermann, Sandra Kröger, Christopher Lord, Christine Neuhold, Alexander Schilin, and the participants of the CERiM Conference 2019 for helpful comments. Fabian Tigges has kindly helped me in formatting the chapter. All remaining errors are my responsibility. The European Union's Horizon 2020 Research and Innovation Programme under Grant Agreement 822419 generously supported work on this chapter.

1 Eurostat, 'Excess Mortality in 2020 Reached its Peak in November—Products Eurostat News—Eurostat' (16 February 2021) <https://ec.europa.eu/eurostat/web/products-eurostat-news/-/ddn-20210216-2?redirect=%2Feurostat%2Fweb%2Fcovid-19%2Fpopulation-health> accessed 19 May 2021.

2 European Council, 'Multiannual Financial Framework for 2021–2027 Adopted' (Press release, 17 December 2020) <https://www.consilium.europa.eu/en/press/press-releases/2020/12/17/multiannual-financial-framework-for-2021-2027-adopted/> accessed 19 May 2021.

3 Alexander Conway, 'EU Rule of Law Policy Brief' (Institute of International and European Affairs 2020).

4 Katharina Holzinger and Frank Schimmelfennig, 'Differentiated Integration in the European Union: Many Concepts, Sparse Theory, Few Data' (2012) 19 Journal of European Public Policy 292, 292.

Dirk Leuffen, *Member State Equality and Procedural Fairness in Differentiated Integration* In: *Redefining EU Membership*. Edited by: Diane Fromage, Oxford University Press. © Dirk Leuffen 2024. DOI: 10.1093/9780191948145.003.0002

a compromise proposal that prevented the use of DI. Nevertheless, the case remains informative in various respects. First, it highlights that the EU27 display strong heterogeneities that do not stop affecting EU decision-making even in times of severe crisis. Second, the case illustrates that support of, or opposition to, DI is rarely principled in nature, but depends on the circumstances and, most importantly, the policies concerned and their expected effects. While Hungary and Poland would probably have appreciated being exempted from the rule of law mechanism, and thereby engaging in exemptive constitutional differentiation,[5] these countries were certainly less keen about the idea of being excluded from the financial resources of 'Next Generation EU'. From their perspective, such a step would have constituted a form of 'discriminatory differentiation'.[6] Third, and linked to the matters already mentioned, the example highlights that DI can be used for blackmailing. However, this is not necessarily the case, and it is not always straightforward to identify who is blackmailing whom when it comes to DI. Is DI an instrument to force states that do not conform to a majority's will, but at the same time do not want to be excluded, into compliance, thereby violating their membership rights and their free choices? Or is it a measure of last resort to escape the blackmailing potential of Member States that block agreements that seem necessary to other (equally free) states to sustain, fortify, and possibly legitimize the EU and its actions? The case thus highlights that DI may raise concerns about domination;[7] however, it is not always clear who is dominating whom.[8] Moreover, there may be instances of 'wrong DI' (and 'right no-DI'), as well as 'wrong no-DI' (and 'right DI'). In other words, sometimes it may be justified on normative grounds to prevent a subgroup of states (I will call them the *differentiators*) from engaging in DI (be that through moving forward with, or opting out of, certain policies). At other times, those against DI (henceforth I will call them the *uniformers*) lack normative grounds for stopping the *differentiators* and thereby preventing DI.

Quite recently, promising attempts have been made to substantively spell out the criteria for when DI is democratically justifiable.[9] This chapter will follow suit on these contributions and build on (internationalist) republicanism by claiming that

[5] Frank Schimmelfennig and Thomas Winzen, 'Instrumental and Constitutional Differentiation in the European Union' (2014) 52 JCMS: Journal of Common Market Studies 354.

[6] Frank Schimmelfennig, 'EU Enlargement and Differentiated Integration: Discrimination or Equal Treatment?' (2014) 21 Journal of European Public Policy 681.

[7] Erik O Eriksen, 'Political Differentiation and the Problem of Dominance: Segmentation and Hegemony: Political Differentiation and the Problem of Dominance' (2018) 57 European Journal of Political Research 989; John Erik Fossum, 'Europe's Triangular Challenge: Differentiation, Dominance and Democracy' (EU3D Research Papers 2019).

[8] For Sandra Kröger, Marta Lorimer, and Richard Bellamy, 'The Democratic Dilemmas of Differentiated Integration: The Views of Political Party Actors' (2021) 21 Swiss Political Science Review 1, '[n]on-domination ... is a two-way street.'

[9] Richard Bellamy and Sandra Kröger, 'A Demoicratic Justification of Differentiated Integration in a Heterogeneous EU' (2017) 39 Journal of European Integration 625; Christopher Lord, 'Utopia or Dystopia? Towards a Normative Analysis of Differentiated Integration' (2015) 22 Journal of European Public Policy 783.

DI must be designed not to violate, but instead honour, the principle of freedom as non-domination (ie the absence of uncontrolled, arbitrary interference in states' choices).[10] When implemented in such a way, DI ensures rather than threatens the principle of Member States'—and thereby citizens'—equality. In other words, DI does not lead to first- and second-class EU memberships.[11] I argue that democratic Member States, through their EU membership, self-bind themselves to associative obligations that call for respecting the other Member States' equality and freedom. The associative obligations derive from but go beyond the text of the Treaties, as they demand honouring non-domination in all types of internal differentiation, including secondary and primary law DI, and extend even to the cooperation of Member States outside the Treaty framework. In particular, associative obligations bind the Member States to respect the other Member States' equality and freedom, which precludes arbitrary interference in their fellow Member States' choices. In other words, as will be elaborated later, they generally owe to each other a fair treatment. However, while I claim that republican principles and norms should apply to other types and even to informal types of DI (as concerning, for instance, secondary law exceptions), there is no straightforward translation of the argument to external differentiation, which concerns states that are not members of the EU.[12] This difference is because the associative obligations do not extend beyond the group of Member States, highlighting once again the core importance of membership as a legally regulated category that comes with rights and obligations. Note that, with respect to the differentiated treatment of Member States and non-Member States, my approach is statist[13] or 'unionist' rather than cosmopolitan.

To avoid arbitrary interference in DI decision-making, the design and implementation of DI will need to conform to notions of procedural justice or fairness (note that I will use these terms interchangeably in this chapter). In particular, the EU organs, but also the Member States, must be given joint control over DI decisions, reflecting the idea of constitutional constraints, so important to Pettit.[14]

[10] Richard Bellamy, *A Republican Europe of States: Cosmopolitanism, Intergovernmentalism and Democracy in the EU* (1st edn, CUP 2019); Cécile Laborde and Miriam Ronzoni, 'What Is a Free State? Republican Internationalism and Globalisation' (2016) 64 Political Studies 279; Philip Pettit, *Republicanism* (OUP 1997); Philip Pettit, *On the People's Terms: A Republican Theory and Model of Democracy* (CUP 2012).

[11] In a resolution passed on 17 January 2019, the European Parliament underlined that differentiated integration should not lead to a 'first- and second-class membership' (European Parliament, 'EU Integration: MEPs Want to End Permanent Opt-outs from EU Law' (*News, European Parliament*, 17 January 2019) <https://www.europarl.europa.eu/news/en/press-room/20190109IPR23023/eu-integration-meps-want-to-end-permanent-opt-outs-from-eu-law> accessed 19 May 2021): 'any form of differentiation initiative that leads to the creation of first- and second-class Member States, or to a perception thereof, would be a major political failure with detrimental consequences for the EU project' (European Parliament resolution of 17 January 2019 on differentiated integration (2018/2093(INI)) [2019] OJ C 411).

[12] see Dirk Leuffen, Berthold Rittberger, and Frank Schimmelfennig, *Differentiated Integration: Explaining Variation in the European Union* (Palgrave Macmillan 2013).

[13] Thomas Nagel, 'The Problem of Global Justice' (2005) 33 Philosophy & Public Affairs 113; Andrea Sangiovanni, 'Global Justice, Reciprocity, and the State' (2007) 35 Philosophy & Public Affairs 3.

[14] Pettit, *On the People's Terms* (n 10).

Moreover, control increases the transparency of DI decisions, which may also foster public awareness of such issues and thereby potentially even strengthen civic 'vigilance'.[15] The important point here is that an agreement on procedural justice[16] is expected to raise the legitimacy of DI. Note that the enhanced cooperation procedure,[17] as laid out in the Treaties—and controlled by the supranational organs[18]—largely corresponds to my understanding of control that is needed for DI's legitimacy; it ensures the freedom of both sides—of those who want to move ahead with deeper integration and those who prefer, or for any other reasons are bound to, the status quo.

Obviously, I am not the first to argue that DI is compatible with the EU Treaties and does not violate the core principles of membership. For instance, Thym[19] has highlighted that DI is an incarnation of the EU's motto 'united in diversity', and also the contributions by Lord[20] and Bellamy and Kröger[21] persuasively show that DI is in alignment with the Treaty goals. In fact, my argument in large part echoes Lord's[22] masterful treatment of the issue, but my approach extends beyond the question of externalities as a source of arbitrary domination. Moreover, it allows for different conclusions to be drawn about internal and external differentiation, and thereby differentiation between EU Member States and non-members.

II. Differentiated Integration Does not Entail Differentiated Membership

As in a well-designed club, EU membership entails equal rights and obligations[23] for the Member States (and thereby, in a democratic understanding, for the citizens).[24]

[15] ibid 5.

[16] Tom R Tyler, 'Social Justice: Outcome and Procedure' (2000) 35 International Journal of Psychology 117.

[17] Steve Peers, 'Enhanced Cooperation: The Cinderella of Differentiated Integration' in Andrea Ott and Bruno de Witte (eds), *Between Flexibility and Disintegration: The Trajectory of Differentiation in EU Law* (Edward Elgar 2017); Daniel Thym, '"United in Diversity"—The Integration of Enhanced Cooperation into the European Constitutional Order' (2005) 6 German Law Journal 1731.

[18] Diane Fromage and Christina Fasone, 'Differentiation and the European Commission' in Stefan Gänzle, Benjamin Leruth, and Jarle Trondal (eds), *Routledge Handbook of Differentiation in the European Union* (Routledge 2022).

[19] Thym, 'United in Diversity' (n 17); Daniel Thym, 'Supranationale Ungleichzeitigkeit Im Recht Der Europäischen Integration' (2006) 41 Europarecht 637.

[20] Lord (n 9).

[21] Bellamy and Kröger, 'A Demoicratic Justification' (n 9); Richard Bellamy and Sandra Kröger, 'Differentiated Integration as a Fair Scheme of Cooperation' (European University Institute 2019) EUI Working Papers RSCAS 2019/27.

[22] Lord (n 9).

[23] see Jan Wouters, 'Constitutional Limits to Differentiation: The Principle of Equality' in Bruno de Witte, Dominik Hanf, and Ellen Vos (eds), *The Many Faces of Differentiation in EU Law* (Intersentia 2001).

[24] Francis Cheneval and Frank Schimmelfennig, 'The Case for Demoicracy in the European Union*' (2013) 51 JCMS: Journal of Common Market Studies 334, 342, 344; Equality is a core component of

Bellamy[25] speaks of 'the TEU [Treaty on European Union]'s meta democratic principle of "equality"', but there are also quite explicit references to equality in the Treaties (cf, for instance, Art 4(2) TEU).[26] In a republican reading, the most important egalitarian good should be '[f]reedom as non-domination'.[27] Pettit, time and again, underlines the 'significantly egalitarian character'[28] of freedom as non-domination.[29] For Pettit, 'someone has dominating power over another, someone dominates or subjugates another, to the extent that 1. they have the capacity to interfere 2. on an arbitrary basis 3. in certain choices that the other is in a position to make'.[30] In *On the People's Terms*, Pettit drops the notion of arbitrariness and, referring to Quentin Skinner's work, rather speaks of 'uncontrolled interference: that is, interference that is exercised at the will or discretion of the interferer; interference that is uncontrolled by the person on the receiving end'.[31] When accepting that equality is important for the EU and that republican principles are well-suited to apply to a demoi-cratic understanding of uniform integration, the question arises whether DI weakens structural equality in the EU.[32]

Functionally defined by de Witte, Hanf, and Vos as 'the facilitation and accommodation of a degree of difference between Member States or regions in relation to

political thought; Pettit, *On the People's Terms* (n 10) 132 underlines that a 'state ought to treat its citizens as equals and . . . that citizens ought to be willing to accept this and to live on equal terms with one another. This assumption is intuitively compelling and is not specific to the republican approach; it is endorsed in every plausible political philosophy'. In fact, political equality is generally considered a foundational criterion of democracy (see Thomas Christiano, *The Constitution of Equality: Democratic Authority and Its Limits* (OUP 2008)); Ronald Dworkin, *Sovereign Virtue: The Theory and Practice of Equality* (Harvard University Press 2000); Erik Oddvar Eriksen and John Erik Fossum, 'Europe's Challenge. Reconstituting Europe or Reconfiguring Democracy?' in Erik Oddvar Eriksen and John Erik Fossum (eds), *Rethinking Democracy and the European Union* (Routledge 2012).

[25] Bellamy (n 10) 102.

[26] Membership at the moment of accession may not fully be completed, but this should only be a temporary phenomenon (see Andrea Ott, 'Differentiation through Accession Law: Free Movement Rights in an Enlarged European Union' in Ott and de Witte (eds) (n 17); Schimmelfennig, *EU Enlargement and Differentiated Integration* (n 6)).

[27] Pettit, *Republicanism* (n 10) 274, 288; Pettit, *On the People's Terms* (n 10) 81.

[28] Pettit, *Republicanism* (n 10) 111.

[29] While Pettit, *Republicanism* (n 10) 117 holds that the 'connection between non-domination and equally intense non-domination is . . . tight', he has no 'objection if others . . . wish to cast the goal explicitly as equally intense non-domination'. Note that while, for John Rawls, *A Theory of Justice* (Belknap Press 1971), structural equality has precedence over material equality, for Pettit the two are inseparable, as the republican conception of freedom as non-domination in fact 'already requires institutions that perform well in regard to values like equality and welfare; thus those values do not have to be introduced as distinct desiderata' (Pettit, *Republicanism* (n 10) 81).

[30] Pettit, *Republicanism* (n 10) 52.

[31] Pettit, *On the People's Terms* (n 10) 58.

[32] It is interesting to note, in this respect, that Pettit, *Republicanism* (n 10) 200 acknowledges that '[t]here should be room in any republican society for dissenting individuals and groups to claim a special treatment under the law. The special treatment allowed should not create the possibility of some individuals exploiting others—and thereby interfering on an arbitrary basis with them through being able to escape the burdens of a system of coercion from which they continue to benefit. But there are a variety of ways in which individuals or groups might receive special treatment, on the basis of conscientious procedural objection, without looking for such an exploitative benefit.'

what would be otherwise common Union policies',[33] or descriptively by Holzinger and Schimmelfennig as an incongruence between 'the territorial extension of European Union (EU) membership and EU rule validity',[34] DI has become a prominent political and legal reality in the EU. While still largely a taboo in primary law during the 1970s,[35] differentiated integration or 'asymmetric non-participation'[36] with respect to primary law has been introduced and sharply extended since the passing of the Maastricht Treaty in the early 1990s. Today only a few policy areas are exempted from some form of internal or external differentiation: internal differentiation means that not all EU Member States participate in certain policies; external differentiation refers to the case of outside states participating in EU policies, as most prominently highlighted by Norway's, Iceland's, or Liechtenstein's membership of the European Economic Area (EEA), and Switzerland's participation in the Schengen regime.[37] Moreover, the impressive dataset presented by Duttle and others highlights that numerous exemptions from EU secondary law have existed since the early beginnings of the European Communities.[38] In addition, the Treaty of Amsterdam established 'enhanced cooperation' as an institutionalized form of differentiated integration,[39] and this was later revised by the Treaties of Nice and Lisbon.[40] In sum, there are many examples of differentiated integration in today's EU.

Elsewhere, my co-authors and I have called the EU a 'system of differentiated integration'.[41] Starting from the observation that the EU was neither a state nor an international organization, we diagnosed that it maintained an 'organizational and member state core but with a level of centralization and territorial extension that vary by function'.[42] Sticking to this characterization, I would claim that DI does not—and, I would add, should not—violate the idea of EU membership. Formal membership of the EU is not incompatible with different forms and manifestations of differentiation; rather, DI can be a means to protect and maintain core principles of the EU, as Lord[43] and Bellamy and

[33] Bruno de Witte, Dominik Hanf, and Ellen Vos, 'Introduction' in de Witte, Hanf, and Vos (eds) (n 23) XII.

[34] Holzinger and Schimmelfennig (n 4) 292.

[35] see Ralf Dahrendorf, 'A Third Europe? Third Jean Monnet Lecture by Professor Ralf Dahrendorf, Director of the London School of Economics' (Archive of European Integration, 26 November 1979) <http://aei.pitt.edu/11346/> accessed 15 May 2021.

[36] Thym, 'United in Diversity' (n 17) 1731.

[37] Leuffen, Rittberger, and Schimmelfennig (n 12).

[38] Thomas Duttle and others, 'Opting out from European Union Legislation: The Differentiation of Secondary Law' (2017) 24 Journal of European Public Policy 406.

[39] Eric Philippart and Geoffrey Edwards, 'The Provisions on Closer Co-operation in the Treaty of Amsterdam: The Politics of Flexibility in the European Union' (1999) 37 JCMS: Journal of Common Market Studies 87; Filip Tuytschaever, *Differentiation in European Union Law* (Hart Publishing 1999).

[40] Daniela A Kroll and Dirk Leuffen, 'Enhanced Cooperation in Practice. An Analysis of Differentiated Integration in EU Secondary Law' (2015) 22 Journal of European Public Policy 353; Peers (n 17).

[41] Leuffen, Rittberger, and Schimmelfennig (n 12).

[42] ibid 10.

[43] Lord (n 9).

Kröger[44] have forcefully shown. I also follow Thym,[45] who has linked differentiation to the EU's motto 'united in diversity'. In line with these authors, I do not believe that graded levels of integration in specific policy areas imply 'graded membership'[46] of the EU. While there can be different degrees of integration into different EU policy regimes, EU membership is dichotomous: you are either in or out.

Non-domination, in the case of DI, must mean that the majority does not dominate the minority, but also that the minority does not dominate the majority. In other words, there may be legitimate and illegitimate forms of DI. When DI is legitimate—ie it contributes to minimizing domination—then the *uniformers* lack justifications for preventing DI. When it is illegitimate, however, the *differentiators* must be stopped.

Lord shows that 'managing externalities can provide . . . a consistent standard for evaluating differential and uniform integration, and for making practical choices between the two'.[47] In particular, he argues that, if 'freedom is defined as absence of arbitrary domination, it will be incomplete without freedom from polluters, monopolists or free riders, or, in short, freedom from externalities'.[48] And, in fact, externalities have been an important component of DI research, at least since Kölliker's seminal contribution.[49] Importantly, domination can result both from DI imposing negative externalities on non-participating states and from non-participating states arbitrarily blocking DI.[50] Lord's focus is on externalities, and the losers may, in principle, receive compensations. However, there can also be other challenges related to DI that cannot be directly translated into an externality framework, but that may very well violate republican principles, eg by violating core community norms. For instance, constitutional differentiations (as the introductory example of Hungary and Poland concerning the rule of law mechanism may highlight) cannot always be directly linked to an externality framework. Kelemen,[51] for instance, objects to rule of law differentiation because he fears a deadly blow to the 'law state' legitimacy and the principle of supremacy of EU law, and thereby to Member State equality.[52] This reasoning conforms to the more general non-domination logic, but I find it harder to link it to the externality

[44] Bellamy and Kröger, 'A Demoicratic Justification' (n 9).

[45] Thym, 'United in Diversity' (n 17); Thym, 'Supranationale Ungleichzeititgkeit' (n 19).

[46] Frank Schimmelfennig, 'Good Governance and Differentiated Integration: Graded Membership in the European Union: Good Governance and Differentiated Integration' (2016) 55 European Journal of Political Research 789.

[47] Lord (n 9) 785.

[48] ibid 786.

[49] Alkuin Kölliker, 'Bringing Together or Driving Apart the Union? Towards a Theory of Differentiated Integration' (2001) 24 West European Politics 125.

[50] Sandra Kröger rightly pointed out to me that the case of free-riding, while being a form of unfairness, probably falls short of domination. Free-riding should, thus, be treated separately.

[51] Roger Daniel Kelemen, 'Is Differentiation Possible in Rule of Law?' (2019) 17 Comparative European Politics 246.

[52] see Federico Fabbrini, 'After the OMT Case: The Supremacy of EU Law as the Guarantee of the Equality of the Member States' (2015) 16 German Law Journal 1003.

framework developed by Lord.[53] I therefore stick to the more general conception that DI must not violate the principle of freedom as non-domination.

Importantly, to intersubjectively establish the costs of DI policies, the different parties and actors need to interact with one another. Such interactions, as part of the system of constitutional constraints, relate to the control dimension inherent in Pettit's later definition of non-domination.[54] Moreover, such interactions, when publicly executed, would enhance contestability.[55] For Pettit,[56] constitutional constraints in combination with 'eternal vigilance'[57] are preconditions for the maintenance of freedom as non-domination. I will claim in the following that an institutionalized system of control may also strengthen public attentiveness in relation to EU affairs.

III. Why Non-domination Applies to Internal but not External Differentiation

Following Pettit[58] and Bellamy,[59] structural political inequalities are minimized when non-domination prevails. In my understanding of the EU, the principle of non-domination should apply to all forms of internal differentiation, even extending beyond the Treaty context proper. However, it need not apply to external differentiation. The reason for this distinction consists in the associative obligations that come with membership, and which make the EU Member States owe more to each other than to outsiders. In particular, EU membership not only entails respecting the fundamental norms enumerated in Article 2 TEU (eg the respect of democracy, the rule of law, and human rights) and the willingness to contribute to the EU's objectives, but Article 122 TFEU (Treaty on the Functioning of the EU), which gained prominence during the COVID-19 crisis, as it paved the way for 'Next Generation EU', invokes a 'spirit of solidarity' between the Member States (cf also Art 222 TFEU and Art 3(3) TEU). Article 4(3) TEU underlines 'the principle of sincere cooperation'. In the Sibiu Declaration of 9 May 2019, the heads of state and government reiterate that the Member States:

> will stay united, through thick and thin. We will show each other solidarity in times of need and we will always stand together. We can and we will speak with

[53] Lord (n 9).
[54] Pettit, *On the People's Terms* (n 10) 58.
[55] Pettit, *Republicanism* (n 10) 183ff. On the importance of democratic control, see also Laborde and Ronzoni (n 10) 288.
[56] Pettit, *On the People's Terms* (n 10) 5.
[57] see also Pettit, *Republicanism* (n 10) 250.
[58] Pettit, *Republicanism* (n 10); Pettit, *On the People's Terms* (n 10).
[59] Bellamy (n 10).

one voice. We will always look for joint solutions, listening to each other in a spirit of understanding and respect.[60]

These examples suggest that EU membership, as part of the EU's constitutional order,[61] entails associative political obligations[62] which extend beyond the formal decision-making procedures and policies contained in the Treaties. Likewise, for Bellamy,[63] the 'normative goal of an EU conceived as an association of sovereign democratic states is to ensure fair terms of cooperation between them'.[64,65]

Therefore, the general principles guiding what democratic Member States 'owe to each other',[66] which I have already summarized as the obligation to respect freedom as non-domination of all Member States, should apply not just to the forms of DI contained in the Treaties, like enhanced cooperation.[67] In fact, the rules regulating the establishment and the implementation of enhanced cooperation are designed to respect core norms of the EU, such as the integration goals and openness to those states which are reluctant to join a new policy at the start:[68] According to Article 20 TEU, enhanced cooperation 'shall aim to further the objectives of the Union, protect its interests and reinforce its integration process. Such co-operation shall be open at any time to all Member States.'[69] Accordingly,

[60] Council of the EU, Press Release 335/19, 9 May 2019.

[61] John Erik Fossum and Agustín José Menéndez, *The Constitution's Gift: A Constitutional Theory for a Democratic European Union* (Rowman & Littlefield Publishers 2011).

[62] Margaret Gilbert, *A Theory of Political Obligation* (OUP 2006) <https://oxford.universitypressscholarship.com/view/10.1093/0199274959.001.0001/acprof-9780199274956> accessed 19 May 2021; Bas van der Vossen, 'Associative Political Obligations' (2011) 6 Philosophy Compass 477.

[63] Bellamy (n 10) 174.

[64] Thomas Scanlon, *What We Owe to Each Other* (Nachdr, Belknap Press of Harvard University Press 1998); Christopher McMahon, *Reasonableness and Fairness: A Historical Theory* (CUP 2016) 21; Jonathan Wolff, 'Fairness, Respect, and the Egalitarian Ethos' (1998) 27 Philosophy & Public Affairs 97.

[65] Arbitrariness has been linked to fairness: for instance, McMahon (n 64) 21 recalls that '[p]erhaps the most familiar approach to fairness in the contemporary literature ties the concept to arbitrariness'. Thus, in *What We Owe to Each Other*, Scanlon (n 64) 212 says that policies that arbitrarily favour one person over others are, in that respect, unfair. And Wolff (n 64) 106 has examined the place of fairness, which he understands as 'the demand that no one should be advantaged or disadvantaged by arbitrary factors', in egalitarian theories of justice. 'We can speak here of fairness as non-arbitrariness (or unfairness as arbitrariness).' In particular, Scanlon (n 64) 212ff argues that policies that 'arbitrarily favor one person over others . . . are in this respect unfair. As I have said, each person has reason to prefer partial principles that would favor him or her. If one of these principles is made binding, with no further reason to support it, then one person's reason for wanting to be favored is given precedence over others' similar reasons, without justification. This is what makes such a choice arbitrary, and makes the principle rejectable. This substantive objection applies to principles that make essential use of proper names as well as to those relying on "rigged" descriptions.'

[66] Scanlon (n 64).

[67] Democratic backsliding may raise concerns about the issue of whether Member States are entitled to intervene in each other's affairs. One could counter that the breaching of democracy not just undermines a key basis of their cooperation, but also violates the principle of citizens' equality.

[68] Thym, 'United in Diversity' (n 17) discusses 'substantive constraints' as well as 'procedural requirements' related to enhanced cooperation in more depth.

[69] Note, however, that the European patent and its establishment in the form of enhanced cooperation was not considered as 'fair' by Italy and Spain, leading to lasting dissensus and a lack of support (see Kroll and Leuffen (n 40)).

the associative rights and obligations of the Member States—not to be dominated and not to dominate—apply to informally negotiated forms of DI (be that with respect to primary or secondary law) or even outside cooperation[70] as well, a prominent example of the latter being the initial signing of the Schengen Agreement in 1985.

At the same time, as the associative obligations of EU membership do not extend to non-EU states, the same principles need not apply to internal and external differentiation. Thus, there is a difference between what the Member States owe to each other and what they owe to outsiders (in particular, those that would be in a position to become members, but that prefer not to—to borrow an expression from Melville's 'Bartleby').[71]

IV. The Citizens, Fairness, and Support of DI

So far, I have focused on a normative treatment of DI. However, the issue is of practical political concern as well. DI has become an integral part of EU politics and the debate on the future of the EU. For example, at least one of the five future scenarios depicted by the European Commission's in its *White Paper on the Future of Europe*[72] relates to DI. The problem is that while DI theoretically offers a way to reconcile the desires of the drivers and brakemen of integration, there remain many concerns against it.[73] The public, in particular, but also partisan actors[74] are strongly divided on DI. Leuffen and others[75] show that there is strong disagreement amongst European citizens about the merits of a two-speed Europe, and there is also evidence that citizens care about the fairness of different forms of DI. In particular, Eurobarometer data reveals differences between equality-oriented and more economically liberal-oriented citizens. Moreover, there are substantive differences between citizens of northern and southern Member States. In particular, citizens of the latter seem concerned about political and economic inequalities or discrimination caused or intensified through DI.[76] On average, only a little

[70] Kroll and Leuffen (n 40).

[71] Future research should inspect possible variation of different types of external differentiation with greater care. For instance, candidate countries which still lack capacities to join the EU may be distinguished from those that would be capable but are unwilling to join. This point has been made to me by Max Heermann and Diane Fromage.

[72] European Commission, 'White Paper on the Future of Europe. Reflections and Scenarios for the EU27 by 2025' (2017).

[73] Rebecca Adler-Nissen, 'Opting Out of an Ever Closer Union: The Integration *Doxa* and the Management of Sovereignty' (2011) 34 West European Politics 1092; Kröger, Lorimer, and Bellamy (n 8) summarize the most important pros and cons related to DI.

[74] Kröger, Lorimer, and Bellamy (n 8).

[75] Dirk Leuffen, Julian Schuessler, and Jana Gómez Díaz, 'Public Support for Differentiated Integration: Individual Liberal Values and Concerns about Member State Discrimination' [2020] Journal of European Public Policy 1.

[76] Adler-Nissen (n 73); Kröger, Lorimer, and Bellamy (n 8).

more than 50 per cent of citizens seem to approve of the concept of a two-speed Europe,[77] and that should be of concern, given that the integration project increasingly hinges on public support.[78]

Therefore, even beyond the normative argument already displayed, it seems politically important to assure that DI does not alienate citizens from the EU. Arguably, lacking perceptions of fairness would lead to contestations of DI. When again following Scanlon's[79] linkage of fairness to non-arbitrariness, and non-arbitrariness to non-domination, assuring the principle of freedom as non-domination in the establishment and implementation of DI may be the best way to sustain citizens' support. The best assurance against domination consists in setting up institutional mechanisms that guarantee a high degree of control. Thus, while structures or outputs are commonly linked to fairness, here I also consider the process as an important fairness component (Pettit,[80] too, stresses the importance of procedural fairness when discussing the need for civility). Elster speaks of 'act unfairness',[81] and Frey and others establish that '[p]rocedural utility means that people not only value actual outcomes, i.e., the what, but also the conditions and processes that lead to these outcomes, i.e., the how. Procedural utility thus represents a completely different approach to human well-being from the standard approach applied in economics.'[82] The process dimensions can be linked to what has been called, in the literature, procedural fairness or procedural justice.[83] Greenberg defines procedural justice as 'the perceived fairness of the policies and procedures used to make decisions'.[84] And this dimension has been shown to be crucial for solving controversies in very different fields, ranging from distributional conflicts to normative issues.[85] Bolton and others go as far as stating that '[p]rocedures are the area where fairness arguably has its largest influence on modern societies'.[86] Levi[87] establishes that perceived fairness increases citizens' willingness to consent even to extreme cases of service, such as, for example, conscriptions and military service.

[77] On different concepts or types of DI, see Holzinger and Schimmelfennig (n 4); Alexander Stubb, *Negotiating Flexibility in the European Union* (Palgrave Macmillan 2002) <http://link.springer.com/10.1057/9781403907615> accessed 27 September 2020.

[78] Sara B Hobolt and Catherine E de Vries, 'Public Support for European Integration' (2016) 19 Annual Review of Political Science 413.

[79] Scanlon (n 64) 212.

[80] Pettit, *Republicanism* (n 10) 246.

[81] Jon Elster, *Nuts and Bolts for the Social Sciences* (CUP 1989) 365.

[82] Bruno S Frey, Matthias Benz, and Alois Stutzer, 'Introducing Procedural Utility: Not Only What, but Also How Matters' (2004) 160 Journal of Institutional and Theoretical Economics (JITE)/Zeitschrift für die gesamte Staatswissenschaft 377.

[83] Tyler (n 16).

[84] Jerald Greenberg, 'Organizational Justice: Yesterday, Today, and Tomorrow' (1990) 16 Journal of Management 399, 402.

[85] Tyler (n 16); Tom R Tyler and Steven L Blader (eds), *Cooperation in Groups: Procedural Justice, Social Identity, and Behavioral Engagement* (Psychology Press 2000).

[86] Gary E Bolton, Jordi Brandts, and Axel Ockenfels, 'Fair Procedures: Evidence from Games Involving Lotteries' (2005) 115 The Economic Journal 1054.

[87] Margaret Levi, *Consent, Dissent, and Patriotism* (1st edn, CUP 1997).

According to Tyler, 'research demonstrates that people are more willing to accept decisions when they feel that those decisions are made through decision-making procedures they view as fair'.[88] In sum, there is abundant evidence in the psychological and behavioural economics literature in support of the claim that procedural justice matters for taking (costly) decisions. For political scientists, there is no doubt that legitimacy is a foundation for the authoritativeness of a state.[89]

I would claim that assuring a high degree of Member State control would strengthen the perceived fairness of the system, and thereby increase citizens' support for DI.[90] The most straightforward way to increase control is to tie all EU Member States into decision-making on DI and give them a say in its design.[91] In particular, the necessary support of the European Commission, as well as of a substantive number of non-participating states, eg through qualified majority voting, would assure a system of constitutional constraints. When assuming that there is a general agreement on fairness and its intrinsic value, this should minimize the potential for inappropriate manipulation of such rules (eg through the construction of package deals). By not granting veto powers to all Member States, the freedom of the more integration-friendly states would be procedurally protected as well.

V. Application: Can an 'À la carte Europe' be a Fair Europe?

In order to illustrate the idea of procedural fairness in DI, I will, in the following, apply the basic ideas which were already spelt out earlier in this chapter to a concept of a so-called 'à la carte Europe', arguably representing the most radical model of DI. This concept or model was already identified in Stubb's[92] early attempts to get to grips with DI. In particular, guided by the three dimensions of (i) time, (ii) space, and (iii) matter, Stubb[93] distinguished 'multi-speed', 'variable geometry', and 'à la carte' models of differentiated integration. Stubb defines an 'à la carte Europe'

88 Tyler (n 16) 117.

89 eg Seymour Martin Lipset, 'Some Social Requisites of Democracy: Economic Development and Political Legitimacy' (1959) 53 American Political Science Review 69.

90 According to the *Webster's New World Dictionary* (2nd College edn, David B Guralnik (ed), Word Publishing Company 1970), 'fairness' and 'fair' both 'derive from the Gothic word *fagrs*', which meant 'pleasing to behold', and in turn from an Indo-European root that meant 'to be content'. (As cited by Benjamin David Steele, 'What is the Origin of our Sense of "Fairness", and of what is Unfair? Children Use those Words a Lot. What do they Mean?', *Quora* <https://www.quora.com/What-is-the-origin-of-our-sense-of-fairness-and-of-what-is-unfair-Children-use-those-words-a-lot-What-do-they-mean> accessed 19 May 2021. Applying this aesthetic concept to the EU, I postulate that DI should be organized in a way that is 'pleasing to behold' from a citizen's perspective. Note also that fairness is among the six values that are cherished by almost all people worldwide, according to Jonathan Haidt, *The Righteous Mind: Why Good People are Divided by Politics and Religion* (Vintage Books 2013).

91 Note that the success of the ingenious Brexit slogan 'take back control' may underline that the concept of control resonates strongly with citizens' desires.

92 Alexander CG Stubb, 'A Categorization of Differentiated Integration' (1996) 34 JCMS: Journal of Common Market Studies 283; Stubb, *Negotiating Flexibility* (n 77).

93 Stubb, 'A Categorization of Differentiated Integration' (n 92).

as a 'mode of differentiated integration whereby respective Member States are able to pick-and-choose, as from a menu, in which policy area they would like to participate, whilst at the same time holding only to a minimum number of common objectives'.[94] Importantly, the radical concept of an 'à la carte' Europe should allow opt-outs, even in relation to already established uniform EU legislation. This has been linked to 'raisin-picking', as an immoral practice of a maximization of gains at the expense of others.

How can the practice of 'opting out' of existing legislation be rendered fair and viable for the other EU Member States? In the wake of the Brexit referendum, Hanno Degner and I have played around with a model which aims at striking a balance between the—in principle legitimate—will of a Member State not to be part of a specific regime and the other EU Member States' similarly legitimate desire to avoid free-riding.[95] In particular, we have proposed that *ex post* opt-outs—mirroring to some extent the enhanced cooperation procedure—would require a qualified majority in the Council and a simple majority in the European Parliament.[96] This system would hinder states from free-riding at the expense of others. If the wishes behind, and the conditions of, an opt-out were to be considered fair, a deal could be reached; in contrast, unfair instances of differentiation would very likely be prevented by this procedure.

In addition, the negotiation process should take place in a transparent context, which would allow the citizens—both amongst the *uniformers* and the *differentiators*—to form their preferences and ideas on the issues concerned. If the process of granting à la carte opt-outs is considered fair—in that it also takes into account the interests and ideas of the pro-integrationist Member States—even such an admittedly rather radical model could, therefore, strengthen the value of EU membership. On the downside, however, in the long run extensive opt-out practices may lead to desocialization, or disintegration cascades that could possibly reduce Member States' will to participate in the production of common goods.[97] At the same time, the possibility of choice could enhance the legitimacy of the EU by imposing fewer constraints on Member States. In fact, in a recent article, Schraff and Schimmelfennig[98] highlight that DI, through extending states' choice set, has

[94] ibid 285.

[95] Dirk Leuffen and Hanno Degner, 'Für Ein Faires Rosinenpicken in Der EU' *Frankfurter Allgemeine Zeitung* (Frankfurt, 3 August 2016).

[96] A similar idea is proposed by Bellamy (n 10) 202, but for him opt-out requests could be blocked by qualified majority in the Council (and an absolute majority in the European Parliament). Moreover, in the Banking Union, Member States also established a double majority—of those in and outside the Single Supervisory Mechanism—for rules applicable to all Member States (see Lord (n 9) 795ff).

[97] Moreover, on the downside, it could be noted that legal fragmentation may be a consequence, leading to a less governable and transparent EU, which, in turn, may decrease citizen support. Sandra Kröger has communicated this point to me.

[98] Dominik Schraff and Frank Schimmelfennig, 'Does Differentiated Integration Strengthen the Democratic Legitimacy of the EU? Evidence from the 2015 Danish Opt-out Referendum' (2020) 21 European Union Politics 590.

the potential to increase the perceived democratic quality of EU decision-making and to strengthen citizens' support. One could, furthermore, expect such decision-making to activate the public debate on the EU, both in the states that desire opt-outs and in those that promote integration, thereby fostering public attentiveness and strengthening the scope for, or the ability of, citizens to contest the decisions they are subject to. In sum, such a system would correspond rather well to the three core republican ideas of (i) freedom as non-domination, (ii) constitutional constraints, and (iii) eternal civic vigilance.[99]

VI. Conclusion

This chapter first shows that DI does not, in principle, violate the concepts of EU membership and Member State equality. Starting from a republican premise, I argue that the most important equality that EU Member States—which in a demoi-cratic understanding translates to the EU citizens as well—should share is freedom as non-domination. DI can be a means to prevent domination, thereby strengthening equal freedom. But Member States are obliged not to arbitrarily interfere in other Member States' choices through DI. Imposing negative externalities on others is one, but not the only, example of arbitrary interference. At the same time, the *uniformers* have the obligation not to dominate the *differentiators* by generally objecting to DI. Second, the chapter argues that the same norms should apply to different kinds of internal differentiation, but not necessarily to external differentiation. The reason for the difference consists in the presence or not of associative obligations acquired through EU membership. The third contribution of the chapter is to move forward practical guidance on how to establish fair practices of DI. In particular, I stress the importance of procedural justice and claim that DI should be decided in a transparent and inclusive way in order to grant control to both sides (those that want to cooperate more closely and those that are more reluctant to do so). Thus, constitutional constraints should be respected, or be established, for the cases of 'outside cooperation' or an 'à la carte Europe'. As a side effect, constitutional constraints may also freshen the public debate on the EU and awaken the contestatory citizenry. In sum, the conception of DI that I present in this chapter seems to fulfil the core ideas of republicanism, namely that freedom as non-domination is assured through constitutional constraints and civic vigilance.[100] For European federalists, my proposition will probably lack ambition, with its strong attachment to the idea of a republican Europe of states.[101]

99 see Pettit, *On the People's Terms* (n 10) 5.
100 see Pettit, *On the People's Terms* (n 10) 5.
101 Bellamy (n 10).

I have not, in this chapter, addressed the question of the EU organs.[102] Nor have I detailed the question of substantive justice that also may be related to DI with respect to certain policy areas. For instance, should states be arbitrarily excluded from redistributive measures, that would represent a clear instance of domination and a violation of these states' membership rights.[103] Ideally, however, this should be prevented by the proposed control mechanism. The question of in which areas DI is more legitimate or problematic should certainly be the object of future inquiries. I hope that the republican approach used in this and other work on the topic may be of help in this respect as well.

[102] see on that, eg Fromage and Fasone (n 18); Max Heermann and Dirk Leuffen, 'No Representation without Integration! Why Differentiated Integration Challenges the Composition of the European Parliament' (2020) 58 JCMS: Journal of Common Market Studies 1016.

[103] Note that an exclusion may be non-arbitrary where a state violates certain criteria, either by not falling into predefined and agreed-on categories of recipient states or regions (eg particularly rich regions may not fulfil criteria of neediness required to be flagged out as states that deserve to receive aid) or by objecting to certain normative criteria, as highlighted by the case of Hungary and Poland with respect to the rule of law mechanism and 'Next Generation EU'.

3

How Differentiated is EMU Membership? The *De Facto* and *De Jure* Constraints of EU Economic Governance

Mark Dawson and Tomasz P Woźniakowski

I. Introduction

From its first establishment, Economic and Monetary Union (EMU) has been described as the 'mother' example of differentiated integration (DI) in Europe.[1] To briefly define the term, EMU refers to the integration and coordination by the EU of the economic policies of its Member States (it is not, therefore, confined to eurozone states). The very notion established in the Maastricht Treaty—of a Union based not always on common obligations but on varied degrees of integration between states—owes much to the EMU example, and particularly to the reluctance of the UK to embrace the Euro project. At the same time, the position of EMU in the overall architecture of the Union has changed significantly since 1993. It is worth, therefore, reflecting on what EMU tells us about the meaning of 'membership' of the European Union in the 2020s.

EMU's original design followed a general logic of using DI as a response to centrifugal tendencies.[2] Two centrifugal forces are particularly important. The first—reflecting the UK's opt-out negotiated at Maastricht—is preference divergence. As a policy field involving the sharing of authority over what political scientists have termed a 'core state power' (with massive fiscal consequences for the states involved), DI in EMU is triggered by the fact that states diverge in their willingness to pool sovereignty over different economic policies.[3]

An equally important second centrifugal force, however, is functional divergence. Different states enter EMU from different starting points, and might require different degrees of fiscal and monetary oversight depending on their economic situation. To give an early example, the entry of states into the eurozone from

[1] eg Francis Snyder, 'EMU—Integration and Differentiation: Metaphor for European Union' in Paul Craig and Grainne de Burca (eds), *The Evolution of EU Law* (OUP 2011).

[2] On general conditions for use of DI, see Frank Schimmelfennig, 'The Choice for Differentiated Europe: An Intergovernmentalist Theoretical Framework' [2019] 17 Comparative European Politics 2.

[3] Philipp Genschel and Markus Jacthenfuchs (eds), *Beyond the Regulatory Polity? The European Integration of Core State Powers* (OUP 2014).

Mark Dawson and Tomasz P Woźniakowski, *How Differentiated is EMU Membership? The* De Facto *and* De Jure *Constraints of EU Economic Governance* In: *Redefining EU Membership*. Edited by: Diane Fromage, Oxford University Press.
 DOI: 10.1093/9780191948145.003.0003

Maastricht onwards was conditional upon their fulfilling strict economic and monetary convergence criteria. To give a more recent one, the monitoring of compliance with conditionality, in the context of EU financial assistance, also speaks to divergence in obligations depending on the fiscal position of the state concerned. Functional and preference diversity thus act as centrifugal forces, establishing differentiated obligations both between states and across the different policy fields EMU entails.

EMU also, however, has strong centripetal forces: forces that have grown in strength as the ambitions of the EMU project have increased. We can again describe these centripetal forces using the vocabulary of preference and functional convergence. In both cases, the context for this convergence is that states both within and outwith the eurozone have high economic interdependencies, and thus externalities that force the coordination of their economic policy decisions.[4] In terms of preference convergence, the euro is more than an economic project but carries a political element, ie it anchors the wider EU policy-making system, with the EU Treaties stating that the euro is the Union's 'single currency'.[5] This has always created fears of being 'left out' of decision-making, encouraging states to 'opt in' even to parts of EMU that they are legally not obliged to join (a prominent example being the decision of a number of non-eurozone states to join the EU's Fiscal Compact, in late 2012).[6]

In terms of functional convergence, states on the outside of certain EMU policies may either wish to, or be forced to, join aspects of EMU at a future date, thus requiring a degree of economic convergence in order to do so. From its inception, the rules of the eurozone have thus been accompanied by an umbrella of further fiscal and other rules designed for all EMU members (such as debt and deficit rules). The nexus between EMU and political union, as well as the inevitable economic interdependencies between EU states, thus act as centripetal forces, making obligations in EMU more rather than less uniform.

The wider argument of this chapter will be that these centripetal forces create an EMU that is less differentiated than it (formally) appears. While the chapter was completed as the COVID-19 crisis began, there is every indication that the changes to EMU as a result of the pandemic will produce further processes of economic convergence in EMU, further eroding the distinction between full and partial EMU membership. The direction of travel is thus contrary to what one might have expected given the increasing widening and deepening of the Union since Maastricht.

The chapter will advance this argument in two main steps. Part II will start with *de jure* differentiation (ie differences in legal status and obligations between Member

[4] On these externalities and their impact, see Aidan Regan, 'The Imbalance of Capitalisms in the Eurozone: Can the North and South of Europe Converge?' [2017] 15 Comparative European Politics 6.

[5] Art 133 of theTreaty on the Functioning of the European Union (TFEU).

[6] George Tsebelis and Hahm Hyeonho, 'Suspending Vetoes: How the Euro Countries Achieved Unanimity in the Fiscal Compact' [2014] 21 Journal of European Public Policy 10.

States within EMU). Here, we will deal with EMU's three main fields: monetary policy, fiscal policy, and prudential/banking supervision. Part III will then examine *de facto* differentiation (ie how EMU obligations are concretely applied and interpreted at the national and EU levels, including in their accountability dimensions). While Part II will examine EMU as a whole, Part III (given its need to empirically investigate concrete implementation of EMU policies at the national policy) will focus on one field of EMU only, namely fiscal policy coordination in the context of the European Semester. We will concentrate on Poland, the largest non-eurozone Member State. As such, it is exempted from some requirements under the Semester: for instance, it does not have to submit draft budgetary plans (DBPs). However, its parliament regularly discusses all major documents of the EU's economic policy coordination and, as such, can hold the relevant executive institutions accountable.

The Semester is a useful case to study *de facto* differentiation, in that it: (i) displays both of the factors of preference and functional convergence/divergence which were discussed earlier in this chapter; and (ii) contains a mixed set of *de jure* obligations, some applicable only to the eurozone, and others to all EU Member States. In the concluding part, we will reflect on what the experience of differentiation of EU membership in the Semester process can tell us about the likely trajectory of differentiation under a 'post-COVID' EMU (a trajectory that seems, again, likely to limit rather than foster differentiation).

II. *De Jure* Differentiation

De jure differentiation refers, of course, to distinctions between the obligations of EU Member States in EMU established through law. We can distinguish between different varieties of *de jure* differentiation in EMU.

The first of these is intra-Treaty differentiation. According to Treaty rules, the default status of EU states is that they are eurozone members unless subject to a derogation emerging from either: (a) an explicit opt-out (like UK/Denmark, under Protocols 15 and 16); or (b) an inability to meet the criteria for admission set out under Article 140 of the Treaty on the Functioning of the European Union (TFEU). Article 139 TFEU exempts derogating states from a number of Treaty obligations in the field of EMU (eg concerning acts of the European Central Bank (ECB) and coercive elements of the Stability and Growth Pact). These differentiated provisions can be seen in light of some of the concepts discussed in this project as a whole. If I am not a member of a given club, there are surely limits on what the club can expect of me, and what I should have to contribute to its maintenance.[7]

[7] On the notion of 'club' governance and its application to debates on DI in the EU, see Giandomenico Majone, 'The European Union Post-Brexit: Static or Dynamic Adaptation?' [2017] 23 European Law Journal 1–2.

Many of the provisions of the EMU chapter, however (eg the obligations to avoid excessive deficits and to coordinate economic policies) continue to apply to all Member States. The Treaties, therefore, require 'participation' in the EMU project, regardless of eurozone membership. Here, two factors are of some significance. The first was already discussed: as all EU states are obliged to (eventually) enter the eurozone, participation in common rules is an important element in preparing states for eurozone membership. The second is that, even if non-eurozone states stay on the outside, economic imbalances in the wider EU (given the common participation of all EU states in a single common market) have the capacity to affect the stability of the eurozone. The Treaty's economic policy chapter, therefore, creates an economic policy framework for the EU as a whole (including a set of common guiding principles under Article 119(3) TFEU), while recognizing that these principles might be institutionalized differently for different Member States.

The second variety is extra-Treaty differentiation: the adoption of international treaties between EU states outside of the EU framework.[8] The Treaty on Stability, Coordination and Governance (or Fiscal Compact); the European Stability Mechanism Treaty; and the Inter-Governmental Agreement on Contributions to the Single Resolution Fund all represent efforts to establish new obligations/capacities for eurozone states. At the same time, they were adopted either because of a reluctance on the part of other Member States to join their provisions (such as the UK, in the case of the Fiscal Compact) or a need to establish a different governance framework for a given EMU policy, with stronger intergovernmental control.

These examples are, however, open to non-eurozone states. This has resulted in far less differentiation than the 'optional' nature of these Treaties for many states would imply. To take the example of the Fiscal Compact, it was eventually signed by all states bar the UK. Equally, the Resolution Fund agreement was signed by all states bar the UK and Sweden. This bears out a point made in the introduction: to the extent that the eurozone is an increasingly important centre of EU decision-making, Member States bear a political cost by excluding themselves from its key programmes. Non-eurozone members have, therefore, often rushed to adopt even relatively burdensome obligations (such as the Fiscal Compact debt brake rule), for fear of being left out of common policies.[9]

A third variety of *de jure* differentiation is below the level of the Treaties, concerning differences in obligations under secondary legislation. In fiscal policy, Article 136 TFEU allows the adoption of specific legislation for the eurozone,

[8] Bruno de Witte, 'An Undivided Union: Differentiated Integration in Post-Brexit Times' [2018] 55 Common Market Law Review 2.

[9] Much of this embrace may, of course, reflect the embedding of the Fiscal Compact in existing EU secondary law, and the lack of real mechanisms of enforcement (thanks to Diane Fromage for this point). On the continued reluctance of Member States to implement the debt brake obligation, see GiovanniBoggero and Pasquale Annicchino, 'Who Will Ever Kick Us Out?': Italy, the Balanced Budget Rule and the Implementation of the Fiscal Compact' [2014] 20 European Public Law 2.

whereas Article 138 also allows specific eurozone-only legislation for participation in the international monetary system. The former legal basis was utilized for the adoption of the 'six-pack' and 'two-pack', designed to strengthen EU fiscal surveillance following the euro crisis.[10] The aftermath of the crisis also saw a series of legislative measures designed to strengthen prudential supervision in the eurozone, laying down a framework for direct ECB supervision (through the Single Supervisory Mechanism (SSM)) of large Eurozone banks.

Here too, however, the framework of secondary law established less differentiation than one might imagine. While the two-pack (given that it contains stronger enforcement mechanisms) applies only to eurozone states,[11] the majority of the six-pack provisions apply to all Member States. In the Banking Union, the main SSM Regulation applies to eurozone states, but can allow the direct supervision of significant institutions in non-eurozone states by the ECB, where agreed under a 'close cooperation agreement' under Article 7 of the SSM Regulation. Banks in such states will not have access to ECB liquidity but are subject to the Banking Union single rulebook (a set of rules applicable across the EU). Both Bulgaria and Croatia entered into such an agreement in October 2020.[12] By joining the Banking Union these states also became participants in the Single Resolution Mechanism for the winding down of large European banks. As a result, only six EU states (Czech Republic, Denmark, Hungary, Poland, Romania, and Sweden) are currently outside both the monetary and banking pillars of EMU.

A final variety of *de jure* differentiation concerns policy coordination and 'soft' non-binding forms of law. It is in the very nature of policy coordination that it is differentiated. Part of the appeal of instruments like the European Semester (and the open method of coordination (OMC), on which it draws)[13] is tied to their ability to achieve common goals, like economic competitiveness or consolidation, through diverse means.[14] The need for flexibility in how common economic goals are reached reflects the significant differences in the basic political economies of EU

[10] For an overview of the applicable Acts, see European Commission, 'Legal basis of the Stability and Growth Pact' (https://economy-finance.ec.europa.eu/economic-and-fiscal-governance/stability-and-growth-pact/legal-basis-stability-and-growth-pact_en#:~:text=The%20legal%20basis%20of%20the,values%20on%20deficit%20and%20debt.) u

[11] Regulation 473/2013/EU on common provisions for monitoring and assessing draft budgetary plans and ensuring the correction of excessive deficit of the Member States in the euro area [2013] OJ L140/11, Art 1(3).

[12] Decision (EU) 2020/1015 of the European Central Bank of 24 June 2020 on the establishment of close cooperation between the European Central Bank and Българска народна банка (Bulgarian National Bank) (ECB/2020/30) (https://eur-lex.europa.eu/legal-content/EN/TXT/?uri=celex%3A32020D1015); Decision (EU) 2020/1016 of the European Central Bank of 24 June 2020 on the establishment of close cooperation between the European Central Bank and the Croatian National Bank (https://eur-lex.europa.eu/legal-content/EN/TXT/PDF/?uri=CELEX:32020D1016)

[13] On the link between the OMC and the Semester, see Mark Dawson, 'New Governance in the EU after the Euro Crisis: Retired or Reborn' in Marise Cremona and Claire Kilpatrick (eds), *EU Legal Acts: Challenges and Transformations* (OUP 2018).

[14] Charles Sabel and Jonathan Zeitlin, 'Learning from Difference: The New Architecture of Experimentalist Governance in the EU' (2008) 14 European Law Journal 3, 289.

states. Recommendations under the European Semester (the so-called country-specific recommendations or 'CSRs') are, therefore, 'country-specific'. The 'hard law' instruments embedded in the European Semester, such as excessive deficit (EDP) and macro-economic imbalances (MIP) procedures, also by design treat states differently depending on their fiscal situation, ie those with higher fiscal risks are subject to additional obligations and monitoring than better performers. EMU law, therefore, creates a policy coordination framework that distinguishes between the obligations of states depending on their economic position and performance.[15]

Again, however, policy coordination is partially aimed at managing diversity, and partially at inducing convergence. A number of instruments in the Semester (eg the Annual Sustainable Growth Strategy) act as centralizing forces, establishing sets of CSRs that tend to produce common patterns across states. As discussed by a number of authors, we see variation in CSRs over time.[16] Yet this variation also reflects common priorities set at the EU level, with CSRs under the Barroso Commission tending towards fiscal consolidation and controls on social spending, and in the Juncker Commission focusing on targeted social investment and structural reform.[17] In this sense, coordination allows for significant differentiation but also carries harmonizing elements, reflecting the overall economic priorities of the Union and EU-level institutions.

In practice, where we see differentiation under EU fiscal policy coordination, it often happens at the level of implementation. In the context of the EDP and MIP, all states are subject to central 'nudging' (even Germany), with little credible threat of the most serious steps (sanctioning) being levelled against anyone (see, eg the continuous finding of 'excessive imbalances' in the Cypriot, Romanian, and Italian cases, without further sanction, even though these states have a poor record in implementing CSRs).[18] The level of compliance with recommendations under the Semester process remains notoriously low, meaning that Member States can escape its harmonizing elements simply by ignoring the most onerous recommendations (and following those that they wished to implement anyway).[19] As we will

[15] We refer to this in other work as asymmetric sovereignty transfer: Mark Dawson, 'The Legal and Political Accountability Structure of "Post-Crisis" EU Economic Governance' [2015] 53 Journal of Common Market Studies 5.

[16] eg Sonja Bekker, 'Hardening and Softening of Country-specific Recommendations in the European Semester' (2021) 44 West European Politics 1.

[17] On this centralizing tendency, see Sonja Bekker, 'Is There Flexibility in the European Semester Process? Exploring Interactions between the EU and Member States within Post-Crisis Socio-Economic Governance' [2016] SIEPS Paper 1; Mark Dawson, 'New Governance and the Displacement of Social Europe: The Case of the European Semester' (2018) 14 European Constitutional Law Review 1.

[18] 'Implementation of the Macroeconomic Imbalance Procedure: State of Play (January 2022)' (https://www.europarl.europa.eu/RegData/etudes/STUD/2022/645735/IPOL_STU(2022)645735_EN.pdf).

[19] eg Konstantino Efstathiou and Guntram B Wolff, 'Is the European Semester Effective and Useful?' [2018] Bruegel Policy Contribution No. 2018/09.

explore in the next section, under soft law processes, formal uniformity can belie significant divergence 'in practice' at the national level.

What can we take from these four varieties of *de jure* differentiation? They illustrate that there is a high level of differentiation in obligations under EMU. Neither Member States nor the EU institutions, however, tend to make full use of the 'right to do things differently' that EMU law provides. This may be for different reasons for different states. An example is the contrast between the Fiscal Compact and the Resolution Fund Agreement: in the former case, non-eurozone states seemed to join out of a fear of being left in the 'outer ring'; in the latter case, non-eurozone states (eg Bulgaria and Romania) joined out of a wish to make use of risk-sharing, and anticipating future eurozone/Banking Union membership. The EU institutions, meanwhile, carry incentives to limit differentiation (ie to assess economic policies through a common method, and to avoid damaging economic spillovers). *De facto* differentiation is thus more limited than it first appears.

Finally, there may be differences in the level of *de jure* differentiation between different areas of EMU. In monetary policy, the distinction between 'ins' and 'outs' is much clearer: either a Member State is part of the eurozone, and thereby subject to the monetary decision-making of the ECB, or it is not. In the other two main fields—banking supervision and fiscal policy—the lines are less clear-cut. In banking, the orbit of ECB supervision has tended to grow as states anticipate future eurozone membership or seek to improve the credibility of their regulatory processes. Fiscal policy retains a patchwork of rules, some of which apply to the eurozone only, and some to all, and all of which are implemented unevenly (with significant Commission discretion) between EU Member States.

III. *De Facto* Differentiation: Poland in the European Semester

What do these preliminary conclusions mean when moving to examine *de facto* differentiation? Before analyzing more systematically the specific case of fiscal policy and the European Semester, we might draw some preliminary conclusions. The first is that these 'layers' of *de jure* differentiation create serious accountability challenges.[20] Accountability relies on the ability of those affected by decisions to challenge those making them. Layering, however, makes the extent of obligations (ie to which rules am I bound?) and the exact 'holder' of authority (to whom am I answerable?) uncertain. A prominent example is the eurozone crisis and the uneasy division of authority between national and transnational institutions.[21] In the

[20] On these challenges, see Mark Dawson, Adina Maricut-Akbik, and Ana Bobić, 'Reconciling Independence and Accountability at the European Central Bank: The False Promise of Proceduralism' (2019) 25 European Law Journal 1.

[21] Paul Craig, 'The Eurogroup, Power and Accountability' (2017) 23 European Law Journal 2–3.

case of financial assistance measures, to whom could an individual affected by state austerity turn to contest decisions affecting them? Their national government, who passed the relevant law? The eurozone Finance Ministers, who agreed conditionality conditions? The ECB/IMF, who oversee its implementation? Or the ESM, who lent the money? We might, therefore, expect differentiation to fray and erode accountability structures, particularly at the national level.

The second preliminary conclusion is that these 'layers' of differentiation are likely to create highly divergent levels of obligation and compliance.[22] States within the eurozone, subject to international treaties, subject to 'hard' sanctioning powers under secondary law, and at the centre of economic policy coordination, are likely to have the highest level of obligation. One would, therefore, expect those states to treat EMU rules as binding standards, and the domestic institutions within those states to scrutinize closely both the policies pursued at EU level and their implementation nationally. Conversely, states outwith the eurozone, and without 'hard' obligations, could be expected to view EMU rules as non-binding, and thus to scrutinize and seek to influence EMU rules more loosely. *De jure* differentiation could, therefore, be expected to lead to real differences in the extent to which eurozone and non-eurozone members take EMU obligations seriously. In the next section, we will explore the extent to which these expectations are borne out.

We will, here, particularly focus on whether these hypotheses are met, ie to what extent are accountability and obligations in EMU 'differentiated', and how do these aspects vary depending on the level of formal obligations (eg regarding the question of whether a state is or is not a eurozone member)?

A. Non-eurozone states in the European Semester

Our analysis supports other findings that place these expectations on their head, ie that the non-euro countries may scrutinize aspects of EU economic governance more than the euro members.[23] We focus our attention on the European Semester, and, more specifically, on the Polish case: a state subject to lighter regulation under the Semester. Poland was not bailed out, and does not participate in bailout funds, such as the ESM. Its parliament, nonetheless, scrutinizes the Semester much more than those of euro countries do. For instance, among nine parliaments which were not involved in the preparation of the economic and fiscal programmes—stability/convergence programmes (SCPs) and national reform programmes (NRPs)—seven were eurozone members.[24] The Sejm (the lower chamber of the Polish

[22] Sylvia Karlsson-Vinkhuyzen and Annto Vihma, 'Comparing the Legitimacy and Effectiveness of Global Hard and Soft Law: An Analytical Framework' (2009) 3 Regulation and Governance 4.

[23] Mark Hallerberg, Benedicta Marzinotto, and Guntram B Wolff, 'Explaining the Evolving Role of National Parliaments Under the European Semester' [2018] Journal of European Public Policy 25.

[24] Oliver Rozenberg, *The Role of the National Parliaments after Lisbon: Potentialities and Challenges* (European Parliament 2017), p. 45.

parliament) usually holds three debates a year concerning the Semester, similarly to the Danish parliament,[25] traditionally seen as a role model in the parliamentary involvement in the EU affairs (Denmark also being a non-eurozone member).

The reports on the relations with NPs that the Commission publishes every year provide only a general number of visits of the Commission per country, without specifying their purpose. Hence, we cannot distinguish how many visits took place in the framework of the European Semester.[26] As a result, we do not have enough existing data on the hearings/meetings with the Commission in the national parliaments (NPs). The other source available is the biannual COSAC report, based on the survey sent to NPs: 27 from 38 parliaments/chambers did not hold any hearings with the Commission related to the Semester. However, this source has one limitation: it concerns only one year (2013). Nevertheless, we can try to estimate the number of meetings with the Commission by using a proxy for which more recent data is available, namely presentations of the Commission's opinions on the DBPs. Even though this concerns the euro area only, it can be used as a proxy for two reasons: first, the Commission's opinion on the DBP is perhaps the most specific document within the framework of the Semester, as it concerns the actual budget, and not fiscal and economic programmes, as is the case with the SCPs and NRPs, and so we can expect that this would be of the utmost interest for the NPs; second, in legal terms, the NPs are provided with a 'right' to invite the Commission to present its opinion to the parliament, which is guaranteed by the two-pack legislation.[27] Hence, we expect that a more solid legal foundation would make it more likely for the NPs to invite the Commission to present its opinion on the DBPs rather than on the other documents, such as Annual Growth Surveys (AGSs), which was later on renamed as Annual Sustainable Growth Survey, or CSRs, where such a solid legal foundation does not exist. Therefore, we can presume that if a parliament would invite the Commission for a discussion, it would do so to discuss the DBP, and so we would not expect that the number of hearings regarding the other documents of the Semester, such as AGSs or CSRs, would be higher than those regarding the DBPs. Strikingly, according to a survey from 2018, only two

[25] Valentin Kreilinger, 'Minimum Standards for Parliamentary Participation in the European Semester' [2019] Policy Paper, Jacques Delors Institut, Berlin <https://hertieschool-f4e6.kxcdn.com/fileadmin/user_upload/20190118_Minimum-standards-Parl_Kreilinger.pdf> accessed 16 November 2020; Elo Raimla, 'Involvement of the National Parliaments in SCPs and NRPs—2014, 2015 and 2016' [2017] European Parliament Directorate-General for Internal Policies, Economic Governance Support Unit <https://www.europarl.europa.eu/RegData/etudes/STUD/2016/497743/IPOL_STU%282016%29497743_EN.pdf> accessed 29 November 2020.

[26] In 2017 there were, in total, 215 visits and meetings of the Members of the Commission with national parliaments: European Commission, 'Annual Report 2017 on Relations between the European Commission and National Parliaments' (2018) <https://ec.europa.eu/info/sites/info/files/law/law-making_process/documents/annual-report-2017-relations-between-european-commission-national-parliaments_en.pdf> accessed 5 January 2021, but this figure dropped to 140 in 2018, and 55 in 2019.

[27] Art 21 of Regulation 473/2013/EU.

parliaments of the eurozone invited the Commission to debate its opinion on the DBP, therefore using the opportunity provided to them by EU law.[28]

B. The case of Poland

It has been shown that, paradoxically, the non-euro Member States discuss the SCPs and NRPs more often than the euro countries do.[29] This section builds on this finding and extends this survey-based analysis to the AGS and Country Reports (CRs), by conducting an in-depth case study of the largest non-eurozone country: Poland. The goal of this part is to assess how the Commission, which drafts both the AGSs and CRs, is held to account by a NP. In order to fully understand the accountability relation, one needs to move beyond the analysis of the introductory statements made by the representatives of the EU institutions in the NPs, which, in the case of the ECB, have been dubbed 'unconventional accountability measures',[30] and to delve deeper into the content of those debates. What was debated, and how it was debated, is crucial for assessing how accountability works (and how accountability is differentiated between states) in practice. For this reason, this study analyzes the content of the hearings to show how the Commission is held to account in the NP.

This element of the chapter seeks to answer the following questions: how did the Commissioner reply to the questions? Did they evade them by providing general answers or shifting responsibility? Or did they reply to all questions and provide detailed answers, without shifting responsibility and accepting demands for the justification of, or change of, conduct? Presenting the content according to the framework of accountability as a chain of interactions allows the reader to learn about how accountability works in practice. In order to allow the reader to better understand accountability as interactions, interactions between the forum and the actor are categorized according to both the definition of accountability and, further, by the topic that was contested, according to four categories: 'A. Request information about the decisions of an actor; B. Request justification for the conduct of an actor; C. Request the actor to change its decision or conduct; D. Request the sanctioning of responsible actors'.[31]

[28] Kajus Hagelstam, Wolfgang Lehofer, and Matteo Ciucci, 'The Role of National Parliaments in the European Semester for Economic Policy Coordination: In-depth Analysis' (European Parliament 2018) 18 <https://www.europarl.europa.eu/RegData/etudes/IDAN/2018/614494/IPOL_IDA(2018)614494_EN.pdf> accessed 14 September 2020.

[29] Mark Hallerberg, Benedicta Marzinotto, and Guntram B Wolff, 'Explaining the Evolving Role of National Parliaments Under the European Semester' [2018] Journal of European Public Policy 25.

[30] Tobias Tesche, 'Instrumentalizing EMU's Democratic Deficit: The ECB's Unconventional Accountability Measures during the Eurozone Crisis' (2018) 41 Journal of European Integration 4.

[31] Adina Akbik, *The European Parliament as an Accountability Forum Overseeing the Economic and Monetary* (CUP 2022).

We offer an in-depth analysis on both the number and content of parliamentary debates on the European Semester. We focus on committee hearings during one term of the lower chamber of the Polish parliament—the Sejm—with Valdis Dombrovskis, the Vice-President of the European Commission (2014–19), responsible for the euro, social dialogue, and the Financial Stability, Financial Services and Capital Markets Union. The Commissioner was twice invited to the Sejm during its eighth term (2015–19). The first occasion was for a debate on 9 March 2017,[32] for the purpose of discussing the AGS, CR, and the Working Plan of the Commission for the coming year. The second debate was on 23 November 2018.[33] As this took place earlier in the European Semester cycle, the CR was not discussed. We analyzed the accountability interactions according to three dimensions relevant for the chain of interactions, which are outlined in the following:

1. Generality/specificity of answers

We expected that the Commissioner would provide rather general answers during the debate, but in fact the Commission showed that it is committed to (unconventional) accountability, as it provided rather detailed answers to almost all questions. The Commissioner did not evade these questions by providing general replies. At the same time, he tried not to get into an open dispute with the Members of Parliament (MPs) criticizing the Commission. Rather, he gave credit to many of his opponents' arguments, for instance by admitting that the convergence process in the eurozone is still ongoing, and that there are challenges for countries wishing to adopt the euro which did not peg their currencies. However, he then usually defended the conduct of the Commission and repeated his arguments, which were substantiated with relevant data. He did not show any sign of changing conduct. Remarkably, his deep knowledge of Poland was even praised by Szlachta, an MP from the governing PiS, who was very impressed, and thanked Dombrovskis for coming to Warsaw.

[32] 'Pełny zapis przebiegu posiedzenia Komisji Finansów Publicznych (nr 182), Komisji Gospodarki i Rozwoju (nr 66), Komisji do Spraw Unii Europejskiej (nr 117) z 9 marca 2017 r... [na temat] informacji Wiceprzewodniczącego Komisji Europejskiej, Komisarza do spraw euro i dialogu społecznego oraz stabilności finansowej, usług finansowych i unii rynków kapitałowych, pana Valdisa Dombrovskisa, na temat sprawozdania krajowego 2017 roku w ramach semestru europejskiego oraz rocznej analizy wzrostu, a także planu pracy Komisji Europejskiej z uwzględnieniem kwestii finansowych oraz gospodarczych' (2017), Kancelaria Sejmu <http://orka.sejm.gov.pl/zapisy8.nsf/0/CA2816CA41494110C12580E60050CF53/%24File/0167008.pdf> accessed 15 October 2020.

[33] 'Pełny zapis przebiegu posiedzenia Komisji do Spraw Unii Europejskiej (nr 246), Komisji Finansów Publicznych (nr 399), Komisji Gospodarki i Rozwoju (nr 134) 23 listopada 2018 r. [na temat] informacji wiceprzewodniczącego Komisji Europejskiej odpowiedzialnego za euro i dialog społeczny oraz stabilność finansową, usługi finansowe i unię rynków kapitałowych Pana Valdisa Dombrovskisa na temat Rocznej Analizy Wzrostu na rok 2019 oraz prezentacją Programu Prac Komisji Europejskiej na rok 2019' (2019) Kancelaria Sejmu, http://orka.sejm.gov.pl/zapisy8.nsf/0/1BFB1A71785B17FEC12583590045FD78/%24File/0380208.pdf accessed 15 October 2020.

2. How interactions fit within the theoretical framework

Around half of the questions raised demanded information, and the other half were almost equally divided between indirect requests for justification and indirect requests for changes of conduct. Not surprisingly, no demands to sanction the actor were raised, as the Sejm has no power to do so. Importantly, only the PiS MPs requested a change of conduct, which was done by providing comments in which they expressed their disagreement with the views of the Commission. Nevertheless, such a clear contestation suggests that change of conduct was desired, even if indirectly (such requests are never made *expressis verbis*). This may be due to the fact that the MPs are aware that they cannot influence the workings of the Commission directly. The fact that only members of the governing party contested the Commissioner by requesting change may be explained by the fact that the Commission assesses—and criticizes—the policies of current governments, and that PiS is more Eurosceptic than the opposition parties (which explains its stance towards euro adoption, and the rather pessimistic views on the EU's economic situation brought by its MPs).

During the 2018 hearing, there were no disagreements between the MPs and the Commission: this was perhaps due to the fact that the CR, in which the implementation of the CSRs are assessed, was not debated, but only the AGS, so the main points of contestation were not subject to discussion. However, compared with the first debate, in the second one there were a couple of follow-up questions, which may indicate that the MPs do not shy away from pushing the Commissioner on certain topics, such as euro adoption in Poland, or the separate euro budget. Hence, on the one hand, there were more follow-up questions, but on the other, there was less contestation.

In general, the Commissioner did not avoid answering the questions, and responded more or less specifically to all the questions raised. Importantly, his answers were generally accepted by the MPs, as only in four cases was there a follow-up question (regarding euro adoption, the Common Agricultural Policy, and cryptocurrencies—all asked by two MPs from PiS). This suggests that the voluntary and unconventional accountability mechanisms that the Commission employs while engaging with a non-eurozone parliament are used not as pro forma instruments, but as tools to bring EU policies closer to national policymakers, and to the public (the protocols of Sejm debates are publicly accessible). Only twice did the Commissioner shift responsibility to other actors, but this was justified by the topics raised—coal and energy policy, and the Multi-annual Financial Framework—which were not part of his portfolio.

A high number of questions requesting information suggests that the MPs may lack good analytical support. This is especially evident in the area of euro adoption, as many MPs, including those from PiS, repeatedly asked about the Commissioner's view on when Poland should adopt the common currency. This indicates that there is insufficient information on the euro adoption process, and that the Sejm should consider establishing an independent research centre (or extending the existing one—Biuro Analiz Sejmowych), which could provide it with analysis on euro-related issues.

3. The distribution of issues between governing party and opposition

We expected that the opposition would have used questions to attack the government, while the governing party would only have picked up the issues that supported the government's policies, and would have contested those in which the Commission had criticized the government.[34] That was the case to a large extent: the MPs from the governing party contested CSRs, such as those suggesting changes to pension reforms. The opposition, to some extent, followed up on the issues which could be used for attacking the government, such as its resistance to joining the eurozone. However, much more questions than expected were asked about 'neutral' issues, such as EU's budgetary plans, by both groups of parties. This implies that MPs are genuinely interested in EU-related topics, and try to play an active role not only in the traditionally 'Polish' areas of interest, such as cohesion funds, but on a much broader range of issues, such as the economic situation in other EU Member States.

Such interactions can also expose the Commission to the topics important to particular Member States, and to differentiate the CSRs in order to reflect the particularities of each country, potentially leading to more ownership and implementation. Interactions with the Council cannot substitute those with NPs, in which members of both governing parties and the opposition can express their contestation. The question of how the opposition uses such an opportunity is, however, a different matter. Indeed, we show that only one-third of all questions were asked by MPs from opposition parties (7 out of 21 in the first debate, and 6 out of 19 in the second debate). The rest of the questions were asked by the members of PiS, who were much more active in the debates with the Commissioner. Clearly, the opposition versus government and the Eurosceptic versus Euro enthusiasts divides played a role in how the parties exercised their unconventional right to hold the Commission to account, but the opposition could make greater use of this opportunity to scrutinize the Commission's conduct.

[34] On the role of interparliamentary dynamics, including the majority party/opposition cleavage, see Ronald Holzhacker, 'National Parliamentary Scrutiny Over EU Issues: Comparing the Goals and Methods of Governing and Opposition Parties' (2002) 3 European Union Politics 4; Katrin Auel, 'Democratic Accountability and National Parliaments: Redefining the Impact of Parliamentary Scrutiny' (2007) 13 European Law Journal 4; Eric Miklin, 'Inter-Parliamentary Cooperation in EU Affairs and the Austrian Parliament: Empowering the Opposition?' (2013) 19 The Journal of Legislative Studies 1; Ronald Holzhacker, 'The Power of Opposition Parliamentary Party Groups in European Scrutiny' in Katrin Auel and Arthur Benz (eds), *The Europeanisation of Parliamentary Democracy* (Routledge 2016); Tomasz P Woźniakowski, Aleksandra Maatsch, and Eric Miklin, 'Rising to a Challenge? Ten Years of Parliamentary Accountability of the European Semester ,(2021) 9 Politics & Governance 3.

In sum, this assessment of *de facto* differentiation shows that, first, NPs can scrutinize the EU institutions in a reasonably effective way, and in so doing may contribute to increasing democratic legitimacy (which should accompany the increasingly powerful role that the EU plays in areas that have traditionally been regarded as the domain of the Member States, such as economic and fiscal policy). The analysis of topics shows that debate time is spent rather effectively by the MPs, as the questions they asked concerned either the area of responsibilities of the Commissioner or the broader topics of economic coordination among EU Member States, such as the proposal of the separate budget for the eurozone, the economic situation in the eurozone countries, or the assessment of the various reforms in Poland (eg pension system reform). Surprisingly, the Eurosceptic PiS MPs were more engaged in those discussions than the members of opposition parties, and they also contested the conduct of the Commission the most. In this way, they acted like an opposition towards a government, as their questions concerned mostly requests for justification and change of conduct, while the opposition members usually asked only less confrontational 'information demanding' questions. Interestingly, many questions related to the topic of the common currency, including its future architecture and the possible benefits of joining the eurozone.

Secondly, this in-depth case study shows that non-euro countries, with fewer sanction options and fewer obligations (eg non-euro states do not have to submit a draft of their budgets to the Commission), are interested in scrutinizing EU economic governance. We focus on the interactions with the Commissioners in Poland even more so because Poland may not avail itself of the legal possibility to invite Commissioners to hearings, contrary to eurozone Member States, which have this possibility under the two-pack. The analysis earlier in this chapter concerns only one Member State. It demonstrates, however, the shaky empirical foundations of the notion that EMU is based on a clear membership-based distinction between eurozone and non-eurozone states. The status of Poland as a possible future member, its political salience, and the opportunity to debate larger European economic policy, led the Polish parliament to engage in a serious accountability-rendering discussion with the EU institutions, thus confirming other literature. This must also be contrasted with studies showing the limited enthusiasm of eurozone states in engaging with the EU institutions in the Semester context.[35] *de jure* differentiation already presents a picture of an EU that is divided on monetary and fiscal questions but, as 'a matter of degree', differentiation at the *de facto* level equally underlines the disadvantages of a categorical approach to EMU membership.

[35] eg Katrin Auel and Oliver Hoenig, 'Parliaments in the Euro Crisis: Can the Losers of Integration Still Fight Back?' (2014) 52 Journal of Common Market Studies 6; Davor Jancic, 'National Parliaments and EU Fiscal Integration' (2016) 22 European Law Journal 2.

IV. Conclusion: Differentiation in the 'Post-Covid' EMU

If EMU is less differentiated, at both *de jure* and *de facto* levels, between 'members' and 'non-members', than the notion of a unified 'eurozone' suggests, this poses a further concluding question. How is this picture of differentiation likely to evolve in the future, particularly as EMU embarks on a new era, following the COVID-19 crisis? Section III above has largely excluded the reforms that took place from 2020 from its analysis (as these changes were, at the time of writing, a moving target). The COVID-19 crisis and other recent developments also, however, present some early lessons.[36]

The first concerns the departure of the UK from the Union, and its impact on EU decision-making. As already discussed, much of the cause of differentiation lies in diversity between EU states, and its impact on amassing support for common policies. The departure of the UK has also meant the departure of the biggest non-eurozone Member State, and one willing to block economic policies for the whole of the Union seen as detrimental to its interests. As a result, the Union was able to adopt a relatively far-reaching and fiscally ambitious response to the COVID crisis (without having to resort to intergovernmental agreements, as in the euro-crisis years). This response came not just from non-majoritarian bodies like the ECB, but from the other EU institutions, most notably the agreement on a significant 'recovery and resilience' fund on top of the normal EU budget.[37] While it remains too early to gauge the significance of the UK's departure, and the budget negotiations revealed a number of other 'awkward partners' (most notably Hungary and Poland, regarding rule of law conditionality in the budget), the removal of a willing veto-player suggests that frictions between an 'inner' eurozone and 'outer' non-euro EU are likely to diminish in the immediate future. This may also be aided by other developments, such as the decision of new members (such as Croatia in 2020) to join the Banking Union and seek eurozone membership.

The second lesson of the COVID recovery is that the substantive principles underlying EMU may be shifting. The eurozone crisis was dominated by a strong narrative surrounding austerity and fiscal responsibility.[38] This narrative was used to justify highly divergent treatment between the EU's north and its southern 'debtor' states (with the latter subject to conditionality and higher levels of fiscal surveillance). As already discussed, this cleavage has been a driver of differentiation (eg as found in higher levels of surveillance for 'debtor' states).

The same cleavages do not seem to have had the same initial resonance during the COVID-19 crisis, as a public health crisis affecting all EU states. After initial

[36] Diane Fromage, 'The Future of EMU Architecture Post-COVID' (2020) 47 Legal Issues of Economic Integration 4.

[37] European Commission, 'Recovery and Resilience Facility' (https://commission.europa.eu/business-economy-euro/economic-recovery/recovery-and-resilience-facility_en).

[38] Nicolas Jabko, 'The Political Appeal of Austerity' (2013) 11 Comparative European Politics 6.

resistance by the 'frugal four', the Council quickly settled on a recovery fund in the summer of 2020, based not on conditionality, but solidarity between Member States (with those most economically affected by COVID receiving the lion's share of benefits from money generated by new EU lending capacities).[39] Most importantly for this chapter, the fund has been distributed to all EU Member States, and not just to eurozone members. At the same time, it has been integrated within existing economic surveillance processes, such as compliance with the European Semester. In this sense, the COVID crisis seems likely to further erode the boundaries between eurozone and non-eurozone members, by creating a set of fiscal instruments that are available to all EU members (but at the same time enmeshed with the existing governance structures of the eurozone).

It would be foolish to predict the future of differentiation in EMU. Yet what was once a common assumption—that the EU would be permanently split between a group of eurozone states and those opposed to further economic integration (what was once called a 'two-speed' Europe)[40]—has been challenged both by recent developments, and by the increasing blurring of the boundaries of eurozone membership. The EMU of the 2020s will be differentiated, but also a common project of all the Union's Member States.

[39] Paul Dermine, 'The EU's Response to the COVID-19 Crisis and the Trajectory of Fiscal Integration in Europe: Between Continuity and Rupture' (2020) 47 Legal Issues of Economic Integration 4.

[40] Jean Claude Piris, *The Future of Europe: Towards a Two-speed EU?* (CUP 2011).

4

Differentiated Integration in EU Foreign, Security, and Defence Policy

Petra Mahnič and Álvaro de Elera

I. Introduction

This chapter addresses the phenomenon of differentiation in the specific area of the European Union's (EU) Common Foreign and Security Policy (CFSP), including the Common Security and Defence Policy (CSDP). After briefly addressing, in Section II, the concepts of internal differentiation (ie the adoption of Union instruments by fewer than all Member States) and external differentiation (ie the adoption of Union instruments with the participation of third states) as they apply in that policy area, we will discuss the legal nature, scope, and limits of differentiation in CFSP on the basis of the existing Treaty mechanisms for differentiation (Section III). Special attention will be paid to actual and possible differentiation through selected CFSP instruments, both political and legal. We will first explain why non-legal acts, which are widely used in the area of CFSP, currently exclude differentiation, and will explore ways to allow for enhanced flexibility through such instruments. We will then discuss existing and possible differentiation through legal acts, and address legal constraints limiting their use in the policy area under consideration. We will conclude with some general observations regarding the particularities and inherent limits of differentiation in the area of CFSP, and propose solutions that would allow for more flexibility and differentiation within the applicable Treaty framework, thereby enhancing the effectiveness of the EU external action in the area of CFSP in situations where consensus for the Union action may be lacking (Section IV).

II. The Concepts of Internal and External Differentiation in the Context of CFSP

The current Treaty framework does not allow for external differentiation, whereby third states are brought into the Union's decision-making, as this would be contrary to the basic founding principles of the EU legal order. By virtue of the principle of decision-making autonomy of the Union institutions, non-Member States'

Petra Mahnič and Álvaro de Elera, *Differentiated Integration in EU Foreign, Security, and Defence Policy* In: *Redefining EU Membership*. Edited by: Diane Fromage, Oxford University Press. © Petra Mahnič and Álvaro de Elera 2024.
DOI: 10.1093/9780191948145.003.0004

participation in the decision-making processes of the Union is excluded. This applies to the CFSP in the same way as to any other policy of the Union.

The principle of decision-making autonomy is inherent to the very structure and institutional setting of the Union. Decision-making powers in the Union, as regards the competences conferred on the Union by the Member States, are themselves conferred on the Union institutions (Article 13(2) TEU). At the same time, participation in the decision-making *within* the institutions results from the membership of the Union as established by the Treaties. The Treaties, in turn, restrict membership in the Union institutions to representatives of the Member States or of the Union citizens.[1] Consequently, persons not representing the Member States or Union citizens—such as, by definition, representatives of third states—are excluded from being members of the Union institutions and, as a result, cannot participate in the Union decision-making.[2] This means that, when it comes to decision-making, there is no grey area between the status of a Member State and that of a third state. The two are mutually exclusive and clearly distinct.

In contrast, internal differentiation, whereby fewer than all Union Member States participate in decision-making, is an inherent feature of the Union legal order, and applies also within the CFSP, be it in relation to the policy area as a whole, a subset of it, or a specific instrument or category of instruments. However, a distinction between two sets of mechanisms applicable in this area is called for. On the one hand, it is possible to speak about differentiated *integration* proper only in relation to the two mechanisms that apply in the CSDP, ie the Treaty-based standing exclusion of Denmark in the elaboration of predefined Union actions with

[1] For the European Parliament, see Art14(2) of the Treaty on the European Union (TEU): 'The European Parliament shall be composed of representatives of the Union's citizens', while Union citizenship is limited to persons holding the citizenship of a Member State (Art 20 of the Treaty on establishing the Euroepan Union (TFEU)). Moreover, the attribution of Members of the European Parliament is limited to the Member States. For the European Council, see Art15(2) TEU: 'The European Council shall consist of the Heads of State or Government of the Member States'. For the Council, see Art 16(2) TEU: 'The Council shall consist of a representative of each Member State at ministerial level'. For the Commission, see Art 17(5) TEU: 'The members of the Commission shall be chosen from among the nationals of the Member States on the basis of a system of strictly equal rotation between the Member States'—this also covers the High Representative, who is, by definition, a member of College and Vice-President of the Commission. For the Court of Justice and the General Court, see Art 19(2) TEU: 'The Court of Justice shall consist of one judge from each Member State' and 'The General Court shall include at least one judge per Member State'.

[2] Paras 48 and 49 of the ECJ's order in Case C-684/20 P *Sharpston v Council*, ECLI:EU:C:2021:486. Answering former AG Sharpston's argument that the Representatives of the Member States had acted ultra vires by allegedly ending her mandate prematurely following the UK's withdrawal from the Union, the Court stated that 'the Conference of the Representatives of the Governments of the Member States merely took note of the consequences necessarily entailed by the departure of the United Kingdom from the European Union.... Since the Treaties ceased to be applicable to the United Kingdom on the date of its withdrawal... pursuant to Article 50(3) TEU, that State is no longer, as from that date, a Member State. It follows... that the ongoing mandates of the members of the institutions, bodies, offices and agencies of the European Union nominated, appointed or elected in view of the United Kingdom's membership of the European Union automatically came to an end on that date.'

defence implications,[3] and the Treaty-inbuilt specific manifestation of enhanced cooperation[4] in the CSDP, the permanent structured cooperation (PESCO) established under Articles 42(6) and 46 of the Treaty on the EU. On the other hand, and as regards the CFSP proper (without CSDP), where the logic of integration that applies to other internal policies is lacking, it would be more appropriate to speak about differentiated *convergence*. The CFSP is not about integration; rather, it is about the convergence of national foreign policy preferences that result in EU positions, where other actors of international law deal with, and perceive, the Union as a separate international actor (see Article 24(2) and the first paragraph of Article 32 TEU, according to which 'Member States shall ensure, through the convergence of their actions, that the Union is able to assert its interests and values on the international scene.'). While the possibility for Member States to avail themselves of enhanced cooperation explicitly covers CFSP matters,[5] and is thus, in principle, legally possible, it is *de facto* not operational in the field. Allowing a number of Member States to go ahead without the others in advancing external policy preferences agreed through enhanced cooperation would defeat the very purpose of the CFSP policy and the credibility of the EU as a 'collective external policy actor'.[6] Therefore, only mechanisms that allow for the adoption of Union instruments constitutive of the *acquis* of the Union, while perhaps not committing all Member States allow the Union to act, are capable of fulfilling the very objective of the policy. As we shall see, this is the case only for the mechanisms of constructive abstention, and for the permanent opt-out for Denmark. A fortiori, any kind of differentiated Union membership, be it on the basis of different rights, such as voting rights, or on the basis of different obligations, such as a differentiated application of the *acquis*, would be completely unsuitable for the CFSP.[7]

Finally, differentiated integration should be distinguished from differentiated *implementation*, whereby Union action is implemented by fewer than all Member States (internal differentiated implementation), or where autonomously fixed

[3] On 20 June 2022, following a referendum on 1 June 2022 on revoking the exemption laid down in Art 5 of Protocol 22 on the position of Denmark, Denmark informed the other Member States that it no longer wished to avail itself of that provision. On this basis, it was clarified that, from 1 July 2022, all references to the position of Denmark based on the thirty-year-old opt-out clause relating to EU defence would no longer apply: Council Decision (CFSP) 2023/994 of 22 May 2023 on the consequences of Denmark informing the other Member States that it no longer wishes to avail itself of Article 5 of Protocol No 22 on the position of Denmark, and amending Decision (CFSP) 2021/509 establishing a European Peace Facility and Decision 2014/401/CFSP on the European Union Satellite Centre ([2023] OJ L135/120).

[4] As detailed in Art 20 TEU and Arts 326–34 TFEU.

[5] Art 329(2) TFEU.

[6] Annegret Bendiek, Ronja Kempin, and Nicolai von Ondarza, 'Qualified Majority Voting and Flexible Integration for a More Effective CFSP? A Critical Examination of the EU's Options' (2018) 25 SWP Comment 7.

[7] In the view of the authors, any kind of differentiated Union membership would also be completely unsuitable in general, ie in other policy fields, for a number of reasons. To mention just one, the institutional and procedural complexity it would entail would be impossible to manage.

policies (ie policies fixed without the participation of third states) may allow, in their implementation, for the participation of actors external to the Union (external differentiated implementation). Both are very common in the area of CSDP, where the performance of CSDP tasks is undertaken using civilian and military assets provided by the Member States, be it for missions deployed outside the Union for peacekeeping, conflict prevention, and strengthening international security,[8] or for the purposes of the progressive framing of the European common defence.[9] The status of Member States not participating in the implementation is, however, unaffected, as they remain part of the decision-making process of the Union. Hence, Union membership is unitary and only implementation is differentiated.

In external differentiated implementation, third states may commit to participation by concluding agreements to associate themselves with the relevant Council decisions, and thus contribute, with assets, to EU-led CSDP missions and operations.[10] In the case of the PESCO established under Articles 42(6) and 46 TEU, a CSDP-specific mechanism of differentiation, discussed further in subsection B of Section III below, third states which, exceptionally and upon assessment of compliance with predetermined requirements,[11] may be invited to participate in a PESCO project, may be granted rights in the implementation thereof. According to Article 4 of Council Decision (CFSP) 2020/1639[12] establishing PESCO, an administrative arrangement may include the scope of involvement of a third state in the decision-making process *within the PESCO project*. The overall status of third states is, however, unaffected by their participation in the implementation of Union measures, as they remain outside the decision-making process of the Union concerning the shaping and adoption of those measures.

In the area of CFSP proper, third states' implementation of Union measures may take place through *alignment* with EU positions. This is very common in the field of restrictive measures, where non-EU European countries are regularly invited by the EU, after it has enacted its own measures, to adopt similar ones. Comparable,

[8] Art 42(1) TEU .
[9] ibid.
[10] For the most recent examples, see Council Decision (EU) 2019/1803 of 18 July 2019 on the signing and conclusion of the Agreement between the European Union and the Government of the Socialist Republic of Viet Nam establishing a framework for the participation of Viet Nam in European Union crisis management operations [2019] OJ L276/1, and Council Decision (CFSP) 2019/1328 of 18 February 2019 on the signing and conclusion of the Agreement between the European Union and the Hashemite Kingdom of Jordan establishing a framework for the participation of the Hashemite Kingdom of Jordan in European Union crisis management operations [2019] OJ L207/1.
[11] Council Decision (CFSP) 2017/2315 establishing permanent structured cooperation (PESCO) and determining the list of participating Member States [2017] OJ L331/57, in its Annex III, determines that, in order to be invited, third states need to provide substantial added value to the project, contribute to strengthening the PESCO and the CSDP, and meet more demanding commitments. See also Council Decision (CFSP) 2020/1639 establishing the general conditions under which third States could exceptionally be invited to participate in individual PESCO projects [2020] OJ L371/3, which in Art 4 defines rights and obligations of third states participating in a PESCO project that may be determined in an administrative arrangement.
[12] Council Decision (CFSP) 2020/1639 (n 11).

but different, is the situation where different subjects of international law decide to coordinate the adoption of similar foreign policy measures, with a view to enhancing their global impact.[13]

III. Differentiated Integration through CFSP Instruments

A. CFSP differentiation mechanisms of general nature

1. Constructive abstention

a) Legal nature

Constructive abstention is a special and unique voting arrangement set out in the second paragraph of Article 31(1) TEU. It is therefore an inherent part of Article 31(1), which is a general procedural legal basis for the adoption of CFSP decisions. Constructive abstention was introduced by the Treaty of Amsterdam in 1997, and remained largely unaffected by subsequent Treaty amendments.[14] It is distinct from a standard, unqualified form of abstention,[15] in that it allows a Member State to qualify its abstention by making a formal declaration, following which it is not obliged to apply a CFSP decision, *but must accept that the measure commits the Union.* By allowing a Member State to distance itself from the Union act, EU action in the area of CFSP is permitted even when such action cannot be reconciled with the foreign policy preferences of all Member States. In a spirit of mutual solidarity, the Member State(s) concerned is/are obliged to refrain from any action likely to conflict with or impede EU action based on that decision. In addition, Article 31(1) TEU establishes that '*if the members of the Council qualifying their abstention in this way represent at least one third of the Member States comprising at least one third of the population of the Union, the decision shall not be adopted*'. This limitation is characteristic of a common foreign and security policy, which should reflect '*an ever-increasing degree of convergence of Member States' actions*'.[16] A Union act

[13] The most recent examples include various packages of restrictive measures against Russia, adopted by the EU in a coordinated manner with G7 countries after the escalation of Russia's aggression against Ukraine in February 2022. Before that, restrictive measures against individuals responsible for serious human rights violations and abuses were adopted by the EU in March 2021, in a somewhat coordinated manner with the US, Canada, and the UK. A similar coordinated action with the same actors took place in response to the detention of journalist Roman Protasevich and Sofia Sapega by Belarusian authorities following the unlawful diversion of Ryanair Flight FR4978, in May 2021.

[14] The only subsequent change related to the calculation of the threshold of abstention beyond which the act could not be adopted.

[15] According to Article 238(4) TFEU '*Abstentions by Members present in person or represented shall not prevent the adoption by the Council of acts which require unanimity*'. The standard absention does not absolve a Mener State from its obligation to apply a decision adopted with its abstention.

[16] According to Art 24(2) TEU, 'the Union shall conduct, define and implement a common foreign and security policy, based on the development of mutual political solidarity among Member States, the identification of questions of general interest and the achievement of an ever-increasing degree of convergence of Member States' actions'.

with a support lower than two-thirds of its members could hardly be regarded as defining a *common* policy, as it would not facilitate a higher degree of convergence.

The invocation of this mechanism requires no justification from the Member State(s) concerned. Nevertheless, linking a declaration to important reasons of national foreign policy would seem to be in line with the Member States' duty to '*work together to enhance and develop their mutual political solidarity*', on which the definition and implementation of the CFSP must be based (Article 24(2)(3) and the first paragraph of Article 32 TEU), and would facilitate the understanding and respect by other Member States of the position(s) of their partner(s). The ad hoc nature of the mechanism entails some further conceptual and practical implications. The fact that differentiation is, in principle, only triggered by a Member State declaration *at the end of the decision-making process* means that there is no difference in their overall status between the Member States that will be committed by the EU action and those that, by virtue of the use of the mechanism, will be exempted from such a commitment. They all participate fully in the decision-making process until the very end, including in the vote itself, which also means that the Member State(s) in question retain(s) the power to shape the EU decision until its final adoption. This is only normal, as constructive abstention is simply a possibility open to Member States that does not detract from their default position as full participants in the definition of the policy at hand. It is to be noted that the declaration by the abstaining Member State(s) will not be reflected in the act itself, thereby causing a certain degree of legal uncertainty as to its very existence. Uncertainty may also arise as regards future evolvement of the EU commitment: could the Member State which used the mechanism participate in subsequent decision-making process concerning acts related to the measure concerned?

While no clear answer to this question is provided by the existing legal framework, the first practical example of the use of constructive abstention suggests that such a Member State could so participate. In 2008, Cyprus decided to invoke constructive abstention in relation to Joint Action establishing the EU Rule of Law Mission in Kosovo (EULEX).[17] This, however, did not prevent Cyprus from participating in, and agreeing to, further instruments relating to the mission in question. A formal declaration on the basis of Article 31(1) TEU was also not resubmitted in relation to Council Decision (CFSP) 2018/856, which amended the same Joint Action.[18] Has differentiation in relation to the establishment of the EULEX mission as regards Cyprus, therefore, tacitly ceased to exist? The voluntary

[17] Council Joint Action 2008/124/CFSP on the European Union Rule of Law Mission in Kosovo, EULEX KOSOVO [2008] OJ L42/92.

[18] Moreover, three Council decisions adopted in the summer and autumn of 2008 concerning the conclusion of an agreement between the EU and three third states at the time (Swiss Federation, Croatia, and the US) on their participation in EULEX Kosovo were, equally, adopted without any (internal) differentiation: Council Decision 2008/666/CFSP [2008] OJ L217/23; Council Decision 2008/887/CFSP [2008] OJ L317/19; Council Decision 2008/814/CFSP [2008] OJ L 282/32.

and ad hoc nature of the instrument would suggest exactly that. The potentially reversible nature of the mechanism is also consistent with the underlying philosophy of the CFSP, which is all about building gradual convergence of Member States' foreign-policy preferences, which are prone to evolving and changing over time. In the case of Cyprus, a resort to constructive abstention was prompted by its concerns over the proper legal basis for the involvement of the EU in Kosovo. Cyprus argued for an explicit decision of the United Nations Security Council (UNSC) for the EU mission in Kosovo.[19] The boundaries of internal differentiation based on the rules governing constructive abstention are, therefore, fluid. The Union is allowed to proceed, without negatively affecting some Member States' sensitivities. For some, this is not only part of the attractiveness of the instrument, but also the maximum differentiation that is politically desirable for CFSP.[20]

Constructive abstention also has no bearing on the financial contributions of the Member State opting out, at least as regards the administrative and operational expenditures charged to the Union budget. In line with the duty of the abstaining Member State to accept that the act commits the EU as a whole, the abstaining Member State will simply have to accept that the EU budget will support the EU action at stake. The situation is different if internal differentiation occurs in relation to acts giving rise to operational expenditure arising from operations having military or defence implications, or if the Council unanimously decides that the EU budget will not support the EU action at stake. In cases where expenditure is not charged to the Union budget, it will be charged to the Member States in accordance with the gross national product scale, unless the Council again unanimously decides otherwise. As for expenditure arising from operations having military or defence implications, the constructively abstaining Member State is, in accordance with the second subparagraph of Article 41(2) TEU, exempted from the obligation to contribute to the financing.

The European Peace Facility (EPF)[21] illustrates well the financial complexity that a differentiated EU action not supported by the EU budget may entail. The EPF Decision 2021 allows Member States to finance interventions under the CFSP that are not to be charged to the Union budget. These include, in particular, common costs of CSDP missions and operations having military or defence implications, and assistance measures for third states or regional or international organizations strengthening their military and defence capacities, including, for the first time in EU history, through the provision of arms to the armed and security forces of third states. Austria, Sweden, Ireland, and Malta had serious reservations about

[19] Points 2 and 3 of the declaration set out in the note indicating the end of written procedure (CM 448/08, dated 4 February 2008).

[20] Ingolf Pernice and Daniel Thym, 'A New Institutional Balance for European Foreign Policy' (2002) 7 European Foreign Affairs Review 381.

[21] Council Decision (CFSP) 2021/509 establishing a European Peace facility, and repealing Decision (CFSP) 2015/528 [2021] OJ L102/14.

measures through which lethal equipment could be provided to third states, and thus were politically unwilling to contribute financially to Union measures which some of them considered incompatible with their neutrality. They were only able to agree to the financial envelope for such future measures due to the possibility of invoking constructive abstention in relation to them. Although this form of opt-out would not normally release them from the obligation to contribute financially to such measures,[22] a political compromise between those Member States and the rest was found, whereby the Council determined that a Member State abstaining in a vote on a Council decision concerning assistance measures allowing for the supply of lethal military equipment is not obliged to contribute to the financing of that assistance measure. In exchange for being exempt from the contribution to the costs, those Member States made a commitment to contribute a proportional additional amount to other assistance measures.[23] In this way, the substitute payment ensures that the overall contribution of those Member States to assistance measures will be in accordance with their share of gross national income. This was important for other Member States, which feared that such derogations would undermine the financial solidarity between Member States, and add an excessive budgetary or financial complexity to the measures. The internal differentiation envisaged by the EPF Decision 2021 is duly reflected in the composition of the committee established by the Decision, under the authority and direction of which the EPF is managed. When discussing the financing of any such operations or assistance measures, the body, otherwise composed of representatives of each Member State, will be composed only of representatives of *contributing* Member States.[24]

The examples of internal differentiation through constructive abstention (EULEX Kosovo; assistance measures for Ukraine, adopted since February 2022;[25]

[22] Such an exemption in accordance with the terms of Art 41(1) TEU exists only as regards 'operations having military or defence implications', although this interpretation is not shared by all.

[23] Recital 21 and Art 5 of the EPF Decision 2021 (n 20). With the latest amendment of the EPF Decision 2021 which established a dedicated amount for Ukraine ('Ukraine Assistance Fund'), this possibility was, as a matter of exception, open to any assistance measure to be financed with the dedicated amount (Article 73(10) of the EPF Decision 20121 as amended) and to all Member States, regardless of the specific character of their security and defence policy as referred to in Article 42(2) TEU (See recital 14 of Council Decision (CFSP) 2024/890 [2024], OJ L 2024/890).

[24] The representatives of non-contributing states may attend without taking part in its votes (ibid, Art11(8)(a)(b)).

[25] Council Decision (CFSP) 2022/338 of 28 February 2022 on an assistance measure under the European Peace Facility for the supply to the Ukrainian Armed Forces of military equipment, and platforms, designed to deliver lethal force ([2022] OJ L60/1); Council Decision (CFSP) 2022/471 of 23 March 2022 amending Decision (CFSP) 2022/338 on an assistance measure under the European Peace Facility for the supply to the Ukrainian Armed Forces of military equipment, and platforms, designed to deliver lethal force ([2022] OJ L96); Council Decision (CFSP) 2022/636 of 13 April 2022 amending Decision (CFSP) 2022/338 on an assistance measure under the European Peace Facility for the supply to the Ukrainian Armed Forces of military equipment, and platforms, designed to deliver lethal force ([2022] OJ L117/34); Council Decision (CFSP) 2022/809 of 23 May 2022 amending Decision (CFSP) 2022/338 on an assistance measure under the European Peace Facility for the supply to the Ukrainian Armed Forces of military equipment, and platforms, designed to deliver lethal force ([2022] OJ L145/

and an assistance measure to support the Nigerien Armed Forces)[26] raise questions as regards the actual reach of that mechanism. Is it really of general application, as its incorporation into the general procedural legal basis in the CFSP seems to suggest, or is its actual applicability limited by political and legal constraints? As we will argue under sections b) and c) below, the latter is true not only for political, legally non-binding instruments, but also for at least two categories of CFSP legal acts: decisions establishing restrictive measures and decisions concerning the conclusion of international agreements with third parties falling within the area of CFSP or having an independent CFSP component (hereinafter 'CFSP agreements by the EU').

b) Scope of differentiation through non-legal acts

Unlike legal acts, political or non-legal acts, often labelled as 'atypical acts', are not expressly mentioned in the Treaties.[27] Such atypical acts are very common in the area of CFSP. This is so not only due to Member States' preference in that area for political, non-binding instruments, but also because the choice of instruments in external relations is often the result of negotiations with third actors, and cannot, therefore, be decided by the Union on its own.[28] Without entering into a systematization of the panoply of such instruments (something that would, in itself, require self-standing research), we will look at whether and how the possibility of differentiation applies to such political acts, distinguishing between two main groups of these: unilateral acts, which the Union issues on its own, and non-unilateral acts, which the Union agrees with other international actor(s).

40); Council Decision (CFSP) 2022/1285 of 21 July 2022 amending Decision (CFSP) 2022/338 on an assistance measure under the European Peace Facility for the supply to the Ukrainian Armed Forces of military equipment, and platforms, designed to deliver lethal force ([2002] OJ L195/93); Council Decision (CFSP) 2022/1285 of 17 October 2022 amending Decision (CFSP) 2022/338 on an assistance measure under the European Peace Facility for the supply to the Ukrainian Armed Forces of military equipment, and platforms, designed to deliver lethal force ([2022] OJ L270/95); Council Decision (CFSP) 2023/231 of 2 February 2023 amending Decision (CFSP) 2022/338 on an assistance measure under the European Peace Facility to support the Ukrainian Armed Forces trained by the European Union Military Assistance Mission in support of Ukraine with military equipment, and platforms, designed to deliver lethal force ([2023] OJ L32/62); Council Decision (CFSP) 2022/2245 of 14 November 2022 on an assistance measure under the European Peace Facility to support the Ukrainian Armed Forces trained by the European Union Military Assistance Mission in support of Ukraine with military equipment, and platforms, designed to deliver lethal force ([2022] OJ L294/25); Council Decision (CFSP) 2023/927 of 5 May 2023 on an assistance measure under the European Peace Facility to support the Ukrainian Armed Forces through the provision of ammunition ([2023] OJ L123/27), etc.

[26] Council Decision (CFSP) 2023/1136 of 8 June 2023 on an assistance measure under the European Peace Facility to support the Nigerien Armed Forces with military equipment designed to deliver lethal force ([2023] OJ L149/81).

[27] Art 288(1) TEU: 'To exercise the Union's competences, the institutions shall adopt regulations, directives, decisions, recommendations and opinions.'

[28] Opinion of AG Sharpston [2015] ECLI:EU:C:2016:781 at fn 58: 'unlike internal Union action, the instruments through which the Union acts externally are not limited to those for which the Treaties expressly provide, establish the form and effects and lay down the procedural steps to be taken.'

i) Unilateral instruments

We will focus on the most frequently used unilateral acts through which the Union exercises its policy-making competences (Article 16 TEU), including in the area of CFSP: Council conclusions and Union Statements.[29] While Council conclusions are the most common means of expressing a policy position on any given matter without resorting to acts provided for in the Treaties, Statements are often issued when a rapid reaction to international developments, or within international organizations, is required. Being atypical acts, they have traditionally been adopted by consensus, irrespective of the policy field (thus including CFSP). Consensus means that a vote is not taken, but all Member States must express themselves in favour of the act, and abstentions are not accepted; in other words, Council conclusions or Union Statements must be supported by all Member States. The argument for resorting to a decision-making process of an intergovernmental nature is that, since these acts are not acts provided for by the Treaties, they are not subject to the procedural rules set out in the Treaty legal bases. Where consensus is not possible, 'Presidency conclusions' (or, exceptionally, 'Presidency statements') have been used, sometimes also mentioning the number of Member States supporting them. These are policy positions issued under the responsibility of the Presidency, and committing only the Presidency itself (and thus not the Union as such), even though often many Member States themselves adhere to such policy positions. They are, however, not considered Union instruments, as those can only be adopted with the consensus of all Member States. The question, therefore, arises as to whether it would be possible to establish an EU policy position in the area of CFSP by means of Council conclusions (or Union Statements) approved by fewer than all Member States.

In our view, this would be possible only if the voting arrangements laid down in the Treaties for the adoption of legal acts in a given policy area were followed also for the approval of non-legal acts. For the CFSP, this would include a possibility to resort to the unanimity-voting rule with constructive abstention, thus allowing for Union positions to be reached while providing flexibility for Member State(s) having fundamental problems with a given position and, therefore, not being able to position themselves in favour of it. The degree of differentiation possible for legal acts would thus be permitted also for non-legal acts. This way of proceeding would follow the logic according to which, even when expressing themselves through atypical acts, the Union institutions are bound by fundamental procedural requirements and institutional balance established by the Treaty framework (Article 13(2) TEU).

[29] In the area of CFSP, the term 'Statement of the High Representative on behalf of the Union' is widely used to indicate that the statement has been approved by the Council, although, properly speaking, all statements made by the High Representative are on behalf of the Union, since this is his/her responsibility under Art 27(1) TEU. A more appropriate term would, therefore, be 'Council Statements' or, since it is within the Council's sole responsibility to establish (CFSP) policy positions, 'Union Statements'.

ii) Non-unilateral instruments

If the logic which was proposed earlier has not yet been tested before the EU courts as regards unilateral acts, it has to some extent been approved as regards non-binding instruments, such as memoranda of understanding or joint statements agreed between the Union and third parties. The European Court of Justice (ECJ), in the *Swiss MoU* case,[30] recalled, as regards the signature of a bilateral non-binding instrument, that in accordance with Article 13(2) TEU, '*each institution shall act within the limits of the powers conferred on it in the Treaties, and in conformity with the procedures, conditions and objectives set out therein*',[31] before holding that the decision to sign such an instrument belongs to the policy-making power of the Council established by Article 16 TEU. Although the Court was not asked to deal with the issue of voting rules within the Council, the reference to the *procedures* set out in the Treaties permits the interpretation according to which Council acts approving the entering into the negotiation of such instruments and authorizing their signature could be adopted on the basis of the voting arrangements set out in the Treaties. If applied in the area of CFSP, this would allow for the use of constructive abstention, thereby allowing for enhanced flexibility within the Union when agreeing such instruments with third parties.

c) Scope of differentiation through legal instruments

Legal instruments comprise legally binding legal acts, which in the area of CFSP are limited to decisions,[32] and legally non-binding legal acts, recommendations,[33] and opinions.[34] For the purposes of our analysis, we will focus on Council decisions in use for establishing restrictive measures, on the one hand, and decisions related to the conclusion of CFSP agreements by the EU, on the other. Both of these have a link to the TFEU— Articles 215 and 218 TFEU respectively—with a clear impact on the scope of possible differentiation.

i) Restrictive measures

Article 215 TFEU provides for two categories of restrictive measures that the EU is empowered to adopt: first, measures of general application to interrupt or limit economic, financial, or other relations with third states; and, second, individual measures against natural or legal persons and groups or non-state entities, adopted in view of their responsibility for activities of concern to the EU, such as terrorism, proliferation of chemical weapons, or cyber-attacks threatening the EU

[30] Case C–660/13 *Council v Commission* [2016] ECLI:EU:C:2016:616.

[31] ibid para 32.

[32] These include, eg, decisions referred to in Arts 22(1), 25(b), 26(2), 28, 29, 31, 39, 41(3), 42(4), 43(2), 44, 45(2), and 46(2)(4)(6) TEU, as well as Art 218 TFEU, a procedural legal basis for the negotiation and conclusion of international agreements.

[33] eg Art 46(6) TEU.

[34] An Opinion by the High Representative is required under Art 46(2) and (3) TEU, and Arts 329(2) and 331(2) TFEU.

and its Member States. The procedure for their adoption of both measures is the same and, in both cases, the existence of an initial CFSP decision adopted on the basis of Article 29 TEU, which empowers the Council to 'define the approach of the Union to a particular matter of geographical or thematic nature', is required.[35] Even if the existence of a CFSP decision is a condition for the adoption of measures under Article 215 TFEU, the two legal acts are legally autonomous from each other, and are adopted pursuant to distinct procedures carried out, in principle, simultaneously.[36]

From the point of view of differentiation through constructive abstention, a distinction between measures directly applied on the basis of a CFSP decision and those requiring further Union measures is important. Prohibitions on importation or exportation of arms and military equipment figuring on the common military list of the EU[37] (the so-called 'arms embargoes'), as well as prohibitions on entering the territory of EU Member States (the so-called 'travel restrictions' or 'visa bans'), fall within the first group, as they are applied by the Member States directly on the basis of a CFSP decision. As a result, these measures are not included in the accompanying regulation adopted on the basis of Article 215 TFEU. By contrast, prohibitions on making funds or economic resources available to certain persons or entities ('asset-freeze measures') or restrictions on trade or services, including prohibition of exports or imports of goods other than military equipment ('economic sanctions'), can only be uniformly and directly applied in all Member States if also adopted in the form of a regulation, which is directly applicable and produces direct effects vis-à-vis EU economic operators. A regulation within the meaning of Article 215 TFEU is, therefore, a *necessary measure* through which full effect is given to the economic and financial restrictions laid down in a CFSP decision at Union level.

Arguably, a Member State's opt-out by virtue of a CFSP constructive abstention could only apply as regards the first group of measures, which reside fully within the sphere of the CFSP. Insofar as a CFSP decision covers economic or financial restrictions subject to the implementation through regulation adopted under Article 215 TFEU, differentiation through a CFSP constructive abstention is precluded, given that, by definition, it cannot apply to non-CFSP legal acts, unless it is accepted that regulation adopted under Article 215 TFEU would not follow a differentiation in the CFSP legal act and would therefore apply uniformly in all Member States, regardless of whether they constructively abstained in the adoption of a

[35] In Case C-548/09 P, *Bank Melli Iran v Council* [2011] ECLI:EU:C:2011:735, paras 71, 73, the Court confirmed that the existence of a Council act previously adopted in the sphere of the CFSP was simply a condition laid down in Art301 EC (the predecessor of Art 215 TEU).

[36] In Case C-72/15, *Rosneft* [2017] ECLI:EU:C:2017:236, para 90, the Court further clarified the distinctive functions of the two types of acts: 'Having regard to the different functions of those two types of acts, the one *declaring* the Union's position with respect to the restrictive measures to be adopted and the other constituting *the instruiment giving effect to those measures at Union level*, ...' (our underlining).

[37] Adopted by the Council on 17 February 2020 [2020] OJ C 85/1.

CFSP decision or not. The economic and financial restrictions adopted by virtue of Article 215 TFEU have a clear link with, and impact on, the operation of the internal market. Asset-freeze measures have an effect on the movement of capital and payments, investment, and access to the EU capital markets. Economic restrictions have an impact on trade and on the exercise of the rights of establishment and to provide services. It is, therefore, clear that the transposition of the differentiation from the CFSP sphere to the framework of these policies would introduce a clear distortion of competition in the internal market to the benefit of an abstaining Member State and to the detriment of the others. Also, an opt-out in the sphere of CFSP cannot offer a basis for objective justification of national derogations, as such derogations from internal market rules are not permitted under Article 215 TFEU.

On that basis, it is, therefore, possible to conclude that as matters stand today constructive abstention is practically available only as regards restrictive measures with no impact on common rules regarding the internal market or trade, ie to arms embargoes and travel restrictions that are not implemented through TFEU measures. However, it remains to be further explored as to whether it is legally acceptable that the link with Article 215 TFEU, which 'serves as a bridge between the objectives of the EU Treaty in matters of the CFSP and the actions of the Union involving economic measures falling within the scope of the FEU Treaty'[38] and which enables CFSP measures to benefit from the effectiveness and direct applicability and effect of non-CFSP instruments, is capable of operating a disconnection from the CFSP-specific differentiation mechanism of constructive abstention, thereby reducing the differentiation possibilities of these CFSP measures.

ii) CFSP agreements concluded by the EU

While limitations linked to possible differentiation through constructive abstention as regards restrictive measures flow directly from the Treaty set-up, similar limitations concerning international agreements may have been set by the ECJ in the *Kazakhstan* case.[39] The Court held there that '*the provisions of Article 218 TFEU themselves take account of the specific features of each field of EU activity, in particular those laid down in respect of the CFSP and reflect in that regard the institutional balance established for each of those fields by the treaties*',[40] and thus rejected the post-Lisbon Council practice of citing, alongside Article 218 TFEU, Article 31(1) TEU as a procedural legal basis when recourse to Article 37 TEU (a substantive legal basis empowering the Union to conclude agreements in the area of CFSP) was also made.[41] A citation of Article 31(1) TEU as an additional

[38] Rosneft [2017], ibidem, paragraph 89.

[39] Case C-244/17 *Commission v Council* [2018] ECLI:EU:C:2018:662.

[40] ibid para 24, as well as paras 23, 28, and 29.

[41] The examples of this practice include Council Decision on the signing and Council Decision on conclusion of the enhanced partnership and cooperation agreement with Kazakhstan (2016/123 OJ L29/1 and 2020/244 OJ L52/1, respectively); Council Decision 2017/248 on the conclusion of the Agreement continuing the International Science and Technology Center ([2017] OJ L37/1); Council

procedural legal basis clearly indicated the applicability of constructive abstention, in line with the ruling in the landmark *Mauritius* case.[42] In that ruling, the Court stressed that the procedure of Article 218 TFEU must, '*because of its general nature . . . take account of the specific features which the Treaty lays down in respect of each field of EU activity*',[43] and underlined the symmetry between the procedure for adopting EU internal measures and the procedure for adopting external measures.[44] It has been argued elsewhere that a possible hermeneutical closure of Article 218 TEU, ruling out the application of constructive abstention in decisions concerning CFSP agreements, may have no impact on the institutional balance.[45]

However, the exclusion of the use of constructive abstention in this context is regrettable for other reasons. In practice, it would mean that a Member State that invoked constructive abstention as regards an EU internal measure would be left without such a possibility in relation to a similar or corresponding external measure, preventing the internal differentiation from being reflected in the external measure. This introduces a risk that a Member State deprived of the opt-out possibility as regards external EU action could vote against an act committing the EU vis-à-vis a third partner, thereby hindering external EU action.[46] But, most importantly, excluding CFSP agreements from the scope of application of the mechanism of constructive abstention reduces the flexibility for the Union in agreeing such agreements through differentiation.

2. Enhanced cooperation

The mechanism of enhanced cooperation enabling a group of Member States to establish cooperation among themselves in the field of CFSP is established by Article 329(2) TFEU. As regards the normative evolution of the instrument, from its extension to the CFSP area with the Treaty of Nice to the latest revisions by

Decision 2016/2232 on the signing, on behalf of the Union, and provisional application of the Political Dialogue and Cooperation Agreement between the EU and its Member States, of the one part, and the Republic of Cuba, of the other ([2016] OJ L337I/1); Council Decision 2016/2118 on the signing, on behalf of the Union, and provisional application of the Strategic Partnership Agreement between the European Union and its Member States, of the one part, and Canada, of the other part ([2016] OJ L329/43); and Council Decision 2016/342 on the conclusion, on behalf of the Union, of the Stabilisation and Association Agreement between the EU and EURATOM, of the one part, and Kosovo, of the other part ([2016] OJ L71/1); as well as Council Decisions 2014/295/EU, 2014/494, and 2014/492 on the signature and provisional application of the association agreements with Ukraine ([2014] OJ L260/1), Georgia ([2014] OJ L261/1), and Moldova ([2014] OJ L260/1).

[42] Case C-658/11, *Parliament v Council* [2014] ECLI:EU:C:2014:2025, para 25.

[43] ibid para 53.

[44] ibid para 56; ECLI:EU:C:2016:435, para 68.

[45] Petra Mahnič, 'The Process of Integration of the CFSP into the Evolving Constitutional Legal Order of the EU: Article 218 TFEU' [2019] Zbrornik Znanstvenih Razprav LXXIX 121.

[46] To note but one example of such a scenario, a Member State wishing to prevent the participation of a third state in an EU CSDP mission or operation, in the establishment of which, by means of an internal EU measure, it had previously constructively abstained.

the Treaty of Lisbon, a reference is made to earlier comprehensive accounts.[47] For our purposes, it is sufficient to mention that despite some early voices referring to the mechanism as the first structured legal basis for differentiated cooperation with a possible bargaining tool function,[48] and as a pragmatic tool for facilitating decision-making,[49] the prevalent subsequent opinion in academic literature as regards its effectiveness has been a negative one. The reasons given refer primarily to procedural constraints,[50] including strict requirements for its application.[51] While its underuse in the area of CFSP in the early days of the mechanism was often attributed to a restricted normative scope,[52] the unanimity requirement for its authorization is usually blamed for the lack of use of the mechanism in the post-Lisbon era. In our view, however, the main reasons for this are the inherent unsuitability of the mechanism for CFSP, and, as regards CSDP, the introduction of a more specific and flexible mechanism (PESCO). A closer look at the conditions of application of this mechanism reveals further constraints, making the instrument virtually inapplicable to the area of CFSP.

To begin with, the rule according to which the acts adopted through enhanced cooperation bind only the participating Member States, and should not be regarded as Union '*acquis which has to be accepted by candidate States for accession to the Union*' (Article 20(4) TEU), must be highlighted. This is perhaps the most debilitating feature for using the mechanism in the CFSP field, as it impedes the necessary uniformity of Union action from an external perspective.[53] First, it implies that positions agreed through enhanced cooperation cannot be regarded as established EU positions to be upheld in international organizations and at international conferences (Article 34(1) TEU), as they would bind only the participating Member States, and hence not the Union. Second, this could, theoretically, result in divergent positions being expressed in international fora by the Member States which participate in the enhanced cooperation and those which do not. A politically counterproductive—and, for Union partners and the

[47] Marise Cremona, 'Enhanced Cooperation and the Common Foreign and Security and Defence Policies of the EU' [2009] EUI WP Law 2009/21; Thomas Jaeger, 'Enhanced Cooperation in the Treaty of Nice and Flexibility in the Common Foreign and Security Policy' [2002] European Affairs Review 7, 297–316.

[48] Jaeger (n 43) 314, 315.

[49] Daniel Thym, 'The Political Character of Supranational Differentiation' [2006] 31 European Law Review 789, argued that it allows 'for limited asymmetrical progress in specific situations when Member States cannot agree on the appropriateness of European action'.

[50] Bruno de Witte, 'The Law as Tool and Constraint of Differentiated Integration' [2019] EUI WP, RSCAS 2019/47, 11.

[51] Steven Blockmans, 'Differentiation in CFSP: Potential and Limits' [2017] Instituto Affari Internazionali 7.

[52] By virtue of Art 27b of the Treaty of Nice amending the Treaty on European Union, the Treaties establishing the European Communities and certain related acts [2001] OJ C080/1, enhanced cooperation was limited to implementation of joint actions (Art 14) or common positions (Art 15), expressly excluding matters having military or defence implications.

[53] Pernice and Tym (n 19) 382.

international community at large, confusing—result, therefore, disqualifies the use of the mechanism of enhanced cooperation for the establishment of positions in the area of CFSP, be this via legal or political acts.

The picture is in no way less complicated for non-unilateral acts, be they international agreements or non-binding instruments. Since the High Representative is not mentioned in Article 20(1) TEU alongside the EU institutions which the Member States engaging in enhanced cooperation may make use of, it is not entirely clear whether (s)he could make a proposal for a Council decision on the opening of the negotiations of an agreement on behalf of a group of participating Member States on the basis of Article 218(3) TFEU[54] or request an authorization to enter into discussions regarding the signature of a non-binding instrument. Our view is that this should not be possible as regards internal instruments that bind only participating Member States, as this would be against the very objectives of the CFSP. Another question is whether a mandate to act on behalf of fewer than twenty-seven Member States could be accepted by the High Representative on an intergovernmental basis, ie outside the Treaty framework. It would seem that entrusting such a task to the High Representative would not be in line with the requirement of the *Pringle* case law[55] that the tasks conferred to the Union institutions or bodies should not '*alter the essential character of the powers*' conferred on them by the EU and FEU Treaties.[56] Accepting a mandate to represent a group of Member States would, in our view, be prejudicial to—if not contradictory with—the power of the High Representative to represent *the Union* for matters related to CFSP and to conduct political dialogue with third parties *on the Union's behalf* (Article 27(2) TEU).[57]

Finally, the requirement that enhanced cooperation must not undermine the internal market nor cause discrimination in trade or distort competition between Member States (Article 326 TFEU) indicates that restrictive measures requiring implementation via regulations adopted on the basis of Article 215 TFEU would, equally, not qualify for enhanced cooperation. While other restrictive measures established exclusively by CFSP acts would not be affected by that condition, they would still have to comply with the requirement of aiming at reinforcing EU integration (Article 20(1) TEU), which would be by no means obvious, as making a divergence among Member States visible in the international arena can hardly be conceived as reinforcing EU integration.

[54] For pre-Lisbon inconsistencies between Art 24(5) TEU, which was interpreted as possibly permitting a sort of 'negative differentiation', and Art 44 TEU, which specified that an enhanced cooperation act was not part of the Union *acquis*, see Jaeger (n 43) 304.

[55] Case C-370/12 *Pringle v Ireland* [2012] ECLI:EU:C:2012:756, paras 158–69.

[56] ibid para 162.

[57] The situation would be different as regards internal tasks, such as, eg, in the context of the mutual assistance clause (Art 42(7) TEU), provided that all Member States agreed.

B. Specific differentiation mechanisms in the area of CSDP

In contrast to the area of CFSP (excluding CSDP), where a degree of differentiation seems to have remained constantly low, differentiation in the area of CSDP has increased since the Treaty of Maastricht. On the one hand, legal initiatives in the defence area had, as a consequence, more differentiation on account of the permanent Danish defence opt-out, at least till its abolishment in June 2022; on the other, changes in primary law prompted more differentiation on the basis of PESCO, introduced with the Treaty of Lisbon, and activated for the first time in 2017. In addition, it is not a coincidence that PESCO was activated only after the Brexit referendum.[58]

1. The Treaty-based opt-out

The defence opt-out, which was agreed as part of a solution to the Danish rejection of the Treaty of Maastricht and then incorporated into EU primary law with the Treaty of Amsterdam,[59] prevented Denmark from participating in the elaboration, adoption, and implementation of *legal acts* with a legal basis in Articles 26(1), 42, and 43 to 46 TEU, when such legal acts have *defence implications*.[60] The opt-out thus covered, in particular, EU military non-executive missions and military executive operations, including possible assistance measures to such operations under the EPF Decision 2021, and participation in the European Defence Agency (EDA) as well as PESCO. Denmark could, however, fully participate in the European Defence Fund, in certain measures under the EPF Decision 2021 (eg the funding of ammunition and weapons for third countries rather than for CSDP operations), in civilian CSDP missions, and in other forms of military cooperation outside legal bases cited in the Protocol on Denmark. The defence opt-out also did not prevent Denmark from participating in discussions and decision-making processes as regards political instruments such as statements, joint communiqués, or Council conclusions, even when they had defence implications, since these political instruments clearly fell outside the scope of the Protocol.

In the same vein as the fact that the mechanism of constructive abstention obliges the abstaining Member State to '*refrain from any action likely to conflict with or impede Union action based on that decision*', the permanent opt-out states that '*Denmark will not prevent the other Member States from further developing their cooperation in the area*'.[61] In addition, when Denmark unilaterally and irrevocably

[58] Following the outcome of the referendum on the UK leaving the EU, in June 2016, the Council adopted conclusions, in October and November of the same year, agreeing to explore possibilities for PESCO, an approach that was endorsed by the European Council of December 2016.

[59] Graham Butler, 'The European Defence Union and Denmark's Defence Opt-out: A Legal Appraisal' (2020) 25 European Foreign Affairs Review 117.

[60] Art 5 of the Protocol No 22 on the position of Denmark.

[61] ibid.

forewent the defence opt-out in 2022, it was obliged '*to apply in full all relevant measures then in force taken within the framework of the European Union*'.[62] This is a clear indication that the differentiated measures adopted without Denmark constitute Union *acquis* and that the Danish opt-out did not hinder the EU's ability to act, with Denmark being obliged not to conflict with Union action in the field.

Another question is whether internal differentiation on this basis has any consequence in the external sphere. Neither practice nor existing case law of the ECJ offers a clear answer to this question. Decisions concerning agreements concluded by the EU with third countries regarding their contribution to the EU military operations and missions do, as a general rule, cite Article 37 TEU as their only substantive legal basis, which would, in principle, exclude the application of the Danish Protocol.[63] Here again, the application of the logic of the *Kazakhstan* case (according to which the provisions of Article 218 TFEU themselves 'take account of the specific features of each field of EU activity, in particular those laid down in respect of the CFSP') would result in the impossibility of using the procedural legal bases for establishing CSDP missions and operations that would trigger the application of the Danish Protocol.[64] As a result, Denmark would be bound to participate in the adoption of any such measures in spite of the Protocol. If, on the other hand, we follow the logic established by the *Mauritius* case, which stresses the symmetry between the procedures for the adoption of internal measures and external measures, the inclusion of the specific CSDP procedural legal bases would appear necessary, thus triggering the application of the Danish Protocol and the exclusion of Denmark from the decision-making process related to the adoption of measures which concern commitments by third states in making military capabilities available to the Union (a commitment that the Danish Protocol expressly excludes for Denmark).

We argue that the second interpretation would be more adjusted to the underlying logic and intended objectives of the Danish opt-out, whereas the first interpretation would result in altering primary law by *de facto obliging* Denmark to participate in the elaboration of certain (external) measures having defence implications, despite the clear exclusion established by the Protocol and clearly applicable to internal measures. This would, in turn, have given Denmark, unwarrantedly

[62] ibid Art 7; Art 1 of Council Decision (CFSP) 2023/994 of 22 May 2023.

[63] Recital 5 of Council Decision 2013/178/CFSP on the signing and conclusion of the Agreement between the European Union and the Republic of Mali on the status in the Republic of Mali of the European Union military mission to contribute to the training of the Malian Armed Forces (EUTM Mali) [2013] OJ L106/1 indicates that the opt-out applied. By contrast, there is no such recital referring to the Danish Protocol in Council Decision 2009/29/CFSP concerning the conclusion of the Agreement between the EU and the Somali Republic on the Status of the EU-led naval force in the Somali Republic in the framework of EU military operation Atalanta [2009] OJ L10/27, nor in the Viet Nam Decision (n 10).

[64] ie Arts 42(4) and 43(1) TEU.

and *nolens volens*, the right to oppose (and, therefore, block) the Union from concluding international agreements of that type with third states.

C. Permanent structured cooperation (PESCO)

Permanent structured cooperation (PESCO) empowers those Member States whose military capabilities fulfil higher criteria and which have made more binding commitments to one another in this area to establish such cooperation within the Treaty legal framework.[65] Not only is the bar for its establishment by the Council lower (qualified majority) than that required for enhanced cooperation (unanimity), but additional flexibility is also provided by a number of specific provisions allowing for a flexible entry into (or exit from) the cooperation, as well as a possibility of suspension of a Member State's participation. The Council may, thus, decide by qualified majority on the participation of any Member State, which, at a later stage, wishes to join (Article 46(3) TEU). Although politically no doubt difficult to use and envisaged as a last resort, a suspension of a participating Member State that no longer fulfils the necessary criteria or is no longer able or willing to meet the commitments referred to in Articles 1 and 2 of the PESCO Protocol is also possible (Article 46(4) TEU). This gives the Council a tool to resolve, again by qualified majority (calculated on the basis of the participating states, with the exception of the Member State in question), a possible stalemate in cooperation due to a Member State joining without the ability or the real ambition to deliver. A vanguard of Member States may thus proceed without being blocked by one reluctant participant. Finally, any participating Member State wishing to withdraw from PESCO is free to do so at any time (Article 46(5) TEU).[66]

As regards the decision-making process, it is noteworthy that the framework is driven by participating Member States, rather than by the Union institutions or services.[67] It was pursuant to the initiative of Member States that PESCO was established in the first place[68] and it is also for the Member States to submit projects they deem useful for the purposes of PESCO. Participating Member States associated with a project ('project members') also agree among themselves, by unanimity, the modalities and scope of their cooperation, including the necessary contributions needed to join the project and governance rules. They also decide on the admission of further participating Member States with participating or observer status.

[65] Arts 42(6) and 46 TEU, and 'Protocol (No 10) on permanent structured cooperation established by Article 42 of the Treaty on European union', which was annexed to the Treaty of Lisbon. OJ C 115 / 2008, p 275–77.

[66] For a comprehensive account of the developments and challenges of PESCO, see Steven Blockmans, 'The EU's Modular Approach to Defence Integration: An Inclusive, Ambitious and Legally Binding PESCO?' (2018) 55 Common Market Law Review 1785–826.

[67] Annex III to PESCO Decision 2017 (n 11)

[68] PESCO was established on the basis of a proposal by Germany, Spain, France, and Italy.

The role of the High Representative is to ensure proper coordination of PESCO with the overall CSDP, manage annual assessments, and provide recommendations identifying the most relevant projects in terms of EU level of ambition and the EU's strategic autonomy. In addition, the High Representative is to be consulted on the establishment of PESCO, and as regards subsequent notifications of Member States wishing to join the cooperation. Furthermore, it exercises the right of initiative in relation to Council decisions related to the participation of third states. The EDA, as regards capability development aspects, and the EEAS (EU Military Staff), as regards operational aspects, together form the PESCO secretariat, a single point of contact within the Union's framework.[69] Unlike in the case of general enhanced cooperation, where the Commission has a prerogative to give its opinion on whether the possible use of the mechanism in a given case is consistent with other Union policies, no such role is envisaged for the Commission in the PESCO mechanism, which is understandable as this mechanism is limited to a specific policy field already defined and agreed at the level of primary law.

The governance in charge of maintaining the coherence and the ambition of PESCO is based on existing structures, ie the specific Joint Foreign Affairs/Defence meeting subformation of the Council, with voting rights reserved to the participating Member States. The so-called PESCO format is also envisaged for Political and Security Committee, Politico-Military Group, and EU Military Committee meetings, allowing for all EU Member States to be present, but 'with the arrangement reflecting that only participating Member States have voting right in the Council'. The possibility of informal meetings taking place among the participating Member States only is also envisaged.

In contrast to the mechanism of enhanced cooperation, no express indication is given as to whether or not acts adopted in PESCO format constitute Union *acquis* for the purpose of acceding States. The voluntary nature of the mechanism, its similarity to the enhanced cooperation mechanism, and the fact that it is based on higher commitments and ability to deliver speaks against this. Recent Council practice could, however, suggest otherwise, as recently adopted Council decisions on the participation of third states in the PESCO Project on Military Mobility attest.[70] These decisions do not indicate the internal differentiation that exists within PESCO, in which twenty-five Member States currently participate. The possible non-participation of PESCO non-participating Member States in the adoption of

[69] Art 3 of Council Decision (CFSP) 2018/909 establishing a common set of governance rules for PESCO projects [2018] OJ L161/37.

[70] Council Decision (CFSP) 2021/749 on the participation of the Kingdom of Norway in the PESCO project Military Mobility [2021] OJ L160/19; Council Decision (CFSP) 2021/748 on the participation of Canada in the PESCO project Military Mobility [2021] L160/106; and Council Decision (CFSP) 2021/750 on the participation of the United States of America in the PESCO project Military Mobility [2021] OJ L160/11.

Council acts is not visible from the acts themselves, as was normally the case for acts triggering the Protocol on Denmark.[71]

Finally, as regards political instruments, there is probably no obstacle to the Council making pronouncements on common matters of interest among the participating Member States in 'PESCO format'. It is, however, less certain whether the Council could approve the entering into discussions (by the High Representative?) on, and signature of, non-binding instruments that the participating Member States may wish to agree in the future with third states or international organizations as regards cooperation on PESCO matters. While it is true that the High Representative is given, by virtue of secondary law, a right to initiative in relation to Council decisions related to the participation of third states in individual PESCO projects, it does not follow from this that (s)he would be entitled to represent the PESCO-participating Member States vis-à-vis third partners. Rather, in our view, the same considerations as those discussed under enhanced cooperation would apply: such a role would be prejudicial—if not contrary—to the power of the High Representative to represent *the Union* in relation to matters related to the CFSP and to conduct political dialogue with third parties *on the Union's behalf* (Article 27(2) TEU).

IV. Conclusions

The overview of the forms of differentiation in the area of CFSP shows a mixed picture. External differentiation is, as a matter of principle, excluded by virtue of the principle of EU decision-making autonomy. Internal differentiation is present to a moderate degree, with the mechanism of enhanced cooperation, although legally possible, seeming unsuitable for the CFSP. It is difficult to conclude whether internal differentiation in the area of CFSP has any spillover effect on relations with third states. On the one hand, there is an indication of the reluctance on the part of the ECJ to allow for the inherent features of the CFSP area to be imported into decision-making procedures of general application, such as Article 218 TFEU (the *Kazakhstan* ruling). On the other hand, the imperative of the decision-making symmetry between internal and external acts (the *Mauritius* ruling) requires that the possibility of constructive abstention could be forlorn in the Union's external action. While the opt-outs are constitutive of the Union *acquis*, differentiation through enhanced cooperation (and, most probably, PESCO) does not result in the creation of Union *acquis*. In the former case, differentiation reinforces the EU's ability 'to seek to advance in the wider world . . . the principles which have inspired its own creation, development and enlargement' (Article 21(1) TEU, first

[71] eg Recital 5 of the Mali Decision (n 63) indicates that the opt-out applied.

subparagraph), as it does not hinder the Union's capacity to act on the world stage. In the latter case, the ability to act externally, ie to cooperate and make partnerships with third actors is offered to a group of Member States (PESCO), rather than to the Union itself. The particularities of the CFSP, which aims at furthering convergence of Member States' actions, with a view to projecting the united position of the EU (ie the EU speaking with one voice) vis-à-vis third actors, is therefore the cardinal explanation for a relatively trivial interest in differentiation in this policy area since its inception.

Moreover, when recourse to the Union framework is chosen, Member States prefer non-legal instruments to legal acts. Even when legal acts are considered (or required by the Treaty), Member States prefer that proposals for a Union act come from the High Representative, rather than exercising their own right to submit proposals under Article 30(1) TEU. The proposals by the High Representative are, however, typically triggered after having previously ascertained the consensus of Member States, which, for reasons explained, does not permit differentiation. The constraints regarding political and legal instruments were, therefore, rightly qualified as 'testimony to [the] enduring strength of the consensus culture inside the Council'.[72] In addition, the use of legal instruments is subject to legal constraints laid down in the Treaties, many of which additionally (and substantially) contribute to the reduction of the scope of potential differentiation in the area of CFSP. Yet, recourse to Treaty-based mechanisms and legal acts remains—as the Council practice currently stands—the only possibility for an acceptable degree of differentiation within the EU framework. The solution for the future could, therefore, lie in attempts at transforming the culture of consensus into the culture of unanimity (allowing for constructive abstention and, in some cases, enhanced cooperation). While this proposition may appear controversial in other policy areas, it makes perfect sense for the CFSP. This would be achievable through a twofold effort, requiring a more active engagement by both EU institutions and Member States.

First, legal instruments could be proposed, be it by the High Representative,[73] or by a group of Member States, without necessarily calling for a prior establishment of consensus. A preceding political process could, however, be used to identify Member States with difficulties linked to proposed initiatives, who could be invited to consider invoking constructive abstention if unable to vote for the Union act when proposed, or to vote for authorization of the enhanced cooperation, even when they themselves were unwilling to join the initiative. Second, the CFSP Treaty-based voting arrangements should be applied to non-binding political acts, which would infuse the possibility for differentiation through constructive abstention. Paradoxically, perhaps, for the politically sensitive area of foreign

[72] de Witte (n 46) 7.
[73] Blockmans, 'Differentiation in CFSP' (n 47) 5.

policy, which is not primarily about rule-making,[74] Treaty-based procedures obviously serve flexibility better than the traditional political process. To conclude, the existing institutional framework, all reservations and shortcomings notwithstanding, does provide for '*the necessary groundwork and foundation upon which a more efficient and effective European policy may be built*'.[75] It would just need to be exploited to the maximum in the directions suggested.

[74] Daniel Thym, 'Reforming Europe's Common Foreign and Security Policy' (2004) 10 European Law Review 19.

[75] Ibid., p. 6.

5

Playing Fast and Loose: Unravelling Membership in the AFSJ

*Deirdre Curtin and Maria Patrin**

I. Introduction

The area of Freedom, Security and Justice (AFSJ) represents a special case of differentiated integration within the European Union (EU). It is a particularly heterogenous and complex area, which covers a broad range of policies, and is characterized by a governance structure in which the EU institutions and a number of agencies both play a role. Under the common umbrella of 'Freedom, Security and Justice' diverse issues converge. On the one hand, there are those related to judicial cooperation in civil law, migration, and asylum and border control (migration policies), and on the other, EU cooperation in criminal matters and policing (security issues). These policy areas were originally put together in the intergovernmental third pillar of the Maastricht Treaty, and over the years have been progressively communautarized. The reason why they were placed together can be understood as a result of the abolition of border controls under the Schengen Agreement. This created a gap in the capacity of Member States to control immigration and cross-border crime, thus raising security concerns and fostering the need for cooperation at the European level.[1] However, as these policy areas have evolved in intensity and reach, and become increasingly complex, two separate policy fields with very different needs and problems have emerged.

The AFSJ has seen an extraordinary evolution as probably the most rapidly growing EU policy ever.[2] However, this evolution has taken place in what can only

* This chapter is the result of common work and reflections. Nevertheless, Maria Patrin has drafted Sections I, III, V, and VI, and Deirdre Curtin has drafted sections II, IV, VII, and VIII. We would like to thank our editor Diane Fromage, as well as Claudio Matera, for helpful feedback and advice. All remaining errors are our own.

[1] Dirk Leuffen, Berthold Rittberger, and Frank Schimmelfennig, *Differentiated Integration: Explaining Variation in the European Union* (Palgrave 2012) 235–36; Joerg Monar, 'Why EU Institutions Matter in Justice and Home Affairs' in Florian Trauner and Ariadna Ripoll Servent (eds), *Policy Change in the Area of Freedom, Security and Justice: How EU Institutions Matter* (Routledge 2015) 4.

[2] Leuffen, Rittberger, and Schimmelfennig, *Differentiated Integration: Explaining Variation* (n 1) 221.

Deirdre Curtin and Maria Patrin, *Playing Fast and Loose* In: *Redefining EU Membership*. Edited by: Diane Fromage, Oxford University Press. © Deirdre Curtin and Maria Patrin 2024. DOI: 10.1093/9780191948145.003.0005

be described as a disorderly and even disconnected manner, with new, at times spontaneous, ad hoc arrangements crafted for different needs and paces of integration. As argued by one of the present authors, the very origins of cooperation in the area were highly fragmented.[3] Progressively, however, legal and institutional practices began to show clear patterns of what could be depicted as 'unity', as some of the original fragments were stuck together.[4] Yet, the process was turbulent and required quite a lot of institutional engineering. With the Amsterdam Treaty, the third pillar was split into two areas with different decision-making regimes (asylum and migration policies were placed in the community pillar, while policing and criminal matters remained intergovernmental). The two areas were subsequently joined up again in the Lisbon Treaty within a single communitarian framework. Nevertheless, there are still many exceptions to the ordinary legislative procedure.[5] As a result, the AFSJ remains intrinsically piecemeal and heterogenous:

> Because of continuing disputes between Member States on JHA institutional issues and the resulting renegotiations of the basic legal framework concerning JHA as set out in the Treaties establishing the EU, the institutional framework for EU JHA law is historically complex, in particular due to its use of different rules over time regarding decision-making, jurisdiction of the EU courts, legal instruments and their legal effect, and territorial scope.[6]

Moreover, the disorderly evolution of EU cooperation in AFSJ favoured a geographically diverse regime, which remains a feature of this domain: 'Fragmentation pertained not only to the structurally seemingly separate inter-governmental "pillars" alongside the previously existing supranational core, but also the inclusion at the Treaty level of an endless array of opt-outs for individual Member States on matters of smaller and greater significance.'[7] This type of fragmentation has, arguably, been resistant to the rationalization process that brought together the different fragments within a more coherent institutional and legal system. This has largely to do with the attitude and practice of certain Member States (including, in particular, the UK, but also Denmark and Ireland) who have demanded and been given, for one reason or another, exceptional measures that fray the unitary idea of membership across the board. Playing 'fast and loose', differentiation as

[3] Deirdre Curtin, 'The Constitutional Structure of the Union: A Europe of Bits and Pieces' (1993) 30 Common Market Law Review 17.

[4] Deirdre Curtin, 'From a Europe of Bits and Pieces to a Union of Variegated Differentiation' in Grainne de Búrca and Paul Craig (eds), *The Evolution of EU Law* (OUP 1999).

[5] For instance, Arts 86 and 87 TFEU on the European Public Prosecutor and operational police cooperation. See later in the chapter for more details.

[6] Steve Peers, *EU Justice and Home Affairs Law: Volume I: EU Immigration and Asylum Law* (OUP 2016) 3.

[7] Curtin, 'The Constitutional Structure of the Union: A Europe of Bits and Pieces' (n 3) 17ff.

unravelling membership has become a predominant, and seemingly even stable, trait within the legal architecture of the AFSJ, including after Brexit.[8]

Three main features of differentiation distinguish the EU integration approach in this area. First, the process of differentiation in a highly complex, fragmented, and sensitive area such as AFSJ has resulted in a variety of regimes and instruments.[9] The AFSJ includes virtually all types of internal and external differentiation. The Schengen and Prüm Agreements are examples of external differentiation that was subsequently integrated back into EU law; AFSJ reveals the most varied and extensive range of opt-outs possible, from the Polish and Czech exemptions from the Charter of Fundamental Rights, to the Danish and Irish opt-outs from AFSJ as a whole; the Treaties provide for special enhanced cooperation procedure in some specific cases, and the establishment of the European Public Prosecutor Office (EPPO) is the first example. Finally, agencies such as Europol have set up different forms of participation for members and non-members, associating non-EU Member States or opt-out Member States in different legal and institutional arrangements.

Second, despite the variety of regimes, differentiation in the AFSJ is often permanent, or, rather, constitutive, especially when it takes the shape of voluntary self-exclusion by some Member States (opt-out). Opt-outs mean non-participation on the ground of substantive disagreement about the objectives of EU integration, or about the involvement of supranational institutions. These choices are often sanctioned by referenda, and future inclusion, although legally possible, is hampered by democratic, constitutional, and sovereignty concerns. This is very different from other forms of variable geometry, which are viewed against the backdrop of future cohesion and ultimate inclusion. For instance, Economic and Monetary Union (EMU), another policy area which is highly differentiated, is open, at least in principle, to all Member States, who are supposed to join the euro sooner or later.[10]

However, the story of the AFSJ is not one of exclusion only. The third feature of AFSJ differentiation is that it is marked by a great interest of outsiders (in the sense of non-participating countries) in certain policies. EFTA countries (Norway, Switzerland, Iceland, and Liechtenstein) participate in the Schengen Agreement, and in other related initiatives. The UK and Ireland have negotiated an opt-in

[8] eg Garner, who speaks of 'new old' intergovernmentalism in this area: Oliver Garner, 'Part Three of the EU-UK TCA—From a "Disrupted" Area of Freedom, Security and Justice to "New Old" Intergovernmentalism in Justice and Home Affairs?' (2021) No 1/2021 Brexit Institute Working Paper Series.

[9] Georgia Papagianni, 'Flexibility in Justice and Home Affairs: An Old Phenomenon Taking New Forms' in Bruno de Witte, Dominik Hanf, and Ellen Vos (eds), *The Many Faces of Differentiation in EU Law* (Intersentia 2001) 113.

[10] See Stefaan Van den Bogaert and Vestert Borger, 'Differentiated Integration in EMU' in Bruno de Witte, Andrea Ott, and Ellen Vos (eds), *Between Flexibility and Disintegration: The Trajectory of Differentiation in EU Law* (Edward Elgar 2017) 209–36, and Mark Dawson and Tomasz P Woźniakowski, in this volume.

scheme, whereby they can select the AFSJ policies in which they want to take part. Finally, Denmark has a full opt-out from AFSJ, but this has not prevented it from finding arrangements in order to be associated to AFSJ cooperation, not least through third-party agreements.[11]

This chapter will investigate the forms and instruments of differentiation in the AFSJ. The deeply entrenched and constitutive nature of differentiation, in terms of both type and intensity, makes the AFSJ a laboratory for different kinds of participation patterns within a single legal framework. Our analysis will show that the overlap of various forms of differentiation creates a space in which the distinction between participating and non-participating Member States, as well as external and EU members, tends to get blurred and diluted within the many different participation patterns. The resulting landscape unveils an unravelling membership with considerable degrees of flexibility possible in practice. The very concept of EU membership finds itself shifting towards a 'nuanced' type of membership, composed of several micro-trajectories of participation which are characterized by permeable and fraying edges. However, instead of creating a new membership status, the patterns of differentiation within AFSJ point, rather, to the possibility of including different forms of—frayed—membership within the common and unitary framework of the EU. We certainly do not advocate the creation of layers of membership, nor are we in favour of an associated membership status; rather, we aim to show how the EU legal framework, through differentiation, can already accommodate a considerable variety of flexible memberships and different ways of 'being members'. The question remains, however, where the limits of this flexibility should lie, taking into account the implications for transparency and accountability of such a fragmented membership framework.

We will proceed as follows. We will first provide an overview of differentiation within the AFSJ in a historical perspective. We will explore some examples of differentiation instruments in AFSJ, including Schengen, cooperation in criminal and police matters (Europol and EPPO), and asylum. The selection of these case studies follows a binary logic that interlaces the variety of policies with the interest of differentiation patterns. In line with the theoretical framework followed in this book, we will focus on the geographical differentiation (horizontal) rather than on the vertical type of policy-related differentiation.[12] Finally, we will consider how Brexit is changing this membership landscape, and what impact it is having on the differentiated integration of the AFSJ. In the concluding remarks, we will provide some reflections on the consequences of differentiation for the future of EU membership more broadly.

[11] Rebecca Adler-Nissen, *Opting out of the European Union Diplomacy, Sovereignty and European Integration* (CUP 2014) 127ff (for the UK) and 14ff (for Denmark).

[12] Leuffen, Rittberger, and Schimmelfennig, *Differentiated Integration: Explaining Variation* (n 1) 11ff.

II. AFSJ: A Policy Area Born Differentiated, Growing over Time

The AFSJ was, from the very beginning, a policy domain with high levels of differentiation. It concerns an area of core state powers which is constitutive for national identity and sovereignty, and is often very politicized.[13] Given its sensitive nature, it was 'born differentiated'. Differentiation was the result of a tension between the eagerness of many Member States to proceed with further cooperation at the Union level and the reluctance of others to relinquish sovereignty in this complex domain.[14] The diversity among national positions made it difficult to progress within the traditional Community framework.[15] Thus, before the Maastricht Treaty, cooperation in the field of justice and home affairs (JHA, as it was then known) was intergovernmental and took place outside of Community law.[16] The first structured form of cooperation, the 1985 Schengen Agreement, took the form of a treaty under international law, originally signed by only five members of the European Communities. The 1992 Maastricht Treaty included JHA into the EU Treaty framework, however it placed it under the third, intergovernmental, pillar of the Treaty on European Union.[17] The Treaty of Amsterdam, which entered into force in 1999, 'comunautarized' immigration and asylum issues, whereas policing and criminal matters remained intergovernmental. Thus, the subject matter of JHA was split in two parts, under two different decision-making regimes,[18] while the Schengen Agreement was integrated into the Community framework. At that point, both the UK and Ireland negotiated the right to opt out of both policy areas, and to maintain their own border-control regime. Denmark was also granted an opt-out from all EU JHA rules.[19]

Since then, any subsequent integration step in the AFSJ has only been possible in connection with derogations given to those Member States who opposed further supranational cooperation. Denmark, the UK, and Ireland accepted the expansion of supranational decision-making that their exclusion from the application of EU law in these fields.[20] These negotiating patterns have remained typical of all further changes in the AFSJ, so that the extension of Community powers

[13] Berthold Rittberger, Dirk Leuffen, and Frank Schimmelfennig, 'Differentiated Integration of Core State Powers' in Philipp Genschel and Markus Jachtenfuchs (eds), *Beyond the Regulatory Polity? The European Integration of Core State Powers* (OUP 2013) 194–95.

[14] Peers, *EU Justice and Home Affairs Law* (n 6) 7.

[15] Papagianni (n 9) 104.

[16] Peers, *EU Justice and Home Affairs Law* (n 6) 8.

[17] At the time it was called 'Justice and Home Affairs'. It was renamed 'Area of Freedom, Security and Justice' with the Lisbon Treaty.

[18] Deirdre Curtin and Ige Dekker, 'The EU as a "Layered" International Organization: Institutional Unity in Disguise' in Paul Craig and Gráinne De Búrca (eds) (n 4).

[19] Peers, *EU Justice and Home Affairs Law* (n 6) 8–9.

[20] Steve Peers, 'The Rise and Fall of EU Justice and Home Affairs Law' in Maria Fletcher, Ester Herlin-Karnell, and Claudio Matera (eds), *The European Union as an Area of Freedom, Security and Justice* (Routledge 2017) 14.

has been accompanied by corresponding derogations and opt-outs for these three states. Again, when the Treaty of Lisbon, in 2009, merged police and judicial cooperation in criminal matters into the main body of the EU, thus making initiatives in this policy domain subject to qualified majority voting and supranational decision-making, the UK and Ireland negotiated a block opt-out with a special opt-in option.[21] They could decide whether to 'opt out' of pre-Lisbon police and criminal justice measures (around 100 measures) or remain bound by them. The UK exercised this block opt-out in 2014, but rejoined thirty-five measures, including participation in EU agencies such as Europol and Eurojust, later that year.[22] Conversely, Denmark rejected, in a 2015 referendum, the option to move towards an opt-out/opt-in regime on the UK model, and has, therefore, maintained its full opt-out regime.[23]

In addition to opt-outs, the AFSJ institutional framework provides for other forms of differentiation. Asylum and migration policies are, in fact, subject to the general regime of enhanced cooperation foreseen by the Treaty of Lisbon. According to Article 20 TEU, a group of at least nine Member States may establish enhanced cooperation between themselves within the framework of the Union's non-exclusive competences. The cooperation must be authorized by the Council as a last-resort measure, and can only take place if cooperation cannot be attained by the Union as a whole within a reasonable time period. Also, it must be open to all the other Member States to join. As the AFSJ is an area of shared competences, enhanced cooperation can, in principle, be established in any of its policies (with the aforementioned legal constraints applying). However, up to now, the general enhanced cooperation provisions have only been used to allow the UK and Ireland to opt into immigration, asylum, and civil law measures after their adoption.[24]

A simplified form of enhanced cooperation can be used in some areas of criminal law and police cooperation, namely those AFSJ policies that were communautarized in Lisbon. This fast-track route allows Member States to proceed with enhanced cooperation with a simple notification to the Commission, the Council, and the European Parliament, without obtaining the prior authorization of the Council. This happens in the policy areas which are still subject to unanimity (on the establishment of the European Public Prosecutor Office (EPPO), and on operational police cooperation), and in the policy areas where Member States can trigger a so-called emergency brake if they consider that a provision affects fundamental aspects of their criminal justice system.[25] As noted by

[21] Protocol No 21 on the position of the United Kingdom and Ireland in respect of the Area of Freedom, Security and Justice [2010] OJ C-83/295.

[22] Deirdre Curtin, 'Brexit and the EU Area of Freedom, Security, and Justice. Bespoke Bits and Pieces' in Federico Fabbrini (ed), *The Law & Politics of Brexit* (OUP 2017) 185.

[23] Steve Peers, *EU Justice and Home Affairs Law: Volume II: EU Criminal Law, Policing, and Civil Law* (OUP 2016) 44.

[24] Peers, *EU Justice and Home Affairs Law* (n 6) 27 and 39.

[25] Respectively, Art 86 TFEU (EPPO), Art 87 TFEU (police cooperation), and Arts 82(3) and 83(3) TFEU (criminal justice systems). For more information on these procedures, see Maria Patrin,

Weyembergh, in those areas 'the simplified recourse to enhanced cooperation serves as a sort of compensation for maintaining exceptional legislative procedures/derogations to the ordinary legislative procedure'.[26] As we will show in more detail later in this chapter, this procedure was used for the first time for the establishment of the EPPO.

Finally, the AFSJ displays a high degree of external differentiation, since non-EU Member States participate in many JHA policies. Because of their association with Schengen, EFTA countries are the closest partners to the EU, and take part in policies ranging from the Dublin system for asylum, to information exchange schemes to combat terrorism and cross-border crimes. After Brexit, the UK must be added to the array of external partners maintaining close ties with the EU's AFSJ. Moreover, other countries, such as the US, Australia, Canada, and the EU-neighbouring countries, are also involved in some AFSJ policies and associated to the activities of Europol, with significant variations amongst their forms of association.

These layers of internal and external cooperation compose a complex system of geometries, with full EU members, opt-out EU members, former EU members, and associated third countries interacting on different levels, and often in similar ways. Across these overlapping layers there is rarely a clear divide between insiders and outsiders, as many other intermediate 'forms' of participation are possible. As noted by Peers, 'the question of territorial scope is what distinguished JHA from other policy areas'.[27] Differentiation and flexibility are thus intrinsically connected with the essence of EU integration in this area. They have come to constitute a 'model' of integration that privileges the vertical deepening of the integration process over the horizontal uniformity of its geographical coverage. In the next four sections, we will review several paradigmatic types of instruments and policies in this regard.

III. Schengen and Prüm: Opting in through Treaty Inclusion

Schengen is a policy area of diverse variable geometries, combining internal and external differentiation in an exemplary way.[28] The 1985 Schengen Agreement was originally signed by only Germany, France, and the Benelux countries. However,

Enhanced flexibility: Special Regimes of Closer Cooperation in Core State Powers, Maastricht Journal of European and Comparative Law, (2024) online first.

[26] Anne Weyembergh, 'Enhanced Cooperation in Criminal Matters: Past, Present and Future' in Robert Kert and Andrea Lehner (eds), *Vielfalt des Strafrechts im internationalen Kontext: Festschrift für Frank Höpfel zum 65. Geburtstag* (NWV 2018) 609.

[27] Peers, *EU Justice and Home Affairs Law* (n 6) 26.

[28] Leuffen, Rittberger, and Schimmelfennig, *Differentiated Integration: Explaining Variation* (n 1) 221.

apart from the UK and Ireland, all the other Member States at that time joined the agreement shortly thereafter. As pointed out in the previous section, the Schengen *acquis*, including measures on the abolition of internal border controls, and on the control of external borders, was integrated within the EU law framework in the Amsterdam Treaty. It originally took the form of a closer cooperation between Member States, so as to allow for the non-participation of the UK and Ireland, but also of Denmark, which, although part of the Schengen Convention, opposed the involvement of the EU supranational institutions in Schengen-related matters. The Schengen *acquis* is today incorporated into the Treaty on the Functioning of the European Union (TFEU) via Protocol 19.[29] Not all Member States are part of Schengen. Apart from Ireland (and the UK before Brexit), Cyprus has not joined, for political and practical reasons related to the Greek–Turkish division of the island.[30] Despite not being a Schengen member, Cyprus is joining the Schengen information system as of July 2023.[31] The most recent EU Member State to join was Croatia, in January 2023. Starting from 2024 Romania and Bulgaria will alsojoin, following the Council's decision to progressively lift controls at the borders .[32] Moreover, many third countries are associated with Schengen, including Norway, Iceland, Switzerland, and Liechtenstein. Finally, Denmark participates only on the basis of an intergovernmental agreement, and not within the framework of Union law. This means that, in this respect, it is formally a third country for this purpose.

The Schengen legal framework is further complicated by the fact that non-participating members, such as Ireland, or the UK prior to Brexit, can opt in to Schengen-related measures, as they did, for instance, with the Schengen Information System (SIS). Protocol 22 annexed to the TFEU, on the position of Denmark, establishes that Denmark can choose whether or not to apply any new measure based on the Schengen *acquis*. This allows Denmark to participate in negotiations for new Schengen-related measures, but without voting rights.[33] Adler Nissen offers interesting insights on how Denmark's peculiar status within

[29] Bernd Martenczuk, 'Variable Geometry and the External Relations of the EU: The Experience of Justice and Home Affairs' in Bernd Martenczuk and Servaas van Thiel (eds), *Justice, Liberty, Security: New Challenges for EU External Relations* (VUBPRESS 2008); Protocol No 19 on the Schengen Acquis integrated into the framework of the European Union [2010] OJ C83/290.

[30] Because Cyprus is divided into a Turkish and a Greek part, Schengen rules and controls are difficult to implement without disrupting the communications and relations between the two parts. Cyprus started the process to become a Schengen member in 2019. As of June 2021, however, the country was not yet ready, according to the Commission, who is conducting the evaluation: Shkurta Januzi, 'EU: Cyprus Not Ready to Join Schengen Zone' (*SchengenVisaInfo*, 3 June 2021) <https://www.schengenvisainfo.com/news/eu-cyprus-not-ready-to-join-schengen-zone/> accessed 30 June 2023.

[31] Council Decision 2023/870 of 25 April 2023 on the application of the provisions of the Schengen acquis relating to the Schengen Information System in the Republic of Cyprus, L113/44.

[32] Council Decision on the full application of the provisions of the Schengen acquis in the Republic of Bulgaria and Romania, Brussels 30 December 2023, 17132/23. . On Croatia's accession, see the Commission's press release 'Euro and Schengen: Croatia Joins the Euro and Schengen Areas' (30 December 2022) at https://ec.europa.eu/commission/presscorner/detail/en/ip_22_7907 accessed 1 July 2023.

[33] Adler-Nissen (n 11) 135.

Schengen translates into participation in practice. She has found that Denmark is mostly treated as a normal Schengen country in the Council circles, since decisions are usually made by consensus. 'As long as it does not create problems, nobody mentions the protocol', she reports a Commission official saying. Indeed, Danish officials do their best not to create problems, in order not to jeopardize this inclusive approach.[34] Such practice allows for effective cooperation between the outsider (Denmark) and the insiders (the other EU Member States), and indeed Denmark has endorsed all Schengen-related measures. Yet, it is questionable from an accountability point of view, as it stretches the mandate given by the Danish people to remain outside of EU law. *De facto* Denmark informally participates in the Council's work; and it participates in a subordinated role, acting 'under the threat of exclusion'.[35]

Schengen's convoluted participation framework, therefore, has important consequences for the concept of EU membership in one of the central EU policy areas, which touches upon the core value of free movement and trickles down in manifold secondary provisions. Not only does Schengen bring together some EU Member States with some non-EU Member States, but it also provides for the possibility for Member States to participate as non-Member States. The resulting landscape does not affect the legal functioning of Schengen within EU law, as the Treaties and other legal provisions regulate in detail the relationship between EU members and associated countries. Moreover, the ECJ has ruled several times on the scope of the opt-out provisions, and on the relationship between EU law and international law.[36] Yet, within this legal framework, some Member States share the same rights and obligations with some non-Member States, rather than with the non-participating EU members.. EU membership is thus built and operates within a larger participation framework, which does not present itself as uniform, but rather as fundamentally heterogenous and porous.

The Court's judgment in *Spain v European Parliament and Council* lays bare the impact of differentiation on the relations between participating and non-participating Member States, as well as the difficulties in dissecting their respective rights and obligations under EU and international law.[37] In this case, Spain had challenged certain provisions of the Eurosur (European Border Surveillance System) Regulation, on the ground that they violated the Schengen Protocol by enabling the UK and Ireland to 'take part' in areas of the Schengen *acquis* when their participation had not been authorized by the Council. In its judgment, the ECJ

[34] ibid 136.

[35] ibid 186.

[36] Cases C-77/05 *UK v Council* [2007] ECLI:EU:C:2007:803 and C-137/05 *UK v Council* [2007] ECLI:EU:C:2007:805. In the latter case, for instance, the Court ruled that the UK and Ireland were not allowed to take part in the adoption of a measure building upon the Schengen *acquis* without having first opted into the related policy area, thus curtailing their cherry-picking prerogatives.

[37] Case C-44/14 *Spain v Parliament and Council* [2015] ECLI:EU:C:2015:554.

acknowledges that the patterns of differentiation, and the varying levels on which they play out, have an impact on the 'status' of Member States and their rights under EU and international law. The judgment is all about whether the UK and Ireland can be placed in a situation 'equivalent' to that of the Schengen Member States, or to that of a third country. Ultimately, the Court observes that 'the implementation of enhanced cooperation inevitably leads to a certain fragmentation of the rules applicable to the Member States in the area concerned',[38] but that limited forms of cooperation with the UK and Ireland can also be allowed in areas of the Schengen *acquis* to which the two countries are not part, provided they are of limited nature, and serve the objectives of the *acquis*: 'The fact that Ireland or the United Kingdom is, with respect to the common framework established by the Eurosur Regulation, in a situation differing from that of the other Member States which could be compared to some extent to that of a third country cannot therefore be regarded as relevant.'[39] The ECJ, in this judgment, adopts a shifting notion of the status of the UK and Ireland that is located between full membership and that of a third country. Although they can be considered as third countries, the UK and Ireland are effectively equated to full members of the Schengen area. Interestingly, EU membership only figures in the background of this distinction.

The 2005 Prüm Agreement has followed a similar trajectory to Schengen. It initially took the form of a closer cooperation between seven EU Member States outside of the EU legal framework. Its main objective was to combat terrorism, cross-border crime, and illegal immigration, by setting up information exchange mechanisms for DNA, fingerprint, and vehicle registration data. As Member States quickly realized that cooperation in this field was useful and necessary, the agreement was turned into EU secondary legislation just a couple of years later, by means of Council Decisions 2008/615/JHA and 2008/616/JHA ('Prüm Decisions').[40] Since its incorporation into EU law, participation in Prüm appears to be more uniform than in Schengen, as the Decisions bind all Member States, except Ireland, which has an opt-out. In addition, Norway and Iceland concluded an association agreement in 2009, whereas Switzerland and Liechtenstein joined the scheme more recently, in 2019.[41]

These shifting patterns of participation are the result of the way Schengen and Prüm were agreed as international law instruments and then integrated into the EU Treaty framework. In this sense, they are exceptional in the EU integration process. They show that such an integration pathway is not without consequences, and that it affects the way we conceive of participation and membership. These regimes function on, and are construed on, the boundaries between internal

[38] ibid para 55.
[39] ibid para 56.
[40] Weyembergh (n 26) 617.
[41] Agreements with Iceland, Switzerland, and Liechtenstein are yet to be ratified: https://eucrim.eu/news/Prüm-cooperation-agreements-switzerland-and-liechtenstein/, accessed 30 June 2023.

participation and external association, unveiling a new flexible approach to the EU membership's status. It is thus constitutive to the very idea of EU membership that it is sometimes scattered and adaptable to varying combinations of participating patterns.

IV. Europol: Third-country Member States in Differentiated EU Agency

After several years of intergovernmental cooperation under the Europol Drugs Unit (EDU), the Europol Convention was ratified in 1998, and became operational in 1999.[42] Europol's main role is to support Member States in preventing and combating serious international crimes and terrorism. Europol's mandate has expanded incrementally over time, while becoming solidly anchored into the EU legal system. The Europol Convention was replaced by a 2009 Council Decision (Europol Decision), providing for financing from the EU budget, and turning Europol into a full EU agency.[43] After the Lisbon Treaty, the 2016 Europol Regulation was adopted, making Europol the epicentre of police information exchange.[44] By the same token, the agency was further embedded into the EU institutional framework through, for instance, increased oversight by the European Parliament and national parliaments.[45]

Europol has been defined 'a hub for differentiated integration'.[46] All EU Member States but Denmark are members of the agency. In addition, Europol has partnership agreements with twenty-two non-EU countries, including the Schengen states Switzerland and Norway, key strategic partners such as the US and Canada, and neighbouring countries such as those in the Western Balkans.[47] Europol's governance model builds upon this vast network of participating countries. Its added value rests precisely with the far-reaching geographical ramification, which allows it to steer resources and information across countries and continents, thus improving the coordination of the fight against cross-border crime.

[42] Council Act of 26 July 1995 drawing up the Convention based on Article K.3 of the Treaty on European Union, on the establishment of a European Police Office (Europol Convention) [1995] OJ C316.

[43] Council Decision of 6 April 2009 establishing the European Police Office (Europol), [2009] OJ L 121..

[44] Regulation (EU) 2016/794 of the European Parliament and of the Council of 11 May 2016 on the European Union Agency for Law Enforcement Cooperation (Europol) [2016] OJ L 135.

[45] For instance, the Joint Parliamentary Scrutiny Group (JPSG) established by the 2016 Europol Regulation (n 47), which associates the European Parliament and the national parliaments in the oversight of Europol's activities.

[46] Camino Mortera-Martínez, Zoran Nechev, and Ivan Damjanovski, 'Europol and Differentiated Integration' (2021) Policy Paper 13 EUIDEA 3.

[47] ibid.

This multilayered participation scheme sets a clear distinction between the rights and obligations of actual Europol members, who can be EU Member States only—and those of the associated countries. Only EU Member States sit in the agency's management board and participate fully in both decision-making and implementation;[48] only they have direct access to Europol databases. In spite of this clear-cut distinction between EU members and third countries, EU membership is not homogenous and appears, again, as rather fragmented. The case of Denmark is paradigmatic, unprecedented, and unexpected. In a 2015 referendum, the Danes voted to opt out of the new Europol Regulation with the result that Denmark was no longer a member of Europol as from 1 May 2017. To ensure future cooperation between Denmark and Europol, the Council played 'fast and loose', simply adding Denmark to the list of 'third states' with which Europol may conclude agreements. This happened in February 2017, right before the entry into force of the new Europol Regulation, which required partnerships between Europol and non-EU countries to be negotiated by the European Commission and approved by both the Council and the European Parliament. The Agreement on Operational and Strategic Cooperation between Denmark and Europol entered into force in April 2017. As a result, Denmark exited from Europol as a full member and rejoined it as an associated third party immediately thereafter. Article 8 of the Agreement allows a representative to be invited on to the Europol Management Board as an observer but does not grant them the right to vote. Denmark's position is particularly awkward as it was, seemingly, a major contributor to the Europol database. Although the Commission considered it 'vital to provide for cooperation between Europol and Denmark on key matters',[49] the Agreement was negotiated against the background of Brexit, and the Commission was very careful not to cross any red lines that could set a precedent for the talks with the UK.[50] The Agreement thus explicitly recognizes the jurisdiction of the ECJ in any decision of the European Data Protection Supervisor, as well as on the validity or interpretation of the Agreement. It is, furthermore, conditioned on an obligation for Denmark to remain bound by the Schengen *acquis*. Following the Agreement, Denmark has lost the possibility to search directly in Europol databases. It can, however, assign up to eight Danish-speaking staff to Europol to handle Danish requests, and to input and retrieve data from Danish authorities in the Europol processing systems.[51] While this is not quite the same thing as the full membership it previously had, it is, nonetheless, a frayed approximation that presumably serves its purpose.

[48] The new Europol Regulation (n 45) states that the management board is to be composed of 'one representative from each Member State and one representative of the Commission'. Each representative has a voting right. The management board can invite non-voting observers to its meetings.

[49] As declared in a LIBE Committee meeting in January 2017. As reported by Curtin, 'Brexit and the EU Area of Freedom, Security, and Justice. Bespoke Bits and Pieces' (n 22) 190.

[50] Mortera-Martínez, Nechev, and Damjanovski (n 47).

[51] Curtin, 'Brexit and the EU Area of Freedom, Security, and Justice. Bespoke Bits and Pieces' (n 22) 189ff.

Arguably, the Danish Agreement could have provided a blueprint for future Europol's cooperation with the UK, whose position is complicated by the fact of no longer being an EU member, and of never having been part of Schengen. The UK had been a member of Europol since its creation in 1998. Europol was among the thirty-five measures that it rejoined following its block opt-out. The UK was probably one of the most active supporters of Europol, and provided a leadership role. In 2018, it was the largest contributor to the agency.[52] For almost ten years, from 2009 to 2018, Europol's director was a British national, Rob Wainwright, and 'the agency has borrowed heavily from British law enforcement and police practices'.[53] After the Brexit referendum, the UK considered its future relationship with Europol as 'a critical priority',[54] yet the country did not succeed in negotiating a close partnership with Europol, although this would, arguably, have been in the interest of both the UK and Europol. The UK did, apparently, make what were described by other Member States as 'impossible demands' over access to the Europol database during the negotiations with the EU.[55] In effect, the UK wished to 'approximate the position of a Member State as closely as possible', in terms of access to Europol's central intelligence database (as well as other EU databases, such as SIS II and PNR). As one German negotiator put it, 'this would not only be cherry-picking on speed but [would] set a fatal precedent'.[56] The negotiations were not helped by a classified report by the Commission, unveiled by the press and picked up on by members of the LIBE European parliamentary Committee, which found that the UK was making improper use of the database by copying classified personal information and sharing it with US companies.[57] In any event, the terms eventually negotiated identified procedural means for intergovernmental cooperation, stopping well short of membership for the UK, but allowing its participation despite its non-retention of the Schengen *acquis*.[58]

The EU–UK Trade and Cooperation Agreement (TCA) of December 2020 governs the relationship between the UK and Europol. Title V of Part 3 of the TCA sets out the main cooperative relations between Europol and the UK. It mainly lays down conditions for the exchange of information and personal data, and provides

[52] Emmanuel Comte, 'Brexit, the "Area of Freedom, Security, and Justice" and Migration' (2020) Policy Brief 3 EUIDEA 4.

[53] Mortera-Martínez, Nechev, and Damjanovski (n 47) 12.

[54] Curtin, 'Brexit and the EU Area of Freedom, Security, and Justice. Bespoke Bits and Pieces' (n 22) 186.

[55] Philip Oltermann and Daniel Boffey, 'UK Making "Impossible Demands" over Europol Database in EU Talks' *The Guardian* (London, 23 April 2020) <http://www.theguardian.com/world/2020/apr/23/uk-making-impossible-demands-over-europol-database-in-eu-talks> accessed 11 July 2023.

[56] ibid.

[57] Shkurta Januzi, 'LIBE Committee MEPs Demand UK Sever All Ties to SIS Due to Abuse' (*SchengenVisaInfo.com*, 16 January 2020) <https://www.schengenvisainfo.com/news/libe-committee-meps-demand-uk-sever-all-ties-to-sis-due-to-abuse/> accessed 11 July 2023; Nikolaj Nielsen, 'UK Unlawfully Copying Data from EU Police System' (*EUobserver*, 28 May 2018) <https://euobserver.com/justice/141919> accessed 11 July 2023.

[58] Garner (n 8).

for the creation of a national contact point in the UK, as well as for British liaison officials seconded to Europol to facilitate exchange of information. The TCA is rather vague as regards the possibility of further extending cooperation in the future. It allows for the conclusion of working and administrative arrangements to complement the provisions of the TCA, while always emphasizing the fact that the UK will not be treated as an EU Member State. Arguably, the TCA provisions between the UK and Europol add a further type of 'cooperation agreement' to the already variegated panoply of agreements with Europol, and it is certainly an agreement that will have to be defined and refined through practice:

> In the interest of mutual operational benefits, the Parties shall endeavour to cooperate in the future with a view to ensuring that data exchanges between Europol and the competent authorities of the United Kingdom can take place as quickly as possible, and to consider the incorporation of any new processes and technical developments which might assist with that objective, while taking account of the fact that the United Kingdom is not a Member State.[59]

Overall, our analysis shows that Europol's membership is multifaceted and can take a variety of forms. Several layers of participation overlap and relationships between these different layers can vary quickly. The very concepts of outsiderness and insiderness appear to be relative. EU members with opt-out regimes are more involved than full members. In this regard, insiders happen to be led by alleged outsiders. However, those outsider leaders can suddenly become non-members. Some, such as Denmark, have withdrawn from Europol only; others, such as the UK, have left the EU for good. This leaves Ireland as the only EU Member State who has an opt-out from the AFSJ but is a full member of Europol. What further blurs the relations between insiders and outsiders is the fact that Europol's EU (or former EU) opt-out members are often more involved, more willing, and better placed to contribute to the agency's work than the 'normal' members. This is a paradoxical feature of differentiation in the AFSJ, whereby countries who opted out of the AFSJ are, ironically, those who are keenest, it seems, on driving cooperation forward in some specific sectors, including police cooperation.

Europol's legal rules and political practice project an ambiguous idea of EU membership. On the one hand, EU membership, especially following Brexit, is upheld as a special, and in some ways privileged, status within Europol, giving access to full institutional decision-making and resources. However, in practice, such a stringent distinction sounds artificial, as the membership landscape seems to be constantly moving, resulting in different combinations and new arrangements.

[59] Trade and Cooperation Agreement between the European Union and the European Atomic Energy Community, of the one part, and the United Kingdom of Great Britain and Northern Ireland, of the other part [2020] OJ L444. Title V Cooperation with Europol.

Opt-out members can become active opt-in members, but can also very quickly turn into third parties, such has been the case with the UK and Denmark since 2019. The ties that bind are loosened and tightened with varying degrees of intensity over time, and depending on the (former) Member State involved.

V. Internal Differentiation through Enhanced Cooperation: The Case of EPPO

The European Public Prosecutor's Office (EPPO) is the first piece of EU legislation in the field of criminal law to have been adopted via enhanced cooperation, or more precisely, following the simplified procedure for enhanced cooperation foreseen by the Treaties in some areas of AFSJ. Article 86 TFEU provides for the establishment of a European Public Prosecutor within Eurojust, to investigate, prosecute, and bring to judgment crimes against the EU budget. As the establishment of EPPO must be agreed unanimously by the Council, Article 86 also sets out that, in the event of disagreement, at least nine Member States can proceed with enhanced cooperation by simply notifying the European Parliament, the Council, and the Commission, without the need of any further authorization. . Such accelerated enhanced cooperation procedure allows for an easier and more effective recourse to differentiated legislation under the specific conditions established by Art. 86 TfEU; it namely only applies to the creation of EPPO[60]

The European Commission issued its proposal for an EPPO Regulation in 2013.[61] However, the proposal was met with scepticism, and was subject to a yellow card procedure from several national parliaments on the ground of subsidiarity concerns. The Commission decided to go forward with the proposal and to maintain it in its original form, but it soon became evident that disagreement was deeply entrenched, and that unanimity would not be achieved. Hence, sixteen Member States notified the EU institutions that they intended to trigger enhanced cooperation. The EPPO Council Regulation was finally adopted on 12 October 2017.[62] So far, twenty-two Member States have joined this closer cooperation. In addition to Denmark and Ireland, who have an opt-out from the AFSJ, Hungary, Poland, and Sweden have also decided not to join the EPPO for the time being. As enhanced cooperation is always open to non-participating Member States, they may decide to join at any time in the future. The EPPO website declares that 'working arrangements with these five non-participating Member States are being

[60] For more information on the procedure, see Patrin (n 25).

[61] For more background information, see Gerard Conway, 'The Future of a European Public Prosecutor in the Area of Freedom, Security and Justice' in Fletcher, Herlin-Karnell, and Matera (eds) (n 20).

[62] Council Regulation (EU) 2017/1939 of 12 October 2017 implementing enhanced cooperation on the establishment of the European Public Prosecutor's Office ('the EPPO') [2017] OJ L283.

established to define how the EPPO will cooperate with them'.[63] Yet, the relation between participating and non-participating states may prove problematic in the case of a new office, which was, furthermore, highly controversial from the start. For instance, there is a difference between those Member States who do not participate on the grounds of their opt-outs (Ireland and Denmark) and the others who did not join the enhanced cooperation. Furthermore, there are several overlaps between the roles of Eurojust and the EPPO, and it may not always be easy to distinguish the level of participation and involvement of the different countries. Finally, Article 86 TFEU provides for the possibility of extending the mandate of the EPPO to cover serious crimes with a cross-border dimension. Such a decision, however, must be taken by the European Council by unanimity, thus also involving the non-participating Member States.[64]

In sum, EPPO is an interesting test case for the use of enhanced cooperation in the AFSJ, and provides some insights on an instrument that keeps differentiation solidly within the Union law framework. Cooperation is anchored to EU membership. However, here again, micro-patterns of participation emerge that could potentially create idiosyncrasies in the way participating and non-participating members relate to each other. These micro-membership issues emerge in the way the several 'types' of memberships overlap. It is interesting, for instance, that Denmark is listed on the EPPO website as the only real opt-out country, whereas Ireland is included within the groups of countries that 'may join any time' because of its opt-in prerogatives.[65]

VI. Asylum Law: Muddled Differentiation despite Zero Tolerance Normatively

The abolishment of border controls, under the Schengen regime, created spillover effects in other policy areas, and notably in the field of asylum. Member States were no longer able to autonomously control migration movements at their borders, as third-country nationals could move freely across the Schengen area. In the absence of coordination, asylum seekers could thus target the countries with the most favourable asylum standards (asylum shopping) or log several applications in different Member States. EU coordination in the field was thus necessary as a 'functionalist' consequence of the free movement of persons.[66]

[63] EPPO website: https://www.eppo.europa.eu/members accessed 11 July 2023.

[64] Weyembergh (n 26) 621–23.

[65] The website states that, 'with the exception of Denmark, it is possible for more Member States to join the enhanced cooperation for the EPPO later': EPPO website https://www.eppo.europa.eu/en/legal-framework last accessed 1 July 2023.

[66] Leuffen, Rittberger, and Schimmelfennig, *Differentiated Integration: Explaining Variation* (n 1) 235.

The Dublin Convention, signed in 1990 and ratified in 1997, followed a similar trajectory to most AFSJ provisions. It was first adopted within an intergovernmental regime, and subsequently integrated in the Community pillar of the Amsterdam Treaty. The Dublin II (2003) and Dublin III (2013) Regulations have thus replaced the Dublin Convention under EU law.[67] These Regulations set out a common framework to decide which Member State is responsible for treating asylum applications, as asylum seekers can file their applications in only one country (in the absence of other criteria, such as family connections, this is the country of first entry). In parallel, provisions on reception conditions and procedures were adopted, to harmonize protection standards and safeguard the rights of asylum seekers.[68]

As with most AFSJ policies, the Dublin system combines internal and external differentiation. Denmark and Ireland (like the UK, before Brexit) enjoy an opt-out regime but have found ways to be associated to EU asylum policies. The opt-in regime allows for Ireland's participation in the Dublin III Regulation but not in most of the accompanying legislation. Denmark has negotiated a parallel agreement to take part in the Dublin system. Moreover, the EFTA countries, which are also Schengen members, have signed association agreements and apply most Dublin Regulations' provisions.

The asylum opt-in regime has been heavily criticized for the 'cherry-picking' approach. Indeed, the opt-out/opt-in scheme allowed Ireland and the UK to participate in the Dublin regime, but not in the legislation providing for minimum protection standards. In practice, they could return asylum seekers to their country of first entrance, but were not bound by the rights-enhancing provisions and the oversight of the ECJ.[69] Brexit has not washed away internal differentiation. Ireland is still implementing selective participation, as the UK departure did not alter its opt-in legal regime. Moreover, from a differentiated integration perspective, the status of Denmark is again particularly problematic. Through its parallel agreement, Denmark takes part in the Dublin system under international law, thus reinforcing the anomaly of an EU member who joins EU cooperation as a third country. As noted by Adler-Nissen, Commission officials are aware of the oddity of such a practice: 'Parallel agreements are extremely artificial: the EC [European Communities] has to do an external agreement with one of its members. This

[67] Regulation (EU) No 604/2013 of the European Parliament and of the Council of 26 June 2013 establishing the criteria and mechanisms for determining the Member State responsible for examining an application for international protection lodged in one of the Member States by a third-country national or a stateless person [2013] OJ L 180.

[68] Current legislation includes the Qualification Directive (2011/95/EU); the Reception Conditions Directive (2013/33/EU); and the Asylum Procedures Directive (2013/32/EU): Nadine El-Enany, 'The Perils of Differentiated Integration in the Field of Asylum' in Bruno de Witte, Andrea Ott, and Ellen Vos (eds), *Between Flexibility and Disintegration: The Trajectory of Differentiation in EU Law* (Edward Elgar 2017) 371–75.

[69] El-Enany (n 69) 367.

cannot stand as a precedent for any future arrangement with any member state', an official was reported to say.[70] The practice is also questionable from a normative point of view, as it has seemingly allowed Denmark to lower the protection standards for asylum seekers while participating in the Dublin scheme.[71] If it is true that the Danish status is equivalent to that of the EFTA countries, the difference is that Denmark is an EU Member State and, despite its opt-out from the AFSJ, shares some common values and standards with the other Member States. EU membership shall play an important role in defining the boundaries of differentiated regimes in policy areas that affect core EU values and fundamental rights.[72]

This is the reason why it has been argued that the field of asylum should be entirely free from differentiation: 'as a field of law which directly affects the rights of individuals in a context in which their physical survival and psychological wellbeing is at risk, the field of asylum law is unlike other competences of the EU where there is scope for differentiated integration'.[73] Indeed, unlike most security-driven cooperation, differentiation in asylum-related policies raises major issues. As these policies are essentially based on the principle of burden-sharing, it is questionable how a structurally differentiated scheme that would go beyond just a few notable opt-outs could provide a viable solution. Schimmelfennig observes that 'differentiated integration in redistributive policies tends to be self-defeating', and that it 'undermines the purpose of integration aimed at the social sharing of risks, burdens and wealth'.[74] Such a scheme was recently advocated by Comte. He proposed centralizing asylum management at the supranational level through an integrated asylum procedure that would take the form of an enhanced cooperation.[75] As appealing as such a proposal is, its feasibility is questionable. A differentiated and centralized EU asylum scheme is likely to be welcomed by the Member States that are most affected by the migration flows, but would hardly find consensus among the others. Indeed, it is often the case that front-line countries advocate for relocation schemes, which are fiercely opposed by Member States that are not on the migration routes (such as the Central and Eastern European Member States).[76] The 2024 new Pact on Migration and Asylum, which is in the process of being adopted at the time of writing, amends several legislative files, including on common asylum

[70] Adler-Nissen (n 11) 141.

[71] Emmanuel Comte, 'The European Asylum System: A Necessary Case of Differentiation' (2020) Policy Paper 3 EUIDEA 11; For recent developments, see Marina Adami, 'Danish Refugee Law Draws Criticism from UN, EU' (*POLITICO*, 4 June 2021) <https://www.politico.eu/article/denmark-refugee-law-asylum-migration-un-eu-international-protection/> accessed 5 July 2021.

[72] Elena Bertolini and Mark Dawson, 'Fundamental Rights as Constraints to and Triggers for Differentiated Integration' (2021) 27 Swiss Political Science Review 637.

[73] El-Enany (n 69) 362–63.

[74] Frank Schimmelfennig, 'The Conference on the Future of Europe and EU Reform: Limits of Differentiated Integration' (2020) 5 European Papers—A Journal on Law and Integration 989, 997.

[75] Comte, 'The European Asylum System' (n 72).

[76] Schimmelfennig (n 75) 997.

procedures, asylum application and migration and asylum management.[77] The new framework, which does not substantially overhaul the Dublin system, provides for a comprehensive and integrated approach to asylum, with no recourse to differentiated regimes. The focus is very much on external borders' control, efficiency of the procedures and cooperation with third-countries. . No mandatory reallocation quotas are foreseen, but the new legislation introduces a so-called solidarity mechanism giving the possibility to Member States to choose between different "participation options": such as relocations, financial contributions, operational support, request deductions, and 'responsibility offsets'. Thus, some sort of differentiation in the form of discretion left to the Member States is internalized and integrated within the legal framework for asylum. Obviouly, such an optional participation falls short of replacing a binding system of burden-sharing, that would not have been endorsed by all Member States and would have probably led to actual differentiation patterns. Arguably, a unitary but less effective solution was preferred to a more incisive but differentiated one.

Ultimately, internal and external differentiation within asylum law reproposes some of the patterns that we have found in other areas of AFSJ. There is no clear distinction between EU members and non-EU members. Denmark, an EU member, acts as a third party; Switzerland, a Schengen country, participates on a more solid basis than Ireland. Internally, Member States are ideologically and politically so divided on the matter that some degree of differentiation happens anyway in practice, and is now possibly being integrated in a future EU asylum policy. However, as we have argued, in the field of asylum this fluid concept of membership is even more problematic than in other policies, as it engages critical concerns about political and human rights. Political elections are won or lost on migration issues. Moreover, asylum raises redistributive issues that can hardly be only tackled through differentiation. By the same token, we are currently witnessing the most severe breaches of human rights precisely in this field. The Union is falling short of guaranteeing adequate protection standards to asylum seekers across its territory and in rescue operations at sea, and this is essentially due to the low level of intrastate solidarity displayed by Member States. The inability to coordinate and the pushback of many countries as regards the reception of asylum-seekers result in poor reception conditions, overload of first-entry countries, and a general failure to ensure effective rescue operations. Frontex, the EU agency which coordinates actions of surveillance and control of the EU external borders, has been repeatedly criticized for not ensuring adequate protection of migrants' rights.[78] One key issue

[77] For an overview of the different legislative files under discussion in the framework of the New Pact on Migration and Asylum, see the Commission's website at https://home-affairs.ec.europa.eu/policies/migration-and-asylum/pact-migration-and-asylum_en#understanding-the-pact-on-migration-and-asylum, last accessed May 2024

[78] In 2012 an own-initiative inquiry of the European Ombudsman pointed to several shortcomings as regards fundamental rights obligations: Special Report of the European Ombudsman in own-initiative inquiry OI/5/2012/BEH-MHZ concerning Frontex. As a reaction, Regulation 2016/1624

in this regard is the fact that, in principle, Member States remain responsible for the surveillance of their external borders. However, surveillance and rescue operations also involve third countries, so that responsibilities are not clearly demarcated, leading to legal-protection shortcomings.

An EU common migration policy that works and is accepted by most, if not all, Member States could help to define EU membership as founded upon solidarity and the respect of fundamental rights. Conversely, continuous disagreement among EU Member States on asylum mattersrisk tearing apart that same notion of EU membership.

VII. Brexit: A Partially Participating Third Country

Paradoxically, the consequences of the UK's withdrawal from the EU are significant precisely in the policy area from which the UK opted out from the very beginning. As we have argued in this chapter, the AFSJ was, for the UK, simultaneously a source of attraction and rejection. The country was unwilling to commit to any EU supranational integration and formally maintained—and even reinforced—its opt-outs from AFSJ. On a practical level, however, the UK contributed greatly to the development of EU cooperation in AFSJ. As acknowledged by the House of Lords, the UK operated as 'a leading protagonist in driving and shaping the nature and direction of cooperation on police and security matters under the auspices of the European Union'.[79] The leadership role of the UK has, undoubtedly, been very instrumental in helping design the foundations of AFSJ, as well as constructing some very important pillars (eg on data retention and recent EU rules on Passenger Name Record (PNR)). Also, the UK contributed substantially in financial terms in many policy areas it opted into (see, for instance, Europol).[80]

The UK clearly faces the future in a different position to its past one. Given the previous highlevel of involvement in some AFSJ policies, withdrawal from the EU may prove very costly, as it has a direct impact on the level of national security.

reforming Frontex and establishing a European Border and Coast Guard (EBCG) introduced a complaint mechanism for potential victims of fundamental rights violations during operations coordinated by Frontex. Nonetheless, the situation remains critical. In 2021, a migrant boat sank on 24 April 2021 in Libyan waters, with over 100 people feared dead. According to many, there were shortcomings in the rescue operations also involving Frontex, and the tragedy could have possibly been avoided: Lorenzo Tondo, 'More than 100 Asylum Seekers Feared Dead after Shipwreck off Libya' *The Guardian* (London, 22 April 2021) <http://www.theguardian.com/world/2021/apr/23/more-than-100-asylum-seekers-feared-dead-after-shipwreck-off-libya> accessed 5 July 2021.

[79] House of Lords, European Union Committee, 'Brexit: Future UK–EU Security and Police Cooperation', 7th Report of Session 2016–17 (HL 2016–17, 77), para 27.

[80] Helena Carrapico, Antonia Niehuss, and Chloé Berthélémy, 'The Consequences of Brexit for the UK and for the Area of Freedom, Security and Justice' in Helena Carrapico, Antonia Niehuss, and Chloé Berthélémy (eds), *Brexit and Internal Security: Political and Legal Concerns on the Future UK–EU Relationship* (Springer International Publishing 2019).

Indeed, one of the UK's biggest concerns during the Brexit negotiations was how to secure further cooperation in some of these areas after withdrawal. The reason is not only the security and well-being of the citizens and residents of the UK, but also the considerable sunk costs incurred by the UK in setting up the existing arrangements (eg on implementing the Prüm decisions), as well as the likely costs of replicating capabilities outside the EU (eg on a Europol-type agency or database). However, post-Brexit EU–UK cooperation has inevitably splintered into 'bits and pieces', even if not all ties are broken. As we have noted already, cooperation between Europol and the UK is, as of now, suboptimal, and the UK's putatively 'impossible demands' were rejected. The 'new old' intergovernmentalism in this area[81] allows for information exchange but makes it contingent upon several conditions and the mediation of liaison offices. As regards data protection, the Commission adopted, in June 2021, two adequacy decisions for transfers of personal data to the UK, under the General Data Protection Regulation (GDPR) and the Law Enforcement Directive (LED).[82] The two decisions recognize that the UK offers levels of protection to personal data essentially equivalent to those guaranteed under EU law. However, there are a number of conditions attached to these positive decisions. First, their time horizon is limited: the decisions are set to automatically expire in June 2025, but they can be extended. Second, Article 3 of the decisions establishes that the Commission will regularly monitor whether the UK continues to ensure an adequate level of protection, and if this is not the case it may suspend, repeal, or amend the decisions. This is an important step for the UK, given the manner in which its own personal data protection for law enforcement purposes preceded, and provided a model for, that of the EU itself.[83] However, it also shows how the UK has passed from a leading role to living under special surveillance.[84]

Brexit is certainly a critical development for the AFSJ. In substantial terms, the UK departure leaves a void that will be hard to fill, and that has potential repercussions for the internal security of both the UK and the EU. Because the contribution of the UK was so important, diminished information exchange and cooperation will, arguably, be detrimental for both sides. In conceptual terms, the UK leaving is equally problematic for the internal cohesion of AFSJ. Different to other policy fields, where the UK simply moves from membership to non-membership, we

[81] Garner (n 8).

[82] European Commission's Implementing Decision of 28 June 2021 pursuant to Regulation (EU) 2016/679 of the European Parliament and of the Council on the adequate protection of personal data by the United Kingdom, C(2021) 4800 final; European Commission's Implementing Decision of 28 June 2021 pursuant to Directive (EU) 2016/680 of the European Parliament and of the Council on the adequate protection of personal data by the United Kingdom, C(2021) 4801 final.

[83] Curtin, 'Brexit and the EU Area of Freedom, Security, and Justice. Bespoke Bits and Pieces' (n 22) 198ff.

[84] Hendrik Mildebrath, 'EU-UK Private-sector Data Flows after Brexit: Settling on Adequacy' (European Parliamentary Research Service 2021) PE 690.536.

have shown that, in the AFSJ, participation and membership are not neatly boxed black and white concepts, but rather they are frayed considerably at the edges. Thus, instead of simply becoming an outsider, the UK is moving along the AFSJ membership spectrum, from the position of a member with opt-outs and opt-ins, to the position of a third country with selected participation options. This, arguably, further adds to the complex range of variable geometries in the AFSJ rather than simplifying it. Also, it is unlikely to contribute positively to the integration potentials of remaining members, given the already high level of internal and external differentiation.[85]

In addition, the UK moves from being an engaged insider to a disempowered outsider. It will almost inevitably, in the future, be forced to 'mimic' rules and regulations without any democratic participation in their content, nor in ongoing and at times fundamental debates on core issues before the ECJ. At the same time, the incredibly attractive potential of cooperation in AFSJ as well as the converging interests of both the UK and the EU to maintain closer ties in this field will likely result in new geometries and participation patterns. Thus, the UK's perambulations from an engaged insider to a disempowered outsider seem to be culminating, for now, in a novel status as a partially participating outsider.

VIII. Conclusion

This chapter has analyzed the AFSJ through the lens of differentiation. It has argued that AFSJ displays a variety of differentiation patterns both in terms of participation geometries and instruments. As the EU has moved into areas that were previously exclusive to the nation state, such as criminal law and border control, a preference by some for 'outsiderness' over full membership has progressively come to the fore, resulting in the emergence of a host of opt-out regimes. At the same time, the transnational nature of migration and security issues has attracted non-EU members (and even EU opt-out members), resulting in extensive external differentiation. There is virtually no policy area in AFSJ which is free from some sort of differentiation. We have argued that this high level of differentiation has created overlapping layers of participation, obscuring the difference between insiders and outsiders. Analyzing the British and Danish opt-outs about fifteen years ago, Rebecca Adler-Nissen found that British and Danish representatives mostly behaved as normal members in the areas in which they participated, transforming themselves from outsiders into insiders. The pragmatic and consensus-oriented norms of the Council's work enabled inclusion instead of exclusion.[86] Yet, with

[85] An exception may be EPPO, whose regime of enhanced cooperation may profit from the UK's departure, as argued by Carrapico, Niehuss, and Berthélémy (n 82) 30.
[86] Adler-Nissen (n 11) 146.

Brexit the situation has changed. The UK is no longer an insider, nor can it be one, and even Denmark has acquired a highly awkward status within Europol as a partially participating insider. Shifting patterns from outsiders to insiders, and from insiders to outsiders, create idiosyncrasies in the concept of EU membership, and define more fragmented and porous boundaries between the internal and external dimensions. Yet, 'the cooperation on AFSJ cannot be easily divided institutionally into the "ins" and the "outs"', as Adler Nissen observed all those years ago.[87]

Although cooperation always centres around EU membership, below the surface the relations between countries seem to fall into many different compositions. Membership becomes flexible and adaptable to fit several scenarios. A well-known example of this phenomenon is the 'special status' granted to the UK (pre-Brexit) and Ireland. Their opt-out regime with pick-and-choose options has been widely criticized because it creates 'different kinds' of Member States.[88] More substantially, varying participation designs micro-membership patterns that affect how EU members relate to each other and to third countries. Under this spotlight, EU membership loses its unitary character and is revealed as a more nuanced and flexible concept. The rough edges of membership in AFSJ allow EU Member States to experiment with new types of relationships and arrangements, integrating a high degree of differentiation. To a certain extent, a flexible approach to membership has the advantage that it can adapt to different integration (and disintegration) paths and modalities. It reveals that there is, formally and informally, no need to create new types of membership. The AFSJ framework can and does incorporate and reshape relations between insiders and outsiders, between opt-out and opt-in countries, and between EU and associated members. As changes in the area have happened, and are happening, rapidly, such flexibility can prove valuable.

The downside is that such a fragmented membership framework raises substantial challenges for transparency and accountability. The fact that it is complicated to distinguish between insiders and outsiders leads to a complex and confusing legal framework with many discrepancies with the actual practice. At the same time, opt-out stigmatization may strengthen the self-perception of the out-members as being different, thus paving the way to further distancing, as happened with the UK.[89] Such convoluted legal arrangements, combined with shifting membership patterns, are also very difficult to hold to account, as accountability fora vary with the specific arrangements. A differentiated regime such as Schengen combines many accountability mechanisms at different levels, involving the European Parliament, and national parliaments of EU Member States as well as those of the associated non-EU countries. For instance, what would be the most suitable accountability

[87] ibid 124.
[88] Weyembergh (n 26) 622.
[89] Daniel Thym, 'Legal Solution vs. Discursive Othering: The (Dis)Integrative Effects of Supranational Differentiation' (2018) Working Paper N. 7, DCU Brexit Institute.

forum for Denmark, an EU Member State who participates in some AFSJ areas as a third country? Ultimately, there is a mismatch between membership and participation that risks making accountability mechanisms very difficult to implement. Overall, membership overlaps blur the lines between supranational and intergovernmental, between in- and out-members, and between EU and international law. The clarity of the institutional framework is affected, and so is the democratic accountability line between the Union's institutions and its citizens.[90]

In sum, AFSJ can function as a laboratory for testing more broadly what EU membership actually means: '*Le caractère presque paroxystique de la coexistence des situations d'opt-out et d'opt-in au sein de l'ELSJ qui sont susceptibles d'être particulièrement éclairantes pour tenter de cerner à quoi renvoie, aujourd'hui, le statut d'Etat membre de l'Union*'.[91] In a context in which participation patterns between EU and non-EU members largely converge, the question is what identifies the substance of EU membership as such? The Brexit negotiations put the matter back on the agenda, as it became clear that the UK lost many of its privileges when it renounced its membership status. After all, despite all the flexibility, EU membership marks the pivot upon which participation patterns can vary. Whereas third countries can be associated under different regimes, only EU membership gives the right to full participation both at the institutional and at the implementation level. Only EU Member States have full control of the decision-making. Finally, EU Member States are usually granted the privilege to experiment with institutional and legal creativity, when full participation is not wished for nor possible (eg the several opt-out regimes). As the UK's withdrawal shows, such privilege is only the prerogative of EU members, and should arguably, in our view, remain so if EU membership is to be meaningful and translate into concrete benefits.

As a final remark, however, we note that a flexible concept of membership fits well within the AFSJ, which is characterized by policies of shared competence in core state powers. It is unlikely to be easily transposable to other policy areas. There is a constitutive danger in playing too much with EU membership. If the boundaries become too permeable, EU membership risks being watered down to a mere aggregate of divergent elements. This is also the reason why a notion of membership allowing for a high degree of differentiation is problematic in areas such as asylum, where fundamental rights are at stake. Admittedly, there is a fine balance between the need for flexibility to adjust to evolving relationships and the imperative of safeguarding the essence of EU membership. Up to a certain point, a flexible approach to membership protects the resilience of the EU itself, allowing for adaptation, especially in sensitive policy areas and in turbulent

[90] Curtin, 'From a Europe of Bits and Pieces to a Union of Variegated Differentiation' (n 4).

[91] Marie Gautier, 'Le Statut d'Etat Membre: L'Etat Membre de l'Union Dans l'ELSJ' in Laurence Potvin-Solis (ed), *Le statut d'Etat membre de l'Union européenne: quatorzièmes journées Jean Monnet* (Bruylant 2018) 419.

times. Yet, the experience of Brexit proves that, if pushed too far, the system may implode, emptying membership of any value and resulting in disaggregation and disintegration.

Annex: Internal and external differentiation in the AFSJ

Internal and external differentiation	Schengen	Europol	EPPO	Dublin Asylum
EU—non participating	(UK), Ireland, Romania, Bulgaria, Cyprus	Denmark	Hungary, Poland and Sweden, Denmark, Ireland, (UK)	
EU—Participating in some areas or associated	Denmark			Ireland, Denmark
Other countries participating	Norway, Iceland, Switzerland, Liechtenstein	Operational Agreements:Norway, Iceland, Switzerland, Liechtenstein, Albania, Bosnia and Herzegovina, North Macedonia, Montenegro, Monaco, Serbia, Colombia, Georgia, Moldova, Ukraine, US, Canada, AustraliaStrategic Agreements:Brazil, China, Russia, Turkey, United Arab Emirates		Norway, Iceland, Switzerland, Liechtenstein

6

Of Bits and Pieces of EU Law in Territories: The Many Shades of European Integration

Stéphanie Laulhé Shaelou and Katerina Kalaitzaki

I. Introduction

The very first provision of the Treaty on the European Union (TEU) clearly states that the contracting parties to the Treaty establish among themselves a Union, 'on which the Member States confer competences to attain objectives they have in common'.[1] To the extent that the attainment of 'objectives Member States have in common' may have been diverse or differentiated throughout the evolution of the European project, as developed in the present edited volume, this chapter intends to provide a renewed analysis of key manifestations of differentiated integration in today's European Union (EU) by reference to Member State territories (the sum of their various parts or areas falling under their jurisdiction) and their possible impact on the re(definition) of EU membership. It is argued that, notwithstanding initial delimitations in the EU Treaties, the concept of EU membership and the principle of adherence to the EU *acquis* have taken on renewed dimensions during the last decades of the 'ever-closer Union'.[2] Throughout the existence of the EU, Member States may have been allowed to expressly opt out from specific areas or policies in initial phases of the European project's construction, while in its more recent stages, newer Member States may be 'exempted' from EU provisions and/or principles at the core of EU law, as a matter of 'necessity', benefiting from temporary transitional regimes and/or more permanent derogations, exemptions, or limitations.[3] At the same time, specific territories, internal or external to the Union, exceptionally remain *de facto* and/or *de jure* integrated in various EU policies. These multiple shades of European integration are probably most perceivable among some of the territories of Member States and parts of the UK territory

[1] Art 1, 1st limb, Treaty on European Union (Consolidated version 2016) OJ C 202, 7.6.2016.
[2] ibid, Art 1, 2nd limb.
[3] Andrea Ott and Kirstyn Inglis, *Handbook of European Enlargement* (TMC Asser Press 2002). Stephanie Laulhé Shaelou, *The EU and Cyprus: Principles and Strategies of Full Integration (vol 3, Studies in EU External Relations)* (Brill/Martinus Nijhoff Publishers 2010). See also Adam Łazowski, in this volume.

Stéphanie Laulhé Shaelou and Katerina Kalaitzaki, *Of Bits and Pieces of EU Law in Territories* In: *Redefining EU Membership*. Edited by: Diane Fromage, Oxford University Press.
DOI: 10.1093/9780191948145.003.0006

particularly, and through their complex relations with EU law. At the same time, the withdrawal clause from the Union has now been acted upon in the context of Brexit, redesigning the landscape for the UK territory, its relationship with the EU, and with Member States, in a set of complex neighbouring relations.

The existing multi-shaded integration of Member States' territories is a testimony that EU membership may involve greater complexity for some Member States than others, while new challenges may arise in the context of the re(definition) of EU membership, possible withdrawals, or future enlargements, potentially further blurring the lines of European integration in multiple directions. This chapter will provide a comparative analysis of specific parts and/or territories of Member States currently subject to renewed interest in their (non-)integration processes, from exceptional/permanent derogations to temporary regimes and vice versa. In Europe, these territories include Greenland and, on the Island of Cyprus, the areas beyond the effective control of the government of the Republic of Cyprus (RoC), as well as the Sovereign Base Areas (SBAs), in addition to parts of the UK territory currently subject to further variations in European integration, namely Northern Ireland (NI) and Gibraltar.[4] In order to shed some light on the whereabouts of these territories in the path of European integration currently unfolding, the chapter will discuss their complex relationship with EU law, identifying common grounds and differences, as well as the implications on these relationships post-Brexit.

The analysis will begin with the evolution of differentiated integration in territories of the Member States that have always had special status under EU law, attributed to the existence of several factors, including their special status within a Member State and/or the occupation of part of their territory by a third state. These special statuses may have created opportunities for differentiated integration towards an ever-closer Union, such as in the cases of the SBAs and Gibraltar (Section II.A), while at other times creating threats to the European integration project, such as in the case of the occupied areas in the RoC not effectively controlled by the government (Section II.B). The analysis will then proceed to assess the legal status of these territories in the post-Brexit period, emphasizing implications on their relationship with EU law. EU membership has, arguably, never been unitary, and Brexit has only exacerbated this phenomenon, constituting the latest case of membership re(definition) substantially affecting European integration, beyond the UK's borders. The assessment will, firstly, focus on the implications for British Overseas Territories, including the SBAs and Gibraltar (Section III.A), and subsequently on the differentiated integration within parts of the UK territory, namely the Protocol on Northern Ireland (Section III.2). Arrangements had to be found for the UK and the EU Member States involved to preserve the effectiveness of EU

[4] For a comprehensive and thorough analysis of EU Member State territories and their status in EU law, see Dimitry Kochenov (ed), *EU Law of the Overseas: Outermost Regions, Associated Overseas Countries and Territories, Territories Sui Generis* (Kluwer Law International 2011).

law in specific parts of UK territory located within/next to EU Member States, to allow their inhabitants to fully enjoy the rights attached to their EU membership. The territories to be assessed in both of the following sections of this chapter constitute specific examples of differentiated integration within Member States, and an illustration of the multi-shaded European integration, contributing to the (re) definition of the concept of EU membership today, which is more nuanced than ever before.

II. The Evolution of Differentiated Integration within the EU Member State Territories: Towards a Multi-shade of European Integration?

The territory of the Member States is to be determined, first, by reference to national constitutional law considerations.[5] As no Treaty amendment is necessary to reflect changes to a Member State's borders, it would be open to a Member State 'to change the territorial scope of the Treaties unilaterally'.[6] There are examples of variations in the territory, population, or internal structure of specific Member States which have been addressed without a Member State's exit from the EU, and without the need to amend the Treaties. Greenland's departure from the then European Economic Community (EEC) did not affect Denmark's membership, although the territorial scope of application of the Treaties changed as a result. Despite being an autonomous territory since 1979, Greenland remains part of Denmark, and has yet to gain independence.[7] The 2014 Council Decision on the relations between the EU on the one hand, and Greenland and the Kingdom of Denmark on the other,[8] promotes 'partnership' aiming to 'preserve the close and lasting links between the partners while supporting the sustainable development of Greenland'.[9] This arguably points in the direction of the 'redefinition' of a Member State's territory, and to differentiated European integration in a sustainable environment, even if Greenland's departure from the EEC could initially have been perceived as threatening the European integration project.

[5] Case C-148/77 *Hansen v Hauptzollamt Flensburg* [1978] ECR 1787, where the Court ruled with respect to the territorial extent of an EU Member State, as set out in the then Art 227 EEC (now Arts 52 TEU and 355 Treaty on the Functioning of the European Union (Consolidated version 2016) OJ C 202, 7.6.2016), that 'the status of the French overseas departments within the Community is primarily defined by reference to the French constitution' [10]; Phoebus Athanassiou and Stephanie Laulhé Shaelou, 'EU Accession from Within? An Introduction' (2014) 33(1) Yearbook of European Law 335.

[6] James Crawford and Alan Boyle, 'Annex A—Opinion: Referendum on the Independence of Scotland—International Law Aspects' in 'Scotland Analysis: Devolution and the Implications of Scottish Independence' (11 February 2013), available at https://www.gov.uk/government/uploads/system/uploads/attachment_data/file/79408/Annex_A.pdfaccessed 1 July 2023.

[7] Phoebus Athanassiou and Stephanie Laulhé Shaelou (n 5) 342.

[8] OJ [2014] L76/1 15.03.2014.

[9] ibid Art 1(2), 1st limb.

The negotiated departure of Greenland in a pre-Article-50-TEU world would appear to confirm that unilateral withdrawal from the EU was, at least originally, neither intended nor implied under the EU Treaties.[10] The 'very fact' that Greenland remained a part of Denmark made it 'necessary that its withdrawal from the EC be a negotiated one',[11] meaning that Denmark could have unilaterally denounced Greenland's participation in the Communities if no consent had been reached for its departure,[12] potentially threatening the European construction project at the time. Following the introduction of 'home rule' in 1979, and the holding of a referendum on membership of the Communities by the Greenlandic government in 1982, the Danish government 'acted upon' the request by the Greenlandic government and requested the Council 'to amend the Treaties in order to allow for the withdrawal of Greenland and its transfer to the status of OCT [Overseas Country or Territory]'.[13] The Danish government entered into negotiations (on behalf of Greenland) with the other Member States, to decide on Greenland's withdrawal, and on its transformation into an Overseas Country or Territory Associated with the Union (OCT). These negotiations gave rise to an amending Treaty on Greenland requiring unanimity,[14] which took effect with Greenland's withdrawal from the EEC on 1 February 1985.[15]

Whether intentional or not, it appears that the Member States' exercise of their territorial sovereignty translates into dynamic forces within the European integration process, creating opportunities and threats that shape the evolution of differentiated European integration.

A. Dynamic forces of European integration in EU Member State territories: opportunities for differentiated integration

Whereas, under international law, each Treaty normally determines its scope of application, the EU Treaties apply to all areas under the sovereignty or within the jurisdiction of the Member States. Post-Lisbon, Article 52(1) TEU sets out a list of Member States, while Article 52(2) TEU refers to Article 355 of the Treaty on the Functioning of the European Union (TFEU) for details on the territorial scope of

[10] Fredrik Harhoff, 'Greenland's Withdrawal from the EC' (1983) 20 Common Market Law Review 13, 28–31.

[11] Matthew Happold, 'Independence: In or Out of Europe? An Independent Scotland and the EU' (2000) 49 International and Comparative Law Quarterly 15, 32; S Blockmans, 'Between the Devil and the Deep Blue Sea? Conflicts in External Action Pursued by OCTs and the EU' in Kochenov, *EU Law of the Overseas* (n 4).

[12] Phoebus Athanassiou and StephanieLaulhé Shaelou (n 5) 342.

[13] EC Bull, Supplement 1/83, 6 (request to the Council) and COM(83) 66 final (Commission's opinion).

[14] Treaty amending, with regard to Greenland, the Treaties establishing the European Communities [1985] OJ L29/1.

[15] Phoebus Athanassiou and Stephanie Laulhé Shaelou (n 5) fn 22.

the Treaties. For its part, Article 355 TFEU is concerned with some specific territories of the Member States (which it partially specifically defines and includes by reference to Annex II as well). EU Treaties are applicable, in theory, to all the territories of the Member States, including overseas or dependent territories, as well as the airspace and maritime waters falling under the sovereignty or within the jurisdiction of the Member States, unless expressly provided otherwise in the Treaties.[16] This includes the European territories for whose external relations a Member State is responsible, as per Article 355(3) TFEU. In the pre-Brexit world, this last category boiled down, in practice, merely to Gibraltar.[17]

The territorial scope of the EU Treaties is, therefore, 'flexible' to the extent that it covers legal relationships located 'within' the EU territory, 'by reason of the place where they are entered into or of the place where they take effect or by reason of a sufficiently close link with the law of a Member State and thus the relevant rules of [EU] law'.[18] For (justifiable) constitutional, historical, economic, political, or other reasons, there may be an intention not to include a specific territory of a Member State in the territorial scope of the Treaties.[19] This could lead to the formal exclusion of a specific territory from the territorial scope of applicability of the EU Treaties, and hence the creation of a principle of territorial exclusion for a specific territory.[20] In this respect, there are numerous examples of territories falling within or beyond the scope *ratione loci* and/or *ratione materiae* of the Treaties and/or benefiting from a specific status with respect to the territorial scope of applicability of the Treaties, including in Europe.[21] To the extent that such regimes are embedded within the fabric of EU law through a process of positive or negative integration, they participate in the European construction project, and this creates opportunities for differentiated integration.

The EU Treaties set out the EU law regime applicable to the Outermost Regions (ORs) and the OCTs, including those away from metropolitan Europe.[22] Article 355(2) TFEU excludes the application of EU law in the territories having special relations with the UK not included in Annex II to the TFEU.[23] Article 355(4) and (5) TFEU deals more specifically with the derogations, exceptions, and exclusions

[16] Stephanie Laulhé Shaelou, 'The Principle of Territorial Exclusion in the EU: SBAs in Cyprus: A Special Case of Sui Generis Territories in the EU' in Dimitry Kochenov, *EU Law of the Overseas* (n 4) 154.

[17] Art 28 and Annex I(I) of the 1972 Act of Accession of Denmark, Ireland and the UK [1972] OJ L73; Declaration No 55 on Gibraltar OJ C 202, 7.6.2016, 356–56, appended by Spain and the UK to the TFEU.

[18] Koen Lenaerts and Piet Van Nuffel, *Constitutional Law of the EU* (2nd edn, Thomson/Sweet & Maxwell 2005) 352–53.

[19] eg Dimitry Kochenov, 'The EU and the Overseas: Outermost Regions, Overseas Countries and Territories Associated with the Union, and Territories Sui Generis' in Dimitry Kochenov, *EU Law of the Overseas* (n 4).

[20] Stephanie Laulhé Shaelou, 'The Principle of Territorial Exclusion' (n 16) 154.

[21] ibid.

[22] Arts 349 and 355 TFEU as well as Annex II TFEU, to which Part 4 TFEU applies.

[23] Art 355(2) TFEU, 2nd limb.

to the territorial applicability of the Treaties. Within this context, several types of *sui generis* territories appear to be excluded, or to derogate from the territorial and/or substantive scope of the Treaties. They are commonly referred to as '*sui generis*' territories to the extent that they do not fit within the usual pattern of the associated and dependent territories.[24] While ORs and OCTs are subject to different legal regimes in the EU, it has been argued that both categories of territory are, in their own way, variations of the principle of 'inclusion' of the whole territory of the Member States into the territorial scope of applicability of the Treaties.[25] These variations occur through different mechanisms: ORs are subject to a (differentiated) exercise of integration into the EU, while OCTs are initially subject to a logic of association which appears to gradually tend towards integration.[26] This seems to be confirmed by the 'passerelle clause' under Article 355(6) TFEU, which enables a switch of status.[27] *Sui generis* territories, on the other hand, have been found to be manifestations of the principle of territorial 'exclusion' from the EU, and to be subject to provisions of *lex specialis* that prima facie exclude them, partially or totally, from the territorial scope of applicability of the Treaties.[28] Of most relevance to this chapter are the (current or former) part(s) or territory/territories of (current or former) Member States located in Europe and affected directly or indirectly by Brexit.

In the pre-Brexit era, the special territories located at the periphery of the EU (of which they may not be part), enjoying a special link with one or more Member States (being the territory of one Member State next to or within another), and being addressed either directly or indirectly in Article 355(2), (3), and (5) TFEU and/or in Protocols, included Gibraltar[29] and the SBAs in Cyprus,[30] both part of the UK territory.[31] From the UK's accession to the EU in 1972 until the Agreement on the Withdrawal of the United Kingdom of Great Britain and Northern Ireland from the European Union and the European Atomic Energy Community of 2019 (Withdrawal Agreement),[32] the application of the EU Treaties was excluded either partly or wholly in these territories on the basis of the Treaties of Accession

[24] Jacques Ziller, 'ORs, OCTs and others after the Entry into Force of the Lisbon Treaty' in Dimitry Kochenov, *EU Law of the Overseas* (n 4).

[25] Stephanie Laulhé Shaelou, 'The Principle of Territorial Exclusion' (n 16) 155.

[26] ibid.

[27] There is, however, no reference to the possibility for Spanish or British territories to benefit from the passerelle clause, which concerns only current OCTs and Ors; Dimitry Kochenov, 'The EU and the Overseas' (n 19) 62.

[28] Stephanie Laulhé Shaelou, 'The Principle of Territorial Exclusion' (n 16) 156.

[29] Art 355(3) TFEU; Art 28 and Annex I(I) 1972 Act of Accession of Denmark, Ireland and the UK [1972] OJ L73; Declaration No 55 appended to TFEU.

[30] Art 355(5)(b) TFEU.

[31] The Channel Islands and the Isle of Man are also covered in Art 355(6)(c) TFEU.

[32] Agreement on the withdrawal of the United Kingdom of Great Britain and Northern Ireland from the European Union and the European Atomic Energy Community OJ [2019] C 384/1, 12.11.2019 ('Withdrawal Agreement').

of the RoC and the Kingdom of Spain.[33] Under the Withdrawal Agreement, the 'UK or its territory' is understood as referring to the UK, Gibraltar, the Channel Islands and the Isle of Man, the SBAs in Cyprus, and the overseas countries and territories listed in Annex II to the TFEU, to the extent that all these territories were previously subject to EU law.[34] In the interim forty-eight years between UK accession and withdrawal, however, the dynamic applicability of the EU Treaties meant there was scope for the territorial, material, and/or personal application of EU law in these territories, whether EU law was initially applicable or not. In their own way, Gibraltar and the SBAs in Cyprus are, arguably, a living and historical illustration of the growing influence of EU law both within and outside the EU's borders. They illustrate all at once the acceptance of a new Member State into the EU, the adjustment to the status of a Member State's territory, the inclusion of a new territory into the EU's scope (material and personal), and/or the continuity of the territorial realm of EU law following UK withdrawal from the Union.

Starting out as the non-EU territory of a Member State (the UK) in a third country (Cyprus) falling completely outside the scope of applicability of the Treaties, the SBAs evolved post-Cyprus' EU accession, and pre-Brexit, to a non-EU territory of a Member State located within another Member State, and partially subject to EU law. In a nutshell, the island of Cyprus (still) finds itself at the crossroads between enlargement and integration.[35] Its European integration remains

[33] Documents concerning the accession to the European Communities of the Kingdom of Denmark, Ireland, the Kingdom of Norway, the United Kingdom of Great Britain and Northern Ireland, Protocol No 3 on the Channel Islands and the Isle of Man [1972] OJ L73/164 (only to the extent necessary to ensure the implementation of the special arrangements for these territories as set out in the Accession Treaty, ie in Protocol No 3; see Art 355(5)(c) TFEU, which does not refer expressly to the Protocol); Act concerning the conditions of accession of the Czech Republic, the Republic of Estonia, the Republic of Cyprus, the Republic of Latvia, the Republic of Lithuania, the Republic of Hungary, the Republic of Malta, the Republic of Poland, the Republic of Slovenia and the Slovak Republic and the adjustments to the Treaties on which the EU is founded—Protocol No 3 on the sovereign base areas of the United Kingdom of Great Britain and Northern Ireland in Cyprus [2003] OJ L 236/940 (Art355(5)(b) TFEU). Art 299(6)(b) EC had been amended by the 2003 Treaty of Accession. Prior to Cyprus' accession to the EU, a Declaration had been appended to the 1972 Act of Accession.

[34] Art 3, Withdrawal Agreement (n 32).

[35] For several reasons, the island has been 'carved up' into various portions. On 16 August 1960, the RoC was established within 97 per cent of the territory of what had previously been the Crown Colony of Cyprus. On the same day, the UK continued to assert sovereignty over two parts of the Crown Colony of Cyprus. These parts were, respectively, renamed the Akrotiri SBA (known under EU Law as the Western SBA) and the Dhekelia SBA (known under EU Law as the Eastern SBA), jointly known as the SBAs. On 16 August 1960, the RoC also acquired sovereignty over four small enclaves of territory within the Dhekelia SBA. On the same day, the UK continued to exercise effective control, but not sovereignty, over numerous retained sites in the territory of the RoC. On 16 August 1974, following the second of the two Turkish invasions of the RoC during the summer of 1974, the armed forces of Turkey declared a ceasefire, having occupied 36 per cent of the territory and 57 per cent of the coastline of the RoC. The declaration of a ceasefire resulted in the formation of the United Nations Buffer Zone along 'the Green Line'. Since 16 August 1974, Turkey has occupied the areas to the north of the Buffer Zone, as well as the small enclave at Kokkina on the north-west coast of the RoC. Since 16 August 1974, the government of the RoC has exercised control over the areas of the Republic to the south of the Buffer Zone. Since 15 November 1983, the occupied area has been *de facto* administered by the so-called 'Turkish Republic of Northern Cyprus', an illegal subordinate administration of Turkey. Credit goes to Dr Klearchos Kyriakides for this brief description of Cyprus, as part of a handout by Prof

incomplete to the extent that parts of the island are excluded from the effective scope of EU law. Firstly, EU law applies in a selective manner to the territory of the SBAs under Protocol No 3 to the 2003 Treaty of Accession, in the context of international law. As previously mentioned, Cyprus is subject to Article 355(5)(b) TFEU with respect to the SBAs and the selective application of EU law there. The main justification for this ad hoc regime framing the British presence on the island under EU law is deemed to be the 'exceptional status' of the SBAs, characterized by their primary non-economic and military use.[36] Suffice to say here that the SBAs are the parts of the Crown Colony of Cyprus, which remained under British sovereignty and jurisdiction on the creation of an independent RoC in 1960.[37] Unlike Overseas Territories, they fall under the responsibility of the UK Ministry of Defence, due to their military nature, rather than the Foreign Office. Although the purposes of the SBAs are, allegedly, solely military, and their boundaries were drawn in 1960 to include the major military installations and exclude villages and towns, as a result of the events in 1974 and other developments over the years, a significant number of Cypriot nationals, in addition to military and UK-based civilian personnel and their dependents, work or live in the SBAs.[38] Although the RoC and the SBAs are two distinct legal entities, each with their own set of laws and institutions,[39] they cooperate closely, use the euro currency, and are not separated by hard borders.[40] The Treaty of Establishment expressly gives to the residents of the Republic freedom of access to and from the SBAs,[41] while preventing and prohibiting the establishment of custom posts or other frontier barriers between them.[42] Accordingly, Protocol No 3 of the 2003 Treaty of Accession provides that the EU Treaties shall not apply to the SBAs, except to the extent necessary to ensure

Stephanie Laulhé Shaelou, Dr Klearchos Kyriakides, and Dr Nasia Hadjigeorgiou, written in the context of President Koen Lenaerts's visit to UCLan Cyprus, located in the bicommunal village of Pyla, on 16 April 2019.

[36] Final Act, Joint Declaration on the sovereign Base Areas of the United Kingdom of Great Britain and Northern Ireland in Cyprus [1972] OJ L73/194.

[37] CA (Civil Division) *R (on the application of Tag Eldin Ramadan Bashir and others) v Secretary of State for the Home Department and Sovereign Base Area Authority* [2017] EWCA Civ 397, [57].

[38] For up-to-date numbers, visit https://www.sbaadministration.org/index.php accessed 1 July 2023 (scroll down). The 'Declaration by Her Majesty's Government regarding the Administration of the Sovereign Base Area mentioned in Article 1 of the Treaty concerning the Establishment of the Republic of Cyprus which remain under the Sovereignty of the United Kingdom', annexed to the British Parliamentary Command Paper within which the Treaty of Establishment and other key texts were originally presented to the British Parliament in July 1960, can be found at https://www.sbaadministration.org/images/agla/Declarations_by_Her_Majesty.pdf accessed 1 July 2023.

[39] The SBAs' Constitution is embodied in the Sovereign Base Areas of Akrotiri and Dhekelia Order in Council 1960, SI 1960/1369 https://www.sbaadministration.org/images/agla/SBAA_Akrotiri_and_Dhekelia_Order_in_Council_1960.pdf accessed 1 July 2023.

[40] Nasia Hadjigeorgiou and Nikos Skoutaris, 'The Status of the Sovereign Base Areas in Cyprus following Brexit' (2019) PRIO Occasional Paper Series 3 https://cyprus.prio.org/Publications/Publication/?x=4272 accessed 1 July 2023.

[41] Treaty concerning the Establishment of the Republic of Cyprus, Appendix O, s 3(1).

[42] ibid ss 2(iii) and 3(7).

the implementation of the agreements set out in the Protocol.[43] The SBAs are included in the Customs Union (CU) territory,[44] which in turn has implications on their borders.[45] Based on close cooperation, Protocol 3 provides for the UK's responsibility in the application of the Union *acquis* in the fields of customs, indirect taxation, and Common Commercial Policy (CCP), despite the fact that the SBAs are considered part of the territory of the RoC for the purpose of obtaining privileged treatment under EU law.[46] After Cyprus' accession to the EU, the SBAs were added to the Principality of Monaco and the Isle of Man as 'territories having their own customs arrangements with Member States of the EU, but nevertheless benefiting from preferential treatments for the exchange of goods as set out in Part Two of the Annex'.[47] As such, the initial objective of 'granting the same treatment to Cypriots living and working on the SBAs as those living and working in the RoC' has entailed obligations under EU law, including at the State level, upholding the principle of sincere cooperation and rights and duties under the Protocol.[48] In the absence of a comprehensive framework for human rights protection in the SBAs under the European Convention on Human Rights,[49] and possibly under the EU Charter, it is argued that individual rights are maintained and further enhanced within the framework of European integration that provides the dynamic forces to the upholding of fundamental rights in the realm of EU law.[50]

The exercise of dynamic forces of European integration can also be observed in Gibraltar, arguably at a more fundamental level in this territory, whose sovereignty is disputed between the UK, Spain, and Gibraltar.[51] Gibraltar, the small but strategically significant outcrop guarding the entrance from the Atlantic to the Mediterranean Sea,[52] is one of the British Overseas Territories acquired by cession. It joined the then EEC together with the UK in 1973, and until at least Brexit, has been subject to derogations to the application of EU law in primary

[43] Art 1, Protocol 3.
[44] ibid Art 2.
[45] ibid Art 5.
[46] ibid Art 7.
[47] Stephanie Laulhé Shaelou, *The EU and Cyprus* (n 3) 155.
[48] For a more detailed appraisal of the application of EU law in the SBAs, see Stephanie Laulhé Shaelou, 'The Principle of Territorial Exclusion' (n 16).
[49] The British government extended the application of the ECHR to the SBAs in May 2004, but not Protocol 1 to the ECHR, meaning that the rights to property, education, and free elections are not available to the inhabitants of the SBAs: Report by the Committee on Legal Affairs and Human Rights, Rapporteur: Mr Andreas Gross, 'Situation of the Inhabitants of the Sovereign Base Areas of Akrotiri and Dhekelia', Doc.11232, PACE, 4 April 2007, 6 http://www.assembly.coe.int/nw/xml/XRef/X2H-Xref-ViewHTML.asp?FileID=11651 accessed 1 July 2023.
[50] On the implementation of human rights instruments, see Stephanie Laulhé Shaelou, 'The Principle of Territorial Exclusion' (n 16) 170–75.
[51] Artur Khachaturyan, 'Applying the Principle of Good Neighbourliness in EU Law: The Case of Gibraltar' in Dimitry Kochenov and Elena Basheska (eds), *Good Neighbourliness in the European Legal Context* (Brill/Nijhoff 2015).
[52] David Baldock, Allan Buckwell, Alejandro Colsa-Perez, Andrew Farmer, Martin Nesbit, and Mia Pantzar, *The Potential Policy and Environmental Consequences for the UK of a Departure from the European Union* (Institute for European Environmental Policy 2016).

and secondary law.[53] As a result, Gibraltar is excluded from the scope of EU policies such as the Common Agricultural Policy, fisheries, turnover taxes, CCP, and the free movement of goods.[54] Spain's accession to the EEC, in 1985, and its approach to Gibraltar in the context of EU membership, did not appear to change its existing derogation status much.[55] As a territory for whose external relations the UK is responsible, British legislation does not apply there, like it does in the SBAs. However, whereas the SBAs are governed by an administration, Gibraltar has a fully autonomous parliament and government, responsible, inter alia, for the transposition of EU law. Initially, Gibraltarians had been excluded from the scope of the European Parliamentary elections,[56] in accordance with the special status granted to Gibraltar under the 1972 Act of Accession regarding rights attached to nationality.[57] This was rectified in the UK,[58] following a landmark ruling from the European Court of Human Rights[59] in which the Court held that the interpretation of EC law by a national court denying the right of representation to Gibraltarians could amount to a denial of the applicant's right to vote as guaranteed by Article 3 Protocol 1 ECHR, and that the applicant was being completely denied any opportunity to express her opinion in electing members of the European Parliament.[60] The new UK Act was subsequently challenged unsuccessfully by Spain before the Court of Justice of the EU (ECJ) on the basis of EU law.[61] This case should be read in conjunction with the case of *Eman et Sevinger*[62] regarding the right of Dutch residents in the OCT of Aruba to vote in European elections. The Court ruled that EU nationals residing in an OCT are subject to a special regime under

[53] Art 28, Act of Accession of 1972, and Appendix I of the Treaty of Accession of Denmark, Ireland and the United Kingdom (1972) OJ L 73, 27.3.1972.

[54] ArturKhachaturyan (n 51) 320.

[55] Joined Cases T-211/04 and T-215/04 *Government of Gibraltar and UK v Commission* [2008] ECR II-3745, [73]–[74], where in respect of the tax regime in Gibraltar, Spain noted that, even if the case of Gibraltar should be distinguished from the autonomous territories of the Basque Country and Navarre, Gibraltar could not acquire an independent tax system of its own, 'since that would imply that . . . Gibraltar would be treated as another Member State, an outcome which the Kingdom of Spain sees as substantially changing the international status of that territory'.

[56] Act concerning the Election of the Representatives of the European Parliament by direct universal suffrage, annexed to Council Decision 76/787/ECSC, EEC, Euratom of 20 September 1976 [1976] OJ L278/1, as amended by Council Decision 2002/772/EC, Euratom of 25 June 2002 and 23 September 2002 [2002] OJ L283/1.

[57] Declaration annexed to the Final Act, 1972 Treaty of Accession on the term 'nationals', as replaced in 1982 following the entry into force in the UK of new legislation on nationality, to the effect that nationals in the UK are: (i) British citizens; (ii) persons who are British subjects by virtue of Part IV of the British Nationality Act 1981 and who have the right of abode in the UK and are therefore exempt from UK immigration control; and (iii) British Dependent Territories citizens who acquire their citizenship from a connection with Gibraltar [1983] OJ C 23/1, 28.01.1983.

[58] European Parliament (Representation) Act 2003, introducing a right for Commonwealth citizens resident in Gibraltar who are not Community nationals to vote and stand as candidates in elections to the European Parliament.

[59] *Matthews v UK* (1999) 28 EHRR 361.

[60] ibid, paras 32 and 64.

[61] Case C-145/04 *Spain v UK* [2006] ECR I-7917.

[62] Case C-300/04 *Eman et Sevinger* [2007] 1 CMLR 4.

Part IV EC Treaty, which means that general provisions of the Treaty are not applicable to them unless specified otherwise, and that, therefore, Articles 189 and 190 EC on the governing of the European Parliament (which Spain argued the UK was in breach of by allowing non-citizens to vote) were not applicable. As a result, Member States could delimit the right to vote, and to participate in European Parliament elections, in accordance with the territory on which nationals of the said Member State resided, provided such territorial restrictions were objectively justifiable.[63]

The upholding of fundamental human rights in EU Member State territories provides fertile ground for the deployment of dynamic forces of 'uniting' European integration, even in the context of threats to the evolution of differentiated European integration.

B. Dynamic forces of European integration in the EU Member State territories: threats to differentiated integration

One threat to European (differentiated) integration relates to the areas of the territory of the RoC not under the effective control of its government, due to the ongoing Turkish invasion and occupation of the island ('the Areas'). As a result of this *de facto* partition, the Union *acquis* is suspended in these Areas, until the Council, acting unanimously, decides on the withdrawal of the suspension.[64] This leads to a situation, unprecedented in the EU, of a Member State not exercising effective control over the whole of its territory.[65] As a result, it is necessary to determine the terms under which EU law applies to the Green Line, including in its 'boundary' with the Eastern SBAs.[66] Across the Green Line, measures taken with a view to promoting the economic development in the Areas fall beyond the scope of Protocol 10, meaning that a special regime is put in place to address the situation there too.[67] Finally, in the event of a settlement of the Cyprus problem, the Council, acting unanimously, would decide on adjustments to the terms of Cyprus' accession to the EU with regard to the Turkish Cypriot community.[68] Protocol 10 sets out an exception to the principles of application of EU law, to the extent that it suspends the application of the EU *acquis* in the uncontrolled part of the Republic of

[63] See Stephanie Laulhé Shaelou, *The EU and Cyprus* (n 3) 202–04, for an analysis of the case law.

[64] Art 1, Protocol 10 to the 2003 Treaty of Accession OJ L 236, 23/09/2003, 0955–0955

[65] For a detailed appraisal of the applicable regime, see Stephanie Laulhé Shaelou, *The EU and Cyprus* (n 3).

[66] Art 2, Protocol 10 to the 2003 Treaty of Accession; In the northern part of the island, where the Government of the Republic of Cyprus does not exercise effective control, EU legislation is suspended in line with Protocol 10 to the 2003 Act of Accession. Since 1974 the ceasefire line (referred to as the "Green Line") has de facto separated the two parts of the island. The Green Line is not an external border of the EU.

[67] ibid Art 3.

[68] ibid Art 4.

Cyprus, until further notice. It is underlined by a powerful supranational decision-making mechanism transferring power from the RoC to the Council to deal with the present and future scope of EU law in the Areas, provided that the Council decides to exercise this power.[69] Any revision of primary law necessary to accommodate any measures taken should, in principle, fall under the special competence of the Council, at the initiative of the Commission, giving them a large 'power of appraisal' and potentially rendering any review by the CJEU 'marginal'.[70] Over time, however, this particular application of the EU decision-making process has given rise to legal rows between the Council, the Commission, and the European Parliament, over proposed instruments of EU law addressing the differentiated application of EU law in the Republic of Cyprus.[71] In the meantime, Protocol 10 still constitutes the main legal instrument of the differentiated integration of Cyprus, as far as its *de facto* partition is concerned, giving a key role to the Republic to play in the determination and maintenance of its own jurisdiction and its own fate within the EU.

Following Protocol 10, the Areas were declared outside the CU, the fiscal territory, and the Area of Freedom, Security and Justice of the Union, while the Green Line could not, and cannot, constitute an external border of the EU. Article 1(1) Protocol 10 provides for the suspension of the Union *acquis*, including the internal market and related policies, and Article 1(2) constitutes the *lex specialis* legal basis for the application of the *acquis* upon an eventual 'withdrawal of the suspension'.[72] Until a settlement is reached, however, Articles 2 and 3 of Protocol 10 provide a legal basis for the regime of the Green Line and the Areas beyond it. More specifically, Article 2 allows for the adoption of secondary legislation to partly replace the suspended rules of the internal market in the Areas. The Green Line Regulation was adopted on this basis,[73] with the aim of facilitating the free movement of persons and goods over the Green Line while allowing the entry of Turkish Cypriot goods into the CU and the internal market. In order to ensure the effectiveness of these rules, their application was extended to the boundary between the Areas and the Eastern SBAs.[74] The Green Line Regulation also governs the crossing of persons, including of third-country nationals (TCNs), with the aim of combating illegal immigration.[75] For the crossing of goods (excluding live animals and animal products, regularly updated), the RoC agreed that goods certified by the Turkish

[69] Stephanie Laulhé Shaelou, 'Market Freedoms, EU Fundamental Rights and Public Order: Views from Cyprus' (2011) 30(1) Yearbook of European Law 298.

[70] ibid 323.

[71] For a detailed account of the 2004–10 period with respect to the notions of direct and indirect trade involving Cyprus, see Stephanie Laulhé Shaelou, *The EU and Cyprus* (n 3) 81–84.

[72] Stephanie Laulhé Shaelou, *The EU and Cyprus* (n 3) 230–31.

[73] Council Regulation (EC) No 866/2004 of 29 April 2004 on a regime under Article 2 of Protocol 10 to the Act of Accession ('Green Line Regulation').

[74] ibid Recital 3.

[75] Stephanie Laulhé Shaelou, *The EU and Cyprus* (n 3) 186–88.

Cypriot Chamber of Commerce, and originating in the Areas, can cross the Green Line freely.[76] The goods are subject to applicable EU safety and phytosanitary requirements, and as long as these goods are to be consumed in the Republic, no import taxes are due. Once the goods enter the Republic, they are considered as Union goods, and are thus subject to value added taxes.[77]

Despite posing threats to European integration, due to its non-conventional application of EU law in some aspects, it could be argued that the Green Line Regulation regime has provided a viable and working framework for the development of intra-island trade relations, and has brought the two communities closer.[78] Its functioning has, however, been subject to questioning,[79] particularly with respect to its effectiveness to enable goods originating in the Areas to penetrate the EU market.[80] Throughout the years, the European Commission has emphasized the need to adopt a regulation that would allow direct trade relations between the Areas and the rest of the Member States, which is firmly opposed by the RoC for reasons of non-recognition of any political entity associated with the Areas.[81] As set out in the Commission's annual reports, in the meantime, functional problems remain.[82] Despite calls for renewed adoption of legal instruments of EU secondary legislation, Protocol 10 has remained, to date, the main legal basis for the particular or differentiated integration of the RoC in the EU, allowing the Republic to shield itself from full liability under the 2003 Treaty of Accession, as it cannot guarantee the implementation and enforcement of EU rules in the territory beyond its control,[83] and allowing it to keep control of its own fate within the EU.[84] On the one hand, the suspension of the Union *acquis* entails more than a mere 'exclusion of liability clause', since it sets out the principles underlying the EU's policy towards the Turkish Cypriot community; on the other hand, however, even if Protocol 10 has been in force since Cyprus' accession to the EU, the suspension

[76] Commission Decision of 7 July 2004 [2004] OJ L272, on authorization of the Turkish Cypriot Chamber of Commerce according to Art 4(5) of Council Regulation (EC) No 866/2004.

[77] Art 4, Green Line Regulation (n 73).

[78] For a full appraisal, see Laulhé Shaelou, *The EU and Cyprus* (n 3).

[79] UK Parliament, Select Committee on European Scrutiny Thirty-Fourth Report on Commission Communication: Annual Report on the implementation of Council Regulation (EC) No.866/2004 and the situation resulting from its application (2008) https://publications.parliament.uk/pa/cm200708/cmselect/cmeuleg/16-xxx/01610.htm

[80] Nikos Skoutaris, 'The Status of Northern Cyprus under EU law' in Kochenov, *EU Law of the Overseas* (n 4) 414.

[81] For a review of the legal and political background and dimensions of direct trade between the Areas and Member States other than Cyprus, see Stephanie Laulhé Shaelou, *The EU and Cyprus* (n 3) 313–20.

[82] See the ninth (SWD (2013) 299 final), tenth (SWD(2017) 261 final), eleventh (SWD(2015) 108 final), and twelfth (SWD(2016) 281 final) annual reports on the implementation of the Council Regulation EC No 866/2004.

[83] Stephanie Laulhé Shaelou, 'Views from Cyprus' (n 69) 327.

[84] For a review of current European legal affairs around Cyprus, see Stephanie Laulhé Shaelou, 'On the 'Edge' of Good Neighbourliness in EU Law: Lessons from Cyprus' in Dimitry Kochenov & Elena Basheska (eds), *Good Neighbourliness* (n 51).

of the application of EU law in that part of the Republic is deemed temporary in nature, preparing the ground for the full application of the Union *acquis* in the Republic upon reunification.

In the meantime, Protocol 10 has also been one of the legal bases for adopting measures towards the economic development of the Turkish Cypriot community, such as the Financial Aid Regulation,[85] whose aim is to facilitate the reunification of Cyprus by encouraging the economic development of the Turkish Cypriot community. If and until such a settlement is reached, Protocol 10 cannot be interpreted as erecting barriers to the individual exercise of fundamental rights by all Cypriot citizens, as the suspension of EU law is territorial in nature, and does not extend to the exercise of individual rights beyond the specific sealed territory.[86] In particular, the rights of Cypriot nationals including the members of the Turkish Cypriot community to move within the Republic of Cyprus and to other Member States, and their rights as EU citizens, cannot be restricted.[87]

Even though dynamic forces of European integration can lead to opportunities and threats within the EU Member State territories, it remains the case that, fifteen years after Cyprus' accession to the EU, the integration of the whole island of Cyprus still constitutes an ongoing challenge for the whole of the EU and the Mediterranean region in a renewed political and legal context, given the lack of diplomatic relations with Turkey. Such opportunities for, and threats to, European integration, some of which have been revived or exacerbated by Brexit, can also be found in other 'troubled territories' throughout the EU.

III. Post-Brexit Framework of the Multi-shaded European Integration

The distinctive arrangements for EU membership in Member States' territories, as already discussed, have been in operation for decades, subject to minor changes, even where such frameworks are deemed temporary in nature. This situation, however, took a new turn following the 2016 Brexit referendum, which eventually resulted in the UK officially withdrawing from the EU on 31 January 2020, with the transition period ending on 31 December 2020.[88] During and after the Brexit negotiations, new challenges arose in the context of the re(definition) of EU membership for several Member State territories. In particular, the withdrawal of

[85] Council Regulation (EC) No 389/2006 of 27 February 2006 establishing an instrument of financial support for encouraging the economic development of the Turkish Cypriot community and amending Council Regulation (EC) No 2667/2000 on the European Agency for Reconstruction ('Financial Aid Regulation').

[86] Laulhé Shaelou, 'Views from Cyprus' (n 69) 327.

[87] ibid. See also European Commission Representation in Cyprus, https://cyprus.representation.ec.europa.eu/about-us/turkish-cypriot-community_en accessed 1 July 2023.

[88] Art 126, Withdrawal Agreement (n 32).

the UK from the Union has had legal and political ramifications in the SBAs in Cyprus, primarily concerning the application of EU law, as well as for Gibraltar, which shares a border with Spain. Further challenges were also created for the UK itself following Brexit, with respect in particular to NI, which shares not only a border but also deep historical and political ties with the Republic of Ireland, as embodied, inter alia, in the Good Friday Agreement (GFA)[89] and the Common Travel Area (CTA).[90] Consequently, among the many issues on the table in the Brexit negotiations was the need for a 'durable arrangement' addressing the 'very specific situations' relating to Ireland/NI, and to the SBAs in Cyprus, and a separate protocol establishing 'the specific arrangements in respect of Gibraltar applicable particularly during the transition period'.[91]

The Withdrawal Agreement, eventually drafted on 19 October 2019, sets out the arrangements for the UK's withdrawal from the Union and considers the framework of the future EU–UK relationship. According to Article 3(1) of the Withdrawal Agreement, the territorial scope of the Agreement must be understood as including, inter alia, the UK, Gibraltar to the extent that Union law was applicable to it before the Withdrawal Agreement was concluded, and the SBAs of Akrotiri and Dhekelia in Cyprus, 'to the extent necessary to ensure the implementation of the arrangements . . . concerning the conditions of Cyprus' accession to the EU, unless otherwise provided in the Agreement'.[92] As such, separate protocols were annexed to the Withdrawal Agreement, relating to Ireland/NI and the SBAs in Cyprus and Gibraltar.[93] As a result, several territories were driven further away or closer to European integration, in the face of renewed aspects of re(defining) EU membership and/or cooperation.

A. Implications for British Overseas Territories

As already discussed in the previous analysis, the legal status of the SBAs in Cyprus under EU law is *sui generis* to the extent that the EU Treaties apply selectively to the remainder of a UK Crown colony, whereas the SBAs are part of the EU's CU, together with the RoC. As an illustration of differentiated integration, the SBAs in fact became the first constituent part of sovereign British territory to officially adopt the euro currency, due to the introduction of the euro in the RoC, and the

[89] Multi-Party Agreement set out in Annex I to the Agreement between the Government of the United Kingdom of Great Britain and Northern Ireland and the Government of Ireland of 10 April 1998.

[90] The UK legal position on the CTA is set out in s 1(3) of the Immigration Act 1971 and s 9(4) of the Immigration Act 1971.

[91] Preamble, Withdrawal Agreement (n 32).

[92] ibid Art 3(1).

[93] ibid Art 182: 'The Protocol on Ireland/Northern Ireland, the Protocol relating to the Sovereign Base Areas in Cyprus, the Protocol on Gibraltar, and Annexes I to IX shall form an integral part of this Agreement.'

fact that Cypriot citizens live in the SBAs.[94] This must now be considered in the context of a post-Brexit world.

The importance of the status of EU law in the SBAs post-Brexit was clear from the beginning of the negotiations between the UK and RoC governments in October 2017, by common understanding that an agreement that would secure the continuity of the exceptional regime applying to the SBAs under EU law had to reached.[95] On the contrary, a potential customs border with the Republic would likely create significant economic, social, and political frictions on the island of Cyprus.[96] The failure to reach an agreement on this point would have meant that the UK would have been in violation of international law, namely of its intention under the Treaty of Establishment 'not to create customs posts or other frontier barriers between the SBAs and the Republic',[97] and not to 'establish commercial or civilian seaports or airport', as explicitly stated in the Withdrawal Agreement.[98]

The separate Protocol on the SBAs in Cyprus, agreed and annexed to the Withdrawal Agreement, aims to protect the interests of those residing and/or working in the SBAs following the UK's withdrawal from the Union, arguably in full respect of the rights and obligations under the Treaty of Establishment.[99] In particular, the aim of the Protocol is to ensure that EU law will continue to apply in the SBAs, as currently provided for in Protocol No 3 of the 2003 Treaty of Accession, with no disruption or loss of rights, especially for the Cypriot civilians living and/or working in the SBAs. This applies to several policy areas, including taxation, goods, agriculture, fisheries and veterinary, and phytosanitary rules. At the same time, the Protocol recognizes the need to provide for specific arrangements for checks on goods and persons crossing the external borders of the SBAs, and the terms under which the relevant provisions of EU law apply to the line between the Areas and the SBAs of Dhekelia (currently provided under Protocol No 10 annexed to the Treaty of Accession).[100]

With respect to the EU's CU, the Withdrawal Agreement states under Article 2(1) that the SBAs shall be part of the CU after the UK's withdrawal from the Union. Therefore, the provisions of Union law on customs and CCP, including provisions on customs controls of specific goods, continue to apply to and in the

94 A Stergiou, 'The Exceptional Case of the British Military Bases on Cyprus' (2015) 51 Middle Eastern Studies 285–300, 285.

95 Hadjigeorgiou and Skoutaris (n 40).

96 ibid.

97 Declaration by Her Majesty's Government regarding The Administration of the Sovereign Base Areas, being those Areas Mentioned in Article 1 of The Treaty concerning the Establishment of the Republic of Cyprus which Remain under the Sovereignty of the United Kingdom, 111 https://www.mfa.gr/images/docs/kypriako/treaty_of_establishment.pdf accessed 1 July 2023.

98 Preamble, SBAs Protocol annexed to the Agreement on the withdrawal of the United Kingdom of Great Britain and Northern Ireland from the European Union and the European Atomic Energy Community 2019/C 384 I/01.

99 ibid.

100 ibid.

SBAs. Post-Brexit, the SBAs are thus added to the list of parts of third countries that belong to the EU's CU.[101] Moreover, the Protocol stresses that goods produced in the SBAs and placed on the market in the CU shall be considered to be goods in free circulation, while all goods intended to be used/exported in/from the SBAs must enter/exit Cyprus through the civilian airports and seaports of the RoC, and all customs formalities, customs controls, and collection of related import duties shall be carried out by the authorities of the RoC.[102] Derogations to these rules apply, inter alia, to goods imported or exported for official or military purposes, or in personal baggage by or on behalf of UK personnel, as well as by other persons travelling on defence or official business, who may enter or leave Cyprus through a seaport or airport in the SBAs.[103] The Withdrawal Agreement also makes clear that the Treaty provisions on the non-fiscal barriers to trade (Articles 34–36 TFEU), other provisions on goods, particularly measures adopted pursuant to Article 114 TFEU, and EU provisions on turnover taxes, excise duties, and other forms of indirect taxation adopted pursuant to Article 113 TFEU, will apply to and in the SBAs.[104] The EU provisions on agriculture and fisheries in Part Three of the TFEU, and acts adopted pursuant to those provisions, are also referred to as applying to and in the SBAs, based on Article 6 of the Protocol.

With regard to the protection of the rights to social security of persons resident or employed in the SBAs, the Protocol annexed to the Withdrawal Agreement does not provide for a specific arrangement post-Brexit, but indicates, rather, that the UK and the RoC 'shall make further arrangements where necessary, to ensure the proper implementation of Article 4 of Protocol No 3 after the end of the transition period'.[105] In other words, the Protocol confirmed the continuity of the pre-Brexit system, namely that persons resident or employed in the SBAs shall be treated as if they were resident or employed in the territory of the Republic for the purposes of the Regulation on the application of social security schemes, and gave discretion to the parties involved as to how to ensure its proper implementation in the future.[106]

Another important topic is the checks on persons crossing the external borders of the SBAs, which, according to Article 7 of the Protocol, will continue to be carried out by the UK.[107] These checks shall include the verification of travel documents, and anyone crossing shall undergo at least one such check to establish their identity. When it comes to TCNs and nationals of the UK, they are only

[101] Art 3, Council Regulation (EEC) no 2913/92 of 12 October 1992 establishing the Community Customs Code (1992) OJ L302/1.

[102] Art 2(2), (3), and (4), SBAs Protocol annexed to the Withdrawal Agreement (n 98).

[103] ibid, Art 2(6)(a).

[104] ibid Arts 2(7) and 3.

[105] ibid Art 5.

[106] Council Regulation (EEC) No 1408/71 of 14 June 1971 on the application of social security schemes to employed persons and their families moving within the Community.

[107] External borders of the SBAs mean the sea boundaries and the airports and seaports of the SBAs, but not their land and sea boundaries with the RoC. 'Crossing points' means any crossing point authorized by the UK authorities for the crossing of the external borders of the SBAs.

permitted to cross the external borders of the SBAs if they following conditions are fulfilled: (i) possess a valid travel document, (ii) a valid visa for the RoC, if required; (iii) are engaged in a defence-related activity, or they are family members of a person who is engaged in such activity and (iv) they are not a threat to national security.[108] In addition, the crossing points of Pergamos and Strovilia, in the Eastern SBAs,[109] shall be treated as part of the external borders of the SBAs, and the UK authorities will conduct the checks on persons crossing, according to the Withdrawal Agreement.[110] This is particularly important considering that the RoC seems to have raised the issue of controlling the external boundaries during the negotiations with the UK, including the checks conducted at the crossing points of the line that divides the island because of the 'age-old conflict'.[111] The UK authorities, however, refused to devolve or share the task of controlling the crossing points with the Republic, which was deemed necessary to the proper functioning of the Green Line Regulation at the end of the transition period. Therefore, as a result of the post-Brexit arrangements in the SBAs, the task of implementing an important EU legislative mechanism—that of the Green Line Regulation—is now entrusted to the authorities of a non-EU Member State, a somewhat incoherent and controversial scenario.[112]

Post-Brexit, the responsibility to implement and enforce EU law in relation to the SBAs was conferred to the RoC with respect to most areas covered by the agreement, and apart from security and military affairs.[113] The cooperation between the RoC and the UK, including in the form of possible future arrangements, is expressly referred to in the Protocol, in order to ensure its effective implementation, particularly with a view to countering fraud and any other illegal activities that affect the financial interests of the Union or the UK. The RoC is, however, obliged to inform the European Commission of any such arrangements before their entry into force.[114] Importantly, Article 12(1) of the Protocol provides that the institutions, bodies, offices, and agencies of the Union shall have the powers conferred upon them by Union law in relation to this Protocol and applicable EU provisions in relation to natural and legal persons residing or established in the SBAs. In particular, the CJEU shall have jurisdiction as provided for in the Treaties. Acts of the institutions, bodies, offices, and agencies adopted in accordance with Article 12(1) shall produce 'the same legal effects with regard to and in the SBAs as those which they produce within the Union and its Member States'.

[108] Art 7(3), SBAs Protocol annexed to the Withdrawal Agreement (n 98).
[109] Boundary between the Eastern SBAs and the areas not effectively controlled by the RoC.
[110] Art 7(6), SBAs Protocol annexed to the Withdrawal Agreement (n 98).
[111] Nasia Hadjigeorgiou and Nikos Skoutaris (n 40).
[112] ibid.
[113] European Commission, Fact Sheet, 'Brexit Negotiations: What is in the Withdrawal Agreement' (14 November 2018) http://europa.eu/rapid/press-release_MEMO-18-6422_en.htm accessed 1 July 2023.
[114] Art 8, SBAs Protocol annexed to the Withdrawal Agreement (n 98).

A Specialised Committee on issues related to the implementation of the Protocol relating to the SBAs in Cyprus was also created,[115] which will be making recommendations to the Joint Committee regarding the functioning of the Protocol.[116] The Joint Committee has the power to amend any references to EU law contained in the Protocol, including the provisions on the crossing points under Article 7(6).[117] At the same time, the European Commission would need to inform the Specialised Committee of any report submitted on the implementation of the Green Line Regulation, and would need to 'consult' with the UK on 'any Commission proposal to adopt an act amending or replacing that Regulation', should the SBAs be affected.[118] The Specialised Committee on issues related to the implementation of the Protocol in the SBAs in Cyprus has published three joint (UK-EU) statements following the three meetings convened since its establishment by the Withdrawal Agreement. The Specialised Committee has reaffirmed, inter alia, its commitment to continued progress in implementing the measures outlined in the Protocol,[119] and has discussed the remaining issues relating to the smooth implementation of the Protocol, which entered into effect at the end of the transition period.[120] It therefore remains to be seen, in the years to come, how effective the implementation of the Protocol will be in the SBAs, with respect in particular to the continued protection of individuals' rights as provided for under EU Law.

The disruptive implications of Brexit extend beyond the SBAs, to other British Overseas Territories—most notably Gibraltar.[121] As discussed earlier, uniquely among the Overseas Territories, Gibraltar lies within continental Europe, and is considered to be a 'European territory within the meaning of [Article 355 TFEU], for whose external relations the UK is responsible', and to which the provisions of the Treaties apply.[122] This territory plays an important role in the UK's global military network, and for NATO, hosting a Permanent Joint Operating Base, signal posts, runway facilities, and a secure harbour, with protection provided by the

[115] Art 165(d), Withdrawal Agreement (n 32).
[116] Under Article 164 of the Withdrawal Agreement, a Joint Committee, comprising representatives of the Union and of the United Kingdom, is established. The Joint Committee shall be co-chaired by the Union and the United Kingdom.
[117] Art 10, SBAs Protocol annexed to the Withdrawal Agreement (n 98).
[118] ibid Art 9(2).
[119] First meeting on 9 June 2020, https://ec.europa.eu/info/publications/joint-statement-following-meeting-specialised-committee-issues-related-implementation-protocol-sovereign-base-areas-united-kingdom-great-britain-and-northern-ireland-cyprus-videoconference_en; Second meeting on 3 December 2020, https://ec.europa.eu/info/publications/joint-uk-eu-statement-following-second-meeting-withdrawal-agreement-specialised-committee-issues-related-implementation-protocol-sovereign-base-areas-united-kingdom-great-britain-and-northern-ireland-cyprus_en accessed 1 July 2023.
[120] Third meeting on 30 December 2020, https://ec.europa.eu/info/publications/joint-uk-eu-statement-following-third-meeting-withdrawal-agreement-specialised-committee-issues-related-implementation-protocol-sovereign-base-areas-united-kingdom-great-britain-and-northern-ireland-cyprus_en accessed 1 July 2023.
[121] Ian Hendry and Susan Dickson, *British Overseas Territories Law* (Hart 2011) 320–21.
[122] *Gibraltar & the UK v European Commission* (n 55), [10].

Royal Gibraltar Regiment and two Royal Navy patrol boats.[123] In the 2016 Brexit referendum to determine the UK's future membership of the EU, Gibraltarians voted to remain in the EU, with the support for 'remain' standing at an overwhelming 96 per cent, on a turnout as high as 84 per cent.[124] Besides a potentially strong dissatisfaction, Brexit also raised political and economic questions for Gibraltar, including 'existential threats' to the economy in the event of a barrier to trade or free movement with neighbouring Spain.[125]

The Gibraltar Protocol, annexed to the Withdrawal Agreement, stressed that any potential negative effect on the close social and economic relations between Gibraltar and the surrounding Spanish territories must be adequately addressed.[126] Contrary to the SBAs, the Withdrawal Agreement acknowledges the need to establish a separate protocol on Gibraltar, applicable only during the transition period,[127] to ensure an orderly withdrawal from the Union in relation to Gibraltar. The Protocol, therefore, ceased to apply at the end of the transition period, with the exception of Article 1 thereof.[128] Article 1 provides for close cooperation to effectively implement Part Two of the Withdrawal Agreement, on citizens' rights, with an emphasis on the rights of frontier workers residing in Gibraltar or Spain, as provided under Articles 24 and 25 of the Withdrawal Agreement. Other than citizens' rights, the Protocol referred to air transport law in Article 2, clarifying that Union law on air transport was only 'applicable to the Gibraltar airport from the date established by the Joint Committee'. Moreover, under Articles 3 to 5, the Protocol provided for guidelines as to the form of cooperation necessary to be established between Spain and the UK during the transition period, in the areas of fiscal matters and protection of financial interests, environmental protection and fishing, and cooperation in police and customs matters, respectively. Finally, the Specialised Committee on issues related to the implementation of the Protocol on Gibraltar, established by Article 165 of the Withdrawal Agreement, is entrusted with the task of overseeing the implementation of the Protocol, including after the end of the transition period for the provisions still in force. Specifically, in the field of citizens' rights, the work of the Committee is based on the deliberations of the coordinating committee, established by the Protocol as a forum for regular discussion between the competent authorities to monitor matters relating to the

[123] J Black, A Hall, K Cox, M Kepe, and E Silfversten, 'Defence and Security after Brexit: Understanding the Possible Implications of the UK's Decision to Leave the EU—Compendium Report' RAND Corporation, 5 March 2017 https://www.rand.org/pubs/research_reports/RR1786.html accessed 1 July 2023.

[124] Joseph Garcia, 'Brexit: A View from Gibraltar' (2016) 105 The Round Table 585–86.

[125] Andy McSmith, 'Gibraltar Faces "Existential Threat" to its Economy if there's a "Hard Brexit" Deal, its Chief Minister Warns' *The Independent* (London, 20 August 2016) http://www.independent.co.uk/news/uk/gibraltar-existential-threat-economy-hard-brexit-deal-eufabian-picardo-a7201211.html accessed 1 July 2023.

[126] Preamble, Gibraltar Protocol annexed to the Withdrawal Agreement (n 32).

[127] Preamble, Withdrawal Agreement (n 32).

[128] ibid Art 185.

commitment to uphold the citizens' rights outlined under Article 1 of the Protocol, including employment and labour conditions.[129]

As already explained, apart from citizens' rights under Article 1, the status of EU law in Gibraltar after the end of the transition period is not provided for in the agreed Protocol. The European Council guidelines of 29 April 2017[130] set out that 'no agreement between the Union and the UK may apply to the territory of Gibraltar without the agreement between the Kingdom of Spain and the UK'.[131] Consequently, the EU–UK Trade and Cooperation Agreement, setting out the future relationship between the two parties, brought into provisional application on 1 January 2021, 'shall not apply to Gibraltar nor have any effects in that territory'.[132] The UK, Gibraltar, and Spain would continue to negotiate arrangements for Gibraltar's future relationship with the EU, seeking the best possible outcome for the people of Gibraltar and the surrounding region. Following intensive discussions between the parties involved, an 'agreement on a political framework to form the basis of a separate treaty between the UK and the EU regarding Gibraltar' was reached on 31 December 2020.[133]

The text of the preliminary agreement arguably represents the biggest shift in Gibraltarian–Spanish relations since Gibraltar's cession to Britain in 1713. To eliminate controls on the movement of people, and all physical barriers, as part of the proposed framework, Gibraltar would in effect be joining the EU's Schengen zone, moving the physical barriers of this zone to Gibraltar's airport and seaport. The future treaty will thus contain provisions to enable the implementation of the most relevant aspects of the Schengen *acquis*, for which Spain, as the neighbouring Schengen Member State, will be responsible, including for the Schengen Borders Code and the protection of Schengen Area's external limits.[134] During a 'reasonable period of implementation' lasting four years, Spain would seek operational assistance from Frontex, the European border agency, to conduct tasks relating to Schengen controls and the protection of external borders. Moreover, to avoid other

[129] Art 1(3), Gibraltar Protocol annexed to the Withdrawal Agreement (n 32).

[130] European Council, Special meeting of the European Council (Art 50) (29 April 2017)– Guidelines, EUCO XT 2004/17, https://www.consilium.europa.eu/media/21763/29-euco-art50-guidelinesen.pdf.

[131] This provision has been recalled in the Council supplementary negotiating directives of 29 January 2018 (XT 21004/18), and in the European Council guidelines of 14 March 2018 (EUCO XT 20001/18).

[132] Art FINPROV.1(3) of the Trade and Cooperation Agreement between the European Union and the European Atomic Energy Community, of the One Part, and the United Kingdom of Great Britain and Northern Ireland, of the Other Part OJ L444, 31.12.2020.

[133] Foreign, Commonwealth & Development Office Press release, UK-Gibraltar-Spain agreement: statement from the Foreign Secretary (31 December 2020) https://www.gov.uk/government/news/uk-gibraltar-spain-agreement-statement-from-the-foreign-secretary accessed 1 July 2023.

[134] María Martín and Miguel González, 'Deal between Spain and UK plans to eliminate Gibraltar border checkpoint' (El Pais, 11 January 2021) https://english.elpais.com/brexit/2021-01-11/deal-between-spain-and-uk-plans-to-eliminate-gibraltar-border-checkpoint.html; https://www.gbc.gi/uploads/lQ4Zi_SCHENGEN_AGREEMENT_PARTLY_PUBLISHED_-_11.01.21.pdf accessed 1 July 2023.

disruptions to the EU's single market, the EU's CU framework will be adapted to Gibraltar for the first time, and the customs checkpoint at La Verja will be eliminated. Gibraltar will, consequently, have to apply 'substantially' the same duties and trade policy measures as the EU, including decisions on customs, excise, and VAT legislation, as well as to share reliable statistics on its imports with the EU.[135] It therefore seems that the treaty to be negotiated will seek to address maximized and unrestricted mobility of persons and goods between Gibraltar and the EU.[136]

Consequently, while trade barriers are increasing between the UK and the EU, the Gibraltar Agreement is a significant move in the opposite direction. As previously discussed, Gibraltar (like Britain) was, pre-Brexit, not a member of the Schengen area. Therefore, the border with Spain was treated as an external border of the Schengen area for the purposes of the Schengen Borders Code, and thus 'systematic checks' were carried out on EU citizens and 'thorough checks' on TCNs.[137] Additionally, customs controls were hitherto conducted by the Spanish authorities, because Gibraltar is not a member of the CU. Brexit has, undoubtedly, provided a fresh opportunity to revisit the application of EU law in Gibraltar. All parties involved soon recognized the importance of avoiding the worst effects in the territory by safeguarding fluidity at the border, for the benefit of all residents of the area, and of the region's shared prosperity.[138] The proposed treaty framework is being criticized as diminishing the UK's practical role in Gibraltar and strengthening that of the EU,[139] yet if eventually implemented it will be done 'without prejudice to the issue of sovereignty and jurisdiction' of Gibraltar, and should safeguard the respective positions of Spain and the UK on this matter.[140] It remains to be seen in the months to come whether these positions will be respected. This will become clear once a mandate to negotiate the new treaty between the EU and the UK is established by the European Commission.

[135] Cristina Gallardo, What the post-Brexit Gibraltar deal means (Politico, 12 January 2021) https://www.politico.eu/article/what-the-post-brexit-gibraltar-deal-means-uk-spain/ accessed 1 July 2023.

[136] HM Government of Gibraltar, Chief Minister's Statement – The New Year's Eve 'In-Principle' Agreement: A Post Brexit Deal for Gibraltar - 946/2020 (31 December 2020), https://www.gibraltar.gov.gi/press-releases/chief-ministers-statement-the-new-years-eve-in-principle-agreement-a-post-brexit-deal-for-gibraltar-9462020-6542 accessed 1 July 2023.

[137] Regulation (EU) 2016/399 of the European Parliament and of the Council of 9 March 2016 on a Union Code on the rules governing the movement of persons across borders ('Schengen Borders Code').

[138] HM Government of Gibraltar, 'Technical Note (1): Getting Ready for the End of the Transition Period' (18 September 2020) https://www.gibraltar.gov.gi/uploads/Brexit%20Page/633.1-2020.pdf accessed 1 July 2023.

[139] Mark Mardell, 'Is Brexit Driving Gibraltar Into Europe's Arms?' (Foreign Policy, 10 March 2021) https://foreignpolicy.com/2021/03/10/is-brexit-driving-gibraltar-into-europes-arms/ accessed 1 July 2023.

[140] Arts 1 and 3 of the Proposed Treaty Framework; María Martín and Miguel González, 'Deal between Spain and UK plans to eliminate Gibraltar border checkpoint' (El Pais, 11 January 2021) https://english.elpais.com/brexit/2021-01-11/deal-between-spain-and-uk-plans-to-eliminate-gibraltar-border-checkpoint.html accessed 1 July 2023.

B. UK territory: Partial withdrawal from the EU?

Besides the position of the SBAs post-Brexit, the arrangements made for the movement of goods and persons across the Green Line came back to the forefront recently. In particular, the Green Line arrangements currently in force on the island of Cyprus are viewed by some as a template for a soft border in the case of NI after Brexit.[141] The case of NI has, undoubtedly, constituted one of the most controversial aspects of the Brexit negotiations, due to the complexity of the political and legal relationship between the UK and the Republic of Ireland. Particular areas of concern included the physical border between NI and Ireland, and threats to NI's peace process as well as Northern Irish citizens' rights.

The Republic of Ireland and the UK enjoy a special travel zone between them, the CTA,[142] which creates an open borders area, and has been the norm (in various forms) since the Irish Free State was founded in 1922.[143] In practice, it allows for freedom of travel across the border between NI and the Republic of Ireland, largely as if no international frontier existed,[144] while British and Irish citizens enjoy additional rights, including the rights to work, access to education and social security benefits, access to health care, and voting rights, in either of the two countries.[145] The CTA has been described as an area within which 'internal borders are subject to minimal or non-existent border controls'.[146] Within the CTA's framework, both countries cooperate to ensure the security of the CTA's external borders, including the sharing of information.

Brexit also posed risks to the peace settlement for NI, which is underpinned by the signing of the GFA.[147] The GFA, an international multi-party agreement, acknowledges the 'birthright' of the people of NI to identify and be accepted 'as Irish or British, or both, as they may so choose'.[148] This birthright creates a distinct body of Irish citizens living within the UK whose rights derive from the GFA, and not from the CTA, and who remained EU citizens after Brexit. However, because

[141] Stavros Zenios, 'EU Borders: Walking Backwards from Northern Ireland to Cyprus' (*Bruegel*, 25 October 2017) http://bruegel.org/2017/10/eu-borders-walking-backwards-from-northern-ireland-to-cyprus/ accessed 1 July 2023.

[142] The Memorandum of Understanding between the Government of the United Kingdom of Great Britain and Northern Ireland and the Government of Ireland was signed in May 2019, reaffirming the commitment to maintaining the CTA and the associated rights and privileges.

[143] B Ryan, 'The Common Travel Area between Britain and Ireland' (2001) 64 Modern Law Review 855.

[144] Ireland Act 1949, s 2; On 11 November 2020, the Immigration Act 1971 was amended by adding 'An Irish citizen does not require leave to enter or remain in the UK' in s 3ZA.

[145] Graham Butler and Gavin Barrett, 'Europe's "Other" Open-border Zone: The Common Travel Area under the Shadow of Brexit' (2018) 20 Cambridge Yearbook of European Legal Studies 252.

[146] Oireachtas Joint Committee on European Union Affairs, Report on the UK/EU Future Relationship: Implications for Ireland (Houses of the Oireachtas (Irish Parliament), June 2015).

[147] Multi-Party Agreement set out in Annex I to the Agreement between the Government of the United Kingdom of Great Britain and Northern Ireland and the Government of Ireland of 10 April 1998.

[148] Art 1(iv), Belfast Good Friday Agreement.

these individuals were born in the UK and have not moved to another EU Member State, they find it difficult to assert that they have activated some of their rights under EU law,[149] while dual Irish/British citizens are not eligible to apply for the EU Settlement Scheme (EUSS) and benefit from the rights conferred therein.[150] Throughout the Brexit negotiations, the EU has repeatedly recognized the 'particular' circumstances of NI, in a post-conflict state, and the need to ensure that there is no diminution of rights post-Brexit. The UK's exit from the EU complicates questions of citizenship, immigration, and rights, because it creates the potential for British citizens to be treated differently from Northern Irish citizens, who will retain the benefits associated with being citizens of an EU Member State.

While agreeing that the solution for NI could not be based on any previous precedent, the UK government's position paper on how to address the unique circumstances of Northern Ireland and the Republic of Ireland, in light of Brexit, initially noted that there were a number of examples where the EU had set aside the normal regulations and codes set out in EU law in order to recognize the circumstances of certain border areas, referring, inter alia, to Cyprus.[151] A working paper from the Brexit Policy Institute also considered possible solutions, including the adoption of a flexible arrangement based on the Cypriot accession model, allowing NI-produced goods to be exported, via the Republic of Ireland, as EU goods.[152] It had also been suggested that the legal arrangements accommodating the Cypriot situation could offer some inspiration if NI (and Scotland) wished to remain in the EU.[153] In particular, the Green Line Regulation, which deals with the *de facto* Cyprus secession line in a soft manner, was discussed, including the fact that goods allowed to cross the line, subject to conditions, should not be subject to export formalities.[154] A similar arrangement could, allegedly, empower the NI authorities to identify goods as originating there, and possibly gain some of the benefits of avoiding a closed Irish border.[155]

[149] Sylvia de Mars and Colin Murray, 'With or Without EU? The Common Travel Area after Brexit' (2020) 21 German Law Journal 815.

[150] *Secretary of State for the Home Department v Jake Parker De Souza* [2019] UKUT 355; Case C–202/13 *McCarthy*, ECLI:EU:C:2014:2450, para 36.

[151] HM Government, 'Position Paper by the United Kingdom: Northern Ireland and Ireland', Policy Papers, August 2017, para 42 https://assets.publishing.service.gov.uk/government/uploads/system/uploads/attachment_data/file/638135/6.3703_DEXEU_Northern_Ireland_and_Ireland_INTERACTIVE.pdf accessed 1 July 2023.

[152] John Doyle and Eileen Connolly, 'Brexit and the Future of Northern Ireland' (2017) Brexit Research and Policy Institute Working Paper no 1/2017, 10 http://dcubrexitinstitute.eu/wp-content/uploads/2017/06/WP-2017-1-Doyle-Connolly.pdf accessed 1 July 2023.

[153] Nikos Skoutaris, 'From Britain and Ireland to Cyprus: Accommodating 'Divided Islands' in the EU Political and Legal Order' (2016) EUI Working Paper AEL 2016/02 http://cadmus.eui.eu/bitstream/handle/1814/42484/AEL_2016_02.pdf?sequence=1 accessed 1 July 2023.

[154] John Doyle and Eileen Connolly (n 153) 10 http://dcubrexitinstitute.eu/wp-content/uploads/2017/06/WP-2017-1-Doyle-Connolly.pdf accessed 1 July 2023.

[155] ibid 11.

On the other hand, Michel Barnier, the EU Chief Negotiator, insisted that the solution for the border between NI and the Republic of Ireland could not 'be based on a precedent'.[156] The Green Line is an example of exceptionalism that needs to be 'normalized', not to become the 'norm', not only to protect a united EU, but also due to the many asymmetries between the cases of Cyprus and NI. Primarily, the RoC is a member of the EU and the Green Line Regulation allows part of its territory which is not effectively controlled by its government to enjoy membership benefits. On the other hand, in the case of the Irish border, arrangements were sought for a territory that is under the control of a non-EU state. At the same time, the areas in the northern part of Cyprus do not have officially recognized State authorities, which makes it hard to ensure effective customs control, issuance of drivers' licences, or vehicle roadworthiness certificates, without EU intervention.[157] Moreover, besides the temporary suspension of provisions regarding the Union's customs and fiscal territory, the areas beyond the control of the RoC are also outside the Area of Freedom, Justice and Security. The government of Cyprus is, therefore, required to 'carry out checks on all persons crossing the line with the aim to combat illegal immigration', and to secure an equivalent standard of protection of the security of the EU with that of the rest of the EU, regarding illegal immigration and threats to public order, and of its economic interest.[158] A country which has been *de facto* divided by force for forty-six years now should not constitute a role model for a border arrangement between a Union Member State and a third country. It should also be remembered that the status quo over the ceasefire line in Cyprus has fed several illegal activities, including smuggling, tax evasion, fraud, and human trafficking.[159]

As such, the Green Line arrangement in Cyprus could hardly constitute a suitable model for the NI arrangement post-Brexit. Cyprus' multi-shaded integration also constituted a point of reference for Scotland, but this time with reference to the SBAs. Ahead of the 2014 Scottish independence referendum, the British media reported that the Ministry of Defence was investigating the possibility of designating Faslane and Coulport Royal Naval Bases as 'sovereign UK territory' in the event of Scottish independence.[160] The model of the military SBAs retained by the UK in the RoC would have been used in such an event. At the time, however, the UK

[156] Zenios (n 142).
[157] ibid.
[158] Nikos Skoutaris, *The Cyprus Issue: The Four Freedoms in a Member State under Siege* (Bloomsbury Publishing 2011) 113.
[159] In 2017, the Eastern Sovereign Base Area (ESBA) authorities recorded an increase in the number of seizures of smuggled goods within the ESBA: 432 seizures were made, compared with 277 in 2016. As in 2016, cigarettes and hand-rolling tobacco were the items seized most frequently: Report From the Commission to the Council on the implementation of Council Regulation (EC) No 866/2004 of 29 April 2004 and the situation resulting from its application covering the period 1 January until 31 December 2017, {SWD(2018) 352 final}.
[160] BBC News, 'Faslane Trident Base could be in the UK after Scottish Independence' (*BBC News*, 11 July 2013) http://www.bbc.com/news/uk-scotland-23265886 accessed 1 July 2023.

government was quick to disown the proposal as neither 'credible [n]or sensible', amid strong criticism from the Scottish National Party and others.[161] Whether the 'SBAs model' would be reconsidered in the event of a second Scottish independence referendum is unclear,[162] but bearing in mind the costs the relocation of these two naval bases would entail for the UK government, it would, for them, be an attractive option to revisit the situation.

The NI Protocol annexed to the Withdrawal Agreement, which came into force on 1 January 2021, aims to protect the GFA and avoid a hard border between NI and the Republic of Ireland, to preserve the integrity of the EU's single market, and to facilitate unfettered access for NI good to the rest of the UK's market.[163] As a result, NI remains part of the UK's customs territory, including for any future agreements with third countries that would cover NI goods.[164] At the same time, however, custom checks and controls apply for goods moving from Great Britain (GB) to NI, in order to ensure that none of those checks are required between NI and the Republic of Ireland. In particular, Article 5(1) of the Protocol states that 'no customs duties shall be payable for a good brought into NI from another part of the UK by direct transport unless that good is at risk of subsequently being moved into the Union'. Therefore, the Protocol sets out the conditions under which goods can move tariff-free between GB and NI, and at the same time move without customs controls between NI and the Republic of Ireland. It similarly sets out that the tariff on goods coming into NI from a country outside the EU should be the UK's tariff, again unless the good is 'at risk' of moving into the EU. This latter provision ensures that NI businesses can benefit from free trade deals that the UK may strike with third countries post-Brexit.[165] Based on Article 5(2) of the Protocol, the Joint Committee decided on detailed criteria for the goods 'at risk' of being shipped on to the EU, for which the EU tariff must be paid, taking into consideration the goods' destination, use, nature, value, and incentive for undeclared movement into the EU.[166]

[161] Nicholas Watt, 'Trident Submarine Base: No 10 Disowns MoD's Faslane Sovereignty Proposal' *The Guardian* (London, 11 July 2013) https://www.theguardian.com/politics/2013/jul/11/trident-base-no-10-disowns-mod-faslanesovereignty; Peter Geoghegan, 'Sturgeon Accuses May of Ignoring Scotland in Brexit Talks' *The Irish Times* (Dublin, 4 October 2016) http://www.irishtimes.com/news/world/uk/sturgeon-accusesmay-of-ignoring-scotland-in-brexit-talks-1.2815398 accessed 1 July 2023.

[162] A McHarg and J Mitchell, 'Brexit and Scotland' (2017) 19 British Journal of Politics and International Relations 512.

[163] Preamble, NI Protocol annexed to the Withdrawal Agreement (n 32).

[164] ibid, Art 3.

[165] Explainer for the New Ireland/Northern Ireland Protocol and the Political Declaration on the Future Relationship 18 October 2019, https://assets.publishing.service.gov.uk/media/5da9fc9f40f0b6598ec84906/EXPLAINER_FOR_THE_NEW_IRELAND_NORTHERN_IRELAND_PROTOCOL_AND_THE_POLITICAL_DECLARATION_ON_THE_FUTURE_RELATIONSHIP.pdf

[166] Decision No 4/2020 of the Joint Committee Established by the Agreement on the Withdrawal of the United Kingdom of Great Britain and Northern Ireland from the European Union and the European Atomic Energy Community, , 'Decision of the Withdrawal Agreement Joint Committee on the Determination of Goods Not at Risk', 17 December 2020.

The UK government has said that the arrangement in NI 'can only be lasting if it has democratic support'.[167] Therefore, Article 18 of the Protocol provides for the right of NI to withdraw its consent from the trading arrangements under Articles 5 to 10, through a consent mechanism compatible with the GFA.[168] The first consent vote is due to take place in December 2024, and the UK government has set out a process for the consent mechanism in a unilateral declaration.[169] If consent is not given by the NI Assembly, the Protocol will cease to apply after two years. The possibility that NI could leave the trading arrangements is, therefore, present, even with the potential that such a decision could result in a hard border. The EU had previously rejected attempts by the UK to include a 'unilateral exit mechanism' for the NI trading arrangements, yet the NI voting arrangements no longer included UK-wide elements.[170]

IV. Conclusions

This chapter has provided a comparative analysis of specific territories of EU Member States currently subject to renewed European integration forces, from exceptional/permanent derogations to temporary regimes and vice versa. These territories included Greenland, the areas beyond the effective control of the RoC, and the SBAs, Gibraltar, and NI, in the post-Brexit context. The chapter firstly discussed the evolution of a differentiated integration in several EU Member State territories that has led towards a multi-shaded integration. The analysis started by focusing on the territories associated with the EU that have demonstrated features of differentiated integration, in which EU law applies in one way or another. These included Gibraltar and the SBAs, both part of the UK territory, which are covered by the territorial scope of EU Treaties, as per Article 355 TFEU, whether directly or indirectly. The analysis continued with the areas not controlled by the RoC, in which the Union *acquis* is suspended, due to the *de facto* partition on the island. Therefore, the full European integration of Cyprus constitutes an ongoing process even fifteen years after its accession to the Union.

[167] Lords Select Committee on the Protocol on Ireland/Northern Ireland, Chapter 13: Democratic Consent (Article 18) https://publications.parliament.uk/pa/ld5801/ldselect/ldeucom/66/6616.htm accessed 1 July 2023.

[168] Preamble, NI Protocol annexed to the Withdrawal Agreement (n 32).

[169] Declaration by Her Majesty's Government of the United Kingdom of Great Britain and Northern Ireland concerning the operation of the 'Democratic consent in Northern Ireland' provision of the Protocol on Ireland/Northern Ireland, https://assets.publishing.service.gov.uk/government/uploads/system/uploads/attachment_data/file/840232/Unilateral_Declaration_on_Consent.pd accessed 1 July 2023.

[170] Jess Sargeant, Northern Ireland protocol: consent mechanism (Institute of Government, 19 December 2019), https://www.instituteforgovernment.org.uk/explainers/northern-ireland-protocol-consent-mechanism accessed 1 July 2023.

The unique frameworks in force faced further complications due to Brexit, which altered the direction of the differentiated integration of several territories, demonstrating once more the rather unconventional and variable processes of integration and EU membership for several Member States. The post-Brexit assessment started with the analysis of the SBAs, for which the UK and the EU aimed for the proper implementation of Protocol No 3 to the 2003 Treaty of Accession and the Green Line Regulation (where applicable) post-Brexit, as well as for the least disruption possible to the application of EU law there. In contrast, the post-Brexit status of EU law in Gibraltar, which is to be agreed beyond the Withdrawal Agreement, arguably constitutes a significant move towards further European integration. In particular, the proposed agreement seems to drive Gibraltar closer to EU policies than ever before, including the EU Schengen *acquis*. Lastly, Brexit has also resulted in internal cases of differentiated integration, with the Withdrawal Agreement adopting a special regime for the application of EU law in NI, creating controversies. According to the relevant Protocol, NI remained part of the UK's customs territory, yet customs checks and controls apply for goods moving from GB to NI, to ensure that none of those checks are required between NI and the Republic of Ireland. The arrangements in NI have been heavily criticized politically and legally, including due to the possibility of the Protocol to cease to apply under the consent mechanism under Article 18, risking not only economic detriments but also threatening peace on the island of Ireland. The various bits and pieces of EU law in territories post-Brexit seem to have exacerbated the many shades of European integration which already existed pre-Brexit, contributing to the (re)definition of what characterizes EU membership today as a multidimensional concept, arguably going beyond a unitary vision of membership as originally conceived in the Treaties. If EU membership and rights associated with it can, in practice, become multidimensional, due to wider contexts or external shocks such as Brexit, a renewed focus is necessary to ascertain the continuity of individual rights as guaranteed under the Union *acquis*, and to truly assess the essence of differentiated integration, facing threats and opportunities at every step of the way, thereby avoiding the dilution of rights and further divisions among the people of Europe.

7

Permanent Derogations and Transitional Arrangements for New Member States: Accession *Condictiones Sine Quibus Non*

Adam Łazowski

I. Introduction

So far, the European Communities (EC), and later the European Union (EU), have expanded seven times, bringing the total number of Member States to the current twenty-seven.[1] Every enlargement round has supplied new qualities and flavours to the European integration project. Yet, at the same time, the new accessions have always come at the price of ever-increasing differentiation within the EU.[2] At the meta level, quite inevitably, the Europe of different speeds became a ricochet of new accessions, and these were one of several contributing factors that led to the creation of various flexibility mechanisms, including the opt-outs for selected Member States,[3] as well as the modus operandi for enhanced cooperation.[4]

[1] In the period 2013–20 the EU comprised twenty-eight Member States. In 1973 the United Kingdom (UK), Ireland, and Denmark joined the EC. They were followed by Greece in 1981, and Spain and Portugal in 1986. The fourth enlargement of the EC (which also amounted to the first enlargement of the newly created EU) took place in 1995, when Austria, Finland, and Sweden joined the ranks. This was followed by the 'big bang' enlargement in 2004, when the EU/EC membership extended to Estonia, Latvia, Lithuania, Poland, Slovakia, Czechia, Hungary, Slovenia, Malta, and Cyprus. The sixth enlargement round took place in 2007, when Bulgaria and Romania completed their rapprochement. Finally, Croatia joined the EU and Euratom in 2013. The number of EU Member States went down to twenty-seven on 31 January 2020 when the UK left the EU and Euratom. See further, on the history of EU enlargements, Allan F Tatham, *Enlargement of the EU* (Wolters Kluwer 2009); Kirstyn Inglis, *Evolving Practice in EU Enlargement* (Brill/Nijhoff 2010).

[2] One may also argue that the three enlargement rounds of the past two decades, and the migratory movements that followed, have had a knock-on effect by contributing to the disintegrative withdrawal of the UK from the EU and Euratom. On the evolving position of the UK on the EU enlargements, see, inter alia, Martin Westlake, *Slipping Loose: The United Kingdom's Long Drift Away from the European Union* (Agenda Publishing 2018) 67–90; Julija Brsakoska Bazerkoska, 'Impact of Brexit on Future Enlargements of the EU: A View from the Balkans' in Adam Łazowski and Adam Cygan (eds), *Research Handbook on Legal Aspects of Brexit* (Edward Elgar 2022) 507–23.

[3] See further, inter alia, Rebecca Adler-Nissen, *Opting Out of the European Union: Diplomacy, Sovereignty and European Integration* (CUP 2014).

[4] See further, inter alia, Steve Peers, 'Enhanced Cooperation: The Cinderella of Differentiated Integration' in Bruno de Witte, Andrea Ott, and Ellen Vos (eds), *Between Flexibility and Disintegration: The Trajectory of Differentiation in EU Law* (Edward Elgar 2017).

Adam Łazowski, *Permanent Derogations and Transitional Arrangements for New Member States*
In: *Redefining EU Membership*. Edited by: Diane Fromage, Oxford University Press.
DOI: 10.1093/9780191948145.003.0007

However, if one reaches for the microscope and looks through its lens at the terms and conditions of each and every accession round, one can see many other faces of differentiation. This is courtesy of wide suites of permanent derogations and transitional arrangements laid down in respective Acts on Conditions of Accession, which are constituent parts of the accession treaties.[5] In this regard, the first

[5] Treaty between the Kingdom of Belgium, the Federal Republic of Germany, the French Republic, the Italian Republic, the Grand Duchy of Luxembourg, the Kingdom of the Netherlands (Member States of the European Communities), the Kingdom of Denmark, Ireland, the Kingdom of Norway and the United Kingdom of Great Britain and Northern Ireland concerning the accession of the Kingdom of Denmark, Ireland, the Kingdom of Norway and the United Kingdom of Great Britain and Northern Ireland to the European Economic Community and to the European Atomic Energy Community [1972] OJ L73/5 (Accession Treaty 1972); Treaty between the Kingdom of Belgium, the Kingdom of Denmark, the Federal Republic of Germany, the French Republic, Ireland, the Italian Republic, the Grand Duchy of Luxembourg, the Kingdom of the Netherlands, the United Kingdom of Great Britain and Northern Ireland (Member States of the European Communities) and the Hellenic Republic concerning the accession of the Hellenic Republic to the European Economic Community and to the European Atomic Energy Community [1979] OJ L291/9; Treaty between the Kingdom of Belgium, the Kingdom of Denmark, the Federal Republic of Germany, the Hellenic Republic, the French Republic, Ireland, the Italian Republic, the Grand Duchy of Luxembourg, the Kingdom of the Netherlands, the United Kingdom of Great Britain and Northern Ireland (Member States of the European Communities) and the Kingdom of Spain and the Portuguese Republic concerning the accession of the Kingdom of Spain and the Portuguese Republic to the European Economic Community and to the European Atomic Energy Community [1985] OJ L302/9; Treaty between the Kingdom of Belgium, the Kingdom of Denmark, the Federal Republic of Germany, the Hellenic Republic, the Kingdom of Spain, the French Republic, Ireland, the Italian Republic, the Grand Duchy of Luxembourg, the Kingdom of the Netherlands, the Portuguese Republic, the United Kingdom of Great Britain and Northern Ireland (Member States of the European Union) and the Kingdom of Norway, the Republic of Austria, the Republic of Finland, the Kingdom of Sweden, concerning the accession of the Kingdom of Norway, the Republic of Austria, the Republic of Finland and the Kingdom of Sweden to the European Union [1994] OJ C241/9; Treaty between the Kingdom of Belgium, the Kingdom of Denmark, the Federal Republic of Germany, the Hellenic Republic, the Kingdom of Spain, the French Republic, Ireland, the Italian Republic, the Grand Duchy of Luxembourg, the Kingdom of the Netherlands, the Republic of Austria, the Portuguese Republic, the Republic of Finland, the Kingdom of Sweden, the United Kingdom of Great Britain and Northern Ireland (Member States of the European Union) and the Czech Republic, the Republic of Estonia, the Republic of Cyprus, the Republic of Latvia, the Republic of Lithuania, the Republic of Hungary, the Republic of Malta, the Republic of Poland, the Republic of Slovenia, the Slovak Republic, concerning the accession of the Czech Republic, the Republic of Estonia, the Republic of Cyprus, the Republic of Latvia, the Republic of Lithuania, the Republic of Hungary, the Republic of Malta, the Republic of Poland, the Republic of Slovenia and the Slovak Republic to the European Union [2013] OJ L236/17; Treaty between the Kingdom of Belgium, the Czech Republic, the Kingdom of Denmark, the Federal Republic of Germany, the Republic of Estonia, the Hellenic Republic, the Kingdom of Spain, the French Republic, Ireland, the Italian Republic, the Republic of Cyprus, the Republic of Latvia, the Republic of Lithuania, the Grand Duchy of Luxembourg, the Republic of Hungary, the Republic of Malta, the Kingdom of the Netherlands, the Republic of Austria, the Republic of Poland, the Portuguese Republic, the Republic of Slovenia, the Slovak Republic, the Republic of Finland, the Kingdom of Sweden, the United Kingdom of Great Britain and Northern Ireland (Member States of the European Union) and the Republic of Bulgaria and Romania, concerning the accession of the Republic of Bulgaria and Romania to the European Union [2005] OJ L157/11; Treaty between the Kingdom of Belgium, the Republic of Bulgaria, the Czech Republic, the Kingdom of Denmark, the Federal Republic of Germany, the Republic of Estonia, Ireland, the Hellenic Republic, the Kingdom of Spain, the French Republic, the Italian Republic, the Republic of Cyprus, the Republic of Latvia, the Republic of Lithuania, the Grand Duchy of Luxembourg, the Republic of Hungary, the Republic of Malta, the Kingdom of the Netherlands, the Republic of Austria, the Republic of Poland, the Portuguese Republic, Romania, the Republic of Slovenia, the Slovak Republic, the Republic of Finland, the Kingdom of Sweden, the United Kingdom of Great Britain and Northern Ireland (Member States of the European Union) and the Republic of Croatia concerning the accession of the Republic of Croatia to the European Union [2012] OJ L112/10.

enlargement round already delivered, albeit partly transient, a Europe of different speeds. In all subsequent EC/EU enlargements, the permanent derogations and transitional arrangements evolved into immanent features of rapprochement, and thus should be considered as *condictiones sine quibus non* of EU accessions. Put otherwise, contemporarily such arrangements of sorts are part and parcel of the enlargement DNA. However, they constitute exceptions to the general principle of immediate effect of EU law in the new Member States.[6] With this in mind, it is no surprise that permanent derogations from the EU *acquis* at the entry stage are only available in extraordinary circumstances. At the same time, at the heart of accession negotiations are various types of transitional arrangements, which, in principle, bring differentiation of a temporary character. Yet, as evidenced in the present chapter, such arrangements for participation in the Schengen *acquis*, and in the Economic and Monetary Union (EMU), are in some cases characterized by a considerable longevity, bordering on permanence.

Bearing in mind the overarching theme of the present volume, the differentiation inextricably linked to the EU enlargements merits a closer look. For this purpose, the analysis that follows is organized in the following fashion. As a starting point, the permanent derogations are presented in Section II. In turn, the notion of 'transitional arrangements' is deciphered. Furthermore, the *raison d'être* and typology of transitional arrangements is elaborated on (Section III). This is followed by an exegesis focusing on transitional periods applicable to, or in new, EU Member States (Section IV). Section V is dedicated to temporary derogations, including safeguard clauses, which—when used—bring time-limited and scope-restricted differentiation. Section VI focuses on rules governing the phasing in of newcomers into the EU institutional framework, and selected EU policies.

II. Permanent Derogations

A. Introduction

As part of the enlargement mantra, the EU repeatedly argues that no permanent opt-outs à la the UK, Ireland, or Denmark are available to the countries queueing for EU membership.[7] This rule, in principle, has been followed throughout all enlargement rounds thus far, and is unlikely to change in the years to come. Its roots

[6] Saulius Lukas Kalėda, 'Immediate Effect of Community Law in the New Member States: Is there a Place for a Consistent Doctrine?' (2004) 10 European Law Journal 102; Saulius Lukas Kalėda, 'Intertemporal Legal Issues in the European Union Case Law Relating to the 2004 and 2007 Accessions' in Adam Łazowski (ed), *The Application of EU Law in the New Member States: Brave New World* (TMC Asser Press 2010).

[7] For instance, Council of the EU, 'Ministerial meeting opening the Intergovernmental Conference on the Accession of Serbia to the EU' available at https://data.consilium.europa.eu/doc/document/AD%201%202014%20INIT/EN/pdf accessed 1 July 2023.

lie in the principle of equality of EU Member States, which underpins the legal order of the EU.[8] This is a two-edged sword: on the one hand, it does not allow for à la carte membership of new entrants; on the other hand, it stops the EU from treating newcomers in a discriminatory fashion by taking some aspects of the EU membership off the menu. The former would potentially arise if the UK were to attempt to rejoin the EU and, at the same time, try to bring back the plethora of opt-outs it had benefited from before Brexit.[9] The latter could be a tempting solution for the Member States to explore in relation to the stalled rapprochement of Turkey. This is not merely an academic proposition. In fact, the politically and legally dubious idea of permanent derogation from free movement of workers, as a bargaining chip to persuade the reluctant EU capitals, has been already toyed with.[10] A strict interpretation of the EU accession *acquis* inevitably leads to a conclusion that neither option is possible, as Article 49 of the Treaty on European Union (TEU), which is at the heart of it, offers only one choice: a full membership.[11] Furthermore, if large-scale permanent derogations similar to the opt-outs currently enjoyed by Ireland and Denmark were to be introduced qua accession treaties, that would potentially amount to the bypassing of Article 48 TEU, which governs the revision procedures for the EU founding treaties.[12] As long as the latter do not provide for a partial membership, the EU is, from the legal point of view, bound to follow its existing mantra. To proceed otherwise would, according to Hillion, expose the EU to actions for annulment as per Article 263 TFEU.[13] This prima facie agreeable conclusion is not without controversy. If such permanent derogations were to be regulated in accession treaties, such requests for judicial review would face challenges of admissibility. As is well known, the accession treaties belong to EU primary law, and are thus not amenable to review under the procedure in question.[14]

[8] See, inter alia, Lucia Serena Rossi, 'The Principle of Equality among Member States of the EU' in Lucia Serena Rossi and Federico Casolari (eds), *The Principle of Equality in EU Law* (Springer 2017); Markus Klamert, 'Article 4 TEU' in Manuel Kellerbauer, Marcus Klamert, and Jonathan Tomkin (eds), *The EU Treaties and the Charter of Fundamental Rights: A Commentary* (OUP 2019); Hermann-Josef Blanke, 'Article 4 TEU' in Hermann-Josef Blanke and Stelio Mangiameli (eds), *The Treaty on EU (TEU): A Commentary* (Springer 2013).

[9] See, further, Adam Łazowski and Adam Cygan, 'In the Footsteps of Albania and North Macedonia: What if the United Kingdom Opts to Re-join the EU' (2024) 43 Yearbook of European Law (forthcoming).

[10] Christophe Hillion, 'Enlarging the Constitutional Order of States' in Anthony Arnull, Catherine Barnard, Michael Dougan, and Eleanor Spaventa (eds), *A Constitutional Order of States? Essays in EU Law in Honour of Alan Dashwood* (Hart 2011) 485, 497.

[11] This equally applied to predecessors of Art 49 TEU, ie Art 98 ECSC, Art 205 EAEC, and Art 237 EEC. See, further, on the evolution of EU enlargement rules, Christophe Hillion, 'EU Enlargement' in Paul Craig and Gráinne de Búrca (eds), *The Evolution of EU Law* (2nd edn, OUP 2011).

[12] See, inter alia, Bruno de Witte, 'Treaty Revision Procedures after Lisbon' in Andrea Biondi, Piet Eeckhout, and Stefanie Ripley (eds), *EU Law after Lisbon* (OUP 2012).

[13] Hillion, 'Enlarging the Constitutional Order of States' (n 10) 497.

[14] Koen Lenaerts, Ignace Maselis, and Kathleen Gutman, *EU Procedural Law* (OUP 2014) 257–302.

It merits attention, though, that in the course of the seven enlargement rounds the Member States agreed to permanent derogations, albeit only in highly exceptional circumstances. Not only does Article 49 TEU stand as a gatekeeper but also, as aptly noted by Kalėda, countries negotiating accession are in much weaker position to make such far-reaching demands at the entry stage. It may be much more effective to do so once their membership materializes, and the new entrants become fully involved in negotiations of secondary legislation, as well as in the treaty revisions.[15] Yet, some permanent derogations being agreed to during the membership talks are not unheard of. The qualifying factors opening the doors for a bit flexibility on the EU side include, for instance, the special status of parts of territory, including the existence of overseas territories or an idiosyncratic relationship between a future Member State and territories for which it is responsible. Special arrangements applicable to the indigenous population of a new Member State may also be decisive for granting a permanent derogation. In order to give these arguments merit, examples of such permanent derogations laid down in the accession treaties are presented in turn.

B. Permanent derogations for parts of territories and indigenous populations

The permanent derogations made their debut in the Accession Treaty 1972. Indeed, they were part and parcel of the terms of the first enlargement of the EC. Three out of the four countries which were due to join the EC together requested bespoke solutions to reflect the special statuses of some territories falling under their general jurisdictions or linked with them in an idiosyncratic fashion. In relation to the UK, this applied to the Crown Dependencies: the Isle of Man, and the Channel Islands.[16] As for Denmark, Protocol 4 to the Accession Treaty 1972 allowed Greenland to maintain a restriction in relation to the right of establishment.[17] A special derogation was also tailored to the needs and unique status of the Faroe Islands.[18] Norway, too, managed to negotiate an opt-out for

[15] Saulius Lukas Kalėda, *Przejęcie prawa wspólnotowego przez nowe państwo członkowskie. Zagadnienia przejściowe oraz międzyczasowe* (Wydawnictwo Prawo i Praktyka Gospodarcza 2003) 225.

[16] The Channel Islands include Jersey, Guernsey, Herm, Sark, and Alderney. Their status in the EU was regulated by Protocol 3 to the Accession Treaty 1972. Together with the Isle of Man they were part of the EU customs union.

[17] In a nutshell, Denmark was permitted to keep its domestic law requiring six-months' residence in Greenland as a condition for obtaining a licence to perform some commercial activities.

[18] In accordance with Arts 25(3), 26(3), and 27(3) of the Act on Conditions of Accession 1972, the three Founding Treaties of the EC did not apply to the Faroe Islands. However, the Danish government had an option to notify its desire to change this state of affairs by 31 December 1975. Detailed arrangements for trade in goods were provided in Protocol 2 to the Accession Treaty 1972. Its Art 4 also envisaged a special status for Danish citizens residing in the Faroe Islands, who were not to be considered Danish citizens for the purposes of EC law. This, as aptly noted by Kochenov, became problematic

Spitzbergen.[19] In 1981, when Greece joined the EC, a non-binding commitment to take into account the status of Mount Athos in the EC decision-making process was made in a joint declaration. This was not, per se, a legal obligation, yet this par excellence gentlemen's agreement was firmly introduced into the legal framework governing the second enlargement.[20] Spain, which followed, together with Portugal, in 1986, negotiated as part of its EU membership deal a special status for the Canary Islands, Ceuta, and Melilla.[21] In the fourth accession round, Finland negotiated a bespoke arrangement for the Åland Islands.[22] Norway, once again, was granted a tailor-made treatment for Spitzbergen, albeit this was not a carbon copy of the arrangement negotiated in the early 1970s.[23] All three Nordic countries which aimed to join the EU in 1995 also agreed with the existing EU Member States that the exclusive rights to reindeer husbandry would continue to be available only to Sami people.[24] In relation to the 'big bang' enlargement of 2004, one should pay particular attention to accession of Cyprus. Although it joined as the entire—though divided—island, the application of EU law has been suspended in relation to Northern Cyprus, the territory of which is not controlled by the authorities in Nicosia.[25] No comparable issues had to be addressed in the next two accession rounds, when Bulgaria, Romania (2007), and Croatia (2013) joined the EU.

In the years following the consecutive enlargements of the EC/ EU, all the already bespoke regimes evolved together with the tailor-made arrangements which had been designed for the selected founding Member States at the time of creation of the EC in the 1950s.[26] Some of the bespoke regimes, however, have become

when EU citizenship was established, with the entry into force of the Treaty of Maastricht. It was due to its personal, not territorial character: Dimitry Vladimirovich Kochenov, 'Article 202' in Manuel Kellerbauer, Marcus Klamert, and Jonathan Tomkin (eds) (n 8) 1574, 1575.

[19] Protocol 5 to Accession Treaty 1972.

[20] Joint declaration concerning Mount Athos, annexed to the Accession Treaty 1979.

[21] Art 25 of the Act on Conditions of Accession, Art 155 of the Act on Conditions of Accession (in relation to non-application of the Common Fisheries Policy), and Protocol No 2 to Accession Treaty 1985.

[22] Protocol No 2 to Accession Treaty 1994 provided specific derogations. To begin with, it permitted Finland to maintain existing legislation (in force on 1 January 1994) envisaging non-discriminatory restrictions on acquiring real property on the Åland Islands. Secondly, some non-discriminatory restrictions to the right of establishment and free movement of services were also permitted. Thirdly, the Åland Islands were made exempt from the application of the EU *acquis* on indirect taxation.

[23] Protocol No 7 to Accession Treaty 1994 effectively provided that EU law would not apply to Spitzbergen. At the same time, it envisaged that territorial waters surrounding Spitzbergen would be considered as falling under the Common Fisheries Policy. Art2(1) of the Protocol granted customs-free import into the EU of coal, briquettes, ovoids, and similar solid fuels made from coal originating from Spitzbergen. Possible extension to other products would be in the hands of the Council of the EU (Art 2(2) of the Protocol). Art 2(4) of the Protocol introduced basic competition rules that were inspired by Arts 101, 102, and 107 TFEU to trade between Spitzbergen and the EU.

[24] Protocol No 3 to the Accession Treaty 1994.

[25] See, inter alia, James Ker-Lindsay, Fiona Mullen, and Hubert Faustmann (eds), *An Island in Europe: The EU and the Transformation of Cyprus* (IB Tauris 2011).

[26] For a detailed appraisal, see, inter alia, Dimitry Vladimirovich Kochenov, 'The Application of EU law in the EU's Overseas Regions, Countries, and Territories after the Entry into Force of the Treaty of Lisbon' (2012) 20 Michigan State International Law Review 669.

redundant with the passage of time. Neither of the protocols for Spitzbergen entered into force, as Norway did not join the EC in 1973, or the EU in 1995.[27] The initial status of Greenland changed in the 1980s, when it effectively withdrew from the EC.[28] Finally, as a knock-on effect of Brexit, the Channel Islands and the Isle of Man ceased being part of the EU customs union, and had their links with the EU severed.[29]

C. Other permanent derogations

The permanent derogations discussed thus far were tailor-made to accommodate territorial idiosyncrasies and, in case of the northern European countries, the indigenous population of Sami. The question remains, though, whether a degree of flexibility is available in other circumstances. As already explained, it is unlikely that the EU itself would request a general permanent opt-out from its flagship policies. What if, however, a desire to benefit from permanent derogation came from an applicant? The experience thus far demonstrates that some room for manoeuvre is on the menu, although it is strictly reserved for extraordinary circumstances. This was the case for Malta, which, due to its housing situation and limited land available for construction, was able to negotiate special derogations from the free movement of capital.[30] In a nutshell, Protocol No 6 to the Accession Treaty 2003 allows Malta to maintain restrictions on the purchase of secondary residences. It is notable that, in the case of some other newcomers in previous and subsequent enlargement rounds, only transitional periods for the purchasing of land or/and acquisition of secondary residences were negotiable.[31] The spectre of permanent derogations also overshadowed the failed accession negotiations of Iceland. Its government expressed a desire to benefit from a dedicated model for its participation in the Common Fisheries Policy. The lack of enthusiasm for this in Brussels was, in all likelihood, a contributing factor to suspension of the accession talks, and soon afterwards, a withdrawal of Iceland's application for EU membership.[32]

[27] For a detailed account of Norway's adventures with accessions to the EC/EU, see, inter alia, Clive Archer, *Norway Outside the European Union: Norway and European Integration from 1994 to 2004* (Routledge 2004).

[28] See, inter alia, Nils Ørvik, 'Greenland: The Politics of a New Northern Nation' (1984) 39 International Journal 932; Frederik Harhoff, 'Greenland's Withdrawal from the EC' (1983) 20 Common Market Law Review 13.

[29] Art 3(1c) EU–UK Withdrawal Agreement (Agreement on the withdrawal of the United Kingdom of Great Britain and Northern Ireland from the EU and the European Atomic Energy Community, [2020] OJ L29/7). On the impact of Brexit on Crown Dependencies, see EU Committee, *Brexit: the Crown Dependencies* (2016–17, HL 136).

[30] Roderick Pace, 'Malta and EU Membership: Overcoming "Vulnerabilities", Strengthening "Resilience"' (2006) 28 Journal of European Integration 33.

[31] See Section IV.G of the present chapter.

[32] Piotr Kobza, 'Accession of Iceland to the EU: A Failure beyond Repair?' (2017) 22 European Foreign Affairs Review 129, 143.

Piecemeal permanent derogations in technical matters are available too. They are usually introduced by means of technical adaptations of secondary legislation made qua the accession treaties (or secondary legislation). While many such adaptations are necessary to make EU legislation applicable to newcomers, and are indeed technical in name and substance,[33] some others introduce tailor-made measures which amount to permanent derogations. For instance, Sweden and Norway negotiated a derogation from the prohibition of the use of oral tobacco products laid down in Article 8a of Directive 89/662.[34] This was subject to a condition that the domestically produced tobacco would not be sold in the other EU Member States.[35] Another example, dating back to the most recent enlargement, is the non-application of rules on acquired rights in midwifery, which are laid down in Directive 2005/38, to several qualifications obtained in Croatia before 1 July 2013.[36] This built on previous arrangements, for instance in relation to professional qualifications obtained in Romania.[37]

III. Transitional Arrangements: *Raison d'être* and Typology

A. Introduction

This section of the chapter focuses on a variety of transitional arrangements which are at the heart of membership talks and, consequentially, of the accession treaties or related secondary legislation. For the sake of clarity, a fitting starting point is to decipher the notion of 'transitional arrangements', which is widely employed in the academic literature, including the present chapter.[38] It is an umbrella term encompassing all transitional measures envisaged in the accession treaties which provide for time-limited and scope-predetermined or *ex post* exceptions from the general rule that all new Member States are required to accept, as of the date of

[33] For instance, regular additions of the legal professions of the newcomers to Directive 98/5 on provision of legal services (Directive 98/5/EC of the European Parliament and of the Council of 16 February 1998 to facilitate practice of the profession of lawyer on a permanent basis in a Member State other than that in which the qualification was obtained [1998] OJ L77/36).

[34] Council Directive 89/622/EEC of 13 November 1989 on the approximation of the laws, regulations and administrative provisions of the Member States concerning the labelling of tobacco products [1989] OJ L359/1.

[35] Annex XV to Accession Treaty 1994.

[36] Annex III, pt 1b to Accession Treaty 2012, inserting Article 43b into Directive 2005/36 (Directive 2005/36/EC of the European Parliament and of the Council of 7 September 2005 on the recognition of professional qualifications [2005] OJ L225/22).

[37] This time, however, the derogations were introduced qua secondary legislation based on the Accession Treaty 2005: Council Directive 2006/100/EC of 20 November 2006 adapting certain Directives in the field of freedom of movement of persons, by reason of the accession of Bulgaria and Romania [2006] OJ L363/141.

[38] Kirstyn Inglis, 'The Accession Treaty and its Transitional Arrangements: A Twilight Zone for the New Members of the Union' in Christophe Hillion (ed), *EU Enlargement: A Legal Approach* (Hart 2004).

accession, the EU *acquis* as well as EU policies, and to be fully involved in the EU institutional framework. In effect, time-limited exceptions are acceptable, but—as already alluded to—some of them are *de facto* quasi-permanent. With all this in mind there are two questions that beg for answers at this stage of the analysis: firstly, why are such transitional arrangements needed? Secondly, what is their typology? Both questions are answered in turn.

B. *Raison d'être* behind transitional arrangements

A cliché as it may be, it is worth emphasizing that accession to the EU not only has political consequences but, first and foremost, is an exercise with profound legal and economic implications. On the date of accession, EU law, including the international agreements with third countries, starts to apply to every newcomer. This, as mentioned earlier, stems from the principle of immediate effect of EU law.[39] By the same token, a new Member State becomes a part of the EU internal market, is covered by the majority of EU policies, and joins the free trade areas created by the EU with countries around the world. However, as all previous enlargement rounds have proven, *ab initio* full participation in all dossiers falling under the competences of the EU is neither possible nor desired. Therefore, the transitional arrangements amount to idiosyncratic balancing acts. On the one hand, they make the new accessions possible, without inflicting the 'enlargement blues' that may be experienced should the rapprochement be delayed; on the other hand, they allow political, economic, and legal concerns of the EU and its members, as well as those of the candidates for EU membership, to be addressed and placated. Thus, the transitional arrangements are destined to serve not only the interests of the newcomers, but also those of the EU and its Member States. There is no doubt that the transitional arrangements discussed in this chapter have made the seven enlargement rounds possible. They have created, to use the words of Inglis, 'a Twilight Zone for the New Members of the Union'.[40] This, however, has come at the price of increased differentiation within the EU itself.

C. Typology of the transitional arrangements

Transitional arrangements have different faces, which makes development of a coherent typology a rather challenging endeavour.[41] Based on the criterion of the legal basis, one may distinguish between transitional arrangements which are

[39] Kalėda, 'Immediate Effect of Community Law' (n 6).
[40] Inglis, 'The Accession Treaty and its Transitional Arrangements' (n 38) 77.
[41] A number of attempts at a typology of transitional arrangements have been made in the academic literature. For instance, Ott divided them into four categories: temporary derogations, temporary

determined in the law and accidental derogations.[42] It goes without saying that, in the name of legal certainty, the former should be the norm, and the latter must be avoided at all costs. Alas, as experienced in the course of several enlargement rounds, delays in the translation of pre-accession EU *acquis* into the languages of the new Member States, and consequential delayed publication of the special editions of the Official Journal of the EU, have made EU legal acts unenforceable vis-à-vis individuals in the legal orders of the newcomers.[43] This was particularly concerning when it affected directly applicable legislation, in particular EU regulations. The first cases of such accidental derogations go back to the accession of Greece in 1981,[44] however a true avalanche was witnessed in the wake of the enlargements of 2004 and 2007.[45] In the case of the 2004 enlargement, the last volumes of the special edition in the languages of the new Member States were published almost two years after the enlargement.[46] For Bulgaria and Romania, approximately 50 per cent of EU *acquis* in their languages was not ready for publication on the date of accession.[47] These accidental derogations, although relatively short-lived, undermined the effectiveness of EU law in the new Member States, and made it inapplicable against individuals, in contravention of the principle of immediate effect of EU law.

All other transitional arrangements were properly regulated in the law and anchored in the accession treaties or secondary legislation. They can be grouped and classified on the basis of different criteria. Taking into account the criterion of the purpose they serve, one should first distinguish transitional periods, which are agreed to ahead of accession and permit phased-in application of EU *acquis* covered by their scope. Traditionally, these serve as tools to placate economic, legal, and political concerns of the EU, and of the newcomers. In general, the transitional

provisions, safeguard clauses, and transitional regimes: Andrea Ott, 'The "Principle" of Differentiation in an Enlarged EU. Unity in Diversity?' in Kirstyn Inglis and Andrea Ott (eds), *The Constitution for Europe and an Enlarging Union: Unity in Diversity?* (Europa Law Publishing 2005) 112.

[42] I borrow this term from Krystyna Kowalik-Bańczyk: Krystyna Kowalik-Bańczyk, 'Polish Transitional Periods relating to Four Freedoms—Temporary Derogations' (2004–2005) 27 Polish Yearbook of International Law 185, 188.

[43] Case C-161/06 *Skoma-Lux sro v Celní ředitelství Olomouc* [2007] ECLI:EU:C:2007:773.

[44] Case C-160/84 *Oryzomyli Kavallas OEE and others v Commission of the EC* [1986] ECLI:EU:C:1986:205.

[45] See, inter alia, Michal Bobek, 'The Binding Force of Babel: The Enforcement of EC Law Unpublished in the Languages of the New Member States' (2006–2007) 9 Cambridge Yearbook of European Legal Studies 43; Krzysztof Lasiński-Sulecki and Wojciech Morawski, 'Late Publication of EC law in Languages of New Member States and its Effects: Obligations on Individuals following the Court's Judgment in *Skoma-Lux*' (2008) 45 Common Market Law Review 705.

[46] Such accidental derogations should be distinguished from transitional arrangements on the language regime, which are determined in the law. For example, for the first three years after the 2004 enlargement, not all legal acts were published in Maltese (Council Regulation (EC) No 930/2004 of 1 May 2004 on temporary derogation measures relating to the drafting in Maltese of the acts of the institutions of the EU [2004] OJ L169/1).

[47] European Commission, 'Monitoring Report on the State of Preparedness for EU Membership of Bulgaria and Romania' COM (2006) 549 final, 32, 51.

periods are specified periods of time after the accession when meticulously listed pieces of EU legislation, or their parts, do not apply either in or to a new Member State. As will be further illustrated, transitional periods may be contrasted with temporary derogations permitting for post-accession suspension of application of selected rules, either because of economic aftershocks caused by the enlargement or as sanctions imposed by the EU for backtracking on commitments made by the newcomer. Finally, temporary arrangements include measures aiming at the gradual introduction of the new Member States into the EU institutional framework and selected EU policies. These, too, may serve economic, legal, or political ends. All of these measures are presented in further detail in the analysis that follows.

IV. Transitional Periods Applicable to/in New Member States

A. Introduction

Transitional periods became part and parcel of the accession process in the course of the first enlargement, in 1973. Since then, each and every accession treaty has provided a set of transitional periods permitting for time-barred exceptions from the general rule that EU law applies to the newcomers in its entirety as of the day of accession. In the early enlargement rounds the EU pursued a model of general transitional periods, supplemented by tailor-made solutions for selected areas of law.[48] As of the 1995 enlargement, the idea of general transitional periods has effectively been shelved, and the centre of gravity has moved to purely sectoral arrangements. The substantive scope and duration of the transitional periods has always been tailor-made to particular EU entrants, whether joining individually or in groups. However, some more universal patterns have also emerged. A good example in this respect are the transitional periods for free movement of workers, which followed exactly the same model in the 2004, 2007, and 2013 enlargement rounds. The evolving variety of transitional periods is also a mirror reflection of two key factors. Firstly, over the past four decades EU law has developed beyond recognition. As aptly noted by Advocate General Bobek, '[a]t present, the scope and breadth of EU law itself is simply unparalleled. Following the completion of the internal market and no fewer than five successive Treaty amendments, it has become difficult to find an area for which EU legislation is not available'.[49] Consequentially, some of the transitional periods featuring in the recent enlargements cover areas which did not fall under the competences of the EC at the time of the first three

[48] Art 9, Act on Conditions of Accession 1972; Art 9, Act on Conditions of Accession 1979.

[49] Opinion of Advocate General Bobek, Case C–561/19 *Consorzio Italian Management, Catania Multiservizi SpA v Rete Ferroviaria Italiana SpA*, ECLI:EU:C:2021:291, para 122.

accession rounds. Secondly, it has become a well-established practice for the EU to advance the economic rapprochement with, and between, the potential Member States well before the membership talks get off the ground. This, in turn, permits for creation of free trade areas ahead of accessions, which makes redundant the comprehensive transitional periods for free movement of goods which were ever so present in the Accession Treaties of 1972, 1979, and 1985. Furthermore, thanks to the evolution of the pre-accession policy, with introduction of conditionality and benchmarking, a lot of adjustments and reforms which initially took place in the early years of EC/EU membership are now required from the future Member States in the pre-accession phase.[50]

Transition periods are not only a thing of the past, however. It is more than likely that they will be key features of future accession treaties.[51] The question remains whether a shift of paradigm will take place. Thus far, transition periods have been considered as exceptions to the general rule that new Member States are bound by the EU *acquis* in its entirety from the first day of membership. Consequentially, their number and scope, by default, had to be limited. This may change with the prospective accession of Ukraine to the EU. As is well known, its application for membership was submitted within days of Russian invasion in early 2022. Ukraine became a candidate country shortly thereafter, and the green light to open accession talks was given by the European Council in December 2023. Bearing in mind the precariousness of the situation, and how EU enlargement has, once again, become a geopolitical issue, the idea of fast-track accession has been floated. In the present author's view, if it is to materialize, then—unlike the previous enlargement rounds—it will have to be subject to a plethora of lengthy transitional arrangements applicable in and to Ukraine. These would be necessary in order not to undermine the post-war economic recovery, on the one hand, and to placate concerns of the sceptical Member States, on the other.

Last but not least, it merits attention that the transitional periods are primarily negotiated during the membership talks and regulated in the accession treaties. However, as is well known, the rapprochement is a long and legally complex exercise. At the end of the negotiations a cut-off date is agreed to. It opens the door to finalization of the accession treaty, and its signing and ratification by the existing Member States, and—in the case of group accessions—at least one acceding country. These final stages take a few years to complete, yet at the same time, the EU functions normally, with new secondary legislation being adopted continuously.

[50] See further on conditionality and benchmarking, inter alia, Eli Gateva, *European Union Enlargement Conditionality* (Palgrave 2015).

[51] At the time this chapter was completed, the list of candidate countries with which accession negotiations were pending included Montenegro, Serbia, North Macedonia, and Albania, while such negotiations were expected to start with Ukraine and Moldova. Membership talks were also, theoretically, ongoing with Turkey, even though they have stalled over the past decade. The other candidate countries with which negotiations were yet to be opened included Bosnia & Herzegovina, and Georgia. Kosovo had the status of a potential candidate.

With this in mind, it is possible, at this stage, to negotiate additional transitional periods for the new EU *acquis*.[52] For this purpose, special *modi operandi* are provided in the accession treaties.[53]

To analyze all transitional periods in the seven accession treaties concluded thus far would surely exceed the remit of this chapter. However, it is fitting to resort to sampling, to elaborate further on some of the phenomena already discussed. The next sections take the reader on a historical journey, offering an overview of transitional periods covering the freedoms of the internal market, EU external relations, and environmental protection.

B. Free movement of goods

Free movement of goods is, undoubtedly, one of the flagship areas of European integration.[54] It has been at the heart of the EC/EU legal framework from the start, even though its emergence was gradual and subject to a transitional regime in its own right. Interestingly, in all seven EC/EU enlargements, transitional periods applicable to free movement of goods were envisaged. However, when the first three accession treaties are juxtaposed with the ones that followed, a major paradigm shift becomes visible. For the purposes of the 1973, 1981, and 1986 enlargement rounds, the EC and the acceding countries opted to be ring-fenced from the potential economic shock waves caused by the enlargements, by providing for a gradual abolition of various barriers to trade, including customs duties.[55] When the UK, Ireland, and Denmark joined the EC in 1973, their economic rapprochement was advanced yet incomplete. Arguably, the same was the case with the EC themselves, where the internal customs duties were abolished in the late 1960s, and the customs union was only just becoming a reality. None of the three countries, or Norway for that matter, had free trade agreements with the EC prior to the accession. Yet, at the same time, the UK, Norway, and Denmark liberalized trade

[52] This opportunity was utilized by Slovenia in relation to Regulation 1228/2003 (Regulation (EC) No 1228/2003 of the European Parliament and of the Council of 26 June 2003 on conditions for access to the network for cross-border exchanges in electricity [2003] OJ L176/1. The regulation in question was adopted on 26 June 2003, ie after the signature but before the entry into force of the Accession Treaty 2003. When requesting a transitional period, the Slovenian government relied on economic argumentation, claiming that application of the proposed rules would have a detrimental impact on the Slovenian energy-intensive industries. The request was granted in Regulation 1223/2004 granting Slovenia a transitional period until 1 July 2007 (Council Regulation (EC) No 1223/2004 of 28 June 2004 amending Regulation (EC) No 1228/2003 of the European Parliament and of the Council as regards the date of application of certain provisions to Slovenia [2004] OJ L233/3).

[53] For instance, in relation to Croatia, Art 49 Act of Conditions of Accession 2012.

[54] See, inter alia, Laurence W Gormley, *EU Law of Free Movement of Goods and Customs Union* (OUP 2009).

[55] As a backup option, the economic safeguard clauses were included, too. See, further, Section V.C. of the present chapter.

between themselves qua EFTA,[56] while the UK and Ireland benefited from a bilateral free trade deal. The end result of the EC accession talks was a set of transitional arrangements envisaged in the Act on Conditions of Accession 1972. To start with, Article 32 of the Act provided for a general gradual abolition of the customs duties on imports, by 1 July 1977 at the latest.[57] A progressive abolition of charges having equivalent effect on imports was also regulated in the Act. The customs duties on exports, and charges having equivalent effect, were due to disappear by 1 January 1974.[58] At the same time, an earlier suspension of any import or export duties was perfectly permissible, as per Article 34 of the Act. The situation was much more complicated politically and economically with the accessions of Greece, Spain, and Portugal. In all three cases, the countries joining the EC were in rather precarious economic positions after the fall of military juntas and dictatorships. Furthermore, the implementation of trade agreements with the EC was not advanced enough to facilitate frictionless trade as of the date of accession. Hence, both of the relevant accession treaties provided for gradual elimination of customs duties, and phased in application of the EU free movement of goods *acquis*.[59]

In subsequent accessions, such temporary regimes were no longer required, as the countries proceeding with rapprochement were, at their respective cut-off points, already benefiting from tariff-free trade with the EU qua the EEA,[60] or tailor-made association agreements.[61] Furthermore, the trade between the Central and Eastern European countries which joined the EU in 2004 and 2007 had already been liberalized thanks to the Central European Free Trade Area.[62] Thus, horizontal transitional periods were no longer desired, and temporary arrangements targeting selected pieces of the EU *acquis* sufficed.[63] Neither Bulgaria nor Romania benefited from transitional periods in the area in

[56] See further on EFTA, inter alia, Georges Baur, *The European Free Trade Association: An Intergovernmental Platform for Trade Relations* (Intersentia 2020).

[57] The basic duty that served as the benchmark for reductions was the duty applied on 1 January 1972. The timetable for reductions was as follows: as of 1 April 1973, the existing duties were due for reduction by 80 per cent. A further four reductions of 20 per cent each were due on 1 January 1974, 1 January 1975, 1 January 1976, and 1 July 1977. See, further, Art 32 of the Act.

[58] Art 37 of the Act on Conditions of Accession 1972.

[59] See further, inter alia, Loukas Tsoukalis, *The European Community and its Mediterranean Enlargement* (George Allen & Unwin 1981); Dudley Seers and Constantine Vaitsos (eds), *The Second Enlargement of the EEC: The Integration of Unequal Partners* (Macmillan Press 1982).

[60] Agreement on the European Economic Area [1994] OJ L1/3. See further, inter alia, Finn Arnesen, Halvard Haukeland Fredriksen, Hans Petter Graver, Ola Mestad, and Christoph Vedder (eds), *Agreement on the European Economic Area: A Commentary* (Hart/Nomos 2018).

[61] Alan Mayhew, *Recreating Europe: The European Union's Policy towards Central and Eastern Europe* (CUP 1998); Andrea Ott and Kirstyn Inglis (eds), *Handbook on European Enlargement: A Commentary on the Enlargement Process* (TMC Asser Press 2002).

[62] See, further, Martin Dangerfield, *Subregional Economic Cooperation in Central and Eastern Europe: The Political Economy of CEFTA* (Edward Elgar 2000).

[63] For instance, Lithuania negotiated a transitional period in relation to Directive 2001/82/EC (Directive 2001/82/EC of the European Parliament and of the Council of 6 November 2001 on the Community code relating to veterinary medicinal products [2001] OJ L311/1).

question. Croatia negotiated a transitional period in relation to Directive 2001/83/EC.[64]

Bearing in mind that the association agreements with the remaining candidate and potential candidate countries of the Western Balkans, Ukraine, Moldova, and Georgia envisage creation of free trade areas with the EU, a comparable approach is expected in the future accession treaties.[65] The same applies to Turkey, which benefits from the customs union for industrial products with the EU (regardless of its ever-shrinking chances of becoming a Member State).[66] Thus, arguably, the era of long transitional periods for the freedom of the internal market has come to an end.

C. External policies of the EU

By joining the EU, new Member States are expected to become fully involved not only in the internal policies of the EU but also in its external activities towards the outside world. This includes, inter alia, the Common Foreign and Security Policy, which is the political arm of the external dimension, as well as the Common Commercial Policy. It is the latter that has considerable legal and economic implications for the newcomers. It is a well-known phenomenon that the EC, and subsequently the EU, have pursued a trade agenda from the early days.[67] As things stood in 2024, the EU and its Member States benefited from a wide web of international agreements with countries around the world. These took different shapes and forms, stretching from comprehensive arrangements for trade, and flanking

[64] As per Annex V, pt 1 of the Act on Conditions of Accession 2011, Croatia benefited from a transitional period for Directive 2001/83/EC (Directive 2001/83/EC of the European Parliament and of the Council of 6 November 2001 on the Community code relating to medicinal products for human use [2001] OJ L311/67).

[65] Stabilisation and Association Agreement between the EC and their Member States, of the one part, and the Former Yugoslav Republic of Macedonia, of the other part [2004] OJ L84/1; Stabilisation and Association Agreement between the EC and their Member States, of the one part, and the Republic of Albania, of the other part [2009] OJ L107/116; Stabilisation and Association Agreement between the EC and their Member States, of the one part, and the Republic of Montenegro, of the other part [2010] OJ L108/3; Stabilisation and Association Agreement between the EC and their Member States, of the one part, and the Republic of Serbia, of the other part [2013] OJ L278/14; Stabilisation and Association Agreement between the EC and their Member States, of the one part, and Bosnia and Herzegovina, of the other part [2015] OJ L164/2; Stabilisation and Association Agreement between the EU and the European Atomic Energy Community, of the one part, and Kosovo*, of the other part [2016] OJ L71/3; Association Agreement between the EU and the European Atomic Energy Community and its Member States, of the one part, and Ukraine, of the other part [2014] OJ L161/3; Association Agreement between the EU and the European Atomic Energy Community and their Member States, of the one part, and Georgia, of the other part [2014] OJ L261/4; Association Agreement between the EU and the European Atomic Energy Community and their Member States, of the one part, and the Republic of Moldova, of the other part [2014] OJ L260/4.

[66] Agreement of 12 September 1963 establishing an Association between the European Economic Community and Turkey [1977] OJ L361/29.

[67] Billy A Melo Araujo, *The EU Deep Trade Agenda: Law and Policy* (OUP 2016).

policies, to sectoral agreements covering, for instance, air transport. For countries joining the EU, this translates into an obligation to bring their own international commitments into compliance with those of the EU and its Member States. In the contemporary pre-accession policy, this amounts to the obligation to terminate all international agreements which are not compatible with EU commitments, especially those falling into the realms of the EU's exclusive external competences. The EU agreements start to apply to newcomers as of the date of accession; however, many of them have to be supplemented by tailor-made protocols negotiated by the EU with the third countries to reflect the changes in the EU's composition. Furthermore, one of the conditions of EU membership is compulsory accession to the European Economic Area (EEA).[68] This is the subject of a separate accession treaty, which is negotiated in the shadows of the EU membership talks.[69] In the cases of Spain, Portugal, Austria, Finland, Sweden, and Norway, the respective accession treaties envisaged an explicit obligation to withdraw from the European Free Trade Association (EFTA).[70]

Contemporarily, any transitional periods for external commitments are, arguably, not negotiable. However, this was not the case during the early enlargements of the EC, when all newcomers were given time after their accession to bring their international commitments into compliance with those of the EC.[71] In the case of the first enlargement, this was one of the most contentious dossiers for the UK, which, as is well known, had special political and trade links with the countries of the Commonwealth.[72] The bone of contention per se was not a handful of early trade agreements that the EC had at the time with third countries, but rather the consequences for trade of the UK's participation in the Common Agricultural Policy (CAP). The latter had considerable impact on the EC's trade with, inter alia, Australia and New Zealand. Not surprisingly, it created a lot of political and economic friction.[73] This explains the transitional periods, for instance, on the application of the EEC Agreement with African and Malagasy states;[74] the EEC

[68] Art 128 EEA.

[69] For instance, Agreement on the participation of the Republic of Croatia in the European Economic Area [2014] L 170/18.

[70] Arts 182 and 369, Act on Conditions of Accession 1985; Arts 61, 78, 104, 130, Act on Conditions of Accession 1994.

[71] See, inter alia, Arts 108–19, Act on Conditions of Accession 1972; Arts 115–23, Act on Conditions of Accession 1979; Arts 177–83 (Spain) and 364–70 (Portugal), Act on Conditions of Accession 1985; Arts 55–62 (Norway), Arts 73–78 (Austria), Arts 97–105 (Finland), Arts 126–31 (Sweden), Act on Conditions of Accession 1994.

[72] The relations with the Commonwealth were one of the reasons for the UK's initial refusal to participate in the emerging EC, as well as the failure of early attempts at accession. See, inter alia, Stuart Ward, 'Anglo-Commonwealth Relations and EEC Membership: The Problem of the Old Dominions' in George Wilkes (ed), *Britain's Failure to Enter the European Community 1961–63: The Enlargement Negotiations and Crises in European, Atlantic and Commonwealth Relations* (Routledge 1997).

[73] See, inter alia, Alexander Downer, 'Australia (and New Zealand) after the 1973 "Great Betrayal"' in Martin Westlake (ed), *Outside the EU: Options for Britain* (Agenda Publishing 2020).

[74] As per Arts 109–15, Act on Conditions of Accession, the agreement in question did not apply to the new Member States from their date of accession until 31 January 1975 (Convention d'association

Agreement with Tanzania, Uganda, and Kenya;[75] and the importation of butter and cheese from New Zealand into the UK;[76] as well as the transitional regime for importation of sugar from countries/territories falling under the Commonwealth Sugar Agreement.[77] Trade with non-EEC states was also one of the crucial topics during the accession negotiations with Greece. The end result was a complex set of transitional periods covering several EU legal acts, permitting the newcomer to gradually abolish quantitative restrictions in trade with non-EEC states.[78] Tailor-made provisions were also negotiated in relation to trade agreements, allowing for additional transitional periods to be determined during the negotiations of post-enlargement protocols to such agreements.[79] The situation evolved in a comparable fashion in the next two enlargement rounds, with a clear phase-out tendency in the case of the 1995 enlargement.[80] As already mentioned, since the 'big bang' enlargement of 2004 no transitional periods in the area in question are available to newcomers. This is unlikely to change in the future, unless special circumstances arise.[81]

D. Free movement of workers

Free movement of workers is traditionally one of the most contentious dossiers in the accession negotiations.[82] This, in particular, has been the case with countries which at the point of entry had a lower gross domestic product (GDP) than the existing Member States. For their citizens, the prospect of free access to the labour markets of other countries has been a very appealing proposition, and frequently one of the main factors driving the public support for accession. Yet, the

entre la Communauté économique européenne et les États africains et malgache associés à cette Communauté [1964] OJ 93/1431).

[75] Agreement establishing an Association between the European Economic Community and the United Republic of Tanzania, the Republic of Uganda and the Republic of Kenya [1970] OJ L282/94.

[76] Protocol No 18 to Accession Treaty 1972.

[77] Protocol No 19 to Accession Treaty 1972.

[78] Arts 115–17 of the Act on Conditions of Accession 1979 and Annexes V–VII to the Accession Treaty 1979.

[79] Arts 118–22 of the Act on Conditions of Accession 1979.

[80] Arts 177–83 (Spain), Arts 364–70 (Portugal), Act on Conditions of Accession 1985; Art 56 (Norway), Art 74 (Austria), Art 99 (Finland), Act on Conditions of Accession 1994.

[81] It is worth noting that a lack of transitional periods may be particularly problematic for Georgia if it wishes to pursue its rapprochement with the EU in the future. Its main trading partners include, apart from Turkey, also Russia and China. Georgia has free trade agreements with Russia and China, neither of which has a free trade agreement with the EU. Therefore, joining the EU and terminating bilateral trade agreements to which Georgia is a party may be detrimental to the Georgian business community. Lack of geographical proximity to EU Member States and poor transport links will, arguably, make it more difficult to change patterns of trade ahead of EU accession. Thus, some transitional periods may be necessary.

[82] See further on free movement of persons, inter alia, Nicola Rogers, Rick Scannell, and John Walsh, *Free Movement of Persons in the Enlarged European Union* (2nd edn, Sweet & Maxwell 2012).

probability of a large influx of migrant workers made alarm bells ring in the existing Member States. To placate these concerns, transitional periods for free movement of workers have become a permanent feature in the accession treaties, starting with the first enlargement in 1973. This is the area in which the differentiation brought by most enlargement rounds is particularly visible.[83]

The accession of the UK, Ireland, Denmark, and Norway did not raise major concerns in the original six Member States of the EC. In fact, it was the UK and Ireland that requested, and benefited from, a transitional period on free movement of workers. This translated into a temporary waiver from the rules laid down in Directive 68/360.[84] Both countries were permitted to retain, until 31 December 1977, the national rules requiring a prior authorization for access to, and taking up employment in, the Republic of Ireland and Northern Ireland.[85] Furthermore, Ireland was permitted, for a period of five years, to limit access to social assistance, in particular to unemployment benefits.[86] Restrictions on the free movement of workers became a matter of serious concern for the existing EU Member States around the time of rapprochement of Greece, Spain, and Portugal. This was reflected in lengthy transitional periods envisaged in both of the relevant accession treaties. In relation to Greece, a seven-year transition concerning application of parts of Regulation 1612/68[87] and Directive 68/360 was provided for.[88] Furthermore, a three-year transitional period for application of selected provisions of Regulation 1408/71 was regulated in the Accession Treaty 1979.[89] It is worth noting that the transitional period worked both ways; put differently, Greece was permitted to introduce restrictions on nationals of the other Member States. A very similar solution, envisaging a seven-year transition, was followed in relation to Spain and Portugal.[90] Interestingly, another layer of differentiation was added by Article 56 of the Act on Conditions of Accession 1985. It allowed Luxembourg and Spain to keep restrictions on movement of workers for an extra three years, ie until 31 December 1995. In the 1995 enlargement, restrictions on free movement of workers were off the agenda. The reason was rather

[83] See, inter alia, Andrea Ott, 'Differentiation through Accession Law: Free Movement Rights in an Enlarged European Union' in de Witte, Ott, and Vos (n 4).

[84] Council Directive 68/360/EEC of 15 October 1968 on the abolition of restrictions on movement and residence within the Community for workers of Member States and their families [1968] OJ L257/13.

[85] Annex VII, s VII of Act on Conditions of Accession 1972.

[86] This transitional period extended to Regulation 1408/71 (Regulation (EEC) No 1408/71 of the Council of 14 June 1971 on the application of social security schemes to employed persons and their families moving within the Community [1971] L 149/2).

[87] Regulation (EEC) No 1612/68 of the Council of 15 October 1968 on freedom of movement for workers within the Community [1968] OJ L257/2.

[88] Arts 44–46, Act on Conditions of Accession 1979.

[89] ibid Art 48.

[90] Arts 55–60, Act on Conditions of Accession 1985.

self-explanatory: all four EFTA countries aspiring for EU membership were, at the time of accession, part of the EEA. Thus, they were fully in sync with the EU *acquis* on movement of people.[91] Not surprisingly, transitional periods on movement of workers were back on the negotiation table in the next three enlargement rounds. Except for Malta and Cyprus, all other candidate countries suffered from lower levels of economic development, and consequentially, there was a risk of mass migrations to the West. As already alluded to, the Accession Treaty 2003 offered a solution which was based on the prior arrangements but, at the same time, was far more nuanced than the transitional periods that had been envisaged for Greece, Spain, and Portugal. In hindsight, it created a paradigm which has been followed since, and is quite likely to be re-employed in the next rounds of enlargement. While it followed the model of seven-year-long transitional periods known from the Mediterranean enlargements, the legal framework became more complex.[92] The existing EU Member States were permitted to restrict access to their labour markets for an initial period of two years, which could automatically be extended for a further three years. If, however, there was a risk of disturbances to the labour markets, a final extension for a further two years was available. However, this final extension would be subject to a formal notification to the European Commission. It is notable that this system applied only to eight Central and Eastern European countries, which joined on 1 May 2004. *Au contraire*, it did not extend to Malta or Cyprus. Furthermore, it allowed the newcomers to maintain adequate restrictions on access to their own labour markets. Finally, the existing Member States, which had opted to liberalize their immigration regimes, were permitted to bring back the restrictions on economic grounds (but only for the remained of the seven year transitional period).[93] As already alluded to, the same model of transitional period was followed in the next two enlargement rounds, and may serve as a paradigm for future accessions.[94]

[91] Still, however, Joint Declaration No 16 on free movement of workers, which was attached to the Accession Treaty 1994, envisaged that, should the Austrian labour market suffer from difficulties, the EU institutions would attend to the matter.

[92] See further, inter alia, Michael Dougan, 'A Spectre is Haunting Europe ... Free Movement of Persons and the Eastern Enlargement' in Christophe Hillion (ed) (n 38); Sergio Carrera, 'What Does Free Movement Mean in Theory and Practice in an Enlarged EU?' (2005) 11 European Law Journal 699; Iris Goldner Lang, *From Association to Accession: How Free is the Free Movement of Persons in the EU?* (Eleven International Publishing 2011); Ott, 'Differentiation through Accession Law' (n 83).

[93] This option was not used vis-à-vis the 2004 entrants. However, when the eurozone crisis hit, Spain was permitted to reintroduce restrictions on Romanian nationals under the terms of the Accession Treaty 2007. See European Commission, 'The Commission Accepts that Spain Can Temporarily Restrict the Free Movement of Romanian Workers', Press release, 11 August 2011.

[94] See further, inter alia, Adam Łazowski, 'And Then They Were Twenty-Seven ... A Legal Appraisal of the Sixth Accession Treaty' (2007) 44 Common Market Law Review 401, 422–25; Adam Łazowski, 'EU do not Worry, Croatia is behind you: A Commentary on the Seventh Accession Treaty' (2012) 8 Croatian Yearbook of European Law & Policy 1, 24–28.

F. Right of establishment and free movement of services

Neither the right of establishment nor the free movement of services have attracted much attention during the accession negotiations thus far. While transitional periods in relation to these were envisaged in several accession treaties, they were not as comprehensive and far-reaching as was the case with the other freedoms of the internal market. The first major transitional period was provided for Portugal, in Article 221 of the Act on Conditions of Accession 1985. The authorities in Lisbon were permitted to maintain restrictions on establishment and services in the travel and tourist agencies sector (until 31 December 1988), and in the cinema sector (until 31 December 1990). In the 1995 enlargement round, Norway was permitted to keep restrictions on ownership of fishing vessels by non-nationals for a period of three years after accession.[95] This, of course, proved to be of no relevance as, following the accession referendum, the Norwegian authorities had no choice but to withdraw their membership application. Interestingly, no horizontal transitional periods for self-employed people were envisaged in the 2004, 2007, and 2011 Accession Treaties. This is particularly puzzling when one takes into account a paradigm shift from employment to self-employment in the economies of several EU Member States. Put differently, bearing in mind the popularity of self-employment, one would expect a corollary transitional period to the already-discussed restrictions on free movement of workers. Without any such period in place, the migratory movements that many old EU Member States had feared started immediately after 1 May 2004. The Accession Treaty 2003 provided only for transitional periods for the posting of workers in selected sectors applicable to Austria and Germany. Similar arrangements were also provided in the Accession Treaty 2005, for Bulgaria and Romania,[96] as well as the Accession Treaty 2011, for Croatia.[97] It should be added that transitional periods from individual pieces of the EU *acquis* were also available. For instance, Estonia negotiated such temporary arrangements[98] in relation to Directive 94/19/EC on deposit-guarantee schemes[99] and Directive 97/9/EC on investor-compensation schemes.[100] In a similar vein, Bulgaria and Romania benefited from transitional periods for application of the latter Directive.[101]

[95] Art 35, Act on Conditions of Accession 1994.
[96] Annex VI, pt 1, Act on Conditions of Accession 2005.
[97] Annex VII, pt 1, Act on Conditions of Accession 2011.
[98] Annex VI, pt 2, Act on Conditions of Accession 2003.
[99] Directive 94/19/EC of the European Parliament and of the Council of 30 May 1994 on deposit-guarantee schemes [1994] OJ L135/5.
[100] Directive 97/9/EC of the European Parliament and of the Council of 3 March 1997 on investor-compensation schemes [1997] OJ L84/22.
[101] Annexes VI and VII, pts 2 of the Act on Conditions of Accession 2005.

G. Free movement of capital

Free movement of capital, being one of the freedoms of the internal market, is also traditionally under the microscope during the membership talks.[102] Starting with the accession of the UK, Ireland, and Denmark, transitional periods for different aspects of capital and payment movements have taken a prominent place in the political discourse, and in the accession treaties. To begin with, all 1973 entrants were allowed to defer the liberalization of some capital movements.[103] When Greece joined, it was permitted to defer liberalization of direct investments for four years after EEC entry. Furthermore, it was authorized to maintain, until 31 December 1985, national rules on real estate investments of its own citizens and residents in other Member States.[104] Spain and Portugal followed suit. Both newcomers were allowed to derogate from a plethora of rules governing the free movement of capital; however, the system of temporary exemptions was much more comprehensive in the case of Portugal than of Spain.[105] For instance, Portugal was permitted to keep, until 31 December 1992, restrictions on transfers relating to real estate investment in other EEC Member States which were applicable to those who resided in Portugal, and whose transfers were not related to the exercise of free movement of workers or freedom of establishment.[106] For the next wave of enlargement, a uniform transitional period for Norway, Austria, Finland, and Sweden was envisaged in the Accession Treaty 1994. All four countries were permitted to maintain restrictions in relation to secondary residences for a period of five years after their accession.[107] Furthermore, Finland was permitted to apply, for an extra year, the rules limiting foreigners from acquisition of Finnish undertakings.[108] In the case of the 'big bang' enlargement of 2004, requests for transitional periods came once again from the newcomers. The *raison d'être* for these was a proper Molotov's cocktail of reality and fantasy. On the one hand, there were justified fears as to the potential popularity of cheap agricultural land and real property. On the other hand, the issue was relentlessly used in the public discourse by anti-EU parties, in particular in Poland and Hungary. In the former case, the prospect of liberalization of capital movements fuelled obsessions that German nationals and companies would rush to purchase land in the parts of Poland which had formed part of the territory

[102] Further, on free movement of capital, see Steffen Hindelang, *The Free Movement of Capital and Foreign Direct Investment: The Scope of Protection in EU Law* (OUP 2009).

[103] Arts 120–26 of the Act on Conditions of Accession 1972.

[104] Arts 49–56 of the Act on Conditions of Accession 1979.

[105] Arts 61–66 (Spain) and Arts 222–32 (Portugal) of the Act on Conditions of Accession 1985.

[106] ibid Art 227.

[107] Art 34 (Norway), Art 70 (Austria), Art 87 (Finland), Art 114 (Sweden) of the Act on Conditions of Accession 1994. It should be noted that the requests for permanent derogations, along the lines of the opt-out negotiated by Denmark after its accession to the EC, was rejected by the EU. See Marc Jorna, 'The Accession Negotiations with Austria, Sweden, Finland and Norway: A Guided Tour' (1995) 10 European Law Review 131, 136–37.

[108] Art 86 of the Act on Conditions of Accession 1994.

of the Third Reich before World War II .[109] The transitional periods provided in the Accession Treaty 2003 varied in time frame and scope. For instance, Poland was permitted to maintain restrictions in relation to the purchase of agricultural land and forests for twelve years after EU accession.[110] In the case of Hungary, the transitional period for maintaining restrictions on access to agricultural land was seven years, with a possibility of extension for a further three years, albeit subject to the permission of the European Commission.[111] It is worth remembering that, at the same time, Malta negotiated the already-discussed permanent derogation on secondary residences.[112] Similar patterns emerged in the subsequent two rounds of enlargement: Bulgaria, Romania, and Croatia successfully negotiated transitional periods for acquisition of land and secondary residences.[113] As is the case with selected other transitional periods discussed in this section of the chapter, some of the arrangements found in the accession treaties concluded thus far may serve as a point of departure, or even a model, in the future enlargements of the EU.

H. Environmental protection

Environmental protection also deserves inclusion in this rather selective *tour de table* of transitional periods, for several reasons. Firstly, it demonstrates how the transitional periods have, over the years, adjusted to developments in EU competences and, consequentially, in the EU *acquis*. At the time of the early enlargement rounds, the EC were not equipped with specific powers to regulate environmental protection. The pivotal change came in the late 1980s, with the approval of the Single European Act.[114] As argued by Sikora, the area in question has, since then, undergone a constitutionalization in EU law.[115] In the accession context, all of this has translated into a web of complex transitional periods relating to the EU environmental *acquis* in the consecutive enlargement rounds. In the 1995 enlargement, the main problem was that the countries joining the EU benefited from higher environmental standards than those provided by the emerging EU secondary legislation. Thus, the transitional period was designed to allow the EU to catch up,

[109] See, further, Janusz Świerkocki, 'Economic Aspects of Purchasing Real Estate by Foreigners in Poland' in Dariusz Milczarek and Alojzy Z Nowak (eds), *On the Road to the European Union: Applicant Countries' Perspective* (Warsaw University Centre for Europe 2003).

[110] Annex XII, pt 4, Act on Conditions of Accession 2003.

[111] ibid Annex X, pt 3.

[112] See, further, Christophe Hillion, 'The European Union is Dead. Long Live the European Union ... A Commentary on the Treaty of Accession 2003' (2004) 29 European Law Review 583, 601.

[113] Annex VI, pt 3 (Bulgaria), Annex VII, pt 3 (Romania), Act on Conditions of Accession 2005; Annex V, pt 3, Act on Conditions of Accession 2011. See, further, Łazowski, 'And Then They Were' (n 94) 425–26; Łazowski, 'EU do not Worry' (n 94) 28–29.

[114] Single European Act [1987] OJ L169/1.

[115] Alicja Sikora, *Constitutionalisation of Environmental Protection in EU Law* (Europa Law Publishing 2020).

rather than, as has been the case since, to permit the newcomers to upgrade their standards after accession.[116] Thus, the following enlargement rounds have brought lengthy transitional periods. The truth of the matter was that full approximation of the national laws of the Central and Eastern European countries with EU environmental rules was simply beyond the means of the State coffers and the budgets of the business community. As an example, one can take a closer look at a randomly picked transitional period available to Croatia as per the Accession Treaty 2011. Croatia benefited from the right to waive the implementation of requirements for collecting systems and treatment of urban waste water as per Directive 91/271.[117] The temporary regime designed by the Accession Treaty provided for a gradual phasing in of the legislation in question, first in relation to agglomerations exceeding 15,000 inhabitants, and then, finally, in relation to small towns and villages where the population exceeded 2,000 inhabitants. In the case of the former, the transitional period expired on 31 December 2018, however as far as the latter is concerned, Croatia had to comply with the Directive by the end of 2023.[118] This, in fact, was a little over a decade after its accession to the EU. No doubt such a lengthy temporary arrangement was dictated by the economic concerns expressed by the Croatian authorities during the accession talks. As argued earlier in this chapter, it was one of the measures that made the EU enlargement possible.

Similar transitional periods can be expected when some or all of the current candidate and potential candidate countries join the EU. At the same time, however, their room for manoeuvre will be a bit more limited, as the obligation to approximate with the EU environmental *acquis* is one of the conditions of participation in the Energy Community, of which they are all members.[119] The situation is rather complex when it comes to Ukraine, Moldova, and Georgia. Their respective association agreements, on top of the Energy Community obligations, already require a large-scale approximation with the EU environmental *acquis*. Thus, should their EU membership materialize, it would, in general terms, reduce the need to ask for transitional periods applicable after the accession.[120] Having said that, one should be mindful of the precarious situation of Ukraine. The Russian full-scale invasion has, apart from anything else, brought environmental damage of unprecedented scale. Hence, renegotiation of existing Ukraine's commitments in the area

[116] See, further, Sanja Bogojević and Mirjana Drenovak-Ivanović, 'Environmental Protection through the Prism of Enlargement: Time For Reflection' (2019) 56 Common Market Law Review 949; Francisco Granell, 'The European Union's Enlargement Negotiations with Austria, Finland, Norway and Sweden' (1995) 33 Journal of Common Market Studies 117, 129.

[117] Council Directive 91/271/EEC of 21 May 1991 concerning urban waste-water treatment [1991] OJ L135/40.

[118] Annex V, pt 2, Act on Conditions of Accession 2011.

[119] See further, inter alia, Dirk Buschle and Kim Talus (eds), *The Energy Community: A New Energy Governance System* (Intersentia 2015).

[120] For instance, in relation to Ukraine, see Michael Emerson and Veronika Movchan (eds), *Deepening EU–Ukrainian Relations: What, Why and How?* (2nd edn, CEPS 2018) 186–97.

in question may prove to be necessary and transitional periods may be requested during the membership talks.

V. Temporary Derogations

A. Introduction

Another category of transitional arrangements which are part of the enlargement *acquis* are temporary derogations. As argued earlier, this group comprises various types of measures which may be taken post-accession, in order to placate negative economic consequences of enlargement or to ensure compliance with membership commitments undertaken during the negotiations. Analysis of all enlargement rounds thus far demonstrates a number of phenomena. Firstly, the catalogue of possible temporary derogations has grown over the years. Secondly, the temporary derogations have largely remained an 'emergency hatch' that one would have recourse to only in extreme cases. In the analysis that follows, temporary derogations tailor-made for particular newcomers are discussed, as the starting point (Section B). This paves the way for an exegesis focusing on safeguard clauses traditionally envisaged in the accession treaties (Sections C and D).

B. Tailor-made individual temporary derogations

Experience of the past enlargement rounds proves that negotiation of tailor-made temporary derogations, which can be triggered after accession, is possible. This may happen when the newcomers or the EU face 'what if?' dilemmas. Put differently, it may be necessary to introduce additional restrictions because a negotiated transitional period has proven to be too short, or a possibility of temporary derogation may be provided instead of a transitional period, only to be used should extraordinary circumstances arise. Thus, these two types of transitional arrangements may be inextricably linked with one another. The Accession Treaty 2003 provided us with very good examples of both. As already mentioned, several newcomers negotiated transitional periods for land and/or real estate ownership. In the case of the Czech Republic, Estonia, Latvia, Lithuania, Hungary, and Slovakia, a recourse to a safeguard clause was available on the expiry of the transitional periods. Qua permissive decisions of the European Commission, a further three-year extension of transitional periods by means of temporary derogations was possible.[121]

[121] Annex V, pt 2 (Czech Republic), Annex VI, pt 3 (Estonia), Annex VIII, pt 3 (Latvia), Annex IX, pt 3 (Lithuania), Annex X, pt 3 (Hungary), Annex XIV, pt 3 (Slovakia) to Act on Conditions of Accession 2003.

At the same time, Slovenia, which did not benefit from a transitional period, reserved the right to employ, in relation to access to its real estate market, the general economic safeguard clause laid down in Article 37 of the Act on Conditions of Accession 2003 for an additional four years (on the top of the three years envisaged therein).[122] Furthermore, while Malta was not covered by the transitional period on free movement of workers, it could have had recourse to a temporary derogation in the event of disturbances to its labour market.[123]

C. Economic safeguard clause

As of the first enlargement of the EC, the accession treaties provided economic safeguard clauses.[124] These could be triggered for a fixed period of time after the enlargement, on the initiative of the existing Member States or the newcomers, to placate negative economic consequences of recent accession. The institution in charge has always been the European Commission. Arguably, the economic safeguard clauses have, for years, played the role of Chekhov's gun: always an essential part of the story, and occasionally used in practice. It should be noted that the economic safeguard clauses have been time-limited, available for at least a three-year period[125] after enlargements.[126] This, as the already-mentioned example of Slovenia and free movement of capital proves, could be subject to variations. The economic safeguard clauses allowed for derogations from the EU *acquis*, which were, however, subject to numerous caveats. Firstly, they could not go beyond what was strictly necessary, in relation to both their scope and their duration. Secondly, priority was to be given to the measures least disturbing the internal market. A good example of the economic safeguard clause in action was Commission Decision 81/988 permitting France to restrict imports of cotton yarn from Greece.[127] While, in itself, it is now largely forgotten, the challenge to its legality has become a classic case on the *locus standi* of individuals to request a judicial review of EU acts.[128]

[122] ibid Annex XIII, pt 4.

[123] ibid Annex XI, pt 2.

[124] Art 135, Act on Conditions of Accession 1972; Art 130, Act on Conditions of Accession 1979; Art 379, Act on Conditions of Accession 1985; Art 152, Act on Conditions of Accession 1994; Art 37, Act on Conditions of Accession 2003; Art 36, Act on Conditions of Accession 2005; Art 37, Act on Conditions of Accession 2011.

[125] In case of accession of Sweden, Finland, and Austria, the economic safeguard clause was available for only one year after accession: Art 152, Act on Conditions of Accession 1994.

[126] For instance, Art 130(1), Act on Conditions of Accession 1979, and Art 379, Act on Conditions of Accession 1985 allowed for the triggering of the safeguard clause for an additional three years in relation to products or sectors in respect of which the accession treaties allowed for transitional periods of equivalent duration.

[127] Commission Decision 81/988/EEC of 30 October 1981 authorizing the French Republic to take protective measures with regard to imports of cotton yarn from Greece [1981] OJ L362/33.

[128] Case 11/82 *SA Piraiki-Patraiki and others v Commission of the European Communities* [1985] ECLI:EU:C:1985:18.

D. Internal market and justice and home affairs safeguard clauses

The internal market and justice and home affairs safeguard clauses have become a common feature, as of the 'big bang' enlargement in 2004. This is for a number of reasons. Firstly, with the creation of the EU, the integration endeavour has expanded to areas not previously envisaged for joint cooperation. Secondly, the political circumstances of the latest three enlargement rounds, required the EU to redevelop the EU pre-accession policy, and to introduce stricter conditionality and benchmarking.[129] At the time of their applications for EU membership, all Central and Eastern European countries, as well as Croatia, were undergoing painful economic, political, and legal reforms as part of their transformation from communist dictatorships to free-market democratic economies. Thus, to placate worries of the then EU Member States as to the sustainability of the reforms being pursued, a number of tools were developed. Firstly, Article 7 TEU was introduced by the Treaty of Amsterdam to play the role of the 'nuclear-button procedure', should one of the Member States act in breach of the fundamental principles underpinning the EU, which are now regulated in Article 2 TEU.[130] Secondly, apart from the already-mentioned enhanced pre-accession policy, the EU Member States decided to introduce into the accession treaties a set of safeguard clauses allowing the EU to discipline the newcomers should they go rogue or simply fail to meet the EU entry criteria. To this end, the Accession Treaties of 2003, 2005, and 2011 envisaged both internal market and justice and home affairs safeguard clauses. Interestingly enough, both were used only in relation to Bulgaria and Romania. They served as the legal bases for Cooperation and Verification Mechanism[131] and, the internal market safeguard clause was used also for air transport.[132] The question remains

[129] Marc Marescau, 'Pre-accession' in Marise Cremona (ed), *The Enlargement of the European Union* (OUP 2003) 9.

[130] Sadly, this modus operandi proved not to be fit for purpose when the authorities in Budapest and Warsaw opted for illiberal democracy. See, further, inter alia, Dimitry Vladimirovich Kochenov, 'Article 7: A Commentary on a Much Talked-about "Dead" Provision' in Armin von Bogdandy, Piotr Bogdanowicz, Iris Canor, Christoph Grabenwarter, Maciej Taborowski, and Matthias Schmidt (eds), *Defending Checks and Balances in EU Member States: Taking Stock of Europe's Actions* (Springer 2021).

[131] This was a monitoring mechanism for rule of law related reforms. See Commission Decision 2006/928/EC of 13 December 2006 establishing a mechanism for co- operation and verification of progress in Romania to address specific benchmarks in the areas of judicial reform and the fight against corruption [2006] OJ L354/56; Commis sion Decision 2006/929/EC of 13 December 2006 establishing a mechanism for coopera- tion and verification of progress in Bulgaria to address specific benchmarks in the areas of judicial reform and the fight against corruption and organized crime [2006] OJ L354/58. For an academic commentary see further, Martina Spernbauer, 'Benchmarking, Safeguard Clauses and Verification Mechanisms: What's in a Name? Recent Developments in the Pre-and Post-Accession Conditionality and Compliance with EU Law' (2007) 3 Croatian Yearbook of European Law and Policy 273.

[132] The safeguard clause was invoked against Bulgaria in order to suspend some benefits stemming from EU transport legislation, and for that purpose the European Commission adopted a regulation (within the meaning of Art 288 TFEU): Commission Regulation (EC) 1962/2006 of 21 December 2006 on the application of Article 37 of the Act of Accession of Bulgaria to the European Union [2006] OJ L408/8. See also Commission Regulation (EC) 875/2008 of 8 September 2008 repealing Regulation (EC) No 1962/2006 [2008] OJ L240/3.

of what the advantage is of having the safeguard clauses alongside the standard set of infringement procedures. Firstly, they allow for a fairly rapid reaction from the European Commission, instead of the rather lengthy preliminary stages of the infringement procedures. Secondly, the suspension of certain benefits of EU law in relation to a newcomer may play a more persuasive role than a declaratory judgment of the ECJ delivered under Article 258 TFEU. Alas, the safeguard clauses have a political flavour, and they are time-limited, which makes them fit for purpose only in extreme circumstances.

VI. Phasing in of the Newcomers to the EU Institutions and Selected EU Policies

A. Introduction

Transitional arrangements extend not only to selected pieces of EU *acquis* but also to the phasing in of newcomers to the EU institutions and selected EU policies. As far as the latter are concerned, the CAP, the EMU, and the Schengen zone deserve particular attention. This sampling has merits, as it permits the encapsulation with full force of many faces of differentiation inherent in the enlargement process. As a starting point, the phasing in into the EU institutional framework is looked at.

B. Institutions

The new Member States become fully involved in the functioning of the EU institutions as of the date of accession.[133] However, one needs to remember that accession does not happen overnight. *Au contraire*, many preliminary steps are taken during the crucial period between the signing of an accession treaty and its entry into force.[134] To begin with, the acceding countries are, as of the first enlargement in 1973, involved in the work of the Council of the EU (and contemporarily also the European Council) as observers. In accordance with agreements traditionally attached to the accession treaties, the acceding countries are covered

[133] Institutional matters are not only subject to accession negotiations, but also form an inherent part of the fourth Copenhagen criterion: the absorption capacity. In the enlargements of 2004 and 2007, reform of the EU institutions was the *raison d'etre* behind the negotiation and ratification of the Treaty of Nice. On the notion of absorption capacity, see further Adam Łazowski, 'Treaty of Lisbon and the EU's Absorption Capacity' (2010) 19 The Polish Quarterly of International Affairs 56.

[134] While participation in some EU agencies is available to non-EU states, the EU regularly makes it clear that countries aspiring to EU membership may not become involved in the EU decision-making prior to signature of an accession treaty. In this respect, one can see a considerable difference between possible future EU Member States and the EFTA countries, which are, to varying degrees, involved in EU decision-shaping. See Sieglinde Gstöhl and David Phinnemore (eds), *The Proliferation of Privileged Partnerships between the European Union and its Neighbours* (Routledge 2019).

by an information and consultation procedure.[135] To this end, they are part of the decision-making process, but without the voting rights. This has at least two advantages. Firstly, they remain fully informed about the draft legal acts in the pipeline, and as noted earlier, this may build a ground for additional requests for transitional periods. Secondly, the information and consultation procedure forces adjustments to domestic European integration coordination structures and procedures; simply put, they need to change gear from the pre-accession to the post-accession mode.[136] This involves a reduction of the role of the main coordinating authority, combined with a further empowerment of line ministries. This final stage of rapprochement affects not only the European Council and the Council, but also the European Parliament. The parliaments of the newcomers are invited to send observers selected from their own benches in a number equivalent to the number of MEPs envisaged in an accession treaty. In the shadows of big politics, the EU institutions, contemporarily in particular the European Personnel Selection Office, commence recruitment of nationals of the acceding states.

Things change dramatically on the date of accession: lock, stock, and barrel, the new Member States become fully involved in the EU machinery, with all the rights and obligations that come with EU membership. To begin with, they gain voting rights in the European Council and the Council of the EU.[137] Furthermore, shortly after their accession, formal appointments are made to all bodies making up the institutional fabric of the EU. These include, inter alia, members of the European Commission, and judges of the Court of Justice and the General Court. The number of Advocates General at the Court of Justice has, traditionally, also increased with consecutive enlargements, although a majority of the new Member States will not immediately have the right to propose nominees for these posts.[138]

The main theme of this chapter merits taking a closer look at the European Parliament. Unlike other key EU institutions, it is exposed to a degree of differentiation in the wake of accession rounds. In five out of the seven enlargements, the newcomers have been given an additional year or two to organize direct elections to the European Parliament. In the interim, national parliaments were required to

[135] For instance, Exchange of letters between the EU and the Republic of Croatia on an information and consultation procedure for the adoption of certain decisions and other measures to be taken during the period preceding accession [2012] OJ L112/108.

[136] On the Croatian experience, see, inter alia, Mirna Vlašić Feketija and Adam Łazowski, 'The Seventh EU Enlargement and Beyond: Pre-accession Policy vis-à-vis the Western Balkans Revisited' (2014) 10 Croatian Yearbook of European Law and Policy 1, 20–26.

[137] Until the reform of the voting modi operandi qua the Treaty of Lisbon, the system of qualified majority voting was based on the allocation of specific numbers of votes to each and every Member State. This, traditionally, was a battlefield during accession talks, as well as the revisions of the EU founding treaties.

[138] The five biggest EU Member States—ie Germany, France, Italy, Spain, and Poland— always have the right to have an Advocate General. The remaining six Advocates General are chosen from the other EU Member States (in alphabetical order) for six-year terms.

appoint their delegates to attend the sessions in Brussels and Strasbourg.[139] While deprived of a direct democratic mandate, these delegates did, however, benefit from full MEP status, including membership of the committees, and voting rights. With direct elections agreed to only in 1976, this had been a non-issue during the first enlargement round.[140] However, in the subsequent enlargement rounds, this was the reality that the European Parliament was faced with. It was, albeit temporarily, composed of directly elected MEPs and nominees coming from the national parliaments of the newcomers. This, inevitably, brought a degree of disruption to the pace of work of the EU's only democratically elected institution. For Croatia, the EU opted to change the modus operandi: Article 19 of the Act on Conditions of Accession imposed an obligation to organize European Parliament elections before Croatia's actual accession to the EU. In practice, this meant that the European Parliament was properly composed as of 1 July 2013, when Croatia joined the ranks.[141] With this, the element of differentiation disappeared. The question remains open of whether the latter model would be employed for any future enlargements of the EU.

C. EU policies

A great deal of temporary differentiation is also visible when it comes to phasing new entrants into selected EU policies. As argued in the Introduction to this Section, and as will be further elaborated, in some cases such arrangements are formally time-limited, yet open-ended. This, in practice, means that they come very close to turning *per facta concludentia* into quasi-permanent derogations.

From the first enlargement round onwards, participation in the CAP has had a prominent position on the agenda of negotiators. Consequentially, all seven accession treaties provided sets of complex transitory arrangements, which allowed for the gradual phasing of new Member States into, among others, trade in agricultural products, production quotas, and subsidies.[142] This placated economic concerns raised, in particular, during the early enlargement rounds. Bearing in mind the differences in GDP between the existing and future EU Member States in the recent enlargement rounds, the accession treaties envisaged gradual introduction of CAP subsidies. Furthermore, some necessary measures were adopted not as

[139] Art 23, Act on Conditions of Accession 1979; Art 28, Act on Conditions of Accession 1985; Art 31, Act on Conditions of Accession 1994; Art 25, Act on Conditions of Accession 2003; Art 24(3), Act on Conditions of Accession 2005.

[140] Arts 10 and 139, Act on Conditions of Accession 1972.

[141] For criticism, see Łazowski, 'European Union do not Worry' (n 94) 14–16.

[142] Arts 50–107, Act on Conditions of Accession 1972; Arts 57–114, Act on Conditions of Accession 1979; Arts 67–153 (Spain) and 233–341 (Portugal), Act on Conditions of Accession 1985; Arts 137–50, Annex I pt V, Act on Conditions of Accession 1994; Annex II, pt 6, Act on Conditions of Accession 2003; Annex IV, Act on Conditions of Accession 2005; Annex III, pt 4, Act on Conditions of Accession 2011.

part of the accession talks but, rather, unilaterally by the EU during the final stages of rapprochement, ie after signature but before entry into force of the accession treaties.[143]

Phasing into the EMU, as well as the Schengen zone, is a different kettle of fish. While both remain a compulsory part of the menu for all newcomers, their integration into both of these policy areas is subject to tailor-made rules, which—commencing with the EU enlargement in 1995—turned into a paradigm that has been consistently followed. While new EU Member States participate from their date of accession in some elements of the EU *acquis* in these areas, the final decisions on introducing the euro as the currency,[144] and on abolition of border controls,[145] are subject to strict conditionality, benchmarking, and, above all, unanimous decisions of the Council of the EU, and thus of the remaining Member States. A cliché as it may be, both decisions have far-reaching economic, security, and political implications. One also has to bear in mind a number of additional factors. Participation in these deep integration areas touches upon the core of state sovereignty. Some of the new states may express no desire to abolish their national currencies. A good example is Sweden, which joined the EU in 1995, but, following the negative results of a referendum, has never introduced the euro as its currency. Some other countries, including Poland and Hungary, have followed similar paths (*sans* plebiscites). Furthermore, for the remaining EU Member States, it is a matter of trust in the newcomers and their authorities. The abolition of border controls without trust in the control of the external EU borders and robust functioning of police and judicial cooperation in criminal matters would be a recipe for disaster. This, as already argued, translates into considerable differentiation that may go on for years and border on permanence, cementing the Europe of different speeds.

VII. Conclusions

Differentiation in the EU is an unquestionable fact. The breadth of the Europe of different speeds is encapsulated in all chapters forming the present book. As argued in the Introduction to this chapter, the seven enlargement rounds of the EC/

[143] For instance, Council Decision 2004/281/EC of 22 March 2004 adapting the Act concerning the conditions of accession of the Czech Republic, the Republic of Estonia, the Republic of Cyprus, the Republic of Latvia, the Republic of Lithuania, the Republic of Hungary, the Republic of Malta, the Republic of Poland, the Republic of Slovenia and the Slovak Republic and the adjustments to the Treaties on which the EU is founded, following the reform of the common agricultural policy [2004] OJ L93/1 (its legality was unsuccessfully challenged by Poland in Case C-273/04 *Republic of Poland v Council of the European Union* ECLI:EU:C:2007:622).

[144] As far as the EMU is concerned, newcomers are considered to be Member States with derogation as per Art 139 TFEU; Art 4, Act on Conditions of Accession 2003; Art 5, Act on Conditions of Accession 2005; Art 5, Act on Conditions of Accession 2011.

[145] Art 3, Act on Conditions of Accession 2003; Art 4, Act on Conditions of Accession 2005; Art 5, Act on Conditions of Accession 2011; Art 4, Act on Conditions of Accession 2011.

EU have brought a fair amount of differentiation, too. Not only has the increased number of Member States forced a plethora of general flexibility mechanisms to be created, but also the terms and conditions of every enlargement have brought large scale differentiation. It is rather clear that accessions of new countries are always followed by lengthy transitional arrangements, making parts of the EU *acquis*, or some of the EU policies, inapplicable for years on end. Arguably, the patchwork of temporary measures resulting from all past accession rounds has created more varied differentiation than all opt-outs or cases of enhanced cooperation put together. This chapter demonstrates that transitional periods may go to the core of EU law, ie the freedoms of the internal market as well as other key EU policies. They have proven to be evolving in sync with the development of EU law. When the Common Market was in its infancy, the newcomers in 1973 were permitted to benefit from the gradual introduction of free movement of goods or trade agreements with third countries. This generous approach is unthinkable now, when the centre of gravity has moved to other areas which have emerged over the years. Apart from environmental protection, discussed in this chapter, such dossiers include food and phytosanitary standards and transport, to name just a few. Furthermore, as of the creation of the euro as a common currency, and the border control-free Schengen zone, we have witnessed long-term derogations from both of these areas of integration. In some cases, the longevity of these derogations triggers a fundamental question of whether they have *de facto* joined a very modest pantheon of permanent derogations. One thing that remains clear is that, until a formal partial membership of some kind is introduced into the EU founding treaties, the official mantra will remain: joining the EU is an 'all-or-nothing' scenario, even if the newcomers are covered by a plethora of transitional arrangements, including a very slow phasing in to the euro and the Schengen zone.

8

Governance Architecture and Prospects for Regulatory Differentiation in the EU–UK Trade Relationship

*Kathryn Wright**

I. Introduction

Following the United Kingdom's (UK) withdrawal from the European Union (EU) on 31 January 2020, the two sides finally reached agreement on their future relationship at the eleventh hour of the transition period, resulting in the Trade and Cooperation Agreement (TCA).[1] This chapter addresses what was one of the main sticking points in the negotiations: the governance arrangements for the EU–UK future trade relationship. These arrangements are central to managing regulatory differentiation. The governance arrangements and level playing field provisions had been one of the principal areas of difference between the two sides' mandates during the negotiations, given the UK's red line on the role of the Court of Justice of the European Union (ECJ) and the EU's concerns about a regulatory competitor on its doorstep. The EU insisted on a single overarching governance structure (contrary to the multiple agreements with Switzerland), a level playing field, and a dynamic means[2] of managing the future relationship as it develops. The UK position changed between the May and Johnson governments in early 2020, to one

* With thanks to Diane Fromage for helpful editorial comments on an earlier draft.

[1] Agreement was reached on 24 December 2020, with the transition period due to end on 31 December 2020. Trade and Cooperation Agreement [2020] OJ L444/14; revised numbering in [2021] OJ L149/10 (TCA). Running to over 2,500 pages, the TCA is made up of seven parts: (1) common and institutional provisions; (2) trade, transport, fisheries, and other arrangements; (3) law enforcement and judicial cooperation in criminal matters; (4) thematic cooperation (in health security and cybersecurity); (5) participation in Union programmes, sound financial management and financial provisions; (6) dispute settlement and horizontal provisions; and (7) final provisions. Part Two on trade, transport, fisheries, and other arrangements comprises six headings: (1) trade, (2) aviation, (3) road transport, (4) social security coordination and visas for short-term visits, (5) fisheries, and (6) other provisions. Each part is further divided into titles. There are also 48 annexes, covering product-specific rules or further definitions, and three protocols (with their own annexes) on administrative assistance and combating fraud in the tax field, on mutual assistance in customs matters, and on social security coordination.

[2] Council of the EU, Annex to Council Decision authorising the opening of negotiations with the United Kingdom of Great Britain and Northern Ireland for a new partnership agreement, 5870/20 ADD 1 REV 3, Brussels, 25 February 2020 (Council Negotiating Mandate), para 149.

Kathryn Wright, *Governance Architecture and Prospects for Regulatory Differentiation in the EU–UK Trade Relationship*
In: *Redefining EU Membership*. Edited by: Diane Fromage, Oxford University Press. © Kathryn Wright 2024.
DOI: 10.1093/9780191948145.003.0008

of no alignment.[3] It based its proposals on precedented arrangements in the EU's existing free trade agreements, with different arrangements for different sectors [4] and only some of these providing for recourse to an arbitral tribunal.

The TCA establishes the overarching governance structure of a Partnership Council (PC), with 18 Specialised Committees (SCs) and 4 working groups. There is no secretariat or administrative authority like the European Free Trade Association (EFTA) Supervision Authority, for example. To some large extent, the governing architecture is a continuation of arrangements under the Withdrawal Agreement (WA)[5] through its Joint Committee (JC). As with the JC, the PC is a high-level political mechanism, albeit one underpinned by a legal framework.[6] Similarly, the PC has a range of oversight tasks, with an emphasis on dispute settlement through arbitration, and with the ultimate sanctions of rebalancing and suspension mechanisms.

However, this overarching institutional structure is only half the story. It does not account for the ground-level functioning of the relationship and implementation of rules, particularly in respect of the level playing field. Another significant aspect of institutional architecture is regulatory cooperation and agencies. While there are some piecemeal provisions on regulatory cooperation in the TCA, the UK was no longer participating in any EU agencies as of 1 January 2021. During the negotiations there was a focus on the political. As the relationship entered a new phase after the end of the transition period, the salience of functionalist perspectives increased. Market access and cooperation are now at least as important as symbolic sovereignty issues, as the practical implications of EU withdrawal have become apparent. Reports of goods held up, couriers suspending deliveries, and confusion over necessary paperwork[7] show that the borders between the UK and the EU, and between Great Britain and Northern Ireland, are not quite

[3] Notwithstanding the Northern Ireland Protocol and the level playing field to which it agreed in the Political Declaration, the UK's approach set out that it '[would] not agree to any obligation for our laws to be aligned with the EU's', nor to the EU institutions having any jurisdiction in the UK: HM Government, *The Future Relationship with the EU: The UK's Approach to Negotiations* (Cm 211, 2020) para 5.

[4] ibid; Prime Minister Boris Johnson's statement UIN HCWS86 on UK/EU relations, made on 3 February 2020, referred to a 'suite of agreements'.

[5] Withdrawal Agreement and Political Declaration [2019] OJ C384 I/01 (WA).

[6] Art 7(2) TCA; regarding the WA, the UK's domestic EU (Withdrawal Agreement) Act 2020, s 34 states that only a Minister can co-chair the JC.

[7] Peter Foster, 'Brexit Forces German Logistics Group to Suspend UK Deliveries' *Financial Times* (London, 13 January 2021) https://www.ft.com/content/27069111-be39-446f-8cf1-ed216400b171 accessed 1 July 2023; Morgan Meaker, 'One in 10 Lorries Turned Back at Border in Post-Brexit Chaos', *The Telegraph* (London, 14 January 2021) https://www.telegraph.co.uk/technology/2021/01/14/one-10-deliveries-uk-eu-turned-back-border-amid-post-brexit/ accessed 1 July 2023; Lisa O'Carroll, '"Absolute Carnage": EU Hauliers Reject UK Jobs over Brexit Rules' *The Guardian* (London, 20 January 2021) <https://www.theguardian.com/politics/2021/jan/20/absolute-carnage-eu-hauliers-reject-uk-jobs-over-brexit-rules> accessed 1 July 2023.

'frictionless'.[8] Regarding the latter, the Windsor Framework has assuaged some problems by easing checks on goods, but does not resolve everything.[9]

As a Member State, the UK was integrated in the EU's multilevel governance system, including EU agencies and regulatory networks. In addition, EU law is embedded throughout the UK's domestic administrative institutions.[10] Monitoring the extent of regulatory differentiation is central to the trade relationship, which invites a strong role for administrative authorities and technocratic expertise in assessing and managing potential divergence as it arises. Placing the discussion in the context of the literature on the EU as a regulator beyond its borders, this chapter considers the significance of functionalist cooperation in regulatory differentiation. It argues that the role of technocratic agencies and softer coordination in networks will be central to the prospects for regulatory differentiation. Further, by examining the UK's singular situation as a former Member State, the chapter contributes to a recharacterization of membership and participation, to be placed alongside the EU's existing models of alternatives to membership with its neighbours and other categories of third states. The shift from internal opt-outs to external differentiation and a new balance of rights and obligations feeds into this picture.

The rest of this chapter analyses the overarching governance arrangements in the WA and TCA, inter-institutional links, the level playing field, and other divergence-minimizing provisions, before exploring the administrative level. It then applies insights from the EU external governance literature to further show why prospects for regulatory differentiation may be limited. The final section draws some conclusions in the context of this volume's themes of internal and external differentiation, membership and participation, and rights and obligations.

II. Overarching Governance Arrangements in the Withdrawal Agreement and Trade and Cooperation Agreement

This section discusses the institutional architecture in the WA[11] and TCA, the overlapping continuation provisions in the WA, and the level playing field, exploring the constraints on regulatory differentiation.

[8] HM Government, *The Future Relationship between the UK and the EU* (White Paper, Cm 9593, 2018) 2 (UK Future Relationship White Paper).

[9] Simon Usherwood, 'Necessary but not Sufficient: The Windsor Framework and UK–EU Relations' (*UK in a Changing Europe*, 8 June 2023) <https://ukandeu.ac.uk/necessary-but-not-sufficient-the-windsor-framework-and-uk-eu-relations/> accessed 1 July 2023.

[10] See also Franklin, Kühn and Trondal, and Ott and Pirker, in this volume, regarding Norway and Switzerland; Ben Rosamond, 'Brexit and the Problem of European Disintegration' (2016) 12 Journal of Contemporary European Research 865, 865.

[11] Alan Dashwood, 'The Withdrawal Agreement: Common Provisions, Governance and Dispute Settlement' (2020) 45 European Law Review 183; Michael Dougan, 'So Long, Farewell, Auf Wiedersehen, Goodbye: The UK's Withdrawal Package' (2020) 57 Common Market Law Review 631

Article 4 provides for the legal effects of the WA to be mirrored in the EU and UK legal systems, including direct effect, the ability of courts to disapply incompatible legislation, and the availability of remedies, including *Francovich* damages. These duties should be interpreted in conformity with general principles of EU law and ECJ case law handed down before the end of the transition period, with 'due regard' to them in the UK after transition.[12]

A. Shared institutions and other inter-institutional links

The JC is the primary means for the overarching governance of the WA, responsible for its implementation and application.[13] The JC is jointly chaired at a political level, for the EU by the European Commission Vice-President, and on the UK side by a secretary of state. It comprises representatives of the EU and UK from diplomatic staff and civil servants. Under Article 164(4) WA, the JC shall seek appropriate ways of preventing problems and resolving any disputes that arise, and adopt decisions and make recommendations by mutual consent. Those decisions are binding on the parties in the same way as the WA itself. It shall also supervise, determine the tasks of, and delegate responsibilities to, the six SCs beneath it.[14] In terms of their composition, the WA only specifies that the respective representatives on the SCs have appropriate expertise with respect to the issues under discussion.[15] These committees are co-chaired by officials from the European Commission and UK government. In practice, the SC on citizens' rights also includes representatives of the EU Member States and of the UK Independent Monitoring Authority for the Citizens' Rights Agreements.[16] The SC on Gibraltar also includes representatives from Spain and other Member States as part of the EU delegation.[17] The JC may change the tasks assigned, dissolve any of the SCs, or establish new ones.[18]

Notably, the JC can amend the WA until the end of the fourth year following the end of the transition period (ie 31 December 2024), provided that such

[12] EU (Withdrawal Agreement) Act 2020, s 5.

[13] Art 164(3) WA.

[14] On citizens' rights, financial provisions, other separation provisions, and the geographical subcommittees on Northern Ireland, Gibraltar, and the Sovereign Base Areas in Cyprus: ibid Art 165.

[15] ibid Art 165(3).

[16] Joint statement following the meeting of the Specialised Committee on Citizens' Rights between the UK Government and European Commission via video conference, 23 February 2021, available at <https://ec.europa.eu/info/publications/joint-statement-following-meeting-specialised-committee-citizens-rights-between-uk-government-and-european-commission-video-conference_en> accessed 26 March 2021.

[17] Statement following the second meeting of the Specialised Committee on Gibraltar between the European Union and the UK Government, 18 November 2020, available at <https://ec.europa.eu/info/publications/statement-following-second-meeting-specialised-committee-gibraltar-between-european-union-and-uk-government_en> accessed 26 March 2021.

[18] Art 164(5) WA.

amendments are necessary to correct errors, to address omissions or other deficiencies, or to address situations unforeseen when the Agreement was signed, to make changes to the rules of procedure of the JCs and SCs and, further, 'take such other actions in the exercise of its functions as decided by the Union and the United Kingdom'.[19] An example of this competence is the Windsor Framework, which sets out new arrangements under the former Ireland/Northern Ireland Protocol and provides for new decisions and declarations of the WA JC.[20] The JC, therefore, has broad discretion to decide its own work in the future, including the operation of the SCs laid down in Article 165 WA. The fact that the JC is to meet (as a minimum) once a year suggests that additional lower-level mechanisms are also necessary to manage aspects of the future relationship.

In terms of dispute settlement, Article 168 WA provides for exclusive recourse to the WA's procedures for disputes arising under the WA. In common with other EU agreements, the process is initiated through consultations and communications within the JC.[21] If there is no mutually agreed solution within three months, the matter shall be referred to an arbitration panel (of five: two from each side, plus an agreed chair).[22] Where a dispute submitted to arbitration raises a question of interpretation of EU law, a reference to EU law in the WA, or the UK's failure to comply with a ECJ judgment to which it is subject under the Treaties or the WA, the arbitration panel must request a ruling from the ECJ. The ECJ's ruling is then binding on the arbitral panel.[23] This arbitration procedure reflects the balance between the EU's imperative to protect the autonomy of EU law[24] and the UK's wish to end ECJ jurisdiction within the UK. Compliance with the arbitration panel's ruling is required within a reasonable period.[25] If this does not happen there is a lump sum or periodic penalty payment, and a further six months to comply. As a last resort, the agreement can be proportionately suspended in full or part (except Part II on citizens' rights) as a retaliation mechanism.[26]

Although the WA is said to deal with separation and 'divorce' only, it is less clear-cut than that: provisions in the WA and the Political Declaration on the future relationship (PD) set the framework for that relationship. . Most obviously, as set out in the Ireland/Northern Ireland (NI) Protocol, subject to the arrangements of the more recent Windsor Framework, NI would continue to follow EU rules in customs, and in areas of the single market necessary to avoid a hard border on the

[19] ibid Art 164(5)(f).

[20] Decision No 1/2023 of the Joint Committee established by the Agreement on the Withdrawal of the United Kingdom of Great Britain and Northern Ireland from the European Union and the European Atomic Energy Community of 24 March 2023 laying down arrangements relating to the Windsor Framework OJ L102/61.

[21] Art 169 WA.

[22] ibid Art 180–81.

[23] ibid Art 174.

[24] Opinion 1/17 *CETA* C:2019:341, Case C–284/16 *Achmea* [2018] C:2018:158.

[25] Art 175–76 WA.

[26] ibid Art 177–79.

island of Ireland. Meanwhile, affecting the whole of the UK, beyond the transition period's 'alignment without membership',[27] several temporal provisions refer to circumstances arising before the end of the transition period, and therefore aim to maintain convergence in the short term. The clearest examples of this are CJEU jurisdiction over citizens' rights until eight years after the end of transition,[28] and the establishment of the Independent Monitoring Authority for Citizens' Rights in the UK (IMA).[29] Relating more directly to trade, there is a general provision regarding administrative cooperation procedures.[30] For public procurement, the relevant EU legislation continued to apply for procedures launched by UK authorities for up to nine months.[31] Regarding State aid granted before end of the transition period, the European Commission has competence until four years after end of transition, and also for proceedings started within that period.[32] Article 98(2) relates to the competent authorities for customs procedures launched up to three years later and Article 99 lays down similar arrangements concerning indirect tax, but up to four years after the end of transition. These examples show the overlap between withdrawal and the future trade relationship.

In terms of judicial procedures, CJEU jurisdiction continues over pending preliminary references and proceedings brought by or against the UK before the end of transition.[33] The European Commission can bring infringement proceedings against the UK for up to four years after the end of the transition period for failure to comply with EU law before 31 December 2020,[34] which it put into practice regarding the proposed UK Internal Market Bill and the UK's breach of its obligations under the NI Protocol.[35]

The WA foresees consistent application and interpretation in the short term through various forms of other inter-institutional dialogue: the European Commission may make submissions to UK courts when these courts are

[27] Kenneth Armstrong, 'Regulatory Alignment and Divergence after Brexit' (2018) 25 Journal of European Public Policy 1099, 1112.

[28] Art 158 WA

[29] ibid Art 159. The JC is to decide after eight years whether the IMA is still needed.

[30] ibid Art 92.

[31] ibid Art 78.

[32] ibid Art 93.

[33] ibid Art 86.

[34] ibid Art 87.

[35] United Kingdom Internal Market HC Bill (2019–21) [177], introduced in September 2020; European Commission, 'Withdrawal Agreement: European Commission Sends Letter of Formal Notice to the United Kingdom for Breach of its Obligations' (Press release, 1 October 2020) <https://ec.europa.eu/commission/presscorner/detail/en/IP_20_1798> accessed 28 February 2021. The controversial clauses were removed, and do not appear in the UK Internal Market Act 2020. However, the European Commission subsequently sent a letter of formal notice to the UK on 15 March 2021, for breach of its obligations under the Northern Ireland Protocol and its good faith obligation under the Withdrawal Agreement: Letter from Vice-President Maroš Šefčovič to David Frost (15 March 2021) <https://commission.europa.eu/publications/letter-vice-president-maros-sefcovic-david-frost-15-march-2021_en> accessed 23 March 2021. This process opened negotiations eventually leading to the Windsor Framework.

considering the interpretation of the WA;[36] the UK may participate, and UK lawyers may represent or assist parties, in relevant proceedings before the CJEU,[37] and the UK's highest courts may maintain a dialogue with CJEU judges. While the form of this dialogue is not specified, it is seen as analogous to the dialogue between the CJEU and the highest courts of the Member States, with a view to facilitating the consistent interpretation of the WA.[38] The UK may also maintain intervention rights before CJEU proceedings in direct actions and participate in preliminary references[39] until all proceedings have become final, and may intervene in cases where the UK is subject to the same obligations as remaining Member States.

For the TCA's future relationship, whereas the EU consistently insisted upon unique overarching governance arrangements on account of the close geographic and economic relationship,[40] the UK negotiating position unveiled under the Johnson government emphasized 'precedented' arrangements,[41] making frequent reference to other free trade agreements. The UK's position by this point was also markedly different in structure to the PD agreed in October 2019. It presented discrete policy areas, with no indication of areas of priority or an overarching scheme.

The EU–UK TCA's eventual overarching governance structure comprises a Partnership Council (PC)[42] and 18 SCs—ten trade committees and eight sectoral committees[43]—and four technical working groups,[44] which can be added to.[45] As with the JC, the PC is co-chaired at a political level, by a member of the European Commission and a UK minister. Decisions in the PC and its committees are to be taken by mutual consent, and they meet at least once a year, or more often at the request of either party. The EU or the UK may refer to the PC any issue relating to the implementation, application, and interpretation of the TCA.

As with the WA SCs, the SCs and working groups should comprise representatives of each party with appropriate expertise,[46] and so are largely staffed by officials

[36] Art 162 WA.

[37] ibid Art 161(3)(b).

[38] ibid Art 163.

[39] ibid Art 90.

[40] Council Negotiating Mandate (n 2); European Commission, Draft text of the Agreement on the New Partnership with the United Kingdom, UKTF (2020) 14, 18 March 2020.

[41] HM Government, *The UK's Approach to Negotiations* (n 3) para 6; Draft UK–EU Comprehensive Free Trade Agreement, 19 May 2020, available at <https://www.gov.uk/government/publications/our-approach-to-the-future-relationship-with-the-eu> accessed 26 March 2021.

[42] Art 7 TCA.

[43] ibid Art 8(1). The trade committees are on goods; customs cooperation and rules of origin; sanitary and phytosanitary measures; technical barriers to trade; services, investment and digital trade; intellectual property; public procurement; regulatory cooperation; level playing field; and administrative cooperation in VAT and recovery of taxes and duties. The other sectoral committees are on energy; air transport; aviation safety; road transport; social security coordination; fisheries; law enforcement and judicial cooperation; and Union programmes.

[44] Art 9 TCA. The working groups are on organic products, motor vehicles and parts, medicinal products, and social security coordination.

[45] ibid Art 7(4)(g).

[46] ibid Art 8(5)–(7).

and civil servants. The SCs' roles include monitoring and reviewing implementation of their respective chapters, exchanging information and best practice, and resolving disputes. In addition, specific tasks of particular committees include, for example, exchange of statistical information (on air transport) and discussing new regulatory measures (on road transport). As with the PC, the SCs are to meet at least once a year. This seems unlikely to replace the intensity of interaction taking place between networks of regulators.

Enforcement through the TCA is based on upon compensatory, remedial, and suspension measures. Persistent lack of compliance with an arbitral ruling may ultimately lead to temporary compensation agreed between the parties, or unilateral suspension of obligations in any area by the complaining party. The horizontal dispute resolution process is through arbitral tribunal, without a role for the CJEU, unlike in the WA.

Where either party is experiencing 'serious economic, societal or environmental difficulties of a sectorial or regional nature . . . that are liable to persist', it may apply proportionate safeguard measures restricted in scope and duration.[47] While these measures should prioritize areas which will least disturb the agreement's functioning, they may ultimately extend to suspending obligations in any area of the TCA. The horizontal dispute settlement mechanism applies to these measures. The other party may respond with 'rebalancing' measures, which should, again, be those that will least disturb the functioning of the agreement.

Unlike the WA, the TCA can be terminated through diplomatic channels, causing it to end twelve months later.[48] Less drastically, either party may request a review of the TCA provisions under the trade heading, to assess whether it 'delivers an appropriate balance of rights and obligations' or whether a modification of its terms is needed.[49] The review process should take place no less than every four years,[50] unless rebalancing measures have been applied frequently, or if they have a material impact on trade or investment, and have been applied for a year.[51] If the review finds a need for modification and year-long negotiations are inconclusive, the parts on trade and transport may be unilaterally terminated.[52] The TCA provides for a general review of its operation every five years,[53] with sector-specific reviews at various stages.

[47] ibid Art 773(1).
[48] ibid Art 779.
[49] ibid Art 411(8).
[50] ibid Art 411(7).
[51] ibid Art 411(5).
[52] ibid Art 411(10).
[53] ibid Art 776.

B. Level playing field governance: regulatory differentiation at a price

The level playing field is a key focus of prospects for regulatory divergence, since it is where public policy considerations interact with trade in goods and services. Despite the UK agreeing to the level playing field provision in the PD[54] and an initial commitment to high standards, non-regression, and a common rulebook on State aid,[55] there was subsequently a marked change in the UK's stance. A significant change in the TCA was the removal of any reference to 'Union' standards, but with continued focus on convergence to international standards.

The TCA emphasizes the regulatory autonomy of the parties: the purpose of the level playing field is 'not to harmonise the standards of the Parties' but the parties are 'determined to maintain and improve their respective high standards'.[56] However, first, non-regression commitments and convergence to international standards set a baseline; and, second, rebalancing measures set out the potential consequences for future divergence.

A non-regression clause on tax matters focuses on limiting the parties' divergence from standards agreed in the Organisation for Economic Co-operation and Development (OECD) rules in place at the end of the transition period. [57] As with the competition chapter, taxation is not subject to dispute resolution mechanisms.[58] Stronger, binding, and enforceable non-regression commitments pertain to labour and social standards (Title XI of the trade heading, Chapter 6), as well as the environment and climate (Chapter 7). In both areas, the EU and the UK have committed not to 'weaken or reduce, in a manner affecting trade or investment between the Parties . . . levels of protection below the levels in place at the end of the transition period, including by failing to effectively enforce' their law and

[54] Political Declaration setting out the framework for the future relationship between the European Union and the United Kingdom [2019] OJ C384 I/02 (Political Declaration), para 77: 'Given the Union and the United Kingdom's *geographic proximity and economic interdependence*, the future relationship must ensure open and fair competition, encompassing robust commitments to ensure a level playing field. The precise nature of commitments should be commensurate with the scope and depth of the future relationship and the economic connectedness of the Parties. These commitments should prevent distortions of trade and unfair competitive advantages. To that end, the Parties should *uphold the common high standards* applicable in the Union and the United Kingdom at the end of the transition period in the areas of state aid, competition, social and employment standards, environment, climate change, and relevant tax matters. The Parties should in particular *maintain a robust and comprehensive framework for competition and state aid control* that prevents undue distortion of trade and competition; *commit to the principles of good governance in the area of taxation* and to the curbing of harmful tax practices; and *maintain environmental, social and employment standards at the current high levels provided by the existing common standards*. In so doing, they should *rely on appropriate and relevant Union and international standards*, and include appropriate mechanisms to ensure effective implementation domestically, enforcement and dispute settlement. The future relationship should also promote adherence to and effective implementation of relevant internationally agreed principles and rules in these domains, including the Paris Agreement' (emphasis added).

[55] UK Future Relationship White Paper (n 8) para 108.

[56] Art 355(4) TCA.

[57] ibid Art 384.

[58] ibid Art 385.

standards.[59] Although the parties shall 'strive' to increase their respective levels of protection,[60] if standards are raised, there is no evolution clause to raise the benchmark from that at the end of the transition period, as the EU had originally included in its negotiating position. International commitments should be used as a reference.[61] In these chapters, disputes are to be dealt with exclusively through the level playing field panel of experts for non-regression areas, as laid out in Articles 408 to 410, rather than the horizontal dispute resolution procedure,[62] but they are subject to arbitration tribunals for rebalancing measures.[63]

If a subsidy causes or seriously risks causing a 'significant negative effect on trade or investment between the Parties', [64] proportionate remedial measures may be imposed to remedy that effect or risk, following a sixty-day period for information and consultation. Priority is given to measures that will least disturb the functioning of the overall agreement. The other party may request an arbitral tribunal, with a thirty-day expedited procedure.[65] Importantly, the request for a tribunal does not have a suspensive effect on the remedial measures.[66] If the arbitral tribunal finds the remedial measure inconsistent or disproportionate, it must cease or be adjusted, otherwise the other party may apply compensation measures through suspension of obligations in any area of the TCA.[67]

Certain aspects of the level playing field—labour and social standards, environment and climate, other instruments for sustainable development—are subject to dispute resolution through initial consultation with civil society groups and international organizations, with a decision taken by a panel of experts. Lack of resolution may still lead to compensation, rebalancing, or suspension of the obligations and the involvement of an arbitral tribunal.

Article 411 on rebalancing encapsulates the parties' regulatory autonomy regarding future policies—but at a cost: 'the Parties acknowledge that significant divergences ... can be capable of impacting trade or investment between the Parties in a manner that changes the circumstances that have formed the basis for the conclusion of this Agreement'. Deviation from the level playing field standards entitles the other party to adopt unilateral rebalancing measures,

> if *material impacts on trade or investment* ... [arise] *as a result of significant divergences* between the Parties ... Such measures shall be restricted with respect to their scope and duration to what is strictly necessary and proportionate in order

[59] ibid Arts 387(2), 391(2).
[60] ibid, Arts 387(4), 391(5).
[61] ibid Arts 387(1), 391(1), Title XI Chapter 8 on sustainable development.
[62] ibid Arts 389(2), 396(2), 407(2).
[63] ibid Art 411.
[64] ibid Art 374(1).
[65] ibid Art 374(9) in accordance with Art 739.
[66] ibid Art 374(9).
[67] ibid Arts 374(12), 761.

> to remedy the situation. Priority shall be given to such measures as will least disturb the functioning of this Agreement. A Party's assessment of these impacts shall be based on reliable evidence and not merely on conjecture or remote possibility (emphasis added).

The concepts of 'material impacts', 'significant divergence', and 'reliable evidence' are undefined, leaving each party to interpret them. It is possible to imagine that there may be material impact on trade or investment which arises for reasons other than significant divergences between the parties, so this could be viewed as a two-part test. Alternatively, the 'significance' of the divergence might be determined by the fact that some degree of divergence has caused a material impact on trade or investment. These interpretations will be debated at political level in the PC (and SCs), as well as through the arbitral tribunals and panels of experts, since the intention to take rebalancing measures must be notified through the PC to trigger consultations.[68] Indeed, in the similar wording regarding remedial measures on subsidies, [69] the PC 'may maintain an illustrative list of what would amount to a significant negative effect on trade or investment'.[70]

Divergence-minimizing mechanisms, aligned with international standards, are also found away from the level playing field provisions. On technical regulations, the parties shall increase convergence with relevant international standards and take into account any changes in the circumstances that have given rise to divergence from them. [71] Similarly, regulatory impact assessments should show how different options relate to relevant international standards, including the reasons for any divergence.[72] On motor vehicles and equipment, if the EU or UK introduces a domestic technical regulation, marking, or conformity assessment procedure, they must identify the parts which substantially diverge from the relevant international regulations and provide justification for the divergence. The domestic measures then need to be self-reviewed at regular intervals at least every five years. [73]

In addition to the governance and dispute mechanisms concerning measures adopted after 1 January 2021, which were already described, some level playing field aspects require domestic implementation and institutions. This includes control of subsidies by an independent domestic authority in the UK, and access to redress for private parties in the EU.[74] Courts must be empowered to prohibit, suspend, or recover subsidies[75] if they have not been granted according to the general

[68] ibid Art 411(3)(a).
[69] ibid Art 374(5), (6).
[70] ibid Art 374(7).
[71] ibid Art 91(7), Arts 92(1)(b) on standards, and 93(3)(c) on conformity assessment.
[72] ibid Art 347(2)(d).
[73] ibid Annex 11 Art 5.
[74] An exception to the general principle in Art 5 that the TCA itself is not to create rights for private parties directly invoked in the domestic legal systems of the Parties.
[75] Art 372–73 TCA.

principles on subsidies (including pursuing a specific public interest objective, remedying market failure, and being granted according to necessity and proportionality),[76] and, if applicable, the relevant principles on particular sectors or types of aid. Details of subsidies are required to be published online within six months, and for tax measures within one year.[77] This would allow the EU or UK to raise any issues within the level playing field SC, or competitors or other interested parties to challenge measures through the courts. There are also requirements to maintain independent authorities and an enforcement system, eg in competition law,[78] telecoms,[79] and energy.[80]

The provisions on labour and social standards and on environment and climate are similar in terms of requiring effective domestic enforcement, including administrative and judicial authorities and proceedings empowered to provide appropriate and effective review, remedies, and sanctions.[81] In environmental matters there is a commitment to cooperation between agencies, but it is looser than on competition and subsidies: 'the Parties shall ensure that the European Commission and the [UK] supervisory bodies regularly meet with each other and co-operate on the effective monitoring and enforcement of the law'.[82]

These complex arrangements are an inevitable result of politically charged trade-offs. References to international commitments inject some neutrality, although in practice those standards will often be based on EU policy leadership. The compensation and suspension mechanisms—ultimately in any area of the TCA—as a last resort create knock-on effects and blur the boundaries between sectors. In the context of triggering unilateral rebalancing measures, as already noted, 'material impacts on trade or investment', 'as a result of significant divergences between the Parties', are rather vague tests, susceptible to divergent—and politically expedient to each side—interpretations. To minimize damaging tit-for-tat disputes, it would be preferable to develop objective measures. This is a further argument for the involvement of sectoral authorities and expertise.

III. Regulatory Extension and the Multilevel Governance Role of Regulatory Agencies and Networks

Below the overarching governance structures of the trade relationship, a significant aspect of institutional architecture is regulatory cooperation and agencies.

[76] ibid Art 366.
[77] ibid Art 369.
[78] ibid Arts 359 and 360.
[79] ibid Art 167.
[80] ibid Art 310.
[81] ibid Arts 388, 394.
[82] ibid Art 395.

Despite its practical importance to the future relationship, this aspect garnered much less attention during the negotiations. As a Member State, the UK was integrated in the EU's multilevel governance structure,[83] including EU agencies and regulatory networks. Administrative authorities and technocratic expertise will play an important role in assessing and managing potential divergence as it arises. Functionalist cooperation through technocratic agencies and softer coordination mechanisms in networks will, therefore, be central to the prospects for regulatory differentiation. Not only are administrative agencies important for assessing the extent of regulatory differentiation, which will often be a technical judgement in a given policy area, but cooperation and mutual interest between them may also make such differentiation for politics' sake less likely.[84]

In the P D the EU and UK committed to make arrangements for appropriate cooperation between regulators on data protection,[85] and to 'explore the possibility' of cooperation between the UK authorities and EU agencies, 'such as' the European Medicines Authority (EMA), European Chemicals Agency (ECHA), and European Aviation Safety Agency (EASA).[86] The mention of these specific agencies indicated the priorities of the UK government, but the wording also denotes the non-exhaustive nature of the list. Notably, even at this point, cooperation rather than membership was the aim, even where the respective agency's founding regulations would allow membership.[87]

Agency membership was no longer explicitly mentioned in the UK and EU negotiating positions by February 2020, and the TCA outcome confirms that position as of 1 January 2021. Alongside no PC secretariat, there is no participation, much less membership, in EU agencies. Instead, the TCA contains piecemeal arrangements, including regulatory cooperation provisions and bilateral links between EU agencies and UK designated regulatory authorities.

The TCA Specialised Sectoral Committees (eg on energy, aviation safety, and transport) and working groups (eg on medicinal products) are not intended

[83] See, eg, Morten Egeberg (ed), *Multilevel Union Administration: The Transformation of Executive Politics in Europe* (Palgrave Macmillan 2006); David Coen and Mark Thatcher, 'Network Governance and Multi-Level Delegation: European Networks of Regulatory Agencies' (2008) 28 Journal of Public Policy 49; Arthur Benz, Andreas Corcaci, and Jan Wolfgang Doser, 'Unravelling Multilevel Administration: Patterns and Dynamics of Administrative Co-ordination in European Governance' (2016) 23 Journal of European Public Policy 999.

[84] On epistemic communities, see Peter M Haas, 'Epistemic Communities and International Policy Coordination' (1992) 46(1) International Organization 1.

[85] Political Declaration (n 54) para 10.

[86] ibid para 23; para 61 regarding EASA; and para 65 regarding the European Maritime Safety Agency. This followed the previous UK position under Theresa May's government, stating its preparedness to '[accept] the rules of these agencies and contribut[e] to their costs, under new arrangements that recognise the UK will not be a Member State', in the UK Future Relationship White Paper (n 8) 8, and the earlier version of the Political Declaration in which the UK would 'consider aligning with EU rules in relevant areas': Council of the EU, 'Draft Political declaration setting out the framework for the future relationship between the EU and the UK', 22 November 2018, XT 21095/18, para 25.

[87] See de Witte on selective membership of Union bodies and Milenkovic on the participation of Western Balkan states, in this volume.

to confer a status comparable to UK participation in EU agencies. This is made explicit with regard to the Agency for the Cooperation of Energy Regulators (ACER).[88] Furthermore, regulatory cooperation activities in particular policy areas are voluntary.[89]

The TCA's piecemeal approach in different policy areas through bilateral co-operation includes information sharing, recognition of existing testing procedures, simplified procedures for EU and UK traders to demonstrate compliance with the other party's rules, and shared commitments to apply international standards. There are various references to links between EU agencies and designated UK regulatory authorities. As laid out in Title X of the trade heading on good regulatory practices and regulatory cooperation, the Specialised Committee on Regulatory Cooperation is charged with rather general obligations: 'enhancing and promoting' regulatory cooperation between the EU and UK, exchanging views, and encouraging EU-UK cooperation in international fora.

There is no overarching provision to notify policy and legislative changes on each side, which would allow review of alignment or divergence over time. However, under the transparency title, Article 335(1) states that 'each Party shall ensure that its laws, regulations, procedures and administrative rulings of general application are promptly published'. The good regulatory practices title contains a general requirement for information on planned 'major' (as understood by each party) regulatory measures to be released at least once a year, and for those measures to include public consultation on drafts and impact assessments.[90] A publicly available register of regulatory measures in force is also required.[91]

More specifically, there are provisions on exchange of information concerning customs legislation[92] and a requirement for legislation to be published through the internet.[93] When developing a major technical regulation which may have a significant effect on trade, there must be a public consultation allowing 'persons of the other Party' to give views on the same terms as those of its own nationals.[94] In aviation safety[95] and in medicinal products,[96] there must be an opportunity to comment on significant changes to laws and regulations.

Article 340(3) on good regulatory practices states that '[n]othing in this Title shall affect the right of a Party to define or regulate its own levels of protection in pursuit or furtherance of its public policy objectives' in a non-exhaustive list of policy areas. While each side has regulatory autonomy, some of these areas, which

88 Art 318(2) TCA.
89 ibid Art 351.
90 ibid Art 345.
91 ibid Art 349.
92 ibid Art 103(2)(a).
93 ibid Art 111.
94 ibid Art 91(8).
95 ibid Art 450(2).
96 ibid Annex 12, Art 10.

include labour conditions and the environment and climate change, clearly link to the level playing field provisions and consequences for differentiation.

In terms of bilateral links, the deepest cooperation between agencies set out in the TCA is in energy and aviation. In energy, transmission system operators are required to request the opinions of ACER and the designated UK regulatory authority.[97] Further, those authorities should 'develop contacts and enter into administrative arrangements as soon as possible'.[98] Some provisions do extend to exchange of information on market monitoring and enforcement.[99] In aviation, in specific investigations and oversight in aviation safety, one party's authority may act as an observer in the other's activities (again, without amounting to 'systematic participation'), exchange information, and provide assistance.[100]

Regarding medicinal products, the TCA provides for the recognition of results of inspections carried out by each side's authorities,[101] but with rights to suspend that recognition, to be discussed in the Working Group on Medicinal Products.[102] Otherwise, each side's authorities shall 'endeavour' to consult each other and cooperate in relevant international bodies.[103] This is a far cry from the level of involvement in the EMA and the UK Medicines and Healthcare products Regulatory Agency.

There is a framework for cooperation on market surveillance and product safety, recognizing 'the importance of building mutual trust based on shared information'.[104] Administrative agencies may also play a role in technical discussions, which can be requested if 'a Party considers that a draft or proposed technical regulation or conformity assessment procedure of the other Party might have a significant effect on trade between them'.[105]

In some areas the TCA itself does not set up cooperation but instead the EU and UK 'encourage' administrative authorities to cooperate with their counterparts, eg on sustainable food systems,[106] on standards,[107] and between customs authorities.[108] The most prominent example is in competition enforcement, where there is explicit reference to subsequent cooperation agreements between each side's authorities, including exchange of confidential information.[109] Similarly, the provisions on subsidies allow for a cooperation framework between the respective

[97] ibid Art 317(3).
[98] ibid Art 318(1).
[99] ibid Art 318(3)).
[100] ibid Art 450(3)–(5).
[101] ibid Annex 12, Art 5(1).
[102] ibid Annex 12, Art 9.
[103] ibid Annex 12, Art 10.
[104] ibid Art 96(1).
[105] ibid Art 97.
[106] ibid Art 86.
[107] ibid Art 92.
[108] ibid Art 119(4).
[109] ibid Art 361.

independent authorities.[110] Significantly, Article 342(3) TCA states that the good regulatory practices title does not apply to regulatory authorities and regulatory measures, regulatory practices, or approaches of the *Member States*, so the TCA is largely silent on the role of regulatory networks in which the UK authorities coordinated with their national counterparts.[111]

The literature on the EU as an external regulator posits that regulatory extension occurs through both political and technocratic institutions, and different modes of governance: hierarchy, competition through the market, coordination, and networks.[112] The interplay of these factors will influence the prospects for regulatory differentiation. 'Territorial extension' may occur not only at country level, but also at the level of business or transactions.[113]

First, the foreign policy mode includes agreements with the EU and legislation referring to third countries, extending regulatory commitments to third-country actors.[114] These dynamics map on to hierarchy and competition. Hierarchy is characterized by coercive, rule-based discipline with implementation and enforcement through public institutions.[115] The overarching governance structures of the TCA could be seen as exemplifying this. Meanwhile, competition implies the behaviour of multinational market actors in continuing to comply with EU rules and norms, even in their non-EU market activities, contributing to the diffusion of EU rules and norms beyond the territory of the EU.[116]

Regarding the element of competition, differences in product standards between jurisdictions lead to increased costs and uncertainty for businesses, since different production lines for products for sale in different countries are inefficient. A *de facto* 'Brussels effect'[117] operates when firms and market actors required to produce goods to EU standards for the EU market rationally decide to comply with those same standards for their other geographic markets. This incentive to over-comply with EU rules is reflected in Bradford's condition of 'non-divisibility of standards', particularly economic (it is less expensive for producers to comply with

[110] ibid Art 371(2).

[111] (emphasis added). Member State authorities are mentioned in competition (Art 361), customs (Art PCUST.15), aviation safety (Annex 30, Art 5(2)(a)), administrative cooperation regarding posting of drivers (Annex 31, s 2 Art 6), and in offshore renewable energy (where a specific new forum is planned under Art 321(2)).

[112] Sandra Lavenex, 'The Power of Functionalist Extension: How EU Rules Travel' (2014) 21 Journal of European Public Policy 885; Armstrong, 'Regulatory Alignment' (n 27).

[113] Joanne Scott, 'The Global Reach of EU Law' in Marisa Cremona and Joanne Scott (eds), *EU Law Beyond Borders: The Extraterritorial Reach of EU Law* (OUP 2019).

[114] Lavenex, 'The Power of Functionalist Extension' (n 112); Joanne Scott, 'Extraterritoriality and Territorial Extension in EU Law' (2014) 62(1) American Journal of Comparative Law 87; Scott, 'The Global Reach of EU Law' (n 113).

[115] Armstrong, 'Regulatory Alignment' (n 27) 1105. See also Kenneth Armstrong, 'Regulatory Autonomy after EU Membership: Alignment, Divergence and the Discipline of Law' (2020) 45 European Law Review 207.

[116] Armstrong, 'Regulatory Alignment' (n 27).

[117] Anu Bradford, 'The Brussels Effect' (2015) 107 Northwestern University Law Review 1.

one standard than several) and technical (where firms cannot produce goods with different specifications for different markets).

This is linked to Bradford's third type of non-divisibility of standards: legal non-divisibility, developed by Scott.[118] Going beyond *de facto* incentives, firm-level territorial extension requires third-country companies to comply with EU law even when they are not producing goods for the EU market. Country-level territorial extension operates to make EU market access conditional upon the content of third-country law, giving rise to the *de jure* Brussels effect. This *de jure* effect occurs when a third country incorporates EU standards into its domestic legislation.[119] The UK did this initially through its EU (Withdrawal Agreement) Act 2018, with the immediate priority of avoiding lacunae in domestic law. Now, the UK's Retained EU Law (Revocation and Reform) Act 2023 aims to identity, remove, and replace EU-derived legislation. This raises questions of whether the pull of EU regulation wears off over time, and on the constraining impact of the TCA level playing field provisions and rebalancing measures.

It is important to bear in mind, however, that rules may be developed not only through governmental rule-making and primary legislation, but at a sectoral level between regulators, and in some cases with stakeholders themselves.[120] This leads us to the second type of institutional interaction, through technical cooperation between sectoral regulatory agencies. This maps onto the modes of coordination and networks. Coordination implies voluntary mutual agreement (such as in mutual recognition mechanisms) without transferring rule-making to an external authority. In the context of the TCA, this would include relatively weak regulatory cooperation measures and the groundwork for unilateral equivalence decisions in data and financial services. Networks imply sharing or production of knowledge among communities of, inter alia, regulators and standard-setting bodies.[121] Here, EU influence is extended through more subtle mechanisms of learning and socialization. Third-country regulators may be co-opted through functionalist extension of EU law and policy on a sectoral or policy area basis.[122]

The role of regulators and administrative institutions is likely to be significant in the trajectory of the EU–UK trade relationship, separately from the high-level political dynamics. As others have noted, the presence of independent regulatory bodies and 'regulatory clashes between jurisdictions creates a demand for cross-national initiatives to "solve" these clashes, whether through formal or informal means'.[123] Transnational executive bodies are, therefore, open for mutual

[118] ibid 17–19; Scott, 'The Global Reach of EU Law' n 113) 32–33.
[119] Scott, 'The Global Reach of EU Law' (n 113) 31.
[120] Adrienne Héritier, 'New Modes of Governance in Europe: Policy Making without Legislating?' (2002) IHS Political Science Series, No 81 on 'policy-making without legislating' through transgovernmental committees and regulatory agencies
[121] See n 83; Armstrong, 'Regulatory Alignment' (n 27).
[122] Lavenex, 'The Power of Functionalist Extension' (n 112) 887, 890.
[123] Henry Farrell and Abraham L Newman, 'Domestic Institutions beyond the Nation-State: Charting the New Interdependence Approach' (2014) 66 World Politics 331, 345.

influence in regulatory coordination.[124] Lavenex finds that external differentiation follows sector-specific functionalist dynamics that are only loosely linked to overarching foreign policy agreements (such as the European Economic Area (EEA), the European Neighbourhood Policy, and the bilateral agreements with Switzerland).[125] Of particular pertinence to the UK's position as a former Member State, institutional path dependencies are significant in extending governance modes beyond the EU's territory, and political structures lack the ability to fully steer them.[126]

The UK will experience mechanisms of European integration even without membership, given the interdependence of the EU and UK markets. As Trondal and Kühn observe, drawing from the position of Norway, civil servants and administrative officials are tightly interwoven into, and influenced by, EU institutions, largely as a result of 'increased institutionalization of the European multilevel administrative system in which national agencies have acquired a larger position as access points for EU agencies'.[127] Their longitudinal data on the domestic context showed that officials had become more integrated into the EU's multilevel administrative system over time, and that '(administrative) integration beyond membership is promoted and nudged by favourable organizational conditions at the domestic level'.[128] Thus, they expect the UK to experience 'silent EEA-ization'.[129] While the UK does not have Norway-style alignment or extension of the EU *acquis* as a 'quasi-member' through the EEA, it starts from a position of even greater integration as a former full EU Member State. While divergence after the UK's Retained EU Law (Revocation and Reform) Act 2023 remains to be seen, EU law is currently embedded throughout the UK's domestic legislation, case law, and administrative institutions. Moreover, withdrawal from the EU will affect the UK's future domestic regulatory architecture, by requiring either the designation of existing authorities or the establishment of new ones: first, it must transfer or duplicate previous EU competences from the EU level; and, second, there are institutional obligations arising from the WA and TCA.[130]

[124] Sandra Lavenex, 'The External Face of Differentiated Integration: Third Country Participation in EU Sectoral Bodies' (2015) 22 Journal of European Public Policy 836, 839

[125] ibid.

[126] S Lavenex, D Lehmkuhl, and N Wichmann, 'Modes of External Governance: A Cross-National and Cross-Sectoral Comparison' (2009) 16 Journal of European Public Policy 813, 813.

[127] Jarle Trondal and Nadja Kühn, 'Governing a Post-Brexit Europe and the Case of Norway: Integration without Membership in an Affiliated State' in Stefan Gänzle, Benjamin Leruth, and Jarle Trondal (eds), *Differentiated Integration and Disintegration in a Post-Brexit Era* (Routledge 2019) 173.

[128] ibid 165.

[129] Stefan Gänzle, Benjamin Leruth, and Jarle Trondal, 'Whither Differentiated (Dis)Integration in a "Post-Brexit Era"?' in Stefan Gänzle, Benjamin Leruth, and Jarle Trondal (eds) (n 127) 243.

[130] New UK public bodies created following Brexit include the Office for Environmental Protection, the Independent Monitoring Authority for Citizens' Rights (IMA), the Trade Remedies Authority, the Office for the [UK] Internal Market (sitting within the CMA), and the UK Office for SPS Trade Assurance, coordinating market access for imports of animals and animal products. The existing Competition and Markets Authority has taken on the subsidy oversight role required by the TCA. In

IV. Conclusions

As of 1 January 2021, the UK and the EU are two distinct regulatory and legal spaces.[131] The TCA recognizes regulatory autonomy—but at a cost. Overarching governance arrangements explicitly aim to constrain regulatory competitiveness. In maintaining a level playing field, much may rest on the interpretation of 'material' impact on trade and investment as a result of 'significant' divergences. Other factors acting to restrain or disincentivize regulatory differentiation include commitments on convergence to international standards (many of which are, in practice, based on EU standards)—and, in some cases, a duty to review adherence and explain any divergences from these—transparency requirements on new regulations, and unilateral equivalence decisions still to be taken. Still other elements may be more organic, including functionalist cooperation in sector-specific policy communities, and the path dependency which comes from the existing deep embeddedness of EU law in the UK. Withdrawal from the EU will also affect the UK's future domestic regulatory architecture.

In terms of governance architecture, the high-level political mechanisms—albeit underpinned by a legal framework—of the WA J C and TCA P C are relatively blunt instruments. The relevance of functionalist perspectives may increase as reality begins to bite. As the relationship moves beyond the transition period, market access and regulatory cooperation may become more important for the UK than (the appearance of) taking back control. The role of networks between regulators, decentralized horizontal coordination, and the existing embeddedness of EU law and standards through administrative institutions, are therefore significant factors. Monitoring and managing regulatory alignment requires technical assessments, putting technocratic executive authorities in a central position. The non-Member State UK, therefore, represents an ideal empirical case study (and case studies in particular sectors) to test and combine the 'Brussels effect' and the external regulatory reach of the EU, and multilevel governance and administrative integration beyond its borders.

It remains to be seen how willing each side (the EU and UK) will be to activate the remedial and rebalancing measures established through the hierarchical discipline of the WA and the TCA—with the ultimate possibility of suspension of obligations and harmful tit-for-tat retaliation—or whether any regulatory

chemicals, aviation, and medicines, responsibilities from the EU level have been taken over by existing authorities: the Health & Safety Executive, the Environment Agency, the Civil Aviation Authority, and the Medicines and Healthcare Products Regulatory Agency, respectively.

[131] European Commission, 'EU–UK Trade and Cooperation Agreement: protecting European interests, ensuring fair competition, and continued cooperation in areas of mutual interest' (Press release, 24 December 2020) available at <https://ec.europa.eu/commission/presscorner/detail/en/ip_20_2531> accessed 7 March 2021.

differentiation will be mediated through coordination and networks. Continued engagement within regulatory networks is likely to be beneficial for both the EU and the UK in terms of coordination, sharing of technical expertise, and opportunities for influence. In making their own decisions on which regulatory standards to adhere to, the economic necessities of businesses will be another important factor in the prospects for divergence.

In the context of the wider themes of this volume, the EU–UK trade relationship and its governance architecture engage questions of membership and participation, rights and obligations, and internal and external differentiation.

Regarding membership and participation, this volume's Introduction suggests that membership also implies full involvement in enforcement procedures. Mapping the scope of external differentiation may require separating consideration of decision-making and enforcement functions. The UK has clearly not been involved in EU decision-making procedures since withdrawal on 31 January 2020, including during the transition period. It is, nonetheless, involved in some enforcement procedures, eg collecting customs duties and carrying out checks on the EU's behalf. There is no membership or lesser participation in agencies, even where a third country is allowed. There is also a distinction between 'membership' and 'participation' in EU agencies. While, under Theresa May's government, UK participation in particular agencies had been the aim, ultimately the Johnson government's change of position meant that this was no longer pursued, even where participation is allowed in the relevant founding regulation of the agency. As noted in this chapter, there are various provisions in the WA and TCA for inter-institutional links between EU institutions and UK authorities. There may also be scope for the UK to remain involved in regulatory networks alongside the European Commission and Member State counterparts—the TCA is largely silent on this, but such practical coordination is likely to be beneficial to both sides.

Being an EU Member State entails 'a series of rights and obligations', including the duty of loyal or sincere cooperation. The balance of rights and obligations came up frequently in the EU–UK withdrawal negotiations, alongside references to 'cherry-picking'. In the final text, the specific wording of 'loyal cooperation' was eventually dropped in favour of the less EU-specific 'good faith',[132] except with reference to the transition period.[133] In the TCA, the level playing field arrangements state that either party may request a review of the TCA trade heading to assess whether it 'delivers an appropriate balance of rights and obligations'.[134] On safeguard measures, which either side may introduce to deal with serious economic,

[132] Art 5 WA.

[133] ibid Art 129(3): 'In accordance with the *principle of sincere cooperation*, the United Kingdom shall refrain, during the transition period, from any action or initiative which is likely to be prejudicial to the Union's interests, in particular in the framework of any international organisation, agency, conference or forum of which the United Kingdom is a party in its own right' (emphasis added).

[134] Art 411(8) TCA.

societal, or environmental difficulties, the trigger for the other party to take proportionate rebalancing measures is if a safeguard measure 'creates an imbalance between the rights and obligations under this Agreement or under any supplementing agreement'.[135]

Following years of internal differentiation, the UK took the ultimate opt-out. Adding to the EU's existing models of close relationships without membership, such as those with the EEA and Switzerland, its unique situation as a former Member State invites reconsideration of the conceptualization of external differentiation along territorial and functional lines. The UK's position represents an opportunity to test, in real time, the EU's external regulatory reach and the significance of institutional architecture.

[135] ibid Art 773(4).

9

Caught in the Balance: Consequences of Associated Membership over Time

*Nadja S Kühn and Jarle Trondal**

I. Introduction

After decades of integration, the European Union (EU) has become tightly interwoven into the societal and political fabric of European nation states. The classical dichotomies of Member States versus non-members, of ins versus outs, and dependent versus sovereign, fall short of expressing the complex reality of differentiation in the EU. This chapter contributes to the study of external differentiation in the EU by investigating the case of Norway. The study examines consequences of associated membership that is characterized by deep integration without formal EU membership. More recently, external differentiation of the EU has been illustrated by the lengthy and complex Brexit negotiation process between the United Kingdom (UK) and the EU.[1]

This chapter argues that an important dimension of association agreements or 'quasi-memberships' with 'third countries' relates to administrative cooperation. Whereas formal membership grants a state political access to EU decision-making arenas and processes, associated membership implies that domestic administrative institutions may participate in certain policy areas of the EU without being politically integrated into the decision-making processes. One consequence is that associated members rely strongly on administrative interaction with the EU administrative system. They may participate in administrative cooperation, such as expert committees or working groups under different EU institutions. Since bureaucratic processes are fundamental providers of political premises,[2] administrative interaction across levels of governance becomes not only an important

* This contribution is financially supported by the Norwegian Research Council ('EURODIV: Integration and division: Towards a segmented Europe') and university allowances. Previous versions of the chapter have been presented at the European Group of Public Administration (EGPA) in Milan, Italy, in 2017, and at the European Union Studies Association (EUSA) in Miami, Florida, in 2022. The authors acknowledge valuable comments from participants at both conferences.

[1] Frank Schimmelfennig, 'Debordering Europe: External Boundaries and Integration in the European Union' (2021) 28(3)Journal of European Public Policy, doi.org/10.1080/135011763.2021.1881589.

[2] B Guy Peters, *The Politics of Bureaucracy* (Routledge 2001); Dwight Waldo, *The Administrative State: A Study of the Political Theory of American Public Administration* (Routledge 1947).

Nadja S Kühn and Jarle Trondal, *Caught in the Balance* In: *Redefining EU Membership*. Edited by: Diane Fromage, Oxford University Press. © Nadja S Kühn and Jarle Trondal 2024. DOI: 10.1093/9780191948145.003.0009

tool for uploading preferences for nation states but may also shape domestic-level processes and policy outcomes.[3] This chapter shows the profound role of public administration in the multilevel governing system of the EU, in which 'third countries' are involved, and how this may influence domestic processes within these countries.

The chapter thus also contributes to studies of the European multilevel administrative system, consisting of strongly interconnected administrative bodies across levels of governance.[4] Administrative capacity-building by stealth at the EU level is seen as challenging administrative autonomy among national governments, particularly within associated 'third countries'.[5] These studies also suggest how an organizationally heterogeneous EU sends a plethora of differentiated 'signals' to national governments, eg how the Council of Ministers (Council) fuels executive coordination within national central administrations whereas the Commission circumvents executive hierarchies and privileges non-majoritarian bodies.[6] This study makes three contributions to the extant literature, as follows:

- Theoretically, the chapter examines how organizational factors shape processes of administrative integration across levels of governance in the EU.[7] An organizational approach emphasizes how organizational factors bias governance processes. By biasing and nudging actors' attention towards certain problems and solutions, certain policy outcomes become more likely than others. Administrative integration, this chapter establishes, is nudged by 'favourable' organizational conditions at the *domestic* level of government. The chapter establishes how the impact of the EU is mediated by organizational variables at the national level.
- Empirically, the chapter examines a case of deep EU integration without formal membership, represented by Norway. Norway enjoys associated membership, as outlined in Chapters 1 and 2 of this volume. To demonstrate how essential parameters of domestic public governance are systematically influenced by the EU even within a non-EU Member State, the chapter presents a novel *longitudinal* dataset consisting of a large-N (N = 3562) questionnaire study collected from among government officials in the Norwegian central administration in three different decades: in 1996, 2006, and 2016.

[3] Morten Egeberg, *Multilevel Union Administration* (Palgrave Macmillan 2006) 2.

[4] Michael Bauer and Jarle Trondal, *The Palgrave Handbook of the European Administrative System* (Palgrave Macmillan 2015) 10.

[5] Philipp Genschel and Markus Jachtenfuchs, *Beyond the Regulatory Polity* (OUP 2014) 10; Jarle Trondal, *An Emergent European Executive Order* (OUP 2010) 8.

[6] Morten Egeberg, Guenther Schaefer, and Jarle Trondal, 'The Many Faces of EU Committee Governance' (2003) 26 West European Politics 19, 40.

[7] Morten Egeberg and Jarle Trondal, *An Organizational Approach to Public Governance* (OUP 2018) 3; Johan P Olsen, 'The Bergen Approach to Public Administration and Political Organization' (2018) 34 Norsk Statsvitenskaplig Tidsskrift 188, 206.

Moreover, the chapter provides novel data from the *core executive* level of government (ministerial departments), and thereby adds to a literature that, empirically, has been dominated by studies of agencies. The data suggest that the EU contributes to reinforcing the administrative state through strong unintended effects. This self-reinforcing administrative bias is amplified by the fact that Norwegian government officials who deal with the EU are also, increasingly, loosely coupled to the political level (low-ranked staff) and tightly interwoven and influenced by EU institutions.

- Finally, the study contributes to a 'public administration turn' in EU studies.[8] Understanding the role of administrative actors in the political-administrative life of the EU has been essential to this turn.[9] The inherent State prerogative of preparing and executing policy has been challenged by the rise of independent and integrated administrative capacities at the EU level. The supply of organizational capacities inside the European Commission—together with the rise of EU agencies—has enabled the executive branch of the EU to act fairly independently of domestic government institutions.[10] Moreover, the organizational capacities of EU-level administrative actors supply them with a capacity to influence non-majoritarian institutions (agencies) at domestic level,[11] even in associated non-Member States such as Norway.[12]

The chapter is structured as follows: the next section presents the case of Norway by outlining both its particular form of association to the EU and key characteristics of the government apparatus. The subsequent section outlines an organizational theory approach to administrative integration beyond full membership. Third, a section on data and methods is included, before presenting and discussing the empirical observations. The chapter concludes with key findings and some suggestions for future research.

II. The Case of Norway

Examining government administration of a non-EU Member State allows us to study external differentiation of the EU and the external effects of EU norms and rules beyond EU borders. Compared with contemporary instances of external differentiation of the EU, Norway is still by far the most strongly integrated EU

[8] Bauer and Trondal (n 4) 9; Egeberg, *Multilevel Union Administration* (n 3) 12; Jarle Trondal, 'The Public Administration Turn in Integration Research' (2007) 14 Journal of European Public Policy 960, 972.

[9] Olsen, 'The Bergen Approach' (n 7) 206.

[10] Morten Egeberg and Jarle Trondal, 'Researching European Union Agencies: What Have We Learned (and Where do We Go from Here?)' (2017) 55 Journal of Common Market Studies 675, 690.

[11] Egeberg, *Multilevel Union Administration* (n 3) 9.

[12] See Bruno de Witte, in this volume.

non-member, through a dense web of agreements and administrative relations.[13] This affiliated status grants the Norwegian central administration the right of interaction and participation vis-à-vis most parts of the EU administration, which in turn paves the way for administrative integration across levels of governance. Moreover, the absence of political representation at the EU level provides fewer incentives for policy coordination within the national government. In consequence, government officials may enter the European policy-shaping stage with unclear and ambiguous mandates, leaving them to rely extensively on discretionary capacities and powers. Thus, it may be contended that administrative integration across levels of governance might go even further in affiliated non-Member States than in EU Member States, due to their exclusion from political representation in the Council. In line with this assumption, this chapter shows how a lack of political representation in the Council (and the European Parliament) mobilizes administrative bias in the national core executive. This denotes that national political leaders are less involved in the handling of EU affairs than the national civil service. Consequently, integration may happen more easily by stealth in affiliated states such as Norway than in EU Member States, even though the official position is not to become a political member.[14]

The launch of the European Economic Area (EEA) Agreement in 1994 marked the beginning of a new area of dense administrative integration between EU institutions and the Norwegian central administration. Yet, the EEA Agreement was considered merely as a *prelude* and *interim period* towards full EU membership.[15] However, following another[16] rejection of EU membership in a national referendum in 1994, the EEA Agreement was to be reintroduced as Norway's foundational connection to the EU in the years to come. Additionally, close historical and cultural ties, as well as shared policy preferences in a host of policy areas, led to subsequent agreements in areas outside the framework of the EEA Agreement (Norwegian government 2012–13), such as the Schengen Agreement and agreements on justice and home affairs, defence policy, and participation in EU programmes. At present, approximately 100 agreements have been agreed between Norway and the EU, with the EEA Agreement being the most encompassing one. In effect, while the *form* of affiliation has remained

[13] Morten Egeberg and Jarle Trondal, 'Differentiated Integration in Europe: The Case of EEA Country, Norway' (1999) 37 Journal of Common Market Studies 133, 142; Sandra Lavenex, 'Concentric Circles of Flexible "European" Integration: A Typology of EU External Governance Relations' (2011) 9 Comparative European Politics 372, 393; Jon Erik Fossum and Hans Petter Graver, Squaring the Circle on Brexit (Bristol University Press 2018) 43; C Franklin, and contrast with the Swiss case analysed by A Ott and B Pirker, in this volume.

[14] Giandomenico Majone, *Dilemmas of European Integration* (OUP 2005) 1ff.

[15] Fossum and Graver (n 13) 1ff.

[16] In a first referendum, held in 1972, Norway rejected membership of the EEC by 53.5 per cent (voter turnout 79.2 per cent). In the second referendum, held in 1994, it rejected EU membership by 52.2 per cent (voter turnout 89 per cent).

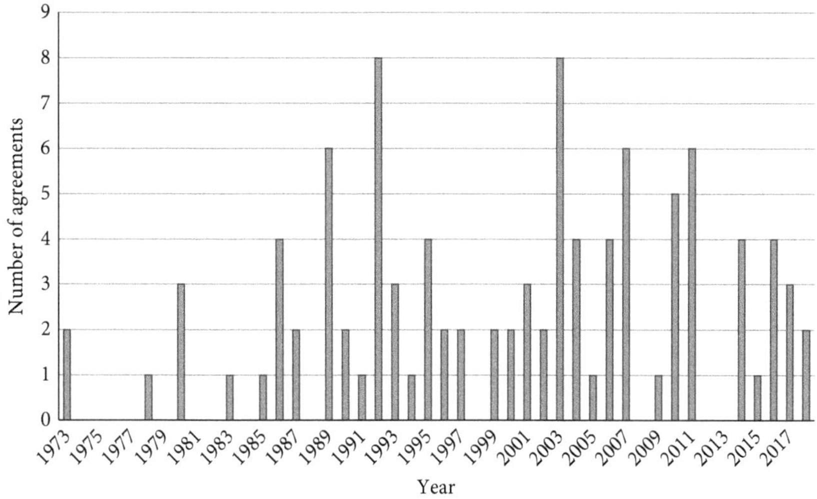

Figure 9.1 Number of agreements between Norway and the EU, by year, 1973–2018
Source: Norwegian Government (2019)

stable during the past twenty years, the *scope* of the affiliation has undergone significant expansion—partly in response to policy progressions in the EU, partly in response to the dynamic character of the EEA Agreement, and partly because of Norway signing

agreements that are sectoral in nature are continuously increasing in number with the EU. In sum, this has increased the subsequent likelihood of Norwegian government institutions and governance processes being profoundly shaped by EU-level institutions and decision-making processes. Figures 9.1 and 9.2 illustrate the dynamic character of the associated membership of Norway.

Figure 9.1 provides an overview of the number of agreements concluded between Norway and the EU each year, and illustrates that this dynamism largely coincides with major Treaty negotiations within the EU, notably the Single European Act, the Maastricht Treaty, the Amsterdam Treaty, the Nice Treaty, and the Lisbon Treaty. Figure 9.2 shows how these agreements have accumulated over time. Overall, both figures suggest a profoundly dynamic character of the associated membership. At the same time, based on the expanding EEA Agreement that ties Norway to the EU's internal market, the *form* of association has remained stable over time.

The *dynamic* character of the EEA Agreement requires Norwegian law to continuously adjust to new EU legislation. The Agreement is based on the premise of *dynamic homogeneity*, and more than 14,000 EU legal acts have been incorporated into the Agreement since 1994. The Agreement covers mostly the single market *acquis*, but also rules from adjacent policy areas, making it the most extensive form of agreement between the EU and a non-member as regards regulatory scope and

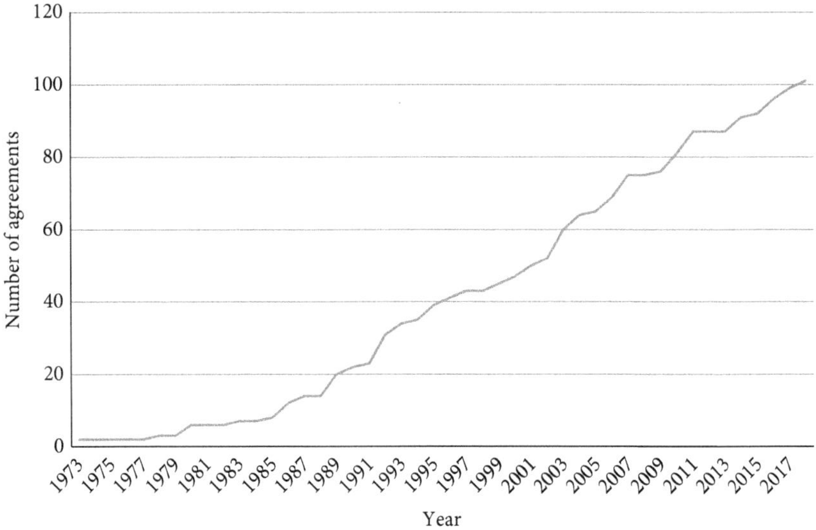

Figure 9.2 Accumulated number of agreements between Norway and the EU, 1973–2018
Source: Norwegian Government (2019)

legal obligations resulting from the contractual relations.[17] At the same time, the Agreement blocks Norwegian governments qua state from political representation in the Council. Nonetheless, whereas Norway's associated status does not grant it formal access to EU decision-making institutions, it provides for *administrative* participation at various stages of the EU's legislative process. Norwegian ministries and agencies are represented in Commission expert committees and comitology committees, attend boards and committees in many EU agencies, are entitled to second national experts to the Commission, and participate in a host of European administrative networks (EANs). Norwegian civil servants are thus granted privileged access to EU-related work and are largely responsible for handling everyday relationships with EU institutions, in upstream processes (the agenda-setting processes) and in downstream processes (the implementation and practising of EU law). Thus, whereas Norway is politically sidelined in EU decision-making processes, the Norwegian central administration is granted access to the EU bureaucratic apparatus quite similar to that of EU Member States.

Analogous to the Commission and EU agencies, the Norwegian central administration is organized according to the principles of purpose and function. From an organizational perspective, this has two substantial implications: firstly, it

[17] Lavenex (n 13) 393; Fossum and Graver (n 13) 43.

encourages sectoral allegiances and integration across levels of governance; and, secondly, it underpins interministerial fragmentation. Moreover, as far as policy harmonization is concerned, the *form* of affiliation does in fact warrant EEA countries the same level of integration as full Member States. Since Norway does not have political representation in the Council, it has been argued that Norwegian sector ministries are likely to be even more strongly affected by the Commission than Member States' ministries,[18] due to a lack of political 'filter' and subsequent political steering. This assumption, however, is beyond the scope of this chapter.

Like most core executives, the Norwegian central administration is organized into core executive ministries and subordinated agencies. The system is characterized by a ministerial primacy whereby subordinated agencies are subject to ministerial control and accountability from the responsible minister, and not primarily from a government collegium. The total number of employees within the central administration[19] has increased from around 13,000 in 1994 to 21,000 in 2015, of which 4,600 are employed in the ministries and the remaining 16,400 are employed in subordinate agencies.[20] While Norwegian ministries are secretariats for the political leadership, with planning and coordinating functions,[21] agencies are mainly responsible for advising ministries and being technical helpers, but are also essential ingredients in the political processes when preparing, implementing, and administering policies.

III. An Organizational Theory Approach to Administrative Integration

Public administration is not a neutral tool in the hands of shifting governments. An organizational approach emphasizes that public administration might have an independent role in its own right. This theoretical framework is grounded on the assumption that internal organizational characteristics of public administration may explain *how* it works and changes. Consequently, organizational variables may help explain how domestic ministries 'adopt' the influence of the EU, and thus how integration may happen even without formal EU membership, and shape the pursuit of domestic public governance.[22]

[18] Egeberg and Trondal, 'Differentiated Integration in Europe' (n 13) 142; Jarle Trondal, 'Beyond the EU Membership—Non-membership Dichotomy? Supranational Identities among National EU Decision-makers' (2002) 9 Journal of European Public Policy 468, 487.

[19] Includes all employees in ministries and subordinate units.

[20] Direktorat for Forvaltning og IKT (Difi), 'Ansatte i staten' (2015) retrieved February 2017 from https:www.difi.no/rapporter-og-nokkeltall-og-statistikk/nokkeltall-og-statistikk/ansatte-i-statenacces sed 1 July 2023.

[21] Tom Christensen and Per Lægreid, 'Living in the Past? Change and Continuity in the Norwegian Central Civil Service' (2009) 69 Public Administration Review 951, 961.

[22] Bauer and Trondal (n 4) 20; Morten Egeberg, Åse Gornitzka, and Jarle Trondal, 'Organization Theory' in Chris Ansell and Jacob Torfing (eds), *Handbook on Theories of Governance* (Edward Elgar 2016) 32, 45; James March and Johan P Olsen, *Rediscovering Institutions: The Organizational Basis of*

Literature harbours competing ideas on the extent to which actual decision behaviour reflects the organization structure within which actors are embedded. These ideas include public choice theories, organizational sociology, and representative bureaucracy, to mention only a few.[23] While some observers ascribe lack of government action to political leaders' lack of will, this chapter advocates that political will is endogenously shaped by organizational positions which also enable (and constrain) action. An organizational approach posits that organizational factors or variables are not merely an expression of symbol politics,[24] but create systematic bias in human behaviour and decision-making processes by directing and nudging choice and attention towards certain problems and solutions, ie making certain outcomes more likely than others.[25] Contemporary organization theory literature focuses on the explanatory power of organizational factors.[26] Two reasons are given for focusing on organizational structure: first, empirical studies demonstrate the systematic and significant effect of organization structure on decision-making behaviour;[27] second, organization structure, compared with other factors that intervene in the policy process, is likely to be more subject to deliberate change, and may thus be an important design instrument of the context of choice in public governance.[28]

An organization structure is a normative structure composed of rules and roles stipulating who is expected to do what, and how.[29] The structure regulates actors'

Politics (Free Press 1989), 5; Morten Egeberg and Jarle Trondal, 'Why Strong Coordination at one Level of Government is Incompatible with Strong Coordination across Levels (and How to Live with It): The Case of the European Union' (2015) 94 Public Administration 579, 592; Johan P Olsen, 'Change and Continuity: An Institutional Approach to Institutions of Democratic Government' (2009) 1 European Political Science Review 3, 32.

[23] William Niskanen, *Bureaucracy and Representative Government* (Aldine 1971), 1 ff; Jon Meyer and Brian Rowan, 'Institutionalized Organizations: Formal Structure as Myth and Ceremony' (1977) 83 American Journal of Sociology 340, 363; Kenneth Meier and K Jureé Capers, 'Representative Bureaucracy: Four Questions' in B Guy Peters and Jon Pierre (eds), *The SAGE Handbook of Public Administration* (SAGE 2012) 420, 431.

[24] Meyer and Rowan (n 23) 363; Nils Brunsson, *The Organization of Hypocrisy* (John Wiley 1989) 5.

[25] Martin Bækgaard, 'The Impact of Formal Organizational Structure on Politico-administrative Interaction: Evidence from a Natural Experiment' (2011) 89 Public Administration 1063, 1080; Luther Gulick, 'Notes on the Theory of Organization' in Luther Gulick and Lyndall Urwick (eds), *Papers on the Science of Administration* (Institute of Public Administration 1937) 3 ff; Thomas Hammond, 'In Defence of Luther Gulick's "Notes on the Theory of Organization"' (1990) 68 Public Administration 143, 173; Richard Thaler and Cass Sunstein, *Nudge: Improving Decisions on Health, Wealth and Happiness* (Penguin Books 2009) 1ff.

[26] Morten Egeberg, 'How Bureaucratic Structure Matters: An Organizational Perspective' in Peters and Pierre (eds) (n 23) 77, 87; Egeberg and Trondal, *An Organizational Approach to Public Governance* (n 7) 3.

[27] eg Tom Christensen and Per Lægreid, 'The Whole-of-government Approach to Public Sector Reform' (2007) 67 Public Administration Review 1059, 1066; Jarle Trondal, 'Governing at the Frontier of the European Commission: The Case of Seconded National Officials' (2006) 29 West European Politics 147, 160; Egeberg, Gornitzka, and Trondal (n 22) 45.

[28] ibid; Thaler and Sunstein (n 25) 1ff.

[29] Richard Scott and Gerald Davis, *Organizations and Organizing: Rational, Natural and Open System Perspectives* (Routledge 2016) 1ff.

access to decision processes, expresses the preferences and ambitions that should be pursued, limits the set of problems and solutions that should be considered relevant, and creates action capacity by assigning roles to portfolios. It shapes decision-making behaviour by offering actors 'a systematic and predictable selection of problems, solutions and choice opportunities'.[30] While an organizational structure does not predict or determine *actual* decision-making behaviour, it makes some choices become more *likely* than others.[31] This happens by regulating actors' access to decision situations, mobilizing attention to certain problems and solutions, structuring patterns of conflict and cooperation (and influencing power relations), and enabling coordination and steering along certain dimensions rather than others. This also implies that organizational factors do not *directly* impact on society; rather, societal consequences are likely to occur *via* and *due to* governance processes.

The next puzzle is why actors tend to follow structures and rules. Bounded rationality[32] is one mechanism that connects role expectations to actual behaviour; organizational structure simplifies actors' cognitive maps by biasing their attention towards a selection of problems and solutions and suggesting ways of connecting them. The idea of bounded rationality holds that decision-makers operate under three key limitations: limited information about possible solutions and alternatives, limited cognitive capacity to evaluate and process information, and limited time to make decisions. Subsequently, actors tend to opt for a selection of satisfactory alternatives rather than optimal ones, and often turn to their proximate contexts and available knowledge to search for appropriate choices.[33] A second mechanism, the logic of appropriateness, thus views human action as driven by internalized perceptions of what is perceived as appropriate in any given situation.[34] Finally, actors may be rule- and role-compliant because it fits their self-interests. Organizations are thus seen as incentive systems that administer rewards and punishments.

In sum, these mechanisms may explain why structural characteristics *of* central administrative institutions bias how the EU 'hits' domestic government institutions. Essential to this chapter is examining how different structural characteristics of core executive institutions matter in this respect. Three such structural variables are outlined in the following: horizontal specialization, vertical specialization, and organizational affiliations.

[30] James March and Johan P Olsen, *Ambiguity and Choice in Organizations* (Universitetsforlaget 1976) 11.
[31] Egeberg and Trondal, *An Organizational Approach to Public Governance* (n 7) 4.
[32] Herbert Simon, *Administrative Behaviour* (The Free Press 1957), 3.
[33] ibid.
[34] James March and Johan P Olsen, Rediscovering Institutions (n 22) 3ff.

A. Horizontal specialization

Horizontal specialization refers to how tasks or portfolios are allocated horizontally *within and between* organizations. Those policy areas that are encompassed by the same organizational unit are expected to be better coordinated than those that are allocated to separate organizational units. Luther Gulick contemplated four fundamental principles of horizontal specialization of tasks within organizations, namely specialization according to (i) territory, (ii) sector/purpose, (iii) function/process, and (iv) clientele.[35] He also emphasized the mutual relationship between specialization and coordination; policy problems that are encompassed by the same organizational unit are more likely to be coordinated than those belonging to separate organizational units. Accordingly, empirical studies show that, while public officials find coordination to work effectively within their own administrative unit or ministry, this holds less across administrative units or ministries.[36] Therefore, the departmental affiliation of policy units could make a significant difference in how governance processes are likely to unfold. In the same vein, cleavages of conflict are also likely to reflect these principles of organizational specialization. For example, specialization according to purpose is likely to mobilize sectoral lines of cooperation and conflict and thereby foster policy consistency within policy areas and ministerial portfolios. We thus expect that public officials who are embedded in organizations that are primarily specialized by purpose are likely to coordinate more strongly *within* their respective policy domains than across such domains. In the case of government ministries, we thus expect that officials embedded in sector ministries will report stronger *intra*ministerial than interministerial coordination.

Public administrative institutions are, moreover, embedded in the EU's multilevel politico-administrative order.[37] Consequently, we hypothesize that organizational compatibilities across levels of governance are likely to shape governing processes. Studies show that organizations that are specialized according to similar organizational principles tend to align more easily across levels of governance than those institutions that are organized according to different principles.[38] Arguably, organizational compatibility in this regard across levels of governance is likely to

[35] Gulick (n 25) 15.

[36] Husseim Kassim and others, *The European Commission of the Twenty-First Century* (OUP 2013) 189.

[37] See, eg Giandomenico Majone, *Regulating Europe* (Routledge 1996) 3; Renaud Dehousse, 'Regulation by Networks in the European Community: The Role of European Agencies' (1997) 4 Journal of European Public Policy 246, 261; David Levi-Faur, 'Regulatory Networks and Regulatory Agencification: Towards a Single European Regulatory Space' (2011) 18 Journal of European Public Policy 810, 829; Morten Egeberg and Jarle Trondal, 'The Case of the European Union' (n 22) 592; Rik Joosen and Gis Brandsma, 'Transnational Executive Bodies: EU Policy Implementation between the EU and Member-state Level' (2017) 95 Public Administration 423, 436.

[38] Maria Martens, *Organized Administrative Integration* (ARENA Report 2010), 1ff.

facilitate allegiances and cooperation *across* levels of governance. Hence, the effects of organizational principles at one level of governance may be conditioned by the degree of organizational compatibility across levels.[39] Essentially, the executive branch of the EU—concentrated at the Commission, and in EU agencies[40]—is specialized according to purpose (sector) and function (process), and thus largely compatible with national central administrations. Commission DGs and their system of expert committees are largely organized similarly to domestic sector ministries (according to purpose). By contrast, domestic ministries of foreign affairs (MFA) are mainly specialized according to territory, and thus are organizationally compatible with the core structure of the Council. This suggests that domestic sector ministries are likely to align with the Commission DGs more than with the Council structure. Moreover, the continuous expansion of scope and content in the EEA Agreement (from 1994 onwards) gives reason to assume that this pattern has been reinforced over time. The following general propositions may thus be derived:

P1: Due to organizational compatibility, ministerial officials in sector ministries are more likely to interact with the Commission than with other EU institutions.

P2: The coordination of EU-related work within domestic central administrations is relatively lower between than within ministries.

B. Vertical specialization

Vertical specialization denotes division of responsibility and labour *within and between* levels of authority. This chapter focuses empirically on the effect of hierarchy *within* ministerial departments. Hierarchies between organizations are likely to mobilize certain decision premises, eg broader policy perspectives in hierarchically superior units than in lower-ranked units. Vertical specialization between organizations implies installing an organizational boundary between a superior and a subordinate unit. Agencification, the process whereby regulatory tasks are transferred from ministerial departments to semi-independent regulatory bodies, is a topical example. The New Public Management (NPM) wave that swept across

[39] Maria Cowles, James Caporaso, and Thomas Risse-Kappen, *Transforming Europe: Europeanization and Domestic Change* (Cornell University Press 2001) 6; Christoph Knill and Dirk Lehmkuhl, 'How Europe Matters. Different Mechanisms of Europeanization' (2002) 3(7) European Integration online Papers (EIoP), available at SSRN: http://dx.doi.org/10.2139/ssrn.302746 accessed 1 July 2023; James March and Johan P Olsen, *Democratic Government* (The Free Press 1995) 44.

[40] Bauer and Trondal (n 4) 16; Egeberg, *Multilevel Union Administration* (n 3) 6.

the Organisation for Economic Co-operation and Development (OECD) states during the 1980s and 1990s was a strong advocate of autonomy, fragmentation, and proliferation of public administration institutions and systems. One result was that vertical specialization, in the form of structural devolution, became a major reform trend across Europe (in public administration terms, agencification; in organizational terms, inter-organizational vertical specialization). This reform has led to semi-autonomous agencies enjoying ever more degrees of autonomy at both the national and EU levels.[41]

Hierarchy within ministries—or intra-organizational vertical specialization—is measured in this chapter by an official's rank within their respective ministry. Studies have demonstrated that leaders identify with a larger part of their organization than those in the lower ranks. Leaders also interact more frequently across organizational units, and are exposed to broader flows of information than their subordinates. Higher-ranked staff in both ministries and subordinated agencies have been shown to be more attentive to political signals than lower-ranked personnel.[42] This implies that leaders are better equipped to take into consideration a wider set of goals, alternatives, and consequences when making choices. Studies show that top-ranked staff tend to identify more frequently than staff in the lower echelons with organizations as a whole.[43] Additionally, these officials are exposed to a broader range of information than lower-level staff, and thus may be more attentive to broader organizational perspectives than lower-ranked personnel.[44] It follows that government officials in the lower ranks are more loosely coupled to the political leadership and have more local perspectives on task execution, compared with higher-ranked staff. This has one important implication: a relative degree of insulation and autonomy from political leadership makes lower-ranked officials more eligible receivers of impulses from EU-level institutions and processes. The following general proposition is derived:

P3: Ministerial officials at higher ranks are *less* likely to be strongly involved in EU-related work and thereby *less* likely to interact with EU institutions compared with officials at lower ranks.

[41] Per Lærgreid and others, 'The Structural Anatomy of the Norwegian State: Increased Specialization or a Pendulum Shift?' in Per Lægreid and Koen Verhoest (eds), *Governance of Public Sector Organizations* (Palgrave Macmillan 2010) 21, 43; Phillipe Bezes and others, 'Understanding Organizational Reforms in the Modern State: Specialization and Integration in Norway and France' (2013) 26 Governance 147, 175.

[42] Tom Christensen and Per Lægreid, 'Living in the Past?' (n 21) 961; Morten Egeberg and Harald Sætren, 'Identities in Complex Organizations: A Study of Ministerial Bureaucrats' in Morten Egeberg and Per Lægreid (eds), *Organizing Political Institutions* (Scandinavian University Press 1999) 105.

[43] ibid.

[44] Egeberg and Trondal, *An Organizational Approach to Public Governance* (n 7) 10.

C. Organizational affiliation

Organizational affiliations consist of primary and secondary structures. A 'primary structure' is defined as the structure to which participants are expected to devote most of their loyalty, time, and energy. A typical example would be a bureaucratic unit like a ministry. A 'secondary structure' is defined as a structure to which participants are expected to be part-timers. Secondary structures include collegial bodies, committees, and networks.[45] It follows that secondary structures are unlikely to shape actors' decision behaviour to the same extent as primary structures. The EU multilevel administrative system comprises a set of interconnected organizations at different levels of authority. Domestic ministerial officials that operate within this frame are likely to be exposed to several behavioural premises from their primary and secondary affiliations. Empirical studies show that interdepartmental committees, regional councils, and public–private governing arrangements enhance interaction and coordination, and build trust relationships among the participants; however, the effects are moderate.[46] Moreover, a *logic of primacy* suggests that the primary affiliation is likely to affect behaviour more extensively than the secondary one.[47] The following general propositions are derived (see Table 9.1):

P4: When taking part in both primary and secondary structures, ministerial officials are likely to attend to and emphasize signals from both structures, albeit most strongly from primary structures.

P5: When in conflict, ministerial officials are more likely to emphasize signals from primary than from secondary affiliations.

IV. Data and Methods

This chapter benefits from a unique dataset on the role of central administration in the public governance process. Over the last thirty years, a group of Norwegian scholars, including the authors, has each decade conducted surveys in the Norwegian central administration (1976, 1986, 1996, 2006, and 2016). The datasets include questions about the civil servants' backgrounds, careers, contact

[45] Morten Egeberg, 'How Bureaucratic Structure Matters' (n 26) 87.

[46] Inger Stigen, 'Avbyråkratisering og Modifisert Forhandling? Om Bruk av Prosjektorganisasjon i Norsk Sentraladministrasjon' (1991) 7 Norsk Statsvitenskapelig Tidsskrift 173, 191; Per Lægreid and others, 'Coordination Challenges and Administrative Reforms' in Gerhard Hammerschmid, Steven Van de Walle, Rhys Andrews, and Philippe Bezes (eds), *Public Administration Reforms in Europe: The View from the Top* (Edward Elgar 2016) 244; Christopher Ansell and Alison Gash, 'Collaborative Governance in Theory and Practice' (2008) 18 Journal of Public Administration Research and Theory 543, 571.

[47] James March, *A Primer on Decision-Making* (The Free Press 1994) 57ff.

Table 9.1 Summary of propositions

Horizontal specialization	*P1*: Due to organizational compatibility, officials in sector ministries are more likely to interact with the Commission than with other EU institutions.
	P2: Due to organizational compatibility, officials in sector ministries are more likely to interact with the Commission than with other EU institutions.
Vertical specialization	*P3*: Ministerial officials at higher ranks are *less* likely to be strongly involved in EU-related work and thereby less likely to interact with EU institutions compared with ministerial officials at lower ranks.
Organizational affiliation	*P4*: When taking part in both primary and secondary structures, ministerial officials are likely to attend to and emphasize signals from both structures, albeit most strongly from primary structures.
	P5: When in conflict, ministerial officials are more likely to emphasize signals from primary than from secondary affiliations.

patterns, priorities, perceptions about power, reforms, and internationalization. From 1996, the surveys included questions about the central administration's relations with the EU. This chapter includes data from the 1996, 2006, and 2016 surveys, providing an overall N of 3562.

The surveys were all sent to 'A-level' officials with a minimum of one year in office. Appointment at this level usually requires a university degree. Hence, the sample is the total universe of 'A-level' civil servants in Norwegian ministries. These surveys represent *the* 'most thorough screening' of the Norwegian central administration, and thus the most comprehensive dataset on the effects of European integration on a national government administration.[48] To allow for comparisons across time, the questionnaires are kept nearly identical over time, with just a few necessary adjustments. Whereas the survey from 1996 was distributed to the respondents by postal mail, the 2006 and 2016 surveys were conducted as online surveys by the Norwegian Centre for Research Data (NSD). All datasets have been stored and made publicly available by NSD. The overall response rate is solid and the total response rates have decreased only marginally during this twenty-year period. The decrease in response rates from 1996 to 2016 may partly derive from a change of survey technology from postal survey to online survey. The main explanation for decreasing response rates is a general fatigue among respondents towards surveys.

[48] Karin Geuijen and others, *The New Eurocrats: National Civil Servants in EU Policymaking* (Amsterdam University Press 2008) 25.

Table 9.2 Sample size and response rates in the ministry surveys, by year

	1996	2006	2016
N	1,497	1,874	2,322
Response rates	72%	67%	60%

Two caveats should be mentioned. First, studies that rely on respondents' own behavioural *perceptions* do not directly observe public governance processes or behaviour. Respondents may thus exaggerate or downplay their own role or the roles of others. Yet, the use of three large-N surveys does substantially increase the likelihood of robust conclusions. Moreover, the use of different indicators of behaviour increases the validity of measurement. Second, the use of cross-sectional data may be biased by variation in perceptions, or the fact that it fails to take into account concurring factors that may influence outcome. Ideally, in order to draw robust conclusions on causal effects, research on developments over time should benefit systematic comparisons of the same individuals over time. Table 9.2 gives an overview of the data.

V. Administrative Integration without Membership

This section demonstrates how the EU contributes to a self-reinforcing administrative bias in the case of associated membership of the EU. The self-reinforcing administrative bias is observed when Norwegian officials actively involved with EU-related tasks become increasingly distant from the domestic political level and are strongly 'Europeanized' by being tightly interwoven in, and influenced by, EU institutions and policy processes.

First, the surveys asked ministerial officials how affected, in general, they were by the EU/EEA/Schengen in their daily work. Table 9.3 displays an overall stability in this regard over time, yet with a small but steady increase during the last decades. Notably, the proportion of respondents reporting being affected to a *very large* or *large* degree increases from 23 per cent in 1996 to 25 per cent in 2006, and 26 per cent in 2016. The proportion of respondents reporting little or no affectedness varied between 54 per cent (1996), 58 per cent (2006), and 51 per cent (2016).[49] From this, we may infer a small but steady increase in the proportion of officials being affected, whereas the proportion of officials reporting no affectedness fluctuates. In the remainder, only those respondents who report being affected (to a fairly small degree or more) by the EU/EEA/Schengen are included in the analysis.

49 Applies combined values.

Table 9.3 Percentage of officials who reported being affected by the EU/EEA/Schengen, by year

	1996	2006	2016
To a very large extent	11	13	14
To a fairly large extent	12	12	12
To some extent	23	18	23
To a fairly small extent	27	21	31
Not affected	27	37	20
N	100 (1,463)	100 (1,704)	100 (1,773)

Table 9.3 reports the degree to which respondents are affected by the EU/EEA/Schengen.

The respondents were asked about their contacts with and participation in EU institutions. Despite an overall low N, Table 9.4 suggests two main patterns: first, we see an overall stability over time in such participation; and second, we observe that organizational affiliations shape participatory patterns (P1). First, while we observe increased contact between sector ministries, the Commission, expert committees, and comitology committees from 1996 to 2006, these patterns remained stable during the most recent decade. This suggests that Norwegian ministries have experienced a *de facto threshold* in their access to the EU administration.[50] Correspondingly, the gap between the sector ministries and the MFA shows a notable increase between 1996 and 2006, and then remains stable from 2006 to 2016. This gap arguably reflects organizational compatibility between sector ministries and the EU administration (P2). This effect is fuelled by the EEA Agreement making the Commission the *main* partner for sector ministries, which in turn tends to bias the access structure for Norwegian ministries vis-à-vis EU institutions. Also worth noting is that, whereas contacts with the Commission remained stable during the most recent decade, sector ministries' corresponding contacts with EU agencies decreased. This may reflect the fact that national agencies have acquired a larger role as the national access points for EU agencies over time.[51] Second, the data show that ministry affiliation matters (P1), since Table 9.4

[50] This observation also reflects fairly low levels of resources invested in EU regulatory governance in the Norwegian central administration, including few resources for influencing the development of new EU rules, in the national adoption of EU rules, and in the amendment of existing EU rules; Regelrådet, 'Innspill til arbeidsgruppen som utreder departementenes EØS-arbeid' (Sekretariatet 15 May 2020), 7ff.

[51] Egeberg and Trondal, 'The Case of the European Union' (n 22) 592.

Table 9.4 Percentage of officials who report contact with* and/or participation in** EU-level institutions, by year and ministerial affiliation (sector ministries (SM)/ Ministry of Foreign Affairs (MFA)) (percentages)

	1996		2006		2016		
	SM	MFA	SM	MFA	SM	MFA	N
Contact with the Commission	68	32	83	17	83	17	100 (115)
Contact with the Council	—	—	—	—	57	43	100 (21)
Contact with the European Parliament	—	—	—	—	22	78	100 (9)
Contact with EU agencies	—	—	90	10	76	24	100 (39)
Participation in expert committee(s)	82	18	95	5	89	11	100 (94)
Participation in comitology committee(s)	86	14	100	0	100	0	100 (21)
Participation in the Council	—	—	—	—	60	40	100 (10)
Participation in committees, boards, etc in EU agencies	—	—	—	—	94	6	100 (18)

* The 'contact' variables combine values 1 and 2 on the following four-point scale: (1) app. every week; (2) app. every month; (3) a few times; (4) never.

** The 'participation' variables apply value 1 on the following three-point scale: (1) several times; (2) once; (3) never.

reveals a difference between staff affiliated to sector ministries and staff affiliated to the MFA. Overall, sector ministries are consistently more involved with EU institutions than MFA staff. Moreover, reflecting compatible principles of organization, officials from sector ministries tend to concentrate their attention towards the Commission, EU agencies, and Commission expert committees, whereas officials from the MFA give more attention to the Council. As already mentioned, these patterns reflect the biased access structure embedded in the EEA Agreement. Table 9.4 reports patterns of contact and participation in EU-level institutions.

Next, respondents were asked about their coordination behaviour. Table 9.5 reveals an overall low level of coordination of EU-related work and an increasing reliance on *intra*ministerial coordination over time. In support of P2, coordination is slightly higher *within* ministries than *between* ministries at all three points of observation. Moreover, the gap between *intra*ministerial and low-level *inter*ministerial coordination increases over time. Since MFA chairs the national high-level interministerial coordination committee, these data also suggest a declining coordinating role of the MFA in EU-related affairs over time. This shows a rising reliance on sector ministries and sector specialists, and a declining reliance on the generalists from the MFA. Also worth noting is the general decrease

Table 9.5 Percentage of officials who have met in ministerial coordination committees, by year*

	1996	2006	2016
Intraministerial coordination committees**	18	18	13
Low-level interministerial coordination committees***	17	15	9
High-level interministerial coordination committees****	5	7	5
N	100 (1,038)	100 (1,056)	100 (1,402)

* The table applies value 1 on a three-point scale: (1) multiple times; (2) once; (3) never.

** These committees are established to pursue intraministerial coordination of EU-related work.

*** These committees are headed by the responsible sector ministry to coordinate across affected sector ministries.

**** This committee is headed by the Ministry of Foreign Affairs to coordinate those dossiers that the low-level interministerial coordination committees do not solve.

in this type of coordination behaviour, particularly from 2006 to 2016. One important caveat should be noted though: although a common assumption is that the primary objective of coordination committees is to coordinate, studies show that the level of *substantial* coordination within such interministerial coordination committees tends to be low.[52] Such committees are to some degree characterized by mutual interministerial information sharing and less coordination of tasks, policies, and positions. Moreover, bearing in mind that EU-affectedness has remained stable over time (Table 9.2), one may contemplate that the decreasing level of observed coordination reflects EU-related work becoming more routinized among ministerial officials, which in turn diminishes their need for formal dialogue through coordination committees. Table 9.5 reports data on coordination behaviour among the respondents.

As proposed (P3), Table 9.6 confirms that officials' rank is negatively associated with interaction with EU-level institutions. Despite an overall low N, these observations unfold consistently over time both with regard to contacts with various EU institutions and participation in EU committees, including those in EU agencies. In other words, coordination vis-à-vis the EU level is largely exercised by low-level bureaucrats, thus reinforcing a politico-administrative gap over time. Interestingly, Table 9.6 shows a 10–15 per cent increase of interaction with EU-level institutions for low-level officials from 2006 to 2016, and a corresponding decrease in similar interaction for medium- and high-level officials on all variables.

[52] Jarle Trondal, 'Administrative Integration across Levels of Governance' (Doctoral dissertation, Department of Political Science, University of Oslo 2001) 157.

Table 9.6 Percentage of officials who report contact with* or participation in** the following EU-level institutions, by year and rank (lower-level officials (L)***/medium- and higher-level officials (MH)**** (percentage)

	1996		2006		2016		
	L	MH	L	MH	L	MH	N
Contact with the Commission	74	26	63	37	76	24	100 (115)
Contact with the Council	—	—	—	—	90	10	100 (8)
Contact with the European Parliament	—	—	—	—	100	0	100 (20)
Contact with EU agencies	—	—	73	27	83	17	100 (39)
Participation in expert committee(s)	78	22	70	30	85	15	100 (94)
Participation in comitology committee(s)	71	29	70	30	86	13	100 (21)
Participation in the Council	—	—	—	—	80	20	100 (10)
Participation in committees, boards, etc in EU agencies	—	—	—	—	72	28	100 (18)

* The 'contact' variables combine values 1 and 2 on the following four-point scale: (1) app. every week; (2) app. every month; (3) a few times; (4) never.

** The 'participation' variables apply value 1 on the following three-point scale: (1) several times; (2) once; (3) never.

*** Lower-level officials include the following ranks: 1996: executive officer, higher executive officer, principal officer, assistant director. 2006: executive officer/adviser, principal officer/adviser, assistant director/adviser. 2016: adviser/senior adviser, specialist director/special adviser or equivalent.

**** Medium and higher-level officials include the following ranks: 1996: director, director general, positions higher than director general. 2006: director/adviser, director general/adviser, positions higher than director general. 2016: director or equivalent, director general, or equivalent.

This provides further support for the assumption of an institutionalization of EU-related tasks and, more broadly, a self-reinforcing politico-administrative gap over time. Moreover, the sheer increase in interaction is also fostered by an increasing number of agreements between Norway and the EU, involving ever more policy areas and ministerial officials in EU-related governance. Table 9.6 reports on how contact and participatory behaviour is associated with rank.

A parallel analysis (Table 9.7) on the effect of rank on coordination behaviour reveals a similar pattern: we observe a negative association between rank and participation in coordination committees and a parallel negative association between rank and those reporting that their ministry's work has been subject to coordination from the Prime Minister's Office, the MFA, other ministries, the parliament,

Table 9.7 Percentage of officials who report the following coordination behaviour*, by year and rank (lower-level officials (L)**/medium- and higher-level officials (MH)***)

	1996		2006		2016		
	L	MH	L	MH	L	MH	N
Participation in intraministerial coordination committee	71	29	62	38	73	27	100 (181)
Participation low-level interministerial coordination committee	83	17	75	25	84	16	100 (116)
Participation in high-level interministerial coordination committee	56	44	55	45	69	31	100 (61)
Modified/changed own ministry's position in EU-related work due to coordination with the Prime Ministers' Office	63	38	48	52	70	30	100 (35)
Modified/changed own ministry's position in EU-related work due to coordination with the MFA	63	37	54	46	73	27	100 (60)
Modified/changed own ministry's position in EU-related work due to coordination with other ministries	65	35	64	37	69	31	100 (82)
Modified/changed own ministry's position in EU-related work due to coordination with the national parliament	83	17	60	40	77	23	100 (20)
Modified/changed own ministry's position in EU-related work due to coordination with the interest groups	76	24	58	42	77	23	100 (27)

*The table applies value 1 on the following three-point scale: (1) multiple times; (2) once; (3) never.

** Lower-level officials include the following ranks: 1996: executive officer, higher executive officer, principal officer, assistant director. 2006: executive officer/adviser, principal officer/adviser, assistant director/adviser. 2016: adviser/senior adviser, specialist director/special adviser or equivalent.

*** Medium- and higher-level officials include the following ranks: 1996: director, director general, positions higher than director general. 2006: director/adviser, director general/adviser, positions higher than director general. 2016: director or equivalent, director general or equivalent.

and/or interest groups. Ministerial officials in low ranks score consistently higher on these variables than their colleagues in medium and high ranks. This finding is also consistent over time, supporting the observation of a self-reinforcing politico-administrative gap. This behaviour, we argue, measures degrees of involvement in

EU work, and not merely coordination as such. It follows that lower-level officials enjoy a more comprehensive view of their ministry's EU-related work compared with higher-level officials. Supporting these findings in greater detail, Table 9.7 displays increased participation in high-level coordination committees, from around 55 per cent in 1996/2006 to almost 70 per cent in 2016. Moreover, from 2006 to 2016 our data show an average of 11 per cent increase in participation of lower-level officials in the three types of coordination committees. A similar pattern can be found when examining modification/change due to coordination with other actors: from 2006 to 2016 we see an average 16 per cent increase in lower-level officials reporting that their ministry's work had been modified or changed due to coordination with other actors. Table 9.7 reports how coordination behaviour is associated with rank.

Table 9.8 examines whether various types of coordination behaviour are mutually supplementary or contradictory and thus deemed important *by the same officials*. To merely probe patterns, Table 9.8 applies two sets of variables from the 2016 survey: the degree to which ministerial officials participate in intra- and interministerial coordination committees (variables 1 to 3) and the extent to which they report that their own ministry's position in EU-related work has been modified due to coordination with various other institutions (variables 4 to 8). The findings suggest that different types of coordination behaviour tend to be *mutually supplementary*, but also that that substantive coordination is weakly associated with participation in coordination committees. From the latter we infer that coordination committees, albeit meeting actively, are not instrumental coordinating devices in EU-related work. Table 9.8 reports on intercorrelations between different types of coordination behaviour.

Next, Table 9.9 illustrates the perceived importance of both primary and secondary structures (P4). Two main findings are displayed: as expected, primary structures are deemed significantly more important than secondary structures; moreover, this pattern is robust over time. The most noteworthy change is the increased importance ascribed to national agencies from 1996 to 2016. This finding reflects the 'agencification' wave in Norway, as in most OECD countries, during the survey period,[53] and the parallel 'agencification' of the EU administration.[54] While Table 9.4 revealed decreasing contacts between sector ministries and EU agencies, Table 9.8 shows a corresponding decrease in perceived importance of EU agencies. This observation reflects the increased importance of national agencies as national access points for EU agencies over time. Studies have demonstrated a propensity for EU agencies to bypass the ministerial level when interacting with the national agencies, which in turn has contributed to an emergent 'direct' multilevel

[53] Koen Verhoest and others, *Autonomy and Control of State Agencies* (Palgrave Macmillan 2010) 6.
[54] Egeberg and Trondal, 'Researching European Union Agencies' (n 10) 690.

Table 9.8 Inter-correlation matrix on coordination behaviour (Pearson's r, 2016 data)

	1)	2)	3)	4)	5)	6)	7)	8)	N
1) Participation in intraministerial coordination committee		.49**	.45**	.16**	.32**	.26**	.17**	.16**	684
2) Participation low-level interministerial coordination committee			.41**	.07	.22**	.25**	.10	.15**	568
3) Participation in high-level interministerial coordination committee				.17**	.31**	.33**	.17**	.19**	396
4) Modified/changed own ministry's position in EU-related work due to coordination with the Prime Ministers' Office					.71**	.62**	.62**	.36**	359
5) Modified/changed own ministry's position in EU-related work due to coordination with the MFA						.73**	.49**	.49**	362
6) Modified/changed own ministry's position in EU-related work due to coordination with other ministries							.53**	.60**	359
7) Modified/changed own ministry's position in EU-related work due to coordination with the National Parliament								.69**	351
8) Modified/changed own ministry´s position in EU-related work due to coordination with interest groups									

administrative system.[55] This may, in turn, have offloaded some EU workload from the ministerial level. Table 9.9 reports data on perceived importance of primary and secondary institutions.

Finally, to probe P5, respondents were asked to reflect on conflict behaviour: they were questioned on how they typically prioritize when conflicts appear between the wishes of their political leadership and the requirements of EU law

[55] Morten Egeberg and Jarle Trondal, 'National Agencies in the European Administrative Space: Government Driven, Commission Driven or Networked?' (2009) 87 Public Administration 779, 790.

Table 9.9 Percentage of officials who report that the following institutions are important* when making decisions on their own policy area, by year

	1996	2006	2016
Primary structures			
Own ministry	95	96	98
Subordinated agencies	53	65	69
Other ministries	64	64	72
National parliament	78	77	80
National government	86	90	91
Secondary structures			
Commission	23	29	22
Council	—	—	14
European Parliament	—	—	12
EU agencies	—	11	9
N	100 (1,043)	100 (1,007)	100 (1,340)

*The table combines values 1 and 2 on a five-point scale: (1) very important; (2) fairly important; (3) somewhat; (4) fairly unimportant; (5) very unimportant; (6) do not know/not relevant.

in their EU-related work. Table 9.10 demonstrates that, when in conflict, most respondents seek to compromise between the wishes of their political leadership and the requirements of EU law. This suggests that ministry officials, not only agency officials (as studied by Egeberg and Trondal),[56] are 'double-hatted' in their EU-related work. Moreover, Table 9.10 illuminates the intrusiveness of the 'double-hatted' national central administrations, since ministry officials seem to serve 'two masters'. This observation is an even stronger probe of the theory of the national 'double-hatted' central administration, given that ministry officials are less likely to 'go to Brussels' than agency officials, simply by being more strongly bound by national ministerial leadership. Among the few respondents reporting being 'single-hatted', their primary structures (the wishes of their own political leadership) are deemed slightly more important than secondary structures (the requirements of EU law). Table 9.10 reports how respondents prioritize in cases of conflict.

VI. Conclusion

This chapter has made three main contributions. Theoretically, it has examined the role of organizational factors in public governance in general and in

[56] Morten Egeberg and Jarle Trondal, 'Political Leadership and Bureaucratic Autonomy: Effects of Agencification' (2009) 22 Governance 673, 688.

Table 9.10 Percentage of officials who report the following priorities if conflicts occur between the wishes of their national political leadership and the requirements of EU law*

	Ministry	Agency
Primarily follow the wishes of own political leadership	11	15
Try to combine the wishes of own political leadership and EU law	84	68
Primarily follow the requirement of EU law	5	17
N	608 (100)	476 (100)

* The table includes those officials that incorporate and/or practice EU legislation within their own policy field. The category 'not relevant/not occupied with such tasks' are coded missing.

administrative integration in particular. Empirically, the chapter has presented data suggesting that administrative integration is promoted and nudged by 'favourable' organizational conditions at the *domestic* level of government. Finally, the chapter has demonstrated how the EU contributes to a self-reinforcing administrative bias in domestic core executives over time. Following the public administration turn in EU studies, one might also envisage that, while a Member State may withdraw from political membership in the EU (eg Brexit), domestic bureaucrats might find themselves continuously participating in EU administrative networks of various kinds. Moreover, the observed mechanism may play out more generally in Member States. The general theoretical idea is captured by the public administration approach to European integration that sees the EU as consisting of interconnected sets of agencies, ministries, and regulatory networks.

Empirically, this study highlights administrative integration in the EU in an associated non-Member State. The data show that ministerial officials involved in EU-related affairs are increasingly decoupled from the political level and are strongly 'Europeanized' by being tightly interwoven in, and influenced by, EU institutions and policy processes. In greater detail, the data consistently display a relatively high degree of interaction between sector ministries and EU-level executive institutions (P1). It also affirms a higher level of coordination *within* than *between* ministries (P2) and that officials of lower ranks are more extensively involved at the EU level than officials of higher ranks (P3). Finally, the importance of primary organizational structures is affirmed (P4) and the data demonstrate strong tendency of 'double-hattedness' amongst ministerial officials (P5). Future longitudinal studies that document continuity and change in patterns of administrative integration are needed.

Appendix: List of ministries in the survey (2016)

Office of the Prime Minister
Ministry of Agriculture and Food
Ministry of Children and Equality
Ministry of Climate and Environment
Ministry of Culture
Ministry of Defence
Ministry of Education and Research
Ministry of Finance
Ministry of Foreign Affairs
Ministry of Health and Care Services
Ministry of Justice and Public Security
Ministry of Labour and Social Affairs
Ministry of Local Government and Modernization
Ministry of Petroleum and Energy
Ministry of Trade, Industry, and Fisheries
Ministry of Transport and Communications

10
Diffusion and Differentiation of EU Norms in the EEA

*Christian NK Franklin**

I. Introduction

European Economic Area (EEA) cooperation offers the most comprehensive model of participation in the European Union (EU)'s internal market for non-EU Member States. The EEA Agreement allows the three European Free Trade Association (EFTA) states party to it (Norway, Iceland, and Liechtenstein) to enjoy a depth and level of integration with the EU far surpassing other forms of co-operation with other neighbouring countries.[1] Allowing three 'outsiders' not only access to, but also full participation in, core parts of the internal market necessarily involves a high degree of diffusion of EU rights and obligations in the EFTA states. And while the EEA Agreement, in theory, seems open to allowing for significant differentiation at the levels of policy-making, implementation, and enforcement of EU law in the EFTA states, as we shall see in this chapter, such differences are largely glossed over in practice.

The present chapter seeks to contribute to the overall aims of the research project by focusing primarily on certain aspects of external differentiation, ie the possibility for certain non-EU Member States to participate in certain EU policies through the EEA Agreement. While providing examples of vertical diffusion and differentiation (ie the level of integration in the different policy areas covered by the EEA Agreement), it will also seek to shed some light on the manner in which EEA and EU membership differ from one another in terms of the EFTA states' involvement and inclusion in the various decision-making procedures governing the EU's internal market. As we shall see, whereas the EFTA States enjoy no say whatsoever in EU decision-making procedures, they participate fully in decision-making and enforcement within the EEA structure.

* Many thanks to research assistant Erling G Hermansen for input in the final stages of completion.

[1] Agreement on the European Economic Area (EEA) [1994] OJ L1/3. Switzerland, although party to the EFTA Convention, is not party to the EEA Agreement. For simplicity's sake, however, the three EFTA states party to the EEA Agreement will hereinafter be referred to collectively as the EFTA states, in line with the definition provided for in Art 2(b) EEA. Further, on Switzerland's relationship to the EU, see Andrea Ott and Benedikt Pirker, in this volume.

Christian NK Franklin, *Diffusion and Differentiation of EU Norms in the EEA* In: *Redefining EU Membership*.
Edited by: Diane Fromage, Oxford University Press.
DOI: 10.1093/9780191948145.003.0010

In the following, Section 2 will start by looking at the scope of the Main Part of the EEA Agreement, and how it has come to be expanded over time, even without formal amendments ever having been made to its provisions. In Section 3, we shall see how the EFTA Court's dynamic development of the fundamental principle of homogeneity has proven key to ensuring a high degree of undistorted diffusion of EU norms in their EEA setting. The integral role played by the mechanism for incorporating new EU legal acts into the EEA Agreement, and the potential to reserve against their inclusion, will then be ventured in Section 4. The chapter will, finally, discuss the impact that the pluralistic system of judicial enforcement of EEA law may be seen to have on the diffusion of EU norms in the EFTA states (Section 5), before providing a few short conclusions (Section 6).

II. Scope of the EEA Agreement: Formal Limitations and the 'Special Relationship'

Rather unsurprisingly, the main barrier to full diffusion of EU rules in their EEA setting lies in the formal limits contained in the terms of the EEA Agreement itself. On the one hand, the main objective of the EEA Agreement is 'to provide for the fullest possible realisation of the free movement of goods, persons, services and capital within the whole EEA, so that the internal market established within the European Union is extended to the EFTA States'.[2] As a result, most of the substantive provisions of the Main Part of the EEA Agreement mirror the rules on the four freedoms and competition (including State aid) rules under European Community (EC) law as they stood when the EEA Agreement was negotiated and signed in the early 1990s.

On the other hand, however, the very use of the term 'fullest possible realisation' denotes that certain limits can and may well exist. The Main Part of the EEA Agreement is subject to certain formal limitations of scope. Several important areas of EU cooperation connected to the internal market project—such as the Customs Union; the Common Commercial Policy; the Area of Freedom, Security and Justice (AFSJ); and agriculture and fisheries—all remain outside of the EEA Agreement. And since the Main Part of the EEA Agreement has not been updated since its entry into force in 1994(!), new EU rules inherently linked to the internal market introduced by subsequent EU Treaty amendments—such as the concept of EU citizenship, through which the free movement of persons has become radically transformed since its introduction by the Treaty of Maastricht, and the EU Charter of Fundamental Rights—are not reflected in its terms either.[3] That does not mean

[2] Case C-897/19 PPU *Ruska Federacija v IN* [2020] ECLI:EU:C:2020:262, para 50. See also, eg Case C-452/01 *Ospelt* [2003] ECLI:EU:C:2003:493, para 29.

[3] Given that formal negotiations on the Maastricht Treaty and the EEA Agreement were being conducted at the same time (from 1990–92), and the Treaty was signed several months before signatures

that the EFTA states do not cooperate on any of these matters with the EU. On the contrary, a wide range of bi- and multilateral agreements have, indeed, been entered into by the EU and the EFTA states (collectively and/or individually) on matters deemed to fall outside the scope of the EEA Agreement. The EFTA states, for example, currently enjoy status as Associate States in Schengen cooperation, and have entered into several agreements with the EU on fisheries and agricultural issues, as well as agreements linking them to the EU's common asylum system and cooperation in both criminal and civil procedural matters.[4]

Notwithstanding the EEA Agreement's formal limitations, there can be little doubting the unique and increasingly dynamic nature of EEA cooperation in practice. Over time, even certain matters not explicitly included in the Main Part of the EEA Agreement have, in one way or another, come to be seen as covered by its scope. Three examples are particularly illustrative of how both the European Court of Justice (ECJ) and the EFTA Court have sought to use various tools at their disposal in doing so.

Firstly, the lack of inclusion of the EU's Charter of Fundamental Rights in the EEA Agreement has been largely overcome, so far, in practice by reference to other legal instruments binding on the Contracting Parties.[5] In situations where the ECJ interprets provisions of the EU Treaties (or secondary EU measures) in light of the Charter, and the EU Treaty provisions in question are replicated in the terms of the EEA Agreement, the latter will usually be interpreted by the EFTA Court in the same manner under reference to either the provisions of the European Convention on Human Rights and/or the constitutional traditions common to the EFTA states.[6]

were (finally) attached to the EEA Agreement, the Contracting Parties to the EEA Agreement were surely all well aware of the imminent arrival of EU citizenship. The fact that the drafters of the EEA Agreement chose not to include any mention of citizenship is, therefore, not insignificant in itself, especially given their foresight in including certain other changes being introduced by the Treaty of Maastricht, such as, eg Art 29 EEA on social security, which includes an express reference to self-employed persons not found in previous versions of the EC Treaties (Art 42 EC), but only added following the Treaty of Maastricht (what is now Art 48 of the Consolidated version of the Treaty on the Functioning of the European Union (TFEU) [2012] OJ C326/47.

[4] eg the EU–Norway/Iceland agreements concerning those two states' association to the Schengen *acquis* ([1999] OJ L176/36), the Dublin system for seeking asylum ([2001] OJ L93/40), the Lugano Convention ([2007] OJ L339/3), and the EU surrender procedure ([2006] OJ L292/2).

[5] For more on this, and some salient examples of the EFTA Court's 'bridging' work in this area, see Halvard Haukeland Fredriksen and Christian NK Franklin, 'Of Pragmatism and Principles: The EEA Agreement 20 Years on' [2015] 52 Common Market Law Review 3 629, 646–50.

[6] Made largely possible thanks to references in the EEA Agreement's preamble to human rights and the social dimension of the internal market. See further, eg Finn Arnesen and Halvard Haukeland Fredriksen, 'Preamble' in Finn Arnesen and others (eds), *Agreement on the European Economic Area: A Commentary* (CH Beck/Hart/Nomos/Universitetsforlaget 2018), para 3. For examples of the EFTA Court's approach, and certain challenges which may well lie ahead (particularly in situations where the Charter rights are not reflected in the ECHR), see Christian NK Franklin and Halvard Haukeland Fredriksen, 'Differentiated Citizenship in the European Economic Area' in Daniel Thym and Dora Kostakopoulou (eds), *Research Handbook on European Union Citizenship Law and Policy* (Edward Elgar 2022), 297–319.

Secondly, the lack of provisions in the Main Part of the EEA Agreement fully reflecting the concept of EU citizenship seems to have been largely overcome by the EFTA Court's apparent establishment of an overarching general EEA legal principle of free movement. Since Articles 20 and 21 of the Treaty on the Functioning of the European Union (TFEU) are not replicated in the EEA Agreement, and whereas the ECJ has used these provisions to create and strengthen rights of free movement and residence for all EU citizens and their family members over the past twenty-five years, either through direct application of these rules and/or interpretations of secondary EU measures in the light thereof, the same tools, and hence methods, simply do not exist under EEA law. It goes without saying, perhaps, but in the event that workers, self-employed persons, or service providers/recipients were deemed as having different rights in the EU and EFTA states, this could seriously undermine the whole idea of an internal market.

In order to bridge the widening gap in this field, the EFTA Court has, therefore, sought to utilize other EEA tools at its disposal to arrive at similar results. In its Advisory Opinion in *Campbell*, the EFTA Court—paraphrasing statements made by the ECJ in several decisions concerning Articles 45 and 21 TFEU regarding the free movement of workers, and EU citizenship, respectively—held that the free movement of workers under Article 28 EEA is (only) 'a specific expression of the general right to move and reside freely within the EEA'.[7] The creation of such a general right stands in stark contrast to the EFTA states' long-standing belief that free movement rights under the EEA Agreement are almost exclusively connected to various categories of economically active persons. The EFTA Court said nothing about the legal basis for this general right, which in the context of EU law is naturally found in Articles 20 and 21 TFEU. Based on the EFTA Court's approach in other cases, however, it seems fair to assume that this new general right under EEA law may be deduced from the various provisions in the Main Part of the EEA Agreement on the free movement of workers, self-employed people, and service providers and recipients, and the many EU legal acts incorporated into the Annexes of the EEA Agreement concerning free movement of other categories of persons, and (more generally) the very purposes and structure of the EEA Agreement.[8] Given the EFTA Court's previous establishment of several unwritten general EEA principles to fill in gaps in the EEA Agreement, and the EFTA states'

[7] Case E-4/19 *Campbell* [2020], EFTA Ct Rep 21, para 48; Case C-457/12 *S and G* [2014] ECLI:EU:C:2014:136, para 45.

[8] See, further, Franklin and Fredriksen, 'Differentiated Citizenship in the European Economic Area' (n 6). The Annexes to the EEA Agreement will be returned to in more detail. Suffice to point out for the time being that the twenty-two Annexes to the EEA Agreement, into which EU secondary measures (regulations, directives, etc) deemed EEA-relevant are incorporated, are deemed 'an integral part' of the Agreement itself. The Annexes are supplemented, in practice, by Protocol 31 on cooperation in specific areas outside the four freedoms. For more on the Annexes and Protocols, see Halvard Haukeland Fredriksen, 'EEA Law in and beyond the Text of the Main Part of the EEA Agreement' in Arnesen and others (eds) (n 6), 124–43.

tacit and sometimes express acceptance of such moves, the development was certainly not unprecedented.[9] It nevertheless clearly broadens the original scope of the Agreement, extending freedom of movement rights to both economically active and inactive persons, and may, therefore, take a while for (at least some of) the EFTA states to fully accept.

Thirdly, the EFTA Court's approaches in dealing with the formal limits to the scope of the main part of the EEA Agreement in the situations already outlined seem to have been bolstered somewhat by the ECJ's recent decision in *IN*.[10] In this case, the ECJ effectively extended its earlier judgment in *Petruhhin*, concerning the protection of EU citizens from extradition to third countries on the basis of Articles 18 and 21 TFEU, to an Icelandic citizen facing extradition to Russia while on holiday in Croatia.[11] Notwithstanding the fact that the EEA Agreement contains no provisions mirroring the EU's AFSJ policy, the ECJ viewed the combined effects of rights afforded to EFTA state nationals under the EEA Agreement, the Schengen *acquis*, and several other agreements between (at least two of) the EFTA states and the EU on the joint asylum system and the European arrest warrant, as rendering the position of the Icelandic citizen in the case 'objectively comparable with that of an EU citizen to whom, in accordance with Article 3(2) TEU, the Union offers an area of freedom, security and justice without internal frontiers, in which the free movement of persons is ensured'.[12]

The ECJ's judgment, which in many ways echoes and justifies the EFTA Court's establishment of a general right to free movement under EEA law, through the use of broader systemic arguments, is rather astonishing.[13] The ECJ has effectively recognized the possibility of other international agreements between the EU and the EFTA states influencing not only the interpretation, but also the very scope, of the EEA Agreement itself. As a consequence, the amalgamation of various international agreements entered into between the EU and the EFTA states can be seen to give rise to specific rights for EFTA state nationals in an EEA setting, based on

[9] For examples of unwritten general principles of EEA law being deduced in similar ways, see Case E-9/97 *Sveinbjörnsdóttir* [1998] EFTA Ct Rep 95, para 47 (principle of state liability for breaches of EEA law); Case E-04/01 *Karlsson* [2002] EFTA Ct Rep 240, para 28 (principle of consistent or harmonious interpretation); Case E-15/10 *Posten Norge v ESA* [2012] EFTA Ct Rep 246, para 86 (principle of effective judicial protection including the right to a fair trial); Case E-14/11, *Schenker v ESA* [2012] EFTA Ct Rep 1178, paras 118ff (access to documents); Case E-26/13 *Gunnarsson* [2014] EFTA Ct Rep 254, para 84 (general principle of equality); and Case E-10/14 *Deveci* [2014] EFTA Ct Rep 1364, para 64 (freedom to conduct a business). For examples of acceptance by national courts in the EFTA states, see the Norwegian Supreme Court's rulings in HR-2005-713-A, HR-2005-1690-P, and HR-2010-2082-A, and the Icelandic Supreme Court's decisions in H.1999 236 and H.2010 79.

[10] *Ruska Federacija* (n 2).

[11] Case C-182/15 *Petruhhin* [2016] ECLI:EU:C:2016:630.

[12] ibid para 58.

[13] See, further, the insightful case annotation by Halvard Haukeland Fredriksen and Christophe Hillion, 'The "Special Relationship" between the EU and the EEA EFTA States—Free Movement of EEA Citizens in an Extended Area of Freedom, Security and Justice: *Ruska Federacija v I.N.*' [2021] 58 Common Market Law Review 3 851.

the EU's AFSJ policy, which find no resonance in the EEA Agreement viewed in isolation.

In view of the *de facto* sidestepping of the EEA Agreement's formal limitations in scope illustrated so far, it is not difficult to understand how EEA cooperation may be seen to differ rather significantly from other forms of third-country affiliation to the EU. As stressed by the ECJ in *IN*, the EEA Agreement underlines the '*special relationship* between the European Union, its Member States and the EFTA States, which is based on proximity, long-standing common values and European identity'.[14] And as illustrated by its very decision in that case, far from being a mere symbolic gesture, the relationship between the Contracting Parties is understood by the ECJ as special enough to warrant the creation of certain indigenous individual rights not included in the text of the Agreement itself.

It is not difficult to understand why these somewhat radical and far-reaching developments have been heavily objected to, especially by Norwegian authorities, in various interventions before both the ECJ and the EFTA Court.[15] What from the outset had been intended (at least seen from the perspective of the EFTA states) as an international agreement focused on economic integration, and structured around a two-pillar model (ie EU and EFTA) designed to preserve the dualist traditions and legislative and judicial sovereignty of (at least the dualist) EFTA states, has over time gradually been transformed into something very different. Today, more than simply providing a 'halfway house' towards EU membership, or a 'cherry-picking' option, the EEA Agreement sees the EFTA states for all practical purposes as fully vested participants in the internal market's increasingly federal structure, entailing rights in most areas fully akin to those afforded to EU citizens and economic actors. The legal and political tensions caused by these developments is further compounded by the fact that the EFTA states obviously enjoy no say in the political and legal decisions made within the EU sphere, to which they are expected to adapt in their EEA setting. Accepting a situation akin to full membership yet with none of the privileges that this entails would, understandably, be difficult to swallow whole, especially from a democratic perspective. Seen from the EU's perspective, however, the comeback to this is probably quite simply that such is the price to be paid for the unrivalled, privileged access to the EU's internal market enjoyed by the EFTA states as compared with other third countries.[16]

[14] *Petruhhin* (n 11), para 50, emphasis added.

[15] Examples before the EFTA Court are rife, eg Report for the Hearing in *Campbell* (n 7) (available at https://eftacourt.int/cases/e-4-19/). For an example from the ECJ, see the arguments put forward by the Norwegian government, as reiterated in Advocate General Tanchev's Opinion in *Ruska Federacija* (n 2), paras 55–60.

[16] See the chapters in this volume dealing with the relationship between the EU and third states, notably the Balkan states (Milenkovic), Turkey (Müftüler-Baç), and the countries that participate in the European Neighbourhood Policy and the Eastern Partnership (Bosse and Delcour).

III. Ensuring the Dynamic Development of the EEA Agreement: The Principle of Homogeneity

As mentioned earlier, the Main Part of the EEA Agreement has not been amended since it entered into force in 1994. Yet even if the many amendments to the EU internal market rules introduced by the Treaties of Maastricht, Amsterdam, Nice, and Lisbon had been included in the EEA Agreement, that fact alone would obviously not have meant that the EEA rules would automatically be interpreted in the same way as they are within the EU. In order to secure a level playing field and reciprocity of rights and duties between the Contracting Parties, and to preserve the sanctity of the internal market project, however, the rules have to be understood and applied in the same way—or, at the very least, lead to the same results in practice. Crucial to the initial acceptance of the EEA legal construct, this led to the introduction into the text of the EEA Agreement of the fundamental principle of homogeneity, which can be seen to take many different forms today.

At its most base level, as indicated in several places in the wording of the EEA Agreement itself, the principle of homogeneity requires identical provisions under EU and EEA law to be interpreted and applied in the same way, with deference to their understanding as a matter of EU law.[17] The EFTA Court has held, in numerous cases, that substantive similarities between provisions will suffice to trigger the principle, even if the provisions themselves are not reproduced verbatim.[18] As a result, although differences between the EU and EEA legal constructs may, exceptionally, be of such magnitude as to require different interpretations,[19] where the provisions are similar in substance they enjoy a strong presumption in favour of homogenous interpretation and application.[20] The EFTA Court has invariably made rather short shrift of any attempts of the EFTA state authorities to rely on arguments based on the intentions of the Contracting Parties as grounds for breaching the principle of homogeneity.[21] The ECJ has, for its part, done the same, in the relatively sporadic cases coming before it that

[17] Arts 1, 6, and 105 EEA, and eg Recitals 4 and 15 of the EEA Agreement's Preamble. Exactly what lies in the EEA principle of reciprocity in this regard is, nevertheless, rather difficult to ascertain in practice, due to potentially divergent views held by the ECJ and EFTA Court as to how strictly its requirements ought to be understood: cf the ECJ's less strict understanding in Case 104/81 *Kupferberg* [1982] ECLI:EU:C:1982:362, para 18, with the stricter understanding of the EFTA Court in *Schenker* (n 9), para 121.

[18] eg *Schenker* (n 9), para 78.

[19] eg Case C–72/09 *Rimbaud* [2010] ECLI:EU:C:2010:645 (free movement of capital).

[20] eg Case E–3/98 *Rainford-Towning* [1998] EFTA Ct Rep 205, para 21; Páll Hreinsson, 'General Principles' in Carl Baudenbacher (ed), *The Handbook of EEA Law* (Springer 2016), 352–53.

[21] eg Case E–2/06 *EFTA Surveillance Authority v Norway* [2007] EFTA Ct Rep 164, para 57, where arguments based on statements made by the Contracting Parties during the negotiations to the EEA Agreement, and subsequent unilateral reservations made by the Norwegian government following its adoption, were deemed irrelevant by the EFTA Court.

raise questions concerning the understanding of provisions in the Main Part of the EEA Agreement.[22]

The EFTA Court has sometimes been accused of unwarranted judicial activism in its development of the principle, and has certainly extended the perceived boundaries of homogeneity through its case law.[23] A more effects-based understanding of homogeneity has developed over time, and was used as a partial basis for the EFTA Court's establishment of an EEA principle of state liability akin to that found under EU law.[24] The EFTA Court's approach here has long since been endorsed by the ECJ in its case law, which almost certainly, in turn, will have contributed to rendering it more palatable to the EFTA states.[25] Perhaps more contentiously, the EFTA Court has also sought to develop a 'procedural branch' of the homogeneity principle, according to which procedural rules contained in the otherwise indigenous EFTA Surveillance and Court Agreement (SCA) were to be understood and applied homogenously with similar procedural rules in the EU Treaties, on the grounds that this was necessary so as to ensure a level playing field for all economic actors under the two pillars of the EEA structure.[26] The extent to which the procedural rules governing the powers and workings of the EFTA Court and the EFTA Surveillance Authority (ESA) are (or even should be) interpreted and applied in the same way as the rules of the EU Treaties governing the competences of the ECJ and Commission is, nevertheless, questionable. As, for example, we shall return to see further in the following, there are substantial differences in the way EEA rules are to be enforced under the EFTA and EU pillars of the EEA Agreement, not least concerning the Advisory Opinion and Preliminary Ruling procedures. It seems rather clear, in any event, that a presumption of procedural homogeneity may be rebutted with greater ease than where identical or similar substantive EU/EEA rules are at stake.[27]

Although designed and developed to ensure that fewer discrepancies might arise between EU and EEA law, it is worth noting how the principle of homogeneity may (somewhat paradoxically) in itself also serve as a differentiating factor between

[22] eg in Case T-115/94 *Opel Austria* [1997] ECLI:EU:T:115:94, where the Court of First Instance rejected pleas by both the Council and the Commission for diverging interpretations of Art 10 EEA and (what is now) Art 30 TFEU.

[23] eg Wennerås, who goes so far as to contend that the EFTA Court has 'expanded the scope of these rules and basically substituted them for a principle of homogeneity *sans frontiéres*': Pål Wennerås, 'Article 6—Homogeneity' in Arnesen and others (eds) (n 6), 210.

[24] *Sveinbjörnsdóttir* (n 9), para 60; *Karlsson* (n 9), para 28.

[25] Case C-140/97 *Rechberger* [1999] ECLI:EU:C:1999:306, para 39.

[26] Agreement between the EFTA States on the Establishment of a Surveillance Authority and Court of Justice (SCA) [1994] OJ L344/3; *Schenker* (n 9), paras 78 and 121; Case E-18/11 *Irish Bank* [2012] EFTA Ct Rep 592, para 122.

[27] A good example is offered by comparing the ECJ's rather restrictive interpretation of the term 'court or tribunal of a Member State' under Art 267 TFEU in, eg Case C-64/16 *Associação Sindical dos Juízes Portugueses* [2018] ECLI:EU:C:2018:117 and Case C-274/14 *Banco Santander* [2020] ECLI:EU:C:2020:17 with the EFTA Court's more liberal (and divergent) interpretation of the identical term under Art 34 SCA in Case E-8/19 *Scanteam* [2020] EFTA Ct Rep 27, paras 44-54.

the two systems. The ECJ has long reiterated the requirements of uniform interpretation and application of EU law in all Member States as a keystone of EU co-operation. Under EEA law, however, the inclusion of the principle of homogeneity instead of uniformity does not seem to have been an arbitrary choice, but rather a specifically tailored means for differentiation in itself. In short, homogeneity allows for a certain flexibility which a stricter requirement of uniformity would not.

This is, firstly, because the application of EEA law in the EFTA states may (but not must) differ, as opposed to the application of EU law at national level in the EU Member States, given the lack of primacy and direct effect under EEA law—at least as these two principles are understood as a matter of EU law. The (quasi-)primacy requirement of EEA law is of a rather different nature as compared to the EU principle of primacy. Unlike the situation under EU law, where regulations are of direct applicability and only directives require implementation at national level, all directives *and* regulations incorporated into the Annexes of the EEA Agreement require national implementation—at least in the dualist EFTA states of Norway and Iceland.[28] The sole provision in Protocol 35 to the EEA Agreement, which is equally binding and of the same legal value as the Main Part of the Agreement, therefore provides that, '[f]or cases of possible conflicts between implemented EEA rules and other statutory provisions, the EFTA States undertake to introduce, if necessary, a statutory provision to the effect that EEA rules prevail in these cases'. National law which implements EEA directives and regulations is, accordingly, to be afforded primacy over all other conflicting provisions of national law, thereby giving precedence to national law which is EEA-conformant over national law which is not. Unimplemented or incorrectly implemented EEA law enjoys no such priority. And as far as direct effect is concerned, the EFTA Court has, on many occasions, confirmed that although the EFTA states naturally remain free to apply such a principle of their own accord, the EEA Agreement does not require direct effect of non-implemented EEA provisions in the EFTA states.[29] The fact that the ECJ's general approach to direct effect of provisions in certain international agreements to which the EU is a party has led it to conclude, in several cases, that provisions of the EAA Agreement may have direct effect under the EU pillar of the EEA, does not change the fact that the same does not hold true for the EFTA pillar.[30] Although the lack of a requirement of direct effect is certainly offset in certain situations through full incorporation in national law coupled with the effects of (quasi-)primacy and/or the inclusion of so-called 'sector-monism' provisions in national statutes, the differences in applicability seem rather plain.[31]

[28] Art 7 EEA: the situation concerning implementation is, naturally, different in the monist EFTA state of Liechtenstein. The updating of the EEA Agreement through the incorporation therein of secondary EU measures is described more fully in Section below.

[29] eg *Irish Bank* (n 26), para 122.

[30] eg *Opel Austria* (n 22).

[31] 'Sector-monism' provisions are provisions in Norwegian statutes which state that international norms binding on Norway shall have precedence over conflicting rules of the statute in question; see

Secondly, uniformity and homogeneity also appear to differ in the EU and EFTA pillars, since interpretations of EEA law may, in fact, differ from interpretations of EU law, yet still lead to a type of homogeneity being achieved. In a rather controversial twist, the EFTA Court—building further on its effects-based understanding of homogeneity—has, in a series of cases in the field of free movement of persons, developed the principle even further so as to require *homogeneity as to the practical outcome* in a case, even if at the expense of *homogenous interpretations* of the EU measures in question.[32]

The cases in question centred on the interpretation of Article 7 of the Citizenship Directive.[33] Notwithstanding the lack of any provisions in the EEA Agreement mirroring Articles 20 and 21 TFEU, the Directive had, given its obvious impact on rights afforded to economically active persons (workers etc), eventually come to be incorporated in full into the Annexes of the EEA Agreement.[34] Subject to a number of conditions, Article 7 provides for a right of residence for up to five years for EEA nationals and their family members on the territory of *another Member State*. The private individuals involved in all three cases were not seeking to enforce their rights against a *host EEA state* to which they had moved, however, but rather against their *home states*. According to several decisions of the ECJ, while no such right flows from the Directive in its EU setting, such a right does flow from Article 21 TFEU.[35] Applying the more traditional understanding of homogeneity (ie interpreting the Directive in the same manner as the ECJ) would have left the EFTA Court unable to afford EFTA state nationals and their family members the same rights of free movement and residence as those which flow from EU law. A different interpretative route was, therefore, sought with a view to arriving at the same result.

In short, the EFTA Court stressed that the line of ECJ case law in question was distinguishable from the cases that it was dealing with, given the differing EU/EEA legal contexts in which the Directive was to be applied.[36] It then proceeded to find that Article 7 of the Directive, interpreted in its indigenous EEA legal context, and within recognized methodological principles, was to be understood as giving rise

Christian NK Franklin and others, 'Norway (including Iceland & Liechtenstein)' in Marleen R Botman (ed) *National Courts and the Enforcement of EU Law: The Pivotal Role of National Courts in the EU Legal Order* (Eleven International Publishing 2020) 340–45.

[32] *Gunnarsson* (n 9); Case E-28/15 *Jabbi v Norway* [2016] EFTA Ct Rep 575; *Campbell* (n 7).

[33] Directive 2004/38/EC of the European Parliament and of the Council of 29 April 2004 on the right of citizens of the Union and their family members to move and reside freely within the territory of the Member States (the Citizenship Directive) [2004] OJ L158/77.

[34] See, further, on the Citizenship Directive's laboured passage into EEA law: Christian NK Franklin, 'Square Pegs and Round Holes: The Free Movement of Persons Under EEA Law' (2017) 19 Cambridge Yearbook of European Legal Studies 165.

[35] Case C-456/12 *O and B* [2014] ECLI:EU:C:2014:135; confirmed in, eg Case C-133/15 *Chavez-Vilchez* [2017] ECLI:EU:C:2017:354; Case C-89/17 *Banger* [2018] ECLI:EU:C:2018:570; Case C-230/17 *Altiner and Ravn* [2018] ECLI:EU:C:2018:497.

[36] *Campbell* (n 7), paras 54–59.

to rights against an EFTA state national's home state, in the same manner as Article 21 TFEU does under EU law.[37] Employing a bold and innovative effects-based understanding of homogeneity, the EFTA Court was effectively stating that similar cases of free movement under the EU and EFTA pillars of the EEA should lead to the same practical outcomes, even if the legal sources leading to these results might differ, and even if such results come at the expense of identical interpretations of a directive under EU and EEA law. Put differently, the need to ensure homogeneity as to results may, therefore, sometimes trump homogeneity as to interpretation, with a differentiated interpretative approach nevertheless leading to the same outcomes being achieved in practice. Whether a requirement of uniformity as understood under EU law would have proven as pliable seems questionable, to say the least. The EFTA Court's willingness to push the boundaries of its understanding of homogeneity has, nevertheless, proven crucial to the overall success of the EEA project, by glossing over the many (and at times rather significant) cracks which have developed between EU and EEA law over time.

IV. Updates and Handbrakes: Incorporating Secondary EU Measures into EEA Law

The fact that the Main Part of the EEA Agreement has been able remain in stasis for thirty years has been offset not only by dynamic and homogenous interpretations of the Agreement's provisions itself, but also by the rather unique mechanism for incorporating new EU secondary measures into its Annexes. One of the key differences between membership of the EU and participation in the internal market through the EEA Agreement is that the EFTA states—beyond certain input during the preparatory stages when the Commission draws up proposals for new EU legislation related to the internal market—do not enjoy formal access to the EU decision-making processes.[38] They do, however, enjoy full participation in decision-making procedures at EEA level.

A consensus-based decision-making procedure set out in Article 102 EEA allows the EEA Joint Committee, as the body responsible for ensuring the effective implementation and operation of the Agreement, to make decisions on the incorporation of EEA-relevant EU legal acts into EEA law.[39] The Joint Committee, which

[37] Christian NK Franklin, 'Pride and Prejudice: Some Reflections on the (In)discretionary Application of Fundamental Freedoms by Norwegian Courts' in Andreas T Müller and Werner Schroeder (eds), '25 Jahre Europäischer Wirtschaftsraum' (2020) 1 Europarecht 225.

[38] The input referred to here may be made in different ways, such as, eg through the EFTA states' participation in expert groups and Commission committees, and the right to submit so-called 'EEA EFTA comments' (drafted by various EFTA Working Groups, and approved by the EFTA Standing Committee) on proposed or upcoming secondary EU measures. For more information, see <https://www.efta.int/eea/eea-efta-comments> accessed 28 May 2021.

[39] The Joint Committee's decisions encompass not only legislative acts (as defined in Article 289 TFEU), but also many delegated/implementing acts, decisions, and recommendations.

comprises the ambassadors of the EFTA states and representatives from the EU's European External Action Service, meets six to eight times a year to discuss which secondary EU measures ought to be made part of EEA law. As a result, there are approximately 5,000 EU legal acts currently in force as part of EEA law today(!), thus in itself bearing witness to an incredibly high degree of diffusion of EU norms in the EFTA states.

Unlike in the EU, where issues of competence (ie who shall/may do what) often dominate legislative initiatives, the key determinant as to which EU norms are to be made part of the EEA Agreement is the question of EEA-relevance (ie whether the secondary measures are sufficiently connected to the workings of the internal market). While such determinations may generally be considered more of a political than a legal issue, working out which secondary measures (or parts thereof) should be incorporated into the many Annexes to the EEA Agreement has undoubtedly become a more complicated task over time. This is not least due to the removal of the three-pillar structure within the EU following the entry into force of the Treaty of Lisbon, and the resulting establishment of a joint set of objectives for all EU action. Where the legal bases of a given secondary EU measure stretch over several policy fields, and one or more of these is deemed more peripheral (or perhaps even outside) the scope of the EEA Agreement, reaching consensus in the EEA Committee may, understandably, prove more difficult. As much was shown when the Citizenship Directive was up for discussion. While certain rights contained therein were undoubtedly directly connected to the free movement of workers, services, and self-employed persons, and hence clearly EEA-relevant, the question remained whether certain novel provisions arguably borne of the EU concept of EU citizenship were not;[40] and if so, how to unravel and untangle any rules which were not unequivocally EEA-relevant without ripping up the entire fabric of the measure itself.

As the Joint Committee reaches its decisions by way of consensus, the two-pillar structure established by the EEA Agreement requires each pillar (ie EU and EFTA) to coordinate its views before meeting to discuss their positions.[41] Although the necessary procedures for ensuring coordination of views were already in place under the EU pillar in light of the various decision-making mechanisms spelt out in the EU Treaties, a new EFTA institution (the Standing Committee of the EFTA States) had to be created following the signing of the EEA Agreement, in order to enable the EFTA states to speak with one voice on behalf of the EFTA pillar.[42] Crucially to acceptance of the mechanism in the dualist EFTA states of Iceland and Norway,

[40] The novel rights of permanent residence in the host state after five years, enhanced procedural safeguards, and broader range of derived rights of residence for third-country-national family members were a particular cause for concern in this regard.

[41] Art 93 EEA.

[42] Agreement on a Standing Committee of the EFTA States of 2 May 1992, available at <http://www.efta.int/legal-texts/committees> accessed 28 May 2021.

the EEA Joint Committee's decisions must then, in turn, be made part of national law.[43] As mentioned earlier, this applies to all EU measures incorporated into the EEA Agreement, including regulations. Since regulations according to Article 7(a) EEA are to be made part of the national legal orders of the EFTA states 'as such' (ie by way of incorporation), their lack of direct applicability will generally pose few problems in practice. EEA law is thereby enabled to keep more or less up to speed with legislative developments in the EU internal market,[44] while at the same time preserving the formal legislative sovereignty of the EFTA states.

The incorporation of new secondary EU measures into the EEA Agreement has thereby allowed the scope of the Agreement to be adapted and expanded over time. In order to understand why this is so, it is important to note here that, unlike in the hierarchical EU legal system, the primary sources of EEA law are not limited to the provisions contained in the main part of the EEA Agreement. Primary rights under EEA law may also stem directly from EU regulations and directives which are made part of the EEA Agreement.[45] A fitting example is provided by the situation as regards retirees and economically inactive persons. From the very outset of EEA cooperation, both of these categories of persons have enjoyed specific rights of free movement and residence stemming directly from former EC directives incorporated into the EEA Agreement, completely untraceable to any provisions in the Main Part of the EEA Agreement.[46]

Given that the incorporation of EU secondary measures hinges on the question of EEA relevance, it stands to reason that certain opt-outs are thereby (at least theoretically) possible. The mechanism is essentially intergovernmental in nature, allowing for a right to block the incorporation of any new EU measures into the EEA Agreement as each individual EFTA state (or the EU, for its part) might see fit.[47] Yet while the threat of using this 'handbrake' has certainly led to a number of drawn-out discussions, delays, and compromises in the EEA Joint Committee, it has never

[43] Art 7 EEA, as interpreted by Iceland and Norway and (tacitly) recognized by the EU Commission ever since the entry into force of the Agreement. The ECJ caused quite a stir in the EEA legal community when it suggested in passing, in Case C-431/11 *UK v Council* [2013] ECLI:EU:C:2013:589, para 54, and Case C-83/13 *Fonnship* [2014] ECLI:EU:C:2014:2053, para 24, that regulations are directly applicable in the national legal orders of (all of) the EEA states by virtue of Art 7 EEA, but the EFTA Court quickly reassured the dualist EEA/EFTA states that this is not the case, eg Case E-15/14 *ESA v Iceland* [2015] EFTA Ct Rep 40, para 32. As the EU side has not pursued the matter in the EEA Joint Committee, the EFTA Court's stand is essentially the last word on the matter.

[44] Albeit with certain understandable delays as compared with implementation in the EU Member States, given the need for separate deadlines for implementation following the Joint Committee's decision.

[45] Franklin, 'Pride and Prejudice' (n 37). According to Art 119 EEA, the Annexes and the EU legal acts referred to therein (as adapted for the purposes of the EEA) 'shall form an integral part of this Agreement'. Thus, there is no formal hierarchy between the provisions found in the Main Part of the EEA Agreement and the EU legal acts referred to in the annexes.

[46] Council Directive 90/365/EEC of 28 June 1990 on the right of residence for employees and self-employed persons who have ceased their occupational activity [1990] OJ L180/28; Directive 90/364 of 28 June 1990 on the right of residence [1990] OJ L180/26.

[47] Art 6(2) of the Agreement on a Standing Committee of the EFTA States (n 42).

been formally exercised by any of the EFTA states. The most likely reason for this seems to be a fear of legal and/or political reprisals by the EU.[48] In situations where difficulties have arisen in the Joint Committee, the Contracting Parties have so far largely managed to reach political agreements to resolve them, thereby avoiding a potential provisional suspension of the affected part of the relevant Annex to the EEA Agreement.[49] In some cases, this has even allowed the EFTA states to negotiate exemptions, amendments, or technical adaptations to the legal acts in question. While technical adaptations are commonplace (eg substituting 'EU Member States' with 'EFTA States', or 'Commission' with 'ESA'), substantive amendments are much harder to come by, and where they do exist, they are usually due to specificities of the individual EFTA states concerned.[50]

On the whole, while the effective 'veto' right and possibility of negotiating adaptations would seem, in theory, to allow for a high degree of differentiation, in practice the level of full diffusion of the EU norms in question is surprisingly high. The consistently high scores posted each year by the EFTA states on the timely implementation of new EEA measures further underlines this conclusion.[51] And crucial to the success and longevity not only of this particular mechanism, but also of the Agreement as a whole, both the EU and the EFTA states seem largely content with how it actually functions in practice.[52]

V. The Pluralistic Nature of Judicial EEA Enforcement

In the decentralized system of EU law enforcement, national courts naturally play a vital role in securing the effectiveness and application of EU (and EEA) law. The same applies as far as national courts in the EFTA states are concerned, in securing the effectiveness and application of EEA law in practice. The role that the EFTA state courts play is arguably even more pivotal, given the lack (at least in certain

[48] Art 102(4) EEA provides for a form of conciliation procedure to be followed in such instances, in the event of failure to reach agreement by which the affected part of the relevant Annex to the Agreement would be regarded as 'provisionally suspended, subject to a decision to the contrary by the EEA Joint Committee'. Exactly what such a provisional suspension would entail—whether it would apply to the entire Annex in question or merely a more distinct part of it—remains unclear in practice.

[49] Art 102(5) EEA. This procedure has been initiated by the EU on a few occasions, but has never been carried through to its conclusion. See, eg Niels Fenger, Michael Sánchez Rydelski, and Titus Van Stiphout, *The European Free Trade Association and the European Economic Area* (Wolters Kluwer 2012), 133–34; and Fredriksen and Franklin, 'Of Pragmatism and Principles' (n 5).

[50] One example concerns, eg the free movement of persons, where Liechtenstein, owing to its size, enjoys far-reaching derogations and exemptions from the terms of, eg the Citizenship Directive (n 33). For more on this, see Ólafur Jóhannes Einarsson, 'Article 31' in Arnesen and others (eds) (n 6), para 30.

[51] ESA's 47th Internal Market Scoreboard of the EFTA States, 18 March 2021, Doc number 1166451, available at https://www.eftasurv.int/esa-at-a-glance/publications/scoreboard/internal-market-scoreboard-47-march-2021 last accessed 1 July 2023.

[52] As often repeated in various statements by the EEA Council, eg Conclusions of the 57th Meeting of the EEA Council, 19 November 2019, EEE 1606/1/19, available at https://www.efta.int/EEA/EEA-Council-1315 last accessed 1 July 2023.

situations) of an ultimate authority on how EU/EEA rules are to be interpreted and applied under the EFTA pillar of the EEA construct. Put quite simply, the EFTA Court does not enjoy the same pinnacled position in its relationship with the national courts of the EFTA states as the ECJ does in relation to the national courts of the EU Member States.

Crucial to understanding how judicial enforcement of EEA law operates, it is important to point out that, since taking part in the EEA was not to involve any transfer of legislative or judicial sovereignty for the EFTA states, the institutional set-up of the EEA is markedly different from that of the EU. While the EFTA states were unwilling (and constitutionally unable) to submit full authority over EEA matters to the EU institutions, the EU for its part could obviously not accept a situation whereby the EFTA states would be free to monitor their own compliance. The compromise reached, therefore, saw the adoption of a unique two-pillar structure for monitoring and enforcement of EEA obligations, with the EU acting collectively under one pillar, and the EFTA states acting collectively under the other. Although several common EEA institutions were established to act as a bridge between the two pillars (such as, eg the Joint Committee mentioned earlier), there is no common court or supervisory body.[53] The Agreement, therefore, presumed the establishment of a system for supervising and enforcing EEA obligations which would be indigenous under each pillar. While the ECJ and the Commission are charged with doing so under the EU pillar, the EFTA Court and the ESA act under the EFTA pillar to this end, under the terms of the SCA. Strong obligations of sincere cooperation between the EU and EFTA institutions (Art 3 EEA and Art 2 SCA) and the principle of homogeneity aim to ensure that EU norms are not distorted when applied in their EEA setting.[54] Indeed, the EFTA Court is even formally obliged by homogeneity requirements to interpret EEA provisions in conformity with relevant rulings of the ECJ.[55]

The nature and complexion of the dialogue between national courts of the EFTA states and the EFTA Court is, nevertheless, rather different to the more hierarchical set-up under the EU legal system. While the EFTA Court's jurisdiction to render Advisory Opinions under Article 34 SCA was modelled on (and consequently looks rather similar to) the Preliminary Ruling procedure under Article 267 TFEU, these are far from the same. Firstly, unlike decisions of the ECJ, the

[53] Indeed, the idea of a common EEA court was ruled out altogether following the ECJ's *Opinion 1/91 (EEA Agreement)* [1991] ECLI:EU:C:1991:490.

[54] For more on the principle of cooperation (or loyalty) under EEA law, see Christian NK Franklin, 'Art 3 EEA' and 'Art 2 SCA' in Arnesen and others (eds) (n 6), 180–96 and 978–80.

[55] Although Art 6 EEA provides that the EFTA Court must interpret EEA provisions in conformity with the relevant case law of the ECJ rendered prior to the date of signature of the Agreement (ie 2 May 1992), the EFTA Court's practice reveals that it has also consistently taken into account relevant rulings of the ECJ after this date, eg Joined Cases E–9/07 and E–10/07 *L'Oréal* [2008] EFTA Ct Rep 258, para. 28. While the ECJ also routinely takes EFTA Court practice into account in its own case law, there is little denying the formal and practical hierarchical relationship between the two.

opinions of the EFTA Court are considered advisory and not formally binding on the national courts of the EFTA states. The Norwegian Supreme Court has reiterated in several cases that it has not only the right, but also a duty, to independently assess whether or not to follow the EFTA Court's opinion in a case.[56] Several decisions of the Norwegian courts further illustrate that they may well be prepared to deviate from an interpretation of EEA law spelt out by the EFTA Court in a given case, especially where they (rightly or wrongly) deem this necessary in order to follow the ECJ's lead.[57] While such apparent reticence in accepting the EFTA Court as the ultimate arbiter of EEA law in the EFTA pillar might well be thought to pose a serious risk of differentiation in how EU norms are interpreted and/or applied under the two EEA pillars, it should probably not be exaggerated too much. It is settled Norwegian case law that significant importance and weight are to be attached to the EFTA Court's views, meaning that the duty to consider the EFTA Court's opinions is not to be taken lightly. The resultant prima facie presumption of following the EFTA Court's opinions may only be rebutted where there are 'special reasons' for doing so.[58] And the threat of infringement proceedings raised by the ESA based, inter alia, on a breach of the duty of sincere cooperation under Article 3 EEA and/or Article 2 SCA will usually also entail an exceptionally high threshold before national courts would consider arriving at a different result in practice.[59]

Secondly, it seems clear from the wording of Article 34 SCA that national courts have no duty to refer questions on the interpretation and/or application of EEA law to the EFTA Court, even when deciding at last instance. The question as to whether an unwritten duty might, nevertheless, be said to exist under EEA law to this end has been the subject of a great deal of academic debate.[60] Suffice to say here that the EFTA states are formally entitled to limit the right to request Advisory Opinions to courts and tribunals against whose decisions there is no judicial remedy under national law.[61] And while never brazen enough to say so directly, it seems quite clear from practice that at least the Norwegian Supreme Court, for its part, tacitly construes Article 34 as not imposing any duty to refer questions to the EFTA Court.

[56] HR-2000-49-B *(Finanger I)* and HR-2013-496-A *(STX)*.

[57] Suggested in *Finanger I* (n 56), and unequivocally demonstrated in *STX* (n 56), LF-2015-187242 *(Fosen Linjen I)*, and LB-2018-141762 *(Netfonds)*; see also HR-2009-1319-A *(Pedicel)*, where the Supreme Court tacitly distanced itself from parts of the Advisory Opinion which the Norwegian Market Council had obtained from the EFTA Court.

[58] *STX* (n 56).

[59] The national Supreme Courts of the dualist EFTA states have expressed as much of their own accord, eg *Finanger I* (n 56); HR-2004-981-A *(Paranova)*; HR-2007-1144-A *(Gambling Machines)*; and *STX* (n 56). For similar pronouncements made by the Icelandic Supreme Court, see eg H.1999 4429 and H.1999 4916.

[60] Compare, eg the views of Carl Baudenbacher, 'The EFTA Court: Structure and Tasks' in Baudenbacher (ed) (n 20), 157, with the more sceptical views of Fredriksen and Franklin, 'Of Pragmatism and Principles' (n 5) 672–73, and Christian NK Franklin, 'Art 3 EEA' (n 54) 195.

[61] Art 34 SCA.

The more limited nature of the Advisory Opinion procedure, as compared with its EU law counterpart, is further reflected in the total number of referrals made, which since 1994 have averaged fewer than five per year from all three EFTA states combined. A review of the past thirty years reveals a very large number of cases where courts (or at least Norwegian courts), faced with issues concerning the interpretation and/or application of EEA law, made no referral to the EFTA Court whatsoever. Of course, in some of these cases, the lack of a referral might be deemed completely unproblematic. This might either be because the issue in question had already been answered by the ECJ and/or EFTA Court in a different case, and the national court had arrived at the same conclusion, or perhaps, even though the ECJ and/or EFTA Court had not provided an answer, they would presumably have arrived at the same answer as the national court in any event. In some of the cases, however, the Norwegian courts' final decisions reveal that seeking some advice on the correct understanding of EEA law might have been preferable.[62] While historically understood as rather frosty, there has (happily) been a thawing in the relationship between particularly the Norwegian Supreme Court and EFTA Court in the past five to ten years or so. Yet, notwithstanding the absence of any duty to do so, it is nevertheless still rather difficult to explain why national courts in the EFTA states do not exploit their *right* to refer questions to the EFTA Court on difficult questions of EEA law more regularly.

Finally, it is worth emphasizing that neither the ESA nor the EFTA Court have any real means at their disposal to ensure that Advisory Opinions are enforced in practice. The same applies as far as the EFTA Court's decisions in direct actions for breaches of EEA law under Article 31 SCA are concerned. Although (unlike Advisory Opinions) these are considered legally binding, and notwithstanding clear obligations under Article 33 to take the necessary measures to comply with any judgment of the EFTA Court, recalcitrant EFTA states cannot be forced to comply. As a result, there is certainly a greater theoretical risk of EU norms being interpreted and/or applied differently at national level in the EFTA states than there is in the EU Member States. How great the risk should, in practice, be considered to be is, nevertheless, open to debate. In most situations where the EFTA states' courts appear unable or unwilling to follow the EFTA Court's lead, matters tend to be smoothed out politically by the ESA and the State authorities in question, often leading to a recalibration of administrative (or other) practice and/or change of national rules to resolve the issue.

[62] The Supreme Court, eg, appears to have been mistaken in its understanding of EU and EEA law in *Finanger I* (n 56) (scope of the principle of consistent interpretation); HR-2012-2213-A *(Personskadeforbundet)* (scope of principle of state liability); and *Gambling Machines* (n 59) (proportionality assessment, reversal of burden of proof).

VI. Conclusions

As we have seen in this chapter, EEA cooperation undoubtedly contains scope for a potentially high degree of external differentiation in the diffusion of EU norms in the EFTA states. Yet such concerns seem largely theoretical: in practice, the various tools which might have been used in order to limit or distort the full transplantation of EU internal market rules are, in fact, rarely utilized by the Contracting Parties. The EFTA states are, further, bound by numerous EEA rights and duties, which, although differing somewhat from their EU counterparts (eg homogeneity/uniformity, (quasi-)primacy), as well as underlining fundamental differences between membership in the EU and participation in the internal market through the EEA Agreement, nevertheless render their status within the internal market project as largely comparable to those of the EU Member States. Crucial to the success of EEA cooperation is that, although the EFTA states do not participate formally in decision-making at EU level, they take full part in the decision-making procedures within the EEA, and in the enforcement of EEA norms in practice. Barring the occasional (political) cut and scar, the diffusion of EU norms through the EEA Agreement has, therefore, proven a largely seamless operation in practice.

The increasingly dynamic nature of EEA law does, naturally, give rise to certain tensions and questions as to how far the cooperative venture actually stretches in practice. While the Agreement is formally limited in terms of its material scope, there can be little doubting the at times rather illusory nature of such limits in practice. Yet, as EU law develops and evolves, so too must EEA law, in order to avoid undermining the internal market project. The EFTA states might well view such a development as upsetting the entire premise of EEA cooperation. Seen from the EU's perspective, however, it is probably best understood as the (admittedly high) price to be paid in order to maintain the very 'special relationship' which has come to exist between the EU and EFTA states over the past thirty years. In any event, given the EU and the EFTA states' oft-repeated statements of apparent contentedness with the overall functioning of the Agreement, and notwithstanding the possibility of revisiting its terms, particularly following Brexit, any discussions on a revision of the Agreement seem doubtful for the foreseeable future.

11

EU Norm Diffusion to Switzerland: EU Policies À la carte and Integration in Pieces?

*Andrea Ott and Benedikt Pirker**

I. Introduction

The present chapter examines norm diffusion in European Union (EU)–Swiss relations, with norm diffusion denoting, somewhat broadly, a practice of transferring EU law norms to a third European country. The term derives from international relations but is in this context understood much broader as taking place 'within countries, among a wide range of public and private actors, and it can lead to the spread of all kinds of things, from specific instruments, standards, and institutions, both public and private, to broad policy models, ideational frameworks, and institutional settings'.[1] From a legal point of view and our understanding, the definition of norm diffusion is much narrower and focusses on the instruments, the rules, laws and its legal interpretation, which are diffused or extended on a third country. This norm diffusion enables a third country—and primarily a European third country—to participate in EU policies, especially in the EU internal market, the Schengen regime, the EU sectoral policies in the form of education and training or aviation, and the sub-institutional EU agencies governing the respective EU policies' implementation. This membership *in* an EU policy will always remain slightly different from membership *in* the EU, based on equality among Member States under the same institutional rights and obligations. Despite this qualitative difference, Swiss literature coined Swiss participation in EU policies as a 'de facto or quasi membership'.[2] However, this 'integration without membership'[3] unfolds

* This text was finalized before this author started work as a legal advisor for the Swiss Federal Department of Foreign Affairs in September 2022. The author is expressing a personal point of view in his academic function. The opinions stated in this text should not be regarded as the official position of Switzerland, or of the Federal Department of Foreign Affairs. Later revisions and updates have been undertaken by Andrea Ott alone, and concern only the last section of this chapter.

[1] Fabrizio Gilardi, 'Transnational diffusion: Norms, ideas, and policies' in Walter Carlsnaes, Thomas Risse, and Beth Simmons (eds) *Handbook of International Relations* (SAGE Publications 2012), 453–47. See for further details on the definition Section 3.1II.A below.

[2] Matthias Oesch, 'Switzerland-EU Bilateral Agreements, the Incorporation of EU Law and the Continuous Erosion of Democratic Rights' (2020) 39 Yearbook of European Law 602–39, 639; Thomas Cottier and André Holenstein, *Die Souveränität der Schweiz in Europa* (Stämpfli 2021) 89.

[3] Marius Vahl and Nina Grolimund, *Integration without Membership: Switzerland's Bilateral Agreements with the European Union* (CEPS 2006).

Andrea Ott and Benedikt Pirker, *EU Norm Diffusion to Switzerland* In: *Redefining EU Membership*. Edited by: Diane Fromage, Oxford University Press. © Andrea Ott and Benedikt Pirker 2024. DOI: 10.1093/9780191948145.003.0011

only under certain conditions set by the EU's political and legal institutions and, at the same time, when being accepted by a third country (in this case, Switzerland) in negotiations and through binding international agreements. Furthermore, these EU conditions have only been refined by the EU institutions after specific bilateral relations were set up, with the Free Trade Agreement (FTA) in 1972[4] and the subsequent bilateral agreements since 1999.[5] Particular difficulties arise from the Swiss political and economic situation when updating the bilateral relations. Switzerland is a close geographical neighbour for whom cooperation with the EU is highly advantageous. However, it is also an affluent state with long democratic traditions and stable institutions to which the 'classic' EU external relations toolbox—eg conditionality—is not easily applicable or acceptable. We note as a core 'red thread' that, in their relations, both parties rely on what we term *de jure* and *de facto* strategies of norm diffusion, but that a remarkable gap in the perception of these relations and their future has emerged, embodied by the 2021 failure of the EU–Swiss draft institutional framework agreement.

The 1972 FTA still determines the current trade relations between Switzerland and the EU. While the other European Free Trade Association (EFTA) members updated their trade relations with the European Economic Area Agreement in 1992,[6] a clear majority of the Swiss cantons, and a narrow majority of the Swiss people, rejected accession to the EEA at the same time. The parallel request to accede to the EU, submitted by the Swiss Federal Council together with most other EFTA countries, shortly before the Swiss vote, is often identified as one of the main reasons for the negative vote; specifically, that the Swiss public perceived the EEA from then onwards exclusively as an interim step towards the—contentious—full membership of the EU.[7] This crucial moment set Switzerland on a different trajectory from the other EFTA countries, which joined the EU (Sweden, Finland, and Austria) or constituted the EFTA members of the EEA (Liechtenstein, Iceland, and Norway).[8] As this contribution nonetheless shows, even in the absence of prospects of EU membership, there is norm diffusion but with certain problems caused

[4] [1972] OJ L300/189. It has, however, been complemented with protocols and later agreements, especially the Mutual Recognition Agreement [2002] OJ L114/369 and the Agreement amending the Agreement between the European Economic Community and the Swiss Confederation of 22 July 1972 as regards the provisions applicable to processed agricultural products [2005] OJ L23/19.

[5] See overview on these agreements at https://www.eda.admin.ch/europa/de/home/bilaterale-abkommen/ueberblick.html accessed 1 July 2023.

[6] [1994] OJ L1/3. See further on this, the chapters by Christian Franklin, and by Jarle Trondal and Nadja S Kühn, in this volume.

[7] For the Swiss government's position, see Jakob Kellenberger, *Wo liegt die Schweiz? Gedanken zum Verhältnis CH–EU* (NZZ Libro 2014) 30–32. The Swiss request to join the EU was only effectively withdrawn in 2016 (relevant letter at https://www.eda.admin.ch/content/dam/dea/fr/documents/bundesrat/160727-Lettre-retrait-adhesion-CH_fr.pdf last accessed 1 July 2023).

[8] On the legal structure of the relations between Switzerland and these countries, see Benedikt Pirker, 'Switzerland and the EEA' in Finn Arnesen and others (eds), *Agreement on the European Economic Area: A Commentary* (Nomos 2018). See also the chapters by Franklin, and Kühn and Trondal, in this volume IV.

by the aforementioned gap in the perception of mutual relations. This discrepancy provides valuable lessons in the discussion about differentiation in membership (eg whether there is a need for associate membership alongside full membership).

In this chapter, we proceed in several steps. First, we set out the evolution of EU–Swiss relations up to 2023, to bolster our claim that both parties speak in different languages about their mutual relations (II.). Second, we explore the concept of norm diffusion and then assess the categories of *de jure* and *de facto* norm diffusion and their practice in EU–Swiss relations. We then set out the reasons which led the EU to emphasize *de jure* norm diffusion, whereas, on the Swiss side, a certain preference for limited *de jure* norm diffusion and more *de facto* norm diffusion has emerged (III.). Finally, we offer reflections on how both parties might rethink their position to find new ground for compromise in future relations (IV.).

II. EU–Swiss Relations: Talking Two Different Languages

After the rejection of EEA accession, Switzerland asked for the opening of negotiations of bilateral agreements covering various areas, in order to gain at least sectoral access to the internal market. The EU agreed to negotiations, and the first set of so-called 'Bilateral Agreements' (Bilateral Agreements I) was negotiated and signed in 1999, covering the free movement of persons,[9] air transport,[10] land transport,[11] public procurement,[12] scientific and technological cooperation,[13] mutual recognition concerning conformity assessments,[14] and trade in agricultural products.[15] As a particularity, the Bilateral Agreements I are linked by a 'guillotine' clause in each Agreement, ensuring that the termination of one Agreement leads to the termination of the other agreements.[16] The EU required this link to ensure that Switzerland could not cherry-pick by declining—eg through a referendum under Swiss law—the Free Movement of Persons Agreement (FMOPA), which Switzerland perceived as more advantageous for the EU than for Switzerland. The second set of agreements ('Bilateral Agreements II'), covering some topics 'left over' from the first set of negotiations and a number of new topics,[17] was signed in 2004. Among the often rather technical subjects,[18] the

9 [2002] OJ L114/6.
10 [2002] OJ L114/73.
11 [2002] OJ L114/91.
12 [2002] OJ L114/430.
13 [2002] OJ L114/468.
14 Also called the Mutual Recognition Agreement (n 4).
15 [2002] OJ L114/132.
16 Art 25(4), Agreement on the Free Movement of Persons (n 9).
17 On the reasons for the topics chosen in this round of negotiations, see Michael Ambühl, 'Bilaterale Abkommen II—Politische Würdigung' in Christine Kaddous and Monique Jametti Greiner (eds), *Bilaterale Abkommen II Schweiz-EU und andere neue Abkommen* (Helbing & Lichtenhahn 2006).
18 eg statistics ([2006] OJ L90/2) or the participation of Switzerland in the European Environmental Agency and the European Environment Information and Observation Network ([2006] OJ L90/36).

Schengen[19] and Dublin[20] Association Agreements are not only particularly important in themselves, but also because they provide a specific system of legal alignment to ensure full-scale Swiss participation in these respective EU legal regimes.

Furthermore, another 'small guillotine clause' links both agreements in their application.[21] Finally, both sides have agreed, since 2005, on a few additional agreements, such as the agreements involving Swiss participation in some EU agencies,[22] and an agreement allowing Switzerland to participate in the police cooperation scheme established by the so-called Prüm decisions.[23] The aforementioned agreements cover a broad range of subjects; hence, it is difficult to categorize them precisely. However, they range from more classic agreements on trade[24] or facilitating trade[25] to partial integration agreements concerning EU internal market law, but also cover the Area of Freedom, Security and Justice (AFSJ),[26] and flanking policies.[27]

However, since Swiss accession became more unlikely, in 2008, the EU's stance towards Switzerland has been toughened. The EU Commission, Council, and European Parliament[28] have critically perceived this enhanced bilateralism.[29] Twenty-seven joint committees govern one-hundred-and-twenty bilateral agreements, and, therefore, 'Byzantine complexity' burdens the design and implementation of these bilateral agreements.[30] As the EU's suggestions of a Swiss EEA

[19] [2008] OJ L53/50.

[20] [2008] OJ L53/5.

[21] Art 15(4), Schengen Association Agreement (n 19) and Art 14(2), Dublin Association Agreement (n 20), each of which provides that the relevant agreement only applies as long as the other agreement applies.

[22] Agreement between the EC and Switzerland on the participation in the European Environmental Agency, OJ 2006 L90/17; Arrangement between the EC and Switzerland on participation in Frontex, OJ 2010 L243/4.

[23] OJ 2019 L187/3. See, further, Matthias Oesch, *Schweiz—Europäische Union: Grundlagen, Bilaterale Abkommen, Autonomer Nachvollzug* (EIZ Publishing 2020) 24–25.

[24] eg the Free Trade Agreement (n 4) and the Agreement on Public Procurement (n12), the latter of which extends the scope of application of the World Trade Organization Agreement on Government Procurement between Switzerland and the EU.

[25] eg the Mutual Recognition Agreement and the Agreement on Trade in Agricultural Products (n 15).

[26] The Agreement on the Free Movement of Persons (n 9), the Agreement on Air Transport (n 10), and the Schengen (n 19) and Dublin (n 20) Association Agreements. On differentiation in the AFSJ, see Curtin and Patrin, in this volume.

[27] Agreement between the EU and the Swiss Confederation on the linking of their greenhouse gas emissions trading systems, OJ 2017 L322/3; eg the Agreement on Scientific and Technological Cooperation (n 13).

[28] eg European Commission, 'Memo on EU–Swiss relations' (Press release), 10 February 2014 http://europa.eu/rapid/press-release_MEMO-14-100_en.htm accessed 1 July 2023; Council of the European Union, 'Council Conclusions on EU Relations with EFTA Countries', Brussels, 20 December 2012, 5–6 http://eeas.europa.eu/norway/docs/2012_final_conclusions_en.pdf accessed 1 July 2023; European Parliament, 'Report (29.6.2010 A7-0216/2010) on EEA–Switzerland: Obstacles with regard to the Full Implementation of the Internal Market' (2009/2176(INI)).

[29] Adam Łazowski, Switzerland, '*' in Steven Blockmans and Adam Łazowski (eds), *The European Union and its Neighbours* (TMC Asser Press 2006) 95.

[30] Marc Maresceau, 'EU-Switzerland: Quo Vadis?' (2011) 49 Georgia Journal of International and Comparative Law 729.

membership or a comprehensive association agreement fell on deaf Swiss ears,[31] other ways of modernizing the governance of these agreements and updating their content have been explored by the EU, and plans hatched to reinforce these by means of conditionality.[32] Whereas some new agreements have been concluded in various technical areas of cooperation,[33] the EU has been unwilling to negotiate new market-access-related agreements[34] until a new agreement providing an institutional framework for the existing and future agreements on Swiss access to the EU internal market is concluded.[35]

After lengthy negotiations in 2018, the draft institutional framework agreement was finalized, but not signed by the Swiss government.[36] After a long phase of internal consultations and increasing criticism from various stakeholders in Switzerland[37] regarding the negotiated agreement, the Swiss Federal Council pulled the plug on 26 May 2021.[38] It declared that substantial interpretation differences between the EU and Switzerland, concerning the application of the EU Citizens Rights Directive, wage protection in Switzerland, and State-aid provisions, prevented any compromise.[39]

Looking at the former draft institutional framework agreement's detrimental perceptions on the EU side as a done deal, while Switzerland still perceived it as a work in progress, it becomes obvious that both sides talked in different languages, and that the EU's policy tools of conditionality have a limited impact on Swiss decision-making.[40] Switzerland, in contrast to former EU member the UK, has

[31] Christa Tobler, 'A Look at the EEA from Switzerland' in EFTA Court (ed), *The EEA and the EFTA Court: Decentred Integration* (Hart 2014) 542, 542.

[32] For the formulation used repeatedly by the Council, see 'Council Conclusions on EU Relations with EFTA Countries', 14 December 2010, para 48, https://www.consilium.europa.eu/uedocs/cms_data/docs/pressdata/EN/foraff/118458.pdf

[33] Agreement between the European Union and the Swiss Confederation on the linking of their greenhouse gas emissions trading systems (n 27).

[34] eg on the 'frozen' negotiations of an agreement on electricity, see Peter Hettich, Simone Walther, and Sabine Schreiber Tschudin, *Schweiz ohne Stromabkommen* (Dike 2015).

[35] Council of the European Union, 'Council Conclusions on EU Relations with the Swiss Confederation', 28 February 2017, para 5.

[36] Text of the draft agreement at: https://www.eda.admin.ch/dam/europa/fr/documents/abkommen/Acccord-inst-Projet-de-texte_fr.pdf accessed 1 July 2023.

[37] For an overview, see Benedikt Pirker and Livia Matter, 'Europarecht: Schweiz–Europäische Union' (2020) 30 Swiss Review of International and European Law 75, 76–82.

[38] Swiss Federal Council, 'No Signing of the EU–Swiss Institutional Agreement' (Press release, 26 May 2021) https://www.admin.ch/gov/en/start/documentation/media-releases.msg-id-83705.html accessed 1 July 2023.

[39] ibid; See further on the regulation of state aids (eg Simon Hirsbrunner, 'Könnte die Schweiz ein Verbot staatlicher Beihilfen verkraften?' (2017) Zeitschrift für Europarecht 60), the relevance of the EU Cititzenship Directive (eg Astrid Epiney and Sian Affolter, 'Das Institutionelle Abkommen—unter besonderer Berücksichtigung der Unionsbürgerrichtlinie' in Alberto Achermann and others (eds), *Jahrbuch für Migrationsrecht 2018/2019* (Stämpfli 2019)), and the regulation of certain flanking measures in Swiss law taken to counter effects of social dumping in the context of the posting of workers (eg Astrid Epiney and Lena Hehemann, 'Die Tragweite des Institutionellen Abkommens im Bereich der Arbeitnehmerentsendung' (*Jusletter*, 8 April 2019)) https://jusletter.weblaw.ch/juslissues/2019/975/die-tragweite-des-in_7172a55398.html__ONCE.

[40] On misunderstandings already during an early meeting in 2018, see Tobias Gafafer, Christoph G Schmutz, and Daniel Steinvorth, '' *Neue Zürcher Zeitung* (Zürich, 22 June 2021), Was beim

never had member status, and has profited from EU integration outside the EU, and is, in contrast to European third countries such as Ukraine, an affluent and stable democracy based on neutrality, federalism, and direct democracy pointing in the direction of a European '*Sonderweg*' (special path).[41] While the Swiss acted as if the bigger entity (EU) should adapt to the smaller unit and respect Swiss sovereignty concerns, the EU took away, from the ongoing Swiss discussion, another confirmation of Swiss desire for integration à la carte. In the direct aftermath of the British decision to leave the Union, the EU felt it had to rebuke cherry-picking by third European states.[42] At the same time, the EU can no longer agree to the tailor-made cooperation of the 1990s and, instead, aims for a standard framework when extending EU policies and structures in the European neighbourhood.[43] This standardized framework is caused by the EU's political and legal conditions, and coloured by the recent negotiations concerning Brexit and European microstates on provision of access to the internal market to third European states. These political and legal conditions translate into the integrity of the internal market and the securing of a level playing field and an effective dispute settlement system to interpret EU law-inspired norms of international agreements integrating third states. The integrity of the internal market, nowadays even broadened to the integrity of the EU's legal order,[44] is understood by the EU as meaning that EU rules come with rights and obligations for third countries, but that a dividing line between members and non-members must remain. It excludes third countries from gaining equal rights in EU institutions, and from having a free choice regarding which EU integration policies they join. This integrity argument is closely connected to the level playing field argument, which underlines that when third countries, and their citizens and businesses, profit from EU rules and free trade with the Union, they should play along with the basic and relevant EU rules and respect the EU's social values and environmental standards.[45] Finally, the Court of Justice of the European Union (ECJ) has sharpened more and more the autonomy of EU law by stressing that the ECJ has the interpretation monopoly over EU law and its

Geheimtreffen zwischen Bern und der EU 2018 passiert ist (nzz.ch). https://www.nzz.ch/schweiz/was-beim-geheimtreffen-zwischen-bern-und-der-eu-2018-passiert-ist-ld.1630710

[41] The Swiss outsider role with an emphasis on sovereignty and neutrality is historically analyzed by Cottier and Holenstein (n 2) 85.

[42] For the reaction of the European Commission to the Swiss decision, see 'Commission Statement on the Decision by the Swiss Federal Council to Terminate the Negotiations of the EU–Swiss Institutional Framework Agreement', Brussels, 26 May 2021 https://ec.europa.eu/commission/presscorner/detail/en/statement_21_2683 accessed 1 July 2023.

[43] Andrea Ott, 'The Building Blocks and Stumbling Stones of the European Legal Space' in Wybe Douma and others (eds), *The Evolving Nature of EU External Relations Law* (TMC Asser Press 2021) 205–29.

[44] European Council (Art 50) Guidelines for Brexit Negotiations, 29 April 2017, European Council (Art 50) guidelines for Brexit negotiations—Consilium (europa.eu).

[45] Ott, 'The Building Blocks and Stumbling Stones' (n 44) 221 with further references.

progeny international norms, and that EU law disputes cannot be withdrawn from the jurisdiction of Member States' courts and the ECJ.[46]

The former draft institutional framework agreement[47] would have covered core market access agreements.[48] The innovating factor, in line with the EU's already-described red lines, would have revolved around approximation and dispute resolution, thus creating a common framework governing the enforcement of rules and safeguarding their consistent interpretation. It aimed to move away from a more static approximation to create an obligation of continuous legal adaptation for Switzerland in the agreements of internal market relevance.[49] And, moving away from a diplomatic and consensus-driven consultation system in the event of conflict,[50] the draft institutional framework agreement foresaw arbitration dispute settlement. However, in line with all recent dispute settlement clauses included in the Withdrawal Agreement with the UK, and in the Association Agreement with Ukraine,[51] the arbitrators would have referred a dispute relating to the interpretation of EU law-related provisions to the ECJ.[52]

Crucially, this overview shows that, despite the seemingly continuous development of the bilateral relations between the EU and Switzerland, there are fundamentally different conceptions of the overall goals to be pursued, and the

[46] ibid 223; eg, for the case law, Opinion 1/91 (EEA) [1991] ECLI:EU:C:1991:490 and Opinion 1/17 (CETA) [2019] ECLI:EU:C:2019:341.

[47] For a comprehensive discussion of the draft agreement, see Christine Kaddous, 'Switzerland and the EU—Current Issues and New Challenges under the Draft Institutional Framework Agreement' in Sieglinde Gstöhl and David Phinnemore (eds), *The Proliferation of Privileged Partnerships between the European Union and Its Neighbours* (Routledge 2019). https://www.eda.admin.ch/europa/de/home/bilateraler-weg/ueberblick/institutionelles-abkommen/informationen-dokumente.html

[48] The Agreement on the Free Movement of Persons (n 9), the Agreements on Air (n 10) and Land (n 11) Transport, the Agreement on Trade in Agricultural Products (n 15) and the Mutual Recognition Agreement (n 4) as core market access agreements. Contrary to the EU's initial position, Art 2 of the draft institutional framework agreement does not mention the old Free Trade Agreement (n 4) or the Agreement on Public Procurement (n 12).

[49] Again with certain possibilities of participation (decision-shaping) in the EU legislative processes and prolonged deadlines to allow direct democratic procedures in the Swiss constitutional system (Arts 5, 12, and 14 of the draft institutional framework agreement).

[50] With the exception of the Bilateral Air Transport Agreement (n 10).

[51] Art 322, Association Agreement with Ukraine, [2014] OJ L161/3; Art 174, UK Withdrawal Agreement, [2020] OJ L29/7.

[52] Notions of EU law reproduced or acts of EU law referred to in the draft agreement must be interpreted in line with past and future case law of the ECJ: see Art 4. On the dispute mechanism, Art 10 states: '2. *Si le comité sectoriel ne parvient pas à trouver une solution à la difficulté mentionnée au paragraphe premier dans un délai de trois mois à compter de la date à laquelle la difficulté a 23.11.2018—Version finale 8 été portée devant le comité sectoriel, la Suisse ou l'Union européenne peut demander qu'un tribunal arbitral règle le différend conformément au Protocole sur le tribunal arbitral. 3. Lorsque le différend soulève une question concernant l'interprétation ou l'application d'une disposition visée dans le deuxième paragraphe de l'article 4 du présent accord, et si son interprétation est pertinente pour régler le différend et nécessaire pour lui permettre de statuer, le tribunal arbitral saisit la Cour de justice de l'Union européenne. L'arrêt de la Cour de justice de l'Union européenne lie le tribunal arbitral.*' On such dynamic homogeneity, see also Benedikt Pirker, 'Dispute Settlement and Interpretation in the Draft Framework Agreement between Switzerland and the EU' (*European Law Blog*, 12 December 2018). https://europeanlawblog.eu/2018/12/12/dispute-settlement-and-interpretation-in-the-draft-framework-agreement-between-switzerland-and-the-eu/

objectives to be employed, to achieve a partial alignment to EU rules and policies by Switzerland. On the EU's side, the initial idea that an approach based on bilateral agreements would lead, ultimately, to the accession of Switzerland to the EU has been abandoned. Instead, the EU mounted pressure on Switzerland to conclude the draft institutional framework agreement, ie an alternative form of close relationship with the EU next to membership, aligning it more with legal features present in more recent cooperations with the UK and Ukraine, and in line with the conditions of third-country participation as sharpened by the ECJ. In particular, the EU aimed to improve the governance structure, and its dynamic adaptation to the evolving EU *acquis*, to overcome the Swiss integration à la carte. On the Swiss side, the bilateral agreements, combined with the strategy of unilateral autonomous adaptation to EU law, has increasingly been considered the ideal option *('Königsweg')*. Piecemeal integration would enable the country to avoid the thorny question of future EU accession, and to continue negotiating tailor-made access to the internal market and participation in EU policies and programmes,[53] even if it is at the price of accepting less popular agreements such as the Agreement on the Free Movement of Persons, or of cohesion payments.[54]

III. EU–Swiss Relations between Norm Diffusion and Norm Transfer

A. Norm diffusion in the European legal space

Despite the severe disagreements between the two sides on the perspective and governance of the existing cooperation, the Bilateral Agreements have been a functioning integration path enabling tailor-made access for Switzerland to parts of the EU's internal market, and to the AFSJ (Schengen and Prüm), as well as its participation in policy-relevant EU agencies and programmes. Norm diffusion or transfer enables the Swiss policy integration. We will, subsequently, analyze how it is defined and employed in the EU–Swiss relations.

Norm diffusion is a term well known to political scientists; often theorized, but very difficult to simplify into a few words. One explanation defines it as a process of interdependent policy-making, and distinguishes between learning, competition,

[53] On the repeated confirmation of this strategy by Swiss voters in various referenda, see Matthias Oesch, *Schweiz* (n 23) 227.

[54] Switzerland provides contributions typically used to enhance cohesion within the EU, and thus paid directly to the new Member States. On the state of the second cohesion payment at the Swiss internal level, see Benedikt Pirker and Livia Matter, 'Europarecht: Schweiz–Europäische Union' (2021) 31 Swiss Review of International and European Law 123, 130–31. For a critical reflection, see Dieter Freiburghaus, *Königsweg oder Sackgasse? Sechzig Jahre schweizerische Europapolitik* (NZZ Libro 2009).

coercion, and emulation diffusion mechanisms.[55] In a famous contribution by Ian Manners on 'normative power Europe', he distinguishes between diffusion by contagion (unintentional diffusion of ideas from the EU to other political actors) and transference through the exportation of EU norms and standards, or by the 'carrot and stickism' of financial rewards and economic sanctions.[56] This categorization has been criticized for ignoring that it relies on compelling incentives such as EU accession or trade advantages. Also, the persistence of power politics cannot be ignored for the EU, as a realist actor in normative clothes.[57] Fitting Switzerland into this concept, Switzerland does not aim to join the Union and, as an affluent third country with stable democratic and institutional structures, is not punished by economic sanctions or rewarded by financial incentives. The limits of EU conditionality are confirmed by the tug of war that unfolded during the discussion surrounding the negotiation results of the draft institutional framework agreement. For example, with the adoption of a new Financial Directive and Regulation (MiFID II/MIFIR), the EU had the option to provide equivalence to third-country traders on the EU financial market. The European Commission was empowered to adopt decisions to grant third-country traders recognition under this secondary law. However, to put pressure on Switzerland, this equivalence of the Swiss legal and supervisory framework applicable to the stock exchanges in Switzerland was granted in December 2017 for only a year, and extended only in December 2018 for half a year, until 30 June 2019.[58] First, financial repercussions for Switzerland were minimal,[59] and secondly, Switzerland 'retaliated' by withholding money under the cohesion fund set up for the new Member States and the enlarged EU, to which Switzerland has pledged to contribute.[60] Another row unfolded before

[55] Fabrizio Gilardi and Fabio Wasserfallen, 'The Politics of Policy Diffusion' (2019) 58 European Journal of Political Research 1245–56.

[56] Ian Manners, 'Normative Power Europe: A Contradiction in Terms?' (2002) 40 Journal of Common Market Studies 235–58.

[57] Kazushige Kobayashi, 'Is Normative Power Cosmopolitan? Rethinking European Unity, Norm Diffusion, and International Political Theory' (2020) 56 Cooperation and Conflict 2, with further references to the literature.

[58] Commission implementing decision (EU) 2017/2441of 21 December 2017 on the equivalence of the legal and supervisory framework applicable to stock exchanges in Switzerland in accordance with Directive 2014/65/EU of the European Parliament and of the Council, OJ 2017 L344/52; Commission implementing decision (EU) 2018/2047 of 20 December 2018 on the equivalence of the legal and supervisory framework applicable to stock exchanges in Switzerland in accordance with Directive 2014/65/EU of the European Parliament and of the Council, OJ 2018 L327/77; Matthias Oesch, *Switzerland and the European Union* (Nomos 2018) para 341.

[59] Elliot Smith, 'How Switzerland's Dispute with the EU over Stocks Prepared it for the Pandemic' (*CNBC*, 10 February 2021). https://www.cnbc.com/2021/02/09/how-switzerlands-spat-with-the-eu-over-stocks-prepared-it-for-the-pandemic.html

[60] Swiss Federal Council, 11 August 2021, 'European Policy: Federal Council Submits Dispatch on Approving Second Swiss Contribution'. It should be noted that Switzerland has never officially acknowledged a clear legal obligation under international law to such cohesion payments: see Benedikt Pirker, 'The Law and Politics of Cohesion: A Comparison between the Swiss Cohesion Payments and the EEA and Norway Grants' in Christa Tobler and Marc Maresceau (eds), *Switzerland and the EU—A Challenging Relationship* (Brill 2023), 276.

extending the application of the Free Movement of Persons Agreement to Croatia and the EU temporarily excluded Switzerland from the EU Horizon 2020 education and training programmes.[61]

Despite these bilateral difficulties, the EU is perceived in the literature as a successful regional rule-maker, exporting the Brussels rules, especially towards its European neighbours in the European legal space.[62] The EU extends its regulatory model and its 'structured network of rules and principles[63] in different forms and under varying conditions. Brussels rules can impact on third countries through unilateral EU legislation with an extraterritorial reach, or by exporting EU rules through bilateral or multilateral agreements.[64] Often, EU unilateral legislation is adopted that has a 'Brussels effect' on third neighbouring countries and their businesses trading with the EU.[65]

This can, for instance, also be highlighted with regard to data protection rules and Switzerland. With the adoption of the EU General Data Protection Regulation (GDPR) in 2018, stricter data protection rules apply in the EU than in Switzerland and remain different since the adoption of the revised Swiss data protection rules in 2023. While it could be disputed whether the novel rules automatically substitute the previous data protection rules applicable in EU–Swiss relations,[66] the stricter rules in force within the EU impact on the Swiss legal order because an equivalent standard of protection is required under EU law (decision on equivalence) if Swiss companies or traders want access to the EU market and its consumers. The impact resulting from the bilateral agreements is more direct and structured. The EU agrees to extend part of its internal market and the Schengen regime, for instance, because the third country adheres to these EU rules and follows the evolution of its *acquis* and the interpretative interpretation of the ECJ. For the latter, Brussels has developed the previously mentioned set of conditions.

[61] 'Status Update: Swiss Participation in the EU Framework Programme for Research and Innovation and Other Related Programmes and Initiatives' https://www.sbfi.admin.ch/dam/sbfi/en/dokumente/2019/02/horizon-europe.pdf.download.pdf/Fact-sheet_Horizon_en.pdf accessed 1 July 2023.

[62] Ott, 'The Building Blocks and Stumbling Stones' (n 44). See, further, Anu Bradford, *The Brussels Effect* (OUP 2021); Joanne Scott, 'The Global Reach of EU Law' in Joanne Scott and Marise Cremona, *EU Law Beyond EU Borders: The Extraterritorial Reach of EU Law* (OUP 2019); Laure Delcour and Elsa Tulmets (eds), *Policy Transfer and Norm Circulation: towards an Interdisciplinary and Comparative Approach* (Routledge 2019).

[63] Case C–621/18 *Wightman and Others v Secretary of State for Exiting the European Union* ECLI:EU:C:2018:999, para 45.

[64] Anne Weyembergh and Irene Wieczorek, 'Norm Diffusion as a Tool to Uphold and Promote EU Values and Interests: A Case Study on the EU Japan Mutual Legal Assistance Agreement' (2020) 11:4 New Journal of European Criminal Law 439–66.

[65] Bradford (n 63).

[66] Anne-Sophie Morand and Selma Duc, 'International Data Transfers and the EU's Adequacy Decisions' (*Jusletter*, 3 May 2021) 1. https://jusletter.weblaw.ch/juslissues/2021/1065/international-data-t_b7cc8e67ab0.html__ONCE&login=false

B. The categories of norm transfer in EU–Swiss relations

Based on the examples given earlier, we can distinguish between norm diffusion or transfer categories. From the norm-receiving-state perspective, the norm-transfer process can be divided into categories: (1) legal approximation or adaptation through binding commitments (*de jure* norm diffusion); and (2) autonomous adaptation by the receiving state and equivalence decisions by the transferring state/EU (*de facto* norm diffusion).[67] In the following subsections, this distinction between *de jure* and *de facto* norm diffusion provides a useful guideline to assess the state of relations between the EU and Switzerland.

1. Legal approximation by binding commitments: *de jure* norm transfer

Legal approximation or harmonization forms a regulatory tool in the EU's internal market. It aims to remove trade barriers between the economic actors to ensure a level playing field between them. It allows for complete or total harmonization, replacing the national rules, as foreseen by Article 114 of the Treaty on the Functioning of the EU (TFEU). However, internal market minimum harmonization is also possible, and is employed, for instance, in the environmental policy under Article 193 TFEU.[68] Member States are permitted to maintain, and often to introduce, more stringent regulatory standards than those prescribed by Union legislation, for the purposes of advancing a particular social or welfare interest, provided that such additional requirements are compatible with the Treaty.[69] Mutual recognition is linked to harmonization but only compares to minimum harmonization insofar as it requires a Member State to admit, on to its territory, goods or services marketed lawfully in the originating Member State.[70] Approximation of laws, as a term and tool in international agreements, is also used in the EU's neighbourhood and accession candidates to export the EU *acquis* to third countries.[71] Approximation varies from a non-binding best endeavours approach, on the one hand, to a sophisticated regime of binding legislative approximation mechanisms set by the Association Agreement with Ukraine, on the other.[72]

[67] Oesch, *Switzerland and the European Union* (n 59) 16–17.

[68] Marcus Klamert, 'What We Talk About When We Talk about Harmonization' (2015) 17 Cambridge Yearbook of European Legal Studies 360–79, 362.

[69] Michael Dougan, 'Minimum Harmonization and the Internal Market' (2000) Common Market Law Review 855.

[70] Marios Costa and Steve Peers, *Steiner and Woods EU Law* (14th edn, OUP 2020) 349–50.

[71] Roman Petrov and Peter Van Elsuwege (eds), *Legislative Approximation and Application of EU Law in the Eastern Neighbourhood of the European Union* (Routledge 2016); Roman Petrov, 'Exporting the *Acquis Communautaire* into the Legal Systems of Third Countries' (2008) 13 European Foreign Affairs Review 31–52.

[72] Guillaume Van der Loo, Peter Van Elsuwege, and Roman Petrov, 'The EU–Ukraine Association Agreement: Assessment of an Innovative Legal Instrument' 10, The EU-Ukraine association agreement : assessment of an innovative legal instrument (eui.eu)

Finally, we find these latter regulatory tools and norm-transfer mechanisms employed within the framework of the Bilateral Agreements.[73] Legal approximation is achieved by the replication of norms, by mechanisms to accommodate change in EU law through obligations of dynamic legal adaptation, by decision-shaping mechanisms, and by judicial interpretations by the ECJ transferred to the Bilateral Agreements via binding clauses. As a starting point, many Bilateral Agreements *replicate EU law* in their very wording, and thereby transfer EU law to Switzerland, a third country, at the moment of conclusion of the agreements. For example, this is the case of the principle of non-discrimination in the Agreement on Public Procurement,[74] and of Annex I of the Agreement on the Free Movement of Persons, which replicates many norms of EU primary law on the free movement of persons. Often, agreements refer to EU secondary legislation, typically in their annexes. Based on the principle of equivalence of legislation, Switzerland must apply these provisions or create equivalent rules, though not necessarily formally identical legal norms, in its domestic law.[75] Due to the broad Swiss approach to direct application of international obligations, this means that EU directives referred to in a Bilateral Agreement can themselves be directly applicable, and are thus not necessarily transposed into Swiss law.[76] Some agreements formulate Switzerland's obligations more strongly, namely to 'implement and apply' EU secondary legislation,[77] whereas there are also cases in which a mere duty to 'take into consideration' such legislation is established.[78] Even in the latter cases, Switzerland tends not to deviate from such norms except for specific reasons.[79]

There are also *mechanisms to accommodate change*. As a matter of principle, Swiss constitutional law does not permit dynamic references, so the agreements must be treated as static.[80] Still, as changes in EU law need to be taken into account, several approaches are foreseen in the Bilateral Agreements. Revising an

[73] The following overview is based on Astrid Epiney, Beate Metz, and Benedikt Pirker, *Zur Parallelität der Rechtsentwicklung in der EU und in der Schweiz—Ein Beitrag zur rechtlichen Tragweite der 'Bilateralen Abkommen'* (Schulthess 2012), 182ff; for a shortened English language version, see Benedikt Pirker and Astrid Epiney, 'The Integration of Switzerland into the Framework of EU Law by Means of the Bilateral Agreements' in Peter-Christian Müller-Graff and Ole Mestad (eds), *The Rising Complexity of European Law* (Berliner Verlag der Wissenschaften 2014) 45–53.

[74] Art 6 of the Agreement on Public Procurement (n 12).

[75] Corinne Schaerer, 'Acquis communautaire suisse—Das für die Schweiz auf Grund der Bilateralen Abkommen vom 23. Juni 1999 relevante Gemeinschaftsrecht (Umfang und Zugang)' (2004) AJP 340, 340 (and fn 16).

[76] Catherine Kropf, 'Multi-Level-Gesetzgebung: europäisches, bilaterales, nationales Recht und wieder zurück' in Felix Uhlmann and Stefan Höfler (eds), *Rechtsetzung im Mehrebenensystem: Gemeinden, Kantone, Bund, EU* (Dike 2020) 93.

[77] eg Art 2(1), Schengen Association Agreement (n 19).

[78] eg Art 2, Annex II of the Agreement on the Free Movement of Persons (n 9).

[79] Stephan Breitenmoser and Michael Isler, 'Der Rechtsschutz im Personenfreizügigkeitsabkommen zwischen der Schweiz und der EG sowie den EUMitgliedstaaten' (2002) AJP 1003, 1013.

[80] Daniel Wüger and Samuele Scarpelli, 'Die vernachlässigten institutionellen Aspekte der Bilateralen Verträge und die Aushandlung eines Rahmenvertrags' in Astrid Epiney, Andrea Egbuna-Joss, and Markus Wyssling (eds), *Schweizerisches Jahrbuch für Europarecht* (Schulthess 2005/2006) 294.

agreement, for example, is possible but typically cumbersome under international law. Consequently, a typical procedure provided for in the Agreements is the power of an Agreement's joint committee to adopt binding decisions to adapt references to EU secondary legislation in the annexes.[81]

Exceptionally, Agreements—and also the former draft institutional framework agreement—may contain *an obligation for Switzerland to adapt its laws dynamically* to new developments on the EU's side. In the Schengen and Dublin Association Agreements, there is an automatic sanction in the form of termination of both agreements in the event of non-adaptation.[82] For the same situation, the Agreement on Simplifying Inspections and Formalities in Respect of the Carriage of Goods and Customs Security Measures[83] provides for the possibility of safeguard measures by the EU which may amount to the suspension of the Agreement.[84]

Some Agreements also provide for decision-shaping mechanisms, due to which Swiss experts are consulted during the preparation of EU legislation,[85] in the sense that they may attend meetings of committees and expert working parties as observers in the areas of law pertaining to the Bilateral Agreements.[86] At the same time, this is only a consultation mechanism and Switzerland has no formal right to vote, with all the democratic legitimacy questions this raises for the Swiss side.[87]

A final legal tool resulting in *de jure* norm transfer or diffusion is *judicial interpretation*. The Agreement on the Free Movement of Persons[88] and the Agreement on Air Transport[89] include provisions requiring that norms identical to EU norms are interpreted by considering the relevant case law of the ECJ prior to the date of conclusion of the relevant Agreement.[90] In this context, it might prove difficult

[81] eg Art 18 of the Agreement on the Free Movement of Persons (n 9).

[82] Arts 15(4) and 7 of the Schengen Association Agreement (n 19) and 14 (2) and 4 of the Dublin Association Agreement (n 20).

[83] [2009] OJ L199/24.

[84] ibid Art 29.

[85] eg Art 52(2), Agreement on Land Transport (n 11).

[86] See also the Arrangement between the EU, Iceland, Liechtenstein, Norway, and Switzerland on the participation by those States in the work of the committees which assist the European Commission in the exercise of its executive powers as regards the implementation, application and development of the Schengen acquis [2012] OJ L103/4. On the practice, see Georges Baur, 'Die EWR/EFTA-Staaten im Schengen/Dublin-System' in Stephan Breitenmoser, Sabine Gless, and Otto Lagodny (eds), *Schengen und Dublin in der Praxis: Aktuelle Fragen* (Dike 2015) 30.

[87] Section III.D.

[88] Art 16(2).

[89] Art 1(2).

[90] On the exact scope of the obligation contained in these norms, see Thomas Cottier and Nicolas Diebold, 'Warenverkehr und Freizügigkeit in der Rechtsprechung des Bundesgerichts zu den Bilateralen Abkommen. Zur Anwendung und Auslegung von nachvollzogenem Recht und Staatsverträgen unterschiedlicher Generationen' in Astrid Epiney and Nina Gammenthaler (eds), *Schweizerisches Jahrbuch für Europarecht/Annuaire suisse de droit européen* (Schulthess 2008/2009) 258ff; Véronique Boillet, *L'interdiction de discrimination en raison de la nationalité au sens de l'Accord sur la libre circulation des personnes* (Helbing Lichtenhahn 2010), 54ff; Thomas Burri and Benedikt Pirker, 'Stromschnellen im Freizügigkeitsfluss: Von der Bedeutung von Urteilen des Europäischen Gerichtshofes im Rahmen des Personenfreizügigkeitsabkommens' (2010) SZIER 165, 172.

to distinguish between 'old' and 'new' case law that is not covered by the relevant norms, particularly where newer case law of the ECJ relies on broader principles developed in earlier jurisprudence.[91] In practice, however, the Swiss Federal Tribunal has clarified in a landmark decision that—as it had already done—based on the relevant interpretative clause it could and would take into account the earlier and later jurisprudence of the Court of Justice in its interpretation of the Agreement on the Free Movement of Persons, so as to achieve the objective of a parallel legal situation, and would only deviate if 'compelling reasons' spoke out against parallel interpretation.[92] As the Swiss courts cannot and do not have to refer questions on EU law-related interpretation to the ECJ, it is clear that the lack of a final arbiter can, nevertheless, lead to deviations in the judicial interpretation of similar norms.

2. Swiss autonomous adaptation and equivalency decisions: *de facto* norm diffusion

In contrast to these legally obligatory forms of norm transfer, the norm-absorbing country can also voluntarily or autonomously adopt rules. *De facto* norm diffusion occurs either where, as explained previously, with the example of the GDPR, the transferring state/the EU takes an equivalence decision, or where despite the absence of a clear legal obligation, the receiving state/ Swiss side decides to adapt on its own to developments in EU law (often called autonomous adaptation (*'autonomer Nachvollzug'*)). *De facto* norm diffusion, to be explored here, typically takes two forms: a judicial and a legislative one.

Apart from the cases mentioned earlier, in which EU law is transposed to the Swiss context based on Bilateral Agreements and the interpretation of such EU norms is regulated by international treaty norms, there are also cases in which Swiss courts decide to interpret Swiss law in a manner that corresponds to parallel norms of EU law. This concerns acts of Swiss law that are considered to be acts of autonomous implementation of EU norms.[93] In a number of cases, therefore, the Swiss Federal Tribunal has adopted a reading similar to interpretations handed down by the Court of Justice, eg in the fields of the law on product liability or copyrights.[94] Nonetheless, as always, there remains a lot of leeway for Swiss courts in interpretation: eg in competition law, the Federal Tribunal has sometimes aligned

[91] Epiney, Metz, and Pirker (n 74) 168–69.

[92] BGE 136 II 5. This possibility to deviate has not been used to date. On the most recent case law of the Court of Justice on the Agreement on the Free Movement of Persons and its interpretation, see Pirker and Matter, 'Europarecht: Schweiz–Europäische Union (2020)' (n 38) 86–87.

[93] On the difficulty of clearly determining this issue in practice, see Francesco Maiani, 'Lost in Translation: Euro-Compatibility, Legal Security, and the Autonomous Implementation of EU law in Switzerland' (2013) European Law Reporter 29, 32.

[94] eg BGE 129 III 335; BGE 136 III 335.

its interpretation with EU competition law,[95] and sometimes taken the opposite approach.[96]

At the legislative level, the Federal Council reacted to the EU's plans to complete the single market of the 1980s by systematically scrutinizing new legislative and administrative acts as to their 'eurocompatibility'.[97] The goal was to ensure, as much as possible, the compatibility between EU norms and Swiss norms, without, however, going so far as to align Swiss laws automatically, as this would have been perceived as too damaging for Swiss sovereignty. This policy has been continued even after the Swiss 'no' to the EEA in 1992, with the goals of avoiding, as much as possible, economic disadvantages and—at least initially—of keeping an open door for all future integration options (such as an EU or EEA accession).[98] A first package of legislation was adopted in 1993; this so-called Eurolex package on, eg consumer protection law and competition law was initially largely planned to be brought into force as part of the accession to the EEA.[99] Ever since, many new acts or revisions of existing legislation have taken into account EU legal developments,[100] focusing not merely on typical cross-border issues, but on all possible areas of legislation, such as data protection.[101] During the legislative process, the Federal Council always prepares an accompanying report for the new (or to be amended) legal act. As required by law,[102] the government must dedicate one chapter of this report, typically done in a 'Europe chapter', to the relationship between the act and European law.

In the case of ordinances enacted by the Federal Council, the Council can even be obliged to take into account EU law when the underlying legislation has been intentionally aligned to EU law and explicitly states so.[103]

In certain cases, there is high economic pressure on Switzerland to align its laws with EU law, namely where the EU grants market access to third countries based on decisions on the equivalency of those countries' legislation to that of the EU.[104] Switzerland is waiting, for example, for the EU's evaluation of the existing

[95] eg BGE 143 II 297.

[96] eg BGE 137 II 119.

[97] Bericht des Bundesrates über die Stellung der Schweiz im europäischen Integrationsprozess vom 24. August 1988, BBl 1988 III 249, 380.

[98] Botschaft über das Folgeprogramm nach der Ablehnung des EWR-Abkommens vom 24. Februar 1993, BBl 1993 I 805, 810.

[99] For further details, see Oesch, *Switzerland and the European Union* (n 59) 141.

[100] There are estimates that between 30 and 50 per cent of all federal acts and ordinances are influenced by EU law more or less directly (Matthias Oesch, 'Die Europäisierung des schweizerischen Rechts' (2012) 50 Zeitschrift für Schweizerisches Recht 13), although it has also been pointed out that the alignment to EU law through autonomous adaptation seems to have been decreasing with regard to legislative precision since the 2000s (Sabine Jenni, 'Europeanization of Swiss Law-Making: Empirics and Rhetoric are Drifting Apart' (2014) 20 Swiss Political Science Review 208).

[101] See Oesch, *Switzerland and the European Union* (n 59) 141–42, with further examples.

[102] Art 141(2)a of the Federal Act on the Federal Assembly (SR 171.10).

[103] eg Art 4(2) of the Federal Act on Technical Barriers to Trade (SR 946.51).

[104] See, generally, Christa Tobler and Jacques Beglinger, 'Gleichwertigkeit, Angemessenheit, Äquivalenz, Adäquanz: Ein Hotspot in den Beziehungen zwischen der Schweiz und der EU im

decision on the equivalency of Switzerland's data protection standards, in light of the country's newly revised law on data protection, which enters into force in September 2023.[105] However, in 2019, the EU decided not to grant equivalency regarding the regulation of stock exchanges, as a means to pressure Switzerland to finally sign the draft institutional framework agreement, leading to vivid political reactions in Switzerland.[106]

A new variant of autonomous adaptation was created in 2010, in the form of the unilateral introduction of the *Cassis de Dijon* principle. Through an amendment of the Federal Act on Technical Barriers to Trade,[107] all products which are lawfully placed on the market in the EEA—ie in areas harmonized by EU/EEA law or regulated by EU/EEA Member States in non-harmonized areas—could be lawfully marketed in Switzerland without having to meet all Swiss regulatory standards. Notably, this form of autonomous adaptation works prospectively—ie for new products—without the need to adapt Swiss laws. As a crucial limitation, however, this unilateral approach cannot provide facilitated market access for Swiss products on the markets of EU/EEA Member States. Moreover, numerous exceptions to the basic principle have been introduced because of various Swiss interests at the internal level.[108]

The advantage of these *de facto* norm-diffusion instruments on the receiving state's side (in this case, Switzerland's) is clear. Instead of the binding, sovereignty-limiting commitments undertaken in the *de jure* norm-diffusion context, at least formally, a state like Switzerland is acting on its own initiative, which can also be used as an argument in the internal public debate on a perceived loss of sovereignty.[109]

C. EU's legal and political conditions requiring *de jure* norm transfer

Having looked at *de jure* and *de facto* norm diffusion in the EU–Swiss context, the reasons for the choice of one over the other by each actor—the EU and Switzerland—needs to be explored.

rechtlichen Kontext' in Astrid Epiney and Petru Zlătescu (eds), *Schweizerisches Jahrbuch für Europarecht* (Schulthess 2020).

105 Pirker and Matter, 'Europarecht: Schweiz–Europäische Union (2021)' (n 55) 130.

106 On the Swiss decision to make the cohesion payment that the EU expects in return for the market access granted under the Bilateral Agreements conditional upon the elimination of such discriminatory measures, see Pirker and Matter, 'Europarecht: Schweiz–Europäische Union (2020)' (n 38) 82.

107 SR 946.51.

108 Some commentators speak of *Cassis de Berne* rather than *Cassis de Dijon*: Thomas Cottier and David Herren, 'Das Äquivalenzprinzip im schweizerischen Aussenwirtschaftsrecht: von *Cassis de Dijon* zu *Cassis de Berne*' in Astrid Epiney and Nina Gammenthaler (eds), *Schweizerisches Jahrbuch für Europarecht 2009/2010* (Schulthess 2010) 275.

109 Section III.D.

The failed draft institutional framework agreement reflects clearly that the EU wanted to bring the bilateral relations in line with certain political, legal, and judicial conditions, namely the integrity of the internal market and the EU court's autonomy in EU law interpretation.

1. Integrity of the internal market and creating a level playing field

These two aspects—the integrity of the internal market and creating a level playing field—are often seen as two sides of the same coin.[110] The former is more an EU inward-looking requirement, often merged with the integrity of the EU legal order and its autonomy. This requirement has, especially in light of Brexit, been carved out as preserving the integrity and proper functioning of the single market. First and foremost a political condition, it implies that 'membership' in the internal market and other EU policies comes with rights and obligations. Third countries do not get equal rights in EU institutions, and have no free choice as to which EU integration policies they join in.[111] Undeniably, the EU has already compromised on this integrity, with EU–Swiss relations being based on an outdated FTA concerning goods and free movement rights for individuals excluding legal persons. So how far can the functioning of this internal market be endangered and the level playing field undermined by the Swiss piecemeal integration?

The factors undermining the integrity can be , for instance, be detected in the post-accession situation since 2004 resulting in an intricate legal regime and differences between EU15/EEA citizens (Austria, Belgium, Denmark, Finland, France, Germany, UK, Greece, Ireland, Italy, Luxembourg, the Netherlands, Portugal, Spain, Sweden, Iceland, Liechtenstein, and Norway); Cyprus and Malta; the EU8 (Czech Republic, Estonia, Hungary, Latvia, Lithuania, Poland, Slovakia, and Slovenia); the EU2 (Bulgaria and Romania); and Croatia. Firstly, Switzerland only aimed for a gradual market access for EU nationals, in accordance with Article 10 of the Bilateral Agreement on Persons, ratified on 1 June 2004. In addition, Switzerland has the option to apply unilateral safeguard measures to once again restrict market access. In three successive protocols (Protocol I , Protocol II, and Protocol III), the accession of the incoming Member States was agreed between the EU and Switzerland, and Article 10 paragraphs 1(a), 1(b) and 1(c) were introduced. When, for instance, Protocol I was introduced, to amend the Bilateral Agreement on Persons, it first needed to be approved by a Swiss referendum, and then it enabled Switzerland to differentiate between the EU15 citizens and the rest of the EU citizens by keeping restrictions for the new EU members (excluding Cyprus and Malta) in place for longer.[112] Hence, EU citizens from the CEEC only

[110] Basic Facts of the Framework of EU–Switzerland relations, EEAS, str_ifa_eu-switzerlandrelations_factsheet_2_1.pdf (europa.eu).

[111] Ott, 'The Building Blocks and Stumbling Stones' (n 44) 221.

[112] Council Decision of 27 February 2006 on the conclusion, on behalf of the European Community and its Member States, of a Protocol to the Agreement between the European Community and its

benefitted from free movement rights four years later than EU citizens from other EU Member States.[113] In addition, restrictions against Romanian and Bulgarian citizens were still in place when Switzerland invoked a general safeguard clause in 2013 under Article 10(4) of the Bilateral Agreement against all EU Member States.[114]

With the 2014 Swiss referendum on free movement rights, the existing Bilateral Agreement on Persons came under more pressure, leading to an unsuccessful Swiss request to revise this Agreement.[115] These developments resulted in different treatment of EU citizens by Switzerland, and in a better treatment of EEA and Swiss nationals in the internal market, compared with EU citizens from the incoming EU Member States. However, this external differentiation could not have been legally challenged despite how problematic it might look. This reverse discrimination against EU citizens, treating EEA and Swiss nationals better than EU8 or EU2 citizens, materializes only on the territory of a non-EU Member State– Switzerland. In addition, this differentiation between EU citizens is already inherent in the EU Accession Treaty: a form of constitutionally mandated differentiation, because the accession treaty and its protocols form part of primary law adapting existing EU law[116] by imposing transitional measures against incoming EU citizens under the 2+3+2 years rule for the existing EU Member States. Nevertheless, it remains politically questionable that the free movement of persons, as a fundamental pillar of the EU internal market,[117] is undermined from the outside, resulting in a complex and intransparent differentiated regime of treatment of persons.[118]

Member States, of the one part, and the Swiss Confederation, of the other, on the free movement of persons, regarding the participation, as contracting parties, of the Czech Republic, the Republic of Estonia, the Republic of Cyprus, the Republic of Latvia, the Republic of Lithuania, the Republic of Hungary, the Republic of Malta, the Republic of Poland, the Republic of Slovenia and the Slovak Republic, pursuant to their accession to the European Union Protocol I to the bilateral agreement, OJ 2006 L89/28-44. In 2007, extension to Bulgaria and Romania was approved, and extension to Croatia was approved in 2016; Oesch, *Switzerland and the European Union* (n 59) para 46.

[113] Croatia will still fall under restrictions until 2023, and the safeguard clause can be involved by Switzerland until 2026, see Oesch, *Schweiz* (n 23) para 154.

[114] Andrea Ott, 'Differentiation through Accession Law: Free Movement Rights in an Enlarged European Union' in Bruno de Witte, Andrea Ott, and Ellen Vos (eds), *Between Flexibility and Disintegration* (Edward Elgar 2017) 146, 171–72; Oesch, *Switzerland and the European Union* (n 59) paras 137–40.

[115] Exchange of letters between Switzerland and the High Representative Ashton, Bundesrat will mit der EU über Personenfreizügigkeit verhandeln, 8 October 2014 https://www.admin.ch/gov/de/start/dokumentation/medienmitteilungen.msg-id-54761.html accessed 1 July 2023.

[116] See also, and further, the chapter by Adam Łazowski in this volume.

[117] Council of the European Union, 'Council Conclusions on a Homogeneous Extended Single Market and EU Relations with Non-EU western European Countries', Brussels, 16 December 2014, para 45; 'Council Conclusions on EU Relations with the Swiss Confederation', 28 February 2017, para 3.

[118] In the 'Council Conclusions on EU Relations with EFTA Countries', 20 December 2012, however, the Council perceived this regime as a breach of the Agreement on persons: 'In particular, the Council deeply regrets that Switzerland has unilaterally re-introduced quotas for certain categories of residence permits for citizens of 8 EU Member States.' 2012_final_conclusions_en.pdf (europa.eu).

The Commission underlined, in 2012, that the 'backbone of the EU's Internal market [is] common rules and standards and a thorough policy on enforcement and governance'.[119] This effective management of the extension of the internal market is better managed by a dynamic adaptation of EU law. The lack of dynamic update and the conditionality applied for more, or even continued, market access, based on signing the draft institutional framework agreement, became immediately visible in relation to Swiss medical devices. The mutual recognition agreement (MRA) between the EU and Switzerland enables frictionless trade in goods, but no longer applies to medical devices since the conclusion of the institutional framework agreement failed. The EU Medical Devices Regulation replaced the previous directive on 26 May 2021. The equivalence of Swiss products belonging to an important Swiss industry export factor is no longer recognized, and the MRA, including the chapter on medical devices, will not be updated, such that this situation will likely endure over time.[120]

The EU's credo is that both sides should benefit from the extension of the EU's internal market *acquis*, as this would ensure a level playing field for businesses and persons.[121] The EU extended free movement in the EU for Swiss citizens but was met with a complex regime of differentiating standards in Switzerland. This differentiated regime is further highlighted by the Swiss flanking measures that EU posted workers face in Switzerland. Immediately in 2006 and after the entry into force of the FMOPA, Switzerland introduced flanking measures for EU posted workers. This is justified by reference to the FMOPA which does not preclude the applicability of laws, regulations, and administrative provisions providing for the application of working and employment conditions to employed persons posted for the purposes of providing a service. However, Switzerland not only protects its higher labour standards for posted workers, to comply with minimum wage and working conditions, but also requires that EU posted workers notify their presence in Switzerland eight days before they provide their services.[122] Both sides have remained at odds over this rule. The EU argues that Switzerland applies stricter rules, not covered by the EU *acquis* (Directive 96/71 concerning the posting of

[119] Communication from the Commission, Relations with the Principality of Andorra, the Principality of Monaco and the Republic of San Marino Options for Closer Integration with the EU, COM/2012/0680 final.

[120] European Commission, DG for Health and Food Services, 'Notice for stakeholder: status of the EU–Switzerland mutual recognition agreement (MRA) for medical devices', 26 May 2021. For the reaction of the Swiss side to mitigate the effects, see Swiss Federal Council, 'No Signing of the Swiss–EU Institutional Agreement' (n 39); Christa Tobler, 'The EU–Swiss Sectorial Approach under Pressure: Not Least Because of Brexit' in Stefan Lorenzmeier, Roman Petrov, and Christoph Vedder (eds), *EU External Relations Law* (Springer Publishing 2021) 107–26, 116.

[121] Council of the European Union, 'Council Conclusions on EU Relations with EFTA Countries', Council meeting, Brussels, 14 December 2019, para 7.

[122] Oesch (n 23), paras 192–96. See also Council of the European Union, 'Council Conclusions on Relations with the EFTA Countries', 20 December 2012, para 35.

workers), to EU economic operators providing services in its territory, and therefore breaches the principles of proportionality and non-discrimination.[123]

Finally, the financial contribution by Switzerland to the accession of new Member States, to reduce economic and social disparities, is seen by the EU as a justified instrument to balance the profits Switzerland gains from access to the internal market, and secure a level playing field for all EU economic actors.[124]

2. Autonomy of EU courts and their interpretive authority

While the conditions described in Section C.1 above can be categorized as political, and lead only at their fringes to legal questions, the autonomy of the EU Courts and their authority of interpretation form a core legal criterion under which third-country integration stands or falls, since the ECJ EEAOpinions 1/91 and 1/92.[125] In these and subsequent opinions addressing the compatibility of envisaged international agreements with EU law, the ECJ has carved out that international agreements can only extend EU rules to third countries when: (1) the ECJ has the interpretation monopoly over EU law and its progeny international rules; and (2) EU law disputes cannot be withdrawn from the jurisdiction of the Member States' courts and the ECJ to an independent arbitration system.[126] This jurisdiction has been interpreted in two directions: one is where the EU participates in international arbitration involving investor-to-state dispute settlement outside the European legal space. The second scenario concerns the extension of EU rules and policies, accompanied by dispute settlement rules, to ensure the effective application of these rules by the state actors. For this latter form of cooperation, relevant for EU–Swiss relations, the Court has carved out very strict rules, and has only approved two dispute settlement systems so far. The first of these is the one in place within the Common Aviation Area, where the ECJ gives the final verdict on the application and interpretation of the Agreement, and the second is the two-pillar system of the EEA, with the EFTA court ruling for the members of the EEA. A third option on which the European court has not yet ruled is found in the Association Agreement with Ukraine (Article 322), and inspired the former draft institutional framework agreement arbitration rules. According to these rules, first

[123] Council of the European Union, 'Council Conclusions on EU Relations with the Swiss Confederation', 26 February 2017, para 6; 'Council Conclusions on EU Relations with the Swiss Confederation' 19 February 2019, para 13.

[124] Council Conclusions, para 7. As mentioned above (n 61 and accompanying text), Switzerland officially does not see itself bound under international law to contribute, and has also withheld cohesion funds to put pressure on the EU.

[125] Opinion 1/91, [1991]ECLI:EU:C:1991:490; Opinion 1/92 EEA, [1992] ECLI:EU:C:1992:189; Opinion 1/00 (ECAA), [2002] ECLI:EU:C:2002:231; Opinion 1/76 *European Laying-up Fund* [1977] ECLI:EU:C:1977:63, where the focus rested on EU competences and the functioning of common policies.

[126] Ott, 'The Building Blocks and Stumbling Stones' (n 44) 222–25.

an appointed arbitration panel would have ruled, and only if the dispute before it concerned EU-related terms would it have to be referred to the ECJ. As this form of arbitration sails below the judicial radar, it is not clear whether it meets the conditions fleshed out by the ECJ autonomy rulings. However, it might also hold little practical relevance, and has to be seen more as a last resort conditionality tool to bring the third country in line with EU law and its interpretation, and prevent the cherry-picking and bickering about the unpopular part of integration, namely, the Bilateral Agreement on the Movement of Persons.

D. Swiss internal factors determining the preference for *de facto* norm diffusion

There is an overall, and seemingly increasing, preference on the Swiss side for limited, tailored *de jure* norm diffusion and more extensive *de facto* norm diffusion, providing more leeway for the norm-receiving third state. The present section explores the internal factors that help explain this Swiss preference.[127]

As one important factor, Swiss observers often perceive approximation as a danger to the domestic political system. They note, in this context, that the Swiss constitution already appears to be rather introverted, and does not regulate explicitly what goals Switzerland should pursue in its foreign policy with regard to the EU.[128]

Additionally, as in many other democracies, in Switzerland certain difficulties arise in reconciling democracy, full national self-determination, and economic globalization.[129] One core difficulty emerges repeatedly: the direct democratic tools foreseen by the Swiss constitution clash with obligations undertaken as part of the relations with the EU (or with international obligations more generally).[130] Citizens may have a say, eg on international treaties in the form of a referendum or on changes to domestic constitutional law through a popular initiative. In practice, however, the costs of a particular constitutional change that violates Swiss

[127] We focus here on standard accounts and leave aside less 'mainstream' views, eg on the threat EU approximation poses to the supposedly unique democratic system of Switzerland (see Oliver Zimmer, *Wer hat Angst vor Tell? Unzeitgemässes zur Demokratie* (Echtzeit-Verlag 2020)), or on an alleged undemocratic conspiracy at the level of the Swiss federal administration to force Switzerland to join the EU (see Carl Baudenbacher, *Das Schweizer EU-Komplott* (Münsterverlag 2019)).

[128] In favour of a new clause in the federal constitution in this regard, see Matthias Oesch, 'Verfassungswandel durch Globalisierung und Europäisierung' in Oliver Diggelmann, Maya Hertig Randall, and Benjamin Schindler (eds), *Verfassungsrecht der Schweiz—Band I Grundlagen* (Schulthess 2020) 177–81.

[129] Dani Rodrik, *The Globalization Paradox: Democracy and the Future of the World Economy* (WW Norton & Company 2011) 184 ff.

[130] See generally on that problem, Johannes Reich, 'Direkte Demokratie und völkerrechtliche Verpflichtungen im Konflikt' (2008) 68 ZaöRV 979.

obligations towards the EU, the non-adoption of new EU law in the context of the Schengen association, or the rejection of a revision of the Agreement on the Free Movement of Persons (eg in the context of EU enlargement) can be prohibitively high; as a consequence, there may remain only one possible (reasonable) answer for Swiss voters.[131] This factual limitation on the effectiveness of direct democratic prerogatives at the national level, combined with the lack of true participation mechanisms at the level of EU law, has been described as a somewhat inevitable process of 'erosion' of democratic rights in the current situation of partial, selective integration chosen by Switzerland under the Bilateral Path.[132]

Moreover, core to the Swiss perspective on the relationship with the EU is the idea—sometimes qualified as an illusion—that the relationship is one of equals, like two countries meeting on an equal footing, and not a complex relationship with a regional integration organization composed of 27 Member States. The Swiss perspective sometimes finds it difficult to accept that a joint project of this size inevitably exerts a certain gravitational pull, and that the imposition of EU rules—ie *de jure* norm diffusion—is to some extent an inevitable part of the deal for Switzerland to be allowed to participate in the project, even if it comes at the cost of a considerable restriction of the country's sovereignty. Observers often note historical factors for this peculiar perspective, namely that the country was spared major devastations during the World War II, resulting in the conviction that autonomy has a strong significance even if it means paying the price for not participating in larger projects.[133]

Generally, there are strong economic reasons for Switzerland to pursue a strategy of approximation with the EU. These factors render *de jure* norm diffusion economically profitable and *de facto* norm diffusion somewhat inevitable. Whereas it appears difficult to put numbers on the effect of *de facto* norm-diffusion efforts in the context of autonomous adaptation, studies have calculated the impact of the Bilateral Agreements or the effects of a fictitious termination of these agreements on future exchanges. For example, one study estimates the yearly added value of the Bilateral Agreements I at about 24 billion Swiss francs from 2018 to 2035.[134] A slightly older study projected that, by 2035, the Swiss gross domestic product (GDP) would be 7.1 per cent lower without these agreements.[135]

Finally, it should also be noted that sceptical views on immigration play a relevant role in Swiss–EU relations, leading perhaps to a certain hesitance towards

[131] On the *de facto* prohibition on terminating the Agreement on the Free Movement of Persons, see Andreas Glaser, 'Wandel der Volksrechte' in Diggelmann, Randall, and Schindler (eds) (n 129) 479.

[132] Matthias Oesch, 'Switzerland–EU Bilateral Agreements' (n 2) 602.

[133] Roland Bieber, 'La Suisse en Europe—une désintégration équilibrée?' in Jörn Axel Kàmmerer, Markus Kotzur, and Jacques Ziller (eds), *Integration und Desintegration in Europa* (Nomos 2019) 194.

[134] Economiesuisse, 'Der Wert des institutionellen Abkommens', Dossierpolitik 04/2019, 5ff.

[135] BAK Basel Economics, 'Die mittel- und langfristigen Auswirkungen der Bilateralen I auf die schweizerische Volkswirtschaft' (2015) 21.

de jure norm-diffusion solutions. There is a history of popular initiatives and referenda on migration topics. For example, the approval of the popular initiative 'against mass immigration' in 2014 caused severe problems in the relationship between Switzerland and the EU (see at III.B.1). At the same time, other initiatives have been rejected, and referenda results favourable to the free movement of persons have been achieved.[136] The picture is thus rather mixed. Nonetheless, as noted above, migration-related concerns in Switzerland were one of the factors sealing the fate of the doomed draft institutional framework agreement deal.[137]

Summing up, numerous factors make norm diffusion an advantageous process for Switzerland, but at the same time favour a *de facto* norm-diffusion approach, even if one may doubt to what extent the formal sovereignty dividend granted by such an approach can withstand power relations and politics, as well as economic realities.

IV. What Future for EU–Swiss Relations?

Both sides have to decide together how to develop their future relations. The final death blow to the draft institutional framework agreement, in May 2021, has emphasized the clash between norm-diffusion concepts and perceptions, as already outlined. It also demonstrates that both sides revert to the policy of pinpricks without severing their ties. The Swiss Federal Council highlighted the shared interests and values of human rights, climate protection, and migration issues, and suggested continuing with the bilateral approach in light of the mutual importance of trade, services, and movement of persons, immediately after the failure.[138] In reaction to the Swiss decision to terminate the seven-year-long negotiation process, the EU Commission was more tight-lipped, emphasizing that a modernization of the Bilateral Agreements would not be possible.[139]

Between March 2022 to March 2024, both sides have moved from exploratory talks to concrete negotiating mandates again.[140] The Commission compromised

[136] Oesch, Switzerland and the European Union (n 59) 162–65..

[137] In particular, the unclear relevance of the Citizenship Directive, which it is feared could bring, among other things, broadened access to social benefits to EU citizens in Switzerland: see n 40 above and accompanying text.

[138] Swiss Federal Council, 'No Signing of the Swiss–EU Institutional Agreement' (n 39): 'Switzerland is also one of the most important trading partners for the EU, ranking 4th for exports of goods, 3rd for services and 2nd for investment. Moreover, the EU has a trade surplus with Switzerland in the order of tens of billions. 1.4 million EU citizens live in Switzerland. In addition, about 340,000 people commute to Switzerland from the EU, and well over 200,000 persons from the EU/EFTA area are subject to registration each year.' Letter from the Federal Council to the President of the European Commission (26 May 2021) (unofficial translation; original text in French prevails) https://www.eda.admin.ch/dam/europa/en/documents/abkommen/20210526-brief-BR-vdL-InstA_EN.pdf accessed 1 July 2023.

[139] Commission Statement (n 43).

[140] Speech by Commission Vice-President Maros Sefcovic on EU–Switzerland relations at the University of Fribourg, 15 March 2023.

by entering the talks based on a Swiss 'package approach' to secure Switzerland's access to the internal market, covering core agreements (the free movement of persons, land and air transport, agriculture, and technical trade barriers), but also open possible negotiations on energy, food safety, and health. However, comparing the negotiating mandates with each other, discrepancies in interests and the well-known red lines of both sides are clearly outlined. When, for instance comparing the wording on the ECJ's role in the dispute settlement, this could be only nuances of formulation or the different languages as outlined above.

Consequently, future negotiations are faced with similar obstacles as the previous discussions. The EU will insist on these familiar red lines, such as the EU's autonomy, represented by the ECJ's role in applying and interpreting EU law, and the integrity of the internal market. The Swiss side, in contrast, speaks of the deepening of ties and pragmatic solutions.[141] Switzerland also stresses the mitigating effect of an autonomous review of Swiss legislation with the 'potential for autonomous amendments to Swiss legislation to stabilize Swiss–EU relations'.[142] These statements again emphasize the Swiss preference for *de facto* norm diffusion over *de jure* norm transfer, which the EU expects and envisions, in contrast, for deepening and updating the relations between the two parties. It will be necessary for both parties to understand each other's perceptions.

In practice, conflicts on the application of Bilateral Agreements were limited, but when they arose they became highly political and could not be resolved easily, as the free movement provisions and the flanking measures demonstrate. The EU claims to have demonstrated flexibility but decisively perceives the Swiss situation as à la carte integration, which countervails the general conditions established for market integration of third European states. More energy may need to be invested in explaining the EU's position and reasons for the strong focus on *de jure* norm diffusion rather than doubling down on it (which one could argue happened on the EU side by relying on creative ambiguity in the Agreement, and expecting that the ECJ would 'resolve' the issue in the EU's favour at a later point in time, as unpopular as such a judicial approach may be perceived in the partner state). On the Swiss side, it needs to be understood that certain elements of rigidity in the EU's *de*

[141] eg the aforementioned Letter from the Federal Council to the President of the European Commission (n 139). Negotiating mandate of the EU Commission,

Directives for the negotiation of institutional provisions in agreements between the European Union and the Swiss Confederation related to the internal market, on an agreement on the Swiss Confederation's participation in Union programmes and on an agreement that forms the basis for the Swiss Confederation's permanent contribution to the Union's cohesion, Brussels 7 March 2024, Doc 7031/24, Swiss mandate, Bundesrat, Definitives Verhandlungsmandat

(gemäss Bundesratsbeschluss vom 8. März 2024), Beziehungen Schweiz–EU: Der Bundesrat verabschiedet das endgültige Verhandlungsmandat (admin.ch).

[142] Swiss Federal Council, 'No Signing of the Swiss–EU Institutional Agreement' (n 39).

jure norm-diffusion process are as unnegotiable as core features of the Swiss constitutional system. Switzerland will, thus, have to deal with features such as the autonomy of EU law, just as the EU has to deal with the elements of direct democracy of the Swiss constitutional order. An exclusive focus on *de facto* norm diffusion will not help. *De facto* norm diffusion has its limits, and its effectiveness will often depend on the other side, eg in cases of equivalency decisions. Close, frictionless cooperation with the EU will only be possible at the price of a certain restriction of Switzerland's sovereignty.

If these lessons are learned, the next step can hopefully be what is normally the next step in this special relationship: the successful negotiation of yet another agreement, and the updating of the existing agreements. For the larger debate about whether there is a need, for example, for associate next to full EU membership, EU–Swiss relations also provide lessons, namely that an à la carte approach may present certain advantages and pitfalls, including *de facto* norm diffusion and selective *de jure* norm diffusion.

12

External Differentiated Integration: The Modalities of Turkey's Opting into the European Union

*Meltem Müftüler-Baç**

I. Introduction

In recent years, the process of European integration has faced turbulent times with uncertainty looming over the United Kingdom's exit,[1] the Western Balkan states' shaky accession process, and the European Neighborhood Policy,[2] with mixed results for countries in the Eastern Partnership and the South Mediterranean.[3] This uncertainty has been further compounded by the Russian invasion of Ukraine in February 2022, leading the European Union (EU) to reassess the status of the Eastern Partnership countries. Turkey represents another third-country associated non-member of the EU, with whom different shades of integration exist. Concepts such as 'variable geometry',[4] 'multi-speed Europe',[5] 'unity in diversity'[6], or 'flexible integration'[7] are utilized to label internal differentiation[8] among the EU members. [9] On the other hand, external differentiated integration[10] is an emerging

* Earlier versions of this chapter were presented at the EUSA conference in May 2019, and the CERIM conference organized at the University of Maastricht in June 2019. The author also gratefully acknowledges research support from the European Commission's H2020 project, InDivEU, grant number 822304.

[1] Stefan Ganzle, Benjamin Leruth, and Jarle Trondal, *Differentiated (Dis)integration in Light of Brexit: What Future for European Integration?* (Routledge 2020).

[2] Meltem Müftüler-Baç, 'European Neighborhood Policy' in Finn Laursen (ed), *Oxford Encyclopedia on European Politics* (OUP 2019).

[3] On these issues, see the chapters by Milenković, Bosse, Delcour, and Wright, in this volume.

[4] Alexander Stubb, 'A Categorization of Differentiated Integration' (1996) 34(2) Journal of Common Market Studies 283–95.

[5] Katharina Holzinger and Frank Schimmelfennig, 'Differentiated Integration in the European Union: Many Concepts, Sparse Theory, Few Data' (2012) 19(2) Journal of European Public Policy 292–305.

[6] Kenneth Dyson and Angelos Sepos, *Which Europe? The Politics of Differentiated Integration* (Palgrave 2010).

[7] Alex Warleigh, *Flexible Integration: What Model for the European Union?* (Continuum 2002)

[8] Christopher Lord, 'Utopia or Dystopia? Towards a Normative Analysis of Differentiated Integration' (2015) 22(6) Journal of European Public Policy 783–98.

[9] Dirk Leuffen, Frank Schimmelfennig, and Berthold Rittberger, *Differentiated Integration: Explaining Variation in the European Union* (Palgrave 2013).

[10] Sandra Lavenex, 'Concentric Circles of Flexible "European" Integration: A Typology of EU External Governance Relations' (2011) 9(4) Comparative European Politics 372–93.

Meltem Müftüler-Baç, *External Differentiated Integration* In: *Redefining EU Membership.* Edited by: Diane Fromage, Oxford University Press. © Meltem Müftüler-Baç 2024. DOI: 10.1093/9780191948145.003.0012

area of scientific inquiry for the European non-members. External differentiation involves non-EU members' agreements[11] with the EU to participate in EU policies,[12] and their incorporation into the EU's *acquis communautaire.* EU Member States opting out of European policies, and non-members' opting in to these policies,[13] form the basis for assessing different aspects of differentiated integration.[14]

Officially a candidate for EU membership since 1999, and negotiating for accession since 2005, Turkey's relations with the EU have been at a rocky stage since 2016. The European Council's declaration on 26 June 2018, stating that 'Turkey has been moving further away from the European Union and that accession negotiations have therefore effectively come to a standstill',[15] attests to the current standstill. Since then, in December 2021, June 2022, June 2023, and October 2023, the European Council has repeatedly reaffirmed this position. This is also why the European Council's statement of 28 June 2018 that 'Turkey remains a candidate country and a key partner in many areas' [16] is the main framework for Turkey–EU relations, instead of a formal accession perspective. There is an increasing emphasis in all EU official documents with regard to Turkey as a key partner, signalling a change in the EU's assessment of Turkey's status in its enlargement policy without a formal declaration. At the same time, internal and external challenges to Turkey's relations with the EU have been compounded. Since 2016, domestically, Turkey has gone through an unprecedented political transformation,[17] with an attempted military takeover in July 2016, a constitutional referendum in April 2017, and the shift from a parliamentary system to a presidential system in June 2018. A consolidation of the presidential system is under way, with increased concentration of power at the executive level, as seen in the elections held in May 2023. Externally, the EU has confronted its own challenges, with Brexit,[18] rising populism, democratic backsliding, the migration crisis, and Euroscepticism in multiple EU Member States, as well as the unexpected consequences of a global health crisis in 2020. The Russian invasion of Ukraine in 2022 and the attacks against Israel in October 2023 further complicated the EU's external challenges with new security threats and enhanced uncertainty in the European periphery.

[11] John Erik Fossum, 'What is the Norway Model? Mode of Affiliation or Political Compromise?' (2019) 90(2) *The Political Quarterly* 266–73.

[12] Frank Schimmelfennig and Sandra Lavenex, 'EU Rules Beyond EU Borders: Theorizing External Governance in European Politics' (2009) 16(6) Journal of European Public Policy 791–812.

[13] Juha Jokela, 'Multi-speed Europe? Differentiated Integration in the External Relations of the European Union', Finnish Institute of International Affairs Report 38 (2014).

[14] Frank Schimmelfennig and Thomas Winzen, *Ever Looser Union? Differentiated European Integration* (OUP 2020).

[15] https://www.consilium.europa.eu/media/35863/st10555-en18.pdf accessed 1 July 2023.

[16] https://www.consilium.europa.eu/en/press/press-releases/2018/06/29/20180628-euco-conclusions-final/ accessed 1 July 2023.

[17] Meltem Müftüler-Baç, 'Backsliding in Judicial Reforms: Domestic Political Costs as Limits to EU's Political Conditionality in Turkey' (2019) 27(1) Journal of Contemporary European Studies 61–76.

[18] Erik O Eriksen, 'Political Differentiation and the Problem of Dominance: Segmentation and Hegemony' (2018) 57 European Journal of Political Research 989–1008.

The interplay of these internal and external factors led to new question marks over Turkey's relations with the EU, and their restructuring into a functional, more transactional format. This restructuring is, unfortunately, coupled with the loss of the political anchor in the process.

Yet, when EU accession negotiations were opened for Turkey in 2005, the political landscape in Turkey and the EU looked promising provided that both sides stayed on course. Turkey's accession, while difficult, seemed likely.[19] Now, in contrast, there is an effective freeze in Turkey's accession process, wherein no new chapters have been opened since 2016. This brings forth the following questions: if Turkey's accession to the EU soon is unlikely, does this signify the end of Turkey's integration into the EU? Or, alternatively, is it possible to conceptualize Turkey's relations with the EU within a different theoretical framework where formal accession might no longer be the only game in town?

The European Commission's March 2017 *White Paper on the Future of Europe* raised precisely this possibility of alternatives to membership for European countries, specifically if 'one or several coalitions of the willing (countries) emerge to work together in specific policy areas'.[20] The future of the EU as one of differentiated integration for its Member States and the non-EU European countries[21] in the European orbit[22] shapes the modalities of Turkey's relations with the EU. The key puzzle is whether Turkey's compliance with the EU *acquis* irrespective of its accession prospects could be labelled as external differentiated integration.[23] While there are multiple works on Turkey's relations with the EU,[24] relatively little has been written on what kind of modalities would emerge in remoulding Turkey's relations with the EU along differentiated integration lines.[25] In response, this chapter proposes that the reformulation of Turkey's relations with the EU seems to fit into a general pattern of loose, transactional relations with the EU's periphery, but also represents a model case of external differentiation.[26] This chapter

[19] Meltem Müftüler-Baç, 'Turkey's Accession to the European Union: The Impact of the EU's Internal Dynamics' (2008) 9(1) International Studies Perspectives 208–26.

[20] European Commission, 'White Paper on the Future of Europe: Reflections and Scenarios for the EU27 by 2025' COM 2017(2025) final.

[21] Erik Eriksen and John Erik Fossum, *The European Union's Non-Members* (Routledge 2015).

[22] Fossum, 'What is the Norway Model?' (n 11); Frank Schimmelfennig, 'EU Enlargement and Differentiated Integration: Discrimination or Equal Treatment?' 2014 21(5) Journal of European Public Policy 681–98.

[23] Meltem Müftüler-Baç, 'Turkey's Future with the European Union: Alternative Modes of Differentiated Integration' (2017) 18(3) Turkish Studies 416–39).

[24] For further studies, see Cemal Karakaş, 'EU–Turkey: Integration without Full Membership or Membership without Full Integration: A Conceptual Framework for Accession Alternatives' (2013) 51(6) Journal of Common Market Studies 1057–73.

[25] Yonca Ozer, 'External Differentiated Integration between Turkey and the European Union: The Customs Union and its Revision' (2020) 21(3) Turkish Studies 436–61; Beken Saatcioglu, 'The EU's Refugee Crisis and Rising Functionalism in EU–Turkey Relations' (2019) 21(2) Turkish Studies 169–87.

[26] Sieglinde Gstöhl, 'Models of External Differentiation in the EU's Neighbourhood: An Expanding Economic Community?' (2015) 22(6) Journal of European Public Policy 854–70.

demonstrates how Turkish relations with the EU fit into the overall theme of the book, ie differentiated integration, in the light of redefining EU membership, and the loss of the political anchor for democratic changes. The chapter analyzes how this pattern of differentiation can be utilized to assess Turkey's relations with the EU. To do so, the chapter presents the Turkish ties with the EU, through its participation in European agencies and programmes, as well as its CUA. This analysis reveals a robust pattern of integration between Turkey and the EU, with Turkey opting into EU policies and observing a high degree of compliance. The chapter assesses the Turkish alignment to the EU rules in trade, with the CUA; its membership of EU agencies; and its opting in to the EU's multiple programmes. However, given the democratic backsliding and ongoing multiple tensions between Turkey and the EU, it remains to be seen whether the functional cooperation can survive as well. The next section addresses the multiple modes of integration that form the basis for Turkey's opting in to the EU policies.

II. Turkey's Functional Cooperation with the EU: An Illustration of External Differentiation

Turkey, as a third-country associate member, has a high degree of functional cooperation with the EU,[27] which takes multiple forms in terms of economic, political, judicial and internal affairs, energy, and environmental cooperation.[28] These forms of functional cooperation evolved because of Turkey's association with the EU since its 1963 association agreement, signed with the then European Economic Community; because of the 1995 CUA for industrial products; and because of its candidacy since 1999, and the accession negotiations which were opened in 2005, enabling Turkey to adopt EU rules and policies prior to, and without, formal accession. For example, in policy areas such as the EU development policy, Turkey is adhering to, and opting in to, the EU development policy, despite its non-member status.[29] The financial incentives and material benefits of associating further with the EU, as Holzinger and Tosun[30] expect to see for third countries, shapes the Turkish alignment to EU rules. Turkey's involvement with the European agencies, its voluntary participation in EU programmes, and its economic integration—as driven by the 1995 CUA—are critical for this alignment.

[27] European Commission, 'Turkiye Report' SWD (2022) final.

[28] Müftüler-Baç, 'Turkey's Future' (n 23).

[29] Damla Cihangir-Tetik and Meltem Müftüler-Baç, 'Turkey's Compliance with the European Union's Development Policy: A Pattern of External Differentiated Integration?' (2018) 40(7) Journal of European Integration 939–59.

[30] Katharina Holzinger and Jale Tosun, 'Why Differentiated Integration is Such a Common Practice in Europe: A Rational Explanation' (2019) 31(4) Journal of Theoretical Politics 642–59.

A. Turkey and European agencies

Turkey's multiple agreements with the EU constitute the basis of its alignment with the EU rules. At the same time, Turkey's inclusion into some European agencies, as mentioned above, emerges as an important component of its differentiated integration. For Lavenex, such participation in EU agencies is an essential component of external differentiated integration.[31] When the Copenhagen European Council in 1993 foresaw the candidate countries' participation in the EU agencies, it prepared the ground for the Commission's Agenda 2000, adopted in 1997, which recommended the inclusion of candidate countries in these agencies as a stepping stone towards their eventual accession, echoing the temporal dimension of differentiated integration, ie alignment to EU rules on the road to accession. The 1998 European Pre-accession Strategy for Turkey,[32] designed prior to Turkey's candidacy, also determined the modalities on how Turkey might be invited to participate in some EU agencies. As a result, Turkey signed a comprehensive agreement with the European Environment Agency (EEA) on 9 October 2000, to fully participate in the EEA.[33] Similarly, on 26 August 2006, Turkey signed an agreement with the European Centre for Drugs and Drug Addiction, and also become a member of that agency.[34] Both agreements are binding international commitments for Turkey. Turkish participation in these two regulatory agencies—the EEA since 2001 and the European Centre for Drugs and Drug Addiction since 2007—reveals how the EU can include non-members in its external agencies. Turkey is a full member of the EEA, but does not possess voting rights in the management board of the agency. Turkey's involvement in these EU agencies as a third party illustrates the expansion of the EU's governance tools to non-members, and is an important revelation for the EU's external differentiated integration through the Turkish case.

B. Turkish participation in the EU's programmes

A major indicator for Turkey's external differentiated integration in to the EU is provided by its voluntary participation in various EU programmes. Turkey has signed multiple agreements with the EU to participate in EU programmes ranging from research and education to Customs Union issues. For example, the Turkish Accreditation Agency joined the European accreditation agency in 2004, and

[31] Sandra Lavenex, 'The External Face of Differentiated Integration: Third Country Participation in EU Sectoral Bodies' (2015) 22(6) Journal of European Public Policy 836–53.

[32] European Commission, COM (98) 124 final. https://eur-lex.europa.eu/EN/legal-content/summary/turkey-s-pre-accession-strategy.html

[33] [2001] OJ L213/112-119: https://eur-lex.europa.eu/legal-content/EN/TXT/?uri=CELEX:52000PC0873 accessed 1 July 2023.

[34] [2007] OJ L323/24-33.

Turkey signed an agreement in relation to the EU's research programme Horizon 2020 on 4 June 2014, granting Turkey full access to that programme.[35] Turkish association with the Horizon Europe programme from 2021 to 2027 has been cemented with an agreement. Turkey is also a full participant in the EU's Customs 2020 programme and Fiscalis 2020: both of the relevant agreements were signed on 16 July 2014.[36] One should note that Turkish participation in the EU's Customs Union programmes dates to 1996, ie to the operationalization of the Customs Union. In addition, Turkey fully participates in the Erasmus+ programme, Creative Europe, and the Programme for the Competitiveness of Enterprises and SMEs (COSME). To further integrate itself into the EU rules, Turkey signed the agreement for the EU Programme for Employment and Social Innovation, Progress and Social Entrepreneurship (EaSI) with the European Commission in February 2015. Again in 2015, Turkey joined the EU's Civil Protection Mechanism and the European Solidarity Corps. In addition, Turkey has become an observer in the EU Energy Community, and in the European Network of Transmission System Operators for Electricity (ENTSO-E), as the 2006 European Energy Community Treaty for the creation of an internal energy market for its participants is open to EU candidates, as well as the European Neighbourhood Policy (ENP) countries. Turkey must apply the EU's rules in all these programmes, and pays directly into the EU budget. For example, Turkey contributes to the EU budget for research and education programmes at the same level as a Member State. Turkey's participation in the EU programmes is essential for enhancing the competitiveness of its universities and enterprises, and liberalizing its multiple sectors. The EU reaps additional benefits from increased mobility of Turkish researchers and students, along with access to a competitive, vibrant consumer economy. The European Commission affirms the Turkish level of preparedness on these aspects of functional integration, and its ability to meet the EU *acquis*, in its 2022 Turkiye Report.[37]

A concrete illustration of Turkey's alignment with EU rules is provided by its involvement in the Common Aviation Area, operationalized in a comprehensive agreement. This agreement encompasses non-EU members' inclusion in the Common Aviation Area, their adoption of EU legislation with regard to aviation, and the liberalization of civil aviation. In June 2016, the European Council authorized the European Commission to negotiate this agreement with Turkey. Turkey already had a horizontal air transport agreement with the EU, signed in March 2010, which allowed any EU airline with whom Turkey had a bilateral agreement

[35] Turkey contributes significantly to the Horizon 2020 programme financially, and is an active partner. For further information, see https://webgate.ec.europa.eu/dashboard/extensions/CountryProfile/CountryProfile.html?Country=Turkey accessed 1 July 2023.

[36] https://ec.europa.eu/taxation_customs/sites/taxation/files/resources/documents/taxation/tax_cooperation/fiscalis_programme/legal_texts_docs/customs_2020_regulation.pdf accessed 1 July 2023, and https://neighbourhood-enlargement.ec.europa.eu/document/download/01ab8823-249c-42d8-b4a7-3bd1f457ff62_en

[37] European Commission, 'Turkiye Report' (n 27).

to fly to Turkish destinations.[38] However, further progress was impeded by ongoing political disputes. For example, a major impediment to further alignment with EU legislation and Turkish integration to the EU Common Aviation Area is that Turkey needs to open up flights to all EU Member States. However, given Turkey's non-implementation of the Customs Union to the Republic of Cyprus, and its non-recognition of the Greek Cypriot government as the representative of the island of Cyprus as a whole,[39] flights between the Republic of Cyprus and Turkey are not possible. This is a significant political obstacle to the technical alignment required by the adoption of the Common Aviation Area's rules, demonstrating the brakes to external differentiated integration posed by political factors. Nonetheless, Turkey began to participate in the European Union Aviation Safety Agency (EASA) in 2013. While the negotiations for Turkey's inclusion into the Common Aviation Area began in 2016, with a view to concluding a comprehensive air-travel agreement, these negotiations were suspended in July 2019 as part of a sanctions package adopted by the Commission, in response to the ongoing disputes between Turkey and the Republic of Cyprus involving drilling activities in the Mediterranean Sea for natural gas.[40] The working arrangements between the Turkish aviation authority and EASA are affected by the ongoing disputes with Cyprus. As the European Commission clearly underlines in its legal reports, further technical progress in transport policy depends on Turkey lifting its restrictions on Cyprus. This constitutes another illustration of the political obstacles impeding the expansion of the EU *acquis* on to third parties.

In another related area for opting in to EU rules, negotiations are under way for an agreement on the exchange of information and personal data between Turkey and Europol, but with limited progress. These negotiations began in November 2018, based on the 2017 Regulation which allows Europol to conclude cooperation agreements with third parties.[41] The negotiations are tied to an international agreement signed by Turkey and Europol in 2004: The Agreement on Strategic Cooperation. As part of the EU–Turkey Joint Action Plan of 2015 for the refugee crisis,[42] Turkey agreed to have a liaison officer in Europol, and the realization of this cooperation rests on the Liaison Agreement between Turkey and Europol,[43] signed on 21 March 2016 precisely for this purpose.[44] However, the most important

[38] https://ec.europa.eu/commission/presscorner/detail/en/IP_10_369
[39] Müftüler-Baç, 'Turkey's Accession' (n 19).
[40] https://www.consilium.europa.eu/en/press/press-releases/2019/07/15/turkish-drilling-activities-in-the-eastern-mediterranean-council-adopts-conclusions/ accessed 1 July 2023.
[41] Regulation (EU) 2016/794 of the European Parliament and the Council of 11 May 2016. https://eur-lex.europa.eu/legal-content/EN/TXT/?uri=celex%3A32016R0794 accessed 1 July 2023.
[42] https://eur-lex.europa.eu/resource.html?uri=cellar:97f62a52-3255-11e6-b497-01aa75ed71a1.0023.02/DOC_2&format=PDF accessed 1 July 2023.
[43] https://www.eumonitor.eu/9353000/1/j9vvik7m1c3gyxp/vk286md3s9xg
[44] https://www.europol.europa.eu/newsroom/news/turkey-and-europol-sign-liaison-agreement accessed 1 July 2023.

bulwark of Turkey's external differentiated integration with the EU is the CUA, the main instrument for Turkish economic integration.

C. Customs Union Agreement

One of the most important instruments for the expansion of EU rules on to a third country's territory is the CUA for industrial products,[45] signed by Turkey and the EU in 1995. While a Customs Union for industrial products was already foreseen in the Turkish Association Agreement, signed in 1963 with the then European Economic Community, yet it needed to renegotiated on its own and formalized with a separate agreement which was finally realized in 1995. The CUA was designed as an important stepping stone for Turkey's possible membership of the EU in the future, a clear illustration of temporal-based differentiated integration. When it became operational in 1996, the CUA allowed Turkey to expand its volume of trade with EU members, but also necessitated a significant layer of alignment with the EU's technical regulations, the common external tariff, and manufacturing rules. Turkey does not have any voting rights in the EU's single market and is only a rule-taker. The Turkish–EU bilateral trade arrangements are multifaceted, since the 1995 CUA for industrial products was accompanied by an Agreement on Coal and Steel (CSA), which entered into force in 1996, and a preferential trade regime on agriculture and fisheries (AFTR),[46] which became operational in 1998. As a result, a significant degree of economic integration has been possible, with close to 50 per cent of Turkish exports destined to reach the EU consumer market, the Turkish share of the EU's overall external trade being about 5 per cent, and the EU's share of foreign domestic investment in Turkey being close to 60 per cent. These are robust indicators of a high degree of economic integration between Turkey and the EU. The Customs Union enabled Turkey's alignment with the EU's trade-based *acquis*, and expanded trade volume between the EU and Turkey. However, it was not without serious problems of its own that necessitated an update and modernization of its terms.

A Senior Official Working Group, composed of European and Turkish officials, was set up on 28 February 2014 to work on the modalities of an update for the Customs Union. Accordingly, the Senior Official Working Group published a detailed report on 27 April 2015, which emphasized the need for an extension of the Customs Union to agriculture, services, and public procurement, along with institutional amendments for dispute settlement, and an update that protects Turkish

[45] Decision No 1/95 of the EC-Turkey Association Council of 22 December 1995 on implementing the final phase of the Customs Union, https://eur-lex.europa.eu/legal-content/EN/ALL/?uri=CELEX%3A21996D0213%2801%29

[46] Decision no 1/98 of the EC-Turkey Association Council, https://eur-lex.europa.eu/legal-content/EN/ALL/?uri=CELEX%3A21998D0320%2801%29&VonAbsatz=2&VonArtikel=15

industrial products from the asymmetrical application of the free trade agreements the EU signs with third countries. On 2 May 2015, EU Trade Commissioner Cecilia Malmström and the then Turkish Economy Minister Nihat Zeybekçi agreed to update the Customs Union to modernize the current agreement by extending it to cover services, right of establishment, public procurement, and agriculture, to some extent like Ukraine's Deep and Comprehensive Free Trade Agreement. As a result, in December 2016, the European Commission proposed to modernize the Customs Union, and to further extend bilateral trade relations between Turkey and the EU to areas such as services, public procurement, and sustainable development. The European Commission report in 2017 indicated various areas where Turkish–EU bilateral trade relations could be improved.[47] In May 2018, the Customs Union Joint Committee between Turkey and the EU met for the purposes of easing the implementation of the Customs Union, with an eye towards its expansion. In March 2021 there was some progress, with an EU Council decision to ask the Commission to intensify talks with Turkish authorities on the Custom Union. Turkey adopted a Green Action Plan in 2021, in preparation for meeting its obligations under the CUA parallel to the EU's Green Deal. The need for modernization of the CUA is tied to the absence of dispute settlement mechanisms, the asymmetry caused by the EU's free trade agreements,[48] and the diverging rights that other non-EU members, such as Ukraine or Moldova,[49] have negotiated through Deep and Comprehensive Free Trade Agreements that allow greater trade concessions compared with the Turkish Customs Union. For example, one of the key aspects of the Customs Union is the absence of agricultural products from its coverage. Trade between Turkey and the EU on agricultural products and fisheries is covered by multiple decisions: first, by the Decision of the EU–Turkey Association Council No 1/98, which was amended by Council Decision No 2/2006; and, second, by the EU–Turkey Association Council Decision No 1/2007, which introduced new tools for processed agricultural products, which were included in the Customs Union's Decisions No 1/95 and No 1/97 on these arrangements. Council Decision No 1/2007 repealed Decision No 1/97 for further trade-related alignment on agricultural products and fisheries. However, more liberalization on these aspects is needed to further integrate Turkey into the single market, as free trade agreements in countries other than Turkey have included agricultural products and services. Yet, despite this apparent need, the update of the Customs Union is being shaped by political concerns. In 2018, the European Council adopted a freeze on talks for upgrading the Customs Union due to political reasons, and the General Affairs Council concluded, in June 2018, that no

[47] European Commission, COM 2016/830 final, https://ec.europa.eu/smart-regulation/impact/ia_carried_out/docs/ia_2016/swd_2016_0475_en.pdf accessed 1 July 2023.
[48] Holzinger and Tosun (n 30).
[49] Gstöhl (n 26).

work could be conducted for the modernization of the Customs Union,[50] similar to the halt on the accession process in 2017. Despite the renewed intensification of talks between the Commission and Turkey in 2021 on the Customs Union, a mandate from the Council depends on unanimous agreement at the European Council. This is because upgrading the Customs Union is not only an economic process but is highly political. The political ramifications are clearly indicated by the European Parliament in its March 2019 statement, as follows:

> Customs Union would further strengthen the already strong ties between Turkey and the EU and would keep Turkey economically anchored to the EU . . . a door should be left open for the modernisation and upgrade of the 1995 Customs Union between the EU and Turkey . . . believes that the upgrade would provide a valuable opportunity for democratic conditionality, positive leverage and the possibility of a roadmap where the upgrade of the Customs Union would go hand in hand with concrete improvements by Turkey on democratic reforms in the fields of democracy, human rights fundamental freedoms as well as the rule of law and towards a true, open space for civil society and pluralism; believes further that the upgrade of the Customs Union would provide an important opportunity for policy dialogue on socially and environmentally sustainable economic development and climate change, as well as on labour rights in Turkey; calls on the Commission to start preparatory work for the upgrade of the Customs Union as soon as the Turkish Government attests to its readiness for serious reforms; calls on the Commission to include a clause on human rights and fundamental freedoms in the upgraded Customs Union making human rights and fundamental freedoms a key conditionality.[51]

Given the need for the European Parliament's final approval of any change in the Customs Union, the political reservations of the MEPs, along with the views of the European Parliament quoted above, indicate that renegotiating the CUA is not going to be an easy feat. At the same time, this freeze on Customs Union upgrade negotiations is a solid illustration of the political aspects shaping the limits of expanding the EU's rules and regulations beyond the EU's territorial space.[52] Nonetheless, there is a pressing need for the CUA's modernization, and the degree of economic integration between Turkey and the EU is a clear empirical validation of their functional cooperation. Yet, as the uncertainty persisted, other problems began to emerge in the implementation of the already agreed upon decisions of the Customs Union. For example, according to the 2019 Commission Report on

[50] https://www.consilium.europa.eu/media/35866/st10519-en18.pdfaccessed 1 July 2023.
[51] https://www.europarl.europa.eu/doceo/document/TA-8-2019-0200_EN.html?redirect accessed 1 July 2023.
[52] Fossum, 'What is the Norway Model?' (n 11).

Turkey, Turkey's level of alignment with the common commercial tariff deteriorated in 2019, when Turkey applied additional customs duties and further diverged from the EU's Generalized Scheme of Preferences. The Commission has reported this divergence and Turkish non-alignment with the EU rules more frequently in all its Turkiye Reports since 2019. While Turkey aligns itself with the free trade agreements the EU concludes with other third countries—eg with South Korea and Canada[53]—there is a significant problem with regard to the asymmetrical opening of the Turkish market to these third parties without a reciprocal opening of the third-party markets to Turkish products. This is a key problem, like the Norwegian lack of influence[54] on EU policies,[55] and the situation whereby third countries like Turkey and Norway become rule-takers. It is also for this reason that the EU is critical of Turkey for having a free trade agreement with Malaysia which is fully implemented, despite the absence of an FTA between the EU and Malaysia. In other words, Turkey is affected by these free trade agreements concluded with third parties, as they erode its own trade preferences and create trade asymmetries both for Turkey's own trade with the EU and with third countries.

This is because Decision 1/95 requires Turkey to comply and align with the EU's free trade agreements with third countries as well as the preferential trade arrangements and the EU's Generalized Scheme of Preferences. There is no space in this arrangement for Turkey to have a say in these decisions; it is not a decision-maker, or in any context a decision-shaper, but a 'rule-taker'. However, Decision 1/95 requires the European Commission to allow Turkish experts' participation in technical committees, as well as to agree that the 'Parties shall, at the request of either of them, consult each other again within the Customs Union Joint Committee',[56] before a decision is taken. Thus, one possible way forward to institutionalize Turkey's economic integration into the EU would be to grant Turkey an observer status in the Trade Policy Committee, allowing Turkey to at least observe the EU's trade negotiations and policy-making. However, the clear need to expand modalities of external differentiated integration with Turkey rests on building institutional mechanisms for dispute settlement.

D. Dispute settlement and external differentiation

Almost all the means of participation that Turkey currently has in multiple EU programmes and its Customs Union require an effective dispute settlement

[53] https://ec.europa.eu/trade/policy/countries-and-regions/countries/south-korea/ accessed 1 July 2023.

[54] Eriksen, 'Political Differentiation' (n 18).

[55] Eriksen and Fossum (n 21).

[56] EU–Turkey Association Council, 'Decision 1/95 of 22 December 1995 on Implementing the Final Phase of the Customs Union (96/142/EC)' [1996] OJ L035.

mechanism. Unfortunately, the institutional mechanisms in the EU remain limited for dispute settlement with third countries. For example, the updated and deepened Customs Union needs to encompass a strengthened mechanism for the settlement of disputes. Even though the Customs Union Joint Committee is expected to resolve the EU–Turkey disputes promptly without political blockage through courts and mandatory arbitration, one of the main obstacles in furthering Turkey's economic integration is dispute settlement for trade-related matters. The importance of dispute settlement in shaping the future of Turkey's relations with the EU and the Customs Union has become explicitly clear in recent years. In June 2017, the European Commission launched an investigation for anti-dumping of low carbon ferro-chrome products originating in Turkey.[57] Similarly, a 2017 case involved trade in uncoated wood-free paper, when Turkey adopted a licensing requirement for its importation.[58] Both cases rested on the argument that such measures were violations of the CUA. Similarly, on 2 April 2019, the EU launched a case against Turkey over measures affecting pharmaceutical producers.[59] The case is based on the Ministry of Health regulations requiring that only locally produced pharmaceuticals could be reimbursed through State insurance plans. According to European Commissioner Cecilia Malmstrom, 'Turkey is discriminating against EU pharmaceuticals producers by forcing them to move production there. This is a clear violation of WTO [World Trade Organization] rules and puts many EU jobs at risk. We hope that we will be able to resolve both cases during the upcoming WTO consultations.'[60] The WTO decided in the EU's favour, and agreed on an appeal award for the EU in 2022.[61] The case is interesting in its context of asking for governmental regulation changes to Turkish health policy, as the reimbursement rules are seen as non-monetary barriers to free trade. However, this issue could be seen as one of the problems of the CUA, as the Agreement did not incorporate a dispute settlement mechanism, and such disputes are, therefore, presented to the WTO and its judicial panels. Turkey has not yet implemented the WTO decision, and is currently appealing this ruling. Nonetheless, the European Commission is expecting Turkey to comply with the WTO ruling for the removal of localization and prioritization in the pharmaceutical sector.

The need for judicial mechanisms for trade-related disputes under the CUA is further illustrated by a recent case on transportation. One of the most important concerns for Turkey is with regard to transportation quotas, transit visas, and motor vehicle taxes on Turkish transportation, which act as a major obstacle to the

[57] https://trade.ec.europa.eu/tdi/case_history.cfm?id=2253&init=2253 accessed 1 July 2023.

[58] https://eur-lex.europa.eu/legal-content/EN/ALL/?uri=CELEX%3A32018D0322 accessed 1 July 2023.

[59] http://trade.ec.europa.eu/doclib/docs/2019/april/tradoc_157821.pdf accessed 1 July 2023.

[60] http://europa.eu/rapid/press-release_IP-19-1952_en.htm accessed 1 July 2023.

[61] https://ec.europa.eu/commission/presscorner/detail/en/ip_22_4670 accessed 1 July 2023.

free movement of goods from Turkey to EU destinations.[62] For example, Turkish trucks on their way to European markets pass through Bulgaria and Greece via the land route, and pass through multiple inspections, thereby losing significant time and money. This is a key concern, as over 40 per cent of Turkey's trade with the EU depends on land transportation, specifically by truck.[63] Road transport quotas operate as significant barriers to trade, and are among the top concerns for Turkish policymakers in any revision talks. Since these matters are the responsibility of the EU Member States, and Turkey does not have freedom of mobility of people, transportation-related matters remain unresolved, obstructing free movement of industrial goods. The Turkish concerns are relevant for any update of the Customs Union. Yet, there are no judicial mechanisms for Turkey to bring its problems to the attention of the EU. The two main mechanisms of Turkish–EU economic integration are the Association Council, established in 1963, and composed of Turkish ministers, EU Member States' ministers, and EU officials (which meets only twice a year) and the Customs Union Joint Committee, established in 1995, and composed of Turkish and EU officials. However, neither of these mechanisms is sufficient for allowing Turkey to participate in decision-making or to bring its concerns for adjudication, as these bodies do not have dispute settlement powers.

A Turkish–Hungarian dispute over transport-related concerns illustrated the critical importance of judicial mechanisms for economic integration. On 6 April 2017, the European Court of Justice (ECJ) adopted a major ruling on the *Istanbul Logistik Limited v Hungarian Administrative Authorities* case.[64] A Turkish company, Istanbul Logistik, brought a case in a Hungarian court against the Hungarian tax authority for imposing

'the tax in question which constitutes a charge having equivalent effect to a customs duty, the imposition of which, in respect of trade in goods between the EU and Turkey, is prohibited by Decision No 1/95 of the EC–Turkey Association Council on the implementation of the provisions of the EEC–Turkey Association Agreement on the final phase of the Customs Union'.[65]

The Hungarian court asked the ECJ for a judgment on the tax's legality, and an interpretation. In response to this request, Advocate General Henrik Saugmandsgaard Øe contended, with regard to the motor vehicle taxes and transit permits, that 'since the exercise of free movement of goods is linked to the

[62] https://www.utikad.org.tr/images/HizmetRapor/stefaniskanutikad_transportlogisticsandsupplychainservicesinturkey-0678.pdf accessed 1 July 2023.

[63] https://ec.europa.eu/transport/sites/transport/files/icf-eu-turkey-road-freight-liberalisation-final-report.pdf accessed 1 July 2023.

[64] Case C–65/16 *Istanbul Lojistik Ltd v Nemzeti Adó- és Vámhivatal Fellebbviteli Igazgatóság* [2017] ECLI:EU:C:2017:770; Court of Justice of the European Union, 'Press Release No 107/17, Luxembourg, 19 October 2017' https://curia.europa.eu/jcms/upload/docs/application/pdf/2017-10/cp170107en.pdf accessed 1 July 2023.

[65] https://eur-lex.europa.eu/legal-content/EN/TXT/?uri=CELEX%3A62016CJ0065_SUM accessed 1 July 2023.

carriage of these goods',[66] these Hungarian government restrictions 'constitute[d] charges that could be seen as equivalent of a customs duty' and '[were] incompatible with that decision, i.e. Decision no 1/95'.[67] This was accepted by the Court of Justice as its own interpretation, and acted as a final verdict on the Turkish concerns of being subjected to unfair taxes and monetary barriers on transportation of goods.

Despite the suspension of both the accession negotiations and the updating of the Customs Union, Turkey has continued its alignment with the EU rules in multiple areas of the *acquis*, as noted by the European Commission. The main barriers for further progress remain the asymmetry in the Customs Union, and the lack of dispute settlement mechanisms, leading to non-alignment or non-implementation. A clear obstacle also remains with regard to Cyprus, and without a solution to the Cyprus problem, Turkish integration in areas such as aviation, external relations, defence policy, Customs Union, and transport policy have suffered setbacks.

III. Institutional Design: A New Pattern of External Differentiated Integration

Turkey–EU relations have witnessed multiple institutional changes since 2015, with bilateral summits featuring heads of states and governments and high-level policy dialogues to devise new modalities of cooperation. It is noteworthy that Turkey's functional differentiated integration to the EU has continued through the establishment of new institutional, mostly novel, mechanisms: high-level dialogues and bilateral summits.[68] The bilateral summits constitute institutional novelties for the enlargement process, for acceding countries such as Turkey, whereby the EU and Turkey utilize a new institutional framework to adopt intergovernmental decisions, as these summits are held mostly between the EU and the EU's strategic partners.

On 29 November 2015, the first of these summits was held in Brussels, where '[t]he EU and Turkey agreed to re-energize Turkey's accession process to the European Union. High-level dialogue between both parties will be reinforced through more frequent and structured meetings including the organisation of summits twice a year.'[69] The main motivating factor for this summit was the migration

[66] *Istanbul Lojistik* (n 61) paras 40 and 73.

[67] https://eur-lex.europa.eu/legal-content/EN/TXT/?uri=CELEX:62016CJ0065_SUM accessed 1 July 2023.

[68] For further information, see https://www.ab.gov.tr/documents-on-turkey-eu-summits_50287_en.html accessed 1 July 2023.

[69] https://www.consilium.europa.eu/en/meetings/international-summit/2015/11/29/ accessed 1 July 2023.

crisis facing the EU. As if signalling the increasingly transactional character of Turkey's relationship with the EU, Donald Tusk, the European Council President at the time, declared at this summit meeting, '[w]e do not expect anyone to guard our borders for us.... But we expect a major step towards changing the rules of the game when it comes to stemming the migration flow that is coming to the EU via Turkey.'[70] This declaration demonstrates the future direction of Turkish–EU co-operation, with an emphasis for stemming the refugee flow. This increasingly functional aspect of Turkey–EU cooperation on the refugee issue is already a subject of major scientific inquiries.[71]

The second bilateral summit was held on 7 March 2016, to strengthen EU–Turkish cooperation on migration and the refugee crisis in parallel with visa liberalization for Turkish citizens. In the bilateral summit of 17–18 March 2016, a joint Turkey–EU statement on Refugees was adopted. Despite the slowing down of meetings dedicated to Turkey's accession negotiations, with the last meeting of the Accession Conference being held on 30 June 2016, which ended with the opening of one more chapter—Chapter 33 on financial and budgetary provisions—leaders' meetings in the form of bilateral summits continued. On 25 May 2017, another bilateral summit was held. However, the most critical meeting turned out to be the Varna Summit between Turkey and the EU, which was held on 26 March 2018. This bilateral summit indicated that the future of this complicated relationship had become functional, when Donald Tusk declared,

> [o]ur meeting today demonstrated that while our relationship is going through difficult times, in areas where we do cooperate, we cooperate well. We reconfirm our readiness to keep up the dialogue and consultations and to work together to overcome current difficulties with a view to unleashing the potential of our partnership.[72]

In the same summit, the European Commission President at the time, Jean-Claude Juncker, indicated that '[w]e should be talking about the areas of interest and ambitions that unite us, not the ones that divide us. Turkey and Europe must move together as only by joining forces we can tackle common challenges.'[73] The emphasis was clearly on partnership rather than accession. This is also how one could see the importance of the Council declaration that

[70] ibid.
[71] Saatcioglu (n 25).
[72] https://www.consilium.europa.eu/en/meetings/international-summit/2018/03/26/ accessed 1 July 2023.
[73] https://eeas.europa.eu/topics/counter-terrorism/42139/turkey-summit-relaunches-open-and-constructive-dialogue_en accessed 1 July 2023.

> [t]he Council reiterates that continued implementation of the EU–Turkey Statement and continued support for partners along the Western Balkans route is required. Further actions are needed to ensure sufficient administrative and enforcement capacity to tackle migration challenges, including combating the smuggling of migrants. The EU will continue its financial support and technical assistance to strengthen cooperation in this field, including through the EU Facility for Refugees in Turkey.[74]

While Turkey's relations with the EU were descending to a different platform, the enlargement priorities of the EU were also being debated at various EU levels. However, the Russian invasion of Ukraine in 2022 brought a new impetus to EU enlargement, especially for Eastern Partnership countries, with a different focus on securitization.

As for high-level dialogues, a series of these set-ups was established to manage Turkish–EU relations,[75] in which decisions on economic, political, energy, and counterterrorism issues would be taken. These high-level dialogues incorporate ministerial meetings where Turkish Ministers of economics, trade, energy, judicial affairs, and interior affairs meet with their counterparts from the European Commission, ie the Commissioners responsible for these portfolios. The main rationale for these dialogues is to expand cooperation modalities, as well as to discuss opening benchmarks for the relevant negotiations chapters. Table 12.1 summarizes the high-level meetings that have taken place since 2015.

However, all ongoing negotiations and high-level dialogues were suspended in July 2019, when the European Council adopted a set of sanctions for Turkey's drilling activities in the Eastern Mediterranean.[76] Accordingly, the European Council stated:

> the Council decides to suspend negotiations on the Comprehensive Air Transport Agreement and agrees not to hold the Association Council and further meetings of the EU–Turkey high-level dialogues for the time being. The Council endorses the Commission's proposal to reduce the pre-accession assistance to Turkey for 2020 and invites the European Investment Bank to review its lending activities in Turkey, notably with regard to sovereign-backed lending.[77]

[74] https://www.consilium.europa.eu/media/35863/st10555-en18.pdf, 11, accessed 1 July 2023.

[75] Müftüler-Baç, 'Turkey's Future' (n 23).

[76] https://www.consilium.europa.eu/en/press/press-releases/2019/07/15/turkish-drilling-activities-in-the-eastern-mediterranean-council-adopts-conclusions/ accessed 1 July 2023.

[77] Council of the European Union, 'Turkish Drilling Activities in the Eastern Mediterranean: Council Adopts Conclusions' (Press release, 15 July 2019) https://www.consilium.europa.eu/en/press/press-releases/2019/07/15/turkish-drilling-activities-in-the-eastern-mediterranean-council-adopts-conclusions/ accessed 1 July 2023.

Table 12.1 High-level Meetings: Turkey and the EU, 2015–20*

Date	High-level Dialogue
16 March 2015	High-level Energy Dialogue Meeting
25 January 2016	High-level Political Dialogue Meeting
28 January 2016	High-level Energy Dialogue Meeting
25–26 April 2016	High-level Economic Dialogue Meeting
8 June 2016	High-level Counterterrorism Dialogue
9 September 2016	High-level Political Dialogue Meeting
25 July 2017	High-level Political Dialogue Meeting
27 November 2017	High-level Transport Dialogue Meeting
28 November 2017	High-level Counterterrorism Dialogue Meeting
7–8 December 2017	High-level Economic Dialogue Meeting
22 November 2018	High-level Political Dialogue Meeting
15 January 2019	High-level Transport Dialogue Meeting
28 February 2019	High-level Economic Dialogue Meeting
16 September 2021	High-level Climate Dialogue
12 October 2021	High-level Dialogue on Migration and Security
30 November 2021	High-level Health Dialogue Meeting
21 April 2022	High-level Climate Dialogue Meeting
11–12 May 2022	High-level Agriculture Dialogue Meeting
15 November 2022	High-level Dialogue on Science, Research and Technology
23 November 2023	High-level Dialogue on Migration and Security

*Author's own compilation from the EU's Progress Reports on Turkey and the Council of the EU websites.

This was a surprising turn of events, as only a few months earlier, on 15 March 2019, the fifty-fourth meeting of the Association Council was held between Turkey and the EU, where the modalities of deepening Turkey's partnership with the EU were further discussed.[78] Similarly to the suspension of talks on the upgrading of the Customs Union, and negotiations for a Comprehensive Air Transport Agreement, the suspension of the high-level meetings demonstrates the role of political factors for technical alignment, on the one hand, and the linkages between

[78] https://www.consilium.europa.eu/en/press/press-releases/2019/03/15/press-statement-following-the-54th-meeting-of-the-association-council-between-the-european-union-and-turkey-brussels-15-march-2019/ accessed 1 July 2023.

Turkey's technical alignment to the EU rules and political conditions, on the other. From the end of 2021 onwards, high-level dialogue meetings in technical areas began to be organized. While high-level foreign policy consultations took place in March 2022 between Turkey and the EU, due to the increased Russian threat to European security, there were no plans for bilateral summits. Turkey's stance on issues such as sanctions against Russia, Syrian civil war, and Libya differed from the EU's stance. Unlike non-EU members such as Norway,[79] Iceland, or Switzerland,[80] the Turkish case highlights the role of political factors as drivers for the EU's external differentiated integration or the lack thereof. Similar issues for assessing the future of the United Kingdom's relations with the EU are becoming increasingly relevant.[81] Furthermore, there is a clear need for judicial mechanisms to resolve cases involving Turkey's compliance with EU laws, addressing Turkey's concerns in terms of the implementation of the EU rules. Both the bilateral summits headed by the Council, and the increased need for judicial tools of redress for Turkey–EU relations, indicate that Turkey's relations with the EU need new institutional designs. If such new institutional mechanisms emerge, this will strengthen the external differentiated integration patterns between Turkey and the EU. The 2005 Negotiations Framework for Turkey stated that, in the event that negotiation talks failed, then 'Turkey would be tied to the EU with the strongest bonds'.[82] Of course, whether these 'strongest bonds' constitute a form of external differentiated integration needs further elaboration, and whether these bonds include new institutional mechanisms remains to be seen. The Russian invasion of Ukraine in 2022, and the Turkish role in providing safe passage for Ukrainian grain,[83] and a neutral place for leaders to meet, turned out to be another illustration of the Turkish role in Europe, from a European security perspective.

IV. Conclusion

This chapter has argued that Turkey's relations with the EU constitute a prime example of external differentiated integration. In an increasing fashion since the 1995 CUA, Turkey has aligned itself to the EU rules with regard to trade. While Turkish economic integration to the EU's single market is not comparable to the EEA's

[79] Fossum, 'What is the Norway Model?' (n 11).

[80] Christian Frommelt, 'In Search of Effective Differentiated Integration: Lessons from the European Economic Area' (PhD dissertation ETH Zurich, 2017).

[81] Benjamin Leruth, Stefan Gänzle, and Jarle Trondal, 'Differentiated Integration and Disintegration in the EU after Brexit: Risks versus Opportunities' (2019) 57(6) Journal of Common Market Studies 1383–94.

[82] European Commission, 'Negotiations Framework: Principles Governing the Negotiations with Turkey' (Luxembourg, 5 October 2005) http://trade.ec.europa.eu/doclib/docs/2007/september/tradoc_135916.pdf last accessed 1 July 2023.

[83] https://www.consilium.europa.eu/media/60872/2022-12-15-euco-conclusions-en.pdf last accessed 1 July 2023.

experiences in its magnitude, there is still a great degree of similarity in terms of the EU's ability to induce third parties to comply with the EU *acquis*. While initially designed for eventual accession to the EU, both the EEA and Turkey's customs union have become permanent, indicating the temporality dimension of external differentiated integration through the acquisition of a permanent status quo. This is particularly important, as the Turkish accession negotiations have reached an impasse. Despite the impasse, the EU is still Turkey's largest trade partner and foreign direct investment donor, and Turkish alignment to EU rules and its participation in several EU programmes have reached a level that would be very hard to reverse.

However, the current political climate between Turkey and the EU does not bode well for the Turkish accession talks to continue. Political will on both sides towards Turkey's accession has reached an all-time low, with no chapters open for the past five years, and the EU's priorities are no longer towards enlargement nor towards Turkey. This does not, however, mean that Turkey is out of the EU's integration project. Instead, the EU is evolving into a multilevel, multilayered polity with different degrees of integration not only within its Member States, but also with non-member European countries. Turkey is tied to the EU in multiple manners, and its future with the EU is still being moulded. Yet, whether to deepen functional cooperation with Turkey—and if so, how—is perceived as a politically adventurous question with potential to harm the EU's credibility. This seems to be the main dilemma for the EU: the question is how to reformulate Turkish–EU relations, on the one hand, and how to engage with alternative forms of integration without harming the EU's credibility, on the other.

This chapter has demonstrated that Turkey presents a case where a third country has voluntarily opted into EU policies, participates in the EU agencies, and engages with the EU, but does not have any participation rights in the EU decision-making mechanisms, or a vote in the decision-making organs of EU agencies. This participation in these EU policies, programmes, and agencies without voting rights indicates that Turkey does not possess any power to shape EU decision-making or rules. This brings forth further questions about the limits of external differentiated integration and the expectations that third countries are rule-takers but not rule-shapers.

This is precisely what brings us to formulate modes of external differentiated integration for cases such as Turkey. Turkish opting into the EU *acquis* is extensive in certain policy areas, and—most importantly—in policies such as common development and aid, Turkey fulfils the EU criteria to an even higher level than most of the EU Member States. To assess the Turkish place in the larger European framework, and to tap into undeveloped areas of further cooperation, would provide a clear indication of the current degree of external differentiated integration. However, technical alignment to the EU *acquis* is not devoid of politics. As this chapter has demonstrated, Turkey's technical alignment to, and adoption of, EU rules—including the update of the CUA—is subject to its adoption of the EU's political criteria as well. While for other non-EU European countries, such as Norway, a political alignment does not seem to be a precondition for the technical adoption of these criteria, for Turkey there is a high degree of overlap. This, in turn, ultimately means that external differentiated integration for Turkeymight not necessarily be an alternative to its accession.

13
The Western Balkans and European Union Enlargement—Exploring Possibilities of Differentiated Integration

*Marko Milenković**

I. Introduction

The Western Balkans (WB) has made significant progress in terms of political, economic, and cultural transformation[1] since the prospects of European Union (EU) membership were offered in the early 2000s. However, the process has been relatively slow, and has been hampered by numerous factors, both on the EU side and among the candidates.[2] There are currently six candidates and potential candidates for membership of the EU in the Western Balkans: Serbia and Montenegro, with whom accession negotiations are well advanced; Northern Macedonia and Albania, who have been granted candidate status by the Council, with negotiations only opened in 2020; Bosnia and Hercegovina, which was granted candidate status only in December 2022; and, finally, Kosovo*, which is also considered a potential candidate by the EU.[3] More than a decade of different successive crises in the EU has sidelined the enlargement process, while the WB countries have undergone

* This chapter was written as part of the 2020 Research Programme of the Institute of Social Sciences with the support of the Ministry of Science, Technological Development and Innovation of the Republic of Serbia, and updated in 2023.

1 Marko Milenković, 'EU Enlargement, Conditionality Policy and Prospects for the Integration of the Western Balkans' in Laura Montanari (ed), *L'allargamento dell'Unione europea e le transizioni costituzionali nei Balcani occidentali* (Editoriale Scientifica 2022) 61–75.)

2 As recently argued by Džankić, Keil, and Kmezić, '[t]he Western Balkans represent a unique laboratory for exploring a wide array of parallel-tracked political processes. Over the past three decades, the region has experienced manifold state disintegrations, violent and non-violent conflict between and within countries, as well as a delayed transition to democracy and market economy.' See Jelena Džankić, Soeren Keil, and Marko Kmezić, 'Introduction: The Europeanisation of the Western Balkans' in Jelena Džankić, Soeren Keil, and Marko Kmezić (eds), *The Europeanisation of the Western Balkans: A Failure of EU Conditionality?* (Palgrave Macmillan 2019) 3.

3 Kosovo, which declared independence from Serbia in 2008, is currently not recognized by five EU Member States (Spain, Romania, Greece, Cyprus, and Slovakia). Kosovo*is, in many international forums and by the EU, referred to with an asterisk, which refers to a note stating: 'This designation is without prejudice to positions on status, and is in line with UNSCR 1244/1999 and the ICJ opinion on the Kosovo declaration of independence.'

Marko Milenković, *The Western Balkans and European Union Enlargement—Exploring Possibilities of Differentiated Integration* In: *Redefining EU Membership*. Edited by: Diane Fromage, Oxford University Press. © Marko Milenković 2024.
DOI: 10.1093/9780191948145.003.0013

political and economic hardship.[4] Altogether, these factors have allowed limited space for the Europeanization, democratization, and development of the region. The influence of, on the one hand, enlargement fatigue among the EU Member States on the legal and political reforms in the region and, on the other, the distant membership prospects for WB countries, are now apparent: accession fatigue has, consequently, emerged. This chapter builds on the premise that it would be prudent to (re-)examine WB EU integration by exploring legal and political alternatives encompassed by the differentiated integration already used widely within or by the Union.[5] This, however, is done having in mind that full membership of the EU for all Balkan candidates would be the best long-term option for the stability of the region and Europe, and that full adherence to fundamental values and firm insistence on core reforms must be at the centre of the (re-)envisaged short- to medium-term vision of the EU for the region.[6]

The study of the external dimensions of differentiated integration is valuable not only for the WB, but also for Turkey, as the largest candidate country with the longest accession process,[7] as well as for countries of the Eastern Neighbourhood, three of which—Ukraine,Moldova and Georgia—were only offered the prospect of membership in 2022 and 2023 respectively. As Müftüler-Baç and Luetgert have put forward, '[w]hile differentiated integration as a concept is applicable to the EU member states' own varying degree of compliance, it is possible to see it as a model of maximizing the EU's integration capacity towards the non-EU European countries in the EU's external neighbourhood.'[8] Over the years, the EU has developed a comprehensive set of engagements with the countries of the Western Balkans region, which can already be understood as a degree of external differentiated integration for the region. The region's participation in, and engagement with, EU programmes, networks, and agencies is an important feature of the EU's approach to the region. [9] The extent to which

[4] For the economic outlook of the region and EU involvement, see Milica Uvalić, 'Economic Integration of the Western Balkans into the European Union: The Role of EU Policies' in Džankić, Keil, and Kmezić (eds), *The Europeanisation of the Western Balkans* (n 2) 207–35.

[5] Marko Milenković, 'Differentiated Integration of the Western Balkans—Emerging Alternative Membership Options?' in Laura Montanari and others (eds), *We, the People of the United Europe: Reflections on the European State of Mind (Atti del Convegno internazionale Udine 28/29 giugno 2022)* (Editoriale Scientifica 2022) 235–47.

[6] Marko Milenković, 'Ukraine War: A Push towards Differentiated Integration for the Western Balkans?' in Jelena Džankić, Simonida Kacarska, and Soeren Keil, *A Year Later: War in Ukraine and Western Balkan (Geo)Politics* (European University Institute 2023) 155–64.

[7] See Müftüler-Baç, in this volume.

[8] Meltem Müftüler-Baç and Brooke Luetgert, 'The European Union's Alternative Models for Maximizing its Integration Strategy for Candidates and Neighbour States: A Process of External Differentiation', MAXCAP Working Paper Series No 35, November 2016, 8.

[9] For the mapping of the trajectories of differentiated integration for the Western Balkans, see Marko Milenković, 'Trajectories of Differentiated Integration for the Western Balkans' in Jarle Trondal, Stefan Ganzle, and Benjamin Laruth (eds), *Routledge Handbook of Differentiated Integration* (Routledge 2022) 551–64.

candidates might be involved with policies or various EU bodies in the absence of membership prospects is also analyzed. It is argued that wider opening of funds and programmes traditionally reserved for Member States might be crucial for the development of the region without the need to provide a full EU membership , which remains unpopular from the perspective of a number of EU states. In other words, other arrangements must be found that could, in the short- to medium-term at least, replace full membership, thus further expanding differentiated integration.

Different (non-)membership options have been on the table for the wider EU neighbourhood for quite a long time. In his widely cited speech from 2002, the then President of the Commission, Romano Prodi, discussed these developments, and referred to the idea of 'sharing everything with the Union but institutions', but did not exclude 'the possibility of developing new structures with our neighbours at a later stage, if necessary'.[10] It may be argued that the Union has not (substantially) taken this road over the past fifteen years; however, numerous trajectories of integration have been established across the European neighbourhood, both with candidates and with those who have (still) not been offered membership prospects. In the context of the successive EU crises and both enlargement and accession fatigue, alternatives for the countries of the region, exemplified by the differentiated integration scenario for the future of EU (as outlined by the European Commission),[11] should be examined. With the Russian aggression against Ukraine in 2022, enlargement has gained new impetus, with new countries from the Eastern Partnership gaining EU membership prospects. Therefore, differentiation and full membership scenarios should both be studied in conjunction with one another, as part of the same process.

This chapter first recalls the evolution of the WB's relationship with the EU over the past two decades (Section II). It then examines the ways in which the WB already participate in EU policies and bodies at present (Section III). The following section assesses possible alternatives to full membership (Section IV). Finally, Section V concludes the chapter.

[10] Romano Prodi, President of the European Commission, 'A Wider Europe—A Proximity Policy as the Key to Stability "Peace, Security And Stability International Dialogue and the Role of the EU" ', Sixth ECSA-World Conference, Brussels, 5–6 December 2002 (SPEECH/02/619), available at http://europa.eu/rapid/press-release_SPEECH-02-619_en.htm accessed 1 July 2023. Even though this referred primarily to Eastern Neighbourhood countries, the value of the concept is equally applicable to the Balkans.

[11] Inter alia, in European Commission, 'White Paper—Future of Europe' COM 2017(2025) final available at https://eur-lex.europa.eu/legal-content/EN/TXT/?uri=COM:2017:2025:FIN accessed 15 February 2021.

II. Two Decades of EU Integration of the Western Balkans—The Rising Relevance of Differentiated Integration

The study of different models of relationships with the EU for WB candidates is specifically interesting amidst the new stage of research on differentiated integration, its surge in the context of Brexit,[12] and the turn in scholarly research towards disintegration and the various paths differentiated integration might take.[13] For decades, differentiated integration has been termed a 'permanent and "normal" feature of European integration'[14] and one of the 'stable characteristics of the EU legal order',[15] and it remains an intriguing theoretical concept.[16] Until recently, there has been little study of WB EU integration prospects from the differentiated integration perspective,[17] both in terms of current engagements and future possibilities. As argued by Flessenkemper and Reljić, '[f]inancial and trading relations, geographical position and political ties already make the Western Balkans *de facto* a part of the EU—but with many disadvantages and no voting rights'.[18] Raik and Tamminen have argued that the increased application of the approach has been seen as a possible way of making future enlargement easier by offering flexibility to the extent of adopting EU norms and creating new models for the partial integration of neighbouring countries that do not wish, or are not ready, to become full members.[19] They distinguish three existing models for extending integration beyond EU borders: the European Economic Area, Enlargement, and the European Neighbourhood Policy (ENP), and offer two possible scenarios—the first being 'membership minus eurozone', which is already in place for some recent EU newcomers, and the second being a 'more radical model of "two-tier integration" [that]

[12] Bruno de Witte, 'An Undivided Union? Differentiated Integration in Post-Brexit Times' [2018] Common Market Law Review 229–32.

[13] Notably, Jarle Trondal, Stefan Gänzle, and Benjamin Leruth, 'Differentiated Integration and Disintegration in the European Union: State-of-the-art and Ways for Future Research', Department of Political Science and Management, University of Agder, ISL Working Paper 2017:1.

[14] Benjamin Leruth and Christopher Lord, 'Differentiated Integration in the European Union: A Concept, a Process, a System or a Theory?' (2015) 6 Journal of European Public Policy 754.

[15] de Witte (n 12) 248.

[16] See, further, Katharina Holzinger and Frank Schimmelfennig, 'Differentiated Integration in the European Union: Many Concepts, Sparse Theory, Few Data' (2012) 2 Journal of European Public Policy 292–305.

[17] Interestingly, as early as 2008, Economides offered the following perspective of the Balkans' integration process: Spyros Economides, 'The Politics of Differentiated Integration: The Case of the Balkans' (2008) GreeSE Paper No 18 Hellenic Observatory Papers on Greece and Southeast Europe.

[18] Tobias Flessenkemper and Dušan Reljić, 'EU Enlargement: A Six Percent Target for the Western Balkans' (*SWP Berlin*, 27 June 2017) https://www.swp-berlin.org/en/point-of-view/eu-enlargement-a-six-percent-target-for-the-western-balkans/ accessed 1 July 2023.

[19] 'The larger the EU becomes, the more tempting the option to turn to a differentiated mode and deepen integration among a core group of the willing, rather than trying to move forward with all member states. Some candidate countries may also be interested in a selective approach, notably by staying out of the eurozone.' See Kristi Raik and Tanja Tamminen, 'Inclusive and Exclusive Differentiated Integration: Enlargement and the European Neighbourhood Policy' in Juha Jokela (ed), *Multi-speed Europe? Differentiated Integration in the External Relations of the European Union* (Finnish Institute of International Affairs 2014) 45–46.

would re-structure the EU institutions so that a clear separation would be established between the inner core of eurozone members and the outer circle'.[20]

Until accession status was formally granted, the EU's relationship with the WB was first governed by a process based on conditionality and focused on Stabilisation and Association (see subsection A below), with negotiations to join the EU substantially underway with only two out of six candidates at present (see subsection B below).

A. The conditionality approach and the prolonged process of Stabilisation and Association

Up until the beginning of the 1990s, previous rounds of EU enlargement were carried out ad hoc, without a set group of criteria to be fulfilled by the aspiring applicants.[21] The rules governing accession have remained limited to date, as there is no specific secondary legislation, but rules and procedures have been developed through institutional practice, with growing pre-entry conditions. The conditions to join the Union, known as the Copenhagen criteria, were broadly formulated only when the EU's enlargement to Central and Eastern European (CEE) countries commenced, in 1993, and conditionality itself has been gradually built up.[22] These criteria were formulated as follows: (1) stable, democratic institutions, the rule of law, respect for human and minority rights (political criteria); (2) a functioning market economy and the ability to withstand competition from EU companies (economic criteria); and (3) the ability to assume the responsibilities of membership (legal harmonization).[23] The institutional capacity criterion was added by the Madrid Council in 1995, as it became apparent that the fulfilment of the three previous criteria would be conditional on having a competent public administration capable of transposing the new rules into the accession countries.[24] These criteria have been further elaborated by the European Council in subsequent years.[25]

[20] However, they also warn that differentiated integration may not only increase flexibility but also the lines of division and inequality between European countries, expressly claiming that it is 'hard to envisage an outer circle of integration that would not be perceived as second-class membership' (ibid 46–47).

[21] For the overview of the procedure, see Milenković, 'EU Enlargement' (n 1).

[22] Othon Anastasakis and Dimitar Bechev, 'EU Conditionality in South East Europe: Bringing Commitment to the Process' (South East European Studies Programme, European Studies Centre, St Antony's College, University of Oxford, 2003) 5.

[23] European Council in Copenhagen 21–22 June 1993 conclusions of the presidency, SN 180/1/93 REV 1. https://www.consilium.europa.eu/media/21225/72921.pdf

[24] MADRID EUROPEAN COUNCIL 15 and 16 DECEMBER 1995 PRESIDENCY CONCLUSIONS, https://www.europarl.europa.eu/summits/mad1_en.htm

[25] For a detailed overview of the development of the enlargement *acquis*, see Allan Tatham, *Enlargement of the European Union* (Kluwer 2009); Christophe Hillion, 'EU Enlargement' in Paul Craig and Gráinne de Búrca (eds), *The Evolution of EU Law* (OUP 2011).

The political, legal, and economic transformation of the WB over the past two decades has mostly been driven by the EU, with no other candidates ever having been subjected to such numerous and challenging conditionality requirements prior to joining. The reason for this is twofold. On the one hand, there is a legacy of conflicts in the region that, even after twenty years, makes post-war reconstruction and reconciliation far more complicated and especially sensitive in comparison with the usual hardships associated with economic transition and transformation towards a market economy which have been typical of CEE countries. On the other is the fact that the WB countries, as the last to join the EU, are being required to undergo a rigorous check test and fulfil a much more extensive set of requirements to join, in comparison with previous entrants. This includes the building up of conditionality requirements based on the experiences of the previous grand enlargement of ten new member states in 2004, and especially the entry into the EU of Bulgaria and Romania, in 2007.[26] These enlargements have shed light on all the risks of the 'unpreparedness' of individual countries for joining, and thus WB societies are being required to undertake 'by-the-book' transformative processes[27] in order to fulfil the requirements.

The Stabilisation and Association Process (SAP) was introduced as an EU integration approach for WB in 1999. Aimed at the whole region, it comprised four components: political dialogue, pre-accession aid, autonomous trade measures, and Stabilisation and Association Agreements (SAAs). As Lavenex has emphasized, the Stability Pact for South-Eastern Europe, and the SAP, both conceived in 1999, 'laid the basis for the dual track approach based on bilateral pre-accession relations and region-building'.[28] Pre-accession aid still remains the main instrument for helping countries in the region and financing various engagements with the EU, while the SAAs form the contractual basis for relations between the countries and the Union. The 2000 European Council, in Feira, confirmed the WB countries as 'potential candidates for EU membership',[29] and as a part of this process the political decision was made in 2003 to enable WB enlargement. Potential candidates can apply for EU membership to, and be approved as a candidate by, the European Council.[30] This decision was taken only a year before the grand enlargement of 2004, and three years before the entrance of Romania and Bulgaria—two countries

[26] For some accounts of unpreparedness for membership, see Dimitry Kochenov, 'Overestimating Conditionality' in Inge Govaere and others (eds), *The European Union in the World: Essays in Honour of Marc Maresceau* (Nijhoff 2014) 541–56; Miroslav Jovanović, *The Economics of European Integration* (2nd edn, Edward Elgar 2013).

[27] Marko Milenković, *State Aid Control in Serbia—EU Conditionality and the Challenge of Institutional Reform* (Wolters Kluwer CEDAM 2019).

[28] Sandra Lavenex, 'Concentric Circles of Flexible "European" Integration: A Typology of EU External Governance Relations' (2011) 4-5 *Comparative European Politics* 372–81.

[29] Council of the European Union, 'Presidency Conclusions', Santa Maria de Feira European Council Meeting, 19–20 June 2000. https://www.europarl.europa.eu/summits/fei1_en.htm

[30] Council of the European Union, 'Presidency Conclusions', Thessaloniki European Council Meeting, 19–20 June 2003, 11638/03. https://www.consilium.europa.eu/media/20847/76279.pdf

that were lagging behind in reforms. However, subsequent to these enlargements, and the negative experiences of those accessions, enlargement fatigue has been more than present in the approaches of the institutions and individual Member States. It is further perpetuated by an increasing and changing conditionality.[31] It is also argued that the conditionality approach has reached its limits, with unpredictable membership prospects.[32]

Against this background, some proposals have been made with a view to changing the accession procedure that are affecting the ongoing negotiations between the EU and the WB; proposals were made firstly by France, and then followed by other Member States, in 2019, on how to bring new dynamism to the process, and these were later reflected in the changing negotiation framework.

B. Accession negotiations—a changing landscape and limited results

Accession to the EU is a lengthy and structured process, with negotiations taking many years, depending on the individual candidate's particular situation.[33] In November 2019 the French government came up with the Non-Paper on Reforming the European Union Accession Process. This document stressed that the process should be based on four principles: gradual association, stringent conditions, tangible benefits, and reversibility. The main idea was to replace the large number (thirty-five) of thematic chapters with several successive stages, with the clear idea that 'the closing of negotiations corresponding to each stage completed by the country would open up the possibility of participating in EU programmes, being involved in certain sectoral policies and, where appropriate, benefitting from certain targeted finance', thus clearly opening the door for EU integration under the differentiated integration regime but still stressing that 'the final objective would be full and complete accession'.[34] The French proposal was countered by an initiative of nine Member States, with a view to avoid negotiation talks with

[31] Numerous disadvantages and particularities of regional relations, especially 'culturalized conditionality', have been dealt with in Miloš Milenković and Marko Milenković, 'Serbia and the European Union: Is "Culturalization" of Accession Criteria on the Way?' in Finn Laursen (ed), *EU Enlargement: Current Challenges and Strategic Choices* (PIE Lang 2013) 153–72.

[32] As was argued by Hillion: 'The EU and its Member States thus used the membership promise as a bargaining chip to influence, if not steer, the structural reforms with a view to ensuring that the newcomers would be as amenable to membership as possible. In becoming itself a key actor of the transformation process, the EU entered uncharted territories of liberal democratic and market economy state-building . . . The inflated and evolving normative basis for enlargement has raised issues of double standards that have consequently undermined the credibility of the Union's commitments to the norms and values it has advocated vis-à-vis the applicants, questioned the legitimacy of its conditionality, and ultimately the effectiveness of the transformation agenda.' Hillion (n 25) 195–96.

[33] Milenković, 'EU Enlargement' (n 1).

[34] Available at Non-Paper Reforming the European Union accession process , November 2019. https://www.politico.eu/wp-content/uploads/2019/11/Enlargement-nonpaper.pdf accessed 1 July 2023.

Northern Macedonia and Albania being prevented from opening while the process was being revamped. They also considered that 'internal EU reform cannot be a precondition for enlargement'.[35]

Following these proposals to revamp the process, the Commission came up with the new enlargement methodology in February 2020, with the idea of 'bringing more dynamism into the negotiating process'.[36] The Commission proposed grouping the negotiating chapters in six thematic clusters: fundamentals; internal market; competitiveness and inclusive growth; green agenda and sustainable connectivity; resources, agriculture and cohesion; and external relations. It envisages a more credible process, involving a stronger political steer and greater involvement of Member States, and greater predictability of the process (hence the six clusters), including enhanced clarity on the conditions and benchmarks to be achieved. This is envisioned to result in the gradual 'phasing in' of candidates into EU policies, and increased access to funding throughout the process, but would also include 'rolling back' in the event of stagnation or backsliding in prospective members. This methodology also offers fewer opportunities to block the advancement of the process due to unanimous voting for the opening and closing of each of the current thirty-five negotiation chapters (which is of utmost importance given the instrumentalization of current accession rules through bilateral conditionality). However, in spite of the revamped methodology, it is expected that enlargement fatigue will continue to dominate the process in the upcoming decade.[37] One of the reasons for moderate pessimism is the fact that the EU integration paths of each of the WB countries have been related to the break-up of Yugoslavia and conflicts in the 1990s.[38] Several EU Member States have blocked individual advancement in integration on numerous occasions over the past fifteen years, and there are no indications that this would not also be the case in foreseeable future. In addition, a lack of commitment of the other side is perceived by both —the EU and Member States on the one hand, and the WB countries on the other. All this will probably lead to a further slowdown of political, economic, and legal reforms. Even though many reforms remain to be undertaken, governments in the region have already made significant efforts to align national legislation with the EU *acquis*, but at least in the short term, a tangible prospect of advancement in EU integration is missing. More concretely, in terms of differentiation, Raik and Tamminen argue that in the context of 'rising popular criticism towards the EU and the strict requirements of the EU enlargement process, the political elites of

[35] See, further, POLITICO, 9 EU countries push back on French enlargement revamp, December 13, 2019https://www.politico.eu/article/eu-enlargement-reform-pushback/ accessed 1 July 2023.

[36] European Commission, 'Enhancing the Accession Process—A Credible EU Perspective for the Western Balkans' COM(2020) 57 final.

[37] See, further, Marko Milenković, 'EU Enlargement Strategy 2020—Paving the Way for Differentiated Integration?' (*Osservatorio OSORIN*, December 2020) https://www.osorin.it/uploads/model_4/.files/54_item_2.pdf?v=1608022440 accessed 15 February 2021.

[38] See, further, Milenković and Milenković, 'Serbia and the European Union' (n 31).

the candidate and potential candidate countries need to balance their actions and political speech between populism and EU compliance'.[39]

EU enthusiasm was revived from 2020 onwards, to a certain extent, by the previously mentioned new negotiation approach, but no clear prospects were given to much of the region, except for Serbia and Montenegro, who were considered to be 'potentially ready for membership in a 2025 perspective', albeit with the clear note that 'this perspective is extremely ambitious'.[40] As already stated a decade ago,[41] the lack of EU prospects will only create more difficulties, as the elites of the countries of the region are not fully motivated to undertake reforms; therefore, conditionality, especially in difficult and challenging fields, may well fail to produce results. As Müftüler-Baç and Luetgert have argued, 'the perspective that all Balkan states, if given the option, would have chosen an immediate and full membership may have changed',[42] which is a clear sign of EU accession fatigue[43] and rising scepticism across the region regarding EU integration, on the part of both political elites and wider populations.[44] As underlined by Belloni and Brunazzo, '[t]he EU is less attractive today than it was in 2003 when it promised an open door policy for the Western Balkan states.'[45] For these very reasons—two mutually reciprocal fatigues (ie WB accession and EU enlargement fatigues)—it is necessary to enhance a more profound quest for alternative future scenarios of (non-)membership for the region, using various approaches and instruments under the differentiated integration approach, at least in the short- and medium-term perspective.

There is an additional consideration that makes different non-membership scenarios plausible for the region, namely the expectations of the EU integration process. For the CEE countries, transition, democratization, and EU integration came after decades under totalitarian communist regimes and isolation from the West. In that sense, the EU was perceived as a long-awaited departure from the communist past, both in terms of economic reforms and political transformation. On the other hand, the majority of the WB population has not been

[39] Raik and Tamminen (n 19) 50.

[40] European Commission, 'Communication From the Commission to the European Parliament, the Council, the European Economic and Social Committee and the Committee of the Regions—A credible enlargement perspective for and enhanced EU engagement with the Western Balkans' COM(2018) 65 final.

[41] Milenković and Milenković, 'Serbia and the European Union' (n 31); Miloš Milenković and Marko Milenković, 'Is Additional Conditionality Preventing EU Accession? Serbian Democratic "Step Back"' (2013) (2) Sociological Review/Sociološki Pregled 189–210.

[42] Müftüler-Baç and Luetgert, 'The European Union's Alternative Models' (n 8) 17.

[43] See, inter alia, European Parliamentary Research Service, 'The Western Balkans and the EU: Enlargement and Challenges', Briefing, September 2016, 12 http://www.europarl.europa.eu/RegData/etudes/BRIE/2016/589791/EPRS_BRI(2016)589791_EN.pdf accessed 1 July 2023.

[44] Indicative data are provided annually by Balkan Barometer surveys conducted by the Regional Cooperation Council. See, further, https://www.rcc.int/seeds/results/2/balkan-public-barometer accessed 1 July 2023.

[45] Roberto Belloni and Marco Brunazzo, 'After "Brexit": The Western Balkans in the European Waiting Room' (2017) 1 European Review of International Studies 36.

awaiting accession to the EU as eagerly as Soviet-style totalitarian states have been since 1989. It was simply never a reality in the former Yugoslavia (Albania represents a notable regional exception here). For the majority of WB populations, EU accession is not perceived as a shield against totalitarianism. It is, rather, an economic project promising a higher standard of living.[46] Bearing that in mind, it would be prudent to examine already existing modalities of cooperation, and models used with other countries opting not to be part of the Union, as well as to consider how some or all of these mechanisms could be utilized to accelerate the Europeanization of the region.

III. Current Modes of External Differentiation for the Western Balkans

This section offers a brief analysis of current modes of cooperation and engagement of the EU with the WB countries, namely comprehensive SAAs concluded, the Energy Community Treaty, current initiatives in the area of transport, and various other engagements in Union programmes, and with EU bodies.[47]

Article 8 of the Treaty on EU (TEU)[48] envisages that the Union will develop a special relationship with neighbouring countries, aiming to establish an area of prosperity and good neighbourliness, founded on the values of the Union, and characterized by close and peaceful relations based on cooperation. The same Article stipulates that 'the Union *may conclude specific agreements with the countries concerned*, which may contain reciprocal rights and obligations as well as the possibility of *undertaking activities jointly*' (emphasis added). This provision in the Treaty of Lisbon is an addition to the long-established basis for association with third countries, present in the treaties since Rome, and now enshrined in Article 217 of the Treaty on the Functioning of the EU (TFEU).[49] Under this Article, the Union may conclude, with one or more third countries or international organizations, agreements establishing an association involving reciprocal rights and obligations, common action, and special procedure. Article 217 TFEU is the principal and flexible legal basis for establishing relations between third countries and the EU. These provisions afford broad opportunities for the inclusion of candidate countries in different Union programmes and initiatives, as can currently be seen. It can also be argued that, even without a treaty revision, the current primary law would allow for a 'sharing everything but institutions' scenario.

[46] Concerns over this important difference, specifically for Serbia, have been raised in Milenković and Milenković, 'Is Additional Conditionality Preventing EU Accession?' (n 42).

[47] In more detail, see Milenković, 'Trajectories of Differentiated Integration' (n 9).

[48] Treaty on the European Union, Official Journal of the European Union, C 202/1, 7.6.2016.

[49] Treaty on the Functioning of the European Union, Official Journal of the European Union, C 326/47, 26.10.2012

The EU is already widely engaged with the WB countries, which makes it possible to examine layers of differentiated integration, as studied in the case of another notable candidate—Turkey—by Müftüler-Baç.[50] The same author also argues that, 'further enlargement of the Union and its multiple links with non-member European countries indicate that expansion of the scope of differentiated integration is, indeed, inevitable'. [51] The same conclusions may be drawn for the WB region .

All the countries of the region have concluded comprehensive SAAs,[52] which not only enable free trade but also envisage comprehensive reforms and alignment with the *acquis* and its subsequent development in a range of important areas (eg competition and State aid, the environment, etc). 'From a legal perspective, the conclusion of an association agreement is disconnected from the procedure for accession to the EU',[53] however for the WB countries such agreements clearly represent politically conditioned, necessary steps on the path to the EU. Up until the entry into force of accession agreements, SAAs remain the main contractual basis for relations between the Union and the countries concerned. In addition to entailing trade provisions, and to providing the wide and privileged access to the EU market for goods from the association countries, they include a set of other legal and political reforms with precise time limits for the implementation of legislative and institutional transformation. This enables the EU Commission to further monitor the progress of reforms in the relevant country during the integration period. It is worth noting that, since Kosovo is not recognized by five EU Member States, its SAA was concluded only between the EU and Kosovo* (and not with Member States), with many specificities compared to classic SAAs.[54] Van Elsuwege and Chamon, in their comprehensive analysis of Association Agreements, identify association as a pre-accession status, association as an alternative to membership, and association as a privileged status of non-EU countries. They further underline that,

[50] The author also argues that Turkey's accession brings forth key questions on the geographical and cultural borders of Europe, the political future of the EU, and the limits of the EU's institutional capacity. The same may be argued for the WB as well. See Meltem Müftüler-Baç, 'Turkey's Future with the European Union: An Alternative Model of Differentiated Integration' (2013) 2 Turkish Studies 416.

[51] ibid 419–20.

[52] Stabilisation and Association Agreements are international agreements between the EU, its Member States, and potential candidates, which primarily focus on trade liberalization and the gradual creation of a free trade area. See, further, David Phinnemore, 'Stabilisation and Association Agreements: Europe Agreements for the Western Balkans?' (2003) 1 European Foreign Affairs Review 77–103.

[53] Peter Van Elsuwege,Merijn Chamon, The meaning of 'association' under EU law - A study on the law and practice of EU association agreements, European Parliament, 2019. https://www.europarl.europa.eu/RegData/etudes/STUD/2019/608861/IPOL_STU(2019)608861_EN.pdf 22.

[54] For a detailed analysis, see Peter Van Elsuwege, 'Legal Creativity in EU External Relations: The Stabilization and Association Agreement between the EU and Kosovo' (2017) 3 European Foreign Affairs Review 393–410.

> [n]otwithstanding the general flexibility regarding the precise scope and objectives of the established relationship, there are also certain limits to what is feasible under the association formula. In particular, the procedural and institutional rights of the associated countries are limited to decision-shaping and cannot involve any rights of representation or decision-making within the EU Institutions.[55]

Another notable example of existing cooperation is the Treaty establishing Energy Community, concluded in 2005 between the European Community and potential WB candidates.[56] This agreement facilitates the creation of a common energy market, and the adoption of the range of energy and environmental standards *acquis*. Subsequently, Energy Community membership has been extended to Ukraine and Moldova, while Turkey has become an observer. This has, therefore, become a specific tool for the gradual integration of both candidate countries and partners from the ENP region.

In the field of transport, the EU, Iceland, Norway, and countries of the WB region also concluded the European Common Aviation Area agreement (the Open Skies Agreement) in 2006, enabling the easier flow of people across the continent. More recently (2017), the Transport Community Treaty was signed in the field of road, rail, inland waterways, and maritime transport, and the development of the transport network between the EU and the Southeast European parties.[57]

Furthermore, countries of the region already participate in a number of Union programmes in areas of research and development, education and culture, youth, civil society development, health, etc, for which framework agreements are concluded between the EU and prospective candidates. A notable avenue of cooperation has also been opened by the so-called Berlin process, initiated by Germany and a group of Member States, facilitating different initiatives in conjunction with the EU integration process. This process has contributed, in particular, to the aforementioned transport agenda, and has led to the creation of regional cooperation initiatives, such as the Regional Youth Cooperation Office,[58] the Western Balkan Chamber Investment Forum (CIF),[59] and the Western Balkan Fund.[60] However, all these initiatives only add to the powerful pull of various structures put in place

[55] Van Elsuwege and Chamon (n 52) 8.

[56] Including Romania at the time. Kosovo, under United Nations administration, was a party from the beginning, as it was represented by the United Nations Interim Administration Mission in Kosovo pursuant to the United Nations Security Council Resolution 1244. See, further, https://www.energy-community.org/ accessed 1 July 2023.

[57] TREATY establishing the Transport Community, Official Journal of the European Union, L 278/3, 27.10.2017.

[58] See, further, http://www.rycowb.org/ accessed 1 July 2023.

[59] Together with the business chambers of Croatia and Slovenia, as EU Member States but former Yugoslav federal units. See http://www.wb6cif.eu/index.html accessed 1 July 2023.

[60] http://westernbalkansfund.org/ accessed 1 July 2023.

over the past twenty-five years to facilitate cooperation and development in the region, with limited success in actually bringing it closer to the EU.

IV. Ways Forward for Europeanization in the Absence of Membership

The multifaceted crisis within the EU is putting significant pressure on the enlargement process. Enlargement fatigue is having a huge impact on legal and political reforms in the region, in the absence of real membership prospects, even leading to accession fatigue in candidate countries, as already outlined. In addition, the ever-growing presence of other powers in the region further endangers the influence of the EU, which is only just beginning to look for solutions to challenges.[61] As Holzinger and Schimmelfennig argue,

> [t]he longevity of opt-outs and exclusions from the European Monetary Union (EMU) and Schengen, the selective integration of non-members that do not want to join or are not allowed to join (as in the European Economic Area, the Bilateral Agreements with Switzerland, or the Customs Union with Turkey), or the establishment and increased use of the Enhanced Co-operation procedure, demonstrate that differentiated integration has also become an important and—most probably—permanent feature of European integration.[62]

In her recent analysis for Turkey, Müftüler-Baç notes that both temporal alignment and policy opt-ins could be envisaged for non-EU members, which could include transition periods for some policies, such as freedom of movement.[63] In her opinion, differentiated integration might involve the inclusion of non-EU countries into the EU's internal market or the adoption of the euro as their national currency.[64] The latter is already the case in Montenegro and Kosovo for various complex reasons, and is tolerated by eurozone members and the EU. However, if implemented by the WB as a whole, it would present a great economic policy challenge for a region struggling to accelerate development and come close to average EU living standards.

The following subsections examine whether the European Economic Area (EEA)/European Free Trade Area (EFTA) model for differentiated integration

[61] See, further, Nina Markovic Khaze and Xiwen Wang, 'Is China's Rising Influence in the Western Balkans a Threat to European Integration?' [2020] Journal of Contemporary European Studies, 234-250; Mariya Hake and Alice Radzyner, 'Western Balkans: Growing Economic Ties with Turkey, Russia and China', BOFIT Policy Brief 1/2019.

[62] Holzinger and Schimmelfennig (n 16) 292–93.

[63] Müftüler-Baç, 'Turkey's Future' (n 49) 419.

[64] ibid.

represents a suitable and feasible option for the WB (subsection A). They also consider whether participation in EU agencies could also constitute an important piece of the puzzle in an alternative EU integration scenario for the region (subsection B).

A. EEA/EFTA as a model for differentiated integration of the Western Balkans—is it a feasible solution?

After several of its former Member States joined the EU in previous rounds of enlargement, EFTA is now comprised of four highly developed countries—Norway, Iceland, Liechtenstein, and Switzerland—with the first three also being members of the European Economic Area (EEA) and part of the internal market, while Switzerland has comprehensive bilateral agreements with the EU. The status of the former three countries implies that they must continuously align with the internal market *acquis* while having limited participation in decision-making, ie only during preparatory stages. As Egeberg and Trondal pointed out in 1999, 'the EEA as a form of affiliation is one of many alternative arrangements that deserves some scholarly attention. Knowledge about such quasi- or semi-membership forms may also attract the interest of practitioners from both countries striving for membership, and countries eager to relax their relationships with the Union'.[65] It is worth noting that these countries do not participate in agriculture and fisheries policies and, more importantly, do not benefit from agricultural funds, but rather contribute annual fees for their privileged partnership status. Furthermore, this position does not entail, in its current form, access to the structural funds that are increasingly needed by the WB region. Finally, in addition to being excluded from decision-making, these rich European countries are 'relatively stable internally and do not need EU membership as a stabilizing factor',[66] which is mostly not the case for the Balkans. In terms of costs, this option would not be greatly onerous for the WB countries, as they have already undertaken, by virtue of SAAs and other agreements, to open up markets for goods, including agricultural products, and to widely adopt the existing *acquis* and adhere to its progressive development in many areas. However, possible alternative integration models should take account of the level of development and provide more aid, comparable to the structural funds available to less-developed Member States. Although an EEA-style agreement has never been proposed by the Commission to any of the associate countries,[67] this

[65] Morten Egeberg and Jarle Trondal, 'Differentiated Integration in Europe: The Case of EEA Country, Norway' (1999) 1 Journal of Common Market Studies 134.
[66] Raik and Tamminen (n 19) 48.
[67] Müftüler-Baç and Luetgert, 'The European Union's Alternative Models' (n 8) 26.

approach should also be considered (with contextual alterations) as a possible viable alternative to membership.

B. European Union agencies as channels of transformation

Decentralized agencies are now an indispensable feature of executive governance in the EU, and there is hardly an area of EU engagement without an agency involved in delivering some of the Union's functions, to the extent that it is hardly possible to govern the Union without them.[68] However, a feature of the agencies mostly neglected by academia is the growing involvement of third countries in them. Different groups of non-Member States engage with decentralized agencies which enable them to participate in the EU regulatory process in various ways. There are different types of third-country involvement across the decentralized agencies of the EU, formally ranging from (full) membership, to (external) partnership, to observer status, and finally to cooperation with (potential) candidate countries. These engagements are, potentially, becoming an important cooperation tool for a post-Brexit United Kingdom, as well as the candidate countries, amid prolonged enlargement fatigue and uncertain membership prospects.[69] The legal basis for third-country membership in agencies, and participation in agencies' activities and programmes, is found in the EEA Treaty,[70] individual treaties between the EU and the third countries (such as Turkish membership in the European Environmental Agency), the establishing acts of the respective agencies, and Council conclusions. Most agencies are open to some kind of involvement of third countries, depending on their founding regulations.

The countries of the EEA—Liechtenstein, Iceland, and Norway—as well as Switzerland, as part of EFTA, are now engaged with seventeen decentralized agencies as members or observers,[71] even though not all of them have the same status or level of engagement with particular agencies. The legal basis that underpins this participation is found in the EEA Agreement,[72] and the EEA/EFTA states' participation in the EU agencies is enabled through decisions of the EEA Joint Committee. Additionally, there are bilateral agreements in place with the EU to facilitate the participation of individual EFTA states in several other EU agencies.

[68] Michelle Everson, 'European Agencies: Barely Legal?' in Michelle Everson, Cosimo Monda, and Ellen Vos (eds), *European Agencies in between Institutions and Member States* (Kluwer Law International 2014) 53.

[69] See also Kathryn Wright on the UK, in this volume.

[70] Agreement on the European Economic Area (OJ No L 1, 3.1.1994, p 3; and EFTA States' official gazettes).

[71] See, further, http://www.efta.int/eea/eu-agencies accessed 1 July 2023.

[72] Under Art 78 of the EEA Agreement, it is envisaged that the Contracting Parties shall strengthen and broaden cooperation in the framework of the Community's activities in a number of fields, in so far as these matters are not regulated under the provisions of other parts of the EEA Agreement. Agreement on the European Economic Area (OJ No L 1, 3.1.1994, p. 3; and EFTA States' official gazettes)

The participation of candidate countries (until recently, Turkey and the WB states) is based on the 1997 Luxembourg Council presidency conclusions, stipulating that agencies in which applicant countries will be able to participate will be determined on a case-by-case basis.[73] This has resulted in all current and potential candidates engaging with a range of EU agencies, simultaneously following different logics of engagement, ranging from ad hoc arrangements, to more stable contractual forms of collaboration, to membership without voting rights.[74] It is necessary to further explore the extent to which this can be used as a membership substitute mechanism within a differentiated integration approach, but it can surely present an important tool for *acquis* transfer and Europeanization of the region.

V. Conclusion: What are the Current Possibilities under EU Treaties?

With the outbreak of the war in Ukraine, the EU enlargement process has gained new impetus but is also becoming much more complex than before. For a number of years, authors warned that the 'European enlargement process in the Western Balkans is in trouble',[75] that the 'EU agenda for the Balkans seems to be in a conundrum', and that 'the countries in the region are diverging from the EU, both on the political and the socio-economic levels, while the EU and the Member States are losing ground and leverage'.[76] For these very reasons, it is necessary for the EU to act decisively, and differentiated integration is the right platform for this, and could enable EU to keep the region on a transformative track while insisting on fundamental reforms.

For a considerable time there have been suggestions that the WB countries should be granted access to the EU's structural funds, be permitted to participate in the EU's financial stability mechanisms, and 'be treated in all other respects as part of the European integration project'.[77] More recently, the idea of a four-step 'stages accession' was promoted, encompassing several steps which candidates would undergo before obtaining full membership rights.[78] As argued by Müftüler-Baç and Luetgert, '[f]or the enlargement countries, differentiated integration might be

[73] Points 21 and 32, Luxembourg European Council, 12 and 13 December 1997, Presidency Conclusions, available at http://www.europarl.europa.eu/summits/lux1_en.htm#enlarge accessed 1 July 2023.

[74] For an analysis of the WB and Turkey, see Michael Kaeding and Marko Milenković, 'Candidate Countries' Engagement with European Union Agencies—Alternative Modes of EU Integration?' (2023) *Journal of Balkan and Near Eastern Studies*, 25(6), 1002–1019..

[75] Belloni and Brunazzo (n 46) 38.

[76] See, further, Matteo Bonomi, 'The Western Balkans in the European Union: Perspectives of a Region in Europe' (Istituto Affari Internazionali Conference, 26–27 June 2017) 1 http://oefz.at/wp-content/uploads/2017/12/Conference-report.pdf

[77] Flessenkemper and Reljić (n 18).

[78] Michael Emerson and others, *A Template for Staged Accession to the EU* (CEPS October 2021).

seen as a stepping stone on the route to accession with Serbia as a prime example here'.[79] That would also require stepping out of current policy frameworks but not necessarily out of funding treaty delimitations. More precisely, each of differentiation options could be covered under the appropriate association mechanism of the Article 217 TFEU, with the possibility of producing the same or similar effects as those aimed at improving the situation in existing Member States. More concretely, the current instrument for pre-accession aid could be broadly extended and utilized for the infrastructural development of the region. This would enable the proper implementation of *acquis* standards in various fields, from environmental protection, to food safety, to transport. Having in mind the geographical position of the region and its interconnectedness with the EU Member States, this could serve the wider interests of the Union. This idea of gradual inclusion into policies has already emerged in a new negotiation framework, and the EU has recently increased investment in the region's infrastructure.[80] While this poses an additional funding challenge in relation to boosting cooperation with the Balkans through programmes, agencies, networks, or revamped funding instruments, for the political reasons already outlined this cooperation must not be sidelined. Even if the WB states are unlikely to become full EU members in the foreseeable future, this should not prevent their integration into policies and programmes, as their involvement in areas such as research, cultural cooperation, and academic mobilityattests.

Possibilities are already on the table, as numerous tangible trajectories of cooperation and integration of the WB region into the EU policies are currently in place. The EU needs to commit strongly in order to remain the key legal and political force in the region, able to transfer its values. However, as these are some of the poorest countries on the continent, with barely consolidated democracies and political institutions, the instruments need to be different from those used with developed European nations that have opted not to be members. As was argued in this chapter, even without full EU membership, participation in agencies, networks, and EU programmes is an important feature of the differentiated integration approach for the region. But that is hardly sufficient, and countries of the WB region need to be more deeply involved with EU policies, legally aligned, and economically integrated. It may also be argued that, even without a treaty revision, the current primary law would allow for the 'sharing everything but institutions' scenario. This can be achieved through the further integration of countries into the internal market, either through the existing EEA structure or by way of re-envisioned Association Agreements. This approach could be more acceptable

[79] Müftüler-Baç and Luetgert, 'The European Union's Alternative Models' (n 8) 6.

[80] For a comprehensive assessment of the plan, see Will Bartlett, Matteo Bonomi, and Milica Uvalić, 'The Economic and Investment Plan for the Western Balkans: Assessing the Possible Economic, Social and Environmental Impact of the Proposed Flagship Projects', Directorate General for External Policies of the Union PE 702.561, May 2022.

to the electorates of Member States not favourable to the formal accession of new members. However, it needs to be accompanied by redesigned structural aid, to create a credible commitment functional in both directions. The latest developments and reinvention of the negotiation framework for Balkan candidates build on the idea of gradual inclusion into the policies of the Union as the accession process progresses, and present a viable option in the foreseeable future. It can, therefore, be concluded that, with clear political steering, it would be possible to bring the current association process to the next level by utilizing existing experiences and possibilities under the founding treaties, so as to enable the stable Europeanization of the region in the absence of the full membership.

14

Democratic Reform and Backsliding in the Post-Soviet Area: What Role for the EU?

Giselle Bosse

I. Introduction

Following the end of the Cold War, many countries in post-Soviet Europe and Eurasia[1] have embarked on implementing democratic reforms. After the initial wave of reforms and an increase in the average level of democracy across the region in the early 1990s, however, the reform process appears to have lost momentum. Between 2006 and 2018, some countries have still shown a significant (Kyrgyzstan) or at least a modest improvement in the quality of democracy (eg Moldova and Georgia) but developments elsewhere in the region, such as in Ukraine or the Russian Federation[2], point to democratic backsliding.[3] This trend presents a particular puzzle considering that the European Union (EU)'s efforts to support the diffusion of democratic norms and values have been considerably stepped up during the past decade, inter alia through the European Neighbourhood Policy (ENP), launched in 2004. In this chapter, I address the question why the pace of democratic reform between 2006 and 2018 has shown such significant variation. A specific focus is placed on the influence of the EU as key factor in the diffusion of democratic standards in post-Soviet Europe and Eurasia, and to what extent differentiated integration of third countries, such as diverse types of agreements or the intensity of political and trade cooperation, impact on EU democratic norm diffusion. The chapter thereby addresses one of the key questions of this volume, namely under what conditions can the EU influence values and norms observed by third countries, in the absence of any membership prospects. This question is particularly pertinent considering that levels of democracy among some of the Central and Eastern European (CEE) Member States of the EU have been declining over

[1] The ENP includes sixteen countries in the EU's neighbourhood, including Ukraine, Moldova, Georgia, Armenia, Azerbaijan, and Belarus, in eastern Europe.

[2] Hereinafter 'Russia'.

[3] This analysis focuses on political developments in post-Soviet Europe and Eurasia between 2004 and 2018. Developments and events that took place after 2018, such as the 2020/21 Belarus uprising, the 2022 Russian invasion of Ukraine or the EU's decisions in 2023 to open accession negotiations with Ukraine and Moldova and to offer EU candidate status to Georgia, are not covered by this analysis.

Giselle Bosse, *Democratic Reform and Backsliding in the Post-Soviet Area* In: *Redefining EU Membership*. Edited by: Diane Fromage, Oxford University Press. © Giselle Bosse 2024. DOI: 10.1093/9780191948145.003.0014

the past decades, in turn raising questions about the EU's ability to ensure a high standard of democracy among its own Member States.

EU democracy-promotion efforts in its eastern neighbourhood gained unprecedented traction after the EU's enlargement to CEE states. As the EU could not enlarge indefinitely, the EU and its Member States were keen on applying the methodology successfully applied to the CEE countries (conditionality and social learning) to encourage democracy and human rights in neighbouring countries further afield.[4] The ENP placed greater and more explicit emphasis on human rights and democracy compared with previous EU initiatives towards countries in its wider neighbourhood, an emphasis mirrored in the EU's Four Common Spaces (2003) with Russia, the Strategy for Central Asia (SCA) (2007),[5] and the Eastern Partnership (EaP) (2009).[6]

Scholars writing on EU external governance, Europeanization, democratization, and area studies have conducted numerous small-N studies examining the role of the EU and other factors in democratic reform processes in selected countries within post-Soviet (non-EU) Europe and Central Asia.[7] Some studies address reform efforts in the ENP or EaP countries more broadly, but focus on very specific (functional) policy sectors only.[8] Variation in democratic reform effort between all thirteen states in the post-Soviet space, and the specific effects of EU democracy promotion on cross-country variation, have not been addressed systematically.

[4] Judith Kelley, 'New Wine in Old Wineskins: Promoting Political Reforms through the New European Neighbourhood Policy' (2006) 44(1) Journal of Common Market Studies 29–55.

[5] The EU SCA includes Kazakhstan, Kyrgyz Republic, Tajikistan, Turkmenistan, and Uzbekistan.

[6] The EaP includes Ukraine, Moldova, Georgia, Armenia, Azerbaijan, and Belarus.

[7] Tina Freyburg and others, 'EU Promotion of Democratic Governance in the Neighbourhood' (2009) 16(6) Journal of European Public Policy 916–34; Mariya Y Omelicheva, *Democracy in Central Asia: Competing Perspectives and Alternative Strategies* (University Press of Kentucky 2015); Nelli Babayan, 'A Global Trend EU-style: Democracy Promotion in "Fragile" and Conflict-Affected South Caucasus' (2016) 7(2) Global Policy 217–26; Fabienne Bossuyt and Paul Kubicek, 'Advancing Democracy on Difficult Terrain: EU Democracy Promotion in Central Asia' (2011) 16(5) European Foreign Affairs Review 639 – 658; Tanja A Börzel and Bidzina Lebanidze, '"The Transformative Power of Europe" beyond Enlargement: The EU's Performance in Promoting Democracy in its Neighbourhood' (2017) 33(1) East European Politics 17–35; Duncan Leitch, 'International Assistance to Democratic Reform in Ukraine: An Opportunity Missed or an Opportunity Squandered?' (2017) 24(6) Democratization 1142–58; Kristina Muhhina, 'Administrative Reform Assistance and Democracy Promotion: Exploring the Democratic Substance of the EU's Public Administration Reform Principles for the Neighbourhood Countries' (2018) 25(4) Democratization 673–91; Rachel Vanderhill, 'Active Resistance to Democratic Diffusion' (2017) 50(1) Communist and Post-Communist Studies 41–51; Michèle Knodt and others, *EU's Policy of Democracy Promotion: Strategies and Impact in Central Asia and the South Caucasus* (vol 7, Nomos Verlag 2018).

[8] Tina Freyburg and others, *Democracy Promotion by Functional Cooperation: The European Union and its Neighbourhood* (Springer 2016); Sandra Lavenex, Dirk Lehmkuhl, and Nicole Wichmann, 'Modes of External Governance: A Cross-national and Cross-sectoral Comparison' (2009) 16(6) Journal of European Public Policy 813–33; Christoph Knill and Jale Tosun, 'Hierarchy, Networks, or Markets: How Does the EU Shape Environmental Policy Adoptions within and beyond its Borders?' (2009) 16(6) Journal of European Public Policy 873–94; Nina Guérin, 'One Wave of Reforms, Many Outputs: The Diffusion of European Asylum Policies beyond Europe' (2018) 25(7) Journal of European Public Policy 1068–87.

The existing literature (across different fields of research) identifies a variety of different potential explanatory factors ('conditions') for democratic reform progress in the EU's neighbourhood, and demonstrates their impact through numerous case studies. Three often-recurring approaches focus on (1) EU-specific factors, (2) domestic factors, and (3) external factors/actors. Yet, the findings of these studies are often contradictory. The aim of this chapter is to disentangle EU democracy-promotion effects, domestic factors, and the influence of other relevant external actors on democratic reform efforts in post-Soviet Europe and Central Asia. This will, in turn, provide key insights into whether different degrees of external differentiation (ie different types of legal agreements with the EU or intensity of economic and political relations with the EU) impact on the EU's ability to influence the values and norms observed by third countries in the absence of the prospect of membership.

The central questions guiding this chapter, therefore, are: *(1) Which factors (or combination of factors) explain the variation of democratic reform effort among the countries in the post-Soviet space between 2006 and 2018? And (2), to what extent can EU democracy promotion be considered a necessary and/or sufficient condition for democratic reforms?*

Based on a theoretical elaboration of the aforementioned three key conditions, I utilize a fuzzy-set qualitative comparative analysis (fsQCA) to systematically compare the thirteen (non-EU) post-Soviet countries, and to identify (combinations of) causal conditions affecting democratic reform outcomes.

The chapter proceeds in four steps: it first conceptualizes and maps democratic reform progress in the thirteen countries (the 'outcome') and then sketches out the relevant conditions for democratic reform progress and the resulting assumptions to be tested. The chapter introduces fsQCA as a method of analysis and outlines the operationalization of the outcome and the conditions. The discussion of the results underlines the role of domestic factors in explaining democratic reform progress. Following the discussion of the findings, the chapter recommends avenues for further research.

II. Variation in Democratic Reform Efforts across the Post-Soviet Area

Since 1991, the year in which most countries in the post-Soviet area (re-)gained their independence, progress in democratic reform has been far from linear. After an initial peak in democratic reforms in the early 1990s, the quality of democracy across the thirteen countries declined sharply in the mid 1990s. Since then, the democracy scores of individual countries show differentiation. Figure 14.1 shows the variation in democratic reform progress among the thirteen countries in the post-Soviet space between 2006 and 2018. The year 2006 was chosen as a

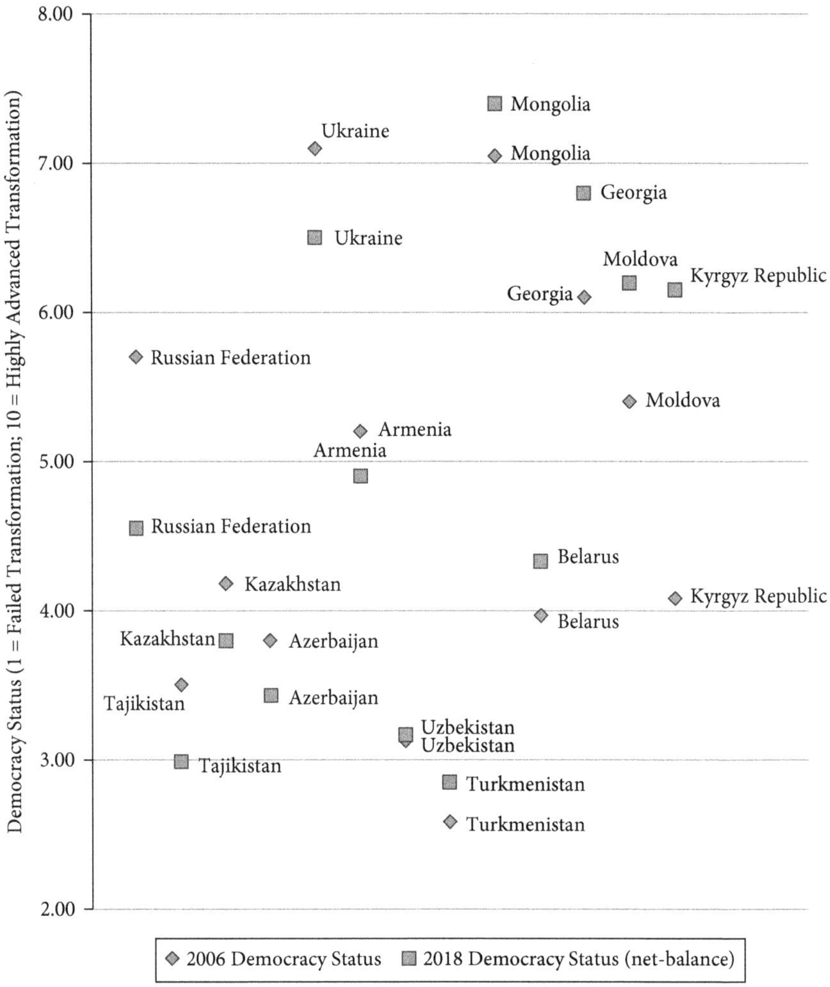

Figure 14.1 Evolution of democracy status scores of countries in post-Soviet Europe and Central Asia

*Source: Bertelsmann Stiftung's Transformation Index (BTI).**

* The 2018 status score is based on the 2006 status score plus the sum of score-point differences from 2006–08, 2008–10, and 2010–12 through to 2016–18. The data, therefore, reflects the 'net balance' of reform progress between 2006–18, taking into account increases and decreases in democracy status scores over the years.

baseline, to account for the considerable time lag that can be expected for the EU's increased committed to democracy promotion (ENP launch in 2004) to have effects on reform efforts in the target countries.[9] Two sets of states with differing outcomes can be distinguished. The first set includes states that show an increase

[9] Frank Schimmelfennig and Hanno Scholtz, 'EU Democracy Promotion in the European Neighbourhood: Political Conditionality, Economic Development and Transnational Exchange'

in democracy scores (Mongolia, Georgia, Moldova, Kyrgyz Republic, Belarus, Uzbekistan, Turkmenistan).[10] The second set comprises states that show a decrease in democracy scores (Ukraine, Russia, Armenia, Kazakhstan, Azerbaijan, Tajikistan).

III. Conditions for Democratic Reforms, including EU Democracy Promotion

The main puzzles addressed in this chapter are why, between 2006 and 2018, democratic reform progress across countries in the post-Soviet space has been differential, and to what extent external differentiation, such as different types of legal agreements with the EU or intensity of political and economic integration, impacts on democratic reform progress in countries that, at the time, had no EU membership perspective. Three broad schools of thought seeking to explain democratization processes and wider reform efforts in the post-Soviet space can be identified. The first and largest group of scholars explains reform progress through the lenses of the Europeanization and related external governance approaches. The Europeanization literature focuses on the adoption of EU rules in post-communist countries which have been offered the perspective of accession to the EU,[11] and also on EU rule transfer to ENP countries.[12] Most scholars see the EU as the main explanatory factor for differences in reform progress across ENP countries. While some focus on EU conditionality and incentives linked to market access and free trade agreements, visa liberalization, or financial assistance,[13] others underline the importance of EU institutional modes of rule transfer, such as hierarchical or

(2008) 9(2) European Union Politics 199. While most scholars use a time lag of one year for influences promoting democracy to come into effect, Schimmelfennig and Scholz (ibid 199) argue that a longer time lag is more appropriate, as it accounts for domestic electoral cycles or popular unrest leading to a change in government.

[10] Despite an increase in democracy scores between 2004 and 2018, Belarus and Turkmenistan remained classified as autocratic regimes.

[11] Frank Schimmelfennig and Ulrich Sedelmeier (eds), *The Europeanization of Central and Eastern Europe* (Cornell University Press 2005).

[12] Michael Emerson, 'European Neighbourhood Policy: Strategy or Placebo?' (2004) CEPS Working Document No 215, 24; Frank Schimmelfennig, 'European Regional Organizations, Political Conditionality, and Democratic Transformation in Eastern Europe' (2007) 21(1) East European Politics and Societies 126–41; Sandra Lavenex and Frank Schimmelfennig, 'EU Rules beyond EU Borders: Theorizing External Governance in European Politics' (2009) 16(6) Journal of European Public Policy 791–812; Andrea Gawrich, Inna Melnykovska, and Rainer Schweickert, 'Neighbourhood Europeanization through ENP: The Case of Ukraine' (2010) 48(5) Journal of Common Market Studies 1209–35.

[13] Inna Melnykovska and Rainer Schweikert, 'Bottom-up or Top-down: What Drives the Convergence of Ukraine's Institutions towards European Standards?' (2008) 8(4) Southeast European and Black Sea Studies 445–68; Esther Ademmer and Tanja A Börzel, 'Migration, Energy and Good Governance in the EU's Eastern Neighbourhood' (2013) 65(4) Europe-Asia Studies 581–608.

network-type modes of governance[14] and types of conditionality.[15] Some works also find that socialization and learning through linkage (eg the density of cross-border contacts, participation in EU programmes, and high-level dialogue) can explain reform progress in neighbouring countries.[16] The impact of EU incentives, conditionality, or socialization mechanisms has, however, also been questioned by many scholars.[17]

A second school of thought contests the importance of the EU as the driver of political reforms in ENP countries, and instead identifies a variety of country-specific domestic factors as key explanatory variables. Scholars have demonstrated the influence of domestic political institutions,[18] veto-players,[19] geopolitical orientation of a government,[20] local perceptions of the EU[21] and the legitimacy of EU norms,[22] or the degree of membership aspiration.[23]

A third school of thought shows the relevance of external factors (and actors besides the EU) on democratic reform processes in the ENP countries. Some scholars show that countries in the ENP are more likely to converge with international democracy norms and standards such as UN conventions, which they perceive as 'more legitimate, fair, and appropriate than EU norms'.[24] These scholars see the EU as an 'amplifier' for international norms,[25] and hence as a sufficient rather than a

[14] Lavenex and Schimmelfennig (n 12).

[15] Gwendolyn Sasse, 'The European Neighbourhood Policy: Conditionality Revisited for the EU's Eastern Neighbours' (2008) 60(2) Europe-Asia Studies 295–316; Tom Theuns, 'Promoting Democracy through Economic Conditionality in the ENP: A Normative Critique' (2017) 39(3) Journal of European Integration 287–302.

[16] Sasse (n 15); Nicholas Ross Smith, 'Europeanization through Socialization? The EU's Interaction with Civil Society Organizations in Armenia' (2011) 19(4) Demokratizatsiya 385; Alexander Warkotsch, 'International Socialization in Difficult Environments: The Organisation for Security and Cooperation in Europe in Central Asia' (2007) 14(3) Democratisation 491–508.

[17] Paul Kubicek, 'The European Union and Grassroots Democratization in Turkey' (2005) 6(3) Turkish Studies 361–77; Frank Schimmelfennig, 'Strategic Calculation and International Socialization: Membership Incentives, Party Constellations, and Sustained Compliance in Central and Eastern Europe' (2005) International Organization 59(4) 827–60; Kelley (n 2); Kataryna Wolczuk, 'Conflict and Reform in Eastern Europe: Domestic Politics and European Integration in Ukraine' (2006) The International Spectator 41(4) 7–24.

[18] Tanja A Börzel and Thomas Risse, 'From Europeanisation to diffusion: introduction.' (2012) West European Politics 35(1) 1–19; Tina Freyburg and others, 'Democracy Promotion through Functional Cooperation? The Case of the European Neighbourhood Policy' (2011) 18(4) *Democratization* 1026–54.

[19] Julia Langbein and Tanja A Börzel, 'Introduction: Explaining Policy Change in the European Union's Eastern Neighbourhood' (2013) 65(4) Europe-Asia Studies 571–80; Melnykovska and Schweikert (n 13).

[20] Laure Delcour and Kataryna Wolczuk, 'Spoiler or Facilitator of Democratization?: Russia's Role in Georgia and Ukraine' (2015) 22(3) Democratization 459–78.

[21] Gawrich, Melnykovska, and Schweickert (n 12).

[22] Esther Barbé and others, 'Drawing the Neighbours Closer ... to What? Explaining Emerging Patterns of Policy Convergence between the EU and Its Neighbours' (2009) 44(4) Cooperation and Conflict 378–99.

[23] Freyburg and others, 'Democracy Promotion through Functional Cooperation?' (n 18); Guérin (n 8).

[24] Barbé and others (n 22) 386.

[25] ibid 383

necessary condition for democratization in ENP countries. Other scholars, and especially those writing on democratic reform efforts in Central Asian countries, demonstrate the importance of external democracy support and a country's relationship with capitalist donors, including but not limited to the EU.[26] More recent works examine the role of 'negative external actors', such as Russia or China, using 'autocracy promotion' strategies to undergird authoritarian regimes or to support anti-democratic political actors or movements in the post-Soviet region.[27]

So far, empirical findings are contradictory and sometimes point in different directions. This can, by and large, be explained by the fact that the vast majority of findings are generated from single or small-N comparative case studies. As a result, it has been impossible to identify generalizable conditions accounting for democratic reform progress in the post-Soviet area. Single or small-N case studies also tend to be limited to demonstrating the influence of one specific explanatory variable. If combinations of conditions on democratic reform progress are examined, it is usually in the context of analyzing single cases.[28]

IV. Explaining Democracy Reform Progress: Combining Sets of Explanations

The three contrasting sets of explanations outlined in the previous section can be reconciled by integrating them into one explanatory model, based on the assumption that only a combination (or different combinations) of several of these factors are decisive for democratic reform progress in countries in the post-Soviet region. In other words, it is assumed that a combination of EU-specific and domestic conditions, as well as external actors and factors, jointly account for differential democratic reform progress across countries in the post-Soviet space.

[26] Oliver Fritz and Gerhard Streicher, 'Trade Effects of Service Liberalization in the EU-Simulation of Regional Macroeconomic Effects for Austria' FIW Research Reports No. 005, 2008.

[27] Thomas Ambrosio, 'Constructing a Framework of Authoritarian Diffusion: Concepts, Dynamics, and Future Research' (2010) 11(4) International Studies Perspectives 375–92; Jakob Tolstrup, 'Studying a Negative External Actor: Russia's Management of Stability and Instability in the "Near Abroad"' (2009) 16(5) Democratization 922–44; Jakob Tolstrup, *Russia vs. the EU: The Competition for Influence in Post-Soviet States* (First Forum Press 2014); Jakob Tolstrup, 'Black Knights and Elections in Authoritarian Regimes: Why and How Russia Supports Authoritarian Incumbents in Post-Soviet States' (2015) 54(4) European Journal of Political Research 673–90.

[28] E.g. Kataryna Wolczuk, 'Implementation without Coordination: The Impact of EU Conditionality on Ukraine under the European Neighbourhood Policy' (2009) 61(2) Europe-Asia Studies 187–211; Julia Langbein and Kataryna Wolczuk, 'Convergence without Membership? The Impact of the European Union in the Neighbourhood: Evidence from Ukraine' (2012) 19(6) Journal of European Public Policy 863–81; Giselle Bosse, 'A Partnership with Dictatorship: Explaining the Paradigm Shift in European Union Policy towards Belarus' (2012) 50(3) Journal of Common Market Studies 367–84; Laure Delcour, *Shaping the Post-Soviet Space? EU Policies and Approaches to Region-Building* (Ashgate Publishing 2013).

A. The impact of EU-specific conditions

I identify two main EU-specific factors that may have an impact on democratic reform progress in the post-Soviet region: the presence of a comprehensive international agreement including 'hard' conditionality, and EU financial assistance for a third country.

On the presence of a comprehensive international agreement, many scholars of international law and politics argue that international agreements positively impact on domestic policy change and democratic reforms.[29] The EU has concluded different types of cooperation agreements with the states in the post-Soviet region, ranging from basic Partnership and Cooperation Agreements (PCAs) to sophisticated and very comprehensive Association Agreements (AAs) including provisions on a Deep and Comprehensive Free Trade Area (DCFTA). These agreements vary in their emphasis on democracy and human rights, as well as on the conditionality they attach to the implementation of, and adherence to, these norms and standards. It can be assumed that:

H1a: The presence of a comprehensive international agreement containing 'hard' conditionality, linking benefits from the agreement to fulfilment of democracy and human rights-related obligations, positively impacts on democratic reform progress.

On EU financial assistance, the literature often identifies international aid and EU assistance in particular as an important determinant of reform progress in third countries.[30] Although the EU does not offer any of the thirteen countries in the post-Soviet region the perspective of membership (often viewed as the most potent reward for domestic reform),[31] it allocates a significant amount of financial assistance to third countries, including for democratic reforms, support for civil society, independent media, and human rights protection. It can be assumed that the higher the amount of EU financial assistance for a third country, the more likely it is to have a positive impact on democratic reform progress (H1b).

H1b: EU financial assistance to a third country positively impacts on democratic reform progress.

[29] Ellen L Lutz and Kathryn Sikkink, 'International Human Rights Law and Practice in Latin America' (2000) 54(3) International Organization 633–59; Kristen B Rosati, 'International Human Rights Treaties *Can* Make a Difference: US Implementation of Article 3 of the United Nations Convention against Torture' (2001) 28 Human Rights 14; Oona A Hathaway, 'Do Human Rights Treaties Make a Difference?' (2002) 111(8) Yale Law Journal 1935–2042.

[30] Joseph Wright, 'How Foreign Aid Can Foster Democratization in Authoritarian Regimes' (2009) 53(3) American Journal of Political Science 552–71; Jac C Heckelman, 'Aid and Democratization in the Transition Economies' (2010) 63(4) Kyklos 558–79.

[31] See also the chapters by Milenkovic and Müftüler-Baç, in this volume.

B. The impact of domestic factors

I identify two major domestic properties as the most relevant for democratic reform progress: prehistory of democratization and level of social capital.

On the prehistory of democratization, path-dependent explanations of democratization gained considerable traction in the 1990s, and are used in studies on 'deviant' cases of democratization (eg Mongolia) in the post-Soviet region.[32] Path dependency suggests a relationship between past levels of democratization of a country and democratic reform progress. This relationship appears to be of particular relevance to countries in the post-Soviet space, of which some emerged from the 'fourth wave' of democratization in the late 1990s displaying a higher quality of democracy than others. It can be assumed that a country's quality of democracy in the late 1990s (when democracy/autocracy levels started to fluctuate less significantly and frequently) had an impact on reform progress in the years thereafter. On this basis, the following hypotheses can be formulated:
H2a: A high level in the quality of democracy of a country positively impacts on democratic reform progress in the following years.

On the level of autonomous social capital, although governments are the principal decision-makers in reform processes, the role of social capital—defined as social networks and norms of reciprocity and trustworthiness that arise from them[33]—is widely considered an important factor in democratization processes.[34] Research on the countries in the post-Soviet region has shown that an active network of civic associations and voluntary organizations plays a vital role in putting pressure on governments to implement democratic reforms.[35] Civil society also acts as an effective watchdog overseeing and monitoring democratic reform progress.[36] A high level of trust among citizens, and favourable historical legacies, are also thought to facilitate democratization.[37] It can be assumed that:
H2b: A high level of social trust and autonomous social capital positively impacts on democratic reform progress.

[32] Renske Doorenspleet and Petr Kopecký, 'Against the Odds: Deviant Cases of Democratization' (2008) 15(4) Democratization 697–713.

[33] Robert D Putnam, *Bowling Alone: The Collapse and Revival of American Community* (Simon and Schuster 2000).

[34] Larry Diamond, *Developing Democracy: Toward Consolidation* (JHU Press 1999); Mark R Beissinger, 'Structure and Example in Modular Political Phenomena: The Diffusion of Bulldozer/Rose/Orange/Tulip Revolutions' (2007) 5(2) Perspectives on Politics 259–76; Robert M Fishman, 'How Civil Society Matters in Democratization: Setting the Boundaries of Post-transition Political Inclusion' (2017) 49(3) Comparative Politics 391–409.

[35] Gabriel Badescu, 'Social Trust and Democratization in the Post-communist Societies' in *Social Capital and the Transition to Democracy* (2003) 120–39.

[36] Susann Worschech, 'New Civic Activism in Ukraine: Building Society from Scratch?' (2017) 3 Kyiv-Mohyla Law and Politics Journal 23–45.

[37] Frank Schimmelfennig and Hanno Scholtz, 'Legacies and Leverage: EU Political Conditionality and Democracy Promotion in Historical Perspective' (2010) 62(3) Europe-Asia Studies 443–60.

C. International external actors

Recent scholarly works have demonstrated the role of non-democratic international actors, such as Russia or China, as factors contributing to democratic backsliding in third countries.[38] Countries can experience different levels of linkages with, or dependencies on, such an external actor, including trade and energy dependence or the presence of an intra- or interstate conflict with the external autocracy promoter. It can be assumed that the higher the level of linkage to an external autocracy promoter, the greater the latter's influence over a government's course of action (H3).
H3: A high level of dependence on an external autocracy promoter negatively impacts on democratic reform progress.

It should, however, be noted that geopolitical balancing can also propel autocratic governments to implement (modest) democratic reforms. The recent developments in Belarus show that increased intrusion into domestic affairs by Russia led Lukashenka to allow more space for independent civil society promoting Belarusian national identity and language.[39]

V. Operationalization and Methods

This chapter applies (fsQCA) to study how different conditions interact and lead to democratic reform progress across the countries in the post-Soviet area. FsQCA is a case-based comparative approach.[40] Qualitative comparative analysis (QCA) is based on two assumptions about causality which make the method especially suited to studying democratic reform progress. First, it helps to analyze which particular explanations (paths or recipes) may equally result in democratic reform progress (equifinality). Second, it holds that the selected conditions only have an effect in combination with other conditions (conjunctural causation). As the aim of the chapter is to analyze the interplay of certain conditions (causal receipt) in order to provide a systematic analysis which provides insights into causal explanations, QCA fits this purpose very well. Moreover, given our limited sample size (n = 13), statistics cannot provide the consistency and strength to deliver robust results.

[38] Ambrosio (n 27); Tolstrup, 'Studying a Negative External Actor' (n 27), *Russia vs. the EU* (n 27); 'Black Knights and Elections' (n 27).

[39] Mikkel Sejersen, 'Democratic Sanctions Meet Black Knight Support: Revisiting the Belarusian Case' (2019) 26(3) Democratization 502–20.

[40] Charles C Ragin, *Fuzzy-set Social Science* (University of Chicago Press 2000); Charles C Ragin, 'Measurement versus Calibration: A Set-theoretic Approach' in David Collier, Henry Brady, and Janet Box-Steffensmeier (eds) *The Oxford Handbook of Political Methodology* (OUP 2008).

In fsQCA, explanations are expressed in terms of necessity and sufficiency. A condition is necessary if democratic reform progress cannot be achieved without it. However, a necessary condition is not always sufficient on its own. A condition, or a combination of conditions, is sufficient only if they result in the outcome, ie democratic reform progress.[41] Two parameters need to be considered when judging whether the (combination of) condition(s) leads to the outcome: coverage and consistency. Coverage is the percentage of the outcome that is covered by the causal recipe, while consistency is the proportion of the sum of the membership scores which the cases have in the particular outcome.[42]

A. Calibration of conditions and outcome

FsQCA is a qualitative method, which helps to describe both the conditions and the outcome as 'sets', ie clusters with a very specific characteristic. Based on the features of a particular case, the researcher assigns to the case a specific membership score in this set. The most basic type of QCA is crisp-set QCA, in which the researcher has to translate all the conditions and the outcome in binary terms (0 and 1). I use a more fine-grained scale, ie four-value fuzzy sets. This provides a more nuanced assessment compared with crisp-set QCA, and helps the cases and causal explanations to be more thoroughly understood. Each condition was assigned scores ranging from 1 to 0, which indicate:

- 1 = if a case is a full member of a set, a high degree of a particular condition.
- .67 = if a case is more in than out of a set, a moderate degree of a particular condition.
- .33 = if a case is more out than in the set, partial (but not full) absence of a particular condition.
- 0 = fully out of the set, absence of a particular condition.

1. Democratic reform progress

Bertelsmann Stiftung's Transformation Index (the BTI) provides scales for countries showing significant improvement in respect to democratic reform (≥ 0.70), improvement (≥ 0.25), and little positive change (< 0.25). Figure 14.2 shows that net democracy scores have declined in six of the thirteen countries (baseline 2006). Accordingly, these countries are considered fully out of the set of countries

[41] Ragin, *Fuzzy-set Social Science* (n 40); Carsten Q Schneider and Claudius Wagemann, 'Standards of Good Practice in Qualitative Comparative Analysis (QCA) and Fuzzy-sets' (2010) 9(3) Comparative Sociology 397–418.

[42] Schneider and Wagemann, 'Standards of Good Practice' (n 41); Carsten Q Schneider and Claudius Wagemann, *Set-theoretic Methods for the Social Sciences: A Guide to Qualitative Comparative Analysis* (CUP 2012).

demonstrating reform progress (categorization 0.0). Of the seven countries which display democratic reform progress, the Kyrgyz Republic, Moldova, and Georgia significantly improved their democracy ratings (≥ 0.70) and have, therefore, been assigned the score of 1.0 (full members of the set). Belarus, Mongolia, and Turkmenistan show improvements (≥ 0.25) and have thus been assigned the score of 0.67. All other countries with unchanged or declining scores are placed outside the set of countries showing reform progress.

2. EU-specific conditions

The level of conditionality is operationalized on the basis of the type of international agreement concluded between the EU and the partner country and the level of EU financial assistance to that country. The presence of an AA including the DCFTA implies a high level of conditionality, and has, therefore, been assigned the score of 1. Comprehensive or Enhanced Partnership Agreements include conditionality clauses but lack the high level of conditionality associated with the DCFTAs (score 0.67). PCAs contain very limited conditionality, and are, therefore, rather more out than in the set (score 0.33), just as countries which have no agreement with the EU (including 'frozen' agreements) are completely out of the set (score 0). The negotiations of the AAs/DCFTAs only started in 2009.

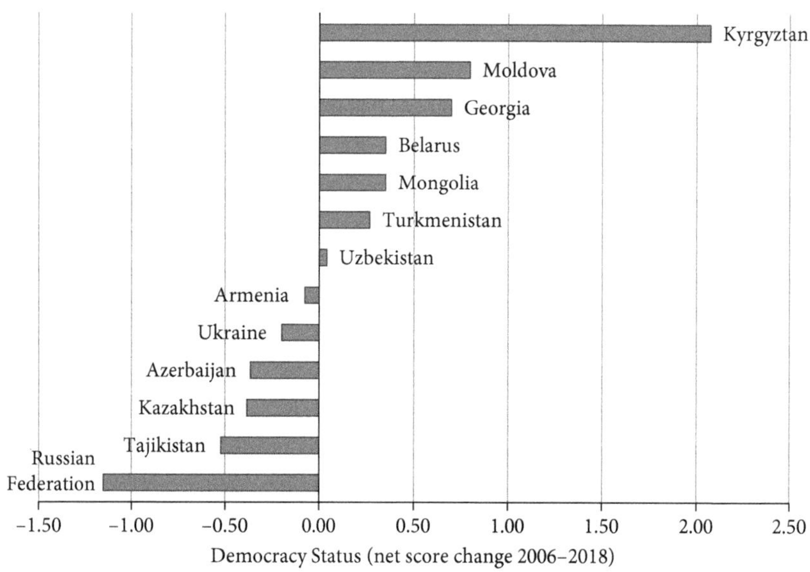

Figure 14.2 Democracy status post-Soviet States 2006–2018: net reform progress
Source: Own compilation. Data from BTI (2019).

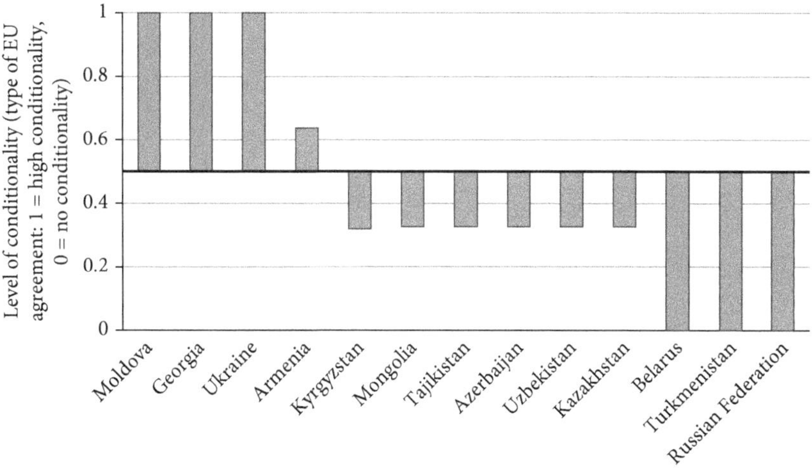

Figure 14.3 Level of EU conditionality
Source: Own compilation.

However, as the EU formally linked the opening of negotiations to democratic reform progress,[43] it can be assumed that conditionality already had effects in the preceding years. Moreover, the conclusion of such an agreement is expected to raise the democracy scores of a country in the following years, thus showing a clear impact on levels of net reform progress overall. Of the thirteen cases analyzed, four (Moldova, Georgia, Ukraine, Armenia) are more in than out of the set 'EU conditionality', ie they have a fuzzy-set membership score higher than 0.5 (Figure 14.3).

Data on EU financial assistance is taken from the European Commission 'EU Aid Explorer' database, which includes financial assistance from the European Commission as well as aid disbursed by EU Member States. Ukraine received the highest amount of financial assistance between 2007 and 2018 (€5.2 billion) while Russia received the least assistance (€2.8 million). Countries which received aid of more than 1 billion euros receive a score of 1, and countries with allocations above 0.5 billion euros receive a score of 0.67 (in the set). Countries receiving under €0.5 billion are considered rather more out than in the set (score 0.33). Figure 14.4 shows that nine countries are more in than out of the set 'high level of EU financial assistance'.

[43] Valeriy Kucheruk, 'Ukraine before the Vilnius Summit: Time to Summarize' (*Euractiv*, 21 November 2013), available at https://www.euractiv.com/section/enlargement-neighbourhood/opinion/ukraine-before-the-vilnius-summit-time-to-summarize, accessed 1 July 2022.

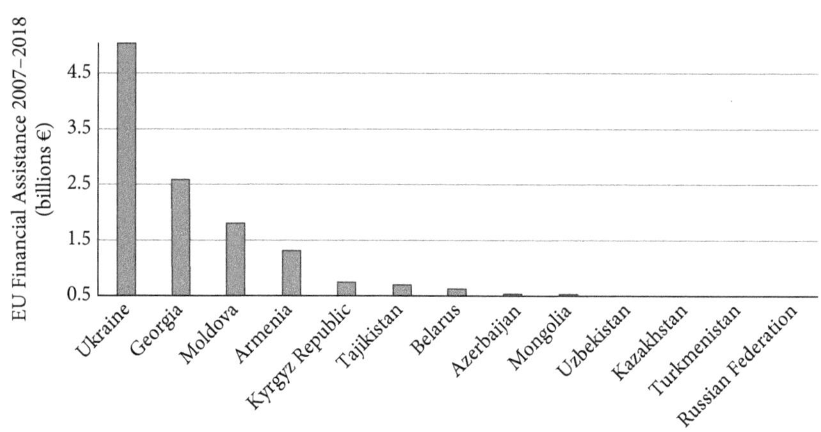

Figure 14.4 Level of EU financial assistance
Source: Own compilation. Data from EU Aid Explorer (2019).

3. Domestic conditions

The calibration for the condition 'prehistory of democratization' is based on the Polity IV dataset.[44] The Polity IV project assigns scores ranging from -10 (fully institutionalized autocracies) to 10 (fully institutionalized democracies). The number of years that a country was ranked a democracy (a score of 6 or above) provides a suitable indicator of its democratic legacy. The time range is from 1992—the first year after the end of the Cold War with complete scores for all countries in the post-Soviet area—until 2005. Countries with over ten years' democratic experience are considered full members of the set (score 1), while countries with less than two years of democratic history are not included in the set. Seven of the thirteen cases are more in than out of the set 'democratic legacy' (Figure 14.5).

Autonomous social capital is measured based on data on political and social integration from 2006–18, from the BTI. Based on expert and public opinion surveys, the index ranks countries according to the extent of: (i) a sense of solidarity and trust among citizens; and (ii) voluntary, autonomous self-organized groups, associations, and organizations.[45] The BTI's definition of social capital goes beyond conventional notions of social capital by capturing the role of 'cultural patterns of interaction'.[46] The role of culture and historical experience is particularly relevant in the context of the post-Soviet space, where 'communist legacies' or

[44] Monty G Marshall, Ted Robert Gurr, and Keith Jaggers, 'Polity IV Project: Political Regime Characteristics and Transitions, 1800–2015', Center for Systemic Peace, 2016, 13.

[45] Bertelsmann Stiftung's Transformation Index (BTI) (2019)24, available at https://bti-project.org/en/methodology, accessed 1 July 2022.

[46] ibid.

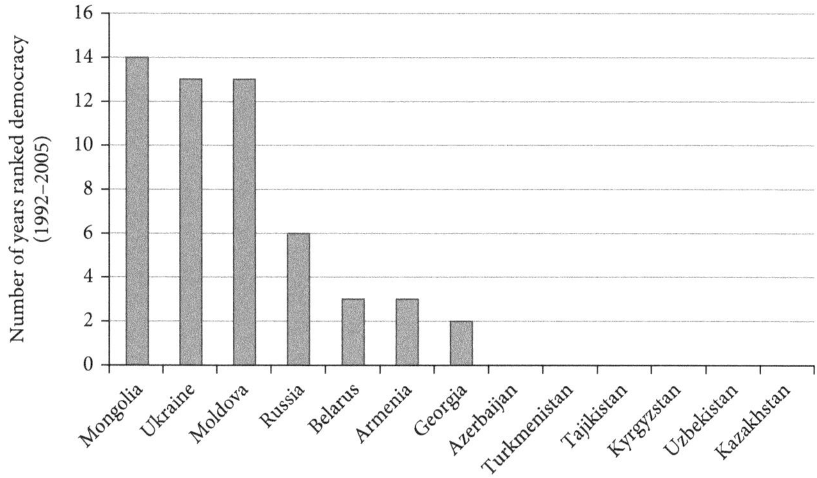

Figure 14.5 Democratic legacy
Source: Own compilation. Data from Polity IV.

'Soviet civic legacies' continue to influence civil society.[47] According to the BTI, countries with a social capital score above 0.25 show improvement (score 1.0). Countries showing limited improvement (below 0.1) or declining scores are, therefore, considered rather more out than in the set 'autonomous social capital'. Of the thirteen cases analyzed, seven can be considered more in than out of the set 'social capital' (Figure 14.6).

4. International external actors

The level of dependence on an external autocracy promoter (here, Russian) encompasses trade, energy, and security dependence. The variable is, therefore, composed of three dimensions. Scores in each dimension range from no dependence (0) to high dependence (1). Trade dependence is operationalized in terms of a country's average annual imports from, and exports to, Russia between 2006 and 2018. Energy dependence is measured based on the external autocracy's average annual share of a country's imports in energy recourses (minerals) between 2006 and 2018. Security dependence is operationalized in terms of: (i) a country's involvement in an interstate conflict in which the external autocracy promoter offers security guarantees; (ii) the presence of a (frozen) conflict in a country involving the autocracy promoter (directly or indirectly); and (iii) the presence of a military base of or joint training/military exercises with the external autocracy promoter in the country. If a country scores a high level of dependence in two, or all

[47] Mark Beissinger and Stephen Kotkin (eds), *Historical Legacies of Communism in Russia and Eastern Europe* (CUP 2014).

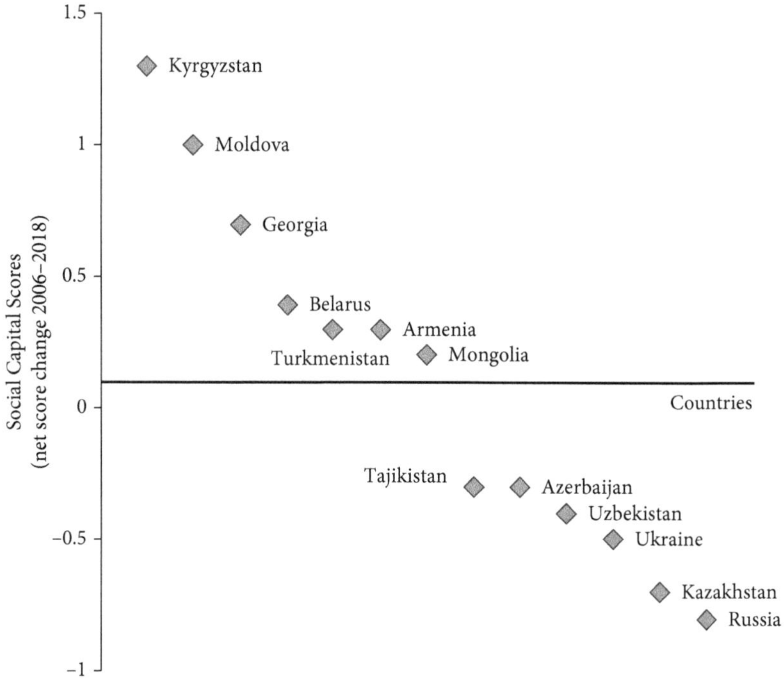

Figure 14.6 Level of autonomous social capital: net score change 2006–2018

Source: Own compilation. Data from BTI (2019).

Notes: The bold horizontal line marks the 0.5 anchor point, i.e. the threshold differentiating between states that our in the set and those that are not.

three, dimensions of dependence, it is considered rather more in than out of the set 'countries dependent on the Russian Federation'. Figure 14.7 shows that eight of the thirteen countries show a high level of dependence and are, thus, included in the set.

For a complete summary of all raw and fsQCA scores, abbreviations, and labels, see tables 14.1, 14.2, 14.3 and 14.4..

VI. Analysis and Results

Instead of studying the net additive effect of variables, QCA studies the necessity and sufficiency of relations between configurations of sets and outcomes.[48] For a condition to be necessary for the outcome, every case that exhibits the outcome

[48] Charles C Ragin, 'Set Relations in Social Research: Evaluating their Consistency and Coverage' (2006) 14(3) Political analysis 291–310; Schneider and Wagemann, *Set-theoretic Methods* (n 42).

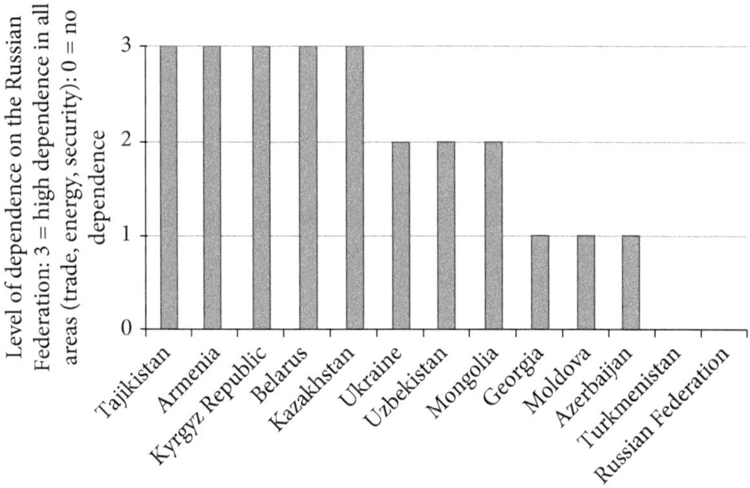

Figure 14.7 Level of dependence on external autocracy promoter
Source: Own compilation. Data from United Nations Statistical Division (2019) and World Bank (2019).

(reform) must also exhibit the particular condition. A sufficient condition is a condition or set of conditions that will produce the outcome. Sufficient conditions are analyzed on the basis of a 'truth table' which displays all logical combinations of all conditions and 'synthetises how many cases adhere to a certain pattern and if they consistently show the same outcome'.[49] If a particular pattern is found to be consistent, these rows are analyzed according to the minimization procedure: 'If two configurations differ in only one condition, but show the same outcome, this particular condition can be eliminated.'[50] The consistency cut-off was set at 0.67 for the analysis of sufficient conditions, and at 0.90 for necessary conditions. These cut-off points are considered adequate.[51]

The analysis of necessary conditions (Table 14.1) for the outcome democratic reform progress shows that social capital is a necessary condition for democratic reform progress (consistency: 0.94, coverage: 0.75). In other words, social capital, including a vibrant civil society and associational culture, is a necessary condition for a country's democratic reform progress. The high coverage indicates that the necessary condition is not trivial.[52]

[49] Ingmar Van Meerkerk, Reinout Kleinhans, and Astrid Molenveld, 'Exploring the Durability of Community Enterprises: A Qualitative Comparative Analysis' (2018) 96(4) Public Administration 658.

[50] Schneider and Wagemann, *Set-theoretic Methods* (n 42) 105.

[51] Ragin, 'Set Relations in Social Research' (n 48); Schneider and Wagemann, *Set-theoretic Methods* (n 42); Van Meerkerk, Kleinhans, and Molenveld (n 49) 658–59.

[52] Ragin, 'Measurement versus Calibration' (n 40).

Table 14.1 Necessary conditions for democratic reform progress

	Democratic Reform		~Democratic Reform	
	Consistency	Coverage	Consistency	Coverage
EU conditionality	0.56	0.53	0.43	0.59
~EU conditionality	0.56	0.41	0.65	0.68
EU financial assistance	0.81	0.54	0.61	0.58
~EU financial assistance	0.37	0.40	0.52	0.80
Democratic legacy	0.56	0.53	0.39	0.53
~Democratic legacy	0.50	0.36	0.65	0.68
Social capital	**0.94**	**0.75**	0.26	0.30
~Social capital	0.12	0.10	0.78	0.95
Dependence on AP	0.62	0.42	0.70	0.67
~Dependence on AP	0.50	0.53	0.39	0.60

Source: Own compilation.

Although the analysis shows that a country's social capital is a necessary condition, it is not, by itself, a sufficient condition. The analysis of sufficient conditions shows which combinations of conditions lead to democratic reform progress. The truth table, created using fsQCA software, clusters all possible logical combinations of conditions and links these to the outcome. Any combination of conditions that is linked to the outcome can be considered sufficient (Table 14.2).

The QCA analysis includes all of the five conditions identified in the theoretical model. Three causal configurations can be seen as sufficient conditions for democratic reform progress in the post-Soviet space. The configurations lead to the following set-theoretic model ('*' signifies a 'logical and' and '+' signifies a 'logical or'):

EUAgreement*EUAssist*Legacy*SocCapital*~DependenceAP
+
~EUAgreement*EUAssist*SocCapital*DependenceAP
+
~EUAgreement*~EUAssist*~Legacy*SocCapital*~DependenceAP
DemocProgress

Table 14.4 shows the intermediate solution, which suggests that countries show democratic reform progress along three causal paths:

Table 14.2 Truth table

	EUCond	EUAssist	Legacy	SocCapital	DependAP	Outcome	Consistency	Cases
1	1	1	1	1	0	1	1.00	Georgia, Moldova
2	0	1	1	1	1	1	0.8	Belarus, Mongolia
3	0	1	0	1	1	1	0.75	Kyrgyz Republic
4	0	0	0	1	0	1	0.67	Turkmenistan
5	1	1	1	1	1	0	0.6	Armenia
6	0	1	0	0	0	0	0.33	Azerbaijan
7	0	0	1	0	0	0	0.33	Russian Federation
8	1	1	1	0	1	0	0.33	Ukraine
9	0	1	0	0	1	0	0.2	Tajikistan
10	0	0	0	0	1	0	0.17	Kazakhstan, Uzbekistan

Source: Own compilation.

Note: Each row presents information about one of the possible combination of conditions. '1' corresponds to the presences of the condition, and '0' denotes its absence. Rows 2, 3, and 4 were assigned the outcome '1' because they do not contain contradictory cases.

Table 14.3 Sufficient conditions for democratic reform progress (outcome)

Solution	Classical	EU-stimulated social capital	Social capital
Cases with membership >0.5	Georgia, Moldova	Belarus,Kyrgyz Republic, Mongolia	Turkmenistan
Consistency	1.00	0.86	0.67
Coverage (raw)	0.31	0.37	0.13
Coverage (unique)	0.25	0.32	0.13
Consistency cut-off		0.67	
Solution consistency		0.86	
Solution coverage		0.75	

Source: Own compilation.

(1) '*Classical path*': EU conditionality applies and EU assistance is available, the country has experienced democratic government during the past two decades, shows improvements with regard to social capital, and dependence on an external autocracy promoter is limited;
(2) '*EU-stimulated social capital path*': EU assistance is offered in the absence of an agreement or 'hard' conditionality, and the country shows improvements with regard to social capital, while displaying a high level of dependence on an external autocracy promoter;
(3) '*Social capital path*': EU-specific factors are absent; there is no previous experience of democracy. Dependence on an external autocracy promoter is limited, while the strength of social capital has improved.

The overall consistency of the model is high (0.86), which implies that few cases contradict the 'subset relational statement of sufficiency'. The overall coverage (0.75) is equally high, demonstrating that a substantial share of the outcome is covered by the respective conditions.

The first configuration, the 'classical path', confirms the expectation that only a combination of EU conditionality and assistance, and an enabling domestic context, as well as limited dependence on an external autocracy promoter, lead to democratic reform progress. More specifically, the first configuration confirms scholarly works which emphasize the interplay between actors at the domestic level and at the external level as essential factors in democratization processes.[53]

[53] Elena Baracani, *Democratization and Hybrid Regimes: International Anchoring and Domestic Dynamics in Post-Soviet States* (European Press Academic Publishing 2010).

An interesting aspect of the first configuration is that EU involvement (conditionality and financial assistance) is found to be a sufficient but not a necessary condition for democratic reform progress. The finding confirms the conclusions of several small-N studies stressing the importance of domestic drivers of democratic reform progress in the post-Soviet space.[54] At the same time, the findings show that the conventional tools of EU democracy promotion clearly played a role in reform progress in countries like Georgia and Moldova between 2006 and 2018, which partly contradicts claims that the EU has 'lost traction' because it 'failed to keep up with larger political and strategic changes within and beyond Europe'.[55] The role of social capital as a necessary condition in the 'classical path' to democratic reform progress marks another crucial finding. Most authors studying the democratization of post-Soviet countries conclude that society at large, and civil society organizations in particular, are only marginal actors in reform progress.[56] It is often argued that civil society is disconnected from society or dependent on external support, and is, therefore, unable to define domestic political dynamics.[57] The first configuration shows that the combination of EU assistance and autonomous social capital, among other factors, leads to democratic reform progress. This suggests that civil society is certainly not a marginal actor, despite (or indeed because) of sustained EU financial support.

The second and third configurations—the EU-stimulated social capital path and the social capital path—also present a number of interesting findings, especially for understanding democratic reform progress or changes in political climate in countries over which the EU has limited influence. Much of the existing literature focuses on explaining the resilience of autocratic regimes such as Belarus or Turkmenistan.[58] Less is known about the conditions which prompt such regimes to introduce (limited) reforms. The second and third configurations suggest that social capital plays a critical role in such reform processes if supported by EU assistance (path 2), but also in the absence of EU support (path 3). The findings point to the important role of civil society as a whole, or business associations more specifically, demanding a (limited) liberalization of the political or economic system. The findings thus draw attention to (limited) improvements of the political climate made by autocratic governments in response to societal demands, albeit

[54] Wolczuk, 'Conflict and Reform in Eastern Europe' (n 17).

[55] Ken Godfrey and Richard Youngs, *Toward a New EU Democracy Strategy* (Carnegie Endowment for International Peace 2019) 1; Alexei Pikulik and Sofie Bedford, 'Aid Paradox: Strengthening Belarusian Non-democracy through Democracy Promotion' (2019) 33(2) East European Politics and Societies 378–99.

[56] Jonathan Wheatley and Elena Baracani, *Georgia's Democratic Veneer: Scraping the Surface* (European Press Academic Publishing 2010).

[57] Di Quirico (n 57) 103–05.

[58] Martin K Dimitrov (ed), *Why Communism Did Not Collapse: Understanding Authoritarian Regime Resilience in Asia and Europe* (CUP 2013); Vitali Silitski, 'Preempting Democracy: The Case of Belarus' (2005) 16(4) Journal of Democracy 83–97; Edward Schatz, 'The Soft Authoritarian Tool Kit: Agenda-setting Power in Kazakhstan and Kyrgyzstan' (2009) 41(2) Comparative Politics 203–22.

often with the intention of securing domestic legitimacy rather than being genuine reform efforts.[59]

Scholarly works on the post-Soviet region also tend to assume that external autocracy promoters, such as Russia, have negative impacts on democratic reform progress in target countries.[60] While the first and third paths to democratic reform progress support this assumption, the second path suggests the opposite: a high level of dependence on an external autocracy promoter forms part of the set of conditions leading to democratic reform progress. Although rarely captured in theoretical works on democratization in the post-Soviet region, Russian pressure on countries in the region frequently has 'reverse' effects, providing incentives for, rather than curtailing, reform efforts.[61] Over the past decade, Belarus, Mongolia, and also the Kyrgyz Republic, have been confronted with increasing pressure from Russia, as the latter attempted to increase its influence vis-à-vis the EU and China. In response, all three countries implemented further reforms, inter alia with the intention of reducing Russian influence by improving economic and political relations with other major, predominantly Western, powers, including the EU (Belarus, Kyrgyzstan) or Japan (Mongolia).

A second QCA analysis was conducted to identify the causal configurations that can be seen as sufficient conditions for the absence of democratic reform progress in the post-Soviet space (for the truth table, see table 14.2.). The configurations lead to the following set-theoretic model:

~EUAgreement*EUAssist*~Legacy*~SocCapital
+
~EUAgreement*~Legacy*~SocCapital*DependenceAP+
~EUAgreement*~EUAssist*Legacy*~SocCapital*~DependenceAP
~DemocProgress

Table 14.4 shows the intermediate solution, which suggests that countries show democratic backsliding along three causal paths:

[59] Peter Burnell, 'Autocratic Opening to Democracy: Why Legitimacy Matters' (2006) 27(4) Third World Quarterly 545–62; Christian von Soest and Julia Grauvogel, 'Identity, Procedures and Performance: How Authoritarian Regimes Legitimize their Rule' (2017) 23(3) Contemporary Politics 287–305; Alexander Dukalskis and Johannes Gerschewski, 'What Autocracies Say (and What Citizens Hear): Proposing Four Mechanisms of Autocratic Legitimation' (2017) 23(3) Contemporary Politics 251–68; Abel Polese, Donnacha Ó Beacháin, and Slavomír Horák, 'Strategies of Legitimation in Central Asia: Regime Durability in Turkmenistan' (2017) 23(4) Contemporary Politics 427–45.

[60] Tolstrup, 'Studying a Negative External Actor' (n 27); Ambrosio (n 27); Peter Burnell and Oliver Schlumberger, 'Promoting Democracy—Promoting Autocracy? International Politics and National Political Regimes' (2010) 16(1) Contemporary Politics 1–15; Rachel Vanderhill, *Promoting Authoritarianism Abroad* (Lynne Rienner Publishers 2013); Oisín Tansey, 'The Problem with Autocracy Promotion' (2016) 23(1) Democratization 141–63.

[61] Delcour and Wolczuk (n 20); Amy Hiscox, 'Modern Mongolia: Geopolitics amid Great Powers' (2018) 13(1) Culture Mandala 1–15; Giselle Bosse, 'Ten Years of the Eastern Partnership: What Role for the EU as a Promoter of Democracy?' (2019) 18(2) European View 220–32.

(3) *'Reverse effect of EU Assistance'*: EU assistance is provided, but an EU agreement and EU conditionality do not apply, the country has no past experience with democratic rule, and social capital is declining.

(2) *'Classical path to democratic backsliding'*: An EU agreement is absent, as are domestic factors conducive to democratic reform progress, while dependence on an autocracy promoter is high.

(3) *'Absence of EU-stimulated social capital'*: The country has experienced democratic rule and is not dependent on an external autocracy promoter. Yet, a linkage with the EU is absent, and levels of social trust and capital are declining.

The overall consistency of the model is high (1.00), which implies that few cases contradict the 'subset relational statement of sufficiency'. The overall coverage (0.48) is moderate, but still demonstrates that almost half of the outcome (absence of reform progress) is covered by the respective conditions.

The first configuration presents an interesting finding about the role and impact of EU financial assistance. The findings show that EU assistance contributes to democratic backsliding in autocratic countries with which the EU has limited contractual relations, and specifically countries which have no previous experience of democratic rule, and where social trust and autonomous social capital are in

Table 14.4 Intermediate solution: sufficient conditions for the outcome absence of democratic reform progress

Solution	**Reverse effect EU assistance**	**Classical path to democratic backsliding**	**Absence of EU-stimulated social capital**
Cases with membership >0.5	Azerbaijan, Tajikistan	Kazakhstan, Tajikistan, Uzbekistan	Russian Federation
Consistency	1.00	1.00	1.00
Coverage (raw)	0.26	0.31	0.13
Coverage (unique)	0.04	0.09	0.13
Consistency cut-off		1.00	
Solution consistency		1.00	
Solution coverage		0.48	

Source: Own compilation.

decline. The finding partly corresponds to a study by Shyrokykh[62] on the negative 'side effects' of EU human rights assistance on hybrid regimes in the post-Soviet space. However, the results of the QCA analysis provide a more nuanced picture, suggesting that the effects of EU assistance vary depending on the combination of other factors, such as social capital or dependence on an external actor.

The second configuration, the 'classical path' to democratic backsliding, confirms the expectation that the absence of a linkage with the EU, combined with a lack of experience with democratic rule and declining levels of social capital, and a high dependence on an external autocracy promoter, is likely to lead to democratic backsliding. The findings correspond to the conclusions of small-N studies examining democratic backsliding in Kazakhstan,[63] authoritarian persistence in Uzbekistan,[64] and the consolidation of autocracy in Tajikistan,[65] during the past decade.

The third configuration—the absence of EU-stimulated social capital—broadly affirms the findings of the first QCA analysis. While EU assistance coupled with increasing levels of social capital (among other factors) leads to democratic reform progress, the absence of both conditions is likely to contribute to democratic backsliding. However, it is worth noting that the third path applies specifically to the case of Russia, which, unlike the other countries in the post-Soviet space, is a major regional power. In the words of Shevtsova, 'there has never in history been a task akin to the democratization of a nuclear superpower with imperialist ambitions'.[66] The findings in the third path should thus be considered in the context of qualitative studies on democratic reform and backsliding in Russia.[67]

VII. Conclusion

The central research question of this chapter addressed the conditions under which countries in the post-Soviet area showed democratic reform progress or democratic backsliding between 2006 and 2018, with a particular focus on the role of the EU and external differentiation among countries without EU membership prospects. Five variables were included in the theoretical model of the chapter: (i)

62 Karina Shyrokykh, 'Effects and Side Effects of European Union Assistance on the Former Soviet Republics' (2017) 24(4) Democratization 651–69.

63 Tika Tsertsvadze and Vera Axyonova, *Trading Values with Kazakhstan* (Universitäts-und Landesbibliothek Sachsen-Anhalt 2013).

64 Mariya Y Omelicheva, 'Authoritarian Legitimation: Assessing Discourses of Legitimacy in Kazakhstan and Uzbekistan' (2016) 35(4) Central Asian Survey 481–500.

65 Andrea Schmitz,*Tajikistan on the Road to Totalitarianism*, No. 10/2019, SWP Comment (2019), available at https://www.swp-berlin.org/10.18449/2019C10, accessed 1 July 2022.

66 Lilia Shevtsova, 'Twenty Years of Postcommunism: What's the Matter with Russia?' (2010) 21(1) Journal of Democracy 152–59.

67 Viatcheslav Morozov (ed), *Decentring the West: The Idea of Democracy and the Struggle for Hegemony* (Routledge 2016).

the level of EU conditionality and (ii) EU financial assistance (EU-specific factors), (iii) democratic legacy and (iv) level of autonomous social capital (domestic factors), and (v) dependence on an external autocracy promoter (external factors).

By applying fsQCA methodology, the analysis identified three causal paths that are sufficient for the outcome 'democratic reform progress'. First, the 'classic path', based on countries' simultaneous membership in the sets '*EU conditionality*', '*democratic legacy*', '*social capital*', and '*no dependence on an external autocracy promoter*'. Second, the 'EU-stimulated social capital path', based on simultaneous membership in the sets '*no EU conditionality*', '*EU assistance*', '*social capital*', and '*dependence on external autocracy promoter*'. And, third, the 'social capital path', based on countries' simultaneous membership in the sets '*no EU conditionality*', '*no EU assistance*', '*no democratic legacy*', '*social capital*', and '*no dependence on an external autocracy promoter*'. Improving levels of social capital, defined in terms of social trust among citizens, cultural and historical legacies, and self-organization in autonomous associations, was found to be a necessary condition.

The analysis also identified three causal paths that are sufficient for the outcome 'democratic backsliding', which show that countries in the set 'democratic backsliding' tend to have simultaneous membership in the sets '*no EU conditionality*', '*no democratic legacy*', '*no social capital*', and '*dependence on an external autocracy promoter*'.

The majority of causal paths confirm the expectation that democratic reform progress in the post-Soviet space between 2006 and 2018 has been the result of a mix of EU conditionality/assistance, favourable domestic factors, and limited dependence on an external autocracy promoter (ie. Russia). At the same time, the analysis resulted in a number of new and partly unexpected findings.

First, the analysis demonstrated that there has not been one, but several, paths to democratic reform progress in countries in the post-Soviet area between 2006 and 2018. The EU, through external differentiation, is neither a necessary nor a sufficient condition for democratic reform progress in and of itself. Rather, EU conditionality and assistance are only sufficient conditions for reform progress in combination with other domestic and external factors. In some instances, for example with regard to democratic reforms in the Kyrgyz Republic and Mongolia, or limited improvements in the political climate in Belarus and Turkmenistan, the absence of an EU agreement was found to be part of the causal path leading to positive change. Also noteworthy is the finding that, in the context of some autocratic countries (Azerbaijan, Tajikistan), EU assistance proved to be an important factor in autocratic consolidation.

Second, all countries in the set 'democratic reform progress' also had simultaneous membership in the set '*social capital*'. This study operationalized social capital in terms of net scores for improvement/decline between 2006 and 2018, thus not in terms of high or low levels of social capital. The results confirm findings of several small-N case studies showing that civil society, especially in the EaP countries, has started to play a decisive role in reform processes during the past decade, encouraged by EU financial assistance.[68] The finding on the positive role of social capital in autocratic countries is, however, controversial. Some authors argue that social trust tends to generate popular support for authoritarian regimes and that 'compliant activism' strengthens authoritarian rule.[69]

Third, the study showed that dependence on an external autocracy promoter such as Russia can lead to democratic reform progress, but only in combination with favourable domestic factors and EU assistance. This finding contributes new insights on the unintentional effects of autocracy promotion.[70]

Overall, this chapter has shown that the EU's role in democratic reform progress in third countries without EU membership prospects is dependent on specific constellations of domestic and external factors impacting on third countries. The level of external differentiation, such as the type of legal agreement concluded with the EU (and associated levels of conditionality), and financial assistance offered by the EU, have been critical factors in democratic reform processes in Moldova and Georgia between 2006 and 2018, both countries without EU membership prospects at the time, yet with clear EU membership aspirations. This suggests that, even though the extent of a formal legal 'opting-in' of a non-EU Member State to EU policies may be limited, a third country's aspiration for membership and sense of 'belonging to Europe' can very well impact on democratic reform progress. This chapter has also shown that, while the EU alone is not a necessary condition for reform progress, it has remained a crucial factor in democratic reform progress in the post-Soviet space, despite the trend of democratic backsliding among several of the CEE Member States. In other words, despite the emerging internal differentiation among EU Member States with regard to upholding democratic standards, the EU remained an important driver of democratic reform progress in the post-Soviet space.

[68] Natalia Shapovalova and Olga Burlyuk, 'Civil Society and Change in Ukraine Post-Euromaidan: An Introduction' in Natalia Shapovalova and Olga Burlyuk (eds) *Civil Society in Post-Euromaidan Ukraine: From Revolution to Consolidation* (Stuttgart: ibidem Verlag, 2018) 11–38.

[69] Alexander Libman and Vladimir Kozlov, 'The Legacy of Compliant Activism in Autocracies: Post-Communist Experience' (2017) 23(2) Contemporary Politics 195–213.

[70] Christian von Soest, 'Democracy Prevention: The International Collaboration of Authoritarian Regimes' (2015) 54(4) European Journal of Political Research 623–38; Thomas Risse and Nelli Babayan, 'Democracy Promotion and the Challenges of Illiberal Regional Powers: Introduction to the Special Issue' (2015) 22(3) Democratization 381–99.

15

Integration without Membership? Achievements and Limitations of Functionalist Cooperation in the EU's Eastern Neighbourhood

Laure Delcour[*]

I. Introduction

The European Neighbourhood Policy (ENP)[1] was launched in 2004 to enhance the European Union's (EU) relations with its new neighbours, in response to increased proximity and growing interdependences after the EU's enlargement. Upon its inception, it emerged as a prominent example of decoupling between the EU's 'territorial' and 'functional' enlargement.[2] On the one hand, the new policy reflected an expansion of the EU's 'legal'[3] (or 'regulatory')[4] boundary beyond its borders. This is because the EU diffuses its own rules, norms, and templates to neighbouring countries, with a view to 'strengthening stability, security and well-being'[5] across the continent. On the other hand, given the 'enlargement fatigue' that developed in the EU after the 2004 enlargement,[6] the ENP remains distinct from accession, and thereby 'precludes the opening of [the EU's] institutional boundary'.[7] This does not

[*] This chapter was written in 2021 and updated in 2023.

[1] ENP countries include Algeria, Armenia, Azerbaijan, Belarus, Egypt, Georgia, Israel, Jordan, Lebanon, Libya, Moldova, Morocco, Syria, Palestine, Tunisia, and Ukraine.

[2] Jan Zielonka, 'The EU and the European Neighbourhood Policy: The Re-making of Europe's Identity' in Tobias Schumacher, Andreas Marchetti, and Thomas Demmelhuber (eds), *The Routledge Handbook on the European Neighbourhood Policy* (Routledge 2018) 144. See also on the ENP, Bosse, in this volume.

[3] Sandra Lavenex, 'EU External Governance in Wider Europe' (2004) 11(4) Journal of European Public Policy 694.

[4] Sandra Lavenex, 'Concentric Circles of Flexible "European" Integration: A Typology of EU External Governance Relations' (2011) 9 Comparative European Politics, 373.

[5] European Commission, 'European Neighbourhood Policy—Strategy Paper' COM (2004) 373 final.

[6] Sandra Lavenex and Frank Schimmelfennig, 'Relations with the Wider Europe' (2006) 44 Journal of Common Market Studies 137.

[7] Lavenex, 'EU External Governance' (n 3).

Laure Delcour, *Integration without Membership? Achievements and Limitations of Functionalist Cooperation in the EU's Eastern Neighbourhood* In: *Redefining EU Membership*. Edited by: Diane Fromage, Oxford University Press.
 DOI: 10.1093/9780191948145.003.0015

exclude, however, a limited degree of 'organizational inclusion',[8] whether as part of EU agencies and programmes or in parallel regional frameworks.

The decoupling between functional/regulatory expansion and territorial/institutional exclusion puts the ENP in sharp contrast to enlargement policy, in which territorial and functional inclusion have always gone hand in hand.[9] In other words, whereas candidate countries adopt and apply EU regulations as part of their preparation to join the EU, such a perspective is absent in neighbouring countries' efforts to approximate their legal frameworks with the EU's *acquis*. However, the functional-territorial disconnect can be observed in other arrangements concluded between the EU and third countries, such as countries participating in the European Economic Area (EEA). Premised upon a broad extension of the internal market[10] to third countries (currently Norway,[11] Iceland, and Liechtenstein), the EEA indeed explicitly served as a source of 'future inspiration'[12] for designing a model of relations with the new neighbours of the EU in 2003–04. Admittedly, in light of the sheer differences in political and socio-economic contexts between EEA and ENP states, the EEA was not envisaged as a blueprint of immediate use for the ENP. Rather, it emerged as a reference point for the level of links that the EU ultimately wants to reach with its neighbours.[13] Therefore, given the long-term nature of the political and economic integration with the EU, the ENP in its current form does not offer either the same degree of organizational inclusion or similarly dense institutional arrangements as those developed with EEA countries.

However, the ENP differs from the EEA in another crucial respect. In sharp contrast to EEA countries that have declined EU membership (sometimes twice, as has been the case for Norway), some of the EU's eastern neighbours (eg Ukraine, Moldova, and Georgia) have expressed their aspirations to join the Union. They have done so from the outset of the ENP and repeatedly ever since, thereby questioning the relevance of the weaker model of integration proposed to them. In the academic literature, the model of relations envisaged by the EU as part of the ENP has indeed been classified as the '"outer circle" of European integration'[14] and,

8 Lavenex, 'Concentric Circles' (n 4)..

9 Zielonka (n 2).

10 The EEA does not include the common agricultural, fisheries, and transport policies, budget contributions and regional policy, or external relations. See Sieglinde Gstöhl, 'Models of External Differentiation in the EU's Neighbourhood: An Expanding Economic Community?' (2015) 22(6) Journal of European Public Policy 858.

11 On Norway, see Franklin, and Kuhn and Trondal, in this volume.

12 Gstöhl (n 10) 854.

13 Upon presenting its vision on how to strengthen the framework for relations with future neighbours, the European Commission indicated that 'the long term goal of the initiatives [presented in the communication] is to move towards an arrangement whereby the Union's relations with the neighbouring countries ultimately resemble the close political and economic links currently enjoyed with the European Economic Area': European Commission, 'Wider Europe Neighbourhood. A New Framework for Relations with our Eastern and Southern Neighbours' COM (2003) 104 final, 15.

14 Frank Schimmelfennig, 'Beyond Enlargement. Conceptualizing the Study of the European Neighbourhood Policy' in Schumacher, Marchetti, and Demmelhuber (eds) (n 2) 19.

therefore, the most distant from the status of EU Member State that some eastern partners aim to reach. According to Sandra Lavenex, the ENP is characterized by 'gradual, process-oriented harmonization' with the EU's *acquis*, and 'more indirect organizational channels' than is the case for closer circles, such as the EEA or candidate countries.[15] At the same time, scholars also agree that the EU's modes of integration with its neighbours have evolved substantially. As an illustration of this dynamic framework, scholarly accounts highlight that the ENP started with a bilateral approach in the early 2000s, then moved to 'the promotion of parallel organizational structures at the regional level',[16] and finally towards a 'hub-and-spoke approach 2.0', in the 2010s.[17] None of these approaches have, per se, shifted the neighbours to closer circles of integration with the EU, and yet the picture of EU relations with many (if not all) ENP countries has changed substantially over the past two decades.

This brief overview of the ENP in comparison to other models of integration with the EU raises key questions: how has the blurring of the 'functional boundaries'[18] between internal and external EU integration operated in practice? In the absence of a membership perspective, what kind of leverage has the EU used to induce domestic change in its neighbourhood, and how far have ENP countries come in adopting and applying EU rules? To what extent is the model of integration underpinning the neighbourhood policy sustainable? And under what conditions can it borrow from, or evolve toward other models?

Focusing on the Eastern Neighbourhood, this chapter delves into the dynamics that have underpinned the ENP since its inception, and asks how the EU's vision of its relations with its neighbours has played out over time. The chapter argues that the ENP (designed as the umbrella framework for EU–neighbours relations) has failed to develop a single model of relations with the EU. Its relevance and sustainability are undermined by the extreme differentiation in neighbours' modes and levels of integration with the EU, which results from partner countries' miscellaneous aspirations and preferences in their relations with the Union, as well as regional developments. While endorsed from the outset as a key principle of the policy, differentiation has grown substantially in recent years, and leads to increasingly contrasting intensities of integration, and in fact different models of relations with the EU.[19] Such a diversity is obvious even at the level of the Eastern Partnership (EaP), the initiative which was launched in 2009 specifically for the EU's eastern neighbours,[20] and which (alongside the Union of the Mediterranean)

15 Lavenex, 'Concentric Circles' (n 4) 397.
16 ibid.
17 Gstöhl (n 10) 864.
18 Lavenex, 'Concentric Circles' (n 8) 372.
19 Laure Delcour and Eduard Soler i Lecha, 'European Policy Mechanisms: Conditionality, Socialisation and Differentiation' in Schumacher, Marchetti, and Demmelhuber (eds) (n 2) 452–53.
20 EaP countries include Armenia, Azerbaijan, Belarus, Georgia, Moldova, and Ukraine.

constitutes one of the two regional subcomponents of the ENP. As detailed in the following sections of this chapter, two of the six EaP countries have, in fact, remained on the sidelines of the policy; by contrast, in terms of legal approximation with the EU trade *acquis*, three other countries have, in fact, come closer to the EU than some of the Western Balkans candidate countries, even before these EaP countries applied for EU membership a few days after Russia's full-scale invasion of Ukraine.[21] Therefore, major fault-lines have emerged within the ENP/EaP, while lines between the ENP/EaP and other models of integration have become increasingly blurred. The recognition of three eastern partners—Ukraine, Moldovaand Georgia—as candidate countries,[22] in particular, shatters the foundations underpinning the EU's external models of differentiation as they were framed in the 2000s.

The rest of this chapter starts with an examination of the functional logic upon which the EU's relations with neighbouring countries are premised (Section II). It offers a comparative analysis of the ENP, both space-wise (ie in relation to other models of integration) and time-wise (ie by capturing the major shifts since the early 2000s). Section III proceeds to scrutinizing partner countries' responses to the EU's offer and highlights a growing divide between countries that have not engaged with the EU's offer and countries aspiring to closer integration with the EU, namely the three EaP-associated countries (Georgia, Moldova, and Ukraine) and (potentially) Armenia. Focusing on the last group of countries, Section IVidentifies the key political challenges raised by the substantial level of harmonization with EU rules, and discusses opportunities for, and obstacles to, further organizational inclusion in EU structures. Section V summarizes the chapter's findings and reflects on the ENP/EaP as a model of external differentiation.

II. From the ENP to the Eastern Partnership and Beyond: An Intensified Diffusion of EU Rules; a (Still) Limited Organizational Inclusion

This section provides an overview of the logic underpinning the ENP since its inception. It argues that the policy, as launched in 2003–04, has been fraught with tensions between, on the one hand, the emulation of existing models of relations with third countries (EEA, enlargement) and, on the other hand, the emphasis

[21] Laurenz Gehrke, 'Georgia, Moldova Follow Ukraine in Applying to join EU' https://www.politico.eu/article/georgia-and-moldova-apply-for-eu-membership/ (*Politico*, 3 March 2022).

[22] European Council, 'Conclusions, 23 June 2022' (Press release) https://www.consilium.europa.eu/en/press/press-releases/2022/06/23/european-council-conclusions-on-ukraine-the-membership-applications-of-ukraine-the-republic-of-moldova-and-georgia-western-balkans-and-external-relations-23-june-2022/ (accessed 25 June 2022); 'Conclusions, 15 December 2023', https://www.consilium.europa.eu/media/68967/europeancouncilconclusions-14-15-12-2023-en.pdf(accessed 10 January 2024)

placed on the role of partner countries in shaping the policy. Such tensions have only increased as a result of the ENP's fuzzy offer and non-binding obligations. In this context, the EaP, launched in 2009 as a subregional component of the ENP, is an important turning point, as it denotes a shift towards 'closer legal relations, going far beyond mere approximation of laws, implying the clear-cut obligations to apply acquis'.[23]

A. The ENP: A fuzzy model of integration

As argued by Lavenex, the launch of the ENP, in 2003–04, reflects an EU 'attempt to tackle interdependencies [with eastern and southern neighbours] through the external projection of internal solutions'.[24] The EU's offer to its neighbours blatantly illustrates the blurring between internal and external EU boundaries, as highlighted in the description of the ENP by the European Commission: the ENP

> envisages enhanced preferential trade relations and increased financial and technical assistance. It also offers neighbouring countries the prospect of a stake in the EU Internal Market based on legislative and regulatory approximation, the participation in a number of EU programmes and improved interconnection and physical links with the EU.[25]

Thus, in its initial version, the ENP drew inspiration from both the EEA model and enlargement policy. On the one hand, the extension of the internal market (premised on the projection of EU rules and templates) was modelled after the EU's offer to the European Free Trade Association (EFTA) countries in the late 1980s, which was designed to mitigate their fears of disadvantages after the completion of the internal market, and which later developed into the EEA.[26] In the case of neighbouring countries, the extension of the internal market was regarded as a major objective, both to offset the negative externalities stemming from the 2004 enlargement (for instance, the disruption of trade and mobility flows between the EU's new Member States and their neighbours) and to 'prevent the emergence of new dividing lines' in Europe,[27] ie between a wealthy enlarged EU and a poorer neighbourhood.

[23] Adam Łazowski, 'Enhanced Multilateralism and Enhanced Bilateralism: Integration without Membership in the European Union' (2008) 45 Common Market Law Review 1436.
[24] Lavenex, 'EU External Governance' (n 3) 695.
[25] European Commission, 'European Neighbourhood Policy' (n 5) 14.
[26] Gstöhl (n 10) 854.
[27] ibid 3.

On the other hand, the ENP—while clearly distinct from accession—directly 'borrowed from the enlargement template'.[28] This is because the EU then regarded enlargement as its 'most successful foreign policy'.[29] Therefore, the key principles upon which the ENP was premised drew upon the enlargement experience. Compared with the previous framework of EU relations with post-Soviet countries, the ENP introduced a broader and more systematic use of conditionality, with the 'prospect of a stake in the internal market'[30] being subjected to effective commitment to 'shared values' and the implementation of domestic reforms.[31] Likewise, the ENP provided new opportunities for interaction in EU–neighbours relations, thereby enhancing the use of socialization as a mechanism complementing conditionality. The major instruments introduced for neighbouring countries were also modelled after the enlargement toolbox.[32] This was the case for the ENP action plans, the key documents negotiated between the EU and each neighbouring country that include a list of priority areas for domestic reforms. In their draft versions, these documents even accidentally referred to the Copenhagen criteria used for candidate countries, thereby reflecting a degree of 'mechanical borrowing' from the accession process.[33] Transfer from the enlargement toolbox was also visible in the introduction of external monitoring (in the form of ENP progress reports, published regularly by the European Commission) and benchmarking, on the basis of which progress in domestic reforms was to be assessed and conditionality was to be applied. Last but not least, the EU extended to the neighbourhood the assistance instruments designed in the 1990s to support domestic transformations in the candidate countries, eg the Twinning and Technical Assistance and Information Exchange instrument (TAIEX).[34]

However, from the outset the ENP's toolbox exhibited important differences from other models of external integration. The rewards offered ('a stake in the internal market') lacked both substance and precision, as the EU neither specified the form and scope of these rewards in the initial ENP documents nor offered

[28] Amichai Magen, 'The Shadow of Enlargement: Can the European Neighbourhood Policy Achieve Compliance?' (2006) 12 Columbia Journal of European Law 405.

[29] European Commission, 'Wider Europe Neighbourhood' (n 13).

[30] ibid.

[31] ibid.

[32] Judith Kelley, 'New Wine in Old Wineskins: Promoting Political Reforms through the New European Neighbourhood Policy' (2006) 44(1) Journal of Common Market Studies 32.

[33] ibid.

[34] TAIEX provides short-term technical assistance through expert missions, workshops, or seminars focused on the approximation of legislation, while twinning provides long-term institutional assistance to public bodies by seconding civil servants and experts from EU Member States. See Elsa Tulmets, 'Is a Soft Method of Coordination Best Adapted to the Context of EU's Neighbourhood?' in Marise Cremona and Gabriella Meloni (eds), *The European Neighbourhood Policy: A Framework for Modernisation?* (2007) EUI Working Papers Law 2007/21, 106; Elsa Tulmets, 'Institution-Building Instruments in the Eastern Partnership: Still Drawing on Enlargement?', Eastern Partnership Review No. 6 (December 2011).

any tangible incentive in the short term (with the exception of increased assistance).[35] Importantly, the EU left the scope of the future 'European Neighbourhood Agreements'[36] open for further specification. Therefore, regulatory convergence, envisaged as part of the action plans in the early years of the ENP, appeared 'process-oriented',[37] ie disconnected from clearly specified end points. Likewise, conditionality remained ill-defined, not least because the ENP action plans lacked clearly defined benchmarks or specific time frames to monitor the reforms to be conducted by partner countries.[38] This made conditionality difficult to apply and amounted to a form of 'conditionality-lite',[39] especially as the link with rewards remained vague. As Casier argues, it was 'unclear which condition an ENP state ha[d] to fulfil in order to get a certain reward'.[40] The fuzziness of both conditionality and the ENP's incentives, as well as the 'open-ended nature of the award under the ENP',[41] are in sharp contrast to both the EEA and the enlargement process.

Being aware of the limited rewards offered as part of the ENP, the EU sought to discursively bridge existing gaps. It introduced the principle of 'joint ownership'[42] in its policy narrative, to emphasize the role of the partner countries in defining and endorsing priorities of cooperation, for instance as part of the ENP action plans. As was made clear by the then Commissioner Verheugen, '[o]ne basic principle behind the ring of friends we are forging is joint ownership. Of course, we cannot impose the policy [ENP] on any neighbour'.[43] In addition, the EU identified differentiation among ENP countries as a corollary of joint ownership: '[priorities] will be defined by common consent and will therefore vary from country to country'.[44] Joint ownership and differentiation were thus encapsulated in the ENP

[35] The European Neighbourhood Partnership Instrument (ENPI)'s financial envelope totalled €11.2 billion for the period 2007–13, ie an increase of 32 per cent compared with the amount available over the period 2000–06 for the MEDA (Mesures d'Accompagnement) and TACIS (Technical Assistance to the Commonwealth of Independent States) programmes. See European Neighbourhood and Partnership Instrument https://neighbourhood-enlargement.ec.europa.eu/document/download/d5cdf670-6d37-4c33-a38f-ae7f2ddb1ce3_en?filename=overview_of_enpi_results_2007-2013_en_0.pdf (accessed 18 January 2021).

[36] Tom Casier, 'To Adopt or Not to Adopt: Explaining Selective Rule Transfer under the European Neighbourhood Policy' (2011) 33(1) Journal of European Integration 44.

[37] Sandra Lavenex, Dirk Lehmkuhl, and Nicole Wichmann, 'Modes of External Governance: A Cross-national and Cross-sectoral Comparison' (2009) 16(6) Journal of European Public Policy 820.

[38] Gwendolyn Sasse, 'The European Neighbourhood Policy: Conditionality Revisited for the EU's Eastern Neighbours' (2008) 60(2) Europe-Asia Studies 303.

[39] ibid 296.

[40] Casier (n 36) 44.

[41] Kataryna Wolczuk, 'Implementation without Coordination: The Impact of EU Conditionality on Ukraine under the European Neighbourhood Policy' (2009) 61(2) Europe-Asia Studies 190.

[42] European Commission, 'European Neighbourhood Policy' (n 5) 8.

[43] Günter Verheugen, 'Towards a Wider Europe: The New Agenda' (2004) Speech/04/141, Prime Ministerial Conference of the Vilnius and Visegrád Democracies, Bratislava, quoted in Elsa Tulmets, 'Can the Discourse on "Soft Power" Help the EU to Bridge its Capability-Expectations Gap?' (2007) 7 European Political Economy Review 212.

[44] European Commission, 'European Neighbourhood Policy' (n 5) 8.

as key principles for enhancing neighbours' receptivity to the EU's policies, norms, and templates.

However, the extent to which different principles and mechanisms could coexist effectively within a single policy framework triggered sharp debates. As argued by Sedelmeier, the combination of different, and sometimes opposite, mechanisms (ie conditionality, on the one hand, and elements of socialization as reflected in the joint ownership principle, on the other) only undermines their respective effectiveness, and thereby results in additional policy tensions.[45] In essence, the emphasis placed on partnership entailed that the EU–neighbours relationship '[was] formally characterised as being one of equals with a set of shared interests'.[46] In the years that followed the launch of the ENP, the EU increasingly stressed the role of joint ownership,[47] which implies that partner countries carry responsibility in policy formulation and application. However, the discursive emphasis on joint ownership was at odds with the EU's role in setting the domestic agenda and deciding upon the size and speed of rewards.[48] Indeed, this use of conditionality entailed an asymmetrical relationship, especially for those ENP countries aspiring to closer ties with the EU (such as Ukraine).[49] The asymmetrical nature of these relations, in turn, hampered joint ownership by the partner countries.[50] Therefore, in the first years of its implementation, the ENP appeared fraught with tensions between different logics: an approach modelled after enlargement and premised on conditionality, and a logic reflecting the fact that, in essence, the ENP is an external policy which needs to engage with local partners to yield influence.

B. The Eastern Partnership: A shift towards deeper integration

The launch of the EaP, in 2009, marked a clear shift in the EU's approach to its eastern neighbours.[51] This is because of three interconnected reasons. First, with the EaP, the EU increased the size of rewards and also made them more

[45] Ulrich Sedelmeier, 'The European Neighbourhood Policy: A Comment on Theory and Policy' in Katja Weber, Michael E Smith, and Michael Baun (eds), *Governing Europe's Neighbourhood: Partners or Periphery?* (Manchester University Press 2007) 201.

[46] Ben Tonra, 'Identity Construction through the ENP: Borders and Boundaries, Insiders and Outsiders' in Richard Whitman and Stefan Wolff (eds), *The European Neighbourhood Policy in Perspective: Context, Implementation and Impact* (Palgrave 2010) 30.

[47] European Commission, 'Strengthening the European Neighbourhood Policy' (Communication to the European Parliament and the Council) COM (2006) 726 final.

[48] Wolczuk, 'Implementation without Coordination' (n 41) 190.

[49] ibid.

[50] Marise Cremona and Christophe Hillion, 'L'Union fait la force? Potential and Limitations of the European Neighbourhood Policy as an Integrated Foreign and Security Policy' (2006) EUI Working Papers Law 2006/39, 22.

[51] The following paragraphs on the EaP are based upon Laure Delcour, *The EU and Russia in Their 'Contested Neighbourhood': Multiple External Influences, Policy Transfer and Domestic Change* (Routledge 2017).

tangible compared with those on offer in the ENP. The EaP's offer consists of four pillars: first, an enhanced contractual framework in the form of Association Agreements (AAs), replacing the Partnership and Cooperation Agreements (PCAs) signed with post-Soviet countries in the 1990s; second, deeper economic integration, with the conclusion of Deep and Comprehensive Free Trade Agreements (DCFTAs); third, visa liberalization—ie the lifting of Schengen visa requirements for citizens from EaP countries once specific conditions have been met; and fourth, increased sectoral cooperation, for instance in the energy area. The upgrading of contractual frameworks to AAs (a decision which was taken during the 2008 EU–Ukraine Summit) is expected to better reflect partners' aspirations to closer integration with the EU than the initially foreseen 'European Neighbourhood Agreements'. This is because the AAs 'leave open the way for further progressive developments'[52] in EU–EaP countries' relations. In addition, in the wake of the mixed assessment of the ENP delivered at the end of 2006,[53] deep economic integration was envisioned as a strong reward that the EU could offer to its neighbours to support them more effectively in the reform process.[54] Indeed, DCFTAs offer enhanced market access by removing import and customs duties and quantitative restrictions, as well as by reducing technical barriers to trade on the basis of partner countries' alignment on EU standards. Likewise, visa liberalization was, undoubtedly, a major expectation of eastern partners vis-à-vis the EU. It represented a key step forward as compared with the earlier visa facilitation schemes offered by the EU, and was, therefore, a key incentive for EaP countries to adopt EU norms and standards in the areas of migration, borders, and mobility. Last but not least, the EaP enhanced the perspectives offered to partner countries for participating in EU programmes and agencies, as well as regional frameworks. This was, for instance, the case in the energy area, in which the EU called both for the completion of negotiations for Ukraine's and Moldova's membership in the Energy Community and consideration of an extension of observer status to other countries; it also encouraged all partners to participate in the Intelligent Energy Europe Programme.[55]

Second, the EaP was a turning point in the EU's approach to legal approximation in its eastern neighbourhood. Unlike candidate countries, the EU does not require homogeneity with its own legal framework from EaP partner states, as these countries lack a membership perspective. Nevertheless, the diffusion of the EU *acquis* as a template for reforms has become much more systematic under the EaP

[52] Council of the European Union, 'Conclusions of the EU–Ukraine summit' (2008) https://www.consilium.europa.eu/ueDocs/cms_Data/docs/pressData/en/er/102633.pdf accessed 4 January 2021.

[53] European Commission, 'Strengthening the European Neighbourhood Policy' (n 47).

[54] European Commission, 'ENP—A Path towards Further Economic Integration Expanding on the Proposals Contained in the Communication to the European Parliament and the Council on "Strengthening the ENP"' COM (2006) 726 final of 4 December 2006.

[55] European Commission, 'Eastern Partnership' (Communication to the European Parliament and the Council) COM (2008) 823 final.

than was previously the case. This has translated into a substantial expansion of both the scope and depth of EU demands for domestic change. For instance, the DCFTAs require partner countries to approximate their legal framework with over 90 per cent of the EU's trade-related *acquis*.[56] In a similar vein, the EU expects EaP countries to adopt and apply a broad range of EU and international standards before eliminating the obligation of Schengen visas. In fact, the scope of EU-demanded reforms is tightly interwoven with the EU's enhanced offer under the EaP.[57] As indicated in the final declaration of the EaP 2009 Prague Summit, 'legislative and regulatory approximation is crucial to those partner countries willing to make progress in coming closer to the EU'.[58] Therefore, in sharp contrast to the ENP, the EaP clearly promotes a result-oriented approach to legal approximation. Contrary to the ENP action plans, legal approximation efforts are geared towards specific goals, namely political association, deeper economic integration, and visa liberalization.[59] Another major difference from the ENP is legal bindingness. In essence, the ENP action plans were political documents, the implementation of which hinged, crucially, on the momentum for reforms in the partner countries, and their administrative capacities. By contrast, legislative approximation provisions under the AAs/DCFTAs are legally binding.[60] Furthermore, in contrast to the PCAs, Association Agreements include specific timetables[61] and dispute settlement mechanisms. As such, and despite the continuous use of the term 'legal approximation', they represent a shift away from approximation understood as a loose process geared towards compatibility of legal frameworks (labelled 'approximation/compatibility'),[62] and towards approximation premised upon deep economic integration (named 'approximation/convergence').[63]

Third, under the EaP, the EU has reinforced its policy mechanisms with a view to facilitating domestic change in line with its demands. On the one hand, with the EaP's multilateral track, the EU has introduced a new framework of exposure to

[56] Alexander Duleba, Vladimir Ben, and Vladimir Bilčíek, *Policy Impact of the Eastern Partnership on Ukraine: Trade, Energy, and Visa Dialogue* (Research Centre of the Slovak Foreign Policy Association 2012) 78.

[57] Peter van Elsuwege and Roman Petrov, 'Setting the Scene' in Peter van Elsuwege and Roman Petrov (eds), *Legislative Approximation and Application of EU Law in the Eastern Neighbourhood of the European Union* (Routledge 2014) 4.

[58] Council of the European Union Joint Declaration of the Prague Summit (2009), 7 May, https://www.consilium.europa.eu/media/31797/2009_eap_declaration.pdf(accessed 9 May 2024).

[59] Guillaume van der Loo, 'The EU–Ukraine Deep and Comprehensive Free-Trade Agreement: A Comprehensive Mechanism for Legal Approximation?' in van Elsuwege and Petrov (eds), *Legislative Approximation* (n 57) 64.

[60] Laure Delcour and Kataryna Wolczuk, 'Eurasian Economic Integration and Implications for the EU's Policy in the Eastern Neighbourhood' in Rilka Dragneva and Kataryna Wolczuk (eds), *Eurasian Economic Integration: Law, Policy, and Politics* (Edward Elgar 2013) 190.

[61] Annexes to the Association Agreements specify the time frames for the implementation of EU-approximated legislation.

[62] Aaron Matta, 'Differentiating the Methods of Acquis Export: The Case of the Eastern Neighbourhood' in van Elsuwege and Petrov (eds), *Legislative Approximation* (n 57) 44.

[63] ibid.

EU norms, relying upon socialization, emulation, and persuasion mechanisms (eg exchange of experience and best practices, presentation of EU legislation). It has also designed new bilateral assistance mechanisms, such as the Comprehensive Institution Building Programmes (CIBs), launched in 2010 with a view to reinforcing eastern partners' administrative capacities in preparation for AAs/DCFTAs. On the other hand, the EU has reinforced the use of conditionality by moving towards *ex ante*, sector-specific conditionality. The tough experience of lengthy DCFTA negotiations with Ukraine in 2008–11 prompted the EU to introduce sectoral conditions that had to be fulfilled before negotiations for DCFTAs could be launched with Armenia, Georgia, and Moldova.[64] Likewise, the Visa Liberalisation Action Plans (VLAPs) handed over by the European Commission to EaP countries detail the measures that have to be adopted and enforced before the EU will lift the Schengen visa requirement.[65]

Therefore, with the EaP, the EU has stepped up its 'transformative engagement'[66] in its eastern neighbourhood. It has laid bare an 'explicit integration objective'[67] that was still fuzzy in the early stages of the ENP. In order to effectively induce domestic change in the region and thereby allow deeper integration, the EU scaled up both the export of its *acquis* and the use of conditionality, which gained prominence compared with the 'partnership' approach. If anything, this shift indicates that the EU regards the diffusion of its norms and templates as the best vehicle to foster stability: its core objective in its neighbourhood. Such a vision is premised upon the previous successful experience of enlargement to Central European countries. This reliance upon the export of the *acquis* is despite the fact that the EaP remains distinct from accession, and offers only partial legal integration. The following section shifts the analytical focus from the EU's offer to policy implementation in Eastern Europe and the South Caucasus. It examines partner countries' responses to the EaP and key developments in EU–eastern neighbours relations.

III. Eastern Partners' Responses to the EU's Offer: A Policy À la carte

The launch of the EaP in 2009 marked a major turning point in the intensification of the relations between the EU and its eastern neighbours. This is because of three reasons. First, the EU clarified and harmonized its policy vis-à-vis all six

[64] Delcour (n 51).
[65] EU–Republic of Moldova Visa Dialogue, 'Action Plan on Visa Liberalization' (2010), available at http://visa-free-europe.eu/wp-content/uploads/2012/03/EU-Moldova-Action-Plan.pdf (accessed 22 April 2021).
[66] Elsuwege and Petrov (n 57) 1.
[67] ibid 5.

countries[68] by embedding in the new initiative policies and rewards that had hitherto been on the table for Ukraine only. Ukraine started negotiations for a new agreement to replace the 1994 PCA in early 2007, and for a DCFTA in February 2008, ie before the EaP was launched. In September 2008, the EU and Ukraine agreed that the new contractual framework would take the form of an Association Agreement.[69] Thus, the EaP's offer draws heavily on the evolution of EU–Ukraine relations, and in fact reflects a generalization, to the region, of the model developed for Ukraine.

Second, given the time horizon needed for implementing the reforms attached to the EaP's key building blocks, the 2009 initiative seemed to usher in a new period of stabilization in EU–eastern neighbours' relations.

Third—and perhaps most importantly—the EaP envisioned the creation of 'a Neighbourhood Economic Community' (NEC) in the longer term,[70] on the basis of a future network of free trade agreements between the EU and its neighbours. The NEC was envisioned as the ultimate step in the process of deep economic integration between the EU and all of its neighbours. However, the EU envisaged two distinct regional paths leading to this Community: one to the east; and a second one fostering integration between Southern Mediterranean partners. [71] Therefore, the EU's narrative illustrated a process of construction of the (eastern) neighbourhood as a specific region in EU foreign policy: one with which a 'special relationship'[72] should develop on the basis of deep economic integration. As was the case in Western Europe at the beginning of the European integration process, increased economic interdependence premised on common trade standards was envisioned as an instrument to promote peace and stability in the EU's neighbourhood. However, in Eastern Europe and the South Caucasus, the EU's attempt at region-building stumbled against the heterogeneity of partne countries' responses to the EaP.

A. The EAP: Limited attractiveness for Belarus and Azerbaijan

From the outset of the EaP, two countries—Azerbaijan and Belarus—remained on the sidelines of the policy and embarked only on selected initiatives.

For Belarus, the launch of the EaP did not mark any significant difference in its relations with the EU. While the country was included in the ENP due to its geographical location at Europe's core, it lacked the contractual framework that

[68] Armenia, Azerbaijan, Belarus, Georgia, Moldova, and Ukraine.

[69] Council of the European Union Joint Declaration on the EU–Ukraine Association Agreement (n 52).

[70] European Commission (n 54) 3.

[71] ibid.

[72] Art 8, Consolidated Version of the Treaty on the European Union [2012] OJ C326/01.

the EU had designed for, and agreed with, post-Soviet countries in the 1990s. As Belarus shifted towards authoritarianism after Aleksandr Lukashenko gained power, the EU never ratified the PCA signed in 1995.[73] As a consequence, political contacts were curtailed and EU–Belarus relations remained covered by the limited (and obsolete) Trade and Cooperation Agreement (TCA) signed in 1989 with the Soviet Union.[74] With the ENP, the EU's policies vis-à-vis Belarus became fraught with tensions between an exclusive approach (on the grounds of breaches of democracy and human rights in the country) and an inclusive logic, premised on Belarus' security importance for the EU (for instance, in terms of border and migration control).[75] While these tensions did not halt with the EaP, they translated into differentiated engagement across policy instruments.[76] Crucially, Belarus' participation in the core pillars of the EaP's bilateral track—the AA, together with a DCFTA—was *de facto* ruled out, as the country was too remote from the political and economic prerequisites underpinning these agreements (namely commitment to shared values, in the case of the AA, and membership in the World Trade Organization (WTO), in the case of the DCFTA). In addition, Belarus (together with Russia and Kazakhstan) joined the Eurasian Customs Union (ECU) in 2010, which excluded the future signature of a free trade agreement with the EU, as the country had transferred its sovereignty to the newly created supranational entity in terms of trade tariffs.[77] Belarus' relationship with the EU deteriorated further as a result of three developments: the brutal crackdown on protesters that followed the rigged 2020 presidential election; the 2021 border crisis with Poland, which was triggered by Belarus' instrumentalization of migrants from the Middle East to create pressure at the EU's external border; and Belarus' role in Russia's invasion of Ukraine, which resulted in new EU sanctions. While it only formally left the EaP in 2021, Belarus had always remained on the fringes of the ENP/EaP.

Unlike Belarus, Azerbaijan had a PCA in force when the EaP was launched. It started negotating an AA in 2010, however without the related DCFTA, as the country is not a member of the WTO and showed little interest in extensive legal approximation with the EU *acquis*. Crucially, the country resisted the EU's political agenda that sought to promote democracy and human rights as part of the

[73] Giselle Bosse, 'Challenges for EU Governance through Neighbourhood Policy and Eastern Partnership: The Values/Security Nexus in EU–Belarus Relations' (2009) 15 Contemporary Politics, 219.

[74] ibid 219–20.

[75] ibid 218–19.

[76] In 2014, the EU started negotiations for visa facilitation and readmission agreements with Belarus, which were signed in 2020. These agreements facilitate mobility from Belarusian citizens to the Schengen area, while engaging with Belarusian authorities in the fight to curb irregular migration.

[77] The only possible exception would be the signature of a free trade agreement between the EU and the Eurasian Economic Union (EAEU), the organization which succeeded the ECU in 2015. However, the possibility of official relations with the EAEU has been ruled out by the EU until the 2015 Minsk Agreement establishing a ceasefire in eastern Ukraine has been fully implemented.

negotiations for an AA.[78] Instead, it developed a selective approach to cooperation with the EU that focused primarily on mutual interests in the energy area. As a result of Azerbaijan's resistance, negotiations for an AA were abandoned in 2013 for a more limited contractual framework, the Strategic Modernization Partnership, inspired by EU–Russia relations.[79]

B. Armenia's difficult quest for complementarity

In sharp contrast to both Belarus and Azerbaijan, Armenia welcomed the EU's enhanced offer as part of the EaP. This is because the 2009 initiative coincided with a period of deep political polarization and economic crisis in the country, as well as enhanced regional vulnerability in the wake of the 2008 Russian–Georgian War. In this difficult context for Armenia, the incumbent authorities and the opposition agreed on the need to modernize the country with a view to reducing its vulnerability.[80] Against this background, the EU was regarded as a key partner in the reform process. After opening negotiations for an AA (in 2010) and a DCFTA (in 2012), Armenia vigorously adopted and started implementing EU templates, so that the country's efforts resulted in the completion of negotiations in July 2013.[81] However, Armenia's reforms in line with EU demands were also premised on two important caveats. Domestically, as the EU placed the emphasis on trade-related conditionality, these reforms entailed limited political costs for the then non-democratic political elites, who therefore embraced the EU's offer and used the centralized political regime to foster change in line with EU demands.[82] Regionally, the AA/DCFTA were perceived as compatible with Armenia's commitments vis-à-vis Russia (the country's major security ally). However, in early September 2013, the then Armenian President Serzh Sargsyan abruptly put an end to the association process and announced that his country would join the Russia-driven Eurasian Economic Union (EAEU), thereby declining to sign an AA/DCFTA. This is because Russia's use of its massive leverage over the country[83] was perceived as a clear signal that Armenia should backtrack from deep integration

[78] Eske Van Gils, 'Azerbaijan's Foreign Policy Strategies and the European Union: Successful Resistance and Pursued Influence' (2018) 70 Europe-Asia Studies 5. See also Bosse, in this volume.

[79] Eske Van Gils, 'Azerbaijan's Foreign Policy Strategies', ibid.

[80] Laure Delcour and Kataryna Wolczuk, 'The EU's Unexpected "Ideal Neighbour"? The Perplexing Case of Armenia's Europeanisation' (2015) 37(4) Journal of European Integration 499.

[81] ibid 497.

[82] ibid 501–02.

[83] In spring 2013, Russia concluded a massive arms sale with Azerbaijan, Armenia's rival over the Nagorno-Karabakh conflict. This was followed by Vladimir Putin's visit to Baku in August, thereby raising fears in Armenia of a Russia–Azerbaijan rapprochement. In summer 2013, Russia also threatened to drastically increase the price of gas sold to Armenia. See Armen Grigoryan, 'Armenia: Joining Under the Gun' in S Frederick Starr and Svante Cornell (eds), *Putin's Grand Strategy: The Eurasian Union and its Discontents* (Central Asia-Caucasus Institute & Silk Road Studies Program 2014).

with the EU. However, despite its coerced accession to the EAEU in 2015, Armenia sought to preserve close links with the EU and negotiated a new agreement that would enhance cooperation while also taking into account the country's EAEU membership.[84] As a result of the latter, the Comprehensive Enhanced Partnership Agreement (CEPA), concluded in 2017 (and in force since March 2021), does not eliminate tariffs and relies on WTO agreements, rather than the EU's *acquis*, as a basis for cooperation in key trade areas, with no 'hard' approximation obligation for Armenia (eg in sanitary and phytosanitary standards (SPS), technical barriers to trade (TBT), and public procurement areas).[85] In other areas, such as services, the agreement envisages mutual access to service markets; this is despite the fact that service liberalization is part of the EAEU agenda. However, in still other areas (such as transport, energy, and the environment) the CEPA goes beyond soft approximation obligations and includes imperative provisions.[86] Overall, despite falling short of the association status, the new agreement substantially expands the scope of EU–Armenia cooperation and reflects a dynamic understanding of legal approximation commitments, which are subject to review and adaptation (based, among other things, upon the degree to which the EAEU agenda is actually fulfilled).[87] Therefore, the CEPA denotes flexibility in determining the pace of cooperation, and in fact reflects the tailoring of the EU's EaP offer to Armenia's specific context: in particular, EAEU membership.[88] With the CEPA, the EU has instilled a new meaning into Article 8 of the Treaty on European Union (TEU) regarding the development of a special relationship with its neighbours,[89] by providing for 'specific agreements' to be concluded with neighbouring countries, which 'may contain reciprocal rights and obligations as well as the possibility of undertaking activities jointly' in order to develop a 'special relationship' with them.[90] In addition to bilateral relations, the EU's engagement as a mediator in Armenia's conflict with Azerbaijan also demonstrates the fluid nature of its relations with Armenia.[91] The

[84] Narine Ghazaryan and Laure Delcour, 'From EU Integration Process to the Eurasian Economic Union: The Case of Armenia' in Roman Petrov and Peter van Elsuwege (eds), *Post-Soviet Constitutions and Challenges of Regional Integration: Adapting to European and Eurasian Integration Projects* (Routledge 2017).

[85] Laure Delcour and Narine Ghazaryan, 'Armenia: A Precarious Navigation between Eurasian Integration and the European Union' in Fabienne Bossuyt and Peter van Elsuwege, *Principled Pragmatism in Practice: The EU's Policy toward Crimea after Russia* (Brill 2021).

[86] ibid.

[87] ibid.

[88] ibid.

[89] Peter van Elsuwege and Roman Petrov, 'Article 8 TEU: Towards a New Generation of Agreements with the Neighbouring Countries of the European Union?' (2011) 36 European Law Review 688–703.

[90] Ghazaryan and Delcour (n 84)

[91] The EU's role as a mediator started in late 2021 under the auspices of the President of the European Council, and increased after Russia's full-scale invasion of Ukraine. In February 2023, the EU also launched a civilian mission in Armenia (EU Mission in Armenia, EUMA), to observe and report on the situation along Armenian borders with Azerbaijan. See Narine Ghazaryan, 'The EU and the Nagorno-Karabakh Conflict: The Forty-four-day War and its Aftermath' (2023) 28(1) European Foreign Affairs Review 53–71.

Armenian authorities' growing criticisms vis-à-vis Russia, and detachment from Russia-driven organizations such as the Collective Security Treaty Organization (CSTO), has resulted in increased security cooperation with the EU. Subject to the country's leaving the EAEU, Armenia's quest for closer ties with the EU may, ultimately, lead to an enhanced contractual framework such as an AA.

C. An offer fully embraced by Georgia, Moldova, and Ukraine

Ultimately, among the six EaP countries, only Georgia, Moldova, and Ukraine signed up to all key elements of the EU's offer. In concluding AAs and DCFTAs in June 2014, the three countries committed themselves to an (unprecedented in the region) wholesale adoption of the EU's *acquis*. he commitment made to approximate their legal frameworks to the *acquis* is wide-ranging, as it encompasses future *acquis*.[92] In addition, most of the legislation that associated countries have to adopt is subject to strict deadlines of implementation. However, the AAs also offer scope for adjustment in some other areas, such as SPS and TBT. In these areas, where adoption of EU standards requires massive reforms and costs to be borne up front by local actors,[93] the partner countries develop their own strategies for implementation on the basis of the priorities mentioned in the AAs.[94] Importantly, such strategies have to be approved by the joint subcommittees set up as part of the AA, which therefore implies the EU's endorsement.[95] In some other areas, such as public procurement, the AAs do not provide for specific deadlines and, therefore, enable the partner countries to sequence reforms over time. Despite these flexibilities, the AAs entail a strict commitment to approximation with the EU *acquis*.[96] The EU has set up new mechanisms to monitor approximation efforts, for instance EU and partner countries' regular progress reports, and on-the-spot expert missions to ensure that approximated legislation is being enforced effectively.[97] In addition, in several sectors, such as SPS or TBT, access to the EU's market (for instance, through a recognition of equivalence for agricultural products) is conditional upon the implementation of approximated legislation. Such 'market

[92] Guillaume Van der Loo, 'The EU–Ukraine Association Agreement: Assessment of an Innovative Legal Instrument' (2014) EUI Working Papers Law 2014/09, 15.

[93] The first comprehensive reforms in line with EU demands were conducted as part of the 'key recommendations' for opening DCFTA negotiations that the EU required from Armenia, Georgia, and Moldova. In SPS and TBT areas, these reforms entailed massive costs, given the sharp difference from Soviet standards, which were still widely used in many EaP countries. See Delcour (n 51).

[94] Kataryna Wolczuk and others, 'The Association Agreements as a Dynamic Framework: Between Modernization and Integration' (2017) EU-STRAT Working Paper 6.

[95] ibid.

[96] ibid.

[97] Van der Loo, 'The EU–Ukraine Association Agreement' (n 92) 13.

access conditionality' is a crucial mechanism to 'tackle the challenges of integration without membership'.[98]

In the energy area, 'enhanced multilateralism', as developed in the Energy Community (EnC) mirrors another approach to integration without membership. Though the geographical scope of the EnC was initially limited to the EU and Western Balkans countries,[99] it has subsequently been expanded to ENP countries. Whereas Armenia has observer status, Moldova, Ukraine, and Georgia joined the Community in 2010, 2011, and 2017, respectively. Designed to foster the creation of an integrated market in natural gas and electricity, the EnC entails approximation with selected EU energy *acquis*. The bulk of approximation is compulsory and entails alignment with EU legislation on regulatory authorities and energy, as well as the environment. However, as is the case for the implementation of EU political and trade rules, the diffusion of the energy *acquis* proves difficult in light of the drastically different contexts in the partner countries. For instance, the creation of independent regulatory authorities has stumbled against rent-seeking practices and State capture, particularly in Moldova and Ukraine.[100] Importantly, the EnC does not have a separate judicial authority that could ensure a uniform application of rules by all the members.[101] As noted by Lavenex, 'in theory it is possible that the European Court, if it was called upon, could establish the principle of direct effect of EU law on the participating non-member States';[102] however, only an Energy Community Court with powers to hear direct actions from the Energy Secretariat and all parties to the Energy Community Treaty would ensure adherence to EU rules.[103]

Overall, developments in EU–eastern partners' relations over the past decade have increasingly questioned the EU's single offer to Eastern European and South Caucasus countries. Only three of the six EaP countries have actually fully embarked on closer legal relations, whether as part of 'enhanced bilateralism'[104] (ie the association process) or 'enhanced multilateralism'[105] (as is the case with the Energy Community). Crucially, differentiated integration within the EaP does not reflect a multi-speed process (whereby all partner countries would move ahead and embrace the EU's offer at their own speeds). This is because some EaP countries (in particular, Belarus and Azerbaijan) have not taken on board the EU's offer of deeper integration by choice. In other words, it is unlikely that the differences

98 ibid.
99 Łazowski (n 23) 1447.
100 Laure Delcour, Antoaneta Dimitrova, and Kataryna Wolczuk, 'State Capture and its Effects on the Implementation of the Association Agreements' (2019) EU-STRAT Working Paper 19.
101 Łazowski (n 23) 1443.
102 Lavenex, 'Concentric Circles' (n 8) 382.
103 Alan Riley, 'Deploying the Energy Incentive: Reinforcing EU Integration in South-East Europe' (2013) CEPS Policy Brief 296.
104 Łazowski (n 23) 1436.
105 ibid.

noted in the scope and depth of relations will remain temporary. This, in turn, undermines the validity of the ENP/EaP as a single model of external integration. It also raises the question of what comes next for the countries that have fully embraced the EU's vision as part of the EaP.

IV. Blurred Boundaries in External Differentiation: From Association to Accession

The progress achieved by the three EaP-associated countries in terms of integration with the EU has not only called into question the relevance of the EU's vision underpinning the ENP/EaP, as the latter is increasingly fragmented; it has also raised the issue of possible bridges between different models of external differentiation, in particular between the ENP and enlargement.

Georgia, Moldova, and Ukraine have long voiced EU membership aspirations. As early as 1996, Ukraine declared accession to the EU as a strategic goal and, two years later, drafted a 'Strategy on Ukraine's Integration with the European Union'.[106] Since the mid 2010s, the associated countries have only become more vocal in asserting their aspirations to join the EU. Georgia's example epitomizes the associated countries' quest for recognition of a membership perspective. During the AA/DCFTA talks, the Georgian negotiating team insisted on the country being recognized as 'Eastern European' in the preamble of the agreement,[107] which enables the country to lodge a future application to the EU, as foreseen under Article 49 of the TEU.[108] Like the agreements signed with Moldova and Ukraine, the EU–Georgia AA also acknowledges 'the European aspirations and the European choice of Georgia'.[109] Four years after signing the AA, the Georgian authorities adopted a 'Roadmap to the EU', a strategy for integration with the EU beyond the AA. This document identifies, as a strategy, enhanced organizational inclusion in EU structures, in the form of sectoral integration, and enhanced participation in EU programmes and agencies. Importantly, the Roadmap also seeks to give further impetus to regulatory inclusion by providing for the screening of Georgian legislation, a key mechanism initiated during the 1990s enlargement process.[110]

[106] Kataryna Wolczuk, 'Integration without Europeanisation: Ukraine and its Policy towards the European Union' (2004) EUI RSC Working Papers 2004/15, 8.

[107] EU–Georgia Association Agreement [2014] OJ L261/5.

[108] Art 49 provides that 'any European State which respects the values referred to in Article 2 and is committed to promoting them may apply to become a member of the Union.' (Consolidated version of the Treaty on European Union OJ C202/43).

[109] EU–Georgia Association Agreement (n 107).

[110] Civil.ge, 'FM Janelidze on Georgia's EU Integration Roadmap' (*Civil.ge*, 20 December 2017) https://civil.ge/archives/218934 accessed 25 March 2021; Kataryna Wolczuk, 'The Development of an Institutional Framework for the Implementation of the Association Agreements in Georgia, Moldova and Ukraine: A Comparative Perspective' (European Parliament AFET Committee, 2018, https://www.europarl.europa.eu/RegData/etudes/STUD/2018/603879/EXPO_STU(2018)603879_EN.pdf, accessed 9 May 2024).

In 2021, the Georgian government went a step further and announced that the country would apply to join the EU in 2024.[111] In the late 2010s and early 2020s, the Ukrainian authorities also expressed their interest for 'sectoral unions'[112] (such as energy, digital, and customs unions, and the internal market) as a mechanism to deepen integration with the EU beyond the AA.[113] This is because all three associated countries have never regarded the AA as an ultimate goal, or even as a durable arrangement, but rather as a step towards EU membership. This was perhaps best illustrated by the 2021 joint letter sent by Georgia, Moldova, and Ukraine to the EU, which called for a 'new, strategic, long-term vision' in EU-associated countries' relations.[114]

Importantly, the associated countries' strategies for enhanced organizational and regulatory integration with the EU have not just been premised on political narratives and aspirations. They have also been based on a comparison with the existing model of relations developed by the EU for current candidate countries, namely those in the Western Balkans.[115] In fact, the AAs concluded with Georgia, Moldova, and Ukraine go beyond the Stabilisation and Association Agreements (SAAs) signed with the countries of the Western Balkans, in terms of both the scope and bindingness of legal approximation. For instance, as noted in a study comparing the two groups of countries, 'in the Serbian SAA the technical barriers to trade are covered by the wording that Serbia "shall seek to promote the use of Community standards", whereas the Moldovan AA has for the same heading an annex of 11 pages listing over 100 EU legal acts to be approximated within given time delays'.[116] The difference in specificity and legal obligations between the two types of agreement is despite the fact that, in sharp contrast to the Western Balkans, the eastern partners did not have a membership perspective until 2022. Crucially, comparisons between the two groups of countries point to the more advanced status of EaP-associated partners in terms of reform implementation, especially with respect to trade and economics. By contrast, despite differences across sectors and countries, accession talks with the countries of the Western Balkans have, overall, been stalling in recent years.[117]

[111] Georgia Today, 'Prime Minister: Georgia is Preparing to Apply for Full EU Membership in 2024' (*Georgia Today*, 6 January 2021) https://georgiatoday.ge/pm-georgia-is-preparing-to-apply-for-full-eu-membership-in-2024/ accessed 28 March 2021.

[112] Michael Emerson (ed.), *Balkan and Eastern European Comparisons: Building a New Momentum for the European Integration of the Balkan and Eastern European Associated States* (CEPS 2021).

[113] The 'EU–Ukraine Policy Agenda within the AA Implementation' includes action plans on energy liberalization, digital liberalization, and transit liberalization, as well as an agenda on justice, liberty and security. See Wolczuk, 'Integration without Europeanisation' (n 106).

[114] Joint letter of Georgia, the Republic of Moldova, and Ukraine on Enhanced Cooperation with the Associated Partners within the Eastern Partnership (11 February 2021) https://3dcftas.eu/library/documents/joint-letter-of-georgia-moldova-and-ukraine-on-enhanced-cooperation-with-the-associated-partners-within-the-eastern-partnership accessed 20 March 2021.

[115] On the Western Balkans, see Milenković, in this volume.

[116] Michael Emerson, *Balkan and Eastern European Comparisons* (n 112)

[117] ibid.

This picture of a growing convergence between EaP-associated countries and the Western Balkans, combined with the increasingly heterogeneous nature of the EaP, has fuelled calls for a revised differentiated integration, in the form of a multi-tier EU that would offer a 'dynamic integration prospect, ranging from a rather "soft" form of membership with limited or partial institutional participation through to ultimately full membership'.[118] Thus, under this configuration, EaP-associated countries would, increasingly, take part in EU structures (including as observers in EU institutions), with the ultimate possibility to become rule-makers if all conditions are met. However, until 2022, such a multi-tier EU was not on the table, as the European Commission had recalled, in 2017, that 'no future accession to the EU is expected in the short-term'.[119]

Russia's full-fledged invasion of Ukraine, in February 2022, drastically changed the picture of EU–eastern neighbours' relations. The European Council's unanimous decision to grant Ukraine and Moldova EU candidate status, and to recognize Georgia as a potential candidate country,[120] constitutes a major turning point, as it charts a completely new course for relations with the associated countries, which had hitherto been constrained by the sheer uncertainty over their *finalité*.

V. Conclusion

This chapter has sought to contribute to the reflection on differentiated external integration by scrutinizing the mechanisms of European integration set up as part of the ENP and their encounter with Eastern European and South Caucasus domestic actors in the absence of a membership perspective. Almost two decades after the ENP was launched, the chapter identifies a variety of integration degrees in the EU's Eastern Neighbourhood. In essence, the EaP appears increasingly fragmented between a group of countries which have embraced the EU's offer and other states which have only selectively (if at all) embarked on this policy. Beyond this observation of a fragmented policy, the chapter sheds light on the multifaceted drivers that shape eastern neighbours' attitudes to the EU. It identifies EU membership aspirations (in the cases of Georgia, Moldova, and Ukraine) and the resonance of EU reform templates (for instance, in the case of Armenia between 2010 and 2013) as key factors explaining domestic change in line with EU demands. By contrast, domestic elites' resistance to EU norms and the policies of other regional powers (eg the creation of an alternative Eurasian integration project, and Russia's

[118] ibid 31.

[119] European Commission, 'White Paper on the Future of Europe: Reflections and Scenarios for the EU27 by 2025' COM (2017) 2025, 8.

[120] European Council, 'Conclusions, 23 June 2022' (n 22). Due to democratic backsliding, Georgia was not granted candidate status, but was recognized as a potential candidate country.

efforts to lure EaP countries into the EAEU) explain the weak resonance of the EU's offer in some other countries, primarily Azerbaijan and Belarus.

Perhaps paradoxically, the growing fragmentation observed in the EaP is intrinsically connected to the inconsistent nature of the ENP as a model of integration. Beyond its borders, the EU is only able to exert its policy leverage (eg through conditionality) to the extent that the partner countries allow it to do so. Whereas the ENP was initially fraught with tensions between the joint ownership principle and mechanisms modelled after EU enlargement policy, the central role of partner countries' aspirations was explicitly recognized in the 2015 ENP revision.[121] However, the differentiation among EaP countries bears critical implications for the EU's models of external integration. In the mid 2000s, the EU clarified its longer-term vision for the ENP, based on an 'economic community [emerging] between the EU and its partners';[122] in other words, a common regulatory space offering a similar degree of market access. Yet, the NEC that was to be premised on a network of DCFTAs has failed to materialize, as a consequence of partner countries' diverse responses to the EU's offer.

This, in turn, questions the relevance and the sustainability of the ENP/EaP as a single model of external integration. In contrast to developments in the EU, where 'most differentiated integration has been "multi-speed" integration, creating only temporary differences in the integration of member states', [123] the differences among EaP countries are likely to persist and even increase. Yet, while it has shifted towards greater flexibility in bilateral relations, the EU has long seemed reluctant to engage in a debate on a complete overhaul of its policy framework.[124]

However, Russia's war in Ukraine abruptly shook up the foundations upon which the EU has interacted with the countries located on its borders over the past two decades. The EU's vision of its periphery was premised upon a dichotomy between future EU members, on the one hand, and countries without any membership perspective in the short- to medium-term, on the other. This vision collapsed abruptly as a result of Ukraine's, Moldova's, and Georgia's applications, which made the dichotomy meaningless. However, the EU has yet to rethink and reshape its strategy vis-à-vis the surrounding regions, including by fully revamping its enlargement policy.

[121] European Commission/High Representative of the Union for Foreign Affairs and Security Policy, 'Review of the European Neighbourhood Policy' JOIN (2015) 50 final.

[122] European Commission, 'Strengthening the European Neighbourhood Policy' (n 47) 5.

[123] Frank Schimmelfennig, 'Is Differentiated Integration the Future of European Integration?' in Björn Fägersten and Göran von Sydow, *Perspectives on the Future of the EU* (SIEPS 2019) 102.

[124] For instance, European Commission/High Representative of the Union for Foreign Affairs and Security Policy, 'Eastern Partnership Policy beyond 2020: Reinforcing Resilience—An Eastern Partnership that Delivers for All' JOIN(2020) 7 final.

Index

For the benefit of digital users, indexed terms that span two pages (e.g., 52–53) may, on occasion, appear on only one of those pages.

Introductory Note

References such as '178–9' indicate (not necessarily continuous) discussion of a topic across a range of pages. Wherever possible in the case of topics with many references, these have either been divided into sub-topics or only the most significant discussions of the topic are listed. Because the entire work is about 'differentiation' and the 'European Union', the use of these terms (and certain others which occur constantly throughout the book) as an entry point has been restricted. Information will be found under the corresponding detailed topics. Cross-references in a form such as 'post-Soviet countries *see also individual countries*' direct the reader to headings in a particular class (e.g. in this case 'Kazakhstan') rather than a specific '*individual countries*' entry.